Spain's First Democracy

Publication of this volume has been made possible in part by a grant from the Program for Cultural Cooperation Between Spain's Ministry of Culture and United States' Universities.

Spain's
First Democracy

The Second Republic, 1931–1936

STANLEY G. PAYNE

The University of Wisconsin Press

The University of Wisconsin Press
114 North Murray Street
Madison, Wisconsin 53715

3 Henrietta Street
London WC2E 8LU, England

Printed in the United States of America

Library of Congress Cataloging-in-Publication Data
Payne, Stanley G.
Spain's first democracy: the Second Republic, 1931–1936 /
Stanley G. Payne.
494 p.   cm.
Includes bibliographical references and index.
ISBN 0-299-13670-1   ISBN 0-299-13674-4 (pbk.)
1. Spain — History — Republic, 1931–1939. 2. Representative
government and representation — Spain — History — 20th century.
I. Title.
DP254.P39   1993
946.081 — dc20   92-56925

For Julia

"The old is dying and the new cannot be born. In the interregnum, a great variety of morbid symptoms appear."

—Antonio Gramsci (1891–1937)

Contents

Illustrations

Tables

Preface

FOR many decades General Franco and his publicists insisted that Spanish society and culture were simply not appropriate for political democracy, which allegedly could never succeed in Spain—a point of view occasionally shared by foreign observers. More than twenty years ago, while Franco was still in power, I suggested in the second volume of my *History of Spain and Portugal* that the record of political liberalism in Spain was not so negative as many had claimed and revealed a definite capacity for representative reform and self-government, though a year earlier I had ended my study of *The Spanish Revolution* with the obvious conclusion that a second attempt at democracy in Spain must avoid the extremism and sectarianism of the 1930s.

Soon afterward, Spain and Portugal pioneered what would eventually become the third great wave of democratization in the twentieth century, laying to rest old cliches about the inability of the peninsular societies to practice democracy. The success of the democratic monarchy subsequently reawakened my interest in the reasons for the failure of the first attempt, and the result is the present book.

I want to thank Juan J. Linz and Robert Kern for their careful reading of this study and their suggestions for its improvement, and I am also grateful to Lydia Howarth for editing the final manuscript.

The illustrations are reproduced courtesy of Información y Revistas, S.A.

Spain's First Democracy

1

The Ordeal of Modernization in Spain

THE emergence and early success of the Second Republic in Spain was the most unusual, and probably the most positive, political event in Europe during the first years of the Great Depression. It contradicted the course of affairs in southern and eastern Europe, where the less developed countries were falling under authoritarian rule. While the political systems of more advanced lands in central Europe were being severely challenged and entering decline, Spanish society embarked on its first complete experience with modern democracy—a dramatic contrast with the perceived direction of European affairs.

Though only a few years were needed to show that the apparent democratic consensus in Spain was doubtful, the early achievements of the Republic were not insignificant and no mere fluke of a separate kind of "Latin American" or "Mediterranean" society. They formed the culmination of two generations of slowly accelerating reform and modernization, which in recent years had made progress in closing part of the gap between Spain and northwestern Europe for the first time in more than a century.

The drama of Spain's history is derived in considerable measure from its location on the periphery of western Europe, the nearest geographic link to Africa and the Middle East. Of all Western lands, only the Iberian peninsula was largely conquered, converted, and acculturated by an oriental civilization, and, of all generally Islamicized territories, it was also the only one to be totally reconquered and reconverted by Christendom. The general notion of "Moorish Spain" and of the semioriental qualities of Spanish culture has lingered since the Middle Ages. In fact, the formal culture and religion of Christian Spain have always been fully Western and Orthodox, and even the language contains fewer Arabisms (less than 2 percent) than many think. During the Middle Ages, however, Spain was frontier territory, and—with the exception of the more typically "Latin" and "European" Catalonia in the northeast—never fully achieved the highest level of western cultural, educational, and economic development.

It was the heritage of Spain and Portugal as crusading frontier societies on the rim of Christendom that enabled them to lead the modern expansion of Europe, beginning in the fifteenth century. This was later accompanied by fuller development of the Spanish economy and the flowering of Spanish education and culture by the latter part of the sixteenth century, catapulting the kingdoms of the Hispanic peninsula from the periphery to a leading role in European life. This dynamic development was halted during the seventeenth century. By the 1650s, both Spain's military strength and economic power had undergone serious decline. Though the Spanish crown long retained the first worldwide empire, it had already become a second-rank European military power.

The seventeenth century was crucial in the emergence of Spanish "backwardness," for, as its economy and cultural life stagnated, Spain generally failed to participate in the "modernization" of science, technology, economic production, commercial relations, and political structures more typical of northwestern Europe (England, Holland, parts of France) during that period. Much more distinctly than in the case of any preceding world culture, the history of Western civilization has been divided into two distinct cycles: the "old regime" of Western Christendom spanning a thousand years from the early Middle Ages to the eighteenth century, and "modernity"— the era of modern science, technology, industrialization, and democratization—from the seventeenth and eighteenth centuries to the present. The German historical philosopher Oswald Spengler once observed that the height of "old regime" culture had been achieved in seventeenth-century Spain,[1] which if correct, would have made Spain the most "typical" or representative Western country for the acme or crystallization of the first millenial cycle of Western culture. There is no obvious way to verify such a broad generalization, but what is more certain is that the rigidified structures of the Spanish old regime were unsuccessful in making the transition to early modernization during the seventeenth century.

The nadir of decline was overcome before 1700, and the eighteenth century was, for Spain, a time of limited development under the new Bourbon dynasty. Both population and gross product increased, but growth was more extensive than intensive, that is, it involved more the expansion of existing structures than the qualitative transformation of cultural and economic activity. At the same time, it would be wrong to discount altogether the educational reforms of the period or the changes in social and fiscal policy that drastically reduced the nominal ranks of the aristocracy by the 1780s.

The era of direct modernization began with the onset of nineteenth-century liberalism, which commenced comparatively early in Spain, collapse of the old regime being induced from without by the Napoleonic invasion of 1808. This enabled a small minority of upper- and middle-class liberals to introduce the liberal constitution of 1812, which in turn was overthrown two years later by the return of the old regime in the person of the exiled king Fernando VII. Six decades of intermittent chaos ensued as the country found itself in a historical trap. The old regime was too weak and its leadership too incompetent to enable it to survive, but the forces of the new liberalism were scarcely any stronger, without the backing of a productive economy or generally literate society. The first three-quarters of the nineteenth century were thus a period of persistent conflict within the elite, in which the military emerged as the almost inevitable arbiter of and direct participant in a political system too weak and divided to function on its own.

The liberal constitution was reintroduced by military revolt in 1820, leading to radicalization and conditions of civil war in the northeast, ended by French invasion to restore absolutism in 1823. A decade later the royal family split over the dynastic succession, traditionalists rallying to the king's younger brother and presumed heir, Don Carlos, while the supporters of his only child, the two-year-old princess Isabel, embraced moderate liberalism to hold the throne. The subsequent First Carlist War (1833–40) was an exhausting conflict between the forces of traditionalism and moderate liberalism, unprecedented in bitterness and duration in western Europe. After the traditionalists were finally defeated, the liberals divided between Moderates and Progressives, with the former winning out during the long reign of Isabel II (1833–68). A more advanced liberal constitution of 1837 was replaced by the Moderate constitution of 1845, which became the standard document of constitutional monarchy in Spain (with a revision in 1876) for nearly a century. Yet even the Moderates were not a modern party, but a loose alliance of elites. Elections under severely restricted suffrage were controlled from Madrid, and Moderate leaders, the queen, and the court coterie normally denied government access to Progressives. Though another military revolt momentarily gave the latter power in 1854, together with the opportunity to introduce the more progressivist constitution of 1855, one more praetorian intervention restored Moderate rule the following year, and in the 1860s, the crown restricted political access even further. This provoked a broad-based military and civilian revolt in 1868, the so-called "glorious revolution," that introduced yet another temporary constitution the following year, accompanied by the principle of universal male suffrage. Greater freedom seemed only to encourage more internecine political conflict, leading to the abdication in 1873 of the Italian prince brought in as Spain's new constitutional ruler. This was followed by an abortive effort to introduce a "Federal Republic" (1873-74), which collapsed of its own weight as various provincial groups tried to set up quasi-independent "cantons." The military once more took the lead in restoring the regular dynasty in the person of the heir to the throne, young prince Alfonso, who reigned as Alfonso XII (1874-85).

The real architect of the Restoration system was its civilian leader, the veteran professional politician (and avocational historian) Antonio Cánovas del Castillo. His goals were order and stability based on moderate elitist liberalism. Under Cánovas two basic political parties emerged, the Conservatives and the Liberals, and for more than three decades they largely alternated in a system of *turno* mediated by the crown. For the first time since the end of the old regime, political stability was achieved and a regular system of access to power was created for competing political elites, though the system was oligarchical and in no sense democratic.

Spain was never engaged in a major international war after 1814, but war was a continuing scourge for the society and economy during the nineteenth century. The Napoleonic war of 1808-14 was followed by a decade of increasingly frustrated colonial campaigns that ended in defeat. There were civil wars in 1822-23, 1833-40, and 1869-76, as well as several minor campaigns against local rebels and a brief international war with Morocco (1859). Spain retained Cuba, Puerto Rico, the Philippines, and other islands in the western Pacific and had no other international ambitions, but these remaining possessions involved her in a ten-year colonial war in Cuba (1868-78), eventually followed by a disastrous three-year campaign (1895-98) that ended in the humiliation and total defeat of the Spanish-American War. All significant remains of the historic empire were lost, only a few small footholds remaining in northwest Africa. Thus altogether Spain spent more years at war than almost any other country during the nineteenth century, and the cost not merely in loss of life (1 percent of the total population was killed in the First Carlist War, and more than fifty thousand in the final Cuban campaign) but also in expense and economic retardation was very great.

Though the Restoration regime could not retain the remnants of empire, it managed to establish a new modus vivendi with the armed forces and remove the military from overt intervention in politics. Even so, the senior military hierarchy remained a privileged elite with virtual autonomy over military administration, seats in the appointive senate, and even occasional participation of senior generals as temporary prime ministers in moments of transition.

The era of convulsive liberalism (1810–74) had been the more difficult because it was a time of only marginal economic growth. From 1800 to 1860 the expansion of Spain's gross domestic product was approximately equivalent to the (relatively slow) population growth, registering no proportionate increase. This had been due only to a small degree to loss of most of the American empire, for recent research indicates that the latter accounted for less than 6 percent of the gross domestic product in its final phase.[2] Nor was this due to "dependency" or exploitation by more advanced powers, for during most of the nineteenth century — particularly during the time of slowest growth — the international terms of trade favored Spain, only turning negative late in the century, at which point the growth rate actually increased.[3] Rather, this doleful economic performance was due to the partial stagnation of agriculture, very limited expansion of industry, and the mounting protectionism of state policy, which sealed off most of the domestic economy, reducing competition, more rapid adaptation, and new export linkages.[4] Thus while Spanish manufactures accounted for nearly 5 percent of the European total in 1800, by 1913 they had fallen to scarcely 2 percent of a much larger international economy.[5]

The sale of most church and common lands between 1836 and the 1880s sucked much of Spain's limited capital into real estate, temporarily bringing the illusion of greater income through the rapid extension of cultivated grainlands until decreasing productivity prompted a search for alternatives. The state also absorbed a considerable proportion of available capital through extensive borrowing, while mounting protectionism discouraged structural transformation. Nevertheless, part of the explanation for retarded industrialization must remain "cultural" — the limited proclivity of Spanish elites to invest in or try to lead new economic enterprises. The end of the old regime did not bring an end to all the attitudes and values of traditional life, and the conversion to a system of private property and capitalist procedures did not in itself generate a very productive bourgeoisie. The tendency to invest primarily in land, urban real estate, and government bonds to the exclusion of riskier new industrial and commercial undertakings remained the norm.

The result was a rather unique Spanish model of nineteenth-century modernization — liberal in its formal institutional structure but in fact elitist and oligarchic, favored by the terms of trade and eventually enjoying a positive exchange balance yet partially closed to the international economy, lacking any active policy of industrial development, oriented toward a semitraditional agriculture that began to grow in productivity and slowly change its structure only after 1860. As a poor south European country, Spain's per capita income was about the same as that of Italy in the middle and later decades of the nineteenth century, with Italy beginning to grow more rapidly only in the 1890s and intermittently adding to its lead through the 1950s.[6]

The first decade of the Restoration regime was comparatively prosperous, and for approximately five years during the mid-1880s, Spain dominated the world wine market, due to the phylloxera epidemic in France. Agriculture expanded during the half century from 1860 to 1910 at a net growth rate of 1 percent a year, while industrial expansion achieved the modest figure of about 2 percent a year between 1830 and 1910. After the change in mining laws in 1854–55, a major surge occurred in copper production, with Spain becoming the leading copper exporter in Europe, while shipments of Basque iron also increased. Catalan textile production led industry for most of this period, benefitting particularly from the broadening of the Cuban market after 1882. Yet a downturn in most of the export areas was noticeable after 1887, as tariff barriers increased almost universally. Spain soon became a leader in that trend through its own steep protective tariff of 1891, which sheltered the home market but did little to encourage new growth. By 1900 industrialization was confined primarily to Catalonia and the Basque country, followed by Asturias and the Valencia region. Textiles and food production amounted to 67 percent of total industrial production, with metallurgy and chemicals together accounting for only 13.68 percent.[7] By 1910 industrial exports amounted to only 7 percent of total industrial production.

Throughout the nineteenth century Spain had a rather low rate of population growth compared with the European norm, due to later marriage, lower overall marriage rates, and higher death rates. By 1900 national population reached eighteen million and was growing more rapidly due to a reduction in the death rate, which nonetheless remained disproportionately high. By 1930 population reached nearly twenty-four million, and by that time a dramatic decline in infant mortality was finally beginning. All the population increase of the early twentieth century was either concentrated in or moved to the cities, or joined the sizable emigration (mainly to Latin America) which by 1912 reached an annual high of 134,000.[8] Urban development speeded up from the 1890s on, and during the early twentieth century the larger centers began to take on the form and manner of typical modern European cities.

During the last decades of the nineteenth century there began a changeover to more intensive export agriculture, centered on wine, citrus products, and olives.[9] The grain producing areas in Castile and León began to lose some of their influence after 1900, while overall wheat production fell from 41 percent of total agricultural output in 1797 to 27.5 percent in 1910.[10] Moreover, the slow transformation of techniques and crops, together with accelerated opportunities for urban employment, brought a decline in the absolute numbers of the male agricultural workforce of about 18 percent between 1900 and 1930, though it still remained proportionately very large and mired in structural unemployment.

It was in this period, soon after the turn of the century, that the basic problems of latifundist agriculture in the south and center came increasingly to public attention. Reformers more and more appreciated the fact that the rural proletariat constituted the largest and most serious social problem of the country. The large estates on which they worked were the product of aristocratic expansion in the late medieval and early modern periods as well as of the transformation of older tenure patterns to capitalist private property in the nineteenth century. The problem was not merely one of equal distribution, for by 1700 there had probably been proportionately more landless farmworkers in England than in Spain,[11] but English largeholdings had rapidly become efficient in technique and often helped to pioneer agricultural modernization, while releasing laborers to man the industrial revolution. In France, conversely, more land had passed directly into the hands of the middle classes and peasantry even before the end of the old regime.[12] Spain had experienced neither the modernizing large domains of England nor the pronounced tendency toward the breakup of large domains as in France.

The amount of land under cultivation increased from 12 million hectares in 1833 to approximately 20 million by 1910 and 22.4 million in the cadastre of 1930. The latter statistic revealed that 7.5 million hectares were concentrated in estates of 250 hectares or more, and approximately another third of the land was held by 1.8 percent of the total number of owners in small medium to large medium properties between 10 and 250 hectares in size, while the remaining third (to be precise, 36 percent) of the land was held by 98 percent of all property owners in smallholdings of less than 10 hectares. In the five latifundist provinces of western Andalusia (Cadiz, Cordoba, Huelva, Jaen, and Seville), large estates amounted to 42 percent of the total.[13] Altogether, 60 percent of the agrarian population of New Castile was landless, and the percentage in Andalusia was even higher. This meant that as much as 40 percent of all those engaged in farmwork in Spain would be completely unemployed for part of the year.

Spain's first major phase of accelerated growth took place between 1910 and 1930. Agriculture continued slowly to expand and to continue its piecemeal restructuring, while industry spurted ahead. During the preceding half century from 1860 to 1910, agriculture, industry, and services had grown at annual rates of 1.5, 2, and 1.6 percent respectively, but from 1910 to 1930 these increased to 1.7, 2.5, and 2.9 percent.[14] During that span of two decades, the Spanish economy for the first time in more than a century began to reduce the distance between itself and the major European countries, according to one measurement cutting the difference between its own proportionate product and those of Britain, France, and Germany by approximately 12.5 percent.[15]

The Struggle for Reform, 1885–1923

Though the self-destructive convulsions of 1868–75 discredited republicanism for more than a generation, the new Liberal Party quickly resumed the politics of reform. Its major achievements were made by the Liberal "long government" of 1885–90 that restored trial by jury, established a formal law of associations which legalized trade unions, completed a new Civil Code, and inaugurated universal male suffrage for the elections of 1890.

The dark side of Restoration politics was its structure of *caciquismo* or "boss-rule" (the term *cacique* being derived from an American Indian word for "chief"). Elections were "made" from Madrid and largely controlled by provincial bosses. Some scholars hold that systems of clientelism and patronage are natural and inherent in south European societies prior to full modernization. Similar mechanisms might have been found in Italy, Greece, and Portugal (and in other countries as well). Certainly apathy remained widespread even after the introduction of universal male suffrage, and some electoral districts were set up as safe *encasillados* ("pigeonholings" or assignments) for whatever candidates those in power might wish to assign. The Conservatives or Liberals did not come to power as a result of elections, but were called to office by the king in order to "make" elections for themselves and guarantee themselves a parliamentary majority for several years. Even in the early years, however, not all opinion was apathetic, so that in the more advanced areas or those with greater political consciousness it was necessary to resort to *pucherazos* (direct vote fraud, or the "cooking up" of elections). After the turn of the century, it became more common to turn to direct vote-buying in some areas, and the distribution of local favors on the eve of elections was always a common practice. Since only one candidate was presented in some districts, a reform measure of 1907 (known as Article 29) endeavored to simplify procedures and eliminate one aspect of controlled voting by stipulating that henceforth candidates running in districts without competition would automatically be declared elected. In this fashion 119 of a total of 404 deputies would be so declared in 1910, the number rising to 146 of 409 by 1923.[16]

For most of the nineteenth century, Spain had led backward southern and eastern Europe in the attempt to introduce advanced modern liberal forms in the absence of a corresponding base of social and economic development. During the 1820s and 1830s Spanish liberalism had served as one of the principal contemporary inspirations for Italian nationalists, Russian Decembrists, and German liberals. Before the close of the century, the Spanish experience would be recapitulated in varying degrees by every other independent state in southern Europe, each of whom encountered many of the same contradictions between politics and society. Though Italy quickly achieved greater stability, no other south European state found it possible to move beyond essentially elitist and clientelistic systems in this era, with the possible exception of Serbia at the close of the century.[17]

In Spain, the fundamental pattern of electoral control would never be altogether broken under the constitutional monarchy. Elections did slowly become more genuine in some of the larger cities, however, and after a few years somewhat broader representation was allowed to third parties, some of them republican. Between 1907 and 1923, these republicans would be allowed to hold between 2 and 4 percent of the seats in parliament, even though registered abstentionism increased after the turn of the century.

"Regeneration" became the keynote for the early twentieth century in response to the national military and imperial disaster of 1898. The fact that other south European countries such as Italy, Portugal, and Greece also experienced humiliation abroad during the 1890s was scant consolation, as the new generation of Spanish leaders sought for keys to accelerate internal modernization. The first of the genre of "disaster" reformist books, Lucas Mallada's *Los males de la patria,* had been published as early as 1890. It correctly defined *caciquismo* not as a cause but as an effect of the social, economic, and educational underdevelopment of the society. Arguably the greatest failure lay in education, where Spain — which once had had proportionately the largest higher educational system in the world — currently maintained either the lowest or one of the lowest per capita budgets in Europe. The weakness of public education was only partially compensated by Catholic schools, which provided much of basic instruction. The literate proportion of the population had risen from perhaps 35 percent in 1877 to only 44 percent by 1900, placing Spain ahead of only Russia, Portugal, and a few regions in the Balkans.[18]

As in Russia, elite culture was much more vigorous, for the Regenerationist era coincided with the modern "Silver Age" of Spanish letters, second only to the "Golden Age" of early modern times. By the 1920s Spanish culture featured such world-class figures as the philosophers Ortega y Gasset and Unamuno, the novelist Baroja, the poets Jiménez and García Lorca, a scientist of the caliber of the histologist Ramón y Cajal, and later painters of the renown of Picasso, Gris, and Miró.

Though Catholicism had lost part of its place in Spanish life, the Church was still an important institution. Liberals had confiscated most of its landed endowments in the 1830s, but the moderate sectors of liberalism had soon reached a modus vivendi with Catholicism, codified in the Concordat of 1851. For the remainder of the nineteenth century, the liberal regime in Spain — particularly under the leadership of the parliamentary Conservatives — was the most Catholic and clerical to be found anywhere in southwestern Europe. The special privileges still enjoyed by the Church and its hostility to innovation made both the Church and clergy a continued target for the left, and also for the regular Liberal Party. Spanish progressivism held that without drastic changes and a sharp reduction in Catholic educational, cultural, and even economic influence, the full modernization and democratization of Spain would never be possible.[19]

Religious identity was sharply divided by region and by social class. Northern Spain, roughly speaking, was Catholic, while the church was much less present and had less following in the south (a difference to some extent stemming from the Middle Ages). Moreover, the clergy largely failed to maintain a presence in the newly expanding cities, so that not merely much of the southern peasantry but also most of the new working class were ceasing to be Catholic. The animosity of middle-class radicals and de-Catholicized workers was amply demonstrated in the great anticlerical riots of the Semana Trágica in Barcelona during July 1909, when the destruction of scores of churches and other religious buildings dramatized the extent to which the Church was blamed for the ills of contemporary Spanish society.[20]

Early twentieth-century Spain was unique in that there was no significant force of Spanish nationalism, while conversely strong new movements of centrifugal regional nationalism had emerged that sought to pull away from the central Spanish state. The absence of Spanish nationalism is explainable by several fundamental features of Spanish history. The dynastic Spanish state was nearly five centuries old and for a long period had been a major power, while in more recent times it was engaged in no major rivalries with or challenges from other European states. Spain faced no stimulus of national unification or major irredentism. Slow modernization also retarded the new interest groups which promoted nationalism in other countries. Moreover, the virtual absence of Spanish nationalism also meant that the main support for a modern rightist and potentially authoritarian brand of politics was lacking.

The classic Spanish monarchy had governed a confederal, not a unitary state, at least prior to the eighteenth century, which permitted the preservation of distinct regional institutions and identities, particularly in the northeastern quarter of the peninsula. Subsequently, the slow rate of modernization made it impossible to subsume all regional identities into a common national identity, as had happened in the case of France during the nineteenth century. Modern Catalan and Basque nationalism thus have their roots in distinctive historical institutions, languages, and identities, but only emerged in the nineteenth century as a consequence of more dynamic patterns of modernization in these regions compared with the Spanish norm. By the early twentieth century modern industry was disproportionately located in Catalonia and the Basque country. Whereas centrifugal regionalism in most other lands stemmed from backward regions that felt left out, in Spain the two most rapidly developing areas produced divergence. In both areas, nationalism was championed especially by the middle classes and initially had scant support among workers, especially the new immigrants from other regions. Since Catalonia was the most modern and dynamic part of Spain, Catalan nationalism began to develop first, emerging as a major force early in the twentieth century. Basque nationalism was slower. Though the Basque Nationalist Party was formed in 1895, it did not begin to gain significant electoral strength until World War I and did not become a powerful force until after the advent of the Second Republic.[21]

In the early twentieth century there were two distinct, competing forms of revolutionary worker movements, anarchosyndicalism and socialism. Bakuninist anarchism entered Spain in 1868, and the combination of anarchism with syndicalism (trade unionism) as an organizational device later produced anarchosyndicalism. A major continuous movement emerged only with the founding of the CNT (National Confederation of Labor) in 1910–11. It became a mass organization by the end of World War I, engaging in numerous acts of *pistolerismo* (political violence) and turbulent strikes. In 1927, a separate Iberian Anarchist Federation (FAI) was organized by hardcore anarchists to ensure the predominance of anarchist ideology and tactics within the broader CNT.[22]

The first Marxist socialist group was organized in Madrid in 1879, but it gained few members. The regular Socialist Party (PSOE) and trade union movement (UGT, General Union of Workers) emerged in 1888. The Spanish party was a fairly typical Socialist organization of the Second International, devoted to trade union activity and the contesting of elections, eschewing revolutionary militancy for tangible gains. For nearly a decade into the twentieth century, it failed to gain a single parliamentary seat, forming an electional "Conjunción" with Republicans only in 1910 that finally placed a Socialist in the Cortes. The issue of Communism and the Third International badly divided the party after 1919. Spanish Socialism eventually opted for the "Two and a half" or Reconstructionist International led by the Austrians, half way between revolutionism and social democracy. Though membership had plummeted by 1923, the party was set on a firmly non-Communist course.[23]

By that point anarchosyndicalism had completely outstripped socialism in labor organization, the CNT becoming Spain's first mass labor movement with nearly a million members, the first and only mass anarchosyndicalist movement anywhere in Europe. Chagrined Marxists attributed this to Spanish backwardness and the small-shop structure of Spanish industry, which did not generate such dense concentrations of workers as in more advanced countries or even as in backward Russia. Yet since Marxism gained mass adherence in certain societies distinctly more backward than Spain, and since anarchosyndicalism was nowhere else as successful in other societies no more advanced than Spain, the argument from sheer backwardness is totally inadequate to explain this phenomenon, for which many other factors must be considered. In Russia, for example, anarchists gained support from Ukrainian peasants and Jewish workers and artisans, both resident in small towns and villages, but also representative of the most individualistic sectors of society. Moreover, in St. Petersburg anarchists were rapidly gaining support in some of the more modern and concentrated industrial areas on the eve of Lenin's coup in 1917.

During the nineteenth and early twentieth centuries, the Spanish state was weak, and indeed more so than in some other underdeveloped countries. The state's lack of penetration made it all the easier for anarchists to conceive of the state as a null or negative factor, the more easily dispensed with, a source neither of progress nor even of decisive power. Moreover, Spanish society had a long historical tradition of localism and particularism, pactist and confederal on the national level and enjoying de facto self-governance on the local level.[24] Anarchosyndicalism developed roots in both the backward agrarian south and in modernizing, industrializing Catalonia. In each case the process was probably encouraged by the broader social and cultural context. In southwestern Andalusia, where anarchism gained the strongest backing, the lower middle classes and workers of the towns had from the mid-nineteenth century been strongly attracted to a radical republicanism that was highly individualistic, egalitarian, and anticlerical, serving to create an environment more propitious for a libertarian movement among the working classes. Moreover, Andalusian anarchists did not appeal merely to the most immiserated but also to a somewhat broader cross section of society.[25] Early twentieth-century Catalonia was rife with individualism and with political particularism on the bourgeois level, a situation not perhaps totally unassociated with the growing libertarianism of workers.

In Spain anarchosyndicalist success was partly predicated on Socialist failure. The latter's UGT was originally founded in Barcelona, long the country's proletarian center, but the Madrid leadership of the movement found Catalonia uncongenial and eventually withdrew to the Spanish capital.[26] Early Spanish Socialism was narrow, rigid, and unimaginative. It quarreled with trade union moderates in Catalonia[27] as well as with incendiary anarchists, and long failed to develop a strategy to reach the largest and poorest proletariat, located not in the cities but in the southern countryside. While the UGT held to the restrictive craft union principle, the CNT in 1919 adopted the *sindicato único* (industrial unionism), maximizing its mobilization potential.

Finally, the anarchosyndicalists of the CNT were more successful in developing a radical syndicalism simply because they were more radical, and also more violent, often practicing violence against workers who refused to join their ranks. Anarchosyndicalist violence and revolutionism became self-perpetuating, creating a self-radicalization of industrial relations that frequently forced the issue and provoked a polarization of worker attitudes and actions that could never have assumed the same form through peaceful trade union means, such as those normally practiced by the Socialists. Anarchosyndicalism thus demonstrated a capacity for revolutionary self-generation that the more disciplined and moderate Marxists simply lacked.[28]

There was in general a slow but growing movement toward organization and regulation in Spanish society after 1900, as social and professional reform entered the official political agenda. An Institute of Social Reform was established under state aegis in 1903 to undertake research and gather information that might encourage improved social conditions.[29] Several government measures to foster limited worker insurance were followed by formation of the Instituto Nacional de Previsión (National Institute of Social Security), a similarly semiautonomous agency to study pension problems and recommend improvements. Though slow, melioration of working conditions developed momentum. In the textile industry the working day was limited by law in 1913 to ten hours (though apparently not enforced) and in 1920 the workday for coal miners was cut to seven hours, while a Ministry of Labor was created in the government that same year. Meanwhile, the country's commercial, industrial, and agricultural interests began to achieve some degree of corporate organization on the eve of World War I, while the small Spanish professional classes and government employees also began to form their own corporate groups.[30]

The last six years of regular parliamentary monarchy (1917–23) were a time of protracted crisis.[31] Neutrality in World War I was accompanied by accelerated economic activity and spot shortages, which in turn produced inflation and rapidly mounting discontent among workers and farmlaborers[32] and among professional middle classes.[33] Leon Trotsky (temporarily exiled to Spain in 1916) advanced the concept that Spain had become the "Russia of the west," a backward society now trapped in hopeless developmental contradictions that was ripe for revolution. This notion also fascinated several leading Spanish thinkers[34] and would reappear more vigorously under the Second Republic. It was momentarily encouraged by the three-pronged crisis of 1917, which made it seem that Spain was teetering on the brink of Russian-style chaos.

In fact, what had developed in Spain during World War I was not so much a revolutionary situation as a crisis of authority.[35] As the largest and most important European neutral, Spain profited considerably from the conflict but was also increasingly divided by it. The split between conservative Germanophiles and the leftists and liberals who backed the Entente was more severe than in any other neutral country save Greece, producing a "civil war of words" and the first great left-right polarization of the century. Conservatives realized that Spain possessed neither the strength nor the geographic opportunity to intervene on the side of Germany, and concentrated successfully on keeping the country neutral, while leftists and liberals pressed for intervention on the side of the Entente. The Conservative government of 1914–15 fell in December 1915 after a minor procedural crisis in parliament, but the succeeding Liberal administration lacked the strength to govern effectively and succeeded only in antagonizing the military.

Three drastic new initiatives appeared during the crisis year of 1917. Much of the army officer corps joined an illicit new officers' organization (a sort of military syndicalism), the Juntas Militares, which fostered insubordination, demanded pay increases, and placed heavy pressure on the government.[36] Catalanists and other progressives outside the two major parties seized the opportunity to convene an autonomous "Parliamentary Assembly" in Barcelona to press for major constitutional reform, but gained no backing either from the military or the more liberal sectors of the establishment parties. Finally, in August the Socialist UGT launched the first serious effort at a general strike in Spain to press for economic improvements and democratic political reforms, but failed to obtain the full backing of the CNT or broad support from labor in general.[37] Each of these initiatives represented separate interests and worked at cross purposes with each other, posing little threat to the established system.

Immediately after World War I ended, difficulties of economic adjustment were exacerbated by two major new problems. One was the outbreak of violent class struggle in the industrial areas for the first time in Spanish history. By 1919 the CNT was a mass movement (with nearly a million members) capable of generating large-scale strikes, accompanied by political killings. Violence had begun in Barcelona in 1917, fomented in part by German agents seeking to disrupt an industrial center that served the Allies. The most reckless sector of the CNT turned to *pistolerismo* (political violence), which was countered by the private vigilantism of an "employers' police," followed in turn by state repression under martial law (wherein regular police employed the *ley de fugas* — "shot while attempting to escape").[38] The appearance of the small new Spanish Communist Party (PCE) only worsened the problem.

Between 1918 and 1920 the intense conflict in industrial centers was compounded by the so-called "Trienio bolchevique" (Bolshevik triennium) in the southern and south-central agrarian provinces. The "trienio" in fact lasted only from the spring of 1918 to the spring of 1920, and featured widespread farmworker strikes and disorders, including numerous cases of arson and destruction of property. Violence against persons was much less common in the countryside, but the farm strikes led on one occasion to the calling out of the Army and raised widespread, though totally exaggerated, fears that landless Spanish farm laborers were seeking to emulate the Bolsheviks in Russia.[39]

The other major new problem was protracted colonial war in Spain's new Moroccan Protectorate. After the debacle of 1898, there had been less support for neo-imperialism in Spain than in any large other European country (or than in many smaller ones). Though minor Spanish economic interests were involved, the main factor that led the government to establish a Protectorate over the northern 5 percent of Morocco in 1913 was probably more defensive than aggressive, to avoid being completely outflanked both geographically and militarily by France and absolutely outdone by all other west European powers. The native kabyles of northern Morocco were hostile and pugnacious. A border conflict there had earlier indirectly provoked a major domestic political crisis in Spain in 1909. After the close of World War I an effort was made to occupy the entire Spanish Protectorate, hitherto largely left in native hands, but the inept Spanish Army suffered a major defeat in the Rif in 1921, followed by two years of humiliating stalemate. The struggle in Morocco was the nastiest and most difficult to be found anywhere in the Afro-Asian world at that time. It led to increasing discord within Spain as civilian politicians hesitated to adopt a more vigorous and costly military policy, while part of the officer corps insisted on vengeance and full conquest. All the while a major demand for an official inquiry into "responsibilities" for the disaster of 1921 was maintained, a campaign which Army commanders feared would lead to the weakening of military institutions.

Amid growing political discontent and alienation, the erstwhile republican parties were unable to present a viable alternative, not so much due to falsified elections (though that continued through 1923) as due to their own lack of prestige and followers. The disaster of the Federal Republic of 1873–74 — four presidents within a year and virtual national civic disintegration — had discredited republicanism for two generations. The first sign of republican revitalization was the support among workers and lower-middle-class voters won in Barcelona in the years after 1900 by the demagogic Radical Republican Party, newly founded by Alejandro Lerroux.[40] Relying on incendiary anticlericalism, its vogue was brief, soon overtaken by the expansion of the revolutionary left and also of Catalanism. A newer, more pragmatic brand of republicanism emerged in the Reformist Republican Party of Melquiades Alvarez in 1914, which stressed basic principles of political reform and democracy more than the installation of a republic.[41]

Broadly speaking, republicanism within the Spanish context stood for direct parliamentary democracy and completion of all the reforms identified with classic middle-class liberalism, including separation of church and state, rapid expansion of education facilities, and basic administrative and institutional reform. Republicans differed among themselves regarding such problems as centralization versus decentralization and showed little concern for state-directed social reform as distinct from civil rights, political democratization, and educational expansion. Nonetheless the Socialist Party entered temporary electoral alliances with some republican groups, on the basis of democratic political reformism, between 1910 and 1918. Even so, the small republican parties proved unable to benefit from the mounting social and political discontent prior to 1923, and the Reformists of Alvarez finally joined forces with the establishment monarchist Liberal Party.

By 1923 the parliamentary system had reached a low point of esteem. The establishment parties were divided and ineffective, while the small oppposition groups lacked strength or legal access. Though a new "Liberal Concentration" was formed at the close of 1922 and fully controlled the elections of May 1923, most adult males in fact did not attempt to vote, and public opinion generally reflected a gulf between the *pays réel* and the *pays officiel*. (See table 1.1.) The atmosphere was one of protracted if low-grade crisis, and amid the general discontent a small number of Army generals seized the initiative to carry out a new *pronunciamiento* that would displace the parliamentary politicians — if no more than temporarily. Led by General Miguel Primo de Rivera, this bloodless revolt, which began on 13 September 1923, was scarcely even resisted by the regular parliamentary government, which seemed eager to resign. The king, Alfonso XIII, presided over a constitutional monarchy in which the ruler was the regulator of access rather than merely the passive spectator to genuine democratic elections. It was always the responsibility of the crown to determine which leader or group should form the next government, since under the system of oligarchic liberalism the next government was not produced by democratic elections, which in fact never occurred. Rather, it was the new government which always conducted and controlled elections to produce a parliamentary majority with which to govern. Since the parliamentary government in fact decided to resign, Don Alfonso invested General Primo de Rivera with the office of prime minister to form a government of his own in order to resolve the crisis and enact necessary reforms, to be followed by resumption of normal constitutional functioning. Though an effort was initially made to cloak this drastic change with a guise of legality, it was in fact an emergency dictatorship and produced the first military dictatorship per se in Spanish history.[42]

Table 1.1. Voluntary and Forced Abstentionism in Spanish Elections, 1899–1923

Year	Registered Voters	Percentage of of Abstentions	Percentage of Voters Affected by Article 29	Total Percentage of Nonvoters
1899	4,273,000	35	. . .	35
1901	4,300,000	33	. . .	33
1907	4,579,000	33	. . .	33
1910	4,650,000	24	29	54
1914	4,714,000	31.2	21.1	52.4
1916	4,754,000	31.5	35.7	67.2
1918	4,720,000	29.6	11.3	40.9
1919	4,720,000	36	19.4	55.4
1920	4,750,000	33.6	17.6	51.2
1923	4,783,000	35.5	35.1	70.6

Source: Miguel Martínez Cuadrado, *La burguesía conservadora (1874–1931)* (Madrid, 1973), 404.

The Primo de Rivera Dictatorship, 1923–1930

The first Spanish dictatorship of the twentieth century did not begin with
an explicit doctrine or ideology, but simply with the goal of saving Spain
from the political oligarchy which had mismanaged it, restoring law and
order and national unity, dealing with financial and economic problems,
and resolving the mess in Morocco. Primo de Rivera himself was a professional officer of solid military credentials, courageous and jovial, who had
developed growing political ambitions in recent years. Yet he denied that
he wished to be a dictator, at first announced that his new "Military Directory" would govern for only ninety days, and insisted that the constitution of 1876 still remained the law of the land.

The easiest problem to solve was that of public order. Martial law quickly
put an end to political violence; little was heard from anarchists and Communists for the next seven years. "Saving Spain from the politicians" proved
much harder to manage, for military officers were scarcely prepared to deal
with complex administrative problems. The ninety days came and went,
but the Military Directory governed for two and a half years, finally giving way in February 1926 to a regular cabinet, composed mainly of civilians, but still led by the temporary dictator.

At first the most intractable problem was Morocco. The Spanish Army
simply lacked the strength and efficiency to put down the insurgency and
occupy the entire Protectorate. During 1924 Primo de Rivera had to carry
out a partial strategic retreat at considerable cost, in order to shorten the
Spanish lines and provide a breathing space in which to reorganize the
combat units. The Rifi leader Abdul Karim then made his fatal mistake
of attacking southward into the French zone as well, provoking joint Franco-
Spanish military cooperation that caught his forces in a vise beginning in
1925. A Spanish amphibious operation occupied the heart of the insurgent
zone, and by 1926 the rebels had been defeated, final mopping-up operations being completed during the next two years.[43]

The dictatorship's other success was economic development. The new
regime rode the crest of the boom of the twenties, which featured the most
rapid industrialization in Spanish history. The expansion of national and
state income enabled the dictatorship to undertake the greatest public works
program ever seen in Spain, beginning the country's modern highway system, and to promote further economic growth.[44] In labor relations, it introduced a system of *comités paritarios* (equal representation committees)
to arbitrate between capital and labor in the negotiation of new contracts.
The Socialist UGT agreed to participate in this system, which benefitted
some sectors of industrial labor but never became nationwide.[45]

The dictatorship's insoluble problem was political reform. Primo at first sought to promote honesty and efficiency in provincial administration by appointing military delegates as overseers, but this created more problems than solutions, and a planned decentralization of local government and administration never took place. In fact the reverse occurred, for the limited autonomy granted to the four Catalan provinces in 1913 (the Mancomunitat) was soon abrogated, leaving both Catalans and Basques increasingly outraged by renewed centralization.[46]

The dictatorship was supported by a kind of civic front, the Unión Patriótica Española (UPE), formed in 1924 and devoted to an amorphous credo based on nationalism, right-wing Catholicism, and strong authority in government, together with corporative principles in economic and political organization. Primo de Rivera seems to have had in mind a political future based on some sort of modern right-wing nationalist force, complemented by a domesticated Socialist Party that might represent organized labor, though in fact his plans were too confused to crystallize in clear-cut alternatives. The dictatorship also emphasized close relations with the Catholic Church, though it was not fulsome in economic support.

After five years an effort was made to approach constitutional reform through the calling of a National Assembly chosen by indirect corporate representation rather than direct elections. Packed with supporters of the dictatorship, it proposed to make partial corporate suffrage a permanent system, reducing the scope of direct elections and greatly increasing the powers of the crown and the central executive. Though the dictatorship had been positively received by most middle-class opinion in 1923, it had completely failed to build any kind of new consensus on behalf of a more authoritarian system as a long-range solution. The proposed constitutional reform of 1928–29 was sharply criticized in the still largely free press and drew little support, ultimately embarrassing both Primo de Rivera and the king before it was quietly scuttled.[47]

The dictatorship had long outlived any utility that it had once possessed and had completely failed to provide a political alternative. By the beginning of 1930 discontent was mounting on every hand. Agriculture was already suffering from the beginning of depression, the budget was heavily in the red, and the peseta had fallen steeply. Even those businessmen who had once supported the regime had become more skeptical, while the Catalan bourgeoisie, particularly, had turned completely against it. The Socialists had grown increasingly distant,[48] while the intelligentsia and Spain's small but vocal university student population had launched strident opposition.[49] For the first time in two generations the republican parties were growing rapidly. Finally, and most decisively of all, the dictatorship had lost the backing of the military, sectors of which had always been cool to it. Primo de Rivera was now suffering severely from diabetes and had become lethargic. The king was increasingly embarrassed by the dictatorship and shrewd enough not to be attracted by any proposed authoritarian constitution. With part of the military actively conspiring against a military dictator, Primo de Rivera consented to a royal request for his resignation at the end of January 1930.

The dictator was gone, but authoritarian rule, after six and a half years, was not so easily disengaged. All rightist alternatives had been discredited, while republican and leftist opposition was growing. The initiative now lay with an increasingly bewildered king, who found it difficult to dismount from the tiger which rightist authoritarianism had become.

2

The Republican Transition, 1930–1931

For decades after the disaster of the Federal Republic, Spanish adults sometimes observed of quarreling children, "This is a republic." During the first years of the twentieth century, only a comparatively small minority of those interested in progress and reform were attracted to republican groups. This began to change after 1925, when the continuation of the dictatorship helped to create the conditions for the broadest expansion of republicanism in Spanish history. Its sudden rise was further assisted by the dictatorship's constant propaganda campaign to discredit the former monarchist parliamentary parties as corrupt and ineffective. The latter had comparatively shallow roots in society and flimsy organization. Their life had been organized around elections and parliamentary sessions; since neither of these existed after 1923, they largely died out over a period of several years. Thus the growing revulsion against authoritarian rule, and the monarchy's association with it, produced a new wave of support among sizable sectors of the intelligentsia and the middle classes previously unattracted to republicanism.

A new orientation was also encouraged by rapid changes in social and economic structure, and to some extent in Spanish culture, in the years between 1915 and 1930. This produced the most rapid proportionate expansion of the urban population and the industrial labor force in all Spanish history. (See table 2.1.) Between 1910 and 1930 industrial employment had almost doubled, from 15.8 percent of the labor force to 26.5 percent. This exceeded the proportionate shift to industrial employment during the great post–World War II boom decade of the 1960s, the only era to equal the 1920s as a period of expansion and modernization.[1] Though agriculture remained the largest single sector, by 1930 the percentage of the active population engaged in agriculture and fishing had dropped to less than half for the first time, having shrunk from 66 percent in 1910 to 45.5 percent in 1930 — a proportionate decline never equaled before or after.[2] Spain

23

Table 2.1. Changes in the Spanish Labor Force, 1920-1930

Sector	Percentage in 1920	Percentage in 1930
Agriculture and fishing	57.2	45.5
Mining	2.3	2.1
Manufacturing	15.6	19.2
Construction	4.1	5.2
Total industry	22.0	26.5
Transportation and communication	2.9	4.6
Commerce	5.9	7.6
Other services	12.0	15.8
Total services	20.8	28.0

Source: *Estadísticas históricas de España Siglos XIX-XX* (Madrid, 1989), 79.

was no longer the overwhelmingly rural, agrarian country that it had been before 1910. Due to urban expansion and the boom in transportation and communication, growth in service employment was even more rapid than in industry, increasing from 20.8 percent in 1920 to 28 percent in 1930. This too was a major indicator of accelerated social and economic modernization.[3]

The total active labor force by 1930 was approximately 8,773,000. Of these, some 2,325,000 were industrial workers, about 1,900,000 farm laborers, and nearly 2,500,000 were engaged in services. There were more than a million smallholders, 700,000 rural renters and sharecroppers, 400,000 small businessmen and artisans, and about 225,000 government functionaries. Relatively large landowners numbered about 12,000, and domestic servants some 350,000.[4]

Major improvements were under way in education. Illiteracy in the adult population dropped by almost 9 percent during the 1920s, again apparently the most rapid improvement within ten years in all Spanish history. Opportunities for women, another basic indicator, were also expanding rapidly. The proportion of women in the labor force grew by nearly 9 percent during the 1920s, while the percentage of women university students nearly doubled from 4.79 to 8.3 in the four years from 1923 to 1927. Moreover, the absolute number of all university students approximately doubled between 1923 and 1930. Though Spain remained seriously underdeveloped compared with northwestern Europe, these rapid changes were producing a new and more modern society that was better educated and increasingly urban, and potentially more attuned to democratization, amounting to what one historian has called "a republican ambiance."[5] They were also producing a much higher level of social and political consciousness and a pronounced revolution of rising expectations, especially among industrial workers and farm laborers. Indeed, these expectations would prove to be of such dimensions that arguably any democratic society which had not yet achieved full modernization would encounter grave difficulty in satisfying them, particularly in a time of incipient depression.

Thus, even though a small minority of right-wing monarchists favored the establishment of a system of royal authoritarianism vaguely analogous to the monarchist dictatorship imposed by King Alexander in Yugoslavia a few months earlier, this was no option for Alfonso XIII and never seriously considered. Civic opinion would not long have tolerated it, and the response would probably have been military revolt. For the king and his advisers, the only viable alternative was to try to ease their way back to the pre-1923 parliamentary system. Since that no longer existed, the transition could not be attempted overnight.

A new temporary government was appointed on 30 January 1930, under General Dámaso Berenguer, a member of the king's own military staff who had held high military posts in the past but had avoided direct involvement in the political controversies of the dictatorship. To initiate a gradual return to constitutionalism, his government quickly reversed major policies of Primo de Rivera. The corporative National Assembly was dissolved, a general political amnesty decreed, and university professors discharged by the dictatorship restored to their positions. In April the legal ban on the anarchosyndicalist CNT was lifted; trade union and strike activity soon increased markedly. None of this was sufficient, however, to win the public participation of the old parliamentary leaders.[6] Berenguer's cabinet was therefore composed of ultra–right-wing monarchists and a few second-rank figures of the old Conservative Party. It represented no broad sector of political society and thus remained hesitant about taking the leap in the dark of new elections.[7]

Some of the more liberal politicians from the old system cobbled together a "Bloque Constitucional," but this was little more than a conversational circle of elites and had no solid basis. At the opposite pole, several figures strongly identified with the dictatorship, such as Primo de Rivera's finance minister, José Calvo Sotelo, organized a new "Unión Monárquica Nacional" designed to lead the way into a more permanent right authoritarian system. This group also remained very small and elitist, though it was flanked by several other tiny, new ultra-rightist organizations.[8]

New republican organizations proliferated rapidly. The only "historical" republican party of any consequence was the Radical Republican Party of Alejandro Lerroux, which had become more moderate with each passing year and had come to stand for a kind of centrist liberal democracy, equidistant between right and left. Conversely the old Federal Republican Party was a shell. More important was the new Republican Action group, formed in 1925 and led by younger intellectuals and professional men, most important of whom was the writer and Justice Ministry department chief Manuel Azaña. This new organization proposed a more radical and leftist kind of reformist republic than did the older Radical Party.

These three formations had been joined by the Catalan Republican Party, originally formed as the left wing of political Catalanism in 1917, to create an informal Republican Alliance in 1926. In fact, the republican organizations were at first not especially active in the opposition to Primo de Rivera, which had been led instead by military figures, reformist monarchist politicians, maverick intellectuals, and university students. They began to enjoy a broad vogue only as discontent reached major proportions in 1929–30. Some of the more extremist republicans split off from the other organizations in 1929 to form a more advanced and Jacobin-type party, the Radical Socialist Republican Party, obviously inspired by turn-of-the-century French terminology. By 1930 Republican Action had constituted itself as a political party, and leading figures of the preceding parliamentary regime such as the former Conservative prime minister José Sánchez Guerra,[9] the Catholic progressive Angel Ossorio y Gallardo, and the Reformist Melquiades Alvarez had publicly declared their loss of faith in the monarchy, while the head of one minor faction of the former monarchist Liberals, Niceto Alcalá Zamora, and Miguel Maura, son of a four-time Conservative prime minister, declared themselves republicans. Together they formed a new conservative republican party, the Liberal Republican Right (DLR), while three of the country's leading intellectuals, led by the world-famed philosopher José Ortega y Gasset, organized a small Agrupación al Servicio de la República (Group for the Service of the Republic).[10]

Republican forces were becoming especially strong in most of the centrifugal regions (though not in the more conservative Basque provinces). The two new leftist Catalanist groups, the ultra-liberal Acció Catalana (Catalan Action) and the extremist Estat Català (Catalan State), were both republican, though the left wing of the former had recently split off as Acció Republicana de Catalunya before the two wings joined once more to form a new Partit Catalanista Republicà in February 1931. A month later they joined with Estat Català to form a new coalition, Esquerra Republicana de Catalunya (Republican Left of Catalonia).[11] In Galicia, regionalist republicans formed their own party (ORGA) while a similar, though somewhat weaker, regionalist republican party was developed in the Valencia region.

The republican groups joined forces in a meeting at San Sebastián on

17 August 1930. Their agreement, later known as the "Pact of San Sebastián," brought together the Radicals, Republican Action, the Radical Socialists, ORGA, the three Catalanist parties and the more conservative DLR, who would be jointly represented by a "Comité Ejecutivo de la Conjunción" (Executive Committee of the Alliance), headed by the moderate Alcalá Zamora of the DLR and dedicated to the direct overthrow of the monarchy. Though no formal document was signed, all parties agreed to subordinate particular interests to the common goal and also pledged to move toward establishment of a broad system of regional autonomy for Catalonia after a republic was established.[12]

The Socialist Party was not at first included. Since its internal conflict over the Third International in 1919–21, the Party had tended increasingly toward moderation. Top leaders had hailed formation of the first democratic Laborite government in England in 1924. Pablo Iglesias, longtime head and virtual founder, had declared that it would undo the damage wrought by Bolshevism, while the veteran UGT chief Francisco Largo Caballero saluted the Laborite victory as the "most important event in the entire history of democratic socialism".[13] In the Spanish context, however, this had been translated into a policy of trade union collaboration with social institutions of the dictatorship. In 1924 UGT representatives had accepted seats on several government-sponsored boards and committees, including Largo Caballero's membership in the Council of State, followed by active participation in the regime's labor *comités paritarios*. Primo de Rivera, in fact, had hoped for even broader collaboration, but the UGT drew only limited benefit from the relationship, its membership growing only marginally from 210,617 in 1923 to a still modest 223,449 in 1927. By 1928 labor unrest was rising, as real wages flattened off. At the 1928 Socialist Party congress the social democrat Indalecio Prieto, the most outspoken opponent of collaboration with the dictatorship, declared, "We have played the fool, as before us the silly Communists who were to a certain degree responsible — through their excesses — for the coming of the dictatorship."[14] Though the Party had then rejected his plea for an end to all collaboration, there were no further initiatives. Yet Socialists were not officially republican, and early in 1930 a police assessment reckoned that they were still a force for stability rather than opposition.

By the middle of the year, the logic of self-interest began to push them toward the republicans, as even the apolitical CNT endorsed the need for a republic and the holding of completely democratic elections and engaged in somewhat vague negotiations with republican leaders. Prieto thus attended the San Sebastián meeting as an observer, and in October the leaders of the Socialist Party and the UGT reached an agreement with the Republican Committee whereby Prieto, Largo Caballero, and Fernando de los Ríos would join the latter as Socialist representatives and the UGT would support the planned republican revolt with a general strike.

Even though Spain had not yet suffered the major effects of the international depression, some sectors of the domestic economy had been under stress for more than a year, and the peseta continued to fall. In this climate the UGT grew rapidly, but after its legalization in April the CNT expanded even more quickly. The UGT tried to keep pace by creating a major new farm laborers federation (FNTT) to organize landless workers primarily in the center and south. By June strike activity from the CNT was spreading rapidly, with UGT rank and file often in support. Bad weather that year hampered the agricultural economy in Andalusia, which became a major focus of labor unrest. According to statistics of the Ministry of Labor, the number of strikes in 1930 increased by more than ten times that of the preceding year (402 to 29), the number of strikers increased fivefold to 247,460, and the number of workdays lost more than tenfold, to 3,745,360. During the summer and autumn the position of the government steadily worsened. All efforts for broader collaboration were spurned by political moderates, and limited efforts at repression by arresting a number of republican figures only increased opposition.

Assured of Socialist support, the Republican Committee converted itself into a self-styled Provisional Government in October. Niceto Alcalá Zamora became prime minister–designate, giving the movement a moderate guise that would hopefully be acceptable to broad sectors, while Miguel Maura, his partner of the Liberal Republic Right, was to serve as minister of the interior. The leading "historical republican," the sixty-six-year-old Alejandro Lerroux of the Radicals, was relegated to the largely decorative function of foreign minister, the left and right of republican politics combining to outmaneuver its center.[15]

The Provisional Government went ahead with plans for revolt, a separate "Military Committee" of republican officers led by the veteran Brig. Gen. Gonzalo Queipo de Llano preparing a military rebellion for mid-December, to be supported by a general strike. The CNT continued to escalate its own strike actions during the autumn but spurned republican efforts toward concerted action. The political attitudes of most army commanders and officers at this point were moderate and also disciplined, so that the republican conspirators were able to generate little support for an overt rebellion. Two young republican firebrands in the garrison of the Aragonese mountain town of Jaca, at the foot of the Pyrenees, nonetheless precipitated action on their own on 12 December, three days before the planned general revolt.[16] Captains Fermín Galán and Angel García Hernández gained control of the Jaca garrison, declared martial law at dawn, and attempted to march on Huesca, the provincial capital, before being stopped by loyal troops.[17]

Three days later, on the fifteenth, the date originally scheduled, a small handful of republican officers led by Queipo de Llano and the famous aviator Ramón Franco[18] momentarily seized control of Cuatro Vientos military airfield outside Madrid and then, gaining no further support, soon flew off to Portugal.[19] There was no accompanying general strike in the capital, due to division within the Socialist leadership,[20] though the UGT initiated large-scale stoppages in major cities of the north and east, in a few areas also gaining support from the CNT. In Alicante the strike briefly turned into an insurrection, and a unit of the elite Legion was called in from Morocco. The whole effort was a complete failure; several members of the Provisional Government were arrested and the rest went into hiding or exile. Galán and García Hernández were soon court-martialed and executed.[21]

This was a pyrrhic victory for the Berenguer government, still as far as ever from gaining any broader centrist or conservative support. The executed rebels were quickly converted into martyrs against monarchist tyranny and, after the government finally announced on 8 February 1931, that parliamentary elections would be held the first of March, republicans, Socialists, centrists, and moderate conservatives all either announced abstention or urged the crown to postpone elections until a more representative government had been formed.

The breadth of this rejection was so great that it became clear to both Don Alfonso and General Berenguer that the government lacked the legitimacy to proceed further. Thus the *dictablanda* or "soft" authoritarian ministry of Berenguer came to an end on 14 February, to be replaced by a more normal government representing at least some civilian political forces. The initial candidates were the leaders of the new Constitutionalist Party, first José Sánchez Guerra and then Melquiades Alvarez, but they were met with continued abstention by most remnants of the old parliamentary parties and were unable to form an effective government. None of the other major figures of the past generation would accept the royal invitation. No better option was found than to appoint an apolitical admiral of the fleet, Juan Bautista Aznar, who formed a very conservative cabinet of establishment politicians of the old guard without any new support. This represented a kind of last stand of the untraconservative circle still loyal to the king, who had run out of alternatives.

The Aznar government first tried to gain a modicum of legitimacy by restoring members of municipal councils and provincial assemblies dismissed by the dictatorship. Elections were momentarily postponed to allow the government to organize itself, and then on 16 March announced in a series of consecutive phases from local to national level. Elections for municipal councilors would be held on 12 April, voting for provincial assemblies (*diputaciones*) would follow on 3 May, full parliamentary elections on 7 May, and a new senate selected on 14 May. The Aznar government was met with a torrent of opposition from university students especially, with the Madrid student body in a state of virtual insurrection after police killed a student on campus, while the strike wave maintained its momentum. Calm returned only to some extent about the end of March, as the electoral campaign began.

The tactic of beginning the return to normalcy with municipal elections was not well chosen from the government's point of view, for the republicans' greatest strength lay in the larger cities. Urban balloting would attract the greatest attention and even before 1923 had been considered the only honest vote, fairly counted and beyond the grasp of rural and provincial *caciques*. Though they did not expect a strong showing in municipal elections to topple the monarchy by itself, the republicans and the left treated the municipal contest as a kind of popular plebiscite, and so did certain government ministers. The monarchists spent considerable time and money to guarantee a large conservative turnout, but their forces were divided, since remnants of the old Liberal and Conservative Parties refused to cooperate fully with the government and rejected the new authoritarian-minded Unión Monárquica Nacional. The old Liberals even hired a new-fangled Madrid advertising firm to improve their image, but the monarchist parties of the former regime had relied on systems of clientage and manipulation that could not be revived overnight. Moreover, the rapid social changes and increase in literacy during the past eight years would make the popular vote that much less easily influenced or manipulated.

Opening of the campaign coincided with the trial by court-martial of Niceto Alcalá Zamora, head of the Republican Committee and Provisional Government, and five other members who had been unable to escape arrest. This event dramatically demonstrated the weakness of monarchist sentiment in the media, among the intelligentsia, and among the urban middle classes in general. The head of the military tribunal actually favored absolution, and the final sentence was a mere token — six months. It was immediately suspended, placing the defendants at liberty. The trial was an overwhelming moral and political victory for the republicans, providing strong momentum for the campaign.

The republican parties and the Socialists stood united, while the CNT, as usual refusing to participate, left its members free to do as they pleased, generally increasing the republican and Socialist vote. The Republican Alliance avoided presenting any specific program, but campaigned vigorously for a decisive vote on behalf of progress and institutional change. Though the first elections took place only at the municipal level, there was little discussion of local issues. The debate centered instead on the future of national institutions.

The campaign raged at high pitch for the two weeks preceding the balloting, producing the most intense mobilization to that point in Spanish history. A news editor in Seville observed that the current contest, "so different from . . . previous elections, reminds us of the methods used in the presidential elections in America."[22] The Socialists in particular were aware of the countercurrent direction of Spanish politics, arguing that it would begin a major new trend in Europe. As Largo Caballero put it: "Our struggle is international as well as national. . . . If we overthrow the monarchy, fascism will also die in Europe."[23] That was altogether unlikely, but the Spanish republican initiative clearly represented a unique new departure in depression-era Europe.

The outcome was everything for which the Republican Alliance could have hoped. With an electoral census that registered 5,440,103 adult male voters, the turnout of 53.56 percent would have appeared small compared to most other west European countries, but in fact was clearly the heaviest participation in Spanish history, with the opportunity for fraud also distinctly less than ever before. Moreover, according to the "Article 29" electoral law of 1907, in districts where only one candidate or alliance presented itself, the existing slate was automatically elected. After the mandatory time for presentation of candidacies had expired on 5 April, the government applied this law, and no contest therefore occurred in districts — mainly rural and northern — in which 20.25 percent of the electorate resided. The actual participation rate for all parts of the country in which there were in fact elections amounted to 67.16 percent of the combined electorate for those districts.

A total of 81,099 municipal council seats were open to election. Monarchist candidates won 34,233 seats, nearly a third of them by means of Article 29 in rural districts. This amounted to 42.2 percent of all seats. Unclassifiable candidates, some of whom were probably monarchists, won 4,813 (5.9 percent), and the Communists, running as Leninist-Stalinist revolutionaries, some 67 seats. The Republican-Socialist alliance thus failed to win an absolute majority over all, but won massively in provincial capitals, where the republicans garnered 44.8 percent of the seats and the Socialists another 16.8 percent, with only 27 percent for the monarchists.[24]

Government leaders were shocked by the outcome and the Conde de

Romanones, minister of foreign affairs and the most influential figure in the cabinet, made a statement to the press before the evening was over that admitted "absolute monarchist defeat."[25] General Sanjurjo, commander of the Civil Guard, told cabinet members that the result would have a great psychological effect on his paramilitary constabulary, who could no longer be relied on "absolutely" to sustain the monarchy. En route to an emergency cabinet meeting the next day, Admiral Aznar replied to a journalist's query: "Is there a bigger crisis than that of a nation which goes to sleep monarchist and wakes up republican?"[26] All but two cabinet ministers agreed that the present administration had no alternative but to resign. As Romanones put it, "The Mauser [standard weapon of the Civil Guard] is an inadequate answer to the manifestation of suffrage."[27]

The members of the republican Provisional Government had expected to do well in the larger cities, but the extent of the victory stimulated them to press for a more rapid takeover than they had ever anticipated.[28] On the thirteenth of April, they issued a statement declaring that the municipal elections had "the value of a plebiscite" and called on the monarchy "to submit itself to the national will."[29] Responding to the Provisional Government's call for public demonstrations, exuberant crowds took to the streets in various provincial capitals and in the larger cities, often singing the "Himno de Riego" (anthem of early nineteenth-century liberalism) and the "Marseillaise."[30]

The king remained calm and at first seemed to believe that several options were still open. Romanones, however, feared that the pretorian tradition of the Spanish army was not at an end and that military units might precipitate an armed revolt. He sent the king a written note on the morning of the fourteenth advising him that "the only solution" was to leave the country as quickly as possible.[31] Don Alfonso soon agreed, although he first proposed to set up a regency council to administer the interests of the crown and to form a constituent government that would hold regular elections and convene a new constitutional parliament.

The Republic was first proclaimed at 6:00 A.M. on the fourteenth by newly elected Republican municipal councilors in the Guipuzcoan industrial town of Eibar (where the Socialists were strong), an action repeated in several other cities during the morning and early afternoon. About 1:30 P.M. the mayor of Barcelona placed the government of Spain's second city in the hands of the left-wing Catalanist Lluis Companys and other newly elected Republican councilors. An hour later the seventy-one-year-old Francesc Macià, head of the militant Estat Català and the larger Esquerra confederation of left Catalanist groups, declared from the provincial government: "In the name of the people of Catalonia I proclaim the Catalan state, under

Lluis Companys, first Republican mayor of Barcelona, carried on the shoulders of his supporters to city hall

the regime of a Catalan Republic, which freely and with complete friendliness urges the collaboration of the other peoples of Spain in creating a Confederation of Iberian Peoples. . . ."[32] Within a few minutes this message was transmitted by radio to all Spain.

In the meantime Romanones had gone to the residence of Alcalá Zamora "with a white flag," as he put it, asking that the Republicans agree to formation of a new Constitutionalist government to hold constituent elections. Alcalá Zamora refused, demanding that the king leave the country "before sunset."[33] By 4:00 P.M., as large, animated Republican crowds were forming in the center of Madrid, General Sanjurjo came to declare his loyalty and that of the Civil Guard to the Provisional Government, while army commanders pointedly refused to take any action in support of the monarchy. Berenguer, now minister of war, admitted that all was lost and D. Alfonso, without formally abdicating, agreed to leave Spain immediately. By 8:00 P.M. Republican leaders had taken over the Ministry of the Interior, from whose balcony on the Puerta del Sol Alcalá Zamora officially proclaimed the inauguration of the Republic in accord with the "national will."[34]

The Provisional Government thus took power peacefully amid general euphoria. The large crowds and exploding popular enthusiasm seemed to indicate that a dramatic popular change was occurring. Republicans hailed the turning toward a progressive and successful modern Spain, free of the contradictions and limitations of the nineteenth century. Comparisons with the French Revolution were often heard, but to the advantage of the Spanish Republic, born without violence. *La Voz*, one of the most ardently Republican newspapers in Madrid, declared, "Spain, the master of its own destiny. The new regime comes in pure and immaculate, without blood or tears."[35]

Such enthusiasm was understandable, but the historical comparison betrayed more than a little confusion. The French Revolution had degenerated into repression and violence only after three years, so that any future parallels with its phase of maximum conflict could be expected only in a later phase, one which was as yet unforeseen. Moreover, the French Revolution both in its initial constructive phase and in its final working out after 1830 had taken the form of elitist liberalism under parliamentary monarchy, the system that had been introduced into Spain as early as 1812 and overthrown, as it turned out for the final time, in 1923. A more exact historical parallel might have been the founding of the Third Republic in France in 1871. The latter, however, had for a decade taken a very conservative form that increased its stability and was far from the mood of the new government and its followers in Spain. The Spanish Republic was indeed based on the ideals of 1789, but was also intended to go beyond liberty, fraternity, and democracy toward some degree of equality, a fundamentally social democratic project of broad reform, reflected in the often deliriously approving mood of large sectors of the ordinary population.

The difficulty that Spain faced in achieving stability and a reasonable degree of consensus under an advanced form of Republican democracy in the early 1930s might be better understood if the relative level of cultural, social, and economic modernization of the country at that time is considered. Though impressive and accelerated progress had been achieved during the generation roughly from 1910 to 1930, this constituted only the first major step in raising Spain to the level of northwestern Europe. In fact, it still remained several entire generations behind. On the basis of civic culture, literacy rates, and economic development, it might be judged that by 1930 Spain was at the level of England in the 1850s and 1860s or France in the 1870s and 1880s. Neither mid–nineteenth-century England nor even France at the beginning of the Third Republic had to face such severe political tests as Spain underwent in the 1930s. Early Victorian England lived under a controlled system of modernizing oligarchy.

Crowd celebrating the advent of the Republic in the Calle de Alcalá, center of Madrid, 15 April 1931

France, after emerging from the second Bonapartist dictatorship, was faced with revolutionary insurrection in only one large city, and that was suppressed with a concentrated ferocity exceeding anything by either side in the Spanish Civil War. Aside from the equivocal experience of the Commune, the working-class movement was very weak in France during the first decade of the Third Republic, but at a similar stage of development in the 1930s Spanish political society was subjected to severe pressures of mass mobilization.

The new Republican project thus bore little comparison either with the French Revolution or the founding of the Third Republic in France. Rather, it represented a significant new departure in liberal democratic and, to some extent, social democratic reformism during an era of fascism and right authoritarianism in central, southern, and eastern Europe. To that extent it marked the second time in little more than a century that Spain had led the way in attempted liberalization. Just as the original Spanish liberal constitution of 1812 and its restoration in 1820 had inspired a generation of liberals in such disparate lands as Italy, Germany, and Russia, so the Second Republic would represent a major new effort in democratic reformism during a decade when the current was running strongly in the opposite direction. The liberals of the early nineteenth century had nonetheless failed, for Spanish society was not adequately prepared for liberal government and the international climate was hostile. Accelerated new development had helped to make possible the breakthrough of 1931, but the danger remained that this same progress might have promoted a kind of developmental trap, stimulating major new demands and mobilization without having completed the growth of the means with which to satisfy them.

The Republican coalition rested on a broad alliance between the Republican left, the Republican center-right, and the Socialists. Head of the Provisional Government and founding prime minister was Niceto Alcalá Zamora, who before 1923 had been the leader of one of the minor factions of the old Liberal Party and was twice minister under the old parliamentary regime. A distinguished lawyer and legal scholar, Alcalá Zamora was a man of considerable culture and a practitioner of the most florid Andalusian rhetoric. He was capable of generating an endless loquacity replete with old-fashioned literary flourishes, a style already becoming anachronistic. Like most Spanish politicians, he had a strong sense of ego and was pronouncedly personalistic in political manner and style, yet he was also a sincere liberal in the nineteenth-century fashion. He had long been a monarchist and veteran of the "old politics" and in 1931 was one of the most recent major converts to Republicanism. His liberalism was combined with a devout personal Catholicism, rare among Republican leaders. This, together with his position as senior leader of the new Liberal Republican Right, the most conservative of all the Republican groups, made him a symbol of Republican moderation and reliability, calculated from the start to reassure conservatives.

Three other moderates also held posts in the first Republican government: Alejandro Lerroux (foreign minister), his chief lieutenant in the middle-class Radical Party, Diego Martínez Barrio (minister of communications), who was head of the Radicals in Seville, and Miguel Maura (minister of the interior), junior co-founder of Alcalá Zamora's party. The Radicals now represented the main force of the Republican center-right and grew rapidly in support among the moderate sectors of the middle classes. The center-right stood for political and to some extent institutional change, but only for a limited cultural transformation. They opposed any drastic social or economic reform. They understood Republican democracy primarily as a liberal democratic political system, as a new and freer set of rules of the political game, but not necessarily a far-reaching project of structural change.

The real fulcrum of the coalition were the parties of the middle-class Republican left, whose concept of the Republic extended well beyond a change in the rules of the political game to embrace a drastic cultural revolution as well as social reform (though the latter goal remained comparatively vague and limited). Their most important group was the Republican Action Party, led by the writer and civil servant Manuel Azaña (minister of war) and Marcelino Domingo (minister of public instruction). Associated with them was the Galicianist ORGA, represented in the government by Santiago Casares Quiroga (minister of the navy), and also the Catalan Esquerra, represented by Nicolau d'Olwer (minister of economics). The most extreme sector of the middle-class left was the new Radical Socialist Republican Party, which sought to pursue more extensive cultural and social, and even possibly economic, reform. The Radical Socialists were represented in the cabinet by Alvaro de Albornoz (minister of public works).

Much was soon to be made of the masonic membership of many Republican politicians. For over a hundred years the Masonic Order had been intensely combatted in Spain by Catholic conservatives, who saw in Masonry the spearhead of liberal anticlericalism. A sizable cross section of Republicans were indeed Masons, but historians would later point out that Masons themselves became increasingly politically divided, in some cases ending up on opposite sides in the Civil War. Spanish Masonry clearly did not represent any monolithic conspiracy,[36] though it is also true that by the second year of the Republic the dominant sector of Madrid Masons would become strongly committed to left Republican politics, in turn provoking considerable resistance among the more moderate members of the order.[37]

The extreme left of the coalition consisted of the Socialists, who had three representatives in the government: Francisco Largo Caballero (minister of labor), Indalecio Prieto (minister of finance), and Fernando de los Ríos (minister of justice). On 22 February, 1930, a joint meeting of the national committees of the Socialist Party (PSOE) and the trade union federation (UGT) had decided by a combined vote of thirty-five to twelve to remain in the coalition and participate as a full ally in the new government. This decision was not subjected to a thorough analysis,[38] but generally held that a fully democratic Republic committed to basic modernization and change would complete the development of "bourgeois democracy" in Spain, eliminate residues of "feudalism" and traditionalism, initiate bold social and institutional reforms, and generally clear the way for a transition to some unspecified model of socialism in some unspecified manner at some unspecified point in the future. Even less than the Republican left did the Socialists identify the new system with formal democratic practice as an end in itself, defining their ultimate goals for the Republic in terms of far-reaching institutional and socio-economic changes.

The decision to participate in the Republican government was approved

The Provisional Government of the Republic, 30 June 1931

for the opening phase of the initial consolidation of the new regime, when the government might be expected to be at its weakest, and did not necessarily extend to permanent participation in "bourgeois reformist" democratic government. Even so, the Spanish Socialist Party had now gone beyond its French counterpart (and earlier model), for the French Socialists still rejected direct government participation in the Third Republic. They had formed victorious electoral coalitions with the middle-class liberals (primarily the French Radical Party) in 1924 and would do so again in 1932, but French Socialists would go no further than to provide parliamentary voting support for ministries made up essentially of middle-class liberals. Among the larger Socialist parties, by 1931 the Spanish ranked second only to the Germans in their degree of democratic collaborationism.

With the exception of the chief moderates — Alcalá Zamora and Lerroux — the Republican leaders and politicians had very little practical political experience. They represented not merely a new generation but also new sectors which had played very limited roles, if any, under the previous parliamentary regime. With the partial exception of the Socialists, they came primarily from the more liberal and radical sectors of the intelligentsia and the professional classes, but had little continuity with the older elites and professionals who had led the old parliamentary system. From the Republicans' own point of view, this was primarily an advantage, for they were uncorrupted with the "old politics," but their inexperience and doctrinaire approach left them with no point of contact with large moderate and conservative sectors of the middle classes that did not share their political goals.

The Republican leaders were impressed by the recent surge in strike activity, much of it at least partially political in intent, and with the exuberant crowds in the streets of the larger cities. What they did not fully grasp, however, was that for hundreds of thousands, indeed millions, of workers and farm laborers the Republic was hailed as the beginning of what was expected to be a great improvement, perhaps a decisive change, in their own situation. Thus the Republic bore not merely the dreams and ideals of middle-class politicians and ideologues, but the diffuse expectations of millions of ordinary Spaniards that a new era of drastic reform had begun.

Though attitudes toward the Republic might vary greatly in different sectors, there was very little overt hostility. From abroad, Alfonso XIII advised his followers to cooperate with the new regime. Judging from the general response, even many of those recorded as having voted for monarchist candidates, or at least of not having voted for Republicans, adopted a relatively benign, if passive, attitude toward the new regime. Initially, the hard-core opposition amounted to no more than 15 percent, probably less, of the electorate. This was composed of the extreme right — the very small Carlist minority, the limited number of diehards of the dictatorship (Unión Monárquica Nacional), and a small residue of ultra-conservative monarchists — plus the revolutionary left of the tiny Communist Party, which rejected the Republic as simply a more up-to-date form of bourgeois repression.

The Provisional Government found itself in a technically revolutionary situation, having been allowed to take over without any resistance and occupying full power without the benefit of legal process. It moved quickly to regularize its constitutional situation, first with a decree on the evening of 14 April temporarily giving Alcalá Zamora the legal power of chief of state (in place of the king) as well as president of government (prime minister). On the following day the official new *Gaceta de la República* published the text of a special Juridical Statute that was promulgated to provide a legal and constitutional code for state and society in the interim before the completion of a new constitution.

The statute contained six basic provisions:

1. It promised a new Constituent Cortes to prepare a democratic constitution based on "norms of justice," to which all acts of the Provisional Government would be submitted for judgement, but in the meantime the

latter reserved *plenos poderes* (full powers) of law and government, "subject to juridical norms."

2. It pledged to prosecute (*a juicio de responsabilidades*) public acts of wrongdoing that had not been prosecuted completely prior to the dictatorship or had been committed by the extraparliamentary governments of 1923–31.

3. It proclaimed complete freedom of belief and religion, implicitly abrogating the Concordat of 1851 that had given the Catholic Church a privileged position.

4. It guaranteed civil rights as well as "syndical and corporative freedom," declaring the latter the "basis of new social law," an explicit pledge to trade unions.

5. "Private property is guaranteed by law. Consequently, it cannot be expropriated except for reasons of public utility and after appropriate indemnity. But this government adopts as a standard of policy that agrarian law must correspond to the social needs of landowning."

6. "The government reserves the right to restrict civil rights by law (*un régimen de fiscalización previa*), subject to parliament when elected."

The statute was a faithful and honest statement of the government's plans. It promised a democratic constitution, while emphasizing that in the meantime it would keep a tight rein on government, and made pledges with regard to trade unions and the need for some kind of property or labor reform in the countryside.

The government declared an amnesty for all existing political prisoners at the same time that it pledged there would be no amnesty for the leaders of the dictatorship. The "Himno de Riego" was proclaimed the national anthem in place of the "Marcha Real" and the red and yellow flag, official since 1785, was altered to a Republican tricolor by addition of a third, purple (*morado*) stripe.

The government's first major problem stemmed from its Catalanist allies. Francesc Macià — tall, lean, fiery-eyed, and white-mustached, an ex-army colonel who looked the spitting image of an elderly Catalan Don Quijote — was now the dominant figure in Barcelona,[39] where he had unilaterally announced on the fourteenth a "Catalan republic" within an "Iberian Federation," none of which was part of the Pact of San Sebastián. He went ahead, also unilaterally, to appoint the chief state officials in Catalonia. Therefore three of the new Republican cabinet ministers hurried to Barcelona, where they emphasized the importance of abiding by the pact, which had promised a Catalan autonomy statute as part of an orderly, not unilateral, constitutional process. A deal was soon cut with Macià, who was not so much trying to subvert the pact as accelerate the process, by which the Catalanists renounced any immediate pretension to a Catalan state in return for the immediate establishment of an autonomous executive power, the Generalitat, in Barcelona for all four Catalan provinces and the power to prepare the terms of their own autonomy statute, subject to a popular referendum in Catalonia and approval by the impending Republican Constituent Cortes. On 21 April Alcalá Zamora signed a decree establishing the Generalitat, which in the interim would have authority over education, public works, finance, and health services.[40] Alcalá Zamora made his first state visit to Barcelona on 27 April and was enthusiastically received, though the beginning of de facto Catalan autonomy was received with hostility in some other regions, where there was talk of a boycott of goods from the "separatist" region.

Aside from a small number of deaths accompanying the abortive revolt and strike of December 1930, introduction of the Republic had been nearly bloodless. Political violence nonetheless quickly reappeared in Barcelona, at the initiative of the local anarchists. Gunmen of the FAI and CNT responded to the restoration of civil liberties in 1931 as they had in 1922, with a series of assaults on their archenemies of the rightist Sindicatos Libres.[41] Within less than a month, twenty-two anti-CNT workers had been shot and killed,[42] but there were no prosecutions and apparently not even any arrests, since the killers were all leftists. It was up to the more responsible editors of the CNT's official Solidaridad Obrera to publish an editorial on 22 April, entitled "It's Time to Stop," calling on CNT and FAI organizational committees to declare "that they are completely opposed to a return to individual atentados, a procedure that is completely inefficient in the material order and in the moral order renders abhorrent those who resort to such tactics." This first new wave of anarchist violence appears to have been brought under control by the anarchists themselves.

During its first weeks the new Catalan government enjoyed a honeymoon in its relations with the CNT. Esquerra leaders were convinced that political violence in the past had stemmed from repressive rightist policies. The police averted their eyes from the initial wave of anarchist violence, and Lluis Companys, the new provincial governor of Barcelona, ordered in May large-scale destruction of district police records, wiping clean the slates of innocent workers, anarchist murderers, and common criminals alike. As head of the new Generalitat, Macià insisted to anarchosyndicalists that "I am your brother."[43] Many cenetistas (members of the CNT) had voted for the Esquerra in the municipal elections, and their prime organ described Macià as "an honest man" with whom they had an "alliance,"[44] though this would soon change.

Leaving Catalonia with its newly established limited autonomy, the Provisional Governnment took over control of all other regions, appointing *comisiones gestoras* (administrative commissions) of Republicans to replace all provincial governments elsewhere. It also replaced all municipal councils in which monarchists held the majority and on 30 April announced that new elections would have to be conducted in all municipalities in which formal protests had been lodged about unfair practices on 12 April (about 5 percent of the total).

There was no general purge of the state apparatus as a whole. Maura, the interior minister, quickly decreed that no regular state functionaries would be dismissed merely for political reasons, and thus the great majority of state employees hired under the monarchy remained in place. Numerous changes, however, were made at the higher levels, accompanied by a mad scramble of erstwhile Republican candidates (among whom were many new aspirants who simply declared themselves Republicans after 14 April). Some effort was made by the government to withstand the new tide of opportunism, but *enchufismo* (cronyism and favoritism) and even nepotism played a role, one of the clearest cases of the latter being the appointment of Aurelio Lerroux, the Radical leader's adoptive son, to a high post in the Telefónica. Maura later confessed to considerable frustration in finding competent appointees:

The [provincial] governors! They were the chief agents of the torture to which I was subjected for the five months that I remained on the rack in the Ministry of the Interior. The governors! Just thinking about them thirty years later gives me goose pimples!

The cream of the crop came to me from the Radical Socialist camp. Marcelino Domingo and Alvaro de Albornoz enjoyed a clientele that was simply unique and indescribable. One would clearly see that all the old elements traditionally resentful of the established order had moved into that party.[45]

During the first months the Provisional Government, in the absence of a parliament, governed by decrees, which subsequently would have to be approved by the Constituent Cortes. In some areas — particularly Labor, Public Instruction, and War — the ministers of the Provisional Government initiated the first steps in what had already been conceived as fundamental and far-reaching reforms. Decrees by the ministers of justice and labor provided security for renters of small agrarian properties (pending a broader agrarian reform), expanded existing legislation on worker accidents and compensation to include farmworkers for the first time, established an eight-hour workday, and extended the scope of labor arbitration committees to the countryside. The minister of public instruction initiated a drastic increase in new school construction, slightly raised teacher salaries, and decreed the beginning of coeducation in secondary schools. The minister of war began a long-range program for reorganization and modernization of the army, reducing the size of the officer corps and changing key aspects of its structure. A decree of 26 May reduced the number of divisions from sixteen to eight. The rank of lieutenant general and all the district captain generalcies were abolished. Plans were announced to promote massive early retirement of redundant officers, to reexamine all merit promotions under the dictatorship, and to close the General Military Academy that was commanded by General Franco. The military reforms, especially, were warmly received by progressive opinion, eliciting dithyrambs, for example, from the philosopher Ortega y Gasset.[46]

It was generally understood that the Republican parties had no higher priority than the secularization of politics and of society, though it was not immediately clear just how far they proposed to go. The first measures touching Catholics were a decree of 2 May forbidding sale or transfer of Church property and another four days later ending obligatory religious instruction in public schools. The Vatican initially counseled the hierarchy to show respect and moderation in dealing with the new regime. *El Debate,* the most prominent Catholic newspaper, recommended cooperation combined with new political mobilization to defend Catholic conservative principles.

The first official Catholic pronouncement under the new regime was a pastoral letter by the Primate, Archbishop Pedro Segura of Toledo, dated 1 May, but generally published in the press only six days later. Segura repeatedly stated that the Church was not committed to any specific form of government, but gratefully saluted the fallen monarchy for its respect for the Church and support of the Catholic religion, a gesture that produced intense antipathy among many Republicans. He called for a "crusade" of prayer and repentance and announced that he expected the new regime to respect the rights of the Church. He also called for "prudent action" by Catholics in the political sphere, urging them to unite in order to elect Catholic delegates to the new Cortes and to oppose those who sought to "destroy religion." The pastoral immediately roused the ire of Republican anticlericals, who naturally considered it a call to political confrontation.

During the first week of May a sharp debate took place in the Catholic press over the proper political course. *El Debate* advised a policy of "accidentalism" and of accepting the lesser evil. The leading monarchist daily *ABC* insisted that only the monarchy could guarantee a Catholic social order. The pragmatists among Spanish conservatives soon laid plans to organize a large movement of "Acción Nacional" that would be "neutral" on the issue of regime but devoted to safeguarding conservative and Catholic interests. For hard-core monarchists, however, this was inadequate, and after a few weeks they made plans to organize a new "Círculo Monárquico Independiente" (Independent Monarchist Circle) and to launch a campaign of propaganda and economic warfare that would rapidly discredit the Republic at home and abroad.

The Provisional Government generally maintained a tight rein on public order and denied the monarchists, or any other force seeking to overturn the new regime, the right to hold public meetings or demonstrations, though closed private meetings were permissible. The first private meeting of the "Círculo Monárquico" was thus authorized by police for a location near the center of Madrid on Sunday, 10 May. Subsequent reports indicated that the monarchist anthem was loudly played through open windows, after which young enthusiasts moved outside onto the sidewalk cheering the monarchy, producing a scuffle with Republican onlookers. The police immediately closed the new monarchist center and arrested numerous participants,[47] but a rumor that monarchists had killed a taxi driver spread rapidly and by mid-afternoon a mob gathered to set fire to the offices of *ABC*. According to newspaper reports, someone fired on the crowd, wounding two, after which the mob attempted to charge the building.

At this point, barely a month into the new regime, a basic problem of public order in early twentieth-century Spain presented itself. Municipal police were weak and quite incapable of serious crowd control. On any major occasion, units of the Civil Guard had to be summoned, but the Civil Guard was a paramilitary national constabulary (originally founded in 1844 on the model of the French Gendarmerie). Designed to maintain order in the countryside, they had no training in restrained crowd control and were normally armed only with Mauser rifles. When the mob rushed the building, the squad of Civil Guards defending it lowered their rifles and fired, killing two and wounding many more.[48] A tragic pattern of crude provocation and brutal retaliation had begun.

That night the government met in the Ministry of the Interior while a mob outside howled for Maura's resignation. Cabinet members were well aware of the anarchy that had consumed the First Republic in 1873–74, and Maura especially was determined to maintain order. He warned that members of the Ateneo, the leading liberal cultural society (of which war minister Azaña was president), were already distributing lists of churches and other religious buildings to be torched the next day. Azaña, however, refused to intervene among his society's members and vigorously led opposition within the cabinet to further use of the Civil Guard.[49]

Soon after the government reconvened on the morning of the eleventh, word came that the threatened *quema de conventos* (burning of religious buildings) had begun. Maura has quoted Azaña as saying on this occasion that "all the convents of Madrid are not worth the life of a single Republican" and as haughtily announcing to his colleagues that he would resign "if a single person is injured in Madrid because of this stupidity."[50] According to Maura, the only other cabinet members who understood the gravity of the situation were the Socialists, Prieto and Largo Caballero, but in view of the attitudes of nearly all the other Republican leaders they were not going to accept any responsibility for calling the Civil Guard. Not only did the government refuse to protect Church property, but it agreed to receive a delegation of the arsonists. Maura then went home and was preparing to resign when he learned that the government had reversed itself. After further information on the continued torching of churches and other religious buildings, the cabinet reluctantly concluded that it must intervene. Instead of authorizing use of the police or Civil Guard, it had decided to declare martial law and call out the army in Madrid! This spastic behavior, first of failing to adopt normal prudent measures and then of overreacting in an excess of violence, would become fairly standard procedure for Republican government.

On 12 May church burnings spread to Seville, Granada, Málaga, Cádiz, Alicante, and other cities in the southeast. Before it was over, more than one hundred religious buildings had been burned or sacked in whole or in part. The attacks were most severe in Málaga (forty-one burnings), the Valencia region (twenty-one), Alicante (thirteen), and Madrid (eleven). There was uncertainty about the identity of the arsonists. In Madrid the initiative had been seized by radical liberals of the Ateneo, who were followed either there or elsewhere by anarchists and Communists. The bulk of the destruction took place in cities where the FAI-CNT was strong. In every case, the disorders were easily brought under control as soon as local authorities made any effort to do so. There were no fatalities, the animus of the mobs being directed against church property, as in 1909, rather than against the persons of the clergy, as in the first anticlerical riots of 1835. In the process, important churches and schools and priceless artwork were destroyed or damaged.[51] Maura was ultimately given carte blanche to deal with future disorders. He fired the national police chief (director general of security), five provincial governors, and numerous lesser employees for negligence, though no effort was made to apprehend and prosecute the hundreds of people who had participated in arson.[52]

The shock effect of the *quema de conventos* on moderate and conservative opinion was great. Even one liberal Republican group, Ortega's "Agrupación al Servicio de la República," released a long statement declaring that the government needed to take more firm and effective action. All this pointed up the need for a modern police force, trained and equipped for orderly crowd control. The only regulation concerning such things in the Civil Guard was the mandatory *tres toques de corneta* (three bugle sounds) before opening fire. This would never do for a democratic Republic faced with increasing social agitation,[53] and on 15 May the government made the initial decision to create a new, more urban national police force. This soon took shape as the dark-uniformed Guardias de Asalto,[54] chosen by strict personnel standards (with a minimum height of one meter eighty centimeters), subject to rigid discipline, and armed with pistols and billy clubs rather than infantry rifles. The new corps of thirty thousand, approximately as numerous as the Civil Guard, was to be ready by the autumn.

The most immediate consequence of the *quema de conventos*, however, was a certain radicalization of reform policy to appease the left. More monarchist militants were arrested, and on 18 May the Bishop of Vitoria was expelled from the country for "subversive" actions. On 22 May the government declared complete religious liberty, while forbidding the further presence of holy images in public schoolrooms (emphasizing that the practice of kissing statues was unsanitary). On 30 May the Vatican demonstrated its displeasure by refusing to accept the credentials of Luis de Zulueta, the new Republican ambassador. On the following day the government retaliated by temporarily suspending *El Debate.* The Spanish Church hierarchy responded by publishing a collective letter of protest on 3 June, insisting that the full and equal freedom of all religions and the proposed separation of church and state violated the Concordat of 1851, while protesting the secularization of cemeteries and the elimination of obligatory religious instruction. The Cardinal Primate, Segura, had fled Spain after 11 May, when the government refused to guarantee his personal security. His comments abroad were highly critical, and one day after his return in June he was arrested and summarily deported. Meanwhile, various incidents took place in provincial towns. In a number of these, new Republican town councils threatened to confiscate Church schools. In August, after the vicar general of Vitoria had been arrested at the border bearing various letters of Segura with instructions to sell items of Church property and place the funds abroad, Segura was forced to resign his archbishopric.

Only a month had been required to bring confrontation, violence, and the entry of the army into the streets under martial law. A clear and promising beginning had begun to cloud.

3

The Republican Constitution

THE Provisional Government promised elections for a new constituent parliament on terms that would break completely the old system of managed or corrupt elections. The new legislature would be unicameral, the senate having been abolished. In place of the old structure of single-member constituencies, so readily manipulated by *caciquismo*, a new electoral law of 8 May established a list system of large multi-candidate districts. This was organized by province on the basis of one seat for every fifty thousand population or fraction greater than thirty thousand, with the further provision that any city with a population of one hundred thousand or more would itself constitute a separate electoral district. Moreover, the Republican government adopted a variation of the Italian Acerbo law, designed to prevent fragmentation. The electoral list that gained an absolute majority in any district was guaranteed 80 percent of the seats in that district, and if the list with the largest vote in a given district gained only a plurality, it was guaranteed 67 percent of the seats. The largest list in a district was by the same arrangement limited to a maximum of 80 percent of the seats, always reserving 20 percent for the minority (second largest total), provided that the latter gained at least 20 percent of the vote. Moreover, every voter had the right not to vote for all the seats in his district and might limit himself to voting for only 80 percent of them. The voting age for men was reduced from twenty-five to twenty-three, with the issue of female suffrage to be decided by the new parliament. Women and clergy would, however, be eligible to run for parliament, and several of both would be elected, producing the first elected women deputies in Spanish history.

The minister of the interior issued categorical instructions that local authorities were in no way to interfere with the electoral process, and there is no doubt that the three Republican elections were by far the most honest and democratic in Spain to that point. Yet irregularities still sometimes occurred, and Republican governments did not entirely refrain from involv-

47

ing themselves in the electoral process. Many senior state administrators stood for election, beginning with the undersecretary of the interior and including numerous director generals of ministries and provincial governors (though not as candidates in the same provinces they were governing).

Partial municipal elections were first held on 31 May in 882 towns, including four provincial capitals, where evidence of corruption had been presented after the 12 April elections had led to monarchist victories. In these partial municipal elections, according to the keenest student of the Republican transition,

. . . the major trend . . . led to an almost complete Republican victory, in a proportion of 8 to 1. But it ought to be pointed out that the "Republican" victory in May like the "Monarchist" victory of April had *caciquista* connotations. In both cases the rival was discriminated against, even "persecuted." . . . The unequivocal result, therefore, was that by the June elections, Republicans had assured their predominance in hundreds of rural Ayuntamientos [municipal councils] by substituting for Monarchist caciquismo their own brand of electoral management.[1]

In several areas an ad hoc "Civil Guard of Republicans" was formed to patrol streets during the campaign, probably deterring opposition.

The Republican-Socialist coalition parties thoroughly dominated the parliamentary campaign, not through repression but through greater militancy and more effective organization. The right was still reeling from the aftershocks of the monarchy's collapse and proved unable to organize. The two principal conservative forces were thus a small new Catholic party called Acción Nacional and a new right-wing Agrarian Party, both concentrated primarily in northern and north-central Spain. Only in the Basque country and Navarre was there effective coordination among rightist groups, and altogether conservative parties presented only 123 candidates, compared with 144 for the Socialists alone and 608 for all the Republican parties.[2] More than a few conservatives quickly tried to turn their coats, sudden Republicanization probably going farthest in Galicia, where former monarchists quickly found new identities. The most blatant effort, however, took place in Colunga (Asturias) where an ephemeral "Republican-Monarchist Party" was formed.[3]

The new system obviously favored multi-party coalitions. In eleven districts where conservative influence remained significant, Republicans and Socialists ran unified lists. In twenty-seven districts there was a primary Republican-Socialist coalition, additionally flanked by smaller allied candidacies that hoped to win the minority seats. In twenty-five districts there was direct electoral competition between Republicans and Socialists, sometimes with two or more Republican parties running in competition with each other as well.[4]

Only four parties loomed as major forces.[5] The Liberal Republican Right (DLR) of Alcalá Zamora and Maura was the most conservative and, as it turned out, the weakest. It stood as the only Catholic Republican party and the one nominally most eager to receive monarchist converts. Yet though it presented 116 candidates, its campaign was not well organized and its national campaign subscription netted only fifty-eight thousand pesetas (about six thousand dollars).[6]

Lerroux's Radical Party occupied the center and quickly became the strongest moderate force, outstripping the Liberal Right in attracting former conservatives and middle-class moderates. Lerroux was fond of declaring that the Republic must be legalistic and moderate, or else would not be at all. His observation may have been correct, but it drew the ire of the left. His own admirers sometimes called him the "Spanish Tardieu," in reference to the current conservative prime minister of France, but the comparison probably exaggerated the extent of his conservatism.

To the left stood the petit bourgeois Radical Socialists, an imitation of its French counterpart in the early years of the century. The Radical Socialists hoped to appeal to workers and often spoke of "social justice" and "transformation of the legal concept of property." Their top leaders, Alvaro de Albornoz and Marcelino Domingo, were doctrinaire and extremist. Albornoz insisted that the Republic should not be conservative "because there is nothing to be conserved," and Domingo, that the new parliament should be "a convention, a stormy assembly."[7]

They were closely flanked by Azaña's Republican Action Party, which spoke little of socio-economic issues but was almost equally doctrinaire.[8] Azaña detested Lerroux's moderation and readiness to compromise even more than his reputation for corruption, inverting the latter's line to stress instead that "the Republic should be radical or cease to exist."[9] Azaña declared that as soon as the Constitution had been completed his party would seek alliance with the Socialists against the Radicals to guarantee a "revolutionary" and "secular" Republic.

At the left of the coalition stood the Socialists, now swelling into a mass movement with a large national trade union base for the first time. Though there was more than a little internal division, the dominant leadership kept the party firmly within the coalition. Largo Caballero, the minister of labor, spoke of a "legal revolution" and asserted that true "extremism would never take root in Spain."[10] The Socialists did not, however, attempt to hide all the differences between themselves and the Republican parties. Feeling the competition of the militantly revolutionary FAI-CNT, their spokesmen also stressed the circumstantial nature of the coalition, intended to hasten the coming of full socialism.

On the local level the alliance sometimes foundered, but not because of the Socialists. The most common divergence was for the other parties sometimes to exclude the DLR because of its conservatism, while in a few cases the Radical Socialists ran alone to avoid joining with the DLR. The most malleable of all were the Radicals, normally willing to ally either with the DLR or the leftist parties, as circumstances dictated.

Minor incidents of violence occurred during the campaign, but there is evidence of only two fatalities, one in the Basque country and the other in Granada. Several more petty incidents occurred. One instance was a Socialist assault on an election meeting of Melquiades Alvarez's new Liberal Democratic Party in Oviedo, which caused only limited damage but led to Alvarez's withdrawal from the campaign in protest.[11]

The elections of 28 June produced an overwhelming triumph for the Republican-Socialist alliance, with numerous individual variations according to districts.[12] The multi-party alliance system, combined with the option for limited voting, made it impossible to calculate the national vote totals for each party with absolute precision, but the closest approximations are presented in table 3.1.

Participation ranged from a low of 56 percent in Ceuta and 61 percent in the province of Almería to a high of 88 percent in Palencia. There was a certain amount of rightist abstentionism, but also no doubt concerning the predominantly liberal orientation of the electorate. The common pattern, already established under the old system before 1923, of higher participation in the north (except for Galicia) and lower participation in the south generally obtained. Though the right gained nearly all its seats in the conservative north, even there most of the vote went for the Republican alliance. The overall rate of abstention was 30 percent, high for some countries but low for Spain. There were no vast changes in participation between the three Republican elections, so it must be recognized that the mood of the electorate as a whole — not just of the core left — was more liberal than it would be in 1933 or 1936. (See table 3.2.)

Despite certain irregularities, this was much nearer an honest and genuinely democratic contest than anything seen before in Spain. Subsequently,

Table 3.1. Party Vote Totals in 1931 Elections

	Average Totals	Maximum Totals
Socialists	1,941,627	2,097,802
Radicals	1,755,948	1,629,507
Radical Socialists	1,283,514	1,487,873
Liberal Rep. Right	793,270	1,104,732

Source: Tusell, *Constituyentes*, 103.

Table 3.2. Parliamentary Seats Won in First Round, 1931

Republican Coalition	
Socialists	113
Radicals	87
Esquerra Republicana	36
Liberal Republican Right	27
Federalists	19
Galicianists	19
Republican Action	16
Radical Socialists	61
Independent Republicans	18
"Al Servicio de la República"	7
Liberal Democrats	4
Total	407
Opposition	
Basque Nationalists	6
Lliga Catalana	2
Agrarian Party	14
National Action	5
Traditionalists	4
Monarchists	1
Misc. rightists	19
Total	51

Source: Tusell, *Constituyentes*, 128.

there were more than a few charges of electoral fraud, and the Comisión de Actas of the new parliament examined the evidence in the more serious cases. Only in the province of Lugo was it judged that there were sufficient proofs to require a new election. The Comisión concluded that in several other provinces minor irregularities had occurred but not of sufficient magnitude to alter the results.[13]

The electoral law provided for a second round of balloting in provinces and districts where no single slate had gained at least 20 percent of the vote. Thus a series of second-round elections subsequently took place in twenty-eight districts. Of the forty-six seats at issue, the Socialists won ten and rightist groups won three, the remaining thirty-three seats going to various Republican parties, slightly more of them being won by the more leftist Republican groups.[14] Results in the second round thus did not differ enormously from the main contest, though a somewhat greater advantage was gained by Republican parties. Altogether, the final composition of the Constituent Cortes consisted of 327 Republicans, 123 Socialists and 54 rightists (including Basque nationalists).

The Socialists and the Radicals were the biggest winners. The PSOE emerged as a mass electoral party for the first time, while conversely, with the relative frustration of Alcalá Zamora's DLR, the Radicals stood as the chief force of moderate Republicanism. Lerroux, having gained 133,789 votes in Madrid and having been elected in four other provincial capitals, became the new hero of the center, who looked to him as the leader who could make the Republic safe for conservatism.

Two weeks after the election, the National Council of the Republican Alliance met on 11 July, and Lerroux and Azaña came to terms, agreeing to form a broad Republican parliamentary bloc of the Radicals, Republican Action, the Federalists, and several other smaller groups. Alcalá Zamora and Maura, given their relatively poor electoral showing, were all the more interested in retaining government office, and the composition of the cabinet was therefore not altered by the electoral outcome.

The Anarchist Offensive

The first challenge that the Republic had to face came from the anarchist left. During the dictatorship the hard-core anarchist affinity groups had organized into a small federation (FAI — Federación Anarquista Ibérica), with the aim of dominating the anarchosyndicalist CNT, which in 1930–31 rapidly expanded once more into a mass movement. The CNT had been the major force behind the strike activity that had pressured the final monarchist governments, but the honeymoon attending the founding of the Republic was brief. Despite the conciliatory policies of the Republican and Catalan governments, minor violence by *faístas* (militants of the FAI) broke out in Barcelona on May Day, and several other minor incidents occurred that month. From the end of April there were major strikes in seven provinces of the industrial north and agrarian south, as well as more numerous smaller strikes. *Cenetistas* undoubtedly played a prominent role in the *quema de conventos* on 12–14 May. As noted earlier, martial law was declared in Madrid on 12 May and soon extended to seven provinces in the south and east, and also to Logroño in the north. By that time disorders were occurring in the southern countryside (though little violence against persons), so that when martial law was lifted in Madrid on 21 May, it was continued in some parts of Andalusia.

The bloodiest incident in the first weeks occurred on the outskirts of San Sebastián on 28 May. Strikers from the neighboring port of Pasajes tried to march into the city but were barred by the Civil Guard, who, when the strikers persisted, opened fire, killing eight and wounding more than fifty,[15] leading to the declaration of martial law in the district. This event, together with the immediately preceding *quema de conventos*, posed the basic dilemmas of the public order problem under the Republic. The regime had begun with good intentions and an effort to placate the anarchist left, but at the same time prudently invoked for itself "full powers." Anarchists were at first permitted, in effect, to murder rightist Catholic workers in Barcelona with impunity, and no effort had been made to control the first arsonists who torched churches. As the matter quickly grew more severe, the government lurched to the opposite extreme, relying on the lethal Civil Guard and even calling out the army. Strikers and demonstrators who would not disperse were then ipso facto declared a free-fire zone. The conflict was doubtless inevitable within the existing context; anarchists rejected social democratic reformism and would not work with government-backed labor arbitration committees (*comités paritarios*), opting for direct action. Thus a general strike in Gerona led to a declaration of martial law in that district on 18 June, and twelve days later similar action was taken in Málaga, after a series of strikes there.[16]

Moderate anarchosyndicalist "constructionists" within the CNT favored more pragmatic tactics. When the CNT's first national congress since 1919 met in Madrid in mid-June, the main issues concerned the policy to adopt toward the democratic Republic and the construction of broader, more organized national labor federations (more similar to the UGT), which could replace local "wildcat" autonomy with more disciplined trade union action. The more moderate anarchosyndicalists wished to support a democratic regime that would guarantee full civil rights, labor freedom, and energetic efforts to implement greater social justice. Though the congress refused to endorse the Republic, it did approve a minimum program drawn up by the moderates to present to the government. The proposal to establish national federations of industry was carried by a heavy vote over bitter FAI opposition, and the leadership of moderates in CNT national offices was reaffirmed.[17]

The membership of the FAI itself was comparatively modest, at first little more than ten thousand, while the CNT claimed eight hundred thousand affiliates by August, but the advocates of direct action rapidly won converts among the new rank and file. *Faístas* preached a vague doctrine of "Libertarian communism" or totally decentralized communalism to be achieved by radical strikes and armed insurrection.[18] The first major labor action after the congress was the calling of a nationwide telephone strike by the CNT's *sindicato único* of phone workers for 4 July, the eve of the convening of the new Constituent Cortes. Service was at first disrupted in such large cities as Barcelona and Seville, UGT workers sometimes serving as strikebreakers. Since the CNT refused to work within the new legal framework of labor relations, Largo Caballero ruled the strike illegal. In the face of increasing labor violence, the first units of the new Republican Assault Guard that was being formed were given orders to "fire without warning," if necessary, and soon two thousand *cenetistas* had been arrested. The CNT's leading voice, *Solidaridad Obrera*, which had proudly declared on May Day that "Spain is the country of revolution without peer in Europe," was by 2 July warning that the new regime was fast becoming "a Republic administered by hangmen and murderers."

El Socialista had already stated on 13 June: "We do not hesitate to say it: All the gangsterism, all the crimes that have been committed in Barcelona, including the *ley de fugas*, are the indirect work of the Sindicatos Unicos. The National Confederation of Labor is a worker organization based on gunmen." And on 9 July:

When the dictatorship came, Catalonia — and especially Barcelona, including the workers — applauded the dictator, because they saw in the new situation the only way of freeing themselves from those dishonorable deeds. Soon after the dictatorship and the monarchy disappeared violence broke out again. In Barcelona everyone is armed; the syndicalists are given to every kind of excess. Where will this situation lead Barcelona?

The Republican *La Voz* lamented on 24 July: "Simply intolerable. The poor, weak Spanish economy cannot resist this continuous assault. Factories are closed. No one builds. Commerce is not sold. Secondary industries languish." Though this dirge was exaggerated, it reflected a common Republican reaction to the anarchist offensive.

Though the anarchists almost by definition could have no allies, their revolutionary stance was paralleled by the tiny Spanish Communist Party. The Eleventh Plenum of the Executive Committee of the Comintern, meeting in April 1931, hailed the definitive crisis of capitalism which was supposedly producing a revolutionary struggle in capitalist countries. Thus the Spanish Communist Party declared war on the Republic, with the aim of replacing it as soon as possible by a "Republic of Worker, Peasant and Soldier Councils," pure Soviet language from 1917.[19]

The only city in which both anarchists and Communists had significant strength was the Andalusian commercial and light industrial center of Seville, where peace had not existed even during the very first halcyon days of the Republic. The fourth-largest provincial capital in Spain, Seville was second only to Barcelona as an arena of labor agitation. By the first weeks of the Republic the CNT numbered approximately twenty-six thousand members — about 30 percent of the labor force — while the Communist CGTU (there called the Unión Local de Sindicatos) counted some fifteen thousand (nearly 18 percent). In 1931 Seville was the nearest thing to a center of Spanish Communism (the Communists having earlier taken over part of the local CNT), which held a monopoly over the dockworkers. By comparison, the UGT at first had only about four thousand members in Seville and did not grow significantly for two more years.

Communist demonstrations in Seville on 14 April had degenerated into mini-riots, while another demonstration the following day managed to engineer a jailbreak. Several gunstores were sacked, and an assault was even attempted on a local infantry barracks, producing much gunfire and one death. Martial law was first proclaimed in Seville on 16 April, the third day of the Republic, earlier than in any other part of Spain. Altogether, there were thirty-four local strikes between April and December, most of them occurring between April and July.[20]

One of the leading Republican generals, Miguel Cabanellas, was dispatched to Seville as district Captain General. He proposed his own solution to labor unrest: economic reform measures to increase employment accompanied by continuation of martial law, prohibition of strikes, closure of CNT and Communist trade unions, and deportation of revolutionaries, labor agitators, and local criminals to Equatorial Guinea. This was too much for the Socialist cabinet ministers to swallow; Cabanellas was eventually replaced and martial law lifted on 15 June.[21]

CNT affiliates in Seville strongly opposed Communists, but, like other regional groups, moved more and more toward the FAI. The major strike wave of June and July began to reach a climax on 18 July, with a violent strike demonstration, leading to a broader walkout two days later and more violence in which one *cenetista* and one policeman were killed. By 22 July it had become a general strike throughout Seville, seconded by the Communists. Martial law, after being lifted for only thirty-seven days, was reimposed and the CNT declared officially closed. Seville city police numbered only forty-nine men. They were totally inadequate to deal with the situation and were reinforced by an ad hoc civil militia. The principal atrocity of the entire strike episode took place in the early hours of 23 July when members of this conservative militia applied the *ley de fugas* to four Communist prisoners in Seville's central park, killing them outright. Later that day artillery was called to blast down a building which housed a bar run by a Communist. All disturbances were ended in Seville on 26 July, after at least twenty people had been killed (sixteen in the city and four in Seville province) and more than twice that number wounded.[22] A parliamentary investigating commission, led by Socialists, later looked into the killings on 23 July, but failed to reach any definitive conclusion.

On 1 August *Solidaridad Obrera* declared that "from now on we know that the Constituent Cortes are against the people. From now on there can be neither peace nor a minute of truce between the Constituent Cortes and the CNT." CNT syndicates did occasionally accept mediation of labor disputes by the civil governor of a given province, as in Catalonia and Cádiz, but the *faísta* line rejecting normal arbitration generally predominated. As the summer wore on, the anarchist leaders who had returned from exile with the coming of the Republic gained increasing support from the most active regional federations.[23] The long, bitter telephone strike was finally settled on moderate terms on 28 August, but one day earlier a new strike wave began in Barcelona when twenty thousand metallurgical workers walked out. Prisoners in a central Barcelona jail rioted and temporarily took it over, after which the Barcelona CNT, demanding the freedom of all its members arrested in recent months, declared a general strike on 3 September. Macià, the head of the Generalitat, who had led a subscription list to raise financial aid for the CNT telephone workers, persisted in his policy of appeasement. He seconded the new CNT demand for release of all its members held prisoner in Barcelona, but local government and police authority lay in the hands of the conservative Catholic Republican civil governor, José Anguera de Sojo (the third provincial governor in five months), who took a hard line and surrounded the local CNT headquarters with the Civil Guard. By the time the strike had ended, at least six people had been killed while many *cenetistas* had been arrested and placed for safekeeping on a prison boat.[24]

September was an agitated month elsewhere, as the general strike in Barcelona was followed by one in Zaragoza, and accompanied by many lesser strikes, sometimes with disorders, spread over at least eighteen provinces and producing several more fatalities. October brought more of the same, with strikes and incidents in at least a dozen provinces and several more political killings. Disorders were most persistent in parts of Andalusia and Extremadura.

Such widespread strikes and frequent violence, both by workers and by the authorities, were part of a dynamic process by which the FAI rapidly reversed the conclusions of the June congress of the CNT and established the hegemony of revolutionary anarchism. *Faísmo* was largely an urban phenomenon, with much less support among rural *cenetistas*, but this provided it with greater leverage. By the end of the summer the fusing of the acronyms — FAI-CNT — reflected a new policy of all out confrontation with the established social order and with the Republic itself.

Moderate CNT leaders found themselves representing a minority, at least in the cities. They took a public stand in the *treintista* declaration of 1 September, so named because it was signed by thirty more moderate figures, led by Angel Pestaña and Joan Peiró. They denounced *faísta* violence and revolutionism, saying flatly that it could lead to a "republican fascism." The *treintistas* stressed the need for labor education, practical trade union organization, sober goals, and a sense of political responsibility, threatening a complete break between their sector of labor syndicalism and revolutionary anarchism, yet the *treintistas* only drew firm support in Valencia and in the key Barcelona suburb of Sabadell, as *faístas* took over *Solidaridad Obrera* and dominated most of the CNT in Catalonia and elsewhere. There were even a few violent street altercations between the two sectors, some *treintistas* accusing the FAI of having the characteristics of a Leninist organization.[25]

Socialist Policy

The contrast between the policy of the FAI-CNT and that of the Socialists was the difference between night and day. During the final months of the monarchy and the first phase of the Republic, party leaders held to the idea that Socialist participation in the government was necessary to stabilize and protect nascent Republican democracy, and that the latter in turn would provide the necessary conditions for moving toward socialism. Associated with this was the predominant conclusion that the "bourgeois revolution" posited by Marxism had never been completed, and that for over a century the country had been living in a kind of halfway house of traditionalism and feudalism comingled with capitalism and a very limited kind of liberalism. This may have been an erroneous reading of Spanish history,[26] for nineteenth-century elitist liberalism had in fact clearly paralleled developments in northwestern Europe, and it confused the Republican middle classes and intelligentsia with the genuine bourgeoisie, which would soon become increasingly antiliberal, but this interpretation provided a theoretical and historical rationale of sorts for collaboration. The Republican breakthrough was certainly good for the UGT, which had had only 277,011 members at the close of 1930 but reached a total of 1,041,539 by June 1932, for the first time rivaling or exceeding the CNT in size.[27]

The issue of continued collaboration was the main theme of the Extraordinary Congress of the party which met in Madrid on 10 July, four days before the opening of the Constituent Cortes. The committee reporting on this question recommended continued collaboration until the Constitution was drafted and the first regular government established. Outside of Germany and Scandinavia, however, European socialist parties still echoed Second International orthodoxy and remained ambivalent on the issue of regular collaboration. The report therefore concluded that "the Party declares itself in principle against participation in power," but that the party should continue to collaborate in the future if necessary to avert the return of rightist forces or a major threat to the new reforms. The pragmatic Prieto, now fully recognized as the head of the social democratic center or right-center of the party, added to this an amendment that empowered the Socialist parliamentary delegation and the party's executive commission jointly to take future decisions about such fundamental problems whenever the situation might change or a new crisis appear.[28]

Opposition to continued participation came from the Madrid philosophy professor Julián Besteiro, who had succeeded the party's founder, Pablo Iglesias, as the central figure in the Socialist leadership after the latter's death in 1925, and from an ultra-left minority, which held that participation and reformism were both hopelessly inadequate and a trap, diverting the movement from its revolutionary goals.[29] Besteiro never wavered from his position that collaboration was wrong for the opposite reasons, because Spanish Socialism was still comparatively weak and immature, and hence would be inevitably compromised, diluted, and diverted from its true goal of building patiently and constructively for a socialist future. Besteiro had earned a reputation as the party's most distinguished Marxist theoretician. He held that Marxist doctrine was an idealistic hypothesis which became a reality in historical development, like the paradigms of scientific theory,[30] but that it was completely impossible to accelerate history artificially, thus reaffirming the one-time Kautskyist orthodoxy of the old Second International.[31] Besteiro urged that the party limit itself to contesting elections and working toward practical social reform in parliament. He had resigned his leadership positions in both the party and the UGT early in 1931, but later accepted the speakership of the new Cortes, hoping that he might facilitate reform legislation. At the July congress, he warned that under the present conditions continued government participation would lead either to the exploitation and dilution of the movement or a premature move toward a Socialist government which would then have to be dictatorial:

If we remain in power, in the long run we either allow ourselves to be taken advantage of by others or we have to exercise a strong hand and become dictators. And I fear a Socialist dictatorship more than a bourgeois dictatorship. We could defend ourselves from the latter; with the former we would ourselves be committing suicide.[32]

His abstentionist motion was rejected by the congress, which voted for Prieto's amended motion 10,607 to 8,362, a relatively close division which indicated that much of the party was not in complete agreement.

The greatest enthusiast of all was the UGT chief, Largo Caballero, in his new post as minister of labor. For the short, blue-eyed, elderly trade union leader, who had devoted all his life to practical organizational matters and labor reformism, this was almost a dream come true. Conversely, he had no patience with the CNT's extremism and refusal to engage in arbitration. On 21 July he demanded that the government take a stronger line on anarchist disorder.[33] By contrast, Prieto, who had initially pushed the collaborationist line and was a more sophisticated and adroit politician, harbored a streak of intermittent pessimism and before the end of year would talk of resigning as minister of finance because of the obstacles involved, while by that time Largo occasionally even speculated about an all-Socialist Republican government.[34]

Drafting the Constitution

The Constituent Cortes was timed to convene on Bastille Day, 14 July, prompting reminiscences of the French Revolution and the French Republics. Its membership was strikingly discontinuous with that of the last parliaments of the monarchy.[35] For the left majority, this was exactly as it should be — a complete break with a corrupt and retrograde monarchist past. In fact, the new assembly was lacking in practical political experience and in wisdom and was also out of touch with significant sectors of Spanish society. The breakdown of the old political organizations and the disarray of the right had left a large conservative and Catholic minority with little representation, and also had the effect of encouraging the Republican and Socialist deputies to believe that they were more representative of Spanish society as a whole than was in fact the case.

The new body was drawn predominantly from the professional and bureaucratic middle classes, who accounted for 81 percent of the membership, led by lawyers (150) and teachers and professors (80).[36] This also included the country's leading intellectuals, for the two most well-known Spanish philosophers, José Ortega y Gasset and Miguel de Unamuno, were both deputies, as were the noted physician and essayist Gregorio de Marañón and Ramón Pérez de Ayala, one of the country's two leading novelists (the latter co-leaders with Ortega of the small "Agrupación al Servicio de la República"). More remarkable was that the political advice and commentary of these sages was generally quite sound and more reliable than that of the leftist majority. Ortega, for example, recommended that the Constituent Cortes avoid rhetoric, vengeance, and counterproductive radicalism, and concentrate instead on pragmatic reform and economic issues.[37] This extremely pertinent advice was largely rejected.

In May Alcalá Zamora had appointed a special Comisión Jurídica Asesora (Advisory Commission) of thirteen members to prepare a constitutional draft project for consideration by the new Cortes. This commission was made up of moderates, who prepared a draft that would create a bicameral legislature and a presidency with broad powers, and who recognized full freedom of religion, including the Catholic Church, which would enjoy a special statute. This was so reasonable and moderate that it was quickly rejected by the Republican government. Instead a new constitutional committee was formed by members of the new Cortes. Chaired by the relatively moderate Socialist law professor Luis Jiménez de Asúa, it was composed of five Socialists, four Radicals, three Radical Socialists, two Catalanists, and seven members from other Republican parties. With both the Socialists[38] and Radical Socialists playing a prominent role, a draft text of 121 articles was completed and submitted to the Cortes on 27 August. Asúa announced it as "leftist but not socialist," "democratic, illuminated by freedom and deep social content." He cited as "maternal constitutions" that had helped to inspire it the Mexican document of 1917,[39] the first Soviet constitution of 1918,[40] and the German Weimar constitution of 1919. It defined the Republic as an "integral state," not a federal one,[41] and declared complete separation of church and state, with dissolution of all religious orders and the nationalization of their properties. Asúa also emphasized that the proposed constitution guaranteed the right to private property even though its goal would be "to proceed gradually to its socialization,"[42] the draft also giving parliament the right to confiscate property without indemnity.

Serious discussion began on 11 September, leading to three months of sometimes heated, often florid, and only occasionally eloquent debate, usually in long sessions that began at 4:00 P.M. and continued intermittently far into the night. The first dispute arose over the attempt of Socialists and Radical Socialists to define the new state in Article 1 as a "Republic of workers," which was not entirely acceptable to all the Republican left. Even more polemical was the dispute over the degree of autonomy that the Republican state would permit, for the Socialists and Azaña's Republican Action wanted to retain a stronger central state that would only grant limited autonomy to special regions. The final text thus read "Spain is a democratic Republic of workers of all classes, organized under a regime of liberty and justice. The powers of all its organs emanate from the people. The Republic constitutes an integral state, compatible with the autonomy of municipalities and regions."

Article 2 established the equality of all before the law, while Article 4 declared Castilian the official language of the Republic, adding that "every Spaniard has the obligation to know it and use it, without prejudice to the rights and laws which the state may grant to the tongues [lenguas] of provinces or regions." Other sections renounced war as an instrument of national policy, divided powers of government into those which were declared within the exclusive competence of the Spanish state (Article 14), those which were in spheres in which the state might legislate but which autonomous regions might administer (Article 15), and certain matters which were declared exclusively under the jurisdiction of any autonomous regions which might be created (Article 16). No agreement was reached concerning abolition of the death penalty, so that issue was omitted.

Article 36, which stipulated the right of all Spaniards twenty-three years or older to vote in elections of universal, direct, and equal suffrage, was highly controversial. The Radicals and the Republican left strongly opposed granting the vote to women because of their alleged conservatism and religiosity. The Radical Socialist Victoria Kent, one of three women elected, went so far as to affirm that "women are backward, reactionary and uncultured,"[43] but conservative feminists of the "Unión de Damas Españolas" proved surprisingly well organized. They presented a petition bearing the signatures of one and a half million women on behalf of the right to vote. An unusual alliance of Socialists and moderates and conservatives carried the issue by a vote of 160 to 121.

The next controversy focused on Article 44, which stated that:

Property in all its forms may be the object of mandatory expropriation in exchange for adequate compensation for reasons of social utility, unless a law passed by the absolute majority of the Cortes rules otherwise. . . . In no circumstance will the penalty of confiscation of goods be imposed.

Narrowly passed, this article was strongly opposed not merely by the small rightist minority but also by the little band of Republican conservatives led by Maura and Alcalá Zamora, and it almost precipitated the latter's resignation as prime minister.

The confrontation over Article 44 formed the prelude to the greatest single conflict, the controversy over separation of church and state. Much of Catholic opinion now accepted formal separation of church and state, yet sought special legislation that would guarantee complete freedom of Catholic worship and education, guarantee complete Church control of its properties, and provide for continuation of the *presupuesto eclesiástico* by which the state paid the salaries of parish priests. Quite conversely, however, the proposed draft declared that "the state will dissolve all religious orders and nationalize their property," and this was followed by a Socialist amendment on 13 October that would permanently ban all religious orders. It created an explosive situation in which even the Republican right threatened to go into opposition.

The final formula was somewhat more moderate. It was developed by Azaña, the firm and resourceful war minister, who had now emerged as the dominant figure of the Republican left. In the most widely quoted speech of the entire constitutional debate, he declared on 15 October: "I form the premise of the problem . . . in this manner: Spain has ceased to be Catholic." By this he did not deny that there were still many millions of Catholics in Spain, but that by the fourth decade of the twentieth century Catholicism had lost its formerly hegemonic role in politics, culture, and society. Azaña added that "on the one hand we have the obligation to respect freedom of conscience," yet insisted that protecting the security of the Republican state came first. Hence "let no one tell me that this is contrary to liberty, because it is a question of public health."[44] Rather than banning all orders, he urged, only the Jesuits need be expelled at that time, while subsequent legislation could be developed to ban all teaching by members of religious orders. There would be no special juridical recognition of the Church with regard to financial support, rights, or properties. These slightly softer terms were acceptable to the Socialists, who withdrew their amendment. The revised Article 26 was approved 175 to 59, provoking the walkout of the rightist minority and also the resignations of the two Catholic Republican ministers, Maura and Alcalá Zamora.[45]

The next article (27) guaranteed freedom of conscience, together with civil jurisdiction over all cemeteries. Article 29 provided for the right of habeas corpus, while further sections recognized the right of all churches to teach their own doctrines as they pleased within their "establishments," meaning church buildings.

Article 71 created the office of president of the Republic, chosen by a special electoral college for a six-year term. The president was empowered to designate a prime minister to lead the government and to ratify a cabinet of ministerial heads proposed by the latter, with the stipulation that a cabinet must have a parliamentary majority to remain in power. The president was given the authority to dissolve the Cortes as many as two times during a presidential term, but the second dissolution would have to be reviewed and approved by the resulting new parliament. If not approved, the president would be deposed (Article 81). He was given only a partial and limited veto power over legislation (Article 83). He could also be impeached and deposed by a three-fifths vote of parliament if found guilty of constitutional violations, or referred to the judgment of the new Tribunal de Garantías Constitucionales for criminal infractions.[46]

This model of presidency was based in considerable measure on that of the contemporary Weimar Republic in Germany and sought a sort of compromise between the American presidential and French parliamentary systems. In fact, as political instability increased after 1933, the de facto authority of the president steadily increased, and would make him axis and arbiter of the government and political system to a significant degree between September 1933 and February 1936.[47]

Section VII dealt with justice, Article 94 decreeing free and fair justice for all by an independent judiciary not subject to political removal, but accountable for their own civil and criminal responsibilities. The system of justice was made more unitary through the abolition of separate military and clerical jurisdiction (except in time of war). Though jurisdictional boundaries between various sections and levels were not fully defined, the system was crowned with a Tribunal Supremo and also a Tribunal de Garantías Constitucionales. The latter would have authority to judge the constitutionality of any legislation referred to it and was also given jurisdiction over the resolution of any conflicts between the Spanish state and any future autonomous regions.[48]

Title VIII, dealing with finance, was drawn in careful detail and specified that all taxes must be voted by parliament. Each year the government would be required to present one single unified budget proposal for parliamentary approval in October. Secondary or exceptional budgets as had been added under the dictatorship were specifically prohibited.

Other sections established lenient terms for divorce by either party to a marriage, provided equal rights for illegitimate children, and pledged that "the state will lend assistance to the sick and aged, and protection to maternity and infancy." The Constitution also recognized the Republic's responsibility "to assure every worker the conditions necessary for a dignified existence," and pledged that "education will be secular, will make labor the axis of its methodical activity and will be inspired by ideals of human solidarity."

The Constitution could be amended by a two-thirds vote of parliament during the next four years and by a simple majority vote after that time. In practice the growing fragmentation of politics would make it impossible to amend the Republican charter at any point.

In most respects, this was a standard liberal democratic constitution of the early twentieth century, influenced possibly more by Weimar than by any other extant document. It departed from other "middle class" parliamentary systems, however, in certain key respects. The Republican Constitution provided greater social guarantees, however vague and general the language, and explicitly addressed the issue of nationalization of property. Its treatment of the Catholic Church (as will be discussed more fully in the next chapter) went beyond separation of spheres, rejected the principle of a free church in a free state, and subjected the Catholic Church (though no other church) to severe restrictions and a measure of persecution, aspects of which—particularly the prohibition of teaching by the orders—would have severe consequences. The Constitution also moved farther in the direction of plebiscitary democracy than was the case with most of its predecessors, even in other democratic systems. Parliament was unicameral and would be elected by universal (not merely male) suffrage.[49]

Most Republicans were pleased with the Constitution, finally approved by the Cortes on 9 December. From the very beginning, however, it was subjected to the most severe criticism from the right and even from part of the center.[50] All Catholic opinion, with only the rarest exceptions, repudiated Article 26, while most conservatives were equally troubled by Article 44. Ortega y Gasset denounced the Constituent Cortes for sectarianism and hollow radicalism as early as 9 September,[51] labeling outspoken Radical Socialist extremists as *jabalíes* (wild boars), a nickname that stuck. He would later characterize the new document as a "lamentable Constitution, without head or tail, nor the remainder of the organic material normally encountered between head and tail."[52] On 6 December, as the Constitution neared completion, he gave a major lecture in Madrid which insisted that it was "necessary to rescue the profile of the Republic. . . . It remains incomprehensible that after the Republic was established so completely and with so little discord, virtually without wounds or suffering, within no more than seven months there is growing throughout the country discontent, vexation, disillusion—in a word, sadness."[53]

Formation of the Azaña Government

After passage of Article 26, Alcalá Zamora, who had resigned in protest, was succeeded as prime minister by Manuel Azaña Díaz, the fifty-one-year old writer and civil servant who held the Ministry of War. As recently as a year earlier, the rise of Azaña could not have been foreseen, but the events of 1931 showed him to be the most striking political personality and real leader of the bourgeois left, hailed by Ortega as the "revelation" of the Republic. Salvador de Madariaga, who often disagreed with Azaña's policies, would later characterize him as "the politician of greatest stature in the life of the Republic."[54]

Azaña had been born of an affluent family in Alcalá de Henares, a provincial town about twenty miles east of Madrid. Orphaned early, he was raised by his paternal grandmother and studied four years in the Augustinian college at El Escorial before gaining a law degree and then a doc-

Manuel Azaña Díaz

torate in law at the University of Madrid. As a very young man with an independent income, he led the life of a literary *señorito* (playboy) for a few years, but collapse of the family estate soon led him to take a position in the civil service. He became a chief clerk in charge of a department (*jefe de negociado*) in the notarial records office of the Ministry of Justice, a position that left him free time to write and later to enter politics. In 1913 he had been active in the new Liga de Educación Política formed by Ortega and others, and the following year he became an early member of Melquiades Alvarez's Reformist Republican Party. He was an outspoken supporter of the Entente during the war and twice unsuccessfully stood for a Cortes seat in the Reformist Party.

His literary work fell into three areas: literary criticism (especially a series of writings on the novelist Juan Valera); belles lettres (one novel and a theatrical drama, with another novel nearly finished by the time of the coming of the Republic); and didactic writing and translations (of which the most notable was his *Estudios de política francesa contemporánea*, though he completed only one volume on military policy). Azaña was very active in the Ateneo, Madrid's leading cultural center, serving several years as secretary and then being elected president in 1930. Thus for some time he had been known in the literary and cultural life of the capital, yet he had never published a truly major work and his writings attracted only limited interest. The mordantly critical Azaña defined himself as a "writer without readers."[55]

His greatest weakness as a politician, together with lack of experience, was probably his personality, which was aloof, acerbic, and arrogant in the extreme. Maura later observed, "The Azaña that I knew in 1930 lacked the most elemental human touch. When he wanted to be amiable he was severe. When he didn't care for someone, he became the prototype of gross behavior." He demonstrated "disdain for everything and everybody, born of the conviction that he was a misunderstood and unappreciated genius," often being "proud, disdainful, cutting without pity or grace, reserved even with those with whom he dealt daily, and pitiless in his judgment of other people and affairs; in a word, intolerable."[56]

Nor was his physical appearance prepossessing. Of medium height, stocky and overweight, bald and rather stooped, with an extremely pallid complexion, he had a glum, normally expressionless, and roundish face highlighted by several large moles, which became a cartoonist's delight. On the rare occasions when he smiled or laughed, he could be quite pleasant with his intimates. The latter were few in number, but very close. Azaña had married only at forty-eight, when he wed the very young sister of his best friend.

Despite tendencies toward intellectual withdrawal, Azaña was at the same time somewhat contradictorily drawn toward public life, in part

because he was a theatrical person who loved stage settings. He once dressed up as a cardinal at a masked ball and tended toward grandiloquence in the public arena. Some of his best writings were in the form of dialogue, almost as if on stage. Reality disgusted him, and at bottom he scorned it; he preferred to recreate it himself. Like many fine artists, he did not notice his own defects and errors; he believed it was the critics and public who were wrong.[57]

It was perhaps not accidental that his closest friend and brother-in-law was a noted theatrical producer.

The experience of the Primo de Rivera dictatorship had crystallized his political ideas and reoriented his activity. Azaña concluded that historic Spanish liberalism had been a failure due to timidity as well as weakness, due to not having been, as he put it, "radical" enough. He would not altogether have agreed with the standard observation elsewhere that politics was the art of the possible, for he believed that Spain possessed a unique opportunity to achieve a dramatic breakthrough and a decisive set of new reforms, which could only be successful if fundamental compromise with conservatism and Catholicism were rejected. One of his biographers has labeled his position "liberal intransigence,"[58] yet the term is not entirely appropriate. Azaña was not liberal in the liberal democratic sense but a radical liberal sectarian. At one meeting in 1930, he spurred his audience with the words "Do not fear to be called sectarian. I am a sectarian,"[59] and this was not mere rhetoric. Azaña was in some respects the last in a long line of radical liberal reformers of Spain's "long nineteenth century," convinced that his predecessors had failed because they had been too timid.

His strength lay in clear, firm ideas that crystallized the goals of the moderate left, in a willingness to lead without a hint of serious compromise or any whiff of corruption, and in his compelling oratorical ability. Maura observed,

The oratory of Azaña resembled no other. It was cold, hard, incisive, monotonous, and lacking tonalities of voice or gesture, but was nevertheless overpowering and fascinating. How many times listening to him from the front benches did I say to myself, "How can the oratory of this man convince, conquer and captivate the masses?" I never figured it out.[60]

His tongue and intellect made him both respected and feared, though his rhetoric eventually became counterproductive.

His famous lapidary and scalding phrases contributed more than a little to the hatred that the right came to feel for him. . . . He offered them with genuine delight and, knowing their effect, like a real masochist with regard to the enmity and hatred they created.

I once asked him the reason for that mania of wounding simply in order to wound, of never missing an opportunity to pour scorn on the opposition, and he replied, "I do it because it amuses me." I am sure that was correct. He positively enjoyed thinking of the effect he was having. Azaña was certainly no ordinary, commonplace character.[61]

But like many intellectuals in politics, he was also characterized by a profound ambivalence. Physically timid and constitutionally averse to violence, he yet was determined never to compromise. His undeniably great political energy and ambition were not boundless, for he lacked the patience, tolerance, and stamina for petty politics necessary during a long period of leadership, and he periodically suffered from deep moods of alienation and a yearning for withdrawal. On the morrow of electoral defeat in 1933, one follower was scandalized to come upon Azaña placidly reading an esoteric history of the Byzantine empire, a millennium removed in time and place.

What Azaña sought was a radical reformist Republic that would end not merely the monarchy but also the cultural and political influence of the Catholic Church and the dominant conservative oligarchies. This would be accomplished through incisive, even intolerant, institutional reform and through a broad new education program. His basic goals were those of nineteenth-century middle-class radicalism, and he sought to modernize Spain and alter its "national character" by completing the cultural revolution of the nineteenth century in the Spain of the 1930s. To Azaña, as to the left in general, the Republic was not so much a form or set of institutions—constitutional democracy and the rules of the game—as it was a specific reform project in church and state, education and government policy.

Like most intellectuals and writers, he was not really interested in economic affairs and had no particular program of economic modernization of the sort that Ortega sought. He seemed at first not fully to realize that in the 1930s the historical framework was no longer that of the nineteenth-century, for new challenges, hopes, and ambitions were creating radically different demands among Spanish workers to which the moderate left could not be indifferent.

There lay a deep irony in this, for Azaña had enough knowledge of basic Spanish society to realize that even in 1931 middle-class progressive Republicanism did not really represent a clear majority of the population, and that alliance with the main organized workers' party—the Socialists— was indispensable for the popular support needed to stay in power. He was much more concerned to maintain alliance with the Socialists than with centrist and conservative Republicans, whose support he felt necessary only during the drafting of the Constitution. The Socialists and the Republican left first began to come to a special understanding in September, when the Socialists decided to accept the basic principle of Catalan autonomy and the bourgeois left in turn indicated support for a more drastic agrarian reform than moderate Republicans favored.

When the anticlerical legislation provoked the resignation of Alcalá Zamora, Azaña became the obvious replacement, since the Republican left had now become the fulcrum of the governing coalition. The Socialists considered the centrist Radicals too bourgeois and basically conservative, while Lerroux and his Radical followers did not hide their increasing distaste for remaining in alliance with Socialists. In the second Republican government formed in mid-October, Azaña combined the Ministry of War with the office of prime minister, switching his Galician ally Santiago Casares Quiroga from the Navy to the key post of minister of the interior (replacing Maura). Though Lerroux remained in the cabinet as foreign minister, his days were numbered. The multi-party Republican-Socialist alliance was in the process of being rapidly reduced to an alliance of the Socialists and the left Republican parties, which would govern for the next two years. This would maintain the "frankly leftist" policies that Azaña insisted would be necessary to firmly establish the Republic.

At the same time Azaña had the practical sense to realize that some of the more extreme gestures of the left in the Constituent Cortes were counterproductive. For example, a special Responsibilities Commission had been created by the Cortes, and subsequent legislation empowered it to investigate and punish abuses of political power under the preceding regime in five areas: (1) Moroccan policy; (2) social policy in Barcelona before the dictatorship; (3) the pronunciamiento of 1923; (4) administrative and political responsibilities of the Primo de Rivera and Berenguer dictatorships; and (5) the Jaca courtmartials of Galán and García Hernández. The government endeavored to moderate this process as best it could, understanding the limited utility of vendettas and the difficulty in many cases of determining "responsibilities." The commission, however, quickly proceeded to arrest twelve men who were either elderly retired generals or comparatively minor civilian bureaucrats, more central targets being dead or in exile. Of the major actors only Berenguer was in prison. Azaña was irritated by the pettiness of the proceedings, which he feared would make martyrs of unimportant personages while yielding no positive result.

On 12 November the Responsibilities Commission entered formal charges against the king. Don Alfonso was accused of "an uncontrollable inclination towards absolute power," though no concrete evidence was produced. Instead, on the basis of "public knowledge," the king was officially convicted of the "crime of high treason" by an overwhelming parliamentary majority. Don Alfonso was officially stripped of all titles and dignities, and all his properties in Spain were confiscated.

The work of the commission continued for another year. Three of its five subcommittees eventually found that they would be unable to bring any indictments. Charges in two categories were finally presented in June 1932 not for any specific crimes but merely for collaboration with the dictatorship and for political responsibilities. These were subsequently heard by a special ad hoc Tribunal de Responsabilidades made up of twenty-one selected Cortes deputies. The sentences were anticlimactic: eight generals and minor bureaucrats were sentenced to twenty years of *inhabilitación* (loss of civil rights). Four civilian and military figures who had played major roles in the pronunciamiento and dictatorship were given stronger sentences, and two other generals in the same category were let off more lightly because they had subsequently collaborated in the advent of the Republic. The only major sentence was levied against Martínez de Anido, the general who had presided over violent repression in Barcelona during 1920–22, who was condemned to twenty-four years of prison and *inhabilitación*.[62]

This scarcely amounted to a savage persecution, but it was nonetheless sectarian vengeance in most instances, since nearly all the accused had been technically obeying the law of the land. It established the precedent that at each turn of the political wheel vengeance would be exacted on the preceding holders of power. Worse than the sentences imposed was the manner of doing it, which violated the Republicans' own promise of independent judicial institutions, since the whole process was carried out by political factions in parliament. Nothing was accomplished, more than a little was lost, and Azaña was entirely correct in his perception that the whole procedure was a mistake.

The Presidential Election of Alcalá Zamora

As the Constitution neared completion in the final days of 1931, the time had come to choose the first regular president of the Republic, who in this initial instance was to be elected by the Constituent Cortes. There were few senior Republican leaders of stature. Some sentiment existed, even among political rivals who sought to neutralize him, on behalf of Lerroux, yet his own Radicals were adamant in not wanting to lose him as active party leader. With Azaña solidly established as prime minister, the only other major candidate was Alcalá Zamora. He had initially played a very active role in parliamentary debate, but often irritated the left, and during the last weeks he adopted a lower profile, especially after his resignation over Article 26, so as not to lose any more supporters. A man of considerable scruple, the white-haired Alcalá Zamora was also vain and ambitious, a product of the old politics who could rarely resist the most extreme forms of highfalutin rhetoric, in his case notable for its plethora of gerunds.[63] His own political group, now renamed the Progressive Republican Party,[64] was very small, so that he had no sizable political constituency of his own that might influence the presidency. His election would reassure moderate and conservative opinion, and he had a better personal reputation than Lerroux. Alcalá Zamora was thus overwhelmingly elected the first regular Republican president on 10 December.

Completion of the Constitution and normalization of political affairs reopened the question of the identity of the Republican coalition, particularly with regard to the Socialists. Some within Azaña's own party did not share his interest in maintaining the alliance with the latter, and at one point he himself concluded that the government would have to become a coalition of Republican parties only. Yet conversely even moderates drew back from expelling the Socialists, whom they now feared to see in the opposition.[65] The result was that when Azaña's government was reorganized for the first time on 15 December, it shifted to the left, with the Radicals, not the Socialists, dropping out. Lerroux and his followers preferred to position themselves as the alternative to a leftist Azaña coalition, moving to what during the course of 1932 became an intermediate position of neither full support nor full opposition. In retrospect, this was a fateful development, for it marked the beginning of the split between moderate and leftist Republicans, a cleavage that continued to grow until it could not be overcome. Once it became clear that the Republican parties could not agree among themselves, it would become increasingly difficult to defend the democratic parliamentary regime from enemies on both the left and right. Depending on one's point of view, the primary blame may be imputed to the moderate Republicans for refusing to come to terms with the Socialists, or to the left Republicans for preferring an alliance with the Socialists to a more moderate policy in concert with the other Republican groups.

Lerroux was replaced as foreign minister by the left Republican Luis de Zulueta. The Catalanist Jaume Carner succeeded Prieto in the Finance Ministry. Prieto moved to the Public Works Ministry, for which he was rather better qualified, and several other ministries changed hands. The government was now composed of the basic "Azaña coalition" of left Re-

Niceto Alcalá Zamora, first prime minister and first president of the Republic, in the garden of his home, summer 1931

publicans and Socialists and ready to prosecute the basic reform program at the heart of the left Republican project.

The Problem of Public Order

Public order had obviously become a major problem, and the first new legislative initiative by the Azaña government was the introduction on 20 October of a proposed "Law for the Defense of the Republic." This stemmed from Azaña personally, who had earlier written in his diary on 20 April: "I propose an energetic policy, that will make the Republic feared."[66] He had used the same language in his inaugural speech as prime minister, declaring that "if the Republic were not respected, the government would make it feared," noting with satisfaction in his diary that night (14 October) that the speech gave "the impression of authority and security."[67]

The bill was partly inspired by the Weimar Republic's Law for the Defense of Democracy, passed in 1925, but despite its strong provisions, in the long run it would be no more successful than its German predecessor in defending democracy.[68] The text specified eleven categories of crime subject to its jurisdiction. These included: (1) incitement to resist or disobey the law; (2) incitement to military indiscipline or conflict between the armed forces and the government; (3) diffusion of news or rumors designed to disturb the peace or the economy; (4) acts of violence against persons or property, and incitement thereto; (5) any deed or statement calculated to cast discredit on the government and its institutions; (6) apology for the monarchy or its leaders, and use of emblems or insignia associated therewith; (7) illegal possession of firearms or explosives; (8) any form of suspension of employment or labor, without just cause; (9) all strikes not announced eight days in advance (unless modified by subsequent legislation), all strikes unrelated to working conditions, and all strikes in which strikers refused to submit to arbitration; (10) unjustified price increases; and (11) lack of zeal or negligence by public employees. The law would be applied by the minister of the interior, who was also given extreme powers of censorship, empowered to prohibit all public meetings, whether political, religious, or social, that might be presumed to disturb the peace, to close all centers or associations that might serve to incite any of the actions specified and to confiscate any weaponry deemed necessary, even if legally owned.[69] Anyone who infringed any of these stipulations might be subject to arrest for an indefinite period, internal exile, or a fine of as much as 10,000 pesetas. There was virtually no provision for appeal from prosecution, the only stipulation being a proviso that anyone arrested or indicted might appeal directly to the minister of the interior if he did so within twenty-four hours of arrest or prosecution. Even this feature was not in the original bill, but introduced as an amendment by the Catholic progressive Ossorio y Gallardo and accepted by the government.[70]

This sweeping measure placed civil rights in grave jeopardy and goes far to reveal the mood of the Azaña government. The only cabinet minister to oppose it was Prieto, who again showed more discretion than his colleagues. Other Socialists also betrayed some uneasiness, realizing that these dictatorial provisions only favored those who could remain in government, but the measure sailed through a Constituent Cortes from which the right had withdrawn, encountering strong opposition only from old monarchist liberals like Santiago Alba and Antonio Royo Villanova, who pointed out that the laws of the parliamentary monarchy had been more liberal. Enforcement would be in the hands especially of the new Assault Guards, most of whose units were now entering service. As the Socialist Vidarte later wrote,[71] the very name of the latter was probably a mistake, reenforcing the new image of an aggressive, heavy-handed Republican government.

The Law of Public Order was authorized to remain in force until dissolution of the Constituent Cortes. As the Constitution neared completion, it became clear that the law contradicted the guarantee of civil rights included in the former, while the Constituent Cortes proposed to remain in legislative power for some time. Rather than trying to resolve the contradiction, the government simply arranged that the law remain in force as an addition to the Constitution. It had gone into effect immediately, a local rightist leader in Zaragoza being sentenced before the close of November to six months internal exile for having made a speech in the provincial assembly (Diputación) attacking the work of the Constituent Cortes. Thus Azaña could boast nearly two years later that he had held in his hands "a power such as few have enjoyed in this country in modern times," and that he had "employed it in putting my foot down on the enemies of the Republic, and that when anyone of them has raised his head above the sole of my shoe, in putting the shoe back on top of him."[72]

The first line of defense in the countryside was still the Civil Guard, units of whom had killed seven people in various agrarian demonstrations in the provinces of Toledo and Salamanca during September. Two more were killed in actions by the Civil Guard in Burgos and in Cordoba province during November, adding to the toll begun in May. Seville remained a major center of disorder throughout the fall. More than half of its salaried labor force was organized, the third highest percentage in the country after Barcelona and Oviedo. A major dock strike in Seville during November led in turn to violent conflict between anarchists and Communists. Altogether, between September and December at least four more people were killed in political and labor disputes there, including one businessman, one anarchist, and two workers accused of strikebreaking.[73] A new CNT strike wave broke out in the last two months of the year, concentrated mainly in northern industrial and southern agrarian provinces. Though all this was strongly denounced by the Socialists, new younger members of the UGT sometimes also joined in the strike activity.

The most notorious new incident occurred on the last day of the year in the small, remote pueblo of Castilblanco in the province of Badajoz in the southwest. Winter was always a time of unemployment and distress for southern farmworkers. Five days before Christmas a peaceful demonstration of unemployed laborers demanding work, organized by the local UGT syndicate, had been broken up by the Civil Guard. The Badajoz provincial leadership of the UGT syndicate then called for a two-day provincial general strike to force recall of the provincial governor (a member of Azaña's Republican Action Party) and the local Civil Guard commander, both accused of complicity with landowners in blocking application of the new Republican labor reforms. Peaceful demonstrations took place on 30 December, but on the following day in Castilblanco the mayor sent the local four-man detachment of the Civil Guard to the village Casa del Pueblo (UGT headquarters) to ask them to call off the second demonstration. When the guardsmen arrived, they found themselves heavily outnumbered by a large group of workers and were taunted by women present. Possibly panicked, the Guardsmen responded in their usual way by opening fire, apparently killing one and wounding two men. Here, however, the four found themselves surrounded at close quarters and they never got off a second round. Infuriated laborers threw themselves on the Guardsmen from all sides, quickly beating and hacking them to death with knives and farm tools. Skulls were crushed and eyes gouged out, with some of the women allegedly dancing over the corpses, leaving a scene that General Sanjurjo, national Civil Guard commander, declared was worse than anything in the Moroccan wars. Widely publicized in the press during the first days of January, Castilblanco sent "a thrill of horror through the country."[74] On the same day as the massacre, a farmworker participating in the strike was shot dead by guardsmen in another part of the province, and in the aftermath many laborers were arrested in Castilblanco, ten eventually being sentenced to life imprisonment.

The start of 1932 was not encouraging, for on 3–4 January there were strikes and disorders in four provinces, including an attack on a local Civil Guard headquarters in Valencia province. Altogether five anarchists and striking workers were killed by Civil Guards during those two days, while a priest was murdered in a separate, apparently political, incident in Bilbao. The primary revenge for Castilblanco was taken by the *Benemérita* (as the Civil Guard was called) on 5 January at Arnedo, a small semi-industrial town in the northern province of Logroño. There workers of a local factory were on strike and had assembled in the public square to protest. A large reinforced Civil Guard unit (twenty-eight men) ordered them to disperse and, after being met with defiant cries, opened fire directly on the crowd, killing possibly as many as eleven (including one child and possibly as many as four women), with many more wounded.[75]

Arnedo was clearly a Castilblanco in reverse, provoking loud protest in the Cortes, though more from the middle-class Radical Socialists than from the Socialists, embarrassed by the severity of the public order problem and the fact that UGT workers had been involved. The government promised full investigation and punishment, and on 5 February replaced Sanjurjo as commander of the Civil Guard with Miguel Cabanellas, one of the minority of formally pro-Republican generals. Sanjurjo was switched to command of the Carabineros (border guards and customs police), who were not normally involved in problems of public order and crowd control.

Numerous incidents followed without respite. On 6 January, the day after the Arnedo incident, the Civil Guard became involved in gunfire against strikers in Calzada de Calatrava, leaving two more workers dead. Several broad strikes in the Basque country protested events in nearby Arnedo, while minor rural disorders continued in Badajoz province. On 17 January a fight broke out in Bilbao in which Carlists and Basque nationalists clashed with Socialists, killing three of the latter. The UGT immediately called a general strike in protest and wrecked the local headquarters of Catholic Action. Before the close of the following day, the government invoked the Law for the Defense of the Republic and closed down many political centers in the Basque country, arresting an undetermined number of Basque nationalists, Carlists, and rightists.

All the while the FAI-CNT was gearing up for its first concerted offensive against the Republic, which began in Valencia province on 18 January with the torching of churches in three towns. The main movement—in FAI planning the start of a revolutionary insurrection—was initiated in two industrial towns in Barcelona province on the nineteenth and by the twenty-first had spread through the Llobregat basin outside Barcelona. *Cenetistas* were able momentarily to take over six small industrial municipalities and in several areas cut the rail lines around Barcelona. A state of revolutionary "libertarian communism" was declared in the mining town of Figols, perhaps for the first time formally in any municipality in Spain. The official

CNT manifesto, released in Barcelona on the twentieth, declared that the Republic had failed to live up to its promises, "with the result that the state is the first enemy of the people."[76]

When parliament opened on the following day, the Azaña government received an overwhelming vote of confidence, 285 to 4. By that point the army had again been called out, and the prime minister informed the Cortes that "The government has no hesitation in declaring that a movement was being prepared for the day of the 25th with the goal of overturning the Republic," adding that the subversives had obtained assistance and instructions abroad "from powers hostile to the Spanish state," perhaps referring to Communist actions which paralleled those of the anarchists. All this, he went on, was pleasing to the "extreme right," but Azaña pledged that he would leave them scant opportunity, boasting that he had given orders to the commanding general in Catalonia "that I am not allowing him more than 15 minutes between the arrival of his forces at the site of the revolt and the extinction of the latter."[77] He added that he was also sending a special General Delegate of the government to the Basque provinces and Navarre to apply the Law for the Defense of the Republic to rightist subversives there.

The main anarchosyndicalist insurrection in Catalonia was quelled by the military and Civil Guard within three days, but flashpoints erupted all over the country in the week that followed. Communists briefly in control of the small town of Sollana in Valencia province were reported to have proclaimed a "soviet republic." Soon more hundreds of anarchosyndicalists had been arrested, as well as a number of Communists, and a special tribunal in Barcelona quickly condemned the leaders and others judged to bear particular responsibility to deportation to a penal colony in Equatorial Guinea. On 10 February a ship left Barcelona with 104 *cenetista* prisoners (including Buenaventura Durruti and the Ascaso brothers), stopping to pick up 15 more prisoners (some of them Communists) in Valencia and Cadiz.

Though all the parties in parliament condemned the insurrection and accompanying revolutionary general strikes — a typically inchoate anarchist "playing at revolution" — three Radical Socialist deputies (one of them Ramón Franco) interpellated the government in parliament on 11 February about the use of the Law for the Defense of the Republic to carry out such swift penal deportations, in their words "an iniquitous act, unknown under the monarchy or the dictatorship," which was technically correct. Casares Quiroga, the febrile and sickly intimate of Azaña who served as minister of the interior, replied that the Republic had faced a major revolutionary threat. In several spots, he said, the insurrectionists had declared the "soviet republic," and he reported that Radio Moscow had publicly announced a struggle for a Soviet Republic in Spain at the same time that news of the outbreak had first reached the Ministry of the Interior.

The country calmed down for a fortnight, only to see more strife in mid-February, with political strikes and disorders in at least seven different provinces. Several more people were killed in these clashes, climaxed by a major incident in Zaragoza on 16 February in which police killed four *cenetistas*. The aftermath of insurrection was not encouraging, for the entire chain of events did not weaken, but actually strengthened, FAI predominance within the CNT, whose moderate secretary, Angel Pestaña, was forced to resign in February.

Press censorship had become so severe that on 19 February Royo Villanova, Unamuno, and others requested in the Cortes that the government simply return to strict application of the old Liberal monarchist press law of 1883, which provided some guarantees against incendiarism and libel but more freedom than the draconian new Republic regulations. Azaña replied stiffly (and misleadingly) that "press regulations provide complete freedom. Anyone can say whatever he wants, provided that he does not attack the Republic in the manner defined by law,"[78] a formula that most dictatorships might have been willing to subscribe to. Subsequently, on 9 March Lerroux, Unamuno, Melquiades Alvarez, Maura, and others urged that at least newspapers which had not been convicted by a specific judicial finding not be suspended arbitrarily by the government. Azaña admitted that the latter's power was "extraordinary" but blamed it on the problems stemming from the preceding regime, which had been a standard excuse for excesses in Spanish politics and government for the past century. The government, he said, was only defending liberty, adding his oft-quoted and scornful phrase, "Ladran, luego cabalgamos" ("The hounds bark, therefore we ride on"), though minutes later he spoke again in an effort to soften the effect of his remarks.[79] Throughout 1932 the prestige of Azaña remained high, as even some moderates continued to hail the one Republican who was universally perceived to be a strong leader. On one occasion, even Mussolini declared, with customary extravagance, that Azaña was the only analogue to fascism in Spain because of the firmness of his leadership.[80]

March and April brought only limited improvement in public order. Violent incidents, bomb explosions, and political strikes were registered in more than twenty provinces, producing at least seven more deaths. Many new rightist political meetings were still being prohibited by law, but rightists were now striking back in attempted disruptions of leftist meetings. Between February and April Republican and Socialist meetings were interrupted and in several cases in ten different provinces were shut down. The spring registered an increase in direct conflict between political groups not of the extreme left, with fistfights and occasional gunfire exchanged between Republicans or Socialists on the one hand and Carlists or other rightists on the other, and in one case between Socialists and Radicals. Politicization was also deepening among university students. The Republican Federación Universitaria Española (FUE), which had dominated the universities in 1930–31, was now being challenged in certain instances by the Federación de Estudiantes Católicos and the Carlist Agrupación de Estudiantes Tradicionalistas. A major brawl between Republican and rightist students took place at the University of Madrid on 6 April, and there were disorders at five universities and colleges that month. Apprehension also increased over the growth of common criminal activity, particularly armed robberies, and on 8 April several deputies sought to introduce a bill that would reestablish the death penalty.

The week from 10 April to 17 April was set aside for festivals and celebrations honoring the first anniversary of the Republic. This gave Azaña the opportunity to show off the luxurious new furnishings of the Palacio de la Presidencia (the prime minister's office and residence) on the Castellana in Madrid. It had been fitted with furniture and art objects from one of the royal palaces. As in the preceding year, the UGT eschewed public marches and demonstrations on May Day, though work stoppage was general. Nonetheless, the press reported violent conflicts in at least seven provinces, resulting in ten fatalities and many lesser injuries.

During the remainder of May, Seville was the principal scene of conflict, with another CNT general strike toward the end of the month. Disorders and riots in prisons, mainly led by anarchists, were a general feature of the spring, with even one disturbance in a leprosarium. This was climaxed by a mass jailbreak of twenty-six prisoners in Cadiz province and the firing of the director general of prisons, the Radical Socialist Victoria Kent (Spain's highest-ranking woman bureaucrat to date) on 5 June.

Altogether the Ministry of Labor registered 139 strikes for the first three months of 1932 and 124 for the three months from April to June. Asturias recorded the greatest concentration for the spring trimester with 35 and overall led in the greatest number of strikers, ahead even of Barcelona, which was second in the number of strikes, while Seville was third for the year in both categories.[81] The Asturian strikes were, however, less frequently political in character, so that the most intense conflict was registered in the CNT strongholds of Barcelona and Seville.

Altogether at least thirteen people were killed in strikes and demonstrations during June and July. The most notorious of the July incidents was

the Communist-inspired revolt of poor farmers and workers at Villa Don
Fadrique in Toledo province, where they dug a sort of trench around their
little town and manned it with shotguns and farm implements to hold out
the Civil Guard. Reinforcements were summoned for the Civil Guard, who
induced the villagers to surrender on the following day after the death of
two of the villagers and one Civil Guard.

The general line of the extreme left in 1932 was that the Republic had
become worse than the monarchy. As a consequence of its incendiary policies, the extreme left had suffered many more fatalities and arrests in little
over a year of the Republic than it had in eight years of overt authoritarian
rule. *El Socialista* commented on 11 June:

Communists and anarchosyndicalists act in such a way that the working class finds
itself in a perpetually desperate situation. Their concept of revolution requires crimes
that make the lives of workers impossible, . . . and workers blame this on the Republic. They insist on wages that cannot be paid, since it is illogical that the total
wages paid in constructing a building amount to the total value of the building.
. . . In large part the unemployment in Seville is due to this. Workers then feel
themselves deceived and hate the Republic, "which condemns them to misery."

The social panorama of Seville, painful as it is for the proletariat, was created
by the tragic radicalism of Communists and anarchosyndicalists. . . . Senseless extremism has resulted in the absurd Seville of today, anarchized and certainly a
powderkeg. But a powderkeg that will blow up only against the proletariat.

The extreme left sought revolutionary domination, but in the process divided organized labor and made a large part of the left the enemy of the
Republic, creating a serious obstacle for the consolidation of democracy.[82]

4

The Republican Reforms

THE Republic inaugurated the most intensive era of reform in Spain since the institutions of liberalism had first been stabilized in the 1840s. The left Republican groups intended to go well beyond the primarily juridical reformism of classic liberalism to remold major aspects of society, culture, and national institutions. This involved the separation of church and state and a severe restriction on Catholicism in order to refashion national character, a broad expansion of education, reform and modernization of the armed forces, regional autonomy, far-reaching labor reforms, intensification of public works, and a basic agrarian reform to benefit dwarfholders and landless farm laborers. Not all the Republican parties agreed on the major aspects and extent of reform in each of these areas, and some of these projects became quite controversial within the Constituent Cortes itself.

Church and State

The charter of religious policy was Article 26 of the Constitution, which read:

> All religious confessions will be considered associations governed by a special law.
>
> The state, the regions, provinces and municipalities will not maintain, favor or support economically any church, religious association or institution.
>
> A special law will regulate the total elimination of the clerical budget within a maximum of two years.
>
> All religious orders will be dissolved who impose, in addition to the three canonical vows, another special vow of obedience and authority different from the authority of the state. Their goods will be nationalized and devoted to charity and education.
>
> Other religious orders will be regulated by a special law to be voted by the Constituent Cortes that will correspond to the following principles:

1. Dissolution of all orders whose activities may constitute a danger to the security of the state.

2. Registration of those allowed to continue in a special registry of the Ministry of Justice.

3. Prohibition of acquiring or maintaining, either in their own name or those of a separate party, any property beyond what can be proved to be necessary to maintain their members and direct fulfillment of their specific activities.

4. Prohibition of the right to participate in industry, commerce or education.

5. Subjection to all the fiscal laws of the land.

6. The obligation to make an annual report to the state on the investment of their assets in relation to the goals of the association.

The property of religious orders is legally subject to nationalization.

According to the Church's own data, in 1930 the Catholic clergy numbered 34,176 priests and more than 60,000 religious of both sexes (predominantly nuns). In addition to guiding the spiritual life of the faithful, they were active in education and charitable activities and were also influential in certain social areas, particularly in family life. Protestants, conversely, remained very few, scarcely one-tenth of 1 percent of the total population.

In addition to separating church and state, the Republican government introduced civil marriage and divorce, pledged to build a completely secular system of state education, end the government's subsidy of the parish clergy, dissolve the Jesuit order, and ban members of the orders from industry, commerce, and education, thus largely eliminating Catholic schools in the long run. The Church's leaders and many Catholic laymen were willing grudgingly to accept the separation of church and state, but they had still hoped to retain certain features of the Concordat, particularly the ecclesiastical subsidy and the freedom of the orders and all other Catholic activities. The government's determination to end the subsidy had the effect of turning the Catholic Church in Spain into a voluntary association of the faithful, to be maintained by individual contributions. Most Spanish Catholics contributed relatively little, so that cancellation of the subsidy was almost harder to accept than separation of church and state. Even more dire in the long run, however, was the assault on the orders and the determination, in effect, to eliminate Catholic education. "These last were an assault on the basic rights of Catholic citizens and through them an intolerable attack on the Church, incompatible, as critics soon pointed out, with the constitution's own liberal principles."[1]

In later years, even supporters of the left would conclude that the radical campaign against the Church was a fundamental mistake, yet the viewpoint of the left Republicans and Socialists in 1931 was that the great majority of practicing Catholics were intransigent enemies of progress and that, in effect, there was no one left to alienate among the Catholic right, since they were all firm enemies of the new Republic anyway. It was certainly correct that the great majority of Catholics were strongly conservative, and that the Church was fully identified with the old order, both politically and economically. In order to establish a radical new Republic, therefore, Catholicism had to be attacked directly and crippled as rapidly as possible. Had the intention been to establish a liberal democratic system of live-and-let-live, a modus vivendi might have been worked out. Such was the goal of Alcalá Zamora and the more moderate Republicans, but the left Republican-Socialist coalition insisted on a radical solution.

Article 26 established only general guidelines for anticlerical policy, specific aspects of which had to be codified in subsequent legislation. Thus a decree of 24 January 1932 dissolved the Society of Jesus and seized its official property. This ended all formal activity of the Jesuits, though individual members were not expelled from the country and might continue to serve in other religious functions. The order withdrew most of its younger personnel from Spain, though in some cities Jesuit schools continued to function as nominally private institutions.[2] As Alcalá Zamora later wrote, this was a destructive measure which generated little financial reward for the government but outraged the feelings of millions of Catholics and presented a totally counterproductive example of disregard for religious freedom and civil rights.[3]

Another decree of 30 January officially secularized all cemeteries, unifying the administration of civil and religious cemeteries and transferring administration of the latter to local municipalities. All external religious funeral ceremonies were subject to regulation by local authorities, which might restrict or forbid them as they saw fit. This was in accord with general Republican legislation forbidding external displays of religiosity. There were numerous instances of local Republican officials imposing fines for outdoor religious activities or even for the wearing of crucifixes in public, and there were even instances in which parish priests were fined for what were considered monarchist allusions in sermons. All this was exasperating to Catholic sensibilities, adding injury to insult. Moreover, other legislation provided that the ecclesiastical subsidy would be ended altogether by the close of 1933, and that in the meantime the meager salaries of parish priests would be reduced from 20 to 30 percent, and that of other clergy by 50 percent, trimming the entire ecclesiastical budget from sixty-seven million pesetas in 1931 to only twenty-two million for the first nine months of 1932.

The Cortes passed a law on 2 February authorizing civil divorce for the first time in Spanish history. The terms were fairly restrictive, requiring evidence of adultery on the part of at least one partner, and in fact produced no sudden rash of divorces, a total of only approximately 3,500 being completed during the two years 1932–33.

Most controversial of all the subsequent legislation was the Law on Confessions and Religious Congregations, first introduced in parliament in October, 1932, because it would determine the extent of limitation on Catholic activity, above all in education. It delimited the rights and functions of all religious personnel and institutions — restricting them mainly to spiritual and liturgical activities, prohibiting all regular educational instruction by members of the clergy (who provided nearly 100 percent of the staff of Catholic schools), and banning most charitable and special remedial programs as well. All church and other religious buildings were declared national property, though religious groups might retain use of them for strictly religious purposes. Religious organizations would also have the right to acquire further property, but only to the extent needed for exclusively religious activities. Any excess was to be confiscated and invested in bonds to assist in retiring the national debt. All clergy were prohibited from engaging in commerce and industry as well as educational instruction, and from using third parties in such activities, all functions of which were to cease by the end of 1933. The law restated the deadline for ending the subsidy, declared church income liable to taxation, and also specified the government's right to veto any appointment to the church hierarchy that it deemed inappropriate.

Many petitions were received from parents' groups and other Catholics on behalf of the religious schools. When the Christian democrat Ossorio y Gallardo inquired who would now conduct schools for the mentally retarded, he was told that the government would. The Republican deputy Federico Fernández de Castillejo lamented, "This project goes against principles cherished throughout the world, such as freedom of thought, of which freedom of education is a consequence,"[4] but the government replied once more that this was a matter of public health. Final terms of the measure required Catholic secondary schools to close on 1 October 1933 and primary schools by the first part of 1934. A vote to cut off discussion carried by 240 to 34, and the law passed on 11 May 1933, by 278 to 50, the Radicals voting with the government coalition. There was much speculation that Alcalá Zamora might refuse to sign the bill, but after a delay of three weeks he did so on 2 June.

The Catholic response was one of scandal and outrage, as lines hardened and positions radicalized. Initially, after the forced resignation of the Primate Cardinal Segura, church leadership had been in the hands of the

Victoria Kent, first Republican director general of prisons and first woman to serve as a senior government administrator in Spain

moderate, pragmatic papal nuncio Msgr. Tedeschini and the moderately liberal Catalan Cardinal Archbishop Vidal i Barraquer.[5] A collective letter of the church hierarchy that was released on 1 January 1932 counselled respect for constituted authority, but condemned the new legislation without qualification and required all Catholics to work constructively for its speedy reversal. Holy Week processions were cancelled in protest in both 1932 and 1933, though in defiance of government edict many external emblems were displayed outside Catholic homes. In 1933, when Good Friday coincided with the second anniversary of the Republic, commercial activity was generally shut down, but the commemoration of the new regime was postponed until the following day. On 2 June, the date of the signing of the Law of Congregations, Vidal i Barraquer released another collective episcopal letter denouncing all interference with Church activities, declaring that the law had made them "an administrative department of the state." On the next day Pope Pius XI issued an encyclical, *Dilectissima nobis*, denouncing the new legislation. Many Catholics set to work to evade its more drastic aspects. Several of the teaching orders proceeded to set up nominally private schools under the nominal direction of Catholic laymen or even some of the former instructors. A new association, SADEL (Sociedad Anónima de Enseñanza Libre), was formed to enable Catholic laymen to take formal responsibility for schools taught by religious in lay attire.[6]

Educational Expansion

One of the greatest obstacles to the modernization and prosperity of Spain and the stabilization of a representative political system was the inadequacy of education. From a land with perhaps the greatest density of Latin schools and institutions of higher learning in Europe in 1600, Spain had fallen within less than a century to the status of educational backwater, and by the middle of the nineteenth century had, together with Portugal, the most illiterate population in western Europe. Most education had been administered by the Church, concentrating on the aristocracy and the middle classes. By the mid-nineteenth century, liberal reforms had secularized and centralized the comparatively small university system and had begun development of a modern public school system, though with woefully inadequate funds. Progress was slow, if relatively steady, but in 1930 at least a quarter of the adult population remained illiterate, while many poor villages, as well as some neighborhoods in larger cities, still lacked schools altogether. (See table 4.1.)

Republican leaders had no higher priority than education, for to them a progressive Republic depended on enlightenment as imparted and guaranteed by secular public schools. Probably the closest precedent had been the "Ferry Laws" of 1881–86 in France, named after a famous minister of

Table 4.1. Illiteracy in Spain (ten years or older)

	1900	1910	1920	1930	1940	1970
Men	36.8	32.1	28.1	19.5	13.8	5.1
Women	54.0	47.5	41.2	32.0	23.2	12.1
Both	45.3	40.0	34.8	25.9	18.7	8.9

Source: Junta Nacional de Alfabetización, in Victor García Hoz, *La educación en la España del siglo XX* (Madrid, 1980).

the Third Republic, which had created a centralized, free, compulsory, secular system of public education. In France, however, the Third Republic's educational system had largely been developed to sustain a middle-class status quo and had rather more modest goals than the Republican program in Spain.[7]

At the beginning of the Republic there were at least 33,000 state schools in Spain, most of them small, enrolling between 1.5 and 2 million students, with another million or so lacking instruction almost altogether. Between 1909 and 1931 the state had built 11,128 schools, an average of approximately 500 per year,[8] a rate which the Republican leaders proposed greatly to accelerate. The projected closing of Catholic schools would, however, exacerbate the problem in the short term. The Ministry of Justice calculated that Church schools enrolled 351,037 students at the primary level and 17,098 secondary students, though Catholic spokesmen insisted that the true figure was much higher.[9] Rodolfo Llopis, the new Socialist director general of primary education, admitted that it was difficult at first to assemble complete data on educational needs. His initial calculation was that the 33,000 public schools were staffed by more than 37,000 teachers, and that meeting the needs of the entire population through the public school system would require 27,151 additional schools and at least that many teachers. The existing shortfall, together with the new gap created by closing Catholic schools, would be filled by maintaining a high rate of expansion — more than 5,000 new schools each year — for the next five years.

Certainly the Constituent Cortes was more sympathetic to educational needs than any parliament in Spanish history. Eighty-eight of its members — nearly one-fifth — were teachers or professors of some sort, though of these only five were primary school instructors and four more primary school inspectors. Adequate funding was another question. A decree of June 1931 delegated authority for primary school construction to municipal councils, who were to set up local commissions to collaborate with the Ministry of Public Instruction. Their financing, however, was limited, stemming from inelastic revenues in the form of property taxes or indirect assessments. The money would basically have to come from the national budget.

Direct state funding for accelerated construction and more teachers was begun early in the life of the Provisional Government, and a sort of five-year plan was adopted by the Cortes in October 1931, projecting the creation of twenty-seven thousand new schools and an equivalent number of new teaching positions, the term "schools" meaning mostly one-room village schools, or sometimes a second room and teacher added to an existing facility. This rate of expansion could not, however, be maintained. Marcelino Domingo, the first minister of public instruction, overspent his budget and was replaced in Azaña's second cabinet by the Socialist professor and social democratic moderate Fernando de los Ríos.

It was also necessary to expand the corps of teachers and upgrade salaries, which were usually miserable. The old Castilian saying "as hungry as a schoolteacher" corresponded to a harsh reality. In 1931 the bulk of government employees were paid at least four thousand pesetas (approximately four hundred dollars) annually, and in some government ministries janitors were paid more than many village school teachers. Only 1 percent of all teachers earned as much as eight thousand pesetas, while in some ministries as much as 25 percent of the staff was paid at least that. Teachers hoped for a minimum salary of four thousand pesetas, which the Republic could not afford.[10]

The goal was a single unified national teaching corps, and in September 1931 a salary of four thousand pesetas was indeed stipulated for all graduates of the reorganized national normal school system, but a decree of the following month raised 6,833 teachers at the lowest level to an annual minimum of only three thousand pesetas (at a time when labor reforms made it possible for unskilled manual laborers to earn more than two thousand pesetas annually, if employed the entire year). Newly recruited teachers, however, were usually paid much more, sometimes as much as seven thousand pesetas.[11] When the question was later raised in the debate over the Law of Confessions as to how the state would find qualified instructors at the secondary level to make up for the closing of Catholic schools, De los Ríos replied that it would provide short, intensive courses to sizable numbers of candidates with *licenciatura* degrees (roughly comparable to the Master's), who would be attracted by the increased salaries. Spain did indeed possess a significant underemployed intelligentsia, and the state teaching corps rapidly increased from 36,680 at the advent of the Republic to more than 46.000 in 1933, but this meant that most of the budget increases had to go for greater salary expenses, the actual rate of school construction falling off during 1932 and 1933. Altogether, the share of education in the national budget was nearly doubled in 1931 and increased further until it reached a level of more than 7 percent overall by 1934. (See table 4.2.) Nonetheless, during a major depression money was not available to meet all needs, and a crash program that sometimes lacked careful planning was not always able to use funds with maximum efficiency.

There was intense resistance from bitter Catholic parents, while in some rural areas other parents who were not particularly Catholic found the

Table 4.2. Budget for Public Instruction as a Percentage of
National Budget

1931	5.69
1932	5.92
1933	6.57
1934	7.08
1935	6.60
1936	6.54

Source: Data from *Anuario Estadístico de España* and
Manual Pérez Galán, *La enseñanza en la Segunda República*
(Madrid, 1975), correlated by Charles F. Gallagher, *Culture
and Education in Spain. Vol. 5, The Second Republic* (American Universities Field Staff Reports, no. 22, 1979).

new emphasis on coeducation of the sexes offensive. A Catholic Federación de los Amigos de la Educación (FAE) had already been organized in 1930, and Catholic mobilization accelerated in 1932 with the organization of a broader confederation of Catholic Parents, though its numbers fell short of the desired membership.[12] As a result of the subsequent victory of the center and right in the 1933 elections, Catholic schools were not in fact closed according to the original schedule, remaining open until after the Popular Front victory in 1936.

Marcelino Domingo would later claim 12,988 "schools" had been created during the years 1931 to 1933, compared with only 3,421 under the center-right in 1933–35.[13] This is misleading. The most careful research has found that fewer than 10,000 new schools were constructed during the entire period of the Republic (see table 4.3).[14] What were sometimes officially termed "schools" seem in fact to refer to *plazas de maestro* (teaching positions), which had apparently been expanded by approximately 14,000 by the time that the Civil War began. Though not quite as impressive as Republican spokesmen made it appear, this was nonetheless a considerable achievement.[15] Had the Republic enjoyed a generation of peace, it might well have trained a new generation more prudent and temperate than its elders.

The Republic generally coincided with the climax of early twentieth-century high culture, the final phase of Spain's modern "Silver Age." Though the years of the Republic were not so distinguished as the second half of the 1920s in literary production,[16] poets such as Federico García Lorca added luster to a literature that already counted such luminaries as the novelist Pío Baroja, the poet Juan Ramón Jiménez, and the playwright Jacinto Benavente, as well as philosophers and essayists of the stature of Unamuno, Ortega, and Madariaga.

Table 4.3. School Construction, 1931–1936

Year	Number of Schools	Increase over previous year
1931–32	35,989	2,543
1932–33	37,072	1,083
1933–34	38,499	1,427
1934–35	40,830	2,331
1935–36	42,766	1,936

Source: See table 4.2.

Republican policy sought to diffuse higher culture more broadly and to make advanced education more readily available. A new kind of extension system called "popular universities," building on an earlier model in Madrid, was created, a special summer university set up in Santander, and a new national Instituto de Estudios Arabes (later to become something of a world center) opened at the University of Granada. Most publicized of all, however, was the formation of "pedagogical missions" to bring modern culture to remote rural areas. These offered mini-museums, theatrical performances (some of them organizied by García Lorca), puppet and slide shows, films, concerts, and traveling libraries.[17] The missions went into operation during the summer of 1933. Though they were later curtailed by shortage of funds, Republican policy succeeded in injecting new momentum into higher education and extension activities.[18]

Azaña's Military Reform

The disarray of the Spanish army had been a major problem for more than a century. Given the weakness of Spanish government, the fragmentation of political forces and the influence of the senior army command as a political arbiter, one reform plan after another had come to naught. Most political figures had little knowledge of the military, but Manuel Azaña had built a reputation as the military expert of the Republican left, especially with his book *Estudios de política francesa contemporánea: La política militar,* published in 1919, and several articles and party position papers of the 1920s. For Azaña, it was, as he once said, "a question of life and death" that the military be brought under control, reformed, and "Republicanized."

As in almost all other things, his model was the French Third Republic, though Azaña insisted that to copy or model was not to imitate. He believed that the French army had suffered from some of the same defects as its Spanish counterpart prior to the French Republican reform that began in 1905. In his somewhat simplistic reading of recent French history, the Third Republic's reform had been a smashing success, transforming the structure, political role, and psychology of the French officer corps. This, of course, ignored its tradition as *la grande muette*, which, unlike its Spanish counterpart, stood apart from politics long before the Republican reform. It also ignored the fact that the French Republican effort to determine military promotions and appointments by political attitudes had led to severe morale problems and had to be abandoned. Finally, it failed to grasp the fact that the political vocation of the Spanish military leaders had stemmed less from any greedy or violent character of their own than from the weakness and division of Spanish civil society.

In the reform which he carried out as minister of war and prime minister, Azaña had two goals: to "Republicanize" the army and to correct its institutional and professional problems, the latter resulting from a backward and inefficient structure, and a woeful lack of modernization in combat readiness. Since effective modernization would cost more than the government could afford, the more practical aim would be structural reform, which was designed to save money in the long run.

Azaña's first priority was to establish control of personnel and appointments, to begin the process of "Republicanization." To this end he began to legislate by decree as soon as he took office. His first decree of 22 April 1931 required all officers to sign an oath of loyalty to the Republic or resign their commissions. Only a minority of officers had actually opposed the coming of the Republic, and of these only six with active appointments chose to resign.[19] Republicanization also required changing the name of the ministry. Primo de Rivera, in imitation of the French style, had changed the name from Ministry of War to Ministry of the Army, but since that alteration had been made by the dictator, Azaña — despite his overweening Francophilia — changed the name back again to Ministry of War, strange nomenclature for a regime that theoretically renounced war as an instrument of national policy, as contradictory as the term "Assault Guards" for the new urban police corps.

Within the ministry Azaña formed a special council of pro-Republican officers as advisors, known to critics as the *gabinete negro* (black cabinet), composed of officers who had not found favor in the preceding regime. Yet he did not fail to recognize the extent of the partisanship and resentment shown by these advisors and so left the monarchist Gen. Ruiz Fornells as assistant secretary of the ministry, as a sort of check and balance.

The method of promotion had been a sore point within the officer corps for many years. Most officers preferred strict seniority, while a minority espoused *méritos de guerra* (combat merits), which rewarded the combat elite and in 1927 had made Francisco Franco the youngest new regular army brigadier in Europe. A decree of May, 1931, restored strict seniority, while a subsequent one of 3 June declared that all merit promotions since 1923 would be subject to review. At the same time, since one goal was to place the army in the hands of more reliable pro-Republican commanders, the 4 May decree also specified that key senior appointments and promotions would still be determined directly by the government (through *elección*, as opposed to *antigüedad*). In fact, nearly all the earlier merit promotions were eventually allowed to stand, and the return to seniority was never fully applied. Though most of the top commands were quickly given to nominally pro-Republican officers, Azaña never found a sound formula to determine promotions as a whole. What his policy did do was to give a strong appearance of political favoritism for the next two years that eventually united many officers in opposition to the ministry.

One of the worst problems was the sheer hypertrophy of officers, who numbered nearly 21,000 for a force of about 118,000 troops and NCOs, something like three times the number needed. Azaña's solution was simple and direct and also quite generous. A decree of 25 April 1931 permitted all officers to elect immediate and complete retirement while retaining full pay for the normal length of their careers. Though this would pay thousands of officers for doing nothing, Azaña judged that this was happening already, and that in the long run drastic reduction of the officer corps would save money. A majority of generals resigned, and at one point Azaña later boasted that half the entire officer corps had accepted retirement under the new regulation, though in fact the number seems to have been closer to 8,000.[20] It did achieve the most drastic reduction in the officer corps in more than a century, though whether it served in any way to "Republicanize" the army is more debatable, for there is impressionistic evidence that it was the more progressivist or leftist minority among the officer corps who were most inclined to leave.

Structural reform began with a decree of 25 May that reduced the number of divisions from sixteen to eight, assigning to each two brigades of infantry (each composed of two regiments), an artillery brigade, and a squadron of cavalry. Approximately half the existing (normally very understrength) military units ceased to exist, Azaña declaring that the reform would save the treasury at least 200 million pesetas a year. A following decree of 3 June also reorganized and reduced the "Army of Africa" in the Moroccan Protectorate. Similarly, the navy was reduced in structure from eleven corps units to five by Azaña's close friend and associate Santiago Casares Quiroga, minister of the navy.

A major target for reform was the system of military justice, condemned as caste-ridden, overweening, and impervious to civil authority. Azaña's very first decree on 17 April abolished the infamous "Law of Jurisdictions" of 1906, which had given military courts the power to prosecute any civilian spokesman or publication judged to have insulted the military. A second decree of 11 May reduced the authority of the military court system to "deeds or crimes essentially military in nature," so that military personnel might be prosecuted in civil courts for any offenses not military in character. (However, military jurisdiction over certain categories of offenses by civilians that violated police norms, such as verbal or other attacks on the police, as well as offenses committed by civilians under conditions of martial law, was not eliminated, in keeping with the government's hardline policy on public order.) The Consejo Supremo de Guerra y Marina (Supreme Council of the Army and Navy) was also abolished and replaced by a special military section of the civilian Tribunal Supremo. In addition, all traditional religious observances in the armed forces were completely abolished.

The seven distinct military academies were reduced to three, though a new one was planned for the Air Corps. The General Military Academy in Zaragoza, created by Primo de Rivera only three years earlier and directed by Francisco Franco, was abolished as tending to foment a narrow caste spirit, while the institution of the Central General Staff, suppressed by Primo de Rivera in 1925, was reestablished. The regional district captain generalcies, dating from the early eighteenth century, were all abolished, as were the ranks of captain general and lieutenant general. Another decree unified the two separate officer rolls of active and reserve officers (the first being products of the academies and the second those promoted from the ranks). All these initial decrees were ratified by the Constituent Cortes in regular legislation passed during August 1931.

Azaña was also concerned to modernize military technology within the limits of the budget, and the principal beneficiary was the air force, as a decree of 26 June 1931 formally constituted the Cuerpo de Aviación as a separate air corps for the first time. Heretofore it had constituted a special "service" within the army that had been officially dissolved by Berenguer at the close of 1930 because of its pro-Republican sympathies. Azaña's action gave it structure and autonomy,[21] and later on 5 April 1933 he created a Dirección General de Aeronáutica to supervise both the Air Corps and civil aviation, under the authority of the prime minister.

Further changes were implemented at a slower pace in the last months of 1931, the year that followed, and in the first part of 1933. One feature of the effort to democratize the army was improved status for NCOs, as in the creation in December 1931 of a new Subofficer Corps, between the regular officers and the lowest ranks of NCOs and troops. It would consist of the four ranks of first sergeant, brigades (*sic*), subassistants (*subayudantes*), and sublieutenants. However, 60 percent of future vacancies in the professional academies would be reserved for subofficers, who, whether by seniority or special examinations, showed the ability to achieve commissions. Ordinary officer candidates entering the academies would henceforth be required to have completed one year of regular university study and six months of service in the ranks.

Another goal was to achieve a more egalitarian system of universal service analogous to the "nation in arms" concept of the French law of universal service of 1905. Basic obstacles, however, stemmed from the fact that the Spanish army neither needed nor could it afford all the recruits available, while the "quota" system by which the wealthier might reduce their military service to six months (or in some cases avoid it altogether) by paying a fee beyond the reach of the lower classes produced about 15 million pesetas a year in revenue. The undemocratic "quota" system was therefore preserved, though beginning in October 1931 Azaña did make a serious attempt to improve material conditions for ordinary recruits by providing better food and barracks.

An inevitably conflicting concern was to save money. The military budget for 1932 was reduced to 390 million pesetas compared with 478 million for the first year of the Republic, most of the saving coming from reduced administrative costs, the elimination of redundant units, and some small reductions in Morocco. Expenditures on maintenance and equipment were, however, very slightly increased, while it was still necessary to pay the salaries of the nearly 9,000 officers and NCOs who had been retired (though these costs were transferred to a different section of the national budget). In fact, regular expenditures rose to 402 million pesetas for 1932 and to 433 million for 1933, but there was no money to permit serious modernization or to raise salaries to levels equivalent to those in other western European armies. The six small arms factories administered by the Artillery Corps were transferred by law in February 1932 to a new Consorcio de Industrias Militares under the Ministry of War, made up of representatives of the government, private industry, and trade unions, but no serious technological modernization could be begun. Altogether, the 1933 budget provided for a peninsular army of 145,000 and an additional force of 35,000 in Morocco, the latter composed of 25,500 Europeans (including 4,000 in the volunteer Legion) and nearly 9,500 Moroccans.

Military reaction was for the most part negative, as expressed particularly in the two military newspapers, *La Correspondencia Militar* and *Ejército y Armada*, and in murmurings in scores of garrisons. Officers demanded to know why the burden of reform and cost reduction in government services should fall primarily on the armed forces, and soon the government announced that there would be equivalent reductions in other ministries. This led to such a storm of protest by civil servants that no such plan was ever developed.

What judgment may be made of the Azaña reform? Like many Spanish politicians of the nineteenth and early twentieth centuries, Azaña had a tendency to talk too much and be carried away by his own rhetoric. Moreover, his acerbic style sometimes seemed to indicate that the most important objective was simply to put the officer corps in its place. As he announced to the Cortes on 1 March 1932, "Now no one speaks of the army, nor does the army itself speak. Everyone in his place."

The words for which he would be most remembered (though inaccurately so) came from a speech in Valencia on 7 June 1931, in which he promised a Republican rally that he would "pulverize" (*triturar*) the system of political *caciquismo* "with the same energy and resolution I have used to pulverize other things no less menacing for the Republic."[22] Later it was supposed by some that this referred to the army, and hence the subsequent references to Azaña's alleged boast of "pulverizing" the military.

Azaña's rhetoric was always stronger than his deeds, for the reform was in fact limited, little modernization was achieved, and the democratization of the armed forces was comparatively modest. There was scant Republicanization in the sense of any extended political purge, and leftists would later blame Azaña for having been too soft and of having altogether failed to purge the officer corps of its most dangerous elements.

Despite severe limitations, this was nonetheless the most serious attempt at reforming the military in more than a century. It neither gutted nor ruined the army, as rightist critics had it, but did manage to rationalize somewhat its organizational structure and improve a few aspects of its functioning. This was all that could be achieved in a short period while enforcing significant cost reductions.[23]

The main failure of the reform lay in public relations, where Azaña's atrocious political style made the new policies seem much more insulting to the officer corps than need have been the case.[24] He himself privately recognized in his diary that he allowed himself to be excessively influenced by his own military clique in making ill-advised appointments, creating the impression that the War Ministry was engaged in political favoritism. At any rate, many officers felt put down by their minister and came to share the idea that the reform was an "attack" on military institutions. Thus began an increasingly adversarial relationship between the military and the Republic that had not existed in April 1931.

The Sanjurjada

The passive attitude of the military during the advent of the Republic had not stemmed from any great enthusiasm for political progressivism so much as from reaction to the failures of the dictatorship, which had compromised and discredited the army, stimulating the military's desire to avoid political involvement. Military men were more conservative than liberal and generally more monarchist than Republican. Once it became clear that the Republic was set on a leftward course and also targeting the army for serious reform, rumors of military conspiracy against the new regime began to circulate as early as June 1931. In the middle of that month two senior, strongly monarchist generals, Emilio Barrera and Luis Orgaz, were arrested, along with two younger officers and six civilian monarchists, though most of the latter were soon released. By the following month a number of other monarchist generals, most of them retired, began to conspire more actively and gained a little financial support from wealthy aristocrats. In August Azaña deported Orgaz and the two junior officers to the Canaries, but he lacked direct jurisdiction over the retirees.

The central military figure during the first year of the Republic was General José Sanjurjo, the "Lion of the Rif," a hero of the early Moroccan campaigns. He had once played a role in the establishment of the dictatorship in 1923, but arguably his relation to the coming of the Republic was more important. Director general of the Civil Guard during the final phase of the monarchy, his refusal to employ the country's only national police against the Republicans after the municipal elections was one of the decisive factors in the fall of the monarchy. The five-foot two-inch Sanjurjo was strictly a man of action with only the most rudimentary sense of politics, and prudently refused the Cortes seat to which he was elected by enthusiastic Republican voters in June 1931. He served as troubleshooter for the Republican government during the initial weeks, being sent to Tetuán to quell a disturbance in the protectorate immediately after the change of regime and then to Tablada airbase near Seville after an abortive semi-anarchist revolt there in June. Yet he was not at all a progressive by conviction and, with his hazy political ideas, it was not surprising that he became the target of maneuvers by a few right-wing Republicans who contemplated a "constitutionalist conspiracy" to restore law and order and to enforce a strict liberal democracy that would avoid all leftist overtones and would largely preclude serious reform. The seventy-year-old Manuel Burgos y Mazo, a veteran politician of the monarchist regime, first approached Sanjuro as early as November 1931,[25] and within two months his efforts were reinforced by Melquiades Alvarez, head of the small Liberal Democratic Party. By the first weeks of 1932 Sanjurjo's name had lost its luster for the government. The "Civil Guard crisis" provoked by the Castilblanco and Arnedo affairs led to demands from the left that Sanjurjo, in effect, be made the scapegoat, and on 5 February Gen. Miguel Cabanellas replaced him as director general.

This was a serious blow to Sanjurjo, who began to show more interest in those who insisted that the Republic needed a drastic change of course. His main contact among top Republicans was Alejandro Lerroux, who had always tried to maintain good relations with the military and who, trying to maneuver two different cards at the same time, had warned Azaña as early as mid-1931 of the danger of military discontent. Lerroux would not become implicated in any military conspiracy, but both Burgos y Mazo and Sanjurjo sought Lerroux's advice and urged him to take a stronger stand against the left.[26] By the spring of 1932 there appear to have existed two or even three distinct lines of conspiracy. While Burgos y Mazo sought to convince Sanjurjo to lead a "constitutional" revolt, retired monarchist generals sought to promote a restoration by coup. It also appears that a handful of senior commanders thought in terms of a strictly military movement to "rectify" the Republic, equidistant in political terms between the "constitutionalist" and monarchist conspiracies.

To establish firmer discipline, the Azaña government passed two new laws. The first, on 9 March 1932, authorized the government to retire any general who had gone six months without active assignment (*en situación de disponible*). It also empowered the government to cancel the salary of any military retiree guilty of any of the wide range of activities proscribed by the Law for the Defense of the Republic and abolished the military political press, now very hostile to the government. The aim was to permit select purging of the senior ranks and also to hit conspiratorial retirees in the pocketbook. A second law, on 16 April, ordered mandatory review of all sentences still in effect that had been decreed by the army's honor courts prior to their abolition by the new Constitution. This was designed to countermand certain decisions earlier made by the honor courts that had had the effect of demoting, or even expelling, left-wing officers. Yet the courts had more frequently punished immoral or dishonorable acts than political opinions, and the new bill roused intense antagonism among officers, who viewed it as an attempt to impugn military honor and further politicize personnel assignments.

By June Azaña was well aware of conspiracy among some senior commanders, and on the night of 7 June he remained awake until 3:00 A.M., waiting further news of a rumored revolt.[27] Though a few more arrests were made, the government had no conclusive proof of conspiracy. Azaña judged correctly that the plotting lacked serious or extensive backing and that the defeat of an abortive coup would strengthen the Republic in the long run. Thus the plotting continued, though, as the son of one of the principals later wrote:

> We do not know if it is entirely correct to term conspiracy an uninterrupted series of interviews, trips, or scarcely disguised café conversations, as one of the witnesses testifies. He relates, "Fraternal luncheons were held around the swimming pool of the Isla de Madrid, where Sanjurjo and Goded used to meet, attended by the former's son Justo and myself as squires. All this was observed from farther off by an officer of the Madrid police."[28]

The conspiracy was weakened by an incident which occurred at a special open-air farewell breakfast (*desayuno de despedida*) for students graduating from the military academies, held at the Carabanchel army base outside Madrid on 27 June. General Manuel Goded, the new chief of staff, concluded his ceremonial remarks with the approximate words "Ahora solo me resta dar un viva a España, y nada más" ("Now there only remains for me to give a *viva España*, and nothing more"). One of the most radically Republican officers in the army, Lt. Col. Julio Mangada (whom Azaña privately dismissed as "crazy") indicated severe displeasure over Goded's attitude and his failure to shout "Viva la República!" leading to an exchange of words with the general which ended with Mangada's military arrest. At that, the latter literally threw a fit, whipping off his uniform jacket and stomping on it.

The matter was immediately brought to Azaña's attention by his pro-Republican military advisers, who apparently insisted that the minister do something about the inferred slight to the Republic. Azaña correctly upheld the arrest of Mangada, but within a few hours relieved the attending divisional and brigade commanders — who had been involved in support of Goded and against Mangada — of their assignments. Azaña respected Goded's ability and did not want to make a martyr of the chief of staff, but Goded then abruptly resigned out of solidarity with the colleagues who had just been relieved. He was replaced by General Masquelet, one of the minority of overtly pro-Republican senior commanders.[29] Since all three generals who were replaced or resigned were connected with the conspiracy, its prospects in Madrid, where all major units were now headed by loyal commanders, were significantly reduced by this incident.

Burgos y Mazo claims to have introduced Sanjuro to officers in the large Seville garrison soon after the beginning of July and later to have prepared a "constitutional Republican manifesto" with which to begin the coup, but in fact Sanjurjo eventually decided to work only with other fellow officers, who were mostly to the right of Burgos y Mazo. When it became clearer during July that Lerroux and the Republican moderates could not force a change in government, plans for a simple pronunciamiento were cobbled together under the nominal overall leadership of the retired General Emilio Barrera, who was senior to Sanjurjo. It is doubtful that many more than a hundred officers were directly involved, but a decision was taken to act rapidly before the government could complete legislation on behalf of a Catalan autonomy statute, strongly opposed by the more right-wing military for "dismembering" Spain. The plan was more that of a nineteenth-century pronunciamiento than a surgical twentieth-century coup d'etat, since the conspirators knew they would probably be unable to seize all of Madrid immediately. However, they hoped to seize a few strong points in the capital while winning complete control of Seville and several provincial capitals. The latter were then to send reinforcement to help conquer Madrid, a scheme bearing some resemblance to the one later adopted in the great conspiracy of 1936. It was assumed that Carlist Navarre would rise in support, but little was done to guarantee it. The basic idea was that comparatively little fighting would be involved, as most of the army joined the revolt and support for the government melted away. As one of the younger conspirators put it, "We never thought that it would come to combat."[30]

The conspiracy in fact quickly became *un secreto a voces* ("an open secret"). A few more preventive arrests were made, and forty-seven people were detained all at once at a monarchist meeting in Madrid. On the morning of 10 August, soon after 7:00 A.M., very small groups of rightist civilians and a handful of troops in revolt began to move on the Ministry of War from opposite directions. Ninety minutes of confused skirmishing followed (with Azaña occasionally peering from around the curtain at an upper window in the Ministry) before larger units of the Civil Guard and Assault Guard suppressed the revolt. About ten were killed, two of them rightist civilians. Meanwhile, the conspirators had sent Sanjurjo to Seville, largest center in the south, in part because it was feared that he might be too pro-Republican and would be best kept away from Madrid. That morning he did manage to rally the Seville garrison, telling them they would quickly be joined by colleagues all over Spain. Instead they were met by a general strike in the city, while loyal units were rushed south to converge on what had become the only focus of revolt. Sanjurjo therefore fled early on the eleventh, surrendering some hours later in nearby Huelva. Because only he had managed to bring out an entire garrison in revolt, the whole affair became known to many as the *sanjurjada*, though in fact he was neither its main organizer nor principal leader. No other garrison seconded him, and the only real fighting took place in Madrid. Though Barrera was flown safely into exile in a private plane, scores of other suspects were arrested, especially in Madrid and among upper-class monarchists. The failed revolt in turn touched off a new round of church-burning by the extreme left, particularly in Seville and Granada.

During the next few months, some 200 officers were brought to trial for armed rebellion. Many took the defense that their duty was to defend the *patria* from all enemies domestic and foreign, including a leftist government in Madrid. The counsel for one general asked why the revolt of the Republicans Galán and García Hernández in December 1930 was deemed justified and that of his client criminal. As the highest-ranking rebel captured, Sanjurjo was condemned to death but, since the government did not want to create a martyr, his sentence was reduced to life imprisonment.[31] The commutation provoked noisy demonstrations from leftist groups, in one of which a worker was killed in Vizcaya. Ultimately 145 officers were deported to Villa Cisneros (just as in the case of the anarchists at the beginning of the year), and some 300 others suspected of complicity were left without assignment or moved to the reserve list. In the aftermath, a total of 128 daily and weekly publications were closed by the government for varying periods.[32] Several policy changes were also made. The Dirección General de Carabineros, which Sanjurjo had headed since February, was suppressed, this constabulary being transferred to the supervision of the Ministry of Finance. A similar step was taken with the Civil Guard, transferred to the Ministry of the Interior, and the Assault Guards were expanded by 2,500 new recruits.

Azaña was naturally pleased with the outcome, which had the effect of breaking a temporary logjam in Cortes, allowing the government to move more rapidly on Catalan autonomy and pass the first land reform bill. He noted with satisfaction that the military had been removed as a factor in the political equation for the first time in more than a century.

Regional Autonomy

Reaction against centralism lay at the root of the Spanish civil wars of the nineteenth century and subsequently gave rise to powerful movements of regional nationalism in Catalonia and the Basque country. Much weaker currents of regionalism had also developed in such diverse areas as Galicia, Valencia, Andalusia, and Aragon. The Catalanist movement was the oldest, the most powerful, and also the most modern, having produced both a major moderate Catalanist party, the Lliga Regionalista, rebaptized in 1933 as the Lliga Catalana,[33] and equally potent left-liberal groups, which with the coming of the Republic had mostly allied as the Esquerra Catalana. Basque nationalism was dominated by the Basque Nationalist Party, founded in 1895 and initially much more exclusivist and separatist than the older Catalanist movement. During the early twentieth century a new generation of Basque leaders had moderated the movement, but to liberals and leftists it remained suspiciously traditionalist, clerical, and rightist.

The left-liberal Catalanists, conversely, strongly supported the Republican movement, and their leaders had participated in the somewhat ambiguous "Pact of San Sebastián," by which the Republican heads had promised to move rapidly toward Catalan autonomy in return for Catalan support of the Republic. The Esquerra leader Macià's premature announcement of a "Catalan state" had precipitated the first Republican minicrisis, as related in chapter 2, resulting in the immediate restoration of the Generalitat, the executive for the medieval Catalan parliament (extinguished in 1713), as de facto regional executive. On 24 May 1931 Catalan municipal councillors elected a provisional legislature (*diputación provisional*) which met on 9 June and immediately appointed a commission to prepare a draft statute of autonomy.[34] There was more than a little apprehension elsewhere in Spain as Macià made statements such as "I am president of a revolutionary and leftist state," and as the Esquerra campaigned in the national parliamentary elections on a frankly demagogic nationalism, replete with one statement about "socialization of land and property,"[35] en route to a sweeping victory.[36]

The text that the Catalan commission prepared by 20 June was nonetheless recognized as moderate on most points, not contesting, for example, the sovereignty of the Spanish state on the much contested point of tariffs. The draft statute was approved by Catalan municipal councillors almost unanimously and submitted to a popular plebiscite on 2 August. Seventy-five percent of the electorate participated, with 99 percent approving the statute, which was presented to the government in Madrid two weeks later. By that point, however, the Constituent Cortes had begun deliberation on the Constitution, postponing consideration of the statute. Moreover, despite the relative moderation of the Catalan draft, certain provisions went farther than the Republican coalition was prepared to go, and it referred the matter to committee at the beginning of 1932.

Basque nationalist leaders tried to move with equal rapidity, calling a meeting of pronationalist mayors of Basque municipalities at Guernica, site of traditional foral oaths, on 17 April 1931, following this up with an assembly of nationalist mayors from the three provinces in San Sebastián on 8 May to initiate plans for an autonomy statute. To head off what it feared might be a conservative nationalist proposal, the new Republican *comisión gestora* (acting provisional government) of Guipuzcoa announced on 7 May the formation of a new commission charged with preparing a proposal of provincial autonomy for the province of Guipuzcoa. The mayors' assembly then moved quickly, authorizing the prestigious Sociedad de Estudios Vascos (Basque Studies Society) to draft a project as soon as possible. It produced a text for a General Statute of the Basque State by 31 May, and, despite certain reservations, Basque Republicans and Socialists agreed to support it.

This proposal, however, was drastically amended by an assembly of municipal delegates, including those from Navarre, which met at Estella (Navarre) on 14 June. It then provided for a high degree of autonomy, restoration of traditional nondemocratic suffrage in internal elections, and total autonomy in church-state relations, including the right to negotiate a separate Basque-Navarrese concordat with the Vatican. Representatives of Navarrese municipal councils met on 10 August to consider a Navarrese statute proposed by the current Navarrese *comisión gestora*, but instead those from municipalities containing 89.5 percent of the population of Navarre voted to include Navarre in the Basque project.

Only in the Basque provinces and Navarre had the forces of the right waged a strong and successful campaign in the recent Cortes elections. This adversarial relationship, combined with the proposed terms of the new statute, produced alarm in the ruling coalition. The Bilbao Socialist leader Prieto warned of a "Gibraltar vaticanista," while the Ministry of War fretted over the danger of regionalist revolt and the possible need to intervene with troops. Indeed José Antonio de Aguirre, head of the Basque Nationalist Party (PNV), did meet with one of the monarchist generals conspiring during the summer of 1931, though they found it impossible to come to terms.[37] On 21 August the government suspended four newspapers in Bilbao, two in San Sebastian, and three in Pamplona, while ordering the occupation (*incautación*) of arms factories in the Basque towns of Guernica and Eibar. Military maneuvers were subsequently held in Vizcaya and in Navarre.

The relationship of the worker parties to regional autonomy was ambivalent. Basque Socialists supported autonomy up to a point, but opposed nationalism as clerical and rightist.[38] The Socialists were also distrustful of Catalanism, while the friendly relations between the new Barcelona government and the CNT soon began to break down.[39] There were, however, small independent socialist and communist groups in Catalonia which strongly supported autonomy,[40] while the Comintern and the Spanish Communist Party sought to exploit regional nationalism to promote the revolutionary process.

The proposed Basque statute was presented to the prime minister on 22 September, but parliamentary debate ended in a decision on the twenty-sixth that the religious clauses were unconstitutional, killing the entire measure. In the weeks that followed, Basque nationalist spokesmen were vocal members of the minority opposed to passage of Article 26 of the Constitution, one of their spokesmen being assaulted in the Cortes by an anticlerical deputy. On 15 October, after passage of the legislation, Aguirre declared that further "reasoning in the Cortes was completely useless,"[41] and the entire *vasconavarra* delegation walked out.

For the Basques, autonomy in church-state relations would have to be abandoned, and that meant in large measure going back to the original approach of the commission from the Sociedad de Estudios Vascos. On 6 November the Republican government decided that the *comisiones gestoras* of the four provinces (including Navarre) should be responsible for a new draft and on 8 December decreed that the new drafting commission be composed of a representative from each of the four *comisiones gestoras* and three representatives from Basque municipalities, though after the Socialists complained of lack of representation three Basque Socialist delegates were added as well. In December, with the Republican Constitution now a reality, the PNV deputies began to rethink their position, demonstrating a conditional reconciliation with the new regime by voting for Alcalá Zamora as president, while the rest of the Catholic minority abstained. By the end of 1931 the *vasconavarra* coalition of nationalists, rightists, and Carlist traditionalists was beginning to break up, as differences between nationalists and Carlists widened. On 20 December Carlist leaders decided not to have anything to do with an autonomy statute prepared primarily by the Republican *comisiones gestoras*. Violent incidents between Carlists and Socialists were by this point increasing, reaching an extreme on 17 January 1932 when three Socialists were killed protesting a Carlist meeting in Bilbao.[42]

The new procedure for a Basque statute required separate assemblies from each of the four provinces to vote on the issue of an *Estatuto único* — a single autonomy statute for all four. These groups met on 31 January 1932 and approved the principle by a ratio of eleven to one, with representatives of eighty-five Navarrese municipal governments voting in favor. The new document was somewhat more limited in scope than its predecessor, but it preserved most aspects of autonomy in internal legislation, social regulation, and economic policy, while leaving greater authority in the hands of the Spanish state in matters of joint interest. There was no mention of a "Basque state," the new autonomous entity being termed "an autonomous politico-administrative unit within the Spanish state" that would be called "País Vasco-navarro" (the Basque-Navarrese country) in Spain and "Euzkadi" in Basque. Citizens would be liable to military service only within the Basque-Navarrese region, save for special training and emergencies, but all religious regulations would conform to those of the Spanish state. The proposed statute upheld the special *concierto económico* for the three Basque provinces and the *convenio* for Navarre with regard to taxation, but would require a new reallocation of the precise burden. Largely due to Socialist insistence, the proposed regional parliament would be made up half of deputies chosen by universal, equal, and proportionate suffrage from each of the four provinces equally, and half from general slates elected within the entire region as a whole (the latter giving somewhat greater voice to the masses of workers in the industrial areas). Each province would enjoy internal autonomy as well, and broad self-government was provided for municipalities.[43]

Opposition to the preceding draft had come from the left; the new text aroused hostility in the right. Carlist objections were numerous and fundamental: the whole project was modernist and ignored the revival of traditional institutions, was geared to a leftist Republic and accepted a Godless anticlerical Constitution, and was criticized for overrepresenting the left and underrepresenting Carlists. An assembly of municipal representatives convened to vote on the new document in Pamplona on 19 June 1932. Those from towns in the three Basque provinces were overwhelmingly in favor, but representatives from 123 Navarrese towns voted against, with delegations from only 109 voting in favor and 35 abstaining.[44] Henceforth Carlist Navarre, by far the most right-wing province in Spain, would become increasingly antagonistic toward the expediencies of Basque nationalism.[45]

Moreover, rejection of the second proposal by Navarre would require drafting of a somewhat different document adjusted to the three provinces of the Basque country alone. Additionally exasperating for nationalists was the fact that withdrawal of rural Navarre began to raise doubts in rural Alava,[46] rightist interests there and elsewhere in the Basque country agitating against the statute. By 1933 nationalism would enjoy strength only in the two northern industrial provinces of Vizcaya and Guipuzcoa.[47]

Meanwhile, in Madrid the Cortes's Comisión de Estatuto had brought in its own draft of a Catalan autonomy statute, broadly similar to the original proposal from Barcelona but with various changes that delimited the extent of Catalan autonomy. Francesc Cambó, the chief spokesman of moderate Catalanism, declared the changes acceptable, but they provoked massive protests in Barcelona. By that time a major reaction had begun in other parts of Spain. Leading Republican figures as diverse as

Lerroux, Ortega, Maura, Melquiades Alvarez, and the more liberal Felipe Sánchez Román all declared that the basic autonomy project was going too far. There were student protests against the Catalan statute at the University of Madrid and in several other cities, while on 27 April the municipal government of Palencia in Old Castile urged that Castilian deputies withdraw from parliament in protest.

Cortes debate began on 6 May and immediately bogged down in a morass of criticism that eventually produced some two hundred would-be amendments and separate motions. Azaña tried to rectify the situation in a long and forceful address on 27 May that carefully distinguished between what would really weaken the state and the Republic's own commitment to a legitimate, though somewhat limited, autonomy. This, however, had little effect and, despite double sessions, parliamentary discussion continued, though with diminishing energy, for most of the summer. The shock effect of the *sanjurjada* on 10 August was necessary to galvanize reformist energies once more, the statute finally being approved on 9 September by a vote of 314 to 24. As a gesture of encouragement to the increasingly frustrated Basques, the signing ceremony which officially put Catalan autonomy into effect took place in the Guipuzcoan capital of San Sebastián, while great celebrations broke out in Catalonia, sometimes accompanied by shouts of "Viva España!"

The statute granted the Catalan government exclusive jurisdiction over civil law and most aspects of internal administration, especially in health, transportation, and welfare. It also received power to administer general Spanish legislation dealing with public works, insurance, mining, forests, agriculture, livestock, social services, and public order, and would share with the Spanish state the administration of taxes and education. Certain key areas such as tariffs, border control, foreign affairs, and the armed forces remained within the exclusive competence of the Spanish state. Catalonia would have its legislature, anthem, and flag, and Catalan and Castilian would be co-official languages within its territory. There would also be a special Catalan appeals court (Tribunal de Casación), with jurisdiction over the areas transferred to the Catalan administration.[48]

Macià's Esquerra federation swept the first elections to the Catalan parliament on 30 November 1932, after which Macià was elected the first regular president of the Generalitat and formed an all-Esquerra cabinet.[49] The transfer of services began shortly afterward. During the next year Macià's administration busied itself with the passage of new regulatory legislation and was especially active in cultural affairs, promoting the use of Catalan, and working to expand education and library services. The improvement of public health facilities, even including some attention to psychiatric services, was a particular achievement. Macià also tried energetically to promote agrarian reform and to encourage rural cooperatives, agricultural experimentation, and agricultural credit. One early source of conflict was taxation, with only one-third of the revenue collected in Catalonia going to the Generalitat.[50]

The third notable nationalist movement, in Galicia, was considerably weaker than either Catalan or Basque nationalism, due at least in part to the underdeveloped rural character of Galicia. Galicianist leftist Republicans had assembled their "Organización Republicana Gallega Autónoma," which formed the key portion of the "Federación Republicana Gallega" of 1930, but this sector was more concerned with Spanish Republican affairs in Madrid than in Galician nationalism, while the "Partido Galleguista" (Galicianist Party) formed at the close of 1931 was much weaker. The first assembly to discuss Galician autonomy met in La Coruña on 4 June 1931 to consider proposals from four different groups. It provisionally adopted the draft prepared by the Federación Republicana Gallega,[51] but this proposal, and a more moderate one that followed, fell victim to opposition both in Madrid and in Galicia. Another assembly that convened in Santiago de Compostela on 3 June 1932 appointed a new commission to prepare yet another proposal, which was ready by the fall. A full assembly of Galician municipal representatives then met in Santiago in December, where the new draft was approved by 76 percent of Galician municipalities, containing nearly 84 percent of the region's inhabitants. The next prescribed step would be a regional plebiscite, but the successive government crises of 1933 would make this impossible, and propitious circumstances did not return until after the elections of 1936.[52]

During 1932 autonomy efforts got under way in several other regions. The "Unión Aragonesa" convened a large assembly in Zaragoza on 26 June, and at a meeting in Valencia on 1 November the mayors from 229 of 263 municipalities in the province voted to proceed with preparation of a statute for the autonomy of the provinces of Valencia, Alicante, and Castellón.[53] On 23 November an "Andalusian flag" was raised before the town hall of Seville to symbolize the mobilization of an Andalusianist movement.[54]

The Labor Reforms

For the Socialists, the two key areas of reform were labor and land ownership. The initiative in the former lay with the labor minister, Francisco Largo Caballero, who sought to exploit the possibilities of Republican reformism to their maximum. That a position of relative hegemony for Socialist trade unionism might be built in a legal and constitutional manner through Republican administration and legislation made it only the easier and more effective. The reformist formula would not only construct a strong new system of binding legislation for Spanish labor but also commit the support of the middle-class left as well, multiplying the potential strength of the party and the UGT by giving both a broader base than they could win on their own. Hence Largo Caballero could confidently declare at the beginning of the Republic that "radicalism," by which he meant violent revolutionism, could have no place in Spain.

He declared to *El Socialista* on 18 April 1931 that he had already thought out "a plan of corporative reorganization."[55] It built on the social legislation of the previous regime, including that of the dictatorship, none of which was revoked, and was explicitly intended to function within a social democratic framework of capitalism. Largo's program recognized that for the time being the Spanish economy would remain "within the orbit of a determined economic system" and that it would not be possible to go "beyond the limits established in the most advanced countries of western Europe."[56]

The core of Largo's reform was presented in eight laws,[57] the basic terms of which he established in a series of decrees during his first three months as minister. Largo's new laws, like other reform decrees of the initial phase, were passed into binding legislation by the Constituent Cortes. These consisted of four laws on labor regulation — the Law of Labor Contracts, of Mixed Juries, of Worker Employment (*Colocación obrera*), and of Worker Intervention — together with basic administrative reforms — restructuring the ministry itself and creating provincial delegations of the ministry — and two laws on organization — the Law of Worker Associations and the Law on Cooperatives.

Largo's first decree, on 22 April 1931, established May Day as national labor day (Fiesta del trabajo), and others followed in comparatively rapid succession. A decree of 7 May initiated a national system of *jurados mixtos* (mixed juries), the joint labor-management arbitration committees first established in limited fashion for industrial labor under the dictatorship. As ratified by subsequent legislation of 27 November, the *jurados* were expanded to all of industry and to agriculture and services as well. Considerable attention was given to simplifying procedures to make them more effective, and much greater funding was assigned to their maintenance. Participating trade unions and employer associations would name their respective jurors for each branch in every local district. The jurors would then have to agree unanimously on a chairman, or else one would be appointed by the ministry, which also named the secretary of each *jurado*.

Even more important was passage of a new Law of Labor Contracts on

Francisco Largo Caballero, first labor minister of the Republic

21 November which reordered existing law with the aim of facilitating collective (that is, trade union) contracts as the basis of labor contracts henceforth. It provided that all contracts and working agreements be brought into full conformity with national labor legislation, particularly with reference to women and to child labor, Sunday rest, the length of the workday, and insurance. The eight-hour day had already been made normative in earlier decrees of 1 and 3 July. Terms of labor regulations in all factories employing fifty or more would have to be written formally, though in small shops more informal relations might continue. General norms for each branch and area would be negotiated through the *jurados mixtos.* Collective contracts would have to be in writing and valid for at least two years, and conditions in which contracts might be terminated were also defined. In general, this may be compared with contemporary German, Scandinavian, and American New Deal legislation in its regulation of collective terms of labor, being modeled to some extent along the lines of the existing norms of the Weimar Republic.[58]

Other laws were directed toward reducing unemployment. One of Largo's initial decrees (28 April 1931) established mandatory hiring of local farmworkers in each district (Términos municipales) before outside workers could be brought in. Another decree (8 May 1931) mandated *laboreo forzoso* — compulsory cultivation — of a certain portion of large estates each year, to mitigate the problems of absentee ownership and of withholding land from cultivation, the law to be administered and enforced by local governments.

The final version of a new bill on Worker Associations was passed on 8 April 1932. It updated existing legislation and facilitated the organization and activity of trade unions. Agrarian unions would also have the power to negotiate collective rent contracts for groups of small farmers.

Administrative reorganization of the Ministry of Labor was not completed until the end of 1932. The major new reform, creation of provincial delegations throughout the country to enforce changes and regulate problems, was intended to make the new policies effective even in the poorest provinces and to facilitate worker organization and representation. This was clearly a step forward for Spanish labor, yet it never went as far as Largo desired, for the full nationwide machinery could not be developed. Within the Republican administrative apparatus, the provincial delegations remained subordinate to the civil governors in each province, and their effectiveness was to a considerable extent determined by the latter.

The most controversial piece of legislation was a proposed "Ley de Intervención Obrera en la Gestión de la Industria" ("Law of worker intervention in industrial management"), presented to the Cortes in October 1931 but due to strong opposition never brought to a vote. This bill represented a Socialist effort to realize initially some of the more radical implications of the Constitution, but it was less far-reaching than it seemed, proposing to establish "management commissions of workers and employees" only in enterprises employing more than fifty. Members of such commissions would have to be affiliates of regularly constituted trade unions and were to have an essentially consultative role in technical aspects of labor. They were not, however, to have a vote on boards of directors nor have any authority with regard to finances or profits. This was not a proposal for true "workers' control," but even so it represented a change of some significance, and was not generally supported by the Republican parties.[59]

A major goal of labor reform was to create a complete and inclusive national insurance system, something which Largo called "el seguro integral." Article 46 of the Constitution dealing with labor was detailed, enumerating among other items that "legislation will regulate insurance for sickness, accidents, unemployment, old age, disability and death; and [will regulate] the work of women and the young and especially maternity rights." An Instituto Nacional de Previsión had existed for more than twenty years but lacked resources to extend insurance coverage broadly throughout the population. Largo moved rapidly to provide farmworkers with the same opportunities as industrial workers, but heavy state subsidies would be required to create a broad national system, and thus the overall achievements were somewhat limited. During the years of the Republic, retirement insurance was extended to an additional 1,300,000 workers, reaching a national total of 5,500,000, well over half the active population of 8,800,000. By 1935 funding for maternity insurance was 12.5 times the level of 1926, though still far from complete. Major strides were made in accident insurance, payments increasing by 300 percent between 1933 and 1935.[60]

The labor reforms constituted an impressive achievement. Organized labor and workers in general were given improved wages, power, respect, and better working conditions such as they had never known before.[61] Much more attention was given the rights and conditions of women workers, even though severe problems remained.[62] The results were most dramatic in agriculture, where wages rose steeply in 1932–33. The terms of the legislation were obviously designed to favor the UGT, but the CNT's common refusal to participate in *jurados mixtos* and other institutions was not the fault of either the Republican government or the Socialists.

There were at the same time severe limits to the accomplishments of the labor reforms. They depended, first of all, on local enforcement, which was often lacking. Provincial Republican officials were normally much more conservative than the Socialists in the Ministry of Labor. Moreover, strong resistance developed among employers within a matter of months, and this was particularly true in rural districts, where an increasing effort was made to ignore or completely sabotage much of the reform. A few aspects, such as the *términos municipales* decree, were simply mistaken, because the latter had scant effect in areas of massive unemployment but otherwise impeded the flow of labor.

For all these reasons, no complete balance sheet can be drawn of the labor reforms. They were generally progressive and salutary and had broadly beneficial aspects, and were especially helpful in improving farmworker salaries. They obviously increased costs, in some areas more than the economy could afford, but were generally beneficial to a struggling and underdeveloped society in time of depression.

Public Works

Development of public works was obviously a major need, first addressed on a larger scale under the dictatorship, which had begun a modern highway system and expanded investment in railroads and hydraulic works. The last regular government of the monarchy, facing mounting debt, had cut back considerably by 1930, while the original Republican program emphasized economic problems considerably less than it did political, institutional, and sociocultural reform'. The first Republican minister of public works, Alvaro de Albornoz, cancelled a large number of previous projects, though in August 1931 he did announce a new program for Andalusia and Extremadura that would spend 423 million pesetas over three years, partly through deficit financing. This targeted road construction and irrigation projects and was designed to combat unemployment in the poorest part of Spain.

The key public works minister of the Republic was Indalecio Prieto, who replaced Albornoz in Azaña's second cabinet of December 1931 and remained in office for twenty-one months. His main emphasis was on hydraulic programs, for which expenditures were nearly tripled by 1933 compared with the last regular monarchist budget. A new National Hydraulic Works Plan for the next twenty-five years was approved in November 1933 (soon after Prieto left office), drawn up under the supervision of Spain's leading irrigation engineer and planner, Manuel Lorenzo Pardo, dismissed by the sectarian and superficial Albornoz but reappointed by Prieto. Whereas new dam construction and irrigation programs under the dictatorship had been relatively decentralized and authorized for those areas most eager for them, Prieto's policy was more broadly national and centralized. It was also directed more toward the south and toward immediate as well as long-term needs, targeting some of the driest and poorest areas where landlords themselves resisted the transition to irrigation. Though it relied on public funding, a new law in 1932 required all landowners, 20 percent of whose land was irrigated, to pay a certain amount for new projects. The goal was to triple the amount of irrigated land within twenty-five years, and the immediate results were impressive. Whereas the dictatorship had nearly doubled the number of dams from twenty-nine in 1920 to fifty-one by 1930, and slightly more than doubled the total volume of water capacity, between 1930 and 1935 a total of twenty-nine more — mostly larger — dams were built, more than tripling the total water capacity.[63]

In 1932 Prieto also began significant new expenditures on railroads, mainly in the north, though over half the cost was to be borne by local government and institutions, and established a new system of state supervisors and inspectors over the still privately owned railroad companies. A major new government offices project, the Nuevos Ministerios, was begun in Madrid to expand modern administration space for twentieth-century government.

Since the fiscally rather conservative Republican administration would not accept more than a comparatively modest amount of deficit spending, there were severe limits to public works expansion. The main achievement was massive growth of the hydraulics program, though the parallel goal of creating enough new public works jobs to offset unemployment was never met.[64]

The Agrarian Reform

There was general recognition that the existence of a large immiserated rural proletariat in the southern half of the country constituted Spain's most important single social problem, but proposals to deal with it varied greatly. The conservative position held that the problem was so severely constrained by technical and economic limitations that no immediate solution was possible; only the most limited funding could be provided for buying up sections of latifundia for distribution, so that the basic problem could be solved only through long-term modernization, which would transform the structure of agriculture and soak up excess labor through urban employment. At the other extreme stood the various groups of revolutionaries, all of whom called for drastic agrarian reform, the confiscation or purchase of the larger properties and their division among farmworkers and dwarf-holders, preferably in the form of collective units. Somewhere in between

Indalecio Prieto

were the attitudes of middle-class Republicans, who believed that agrarian reform should be pursued but were not necessarily willing to make great sacrifices to provide adequate funding and certainly did not believe in collectivized agriculture.[65]

Though the problem was severe, its dimensions were much the same as in the southern half of Italy and Portugal, and did not reach colonial or third-world dimensions. For example, in Mexico in 1940, even after the Cárdenas reform, holdings of more than one thousand hectares occupied in toto 61.9 percent of the country's land surface, while the equivalent statistic for Spain was about 5 percent.[66]

Tiny dwarfholdings were just as characteristic of Spain as were large latifundia, the former being mainly concentrated in the north. Technically the bulk of all land units — nearly forty-two million out of a national total of slightly more than fifty-four million in 1959 — were tiny possessions of less than one-half hectare (about an acre), with one family sometimes holding a number of different dwarf plots. Altogether these amounted to less than 11 percent of all cultivated area in Spain. Units of between one-half and one hectare totaled nearly 6,900,000 and in toto amounted to another 10 percent of cultivated land, while those from one to five hectares numbered 4,243,122 and nearly 18 percent of cultivated land. In 1959 there were 596,035 holdings between five and ten hectares, amounting to only 8.3 percent of cultivated area, and only 439,404 "middle farms" between ten and one hundred hectares that added up to about 25 percent of the cultivated area. Very small properties under ten hectares thus amounted to 99.1 percent of all holdings.[67]

There were about fifty thousand larger holdings of more than one hundred hectares and slightly more than one thousand true latifundia of more than one thousand hectares. This total of slightly more than fifty-one thousand larger holdings occupied about 35 percent of all cultivated land (the true latifundia amounting to only 5 percent of the total), though they constituted 53.5 percent of all landed property, containing proportionately more uncultivated area.[68]

The problem was not the size of holdings alone, but even more the technical inefficiency of most of Spanish agriculture, compounded by frequent absentee ownership on large estates and a lack of alternatives for underemployed and immiserated laborers. The aristocracy was no more than a part of the issue, since it owned only 6 percent of the land. Ownership of most larger properties was comparatively recent in origin, the bulk of land titles dating from the mid-nineteenth century and a significant minority from the early twentieth century. More significant was the fact that, given a protected home market and a bountiful supply of cheap labor, there was limited rational incentive for most larger proprietors to modernize their techniques, even though in certain regions there had been slow, steady improvement since the late nineteenth century.

The matter was further complicated by the considerable political and cultural gulf between the agrarian populations of the northern and southern parts of the country. Propertied families — small proprietors, middle-class owners, and wealthy latifundists combined — comprised 60 percent of the agrarian population of northern and central Spain, and even more in the northern third alone. This gave northern and even part of central Spain a more conservative political complexion, reinforced by the extended Catholic religious identity and culture of most of the rural population.

In the south, by contrast, propertied agrarian families amounted to slightly less than a third of the rural population. Spain's 1,900,000 landless adult male farmworkers were mostly, though by no means exclusively, concentrated in the south, where as late as 1956 they accounted for 43.3 percent of the active rural population.[69] Not merely was the southern agrarian population much less propertied and generally poorer, but it had also become increasingly alienated from the hitherto established religion, heightening the sense of antagonism toward the existing order. A slow but steady increase in the south's share of total Spanish population, due mainly to a lower emigration rate, only added to chronic unemployment and the general malaise. Though Spanish argiculture was in general slowly modernizing, the overall plight of the 1.9 million farmworkers and the lower strata of the 700,000 small renters and sharecroppers — subject to very low wages or comparatively high rents, or both, and to insecurity of leases or sharecropping arrangements — was improving very little.

Agitation and strike activity among farmworkers had first reached notable proportions in 1903–4, then diminished only to reemerge stronger than ever in the so-called *trienio bolchevique* of 1918–20. The slightly meliorated conditions of the early and mid-1920s, combined with increasing literacy and renewed organization and agitation, raised the consciousness of much of the southern poor. This development was only accentuated by the effects of the agricultural pre-depression, which began with a general price decline in 1927, and was soon followed by a reduction in the area cultivated and clearly increased unemployment as early as the spring of 1929. Bad weather during 1930–31 only heightened the agrarian crisis,[70] but the coming of the Republic suddenly brought new hope. The new regime thus coincided with a deepened sense of indignation and a sudden leap in expectations, producing more volatile conditions than ever before.

The Republican leaders generally acknowledged that something must be done, while Socialists insisted that it be given high priority. But there was no agreement whatever as to the solution, and there were no easy options. As Edward Malefakis observes:

Spain lacked all the advantages that have facilitated land reform in other nations. In contrast to the new continents of North and South America, neither the state nor the municipalities possessed arable land that might be delivered to the peasantry by executive fiat and without expropriation. In contrast to Greece in the 1920s or to revolutionary France, so little land belonged to the Church that the alternative route whereby the expropriation of individual property might have been avoided was also closed. In contrast to Rumania in 1918 and Algeria in 1963, no important quantities of land belonged to foreigners, so that none of the repercussions that would follow expropriation of personal property could be safely diverted outside the political framework of the nation. Nor did enough land in Spain belong to the nobility for significant agrarian reform to be possible on the basis of an antiaristocratic crusade alone. If land were to be distributed to the peasantry, there was only one group from which it could be taken; the bourgeois owners who in most essentials were fully integrated into the political structure of the nation and could not be expropriated except at the cost of attacking some of the basic principles of that structure.[71]

The Provisional Government moved quickly by decree to bring some relief to rural renters and underemployed laborers. A measure of 29 April 1931 protected renters from having their leases suddenly cancelled, while from the Ministry of Labor Largo Caballero decreed the eight-hour day, began the expansion of *jurados mixtos,* and imposed the controversial decrees of *términos municipales* to preserve local labor opportunities for the local population, and *laboreo forzoso,* requiring large owners to follow "uses and customs" in keeping a reasonable amount of their area under cultivation or see an equivalent proportion of their land turned over to associations of workers.

The first approach to agrarian reform was the naming of a Comisión Técnica under the distinguished liberal jurist Felipe Sánchez Román, which presented a draft to the Constituent Cortes on 20 July 1931. It proposed to settle from fifty to seventy-five thousand landless families per year for twelve to fifteen years on land taken only from the larger holdings. There was to be no expropriation without reasonable compensation, though it was recognized that this might cost as much as 7 percent of the annual state budget. The draft proposed to finance most of program by a tax on larger owners. This was a coherent, technically sound, and straightforward proposal, but it met stiff opposition from conservatives and was not supported by the Socialists, who wanted even more.[72]

Sánchez Román's proposal was therefore replaced by an alternative drafted by Alcalá Zamora, which proposed to concentrate especially on aristocratic and absentee holdings. The Cortes committee on agriculture, which amended the bill in October, made its terms much more sweeping. The revised bill provided no exemption for directly cultivated lands, no compensation for expropriation of noble lands stemming from traditional seigneurial domain, and compensation for other lands at little more than one-third to one-half of market value. This measure had been almost as important as the passage of Article 26 in provoking Alcalá Zamora's resignation as prime minister. In reaction, two more moderate bills were advanced by Diego Hidalgo of the Radicals (despite their name, the most conservative of all Republican parties on economic issues) and Juan Díaz del Moral (a noted writer on southern agrarian themes) of Ortega's Agrupación al Servicio de la República.[73] These proposals were categorically rejected by the Socialists, who succeeded in having the main bill reported to the Cortes on 26 November with its more radical features accentuated. Yet Azaña's coalition lacked the strength to carry the legislation through parliament as a whole, and this controversy became a major factor in the Radicals' withdrawal from the government in December.[74]

The extent of opposition led the government to produce yet another, somewhat more moderate, version that was referred to committee on 24 March 1932. Its debate became the principal legislative drama of the summer of 1932 (overshadowing even the Catalan statute), with approximately three-fourths of Cortes discussion between 10 May and 9 September devoted to it. As in the case of Catalan autonomy, the logjam was finally broken by the catharsis of the *sanjurjada*, which reenergized the government while weakening the opposition. On 8 September Azaña himself made a major speech on behalf of the agrarian reform for the first time, and the following day all the main Republican parties (including the Radicals) joined to pass the bill by the overwhelming vote of 318 to 19. Only the Agrarians voted against it, but more than a quarter of the deputies—130 in all, including Ortega and his small group—abstained. The government also added an amendment blaming the high aristocracy, the *grandes*, for the recent revolt, even though only two of thirty-one aristocrats arrested in connection with it were *grandes* and there was no evidence whatever that the majority of *grandes* were involved. The amendment punished them by confiscating without compensation all *grande* lands subject to the terms of the new legislation, though they would be allowed to keep forest and pasture lands and a minor portion of their cultivated land. Azaña declared that the Republic was "revolutionary" and must adopt standards of revolutionary justice: thus it was irrelevant (in a typical expression of *azañista* logic) whether individual *grandes* had anything to do with the revolt; the economic power of the monarchist right must be broken, and such confiscations would constitute a cost-free start for the agrarian reform.

The Agrarian Reform Law of September 1932 was extremely complex but generally milder than the land reform laws of eastern Europe in the preceding decade. Since compensation would be provided for all but *grande* land and the principle of private property was respected, with varying limits for the amount subject to expropriation in the different categories, it was a genuine reform rather than a revolutionary act. The law defined thirteen different categories of expropriable land, with maximum limits not subject to expropriation varying from 100 to 150 hectares for vineyards to 300 to 600 hectares for grain lands (the most common category) to 400 to 750 hectares for pasture lands that were partially cultivated. Additional provisions made it possible to lower the exclusionary limits in certain cases, the most important of these applying to *ruedo* (or adjacent) lands that neighbored rural villages and towns, making liable to expropriation all uncultivated lands within two kilometers of inhabited villages in excess of land assessed at 1,000 pesetas in value (equal to about 20 hectares in grain land) for each owner within that municipality. This satisfied a demand of the Socialists, who hoped to make collective farming more attractive by providing sections of large estates directly adjacent to inhabited areas. Only four kinds of properties were subject to complete expropriation: land stemming from seigneurial domain, permanently rented land, land in generally irrigated zones that had not been irrigated, and land judged to be inadequately or very badly cultivated. Complex provisions defined such cases to safeguard due process and objectivity. Hardly any of these features were novel, all having been presaged by the variety of agrarian reform proposals developed since 1907. Moreover, the maximum total for each owner that would be free from expropriation would not be computed on the basis of each individual's total landholdings throughout the country or even in one province, but only within each municipal district. Land to be categorized as directly cultivated (a very flexible term) would earn its owner an additional premium of up to 33 percent more on his maximum limit in each municipality not subject to expropriation, and thus altogether the bulk of the farmland in the country was safeguarded from liability.[75]

The law would have drastic effects only in the latifundia districts of the south and south-center, where in some municipalities 50 to 60 percent or even in a few cases 70 percent of the land might be subject to expropriation. In the three leading latifundia provinces as a whole, this might include 46.3 percent of cultivated land in Badajoz, 46.6 percent in Cordoba, and 52.8 percent in Seville. Yet even here there were so many individual limitations that the actual amount of land likely to be expropriated was in fact considerably less. Moreover, the lease clause concerning expropriation of permanently leased land was restricted to the latifundia districts, while the traditional small rental units of central and northern Spain were excepted.

Yet in other ways the effect of the law's complex provisions was paradoxical, for the vast majority of the holdings technically required to be registered and potentially liable to some degree of expropriation were neither latifundia nor even located in the main latifundist provinces. When the inventory of landowners who might be subject to expropriation was completed in 1933, it contained 79,554 names, more than two-thirds of them in central and northern Spain rather than in latifundist districts, even though the majority might not in fact be very much affected by expropriation. Had the inventory been restricted to the eleven most heavily latifundist provinces, only 20,469 owners would have been potentially involved. Moreover, of 879,371 units of land potentially affected, only 17.6 percent were located in the eleven latifundist provinces. Nearly all provisions save the lease clause applied equally to all regions because of the Socialist insistence that the bill be as uniform and far-reaching as possible. In the small mountainous municipal districts of the north and in the heavily cultivated Mediterranean areas of the east, the exemptions from the lease clause were overweighed by the effects of the *ruedo* clause, for the existence of numerous small municipalities in these districts resulted in nearly half of all land being categorized as *ruedo* land. Even in the south, there was a considerable number of medium and even rather small holders who, thanks to the intricate terms of the reform, would actually be liable to having a higher proportion of their total holdings expropriated than would be the case with most latifundists, due to the consequences of the lease and *ruedo* clauses and the absence of cumulative totals for each large owner.[76]

Thus, while only ten to twelve thousand genuine largeholders existed, the potential terms of the reform targeted in theory as many as nearly eighty thousand owners. Nearly nine hundred thousand farms could potentially be involved, when the number of truly large ones was between thirty and forty thousand. The Socialists had accepted what was in most respects a very moderate reform, but insisted that it be applied very broadly, rousing the enmity of medium and small holders. Conversely, the chief opponents worked especially to protect most of the property of the large medium and large holders, while ignoring the interests of medium and small-medium farmers.

Though only certain large domains of *grandes* were to be confiscated outright, terms of compensation would vary greatly. A very complex set of formulae provided that owners of small and medium properties would receive 20 percent of the full value in cash and eventual compensation of 67 percent, the balance in ten-year bonds bearing 5 percent interest. Holders of the largest properties would initially receive only 1 percent in cash and eventual compensation amounting to only 28 percent. Yet once the assessment was completed, it appeared that the most extreme provisions of limited compensation would affect few. No more than 99 of 262 grandes would undergo the most extreme provisions, since the majority did not own enough land in the indicated categories in individual districts, and the holdings involved would amount to less than six hundred thousand hectares, capable of accommodating little more than sixty thousand landless families — a tiny minority of those in need. If the expropriations went forward according to regulation, most of the land would have to come from other owners and smaller properties claiming a higher rate of compensation, greatly increasing the burden to the state. Moreover, the government also agreed to pay off existing mortgages on units expropriated and compensate for current crops and cultivation, raising costs further.[77]

The law granted priority to farmworkers without any land as beneficiaries of the allotments made available. At Socialist insistence, second priority was given to already existing agrarian workers' societies that had been formed at least two years earlier (in most cases, by the UGT).[78] Third priority went to holders of farms of less than ten hectares, while the lowest priority for new land was given to small tenants and sharecroppers who rented units of less than ten hectares. The latter feature was meliorated by the fact that tenants who had worked the same land in units of less than twenty hectares for six years or more were guaranteed emphyteutic (life-term) tenure, and this would also apply to tenants of larger units who had worked them for thirty years or more. Final ownership of all agrarian reform properties would remain with the state and not pass directly to farmers, a feature which provoked much criticism. An Institute of Agrarian Reform with its own executive council and provincial juntas was created to administer the reform, and provision was also made for a National Agrarian Bank to provide credit for the beneficiaries and assist other needy small farmers.[79]

The result was a program that was extremely complicated, basically inadequate to accomplish the goals sought by its initial promoters and desperately underfunded. So little money was available that, as indicated in table 4.4, after more than two years only 12,260 families had been settled, so miniscule a number as scarcely even to constitute a beginning. The primary defects were the determination of the Socialists to apply it to the entire country, even to regions where it was inappropriate, the categorical

Table 4.4. Land Expropriated and Occupied under the Agrarian Reform Law
to 31 December 1934

	Number of estates	Extension (in hectares)	Proprietors established
Expropriated	468	89,133	8,609
Occupied	61	27,704	3,651
Total	529	116,837	12,260

Source: Institute of Agrarian Reform, *Agrarian Reform in Spain* (London, 1937), 29.

refusal to grant direct ownership, and the rejection of any program of fiscal redistribution, whether through an income tax or a surtax on larger properties, to finance it. Thus the reform fell between two stools, the Socialists seeking to extend it and the middle-class Republican left remaining too lukewarm about basic economic changes to give it the support and financing to make it effective. The rightist opposition was therefore more successful in the defense of its interests in this area than in any other. As one Republican leader would later write, the weakness of the reform won no new supporters to the defense of the Republic, but the fact that it existed at all, and with such complicated terms, gained the Republic new enemies on the center and right.

The Republican Reforms in Perspective

The reform legislation of 1931–33 represented a significant, often impressive attempt to come to grips with some of the crucial problems of democratization and modernization in Spain. There were major achievements in new school construction, expansion of the state teaching corps, labor reform and modernization, and a more creative program of public works, directed toward the south and toward future economic growth. Though limited, Azaña's military reform was the most extensive, and in some respects the best conceived, in more than a century. For the first time a major breakthrough was made in regional autonomy, indispensable for the development of a stable modern democracy in Spain. Moreover, the new system greatly expanded women's rights. Article 25 of the Constitution specified there would be no restriction of legal privileges by sex, while subsequent legislation established liberal terms for divorce and abortion.[80]

Yet some of the key reforms were badly flawed in goal or design and ultimately counterproductive. The anticlerical obsession which insisted that mere separation of church and state was inadequate, that Catholicism must be persecuted and Catholic education eliminated, was a fundamental mistake that can never be justified simply by reference to the preceding record of the Church. Azaña himself to some extent recognized the contradiction involved in trying to build a democracy on the basis of denial of rights, though he insisted that this was necessary for "public health." The consequence was to begin a process of political polarization and the growth of a new Catholic right hostile to Republican democracy. It also to some extent vitiated the educational expansion, because many of the new schools would be needed merely to replace the Catholic institutions which were to be arbitrarily suppressed.

The Republican platform stressed above all the completion of the nineteenth-century liberal reform of democratization, secularization, and cultural revolution, but almost by definition this was inadequate to deal with all the problems of the twentieth century. Ortega and a few others drew attention to the absence of a coordinated economic policy to achieve economic expansion and modernization, without which basic problems could never be resolved. The middle-class Republicans simply lacked economic goals, and they failed even to give attention to fiscal reform and more progressive taxation. The Socialists dwelt much more on social and economic issues, and Prieto and Largo, in quite different ways, can be seen as developmental and modernizing ministers. Yet the ultimate Socialist concern was with redistribution and, to some extent, with fostering collectivism rather than with modernization and increased productivity. The latter, admittedly, were not the prime goals of most European political groups in the 1930s.

Even some of the more positive reforms, such as Catalan autonomy and the reordering of the armed forces, involved significant negatives. The terms of the autonomy statute were basically fair and reasonable; partly for that very reason they did not fully satisfy left Catalanists and therefore would prove inadequate to weather the first major crisis in 1934. At the same time, the relative success of Catalanism was provoking an opposite reaction among the military and other sectors of the right, where a new counteractive right-wing Spanish nationalism was beginning to grow. Though the military reform was much more positive than negative, what it achieved was limited, and the style of Azaña's leadership was itself counterproductive. Also it may have been a mistake to spend as much on the military as was in fact done. The funding might have been better spent on education or public works.

Aside from religion, the most problematic of all the reforms was the agrarian problem, which involved major economic interests and revealed the extent of the division of political and social groups. None of the regular Republican parties was truly committed to a sweeping restructuring of property, nor is it clear how much good a massive expansion of the number of small farm proprietors would have accomplished. Quite aside from the fundamental division of priorities between middle-class Republicans and Socialists, there was the most limited provision for financing and credit, for modernization and productivity, the keys to any real improvement. The reform was largely conceived as a rather punitive zero-sum game. While alienating most landowners, the limited reform was not really convincing to poor renters and laborers. In some cases it may have encouraged the expression of resentment, as in the rural disorders which increased in the province of Badajoz during the final three months of 1932.[81]

It has been said that the Second Republic tried to solve too many problems and execute too many reforms all at once, inevitably overloading the system. There is some truth to this. The nearest thing to a model that Republican leaders had was the fin-de-siècle reformism of the French Third Republic, but in fact the sequence of events and structure of problems was very different in Spain. The French Republic was inaugurated after the fundamental breakthrough into modern industrialization and technical growth had already been achieved in the decades 1840–70. The first decade of the French Republic was devoted primarily to political consolidation without far-reaching structural, cultural, institutional, or social reform. French Republican reformism then only got underway during the 1880s, concentrating on education and health, with some attention to housing, working conditions, and mutual aid. The pace was much more careful and measured, involving a lengthy second phase of the Republic's history.[82] Church and state were separated in 1905, only after the Republic had existed for three and a half decades and was firmly consolidated. And even in France the politicization of military policy after 1900, of which Azaña thought so highly, was seen to be mistaken and subsequently greatly moderated.

The Second Republic in Spain much more nearly followed the pattern of the Portuguese Republic that had been inaugurated in 1910 and had proceeded immediately to a drastic separation of church and state. During the sixteen years that ensued, it compiled the sorriest record in Europe for factional strife and instability. Needless to say, however, no Spaniard would stoop to learn a lesson from the maladies of the Portuguese. From Azaña's perspective, the Portuguese had simply failed to be sufficiently authoritarian and radical.

Though liberalism had come early, full democratization had come late to Spain, which therefore had more problems to solve all at once, but this is inadequate to explain the failure of the Republicans to conceive a broad national platform for progress that a clear majority could support. Partial and uneven modernization had already fragmented the society both culturally and politically. With the exceptions of their efforts to overcome the regional cleavage and to foster public works, the Republican reforms tended to reflect that fragmentation rather than provide the means to overcome it.

The practical alternative might have been a majority Republican middle-class coalition on behalf of political democratization and economic modernization, eschewing drastic attempts at cultural and institutional revolution in the short run, and with a more modest social program. This basically was the proposal of such diverse personalities as Ortega, Lerroux, and Alcalá Zamora — in whole or in part. It would have had to face stronger initial opposition on the left but might have incorporated the moderate right. There is no guarantee that it would have succeeded, but its failure could scarcely have been worse than what ultimately took place.

The reformist coalition that actually ruled — composed of left Republicans and Socialists — was too weak and unrepresentative, and also too mutually contradictory to succeed. The Socialists for two years fooled themselves into believing that they had gained a strong ally in the progressive bourgeoisie, whereas Republican Action and the Radical Socialists merely represented the radical petit-bourgeois intelligentsia and limited sectors of the middle classes, though probably not the majority thereof. One consequence was to throw too great a burden on the Socialists. For the Republican left, the Socialists were the bearers of the broad popular support necessary to make a kind of radical democracy succeed. Though relatively effective in the 1931 elections, the Socialists were not strong enough to play that role, especially in the face of revolutionary competition from the anarchosyndicalists and the extreme expectations of much of Spanish labor.

The reforms of 1931–33 were thus the triumphs of a season, but both inadequate in some respects and counterproductive in others. It was not so much that the governing coalition tried to do too much, for much needed to be done. The main problem lay rather in that this package of partially liberal, partially leftist reforms was politically contradictory and unviable, satisfying neither the middle classes as a whole nor the working sectors as a whole. In the face of this mounting discontent, the alliance soon fragmented and went down to defeat before the reaction of moderates and conservatives.

5

Waning of the Left Republican Coalition

SUPPRESSION of the *sanjurjada*, followed in less than one month by completion of the basic reform program, raised the Republican alliance to its zenith of power and achievement. It had triumphed over all opposition and had no serious rival. The government's position appeared so dominant that even Lerroux (momentarily under a cloud because of rumors of complicity with Sanjurjo) stressed that the Radicals, though outside the ruling coalition, were also in the broader sense left Republicans. Its strength waxed even in the press, as the new owners of Madrid's leading Republican dailies lined up strongly behind the Azaña administration.[1]

Yet the government remained a coalition, and there lay the rub. The problem was twofold, concerning the future of alliance with the Socialists on the one hand, and the interparty unity of the Republican groups on the other. In a speech at Santander on 30 September Azaña publicly raised the question of the future of left Republican power, recommending formation of a broad confederation that could provide a basis for Republican government after the present administration's work was finished and the Socialists had dropped out. Response was generally favorable, though there were obstacles. The only casualty was Ortega's Agrupación al Servicio de la República, never a truly "left" Republican group, whose members had either voted against or largely abstained on both the Catalan and agrarian bills. Its dissolution was announced on 13 October. Eventually a new confederation, FIRPE (Federación de Izquierdas Republicanas Parlamentarias), was announced on 23 December, bringing together the left Republican parties who between them held at least 30 percent of the seats in the Cortes.[2] Only a few months would be needed, however, to show that the apparent unity was somewhat illusory and that the potential for serious division remained even within the left Republican groups.

125

Azaña was now at the height of his nominal power, but his personal attitudes and feelings remained covertly ambiguous. He had written in his diary on 20 August that

> My situation is dramatic. Every new event ties me more tightly to power, where I do not wish to be, and the more it makes me stand out above the others, the heavier is the weight placed upon me. I find it frightening to reflect that right now I have no possible substitute who could satisfy the Republicans and carry on government leadership. Where will all this lead us?

The question was the more pertinent because there was no vision of a broader democratic system of coexistence that might satisfy all the major social and political forces. Azaña and most of his colleagues continued to conceive of Republican politics as a zero-sum game in which their particular project was consubstantial with the Republic itself and could brook no division of power.

This was illustrated dramatically, and almost comically, in a Cortes debate over judicial independence on 23 November. During the past year the minister of justice had retired several hundred judicial officials — magistrates, judges, and prosecutors — for overtly Catholic identities or monarchist sympathies, sometimes for having made promonarchist remarks in a private capacity, in a few cases for still using aristocratic titles, and on one occasion for having harbored a Jesuit. Thus the Radicals and Agrarians introduced a bill to require the government to move as rapidly as possible toward creating the Tribunal de Garantías Constitucionales that had already been proposed in the Cortes. The basic problem was illustrated by the debate between Azaña and the new Catholic rightist leader Gil Robles:

AZAÑA: . . . We hear protests against changes in judicial personnel and the charge: "The independence of the judicial power is endangered." No. Why not? In the first place, I don't know what the judicial power is. Here is the Constitution. I do not govern with books of texts, or articles, or with philosophical and doctrinal treatises. I govern with this little book — the Constitution — and I say that they should look for the judicial power in this book and see if they find it. There is a great and important difference between saying "judicial power" and saying "administration of justice"; they are worlds apart in the concept of the state. Independence of the judicial power? According to what? Independence from whom?

GIL ROBLES: From the government, from the interference of the government.

AZAÑA: Well, I do not believe in the independence of the judicial power.

GIL ROBLES: But the Constitution says so.

AZAÑA: The Constitution may say whatever it wants; I say . . .

GIL ROBLES: Article 94.

AZAÑA: What I say is that neither the judicial, nor the legislative, nor the executive power can be independent of the national public spirit, and, even
less, hostile to the public spirit that informs the entire state.

GIL ROBLES: That was what Primo de Rivera used to say.

AZAÑA: Well, Primo de Rivera had to be right some time. What cannot be permitted functionaries of any class, whether they wear judicial robes or
not, is to sit behind a desk and conduct business with the goal of contradicting the will of the political majority and of the state.

The proposal was defeated by 142 to 100, marking the first time that the
Radicals voted directly against the government.[3]

The Second Anarchist Offensive

The destruction, deaths, and defeat that had met the first FAI-CNT offensive against the Republic and Spanish capitalism in 1931–32 had not
discouraged anarchist revolutionaries. Though they complained that Republican police measures were "worse than the monarchy," the degree of
repression had in most instances been comparatively mild, and most anarchist cadres remained intact. Moreover, organized labor had made impressive gains since the fall of the monarchy. Though this was mainly due
to Socialist reformism within the Republic, it also had the effect of encouraging CNT militants to greater efforts. Thus 1932 had been a year of
overall radicalization of the FAI-CNT, with moderates systematically purged
and anarchist revolutionary militance dominant within most sectors of a
labor movement that now counted nearly a million affiliates.

There were numerous strikes during September and October 1932, accompanied by bomb explosions in five major cities and arson or other attacks on churches in nine cities, again particularly severe in Seville. One
small town in Huelva province was briefly taken over by the FAI, and at
least five workers were killed during these two months, mostly in clashes
with the police.

Not all worker disorders stemmed from anarchists. Through the autumn
there were increasing complaints of "anarchy" in the countryside of Extremadura and in the provinces of Seville and Jaén, with reports of inva-
sions of farmland in four southern provinces as well as Zaragoza, Toledo,
and Avila. In some of these districts the UGT was clearly predominant
and Socialist farmworkers were involved, and in the southwest there was
evidence that some of the local Casas del Pueblo had seized the initiative
in their own interpretation of the *laboreo forzoso* decrees. Passage of the
agrarian reform legislation had only stimulated militant farmworkers to

direct action, and this in turn led to two interpellations in the Cortes. The pro-Azaña *Ahora* lamented on 12 November:

> As a result of irresponsible and demogogic propaganda, a state of veritable anarchy has been created in the Extremaduran countryside that makes normal agricultural work impossible. Bloody clashes and daily incidents make private property in some parts of Extremadura meaningless. Authority loses prestige more and more each day while the audacity of those who promote disorder grows steadily.

During the second half of November general strikes were attempted in six provincial capitals, beginning with Seville on the sixteenth. The most important labor stoppage since the beginning of the Republic, however, was the walkout of thirty thousand Asturian coal miners, which started on the fourteenth. Depression conditions had created a surfeit of coal and had reduced the work week for those still employed to four days or less. The strike was an embarrassment for the UGT, and the government finally agreed to purchase a hundred thousand tons—nearly a third of the current surplus—but complete calm was not restored in Asturias for nearly a month. Another sizable UGT strike began in Salamanca on 5 December and soon spread beyond the city. The national leadership of the UGT in Madrid did all it could to end these stoppages, though unemployed UGT workers were demanding very high dole payments for all without work. When UGT railworkers threatened a paralyzing national rail strike unless they received major concessions, the Socialist minister of public works, Prieto, took an outspoken stand against them on behalf of the national public interest.

Minor acts of political violence continued during the final weeks of 1932. Antileftist forces were now more aggressive. A Socialist was killed by Basque nationalists in Vizcaya and two others by rightists in Orense and in Ciudad Real, while the Socialist mayor of a small town was killed in Cordoba province. Two policemen were killed in Valencia province, and a judge in Cordoba province. For all these killings, there were only a limited number of arrests and very few convictions.

The FAI's goal was another revolutionary insurrection, accompanied by a greater effort at coordination and planning than in January 1932. The initiative was taken by Juan García Oliver and his *cuadros de defensa* of the FAI who hoped to spark simultaneous revolts in industrial districts and small towns mainly in Catalonia and Andalusia, but also including other areas of the northeast and east. At the last minute the CNT railway confederation decided not to participate, and to the end there remained confusion as to whether the national committee of the CNT was actually supporting the effort. In the final days of 1932, FAI-CNT prerevolutionary activity was evident, with bomb explosions in a number of cities. By the third of January the police had discovered small bomb factories in Zaragoza and San Sebastián, two caches of bombs in Barcelona, and one in Valencia. A variety of minor disorders broke out in widely scattered spots during the first week of January, while in Alcalá de Henares there began the court martial of six soldiers and several civilians accused of participating in a Communist conspiracy.

The new mini-insurrection began at dusk on 8 January 1933. The main assaults were launched by armed anarchists against police stations and military installations in Barcelona, as well as in at least seven other localities in Catalonia. Several feeble attacks on military barracks in Madrid were easily beaten off. At least eight people were killed in Barcelona, including two policemen. The most extensive bloodshed occurred in a FAI assault on army barracks at Lérida, where five *faístas* and one soldier were killed. Several more people were killed in other incidents in Catalonia. That night more than twenty bombs were exploded in Valencia, and several pueblos in the surrounding province were momentarily taken over by the FAI, who slew five Civil Guards in one of them. Other disorders occurred in Seville, Zaragoza, Málaga, Gijón, and several other cities.

The government was relatively well informed and on the following day (9 January) declared martial law in the provinces most affected. It closed the offices of CNT syndicates throughout Spain and began plans for new legislation to create a special penitentiary in the African territories. Conflicts persisted in the Barcelona and Valencia districts, and there was an attempted general strike in Granada, but by the eleventh order was generally being restored, even though minor disturbances continued. Altogether more than eighty people were variously reported killed, mostly would-be insurrectionists, though no complete statistics were ever released by the government.[4] The hoped-for mass support never materialized. This was another example of Spanish anarchists "playing at revolution," engaging in small scattered, often isolated risings that had no chance of success. Nonetheless, the FAI-CNT assaults on the Republic and on Spanish society had been persistent, the most extensive attack from any quarter on a new regime in Spain since the last Carlist war.

The effect on both the FAI and CNT was destructive. In addition to the hundreds arrested and heavy fines levied against the main anarchist publications, popular support declined. The FAI began to lose members, and soon about one-third of the CNT's membership had dropped out.

Casa Viejas

The great drama of the January 1933 insurrection did not occur in any FAI center such as Barcelona, Zaragoza, or Valencia but in the pueblo of

Casas Viejas in Cadiz province of the far south. A fairly typical, poverty stricken, small Andalusian town, Casas Viejas had a population of some two thousand including nearly five hundred *braceros*, of whom it was said that scarcely more than a hundred had reliable employment. Of six thousand hectares of cultivable land in its districts, little more than two thousand were sown in certain years. Though the FAI-CNT paid much less attention to the countryside than to industrial areas, Casas Viejas was one of a number of Andalusian pueblos where plans had been made to second the anarchist insurrection in the northeast. Thus at dawn on the eleventh, as the insurrection was dying down elsewhere, the anarchosyndicalists among the Casas Viejas *braceros* — a fairly high proportion of the total — took over the little pueblo, declared "libertarian communism," destroyed municipal records and surrounded the small building housing the four local Civil Guards, fatally wounding two of them. Around noon a dozen Civil Guards arrived from Medina Sidonia, the nearest center, and quickly cleared the town, discreetly firing their rifles in the air to avoid unnecessary casualties. Four or five insurrectionists were taken prisoner, including at least one involved in the attack on the Civil Guards. He was severely beaten and made to reveal the identities of other participants. Meanwhile, morale had plummeted among the would-be insurrectionists after the arrival of the first reinforcements, and nearly all the morning's rebels had fled the pueblo for the countryside.

About 5:00 P.M. the police were further reinforced by a second detachment of twelve Assault Guards and four more Civil Guards. They cautiously explored the town and about dusk approached the thatch-roofed hut of a septuagenarian charcoal maker, Francisco Cruz Gutiérrez, known by his nickname of "Seisdedos" ("Sixfingers"), whose two sons and son-in-law had clearly been implicated. All three of the latter were inside the hut with other family members, and when a Civil Guard entered the doorway he was shot dead with a shotgun blast. The hut was surrounded but difficult to fire at because it was located in a depression, while the Assault Guards had no rifles. The *campesinos* (peasants) within were good shots, while other insurrectionists from nearby knolls and rooftops also fired at the police, wounding several. Between 10:00 and 11:00 P.M. a few more guards arrived with a machine-gun, which, however, would not fire.

Finally about 2:00 A.M. forty more Assault Guards arrived under Captain Manuel Rojas. They were part of a full company sent from Madrid to Jerez the preceding night, who had spent all day patrolling Jerez and now, without genuine rest for nearly forty-eight hours, were ordered on to Casas Viejas. Rojas later testified that the Dirección General de Seguridad had given direct orders that all resistance must be snuffed out that

Assault Guards besieging the hut of Seisdedos in Casas Viejas, 11 January 1933

night, even if it meant burning houses. The machine-gun was repaired and managed to drive off most of the surrounding snipers, after which a tele-gram arrived from the provincial governor directing them to destroy the hut if necessary to end the resistance. The *choza* was fired, its thatch roof lighting up like a torch. A young woman and boy were allowed to escape, but all remaining inhabitants died either of bullet wounds or incineration. Altogether, they numbered four local anarchosyndicalists involved in the previous morning's assault, the elderly "Seisdedos" and one other young man, and two women. During the siege, one guard had been killed and a number wounded.

By daybreak the weary guards were consumed with anger and frustra-tion. A sweep was made of the pueblo to arrest anyone else who might have been involved. One elderly man was shot and killed in the search and twelve young men were arrested (probably in most cases innocent, since the active insurrectionists had largely fled upon the approach of po-lice reinforcements the preceding day). The dozen (mostly very young) prisoners were herded to the embers of the hut to view the bodies of the fallen. Rojas later testified that one or more made an insolent gesture, at which the guards opened fire, quickly shooting down all twelve. Altogether twenty-two civilians died in Casas Viejas, twelve of them summarily executed in cold blood, while three guards (counting the two who later died of wounds) perished.[5]

For a fortnight no news appeared save the limited official version that some twenty anarchists had been killed in an insurrection in Cadiz province. After a short time, however, the surviving anarchist press began to carry a different version nearer the truth.[6] The government vigorously defended its strong line, Azaña lamenting in his diary on 15 January that "nobody wants to obey, except by force."[7] After the Cortes reopened on 1 February, the opposition began to question the government's policy, and on the following day the dissident Radical Socialist Balbontín charged that the police action at Casas Viejas was worse than anything under the monarchy. On 15 February the Radical Party initiated a policy of systematic parliamentary obstruction. Since the government denied an investigation, seven opposition deputies journeyed to Casas Viejas on their own and reported many of the facts to the Cortes on 23 February. On the following day one deputy charged that this was much worse than the notorious Francisco Ferrer execution of 1909, which became an international cause célèbre but was at least done by due process of law. Thus the government had little alternative to naming an official parliamentary investigating commission on the twenty-fourth.

On 7 March, after one Assault Guard lieutenant had revealed the truth and after Rojas made a partial and secret confession to the government, Azaña announced the resignation of Arturo Menéndez, director general de seguridad, and that Rojas and his chief lieutenant had been relieved of duty. The commission then reported to the Cortes that the facts were substantially as charged but that there was no evidence that any member of the government had been involved. The government in turn insisted that elsewhere members of the police had been unnecessarily sacrificed to avoid civilian casualties and that the guards in Casas Viejas had been fired on by numerous snipers during the night of 11–12 January, both of which claims were correct.

Rojas and other Assault Guard officers stoutly maintained that Menéndez had given them categorical instructions to make examples of the rebels and that they wanted "neither prisoners nor wounded," while a General Staff officer assigned to Azaña's Ministry of War claimed that he had received orders directly from Azaña in terms of "Neither prisoners nor wounded. Shoot them in the belly." The latter probably constituted perjury on the part of the captain, but there was considerable circumstantial evidence that Menéndez had issued unusually stern orders. Rojas was eventually brought to trial in May 1934, convicted, and sentenced to twenty-one years in prison,[8] the only member of the security personnel effectively prosecuted for police atrocities under the Republic until 1936.

The Cortes had eliminated the death penalty on 6 September 1932 and reduced the term of life imprisonment to twenty years, but the government remained determined to enforce a firm policy against subversion. Casas Viejas was the worst of several police atrocities under the left Republican coalition and was strongly denounced by the center, right, and extreme left, though the government survived a vote of confidence with the abstention of the opposition. What particularly shocked the public was that the harshest treatment had been dealt an inconsequential group of miserably poor, possibly illiterate, farmworkers in the deep south, while the more sophisticated anarchist leaders and skilled workers of the industrial northeast, who were the major insurrectionists, were treated much more carefully. In addition, the government's policy of creating a new corps of Assault Guards to ensure more humane police control seemed to have backfired, since it was they who had been the main perpetrators.

The government forces, of course, saw themselves as more sinned against than sinning, for no government of the monarchy had drawn such an extreme and sustained assault from anarchists and communists as had the democratic Republic. In an underdeveloped country now undergoing rapid modernization, political democratization had the effect of stimulating the extreme left to ever more extensive and violent efforts, creating the seeming paradox that the freer and more modern the society became, the more intense appeared to become its social and political contradictions.

Moreover, suppression of the January insurrection provided only a temporary respite from disorder, which reappeared within a few weeks. Bombs were exploded in at least a score of cities between March and June, and three Civil Guards were killed on Gomera island in the Canaries on 23 March. There seems also to have been an increase in common crime, making it harder to distinguish political violence from criminal violence.

Between February and June the CNT attempted general strikes in at least nine medium- or large-sized cities and among peasants in Seville province, and many more ordinary strikes, perhaps the most notable of which was one by miners in Asturias, beginning on 7 February to protest layoffs. The Socialists declared a nationwide general strike for 1 May, as in the preceding year, simply as a gesture of observance. On that day the UGT refrained from marches or demonstrations out of respect for Socialist participation in the government, though the CNT and Communists did all they could to compensate. Three days later (4 May), the Basque nationalist Solidaridad de Obreros Vascos (SOV, Basque Workers Solidarity) declared a general strike in the Bilbao district on the occasion of a visit by Azaña, and seventy-one imprisoned nationalists began a hunger strike.

The CNT, in turn, decided on its first major action since January, a new nationwide protest strike to seek the release of hundreds of jailed anarchosyndicalists. This commenced on 8 May, with disorders and bomb explosions in Madrid, Barcelona, Bilbao, Seville, and Asturias. It brought many workers off the job in those districts and became a virtual general strike in La Coruña and Salamanca, spreading further on the ninth. That day three persons were slain in Madrid (two of them policemen) and one in Alicante, while two Civil Guards and three strikers were killed in Játiva. This affair generally lasted three days, with minor disturbances in widely scattered spots, and a particularly high degree of disorder in Valencia. Altogether another two thousand workers were arrested. Crowded conditions and political agitation produced considerable unrest in jails, and a mass escape was engineered from one prison in Valencia.

Agrarian unrest remained intense in the southwest, with numerous complaints over invasion of farmlands, cutting of trees, killing of cattle, and burning of crops. There were several gunfights in Badajoz province in February, with a number of deaths. On 1 March the Asociación General de Ganaderos (Stockmen) declared that the value of livestock in the province had declined by a third due to widespread cattle killings, though this was doubtless an exaggeration. The mayor of a small town in Córdoba province was reported to have been killed, allegedly by a Socialist, on 25 March, while two men identified as "invaders" of farmland were killed in Seville province in April, and a week later a priest in Ciudad Real who was identified as an administrator of rural property was reportedly slain. These and other deaths are best narrated as macrostatistics, since the exact circumstances and responsibilities were often in doubt. On 8 May two thousand protestors from Seville arrived in Madrid to protest "economic anarchy" in the south. Twelve days later Pedro Caravaca, the secretary of the "Federación Económica de Andalucía" who had organized the protest, was shot and killed in a street in Seville; the minister of the interior subsequently attended his funeral there. The "Federación Patronal" (Employers Federation) of Madrid later published statistics on "social crimes" during the first half of 1933, charging that these had produced 102 deaths and wounded 140 others. If the loss of life in the January insurrection was included, this was probably an underestimate.

The Government Weakens

The effect of Casas Viejas and the continued disorder was not merely to encourage the opposition but also to stimulate division within the Republican alliance. The broad union of the Republican left attempted by the FIRPE soon proved abortive, as many of the once incendiary Radical Socialists moved either to more moderate positions or adopted attitudes more critical of the government. Azaña's response was quite the opposite, for now the coalition with the Socialists seemed to him more important than ever. In a major speech at Madrid on 14 February, he declared that since "all modern societies are in the process of vertiginous transformation," it was vital "that if at all possible our country carry out a profound transformation of society, sparing us the horrors of a social revolution,"[9] indicating his own movement to a more strongly social democratic reformist position than heretofore.

The main attention in early spring was on elections to approximately 19,000 seats in 2,478 municipal councils — amounting altogether to about 10 percent of Spain's total and located primarily in the conservative north — where elections had been uncontested in 1931 and where since the start of the Republic these positions had been taken over by centrally appointed *comisiones gestoras*. Gil Robles asked the government formally to suspend the Law for the Defense of the Republic during the campaign, since, according to its sweeping terms, any criticism of the government might bring severe punishment. After Azaña refused, a motion to suspend the law failed in the Cortes by a vote of 132 to 87. During the campaign conservatives made a number of allegations about curtailment of electoral freedom and minor assaults from the left. All the while the Radical Party was engaged in its own campaign of opposition, complaining that for two years the government had shown systematic favoritism to the UGT (which was of course true) and that local officials in fact themselves fomented agrarian disorders in the south and southwest.

The partial municipal elections of 23 April resulted in the government's first clear-cut defeat. Of the 19,000 council seats, the government parties won only 5,048 (1,826 of them Socialists), the right an approximately equal number (some 4,000 of them Agrarians), while moderate and independent Republicans outside the government did best of all, with about 6,000, the remaining approximately 2,500 going to various independents of all hues and to unclassifiable local elements.[10] The right had made a comeback, yet opinion even in the conservative north was not deserting Republicanism, but broadly endorsing a more moderate or conservative brand of Republican democracy. Azaña tried to shrug it off, dismissing these primarily northern municipalities as what in eighteenth-century England were called "rotten boroughs," thoroughly manipulated and controlled.

These were the circumstances under which the final terms of the Law on Religious Congregations were passed by the Cortes on 11 May and reluctantly signed by Alcalá Zamora on 2 June. There were new cases of arson or attempted arson against religious buildings in more than a score of towns during May and June, though Catholic spokesmen pointed with pride to the number of religious displays hung from private homes in Madrid and other cities in conjunction with the Feast of the Sacred Heart on 23 June. By this point more and more Republicans evinced doubt concerning the wisdom of the strict enforcement of the ban on public religious displays that had resulted in so many petty fines during 1931–32.

With the position of the government clearly weakening, Azaña proposed a truce to Lerroux and the Radicals — the only important opposition Republican party — in order to complete basic Republican legislation. This the Radicals denied, though they did vote with the government in a new law on 7 June to create a Tribunal de Garantías Constitucionales, which would serve as a court of appeal regarding the constitutionality of future legislation. Over the protest of the opposition, the new law specifically exempted legislation of the current Constituent Cortes from constitutional review.

The prestige of the governing alliance was slightly weakened further by the hostility of some of the nation's leading intellectuals, who held Cortes seats. Luminaries such as Ortega y Gasset and Unamuno had first begun to criticize the government with the drafting of some of the more extreme features of the Constitution in the autumn of 1931 and had become more outspoken in their hostility a year later. Unamuno declared in a speech before the Madrid Ateneo on 28 November 1932 that, "I don't care if they call me a rightist," since "all the evils of the old regime continue." He later told the press that the present Republican government was maintaining the "dictatorship of a parliamentary majority" and in fact waging "civil war."[11] Ortega, having dissolved his own political group, continued to criticize the government for sectarianism, and during the spring of 1933 gave a number of speeches in various parts of the country about the need for a grand national unity party that could end discord and concentrate on necessary tasks of modernization. He would declare in October that

the Republic uses old ideas that have been retired in all other countries. It is lamentable that the Republic, which might have taken advantage of its marvellous installation to carry out a great new work, has instead relied on programs and postulates of the nineteenth century, without being able to create a new ideology or politico-social philosophy of its own.[12]

This critical attitude was increasingly reflected in the Madrid liberal press. El Sol, La Voz, and Luz, hitherto supportive of Azaña, underwent further changes in administration and by mid-1933 were strongly attacking the government for one-sidedness, sectarianism, and divisiveness. Ortega's seemingly elitist approach won him little direct political support, but rejection by leading intellectuals and the Madrid liberal press further tarnished the fading luster of the ruling coalition.

Cabinet Realignment

The cabinet was facing reorganization due to the growing dissension among the Republican parties and more specifically to the fatal illness of Jaume Carner, minister of finance, suffering from terminal throat cancer. Azaña had been forced to supervise Carner's ministry since 24 February, a situation that could not long continue. After passage of the major new legislation that was completed in the first days of June, he approached the president to gain the required approval for appointing a new finance minister. Alcalá Zamora, however, had become increasingly restive with the coalition, which he basically opposed, and for several weeks had conducted conversations with leaders of the more moderate Republican groups, with a view toward the formation of a more conservative coalition that might replace Azaña.[13] Thus, rather than accept the replacement of the finance minister as Azaña requested, the President chose to treat the matter as a full cabinet crisis and to "open consultations" with a long list of twenty Republican party leaders, including leading intellectuals such as Ortega, Unamuno, and Marañón, now known for their critical attitudes. Most of them recommended a broadening and balancing of the existing coalition, shifting it farther to the right.

Aside from Azaña, the only other party leaders with a real chance at forming a government were Prieto of the Socialists and Marcelino Domingo of the Radical Socialists. Both failed in the endeavor. In Prieto's case, Alcalá Zamora indicated that he would expect the return of the Radical Party to create a balanced coalition, but the Socialist executive commission and parliamentary group vetoed any negotiation with the Radicals, leaving no alternative to the continuation of Azaña, who announced his new cabinet on 13 June. The economist and financial executive Agustín Viñuales became minister of finance, the Catalan Esquerra entered the cabinet as Lluis Companys was made minister of the navy, and the small Federal Republican Party was brought into the coalition, with one of its leaders assigned to the Ministry of Industry and Commerce.

The price of Federal Republican support was termination of the draconian Law for the Defense of the Republic. A new Law of Public Order was approved by the Cortes on 25 July. It covered many of the same provisions as the old law but in a more qualified manner. The new law defined three different states of legal exception. The first and mildest, designated a "state of prevention," might be imposed for a maximum of sixty days without

suspending constitutional guarantees and bore greater similarity to legislation of 1867, during the most repressive phase of the Isabeline regime,
and to that of the dictatorship than to the juridical norms of the constitutional monarchy. It enabled the government to ban meetings and publications, prohibit travel, and intervene in commerce and industry.

The second category, the "state of alarm," could be declared by the council
of ministers whenever "state security" required and authorized personal
arrest, the entry into private homes, and temporary exile of up to 250
kilometers from the place of residence. The third and most severe category
was the "state of war," or martial law, in which command passed to the
military without provision for the formation of joint "consejos de guerra"
(war councils) of civilians and officers, as under the legislation of the constitutional monarchy. In addition, the Law of Public Order authorized formation of *tribunales de emergencia* to be composed of provincial judges
empowered to deal summarily with all crimes against public order under
the states of prevention and alarm.[14]

This legislation was passed without strong opposition, and the new
powers were first invoked to impose a state of prevention in Seville from
18 August to 18 October. Henceforward, one or another of the various
states of exception would be in effect for some part of Spain, and in certain periods for the entire country, almost every day until the start of the
Civil War.

On 26 July, one day after approval of the new Law of Public Order,
the Cortes passed by an overwhelming vote of 244 to 4 a measure limiting
the scope of trial by jury. It excluded from the jurisdiction of jury trials
all crimes against the Cortes or its members, against the government or
the existing form of government, as well as murder, arson, terrorism, armed
robbery, and the use of explosives. Lest this be considered illiberal, the
Radical Socialist minister of justice Alvaro de Albornoz told the parliament: "I do not in any way share the liberal and democratic ideas of the
nineteenth century. I declare before the Chamber that every day I am less
liberal and democratic and each time have less to do with those liberal
and democratic cliches [*tópicos*]. . . . For me there is no law save in the
state and by the state." He justified this position by saying that in eleven
cases of crimes of sedition or rebellion brought before a grand jury in Bilbao in 1932, not a single indictment had been filed.

Socialist Ambivalence

Despite underlying uncertainty, Socialist commitment to the Republican
coalition actually increased during 1932 and the first part of 1933. The

thirteenth congress of the PSOE was held from 6 to 13 October 1932, and the motion to continue participation, once led by Prieto, was approved by representatives of sections with 23,718 party members to 6,356, a stronger margin than in the preceding year. Though a bitter dispute ensued over responsibility for the failure to provide effective support for the abortive Republican revolt of 1930, leaders were relatively united over short-term goals. Even Besteiro conceded that withdrawal from the coalition was not immediately advisable. In a narrow vote, Largo Caballero won the presidency of the party executive commission over Besteiro by a vote of 15,817 to 14,261. The UGT congress, which opened the day after the party congress closed, resulted in a major triumph for Besteiro, who was elected president of the Union's executive commission.[15] The nearest thing to a quasi-dissident left wing was represented by the Socialist Youth (JS). At their national congress in February 1932 they had endorsed virtual elimination of the defense budget, withdrawal of all troops from Morocco, and drastic reduction of the armed forces. The Socialist Youth had also petitioned the party leadership to begin formation of Socialist paragovernmental organisms that would later replace the ministries of the "bourgeois regime."[16]

The enormous increase in the UGT during 1930–32 had converted it into the fulcrum of the movement, since Unión membership had swelled to nearly twenty times that of the Socialist Party, which by comparison remained rather small and elite. By mid-1932 the farmworker FNTT had reached a membership of 445,000, or nearly half the total. This, however, represented a new, backward, relatively untrained, and volatile group of laborers, distinct from the skilled and semiskilled industrial workers who had previously made up the bulk of the Unión, and among older and moderate leaders there was growing concern that the flood of illiterate or semiliterate farmworkers would seriously distort the character of the movement. Similarly, the greatest growth in party membership had come in Andalusia, which now had the largest number of affiliates of any region.[17]

The initial labor reforms of 1931–32 had generated great enthusiasm, but this changed to greater frustration by the summer of 1932, when it became clearer that the government lacked the mechanisms to enforce all the new regulations, particularly in the rural areas. There was a decline in the amount of land cultivated in 1931 because of economic conditions and to some extent because of the reforms. By mid-1932 a considerable number of *arrendatarios*, the large-scale renters and middlemen, who actually managed much of the land on the large southern estates, were reducing their operations, claiming that wages had reached uneconomic levels. Both sides were dissatisfied, for market conditions made it hard for landowners to make much money, while the reduction in cultivation made it even more difficult for laborers to find employment, so that higher wages were of no benefit to some. Many of the smaller landowners suffered severely, and by 1932 there were sometimes concerted efforts to avoid complying with the terms of the labor reforms. According to statistics presented by the Ministry of Labor, 83 percent of all infractions or complaints of infractions of labor regulations during 1932 had to do with those committed by employers.[18]

The revolution of rising expectations that had set in earlier was turning in many regions to disillusionment and even bitterness and anger, under the joint impact of the depression and employer resistance. Coal miners in Asturias were outraged over their loss of jobs and reduction in working time while the country was still importing cheaper, higher quality British coal, and the UGT leadership was not always able to keep them in line, despite the UGT position that strikes during a depression and under a Socialist minister of labor were counterproductive.[19] Dissident railworkers set up their own rival railroad union and tried to foment a large strike. The national UGT leadership stood firm, avoiding the strike but losing several thousand members. In Salamanca, where UGT farmworkers complained that the jurado system was not really working and that arbitrated wage rates were not being fully paid, a brief general strike could not be avoided in mid-December, 1932.[20] Although UGT leaders soon managed to bring the strike to an end, they were nonetheless becoming increasingly worried by the rivalry and extremist tactics of the CNT, whose steady pressure on the Socialist unions was becoming harder to ignore. Even at the recent party congress that had reendorsed participationism, some of the top party leaders hedged their position, with Largo Caballero stipulating that the party "is not [merely] reformist, nor is that the spirit of its members. And the history of the party is there to demonstrate it, showing that legality has been broken when that suited our ideas. . . . No one intends to revise our doctrines. This is now merely a question of tactics."[21]

Though about two-thirds of the new settlements arranged by the *jurados mixtos* were still categorized as favorable to the workers,[22] strike activity increased markedly in 1933, as indicated in table 5.1, and more UGT syndicates were becoming involved. The growth in strikes had several causes, one being that a large proportion of the new contracts negotiated in 1931 were two-year agreements up for renewal during 1933. Constant incitement by the CNT was another factor, to which must be added mounting unemployment (see table 5.2) as Spain entered the trough of its depression (see chapter 6), workers' frustration over the practical limitations of the *jurado* system and effective implementation of new regulations, and

Table 5.1. Spanish Strike Statistics

	Number of Strikes	Workers on Strike
1930	402	247,460
1931	734	236,177
1932	681	269,104
1933	1,127	843,303

Source: *Anuario Español de Política Social 1934–35* (Madrid, 1936).

increasing eagerness simply to seize the initiative before things got seriously worse again. Hence the seeming paradox that as the depression deepened, strike actions more than doubled and the number of workdays lost zoomed from 3,589,473 in 1932 to 14,440,629 in 1933.

Protests from employers and landowners mounted, with increasing complaints about direct action by Socialist farm laborers and renters in the south. The *laboreo forzoso* ruling was extremely cumbersome to implement legally, requiring several different steps and phases. Increasingly, laborers, sharecroppers, and renters took things into their own hands and sometimes torched the barns of owners whom they found uncooperative. Landowners sometimes used violence in return, firing in certain instances on trespassers or suspected arsonists.[23] During the summer of 1933 the Republican provincial governor of Badajoz resigned, alleging, among other things, that Socialist mayors in the pueblos refused to cooperate to maintain law and order. All the charges and countercharges are impossible to validate in detail. In gross statistics, agricultural output declined somewhat in 1933 compared with the preceding year, but the main factor was doubtless meteorological; proportionately the harvest in the south compared well with that in the north.

The Socialist role in government became largely defensive during the spring and summer of 1933, one of trying simply to maintain the existing situation. Party leaders were aware that the government in general and

Table 5.2. Growth in Unemployment, July–December 1933

	Agricultural Unemployment	Total Unemployed
July	341,018	544,837
August	387,570	588,837
September	395,253	611,701
October	368,106	586,105
November	391,205	603,995
December	414,690	618,947

Source: *Anuario Estadístico de España 1933–1934* (Madrid, 1935).

the Socialist strategy in particular were facing grave obstacles. To Besteiro this simply meant that the time had come to withdraw from the government. To Prieto it meant that the party must follow an even more pragmatic policy. To Largo Caballero, however, it meant the continuation of the coalition in power as long as possible while maintaining a willingness to consider a fairly drastic alternative if necessary. In a major speech in Madrid on 23 July, Largo insisted once more that "We are going to conquer power within the Constitution and under the laws of the state," but also warned of the danger of "fascism"—meaning the growth in power of the right—now a major new concern. This might make it necessary to seize power through direct action. He reminded his nominally Marxist audience that Marx had declared categorically that a dictatorship of the proletariat was inevitable in consolidating a socialist society and that, even though it would probably still be possible to win control of the government by parliamentary means, liberal democracy alone would never completely suffice. The ultimate dictatorship of the proletariat should be exercised with as little violence as possible, but that would depend on the degree of resistance.[24]

In the following month the top Socialist leaders had the opportunity to define their policy preferences in addresses before the Socialist Youth summer school at Torrelodones. Besteiro spoke first and was coldly received by the young radicals. A month earlier he had pointed to the responsibility of Italian and German socialists in provoking the bourgeoisie into fascism through the premature growth of socialist power, even though in Germany this growth had mainly taken the form of parliamentary government participation.[25] At Torrelodones he warned against extremism, declaring that "if a general staff sends its army into battle in unfavorable circumstances, then it is fully responsible for the consequent defeat and demoralization," adding that "it is often more revolutionary to resist the collective madness than to allow oneself to be carried along by it."[26]

Prieto was less challenging but warned that there were definite limits to what Spanish Socialism could achieve at the present level of development and given the changing relations of political forces in Europe and Spain. He stressed the fallacy of comparisons made by the left wing of the party between Russia in 1917 and Spain in 1933. In Russia most political institutions had already collapsed before the social revolution began; in Spain the government, church, and armed forces were intact, while the bourgeoisie was much stronger than in Russia.

Ever since the closing months of 1932 Largo Caballero had been increasingly aware of the radicalization of worker sentiment and the need to accommodate it. In his address at Torrelodones he once more defended government participation, which he termed orthodox Marxism, referring to a letter of Engels to Kautsky in 1875 in which the former stressed that a democratic republic was the specific political form that would lead to the dictatorship of the proletariat. "I myself have always had the reputation of being conservative and reformist, but people have gotten this mixed up," he said, stressing that "today I am convinced that it is impossible to carry out Socialist tasks within bourgeois democracy."

Let us suppose that the moment of attempting the installation of our regime arrives. There are those, not only outside our ranks but within them as well, who fear the need to establish a dictatorship. If this is the case, what would our situation be? For we cannot renounce our goal nor can we tolerate any act that might impede the achievement of our aim.

He quoted Marx once more to the effect that the ultimate transition to socialism could not be carried out by other means than the dictatorship of the proletariat. With regard to the only existing model, the Soviet Union, he declared that he did not agree with Soviet foreign policy, but that he fully agreed with Soviet domestic policy.[27] All this was said at the height of the genocidal campaign against the Soviet peasantry, revealing probably not that Largo preached mass murder but that he was quite ignorant of what he was talking about. The old trade union leader had now entered heavy political waters that his mental and emotional faculties simply did not permit him to navigate, but he told the young militants what they wanted to hear and at this point the first cries of "Viva el Lenin español" ("Long live the Spanish Lenin") were heard.[28]

The dilemma facing Spanish industrial relations in general and the Socialists in particular was illustrated by the radicalization of organized labor in Madrid during 1933. The Spanish capital had never been a major industrial center. Aside from commerce and government, the largest sector of employment was provided by the construction industry, which had been greatly stimulated by the expansion of both public works and private construction during the 1920s. This brought in many new workers from rural areas, and despite their often limited skills they had been largely organized by the UGT, which enjoyed as much of a monopoly over labor in Madrid as did the CNT in Barcelona. Under the Republic, trade union organization had reached a new high, with the majority of workers in Madrid now organized, but thanks to the UGT predominance the capital had been little troubled by major strikes or labor disorder during 1931–32.

By 1933 unemployment in the Madrid construction industry had reached 30 percent or more. For the first time the CNT made a major effort to organize workers in a significant sector of the Madrid economy, appealing especially to unemployed *peones* (unskilled laborers). Its goal was to obtain full recognition from the major employers and break the UGT monopoly of hiring at new construction sites. In September, as the Azaña government foundered, the CNT's Sindicato Unico de Construcción (SUC) began a strike of five thousand construction workers that spread rapidly and lasted three weeks, despite energetic UGT efforts to break it. Ironically the Republican *jurado* system had achieved major gains in economic benefits for Madrid construction workers, but the depression had forced so many layoffs that thousands of workers were ripe for radicalization. The SUC won its strike not so much in economic terms as in achieving equal bargaining rights with the UGT, bypassing the official *jurado*. The UGT's legalist and reformist tactics had been *desbordadas*, outflanked by anarchosyndicalist direct action. Now there was strong pressure from young UGT workers and shopfloor leaders to emulate the same tactics, with the result that the *jurado* arbitration system in the capital would never fully recover.[29]

Fall of the Azaña Coalition

The growing strength of the opposition, increased social unrest, and uneasy internal relations among key sectors of the coalition indicated by midsummer that the government's days were probably numbered. The basic legislation of the original Republican project had now been completed, and vocal elements among the Socialists and, even more so, among the left Republicans were now questioning the need or advisability of maintaining the coalition. Parliamentary activity declined precipitously in August, with most sessions devoted to tedious technical details of new legislation on farm rentals amid sweltering temperatures and such poor attendance, even by deputies of the majority, that frequently no more than forty or fifty members might be found in the chamber. Already by the end of July both Alcalá Zamora and Azaña, as well as the leaders of several key Republican groups, were taking soundings about the formation of a new government of "Republican concentration," excluding the Socialists.

The most dissident sector within the government was the Radical Socialists, largest of the left Republican parties, which was undergoing a swing toward the center and expressed increasing antipathy toward the Socialists. A small Izquierda Radical Socialista had split off the preceding year, and in the late summer of 1933 the party was virtually torn apart by a power struggle between the centrists, led by the veterinarian Félix Gordón Ordás[30] (termed satirically by some "the Marañón of the veterinarians"), head of the Alianza de Labradores (middle-class farmers' alliance), and the left-center, led by Domingo and Albornoz. After a raucous extraordinary congress in late September, Gordón and the centrists gained control, after which Domingo and the left-center formed their own Partido Radical Socialista Independiente.[31] This three-way split virtually nullified the Radical Socialists as a political force. Meanwhile the tiny Federal Republican Party was also soon to split in three, all this underscoring the fissiparous character of the Republican organizations.

The government suffered another defeat in the formation of the recently authorized Tribunal de Garantías Constitucionales. Twenty of the thirty-five members of the constitutional court were either chosen by the Cortes, automatically designated ex officio, or selected by the Colegio de Abogados (national bar association) and university faculties, but fifteen members were elected at large on a regional basis by municipal councils throughout Spain. The balloting was held on 3 September, with parties in the government winning only five seats, while the opposition parties, led by the Radicals, won ten, doubling the vote totals of the government forces. This defeat seemed to confirm the thesis of the opposition that the government no longer reflected public opinion, though had the original coalition of 1931 been maintained, it would have triumphed easily, the Radicals having won nearly 30 percent of the vote themselves.

When the Cortes reopened three days later, Azaña denied that the election of a judicial body could be considered a vote of political no-confidence. The government easily won a parliamentary vote by 146 to 3, yet the abstention of the majority of the deputies appeared to undermine its position further. Though his own ambivalence was growing,[32] Azaña felt that he could not give up, if for no other reason than that a more conservative administration or new elections, or both, would probably weaken the left. Alcalá Zamora asked him a series of critical questions and, concluding that the existing majority was too shaky to endure, decided to withdraw his confidence from the existing coalition and open consulations for a new, broader, and more moderate cabinet, led by Lerroux. The Radical leader was more than willing and tried unsuccessfully to interest independent moderates, such as Ortega, Marañón, and Sánchez Román, to join a cabinet. Meanwhile the outgoing coalition was defeated in yet another opinion forum in the intra-institutional elections for the Colegio de Abogados and the universities on 10 September, just as earlier conservatives had won elections at the close of May for the governing committees (juntas) of the Academia de Jurisprudencia and the Colegio de Médicos (Physicians College). By 12 September Lerroux was able to announce formation of a new government of Republican concentration, made up of five other Radicals, five representatives of the various left Republican parties, and one independent Republican. He announced a program aimed at cancellation of the *términos municipales* law, reduction of both taxes and expenditures, reappointment of functionaries fired for political reasons, and suspension of the diplomatic relations recently established with the Soviet Union. Meanwhile labor disorders and disturbances in the southern agricultural provinces continued, with more than fifty cases of agrarian arson reported in Cádiz province alone during the summer. The Socialists harassed the new government every step of the way, and some of the left Republicans began to turn away from their new alliance. On 3 October Lerroux's government was voted down in the Cortes, the outgoing prime minister and Azaña exchanging bitter remarks.

Alcalá Zamora found it difficult to put together any alternative administration. He hoped that an independent Republican moderate might be able to form a coalition that would not attract so much hostility from the left, but no such leader was available. The President was eager to avoid the alternative — dissolution of parliament and new elections — since the Constitution allowed him only one regular dissolution during a presidential term, but it became clear that the only option was a temporary caretaker coalition whose task would be to convene elections. Thus a broad coalition of all Republican groups under Lerroux's chief lieutenant, Diego Martínez Barrio of Seville, was announced on 9 October, and on the following day the Cortes was officially dissolved, new elections being scheduled for 19 November.

The first major phase of the Republic had now come to an end. It had achieved much, enacting major and far-reaching reforms. The Azaña government had also made major errors, governing sometimes harshly and severely and unnecessarily antagonizing the opposition, particularly on the moderate right. Catholic opinion had been treated outrageously, too much money was still being spent on the army, and the persecution of Catholic education negated much of the effort to expand education. Major labor reforms had been executed, but the agrarian reform had become so confused and contradictory that it would lead only to frustration. Even left Republicans adhered to a conservative fiscal and economic policy, where technical limitations and political contradictions abounded. The new regime had been subjected to an unprecedented assault from the anarchist and Communist left, while a rightist reaction was growing rapidly. Status rivalries between the major Republican politicians had become extreme, obscuring common interests and goals and revealing a basic weakness of Republican political culture. The main ally of the left Republicans, the Socialists, were also now alienated and veering toward the more extreme left.

Azaña's basic strategy, the left-center alliance between left Republicans and Socialists, had failed. The principal alternatives were a center Republican coalition, excluding all the worker left as well as the non-Republican right, as suggested by Gordón Ordás and, more vaguely, by Ortega, or Lerroux's subsequent strategy of a center-right coalition, to incorporate and democratize the moderate non-Republican right. Whereas the moderate Republicans had rejected the left-center alliance, their ideal alternative of a broad center Republican alliance was not viable, not so much because of the opposition of the Socialists but because of the refusal of most of the Republican left. Yet the aim of a center coalition was the only strategy which did not involve insuperable contradictions, such as those already revealed by the left-center alliance and subsequently to be revealed by a center-right coalition. There is of course no proof that a center Republican coalition would have had a sufficiently broad base to endure, though it just might have succeeded by encouraging basic political democratization and moderate social reform, while conciliating Catholic opinion. Such a course would have been highly complicated and would have required much tact and cooperation. Perhaps it would simply have exceeded the emotional possibilities of the ambitious, highly personalistic, and vain middle-class Republican politicians, who in some ways exhibited much more the traditional vices of nineteenth-century Spanish politics than the new progressive spirit which they invoked with rhetorical regularity. Such an alternative, however slim its chance of success, might have been the only hope of consolidating a democratic system during the depression decade. Henceforth Republican politics would lie increasingly at the mercy of extremes.

6

Economic Policy and Performance

IT was the Republic's misfortune to coincide with the great world depression, and from this obvious fact it is easy to conclude that political and social conflict in Spain was fueled to a large degree by the depression's impact. Conversely, a number of historians and commentators from Jaime Vicens Vives[1] and Gabriel Jackson on have pointed out that the proportionate effect of the depression in Spain was less than in many other countries and that the main sources of conflict were political and ideological, and also structural and historical, but not primarily due to the depression itself. This contention is to some extent correct. Absolute unemployment was not as great in Spain as in heavily industrialized lands, and social and political conflict stemmed in good measure from direct political stimuli whose rhythm was not determined in any simple way by current economic performance. Nonetheless, Spain was not at all immune to depression, and the new economic pressures increased social distress in a way that cannot be considered unrelated to the conflicts that developed.[2]

The preceding decade of the 1920s had been the greatest boomtime in all Spanish history, with rapid increases in industrial development and service employment and a significant growth in exports, so that 1930 probably constituted the year of maximum export volume ever recorded, even more than the previous high points of 1913–18. By 1930 agricultural employment was declining relatively rapidly in proportionate terms and at 45.5 percent now included less than half the labor force (though these proportions would not change again significantly for a quarter century), with agriculture producing only 40 percent of the national income. The industrial labor force had grown to 26.5 percent of the total, and industry produced approximately 34 percent of national income. Though most Spaniards still lived in rural districts and small towns, urbanization was growing rapidly.

The Spanish economy was sheltered to some extent by its limited reli-

148

ance on the external market. Though national production fell sharply in 1930, this was due to very bad weather for agriculture and the loss of agricultural export markets, since industrial production actually increased. (See table 6.1.) The depression proper began to impact the industrial economy only in 1932, but the gross domestic product actually rose, due to the recuperation of agriculture under the Republic. By 1935 industry had regained its levels of 1929–31, but major aspects of agriculture were suffering due to loss of markets.

Spanish producers were already protected by one of the highest tariff walls in the world.[3] Though the main export sectors of agriculture — wine, citrus, olives — underwent serious decline, those sectors producing primarily for the domestic market — especially wheat, but also vegetables — did comparatively well, with outstanding wheat harvests in 1932 and 1934. At the trough of the depression in 1933, there was a 7 percent decline in agricultural prices, but much of that loss was regained in the following year. Moreover, the slow but fairly steady modernization of agricultural production that had been under way for the past half century continued at about the same rate during the depression years.

Basic industries such as metallurgy, mining, cement, chemicals, and energy had grown more rapidly than the economy as a whole in the 1920s, but then fell more than the average in 1932–33. Metallurgy and mining suffered especially, with metallurgy declining at least 50 percent by the end of 1933. Construction was also seriously affected in many areas, though not in all. The textile industry suffered less, perhaps buoyed by the increase in real wages and purchasing power under the Republic. By 1935, however, industrial production had nearly recovered, thanks to the maintenance of demand and more state credit for construction.

Exports had come to account for about 8 percent of gross domestic product during the main part of the 1920s and almost 10 percent by 1930

Table 6.1. Fluctuations in Economic Production (100 = media of 1900–1930)

	Agriculture	Industry	Total Production
1929	129.6	141.9	134.5
1930	99.4	144.0	117.2
1931	101.9	146.1	119.6
1932	129.1	132.8	130.6
1933	122.2	122.1	122.2
1934	127.2	134.4	130.1
1935	113.2	142.4	124.9
1940	75.6	96.0	83.8

Source: L. Benavides, *Política económica en la II República española* (Madrid, 1972), 268.

(nearly 84 percent of that in foodstuffs and raw materials). By 1933 the volume of trade for some products declined as much as 75 percent and barely accounted for 4 percent of the national product by 1935. Exports and imports combined had amounted to 23 percent of domestic product during 1929–30 but to only 12 percent by 1934. After World War I, the only year in which Spain had enjoyed a favorable trade balance had been 1919. The coefficient of coverage had been an average of 83 percent for the years 1926–31, but this figure dropped to only 60 percent for 1932–35 as imports were not reduced as much as exports fell. The export decline was sharpest in certain minerals such as lead, followed by wine and olive oil, but citrus exports experienced a lesser decline and the foreign market for Spanish almonds remained steady. The government was able to complete several individual trade and barter agreements, which slightly eased the situation. The most important was a 1933 trade agreement with France that established reciprocity and certain mutual tariff reductions. Barter agreements were negotiated for Soviet oil and Argentine wheat, but in other respects the tariff was increased against a few countries. (See table 6.2.) In general, however, an already high tariff wall was not raised further, national income was sustained in terms of overall domestic purchasing power, and by 1932 the peseta had not merely been stabilized but in fact slightly revalued, all of which contributed to import demand.

The principal political controversy connected with international commerce stemmed from the sizable grain imports authorized during 1932 to compensate for the apparent shortage resulting from the poor Spanish harvest of 1931. The government did regulate minimum grain prices in the interest of Spanish farmers, and by 1932 grain growers insisted that this should be raised because of the reduced harvest and wage increases. Though the Ministry of Labor did help to negotiate certain lower wage adjustments to save the 1932 harvest, it also authorized the importation of nearly 300,000 tons of grain between April and June of that year. Grain prices reached

Table 6.2. Proportionate Volume of Foreign Commerce

1929	100
1930	100.5
1931	73.8
1932	52.5
1933	54.5
1934	58.0

Source: Servicio de Estudios, Banco de España, *Ritmo de la crisis económica española en relación con la mundial* (Madrid, 1934), 40–41.

their high point in July, at which time a large amount of domestic grain that had been withheld was dumped on the market, sending prices downward. All this was accompanied by a fine wheat harvest in 1932, which by the autumn had driven grain prices to their lowest point in years. The Ministry of Agriculture was roundly denounced for authorizing excessive imports.[4] This affected not merely large grain producers but even more small farmers, for the majority of small farmers and renters produced at least a certain amount of grain, and the market did not restabilize for them until 1934–35.

The dictatorship had followed an expansionist economic policy, though this had eventually produced major deficits and a weakened currency. The Republican leaders were pledged to honest unified accounting in place of the dictatorship's budgets and sought to avoid major debt, yet they could not reject certain reflationary policies in the midst of the depression. Thus the coming of the Republic did not mark a drastic break in overall economic policy, for the real change had come in 1925–26, as the Spanish government's traditional low-intervention policy had been changed under Primo de Rivera.

Indalecio Prieto, the first Republican finance minister, was faced with formidable problems, for the initial reaction to the new regime was a mild financial panic with some flight of capital and a temporary further 20 percent decline in the value of the peseta.[5] He took energetic measures to halt the peseta's decline, declaring immediately after taking office: "I am not here as a Socialist but simply as Minister of the Treasury."[6] Though his effort to return Spain to the gold standard soon failed, the peseta, which had fallen from 9.09 to the dollar at the Republic's inauguration to 11.86 by 16 January 1932, did begin to revalue slightly during the course of 1932. Prieto was also able to assert somewhat greater government control over the privately owned Banco de España.

Taxes were generally low, and the Republican leaders were little inclined to raise them. José Calvo Sotelo, the finance minister of the dictatorship, had raised rates slightly and made the structure a little more progressive in a reform of 1926–27, but the sizable increase in state revenue after that time was due primarily to greater efficiency in collection.[7] Jaume Carner, who succeeded Prieto, added a modest surtax on certain existing taxes, but the new income tax was quite modest. Voted late in 1932 to apply in 1933, its bracketing started at 1 percent and increased to 6.8 percent on incomes between one hundred thousand and one million pesetas. For incomes over one million, the first million was taxed at 7.7 percent, and all the remainder at 11 percent.[8] This may have increased total tax pressure by some 10 percent.

Government spending under the Republic was moderately expansionist, resulting in steady deficits. The biggest increases were for education, the police, and hydraulic development. Between 1930 and 1933 the budgets of both the Ministries of Education and of the Interior grew approximately 50 percent, the increase for the latter always outpacing the former. The largest proportionate jump was in hydraulic development; Primo de Rivera had never invested more than 60 million pesetas annually in dam construction, but Prieto spent approximately 80 million in 1932 and 175 million in 1933. Significant increases also took place in debt financing and personnel (especially military retirements), and social expenditures generally rose further in 1933. Thus the total budget passed 4 billion pesetas for the first time in 1932, having risen 12 percent in two years and steadily increased. Deficits were hardly a novelty in Spanish government. Those of the Republican administrations began at 373 million for 1931, increasing to 535 million in 1932, 616 million in 1933, and 812 million for 1934.[9] Budget deficits were financed rather easily through short-term bonds at 5 percent (some for only twenty-four months). Payment and redemption schedules were scrupulously honored, helping to maintain the value of the peseta.[10] Given the problems facing them, the Republican administrations can hardly be accused of extravagance, though opposition spokesmen liked to dwell on the number of fancy Chrysler limousines imported for government officials.

In fact, the emission of state securities declined during the first year of the Republic, only regaining and exceeding the level of the last year of the monarchy by 1932, at which point the money supply actually began to decline, as indicated in table 6.3. Overall the Banco de España raised the rediscount rate slightly,[11] the very reverse of a reflationary policy. The Republican and Socialist leaders, with few exceptions, had only rudimentary economic ideas, and Keynesian theory or broad reflationary strategies were beyond them.[12] Even the Republican left thought primarily in terms of holding down the deficit and trying to create a few more jobs through

Table 6.3. Increase in Bank Notes in Circulation (1913 = 100)

1929	231.9
1930	239.7
1931	267.5
1932	259.9
1933	255.2
1934	249.5
1935	248.5

Source: Benavides, *Política económica*, 251.

public works. The Socialists, when pressed, could add nothing to this but redistribution through heavy taxation and one-sided wage settlements, or outright confiscation. There was little interest in providing cheaper credit or subsidies to faltering businesses, so that the antipathy between government on the one hand and business and industry on the other soon widened, even as workers were growing more radically disenchanted. As was common in other countries, an effort was made to reduce the cadres of public functionaries, normally criticized for redundancy and inefficiency, and to achieve greater productivity by salary increases in certain categories,[13] though it is not clear that much was accomplished.

Thanks to the partial insulation of the national economy and to Republican labor policies, the increase in real wages which had been a significant feature of the 1920s actually continued during the depression. Real wages had advanced an approximate average of 2 percent annually from 1923 to 1929, and according to one computation increased 2.9 percent for the year 1930. During the next three years real wages overall advanced at least 7 percent more — and even more rapidly for farmworkers (see table 6.4) — though in toto they fell back at least 3 percent (possibly more) between 1933 and 1935.[14] Nominal wage increases could be directly translated into real gains because they took place amid generally stable prices. Moreover, such a computation does not take into consideration the considerable improvement in fringe benefits and working conditions during the first two years of the Republic.[15] Thus, despite mounting unemployment, per capita income held steady, as indicated in Table 6.5.

The return on capital did not remain constant, but despite the rising complaints — in some quarters reaching hysteria — concerning the ruinous effects of Republican policies, profits in most sectors did not fall disastrously, though such areas as mining and metallurgy were indeed hard hit. The stock market declined, but the overall rate of bankruptcies does not seem

Table 6.4. Farmworker Wages in Córdoba Province, 1930–1934

| Type of Work | Wages for Eight-Hour Day | | | |
	1930	1932	1933	1934
Picking olives	5.50	6.50	5.85	5.75
Seeding by hand	6.00	9.00	8.10	8.10
Threshing by sickle (7 hrs.)	. . .	9.40	8.50	9.00
Threshing by scythe (6 hrs.)	. . .	11.00	9.90	10.40
Hoeing olive groves	4.50	5.75	5.25	5.25
Unspecified	3.75	4.75	4.25	4.25

Source: M. Pérez Yruela, *La conflictividad campesina en la provincia de Córdoba 1931–1936* (Madrid, 1979), 179.

Table 6.5. Per Capita Income (in pesetas)

1929	1,092
1930	1,033
1931	1,020
1932	967
1933	1,078
1934	1,078
1935	1,033
1939	729
1940	819

Source: Benavides, *Política económica*, 251.

to have increased greatly, even though many more companies had at times to suspend payments. Interest income was not drastically reduced, though the real interest rate went down somewhat. Declared bank profits, which had averaged 16 percent from 1923 to 1930, fell to 11.6 percent from 1931 to 1935, scarcely a calamitous cituation.[16] Overall the declared profits of major enterprises, save in a few of the worst sectors, held fairly steady, while in toto agricultural income generally rose in both 1932 and 1934. The *Anuario Financiero* for 1933 (generally the trough of the period) showed that only a minority of firms registered profits significantly below those of the preceding year, while a few were well ahead. Total savings in bank and savings associations increased steadily from approximately 4 billion pesetas in 1929 to 5,227,405,335 pesetas in 1934.[17] The number of new motor vehicles registered dropped from a high of 37,335 in 1929 to a low of 11,105 in 1932, but rebounded rapidly the next year and reached 26,064 in 1935.[18]

The main cause of suffering for the ordinary population was therefore unemployment, which mounted steadily throughout the entire Republican period. (See table 6.6.) Unemployment continued to increase even as the general economy and production improved because of loss of export

Table 6.6. Total Unemployment

	Complete Unemployment	Partial Unemployment	Total
January 1932	. . .	. . .	389,000
June 1932	. . .	. . .	446,263
July 1, 1933	285,900	258,900	544,800
October 1933	348,200	237,900	586,100
December 1933	351,800	267,000	618,900
January 1934	381,200	243,900	625,100
February 1934	378,100	230,600	608,700
March 1934	416,300	250,300	666,600
December 1934	406,743	261,155	667,897

Sources: Various, compiled in J. Hernández Andreu, *Depresión económica*, 175.

markets, increased labor costs, and concern for rationalization and higher productivity, all natural consequences of the depression, of Republican reforms, and of the steady if slow modernization of the economy. Unemployment reached its zenith at 821,322 in June 1936, when it included approximately 10 percent of the active population. Since Spanish statistics also included those who had limited part-time employment, absolute unemployment probably never went beyond 7 percent, a modest figure compared with Germany or the United States. In Spain, however, there were scarcely any unemployment benefits. Largo Caballero was not able to accomplish much on this score during 1931–33 because of the dearth of funds, though a national unemployment insurance system was begun in 1931. It never received the support of as much as one-half of 1 percent of the national budget. Thus in February, 1933, only 2.4 percent of all those listed as completely unemployed were receiving any compensation, and even that was for only 60 percent of their normal wage for a maximum of sixty consecutive days in one year.[19]

Unemployment was particularly bad in industries such as mining, metallurgy, and (less constantly) construction, but the bulk of it was concentrated in agriculture. With approximately 45 percent of the active population engaged in agriculture (and much of it underemployed even in comparatively good times), the agrarian share of unemployment rose from 58 percent at the beginning of 1932 to 65 percent in 1936.[20] Since over half the active agrarian population had some land of its own and would have been less likely to figure in such statistics, the actual incidence of unemployment among landless laborers was obviously much higher than the national average. By 1934 one spokesman reported unemployment rates of 46 percent among farmworkers in the province of Jaén, 39 percent in Badajoz, and 36 percent in Córdoba.

The traditional safety valve of emigration became almost totally blocked. In 1928 thirty-three thousand Spaniards had emigrated to Argentina alone, but with the depression this movement actually went into reverse. By 1935 there had been a net return of approximately two hundred thousand, while within the country young laborers who had earlier been moving to the cities in search of work were sometimes coming back to the pueblos, as well.

Thus though the proportionate impact of the depression in Spain was milder than elsewhere and the absolute unemployment statistics comparatively modest, the poorest sector of the population was extremely hard hit, and actually suffered more than unemployed workers in, for example, Germany, where the national unemployment rate was much higher. These pressures did not create the social and political conflicts of the Republican years, but they intensified them and increased their bitterness.

7

Foreign Policy

FOREIGN policy was never a prime concern of Republican leaders, for two basic reasons. For well over a century, since the Napoleonic wars, Spain had been the great neutral of western Europe, unthreatened by and for the most part uninvolved in major power struggles. Moreover, there was neither significant desire nor capacity to change this state of affairs, while conversely most political leaders remained totally absorbed by ever more pressing and conflictive internal problems. Unlike the situation in nearly all the weaker and more underdeveloped countries of southern and eastern Europe, nationalism was neither a significant force nor a problem for Spain. Though Spanish society was economically underdeveloped, the Spanish state was one of the oldest continuously existing states in the world and had been militantly expansionist long before modern nationalism ever existed. Once the historic empire had been lost, the country had become self-absorbed in internal struggles and was never in serious danger from any other power. The ideology of the right consisted of diverse variants of Catholicism, conservatism, and traditionalism, all largely indifferent to the romantic and radical strains of modern nationalism, while the left was fixated on internal political and social issues. The very slowness of economic development prior to World War I discouraged the growth of new nationalistic social and economic interests. When Spain had become reinvolved with modern imperialism through the establishment of the small protectorate in northern Morocco, the main motivation was more defensive than offensive, to avoid being completely outflanked geographically by French expansionism. That the most active expressions of nationalism were the centrifugal forces of Catalanism and Basqueism were themselves eloquent testimony to the weakness, indeed the virtual nonexistence, of any clear sense or movement of Spanish nationalism.[1]

Republican progressives had certain distinct notions and preferences in foreign affairs, nonetheless. They were generally pro-French in support of the senior democratic republic in Europe, the nearest thing to a model they had. They had almost all supported the Entente during World War I and thus generally backed the quasi-democratic status quo fostered by the great powers in western Europe and in association with the League of Nations. They also tended to blame the monarchy for having, as Azaña and others claimed, no real foreign policy, leaving Spain an idle nullity in the concert of powers. Therefore Azaña stressed that the new regime must overcome "that spirit of shrinkage and withdrawal"[2] characteristic of the monarchy and make Spain's voice felt once more, though essentially on the side of an active and progressive neutralism that projected no drastic ambitions on the international scene.[3]

Like most of his colleagues, Azaña was absorbed by domestic affairs, so that the principal spokesman for Republican foreign policy was the sophisticated internationalist Salvador de Madariaga — an intellectual, scholar, and essayist who wrote fluently and almost interchangeably in Spanish, French, and English. Sometimes seconded by Ortega, Madariaga was the chief proponent of Europeanism under the Republican government, which meant the encouragement of unity within diversity, under the mantle of the common western humanist and progressivist heritage.[4]

Only a moderate liberal himself, Madariaga was well aware that the Republic potentially constituted "the most advanced regime in Europe after Russia" and should therefore play a distinct role in promoting peace and harmony. He and other Spanish liberals considered this also appropriate in the grander sense of historical tradition, making it possible to put into practice the principles of international law first codified by Spanish theorists, such as the sixteenth-century giants Francisco de Vitoria and Francisco Suárez. Even earlier, the great Catalan theologian and philosopher Ramon Llull had proposed an international assembly to deal with Europe's problems in the late thirteenth century. By 1931 the Carnegie Fund was supporting an "International Vitoria-Suárez Association" to complement the society that already existed in Madrid,[5] and a major international celebration of Vitoria and his writings was held at the University of Salamanca in 1933.

The post of foreign minister was considered far from the most important in the numerous Republican administrations. Beginning with Lerroux in 1931 (who, despite his name, did not even know much French, much less any other foreign language),[6] the foreign ministers lacked either experience or aptitude (or both) and were frequently changed, ten different figures holding the post in a little more than five years. An effort was made to appoint well-qualified Republican ambassadors to the major capitals, but, despite a number of initial resignations, the main cadre of conserva-

Salvador de Madariaga, photographed while being interviewed by the BBC

tive monarchist aristocrats stayed on and continued to constitute the basic Spanish diplomatic corps. A portion of the most overtly monarchist members of the diplomatic service was purged after the *sanjurjada*, even though adequate replacements were not always available. The comparatively low status of foreign affairs and general lack of interest was reflected also in the lack of discussion of foreign policy issues in the Cortes.

These attitudes shaped the role of Madariaga, who was first made ambassador to Washington in May 1931, but soon went to Geneva, where he served as de facto (though never official de jure) Spanish representative before the League of Nations for nearly five years. The League was particularly important for Madariaga and for most of the Republican leadership, who in fact wrote the League directly into the new Constitution. Article 6 declared that "Spain renounces war as an instrument of national policy," while Article 77 stipulated: "The President of the Republic is not empowered to sign a declaration of war except under the conditions prescribed by the Pact of the League of Nations and only after all defensive measures that do not have a warlike character have been exhausted."

Any decision to declare war would have to be not only voted by the Cortes but have followed all procedures and provisions for arbitration established by the League.

The basic principles of an active neutrality, as understood by Madariaga, would be to work to strengthen the League, to cooperate with Britain and France, to stress equal or even more cooperation with the smaller west European democracies (whose power and interests were presumably more fully equivalent to those of Spain), to maintain close cooperation with Latin American countries and with Portugal, and to continue to assert in a constructive manner Spain's right to Gibraltar.[7]

Spain's election to the Council of the League of Nations was the occasion for Madariaga's transfer to Geneva, and thus he was presiding when the issue of Japanese aggression in Manchuria was brought before the League in January 1932. He was so outspoken in his denunciation of the Japanese invasion — at a time when other west European powers were inclined to overlook it — that Madariaga was soon given the sobriquet of "Don Quijote de la Manchuria." This position somewhat annoyed the British delegation but won the respect of the smaller European democracies and of some of the Latin American delegations.[8]

Madariaga worked with at least a modest degree of success to develop a sort of entente among the smaller European democratic "group of eight," made up of the six standard neutrals (Spain, Switzerland, Holland, and the three Scandinavian states), plus Belgium and Czechoslovakia (though these last two withdrew from the unofficial group after Germany left the League in October 1933). This was directly encouraged by Luis de Zulueta, left Republican foreign minister from December 1931 to June 1933, the longest tenure of any Republican foreign minister. The tandem Zulueta-Madariaga provided the strongest foreign policy leadership the Republic was to know.

Thus Madariaga served on the Commission of Twelve that investigated the invasion of Manchuria, chaired the Aviation Committee at the International Disarmament Conference that met in February 1932, was one of the official mediators in the Chaco War between Bolivia and Paraguay and also in the border dispute between Peru and Colombia, and later presided over the League committee that recommended sanctions against Italy for the invasion of Ethiopia. Madariaga propounded the goal of world disarmament and eventually a sort of world federal state. At the 1932 conference he proposed suppression of military aviation and the creation of an international civil aeronautics commission, together with the initiation of general disarmament through mutual reductions of all military budgets.[9] This did not generate any particular enthusiasm among Spanish political opinion, which was little interested in foreign affairs, eager to resent the prominence of a unique personality such as that of Madariaga, and frequently dismissive of his "quixotic" proposals.

Between 1931 and 1934 Spain did possess a rather greater moral authority in Geneva than its economic or military strength would have otherwise commanded. The goal was nominally to become somewhat more independent of the two dominant powers, Britain and France. This was, of course, hardly favored in London and Paris, British diplomats fearing that Madrid would move closer to Paris,[10] and the French that Madrid might become more purely independent. When the chips were down, however, Spanish diplomacy could not avoid — and did not seriously seek to avoid — aligning itself with Paris and London on the major issues. Together with the United States, they were Spain's main economic trading partners, and, despite the issue of Gibraltar and tensions with France over Morocco, there were no major active antagonisms at issue. Conversely, it was mainly politicians of the right who sought to encourage closer relations with Germany, both before and after Hitler came to power, emphasizing that historically there had never been conflict between Spain and Germany. Yet, by the same token, there was no convergence of interests, especially after January 1933.

The French press, which was for the most part relatively conservative, was initially somewhat hostile to the Republic and loved to dwell on each report of internal division or social disorder within Spain, while showing considerable friendliness toward the king, who for some years took up residence in Paris. This began to change in 1932, however, as the French left-center began to develop greater cohesiveness and assertiveness, winning the French elections of 1932. During the latter part of that year the French press grew less hostile, and Eduard Herriot, the Radical Party prime minister, decided to try to mend fences with an official state visit in October 1932. This was not initially well organized nor altogether warmly received in Spain, though it ended with moderate success, producing a reasonably constructive new commercial treaty as well as two minor agreements. Later a special arms purchase agreement was signed with France in December 1935.

Deepening of the economic depression brought difficulties with all major trading partners, exacerbated by the Republic's new regulations (especially with regard to labor) and further commercial restrictions. Problems were more severe with the United States than with Britain or France, due in large measure to a tougher American line.[11]

The major active irritant in relations with the chief European powers was not British possession of Gibraltar (which, although protested, was never actively combatted), but the terms governing the enclave of Tangier in the Moroccan Protectorate. Despite its location near the center of the Spanish zone and immediately across from the peninsula, Tangier was an international free city under a multipower government in which French interests were favored over those of Spain. The existing international statute would expire in May 1936, and during the preceding two years the center-right administration in Madrid sought a more favorable revision. This was opposed by the French government and not supported by Britain and Italy, the other powers in the international governing commission. It was one of the few foreign policy issues actually debated in the Cortes, but the correlation of power involved revealed once more that Spain could hardly prevail in a contest with a major power unless supported directly by another major power. The new agreement signed in Paris in November 1935 granted Spain only limited concessions, though the terms were somewhat less unsatisfactory than before.[12]

In general, Republican policy toward the Moroccan Protectorate was to accept the status quo, which by 1931 generally enjoyed the acquiescence of the native population. Within Spain, only the revolutionary left proposed the independence of Morocco.[13] Some effort was made to rationalize and modernize certain aspects of administration, which was centralized under a civilian High Commissioner, and an attempt was made to reduce expenditures. Though the Spanish occupation was generally accepted by Moroccans, nationalist sentiment was growing and there were minor disturbances and demonstrations in 1931, 1933, 1934, and again in June 1936. Spanish policy was to reenforce the authority of the more conservative native Moroccan leaders and gently repress overt new political activity.

In 1934 the center-right government of Lerroux became more assertive and, on 19 April, announced that a very small Spanish expedition under Col. Capaz (sometimes styled "the last of the conquistadores") had officially occupied the small Atlantic coastal enclave of Ifni in the main French protectorate. This was virtually uninhabited territory, to which Spanish rights had been recognized by various agreements with Morocco and other states between 1767 and 1884. The Azaña government had earlier favored its occupation, and so the expedition was made by Capaz, Delegate for Indigenous Affairs in the regular Spanish Protectorate farther north. Similarly, further steps were taken to extend effective military occupation of the Spanish Sahara, immediately to the south of French Morocco, where nomad raiding across the border had led the French government to explore the possibility of its own acquisition of the territory.

A major goal of Republican policy was to create closer relations with Latin America. Article 24 of the Constitution guaranteed preferential treatment for all Latin Americans (including Brazilians) and Portuguese and provided that all nationals of those countries residing in Spain could gain Spanish citizenship without losing the citizenship they already possessed. In 1931 there were approximately three million people with Spanish citizenship living in Latin America, concentrated especially in Argentina and Cuba. The existing Spanish legations in Mexico and Brazil were elevated in status to full-scale embassies, and the Cortes voted creation of a Centro de Estudios de Historia de América, the first such center in Spain, at the University of Seville. Madariaga was active in attempting to mediate the Chaco dispute, and Spanish diplomacy did succeed in helping to resolve a few minor quarrels. In Geneva Madariaga took the initiative on various matters of interest to Latin American countries, and there was at least some tendency on the part of several Latin American delegations to follow his lead there. On the other hand, economic relations with Latin America were limited, due essentially to noncomplementary economies, with Spain generally enjoying an unfavorable balance of trade. Julio Alvarez del Vayo, the ambassador to Mexico during the first Republican biennium, was particularly active, while Spain perhaps enjoyed closer relations with Chile than with any other single Latin American country. Talk of some sort of pan-Hispanic federalism already existed before the Republic, though too many practical obstacles existed for any serious initiative in this regard.[14]

Great power issues became increasingly difficult from 1933 on. The last major diplomatic step taken by the Azaña administration was to complete mutual diplomatic recognition between the Spanish and Soviet governments in July 1933, though they only exchanged minor representatives and did not establish full-scale embassies. This relationship was then frozen by the center-right, and the first official Soviet ambassador arrived only after the beginning of the Civil War.

The growth of conservative political strength after 1933 brought new foreign policy preferences. Catholic opinion sought to draw Spain farther away from British and French policy, and toward a strict neutrality in great power disputes. Mussolini's basic stance toward the Republic was hostile,[15] and the development of the French appeasement policy toward Italy in 1935 seemed to be conducted at the expense of third parties, such as Spain, in Africa. Though no Spanish interests were directly threatened, the fact that Spanish interests and opinion were being thoroughly ignored provoked resentment and one of the Republican Cortes's few foreign policy debates. The result was a slight shift in Spain's general alignment, slightly closer to Britain — who might show some support for Spain's position vis-a-vis Tangier and otherwise tended to guarantee the status quo — and also a very slight movement in the direction of Nazi Germany, from whom the center-right government briefly contemplated an arms purchase. The Spanish government was one of five whose representatives supervised the Saar plebiscite in Germany that year.

The major concern of late 1935 was the Italian invasion of Ethiopia and the ensuing League of Nations economic embargo against Italy, which was strongly backed by Madariaga. The Spanish government supported League sanctions but announced strict neutrality in the event of a wider war, a position concurred in by nearly all domestic political forces. Rightists, however, asked for absolute neutrality and nonparticipation in the sanctions.

The tensest relationship for Spain was that with neighboring Portugal, a country which was traveling in a different political direction. While Spanish politics were becoming radically democratic, the dictatorship introduced by the Portuguese military in 1926 was taking firmer, more institutionalized form under Salazar's "Estado Novo" in 1931–33. The Portuguese had feared possible Spanish intervention for well over half a millennium, so that the "perigo espanhol" (Spanish danger) had become a fixture of their attitudes, revived in the years after 1910 when several attempts were made by Portuguese monarchists on Spanish soil to organize incursions against the nascent Portuguese republican regime of 1910–26. Relations had improved under the Spanish dictatorship, which made a serious effort to stimulate friendly and respectful contacts, especially after the introduction of a parallel authoritarian regime in Portugal.[16]

As events had it, the inauguration of the new Spanish Republic coincided with a series of armed revolts in overseas Portuguese territories (Madeira, the Azores, Guinea), beginning on 4 April 1931.[17] Lisbon authorities feared there might be some connection. The new Spanish Republican press was very critical of the authoritarian Portuguese regime, and Portuguese oppositionists congregated in Spain with complete freedom of movement. A number of them concentrated on the Spanish frontier at the time of later Portuguese revolts in August and December, so that the Portuguese government asked that they be restricted from operating within one hundred kilometers of the border. On 28 August 1931, Portuguese emigrés threw a bomb into the Portuguese embassy in Madrid, and in this case Spanish opinion was one of abundant sympathy and regret for the ambassador.[18]

The Azaña government made little effort to disguise its hostility toward the Portuguese regime and did what it could to encourage the latter's overthrow, waging what the leading Spanish historian of the problem calls a *guerra oculta* ("hidden war") against the Salazar government. Ramón Franco, briefly the director general of aviation under Azaña, provided arms to assist the Portuguese revolt of August 1931, while Azaña himself as minister of war authorized economic support for the Portuguese officers and troops who were allowed to flee into Spain after the revolt failed. In June 1932 a shipment of German arms purchased by Portuguese rebels was allowed to be unloaded in Bilbao, and later the Bilbao shipbuilder and businessman Horacio Echevarrieta arranged to finance a larger arms purchase for the oppositionist Portuguese Democrats. When he alleged lack of funds to go through with the deal, Azaña authorized the Consortium of Military Industries to sell the arms to Echevarrieta on credit for export, so that he could pass them on to the Portuguese opposition. A contract was signed in October 1932, but the weapons never made it beyond Cádiz, where they were deposited in storage (later to be reacquired by the Spanish Socialists for their 1934 insurrection). The basic facts were eventually brought to light in a Cortes debate in March 1935.[19]

After inauguration of the Republic some Spanish rightists also took refuge in Portugal, but the Lisbon government discreetly refrained from giving them overt assistance against the Republican regime. As the Spanish historian De la Torre says,

It seems to me that the range of activities of Spanish political emigrés in Portugal and of the Portuguese in Spain cannot be compared in any way, nor were the respective attitudes of the authorities in the two countries at all equivalent. . . . In so far as I have been able to determine, in Portugal there were neither the contraband arms nor the conspiratorial frontier action that occurred on the other side of the border.[20]

One advantage that the Portuguese regime did derive from this situation was the opportunity to use evidence of a genuine "Spanish danger" to its own propaganda advantage with conservative sectors of Portuguese opinion. Beyond that, in April 1933 President Alcalá Zamora managed to convince the Azaña administration to offer firm support to Lisbon against mounting international pressures on the Portuguese colonies from South Africa and the possibility of a new Anglo-German entente at Portugal's expense. After formation of a new center-right government in Madrid at the close of 1933, relations improved markedly. Lerroux repeated assurances of support for the Portuguese colonies when first prime minister in September 1933 and then again in a speech in 1935. The high point of good relations came with the official visit of the Portuguese foreign minister, Armindo Monteiro, to Madrid in 1935, amid speculation in the Portuguese press about the possibility of an official peninsular alliance between the two states (which would be carried out by Franco a few years later). Amid the harmony of 1935, efforts were made to reach a full new understanding with Portugal through a commercial treaty and another of nonaggression, though these negotiations were never completed.[21]

The situation was dramatically reversed after the Popular Front electoral victory in February 1936. Given the record of the first Azaña administration and the heightened belligerence of the Spanish left, authorities in Lisbon genuinely feared some sort of attack or revolutionary outburst mounted from Spain. In fact, the leftist government in Madrid was now thoroughly correct, and Azaña carefully assured the Portuguese ambassador that his government had nothing to fear from Madrid, which considered its representation in Lisbon its "most important embassy." Azaña, of course, was unable to restrain the revolutionary left, whose militants sent a series of threats against personnel in the embassies of Germany, Italy, and Portugal. As the situation in Spain deteriorated, the German ambassador was ordered away to Paris by his government, and representatives of the embassies of Britain, Germany, Holland, Argentina, and Sweden were reported to be meeting in Madrid to discuss the problem of diplomatic asylum in the event of an emergency.[22] Emigré Portuguese oppositionists once more became active on the Galician and Extremaduran borders, while a broader meeting of Portuguese opposition groups was held in Madrid in May. By that point the Portuguese government was thoroughly alarmed and no longer made much effort to restrain the activities of Spanish rightists plotting against the Republican regime from Portuguese exile. Though relations between Lisbon and Madrid remained formally correct, they had become more tense than at any time in more than a century, presaging the explosion about to be detonated in Spain.

8

Resurgence of the Right, 1933–1934

THE reorganization of the right took two and a half years to reach full stride. The lack of modern new rightist political organizations at the beginning of the Republic and the general discrediting of the right by the dictatorship and the final phase of the monarchy impeded its effort to regain power. Only after the completion of a left-liberal constitution did a serious reaction get underway, fed by the continuing disorders and the reformist legislation that followed. The realignment basically was composed of four different, though somewhat interrelated, categories: political Catholicism, the monarchist forces, reorganization of militant new business interests, and the emergence of a new fascist movement.[1] Of these by far the most important was the emergence of mass political Catholicism, something never before accomplished in the modern history of Spanish parliamentary regimes.

Despite the strongly conservative, not to say frequently reactionary, position of Catholic opinion and the Church since the fall of the Old Regime, the only officially Catholic party of any consequence had been nineteenth-century Carlist traditionalism. Contrary to much opinion, however, the modern Spanish Church was never wedded to Carlism. For most of the nineteenth and early twentieth centuries, the main protector of Catholic interests had in fact been the monarchist Conservative Party, ever since its antecedents in the Moderate Party of the 1830s and 1840s. Church leaders had never endorsed the liberal parliamentary system at any point during the nineteenth century but tended to accept a de facto situation whereby the Conservative Party preserved for the Church a position of greater privilege than in any other west European country, and in any other sizable Catholic European country save possibly Hapsburg Austria. A few efforts were made from time to time to organize specific Catholic political forces, ranging from the extreme right to the first Spanish Christian democratic party in 1922, but none of these endured, in good measure because, prior to 1931, there was no particular need for a new confessional Catholic party.[2]

As explained in chapter 3, most Catholic leaders hoped that some sort of reasonable modus vivendi might be achieved with the Republic, but each passing month made it clearer that strong new political representation would be required. This could no longer be left to the monarchist Conservatives since the latter had become a null factor. The only viable alternative would be the creation of a mass new right-wing political organization in modern form that would work within the parliamentary system. Only a few days after the founding of the Republic, *El Debate*, the most sophisticated and influential Catholic newspaper in Spain, declared that Catholics must unite under the principles of "Religion, Fatherland, Order, Family and Property." Though these were exactly the same principles supported by the monarchist right during the preceding year, Cardinal Pacelli telegrammed Archbishop Vidal i Barraquer that Spanish Catholics in 1931 must follow the example of Bavarian Catholics in 1919 after the fall of the monarchy,[3] while Angel Herrera, director of *El Debate*, invoked that of the monarchist Marshal Hindenburg, who accepted the presidency of the German Republic out of patriotic duty. This did not necessarily involve the full acceptance of liberalism, either ideologically or politically. During the past two generations the basic Catholic position both in politics and economics had become conservative corporatism, which was explicitly endorsed for economic policy in Pope Pius XI's encyclical *Quadragesimo Anno*, issued in May 1931.

The main new Catholic group formed for the first Republican elections was Acción Nacional, based especially in conservative northern central Spain. It was able to elect a handful of delegates to the Constituent Cortes, and its principal leader, the eloquent, mentally nimble, young university professor, José María Gil Robles, soon began to make a reputation as the chief parliamentary spokesman for the right. His interpellations wrung noteworthy admissions from the prime minister, as in an exchange on 9 March 1932, when he protested the arbitrary closing of a Catholic newspaper for expressing opposition opinions:

GIL ROBLES: Does the government have one standard for political friends and
              another for enemies?
AZAÑA: Obviously![4]

After the government forced it by decree to change its name in April 1932, the party held its first national assembly as Acción Popular in October of that year.[5] It was pledged to work legally within the system and rejected violence but adopted an officially "accidentalist" position on the form of government, declaring that it would tolerate diverse opinions among its members. The basic position of the leadership was that monarchism was inadequate as a political banner, but as Gil Robles admitted years later in his memoirs, "In theory I was and am a monarchist," and "the immense majority of those affiliated with Acción Popular were decidedly monarchist."[6]

Not all Catholic opinion was so monarchist, however, and there was a strong tendency to organize around regional groups. Acción Popular therefore soon joined with a variety of other Catholic political organizations to form a large new umbrella party, the Confederación Española de Derechas Autónomas (CEDA—Spanish Confederation of Autonomous Rightist Groups), which convened its first national congress in Madrid on 28 February 1933. Delegates claimed to represent a total of 735,058 members, at a time when Azaña's Acción Republicana numbered some 130,000. Azaña may have been to some extent correct when he claimed that Spain as a whole had ceased to be Catholic, but more Spaniards still believed in Catholicism than in any other single creed or ideology. Militant Catholics made up no more than a large minority of Spanish society, but with most of them organized by the CEDA, the latter was in a position to become the largest single force in the country, as demonstrated in the next two Republican elections. Catholicism was particularly effective in the political mobilization of women, who were said to comprise 45 percent of the CEDA's membership in Madrid, which, if correct, was by far the highest proportion of feminine membership in any major group.

The controversy that soon developed over the CEDA had to do with its true identity and real intentions. Moderate Republicans hoped to win it for a moderate liberal republic of equal rights for all. Left Republicans and the worker left categorized the CEDA as the Trojan horse of rightist authoritarianism, "objectively fascist," and the controversy has continued in historiography down to the present time.[7]

In fact, it seems fairly clear that the CEDA's basic intentions were to win decisive political power through legal means — the exception being an ill-defined "emergency" situation — and then to enact fundamental constitutional revisions that would protect religion and property and alter the basic political system. The CEDA was neither a truly democratic party, as some of its friends and allies hoped, nor was it in any genuine or categorical sense "fascist," as its enemies charged. The CEDA's platform was that of Catholic corporatism, not merely in economic structure but also in political organization. Though the chief CEDA spokesmen were usually coy in defining their long-term goals, their aim was neither a fascist state nor restoration of the monarchy, but a corporative and conservative Catholic Republic, reordered by corporative representation that would mean some

José María Gil Robles, leader of the CEDA

limitation of direct democratic rights. This would be far from the Republic of 1931–33, but it was not the Mussolinian or Hitlerian state that its
enemies charged. If there was a model for the CEDA (and a major Spanish
party had been capable of taking the Portuguese seriously), it might have
been the conservative and authoritarian "Estado Novo" in neighboring Portugal. By 1934 the one new authoritarian regime that *El Debate* and *cedistas*
unreservedly endorsed was the new Catholic corporative state of Dollfuss
and Schuschnigg in Austria, which wrote God into the first article of its
constitution.

Though *El Debate* and other publications associated with the CEDA
sometimes carried favorable articles on Fascist Italy, Gil Robles went to
some lengths to distinguish the movement from fascism. Fascism, in fact,
in the sense of arbitrary state power, was a charge sometimes leveled by
Catholic deputies in the Constituent Cortès against the Azaña administration. The Catalan Christian democrat Carrasco Formiguera referred to
what he called Azaña's "fascist concept of the state," the old Liberal politician Royo Villanova termed the new regime a "fascist republic," and Basque
nationalist spokesmen would call the 1933 education bill an expression
of "Gentilean etatism" (referring to Mussolini's first education minister)
and "pure fascism."[8]

The CEDA's position on fascism and authoritarianism seemed equivocal. Gil Robles visited Rome at the beginning of 1933 and in September
attended the Nazi Party rally at Nürnberg, while Angel Herrera later trav-
eled to Germany in May 1934. Yet Gil Robles insisted that the CEDA rejected statism, whether Communist or fascist, and early in March 1933
declared: "One does not fight against Marxism with Hitlerian militias or
Fascist legions, but with an advanced social program,"[9] reiterating this stance
at a party rally in Barcelona on 21 March. *El Debate* never directly endorsed Mussolini or Hitler, as became the tendency with the extreme right-
wing press, but its treatment of them was always more favorable than unfavorable,[10] and by the autumn of 1933 Gil Robles was declaring that much
could be learned from them, though he always avoided any clear-cut endorsement. His most sinister remarks were made in a major campaign
speech in Madrid on 15 October: "We want a totalitarian fatherland, and
it always surprises me that we are asked to look for novelties abroad, when
a unitary and totalitarian polity already exists in our own glorious tradition," referring to the new concept adopted by ideologues of the radical
right in recent years that the unified monarchy of Fernando and Isabel,
which had created the Spanish state in the fifteenth century, was itself
somehow a "totalitarian regime" (in fact, a gross misreading of Spanish
history). He went on: "We must have integral power. We will not be bound

by archaic forms in the accomplishment of our ideals. When the time comes, parliament must either submit or disappear. Democracy will be a means, but not an end. We are going to liquidate the revolution."[11] The ambiguity of the CEDA with regard to fascism was symbolized by the official salute of their youth movement, Juventudes de Acción Popular (JAP—Youth of Popular Action): the right arm was raised only halfway, then drawn back across the chest.

The Monarchist Realignment

It was only natural that a semimoderate rightist movement like the CEDA win the bulk of middle-class Catholic and conservative opinion. By definition, the conservative middle classes wanted to avoid trouble, and a technically legalistic alternative reflected their habits and values. Small groups of the more extreme monarchist right, however, could not accept the CEDA's relative moderation. While most ordinary monarchists followed the CEDA,[12] a smaller sector of doctrinaires organized a more clear-cut solution for the radical right.

This formed around a journal called *Acción Española* that began publication in December 1931. The activists of *Acción Española* were drawn from three areas: former followers of the monarchist Conservative leader Antonio Maura, the more ultra-conservative wing of social Catholicism, and Carlism. Each of these earlier Spanish sources had been superseded in the thinking of the new group, for classical *maurismo* had been too legalistic and parliamentarian, the nascent Spanish social Catholicism of the early 1920s too heterogeneous, squeamish, and even democratic,[13] and Carlism too reactionary and backward-looking.[14] Financial backing came from wealthy conservatives, above all the well-organized Bilbao industrial-financial elite.[15]

The very title of *Acción Española* made the inspiration of the French Maurrasian radical right obvious. Italian Fascism was a more distant secondary influence. Chief foreign collaborators were members of Action Française, followed by Portuguese Integralists and National Syndicalists and a few Italian Fascists. *Acción Española* generally approved of Hitlerism but criticized the German movement for its secularism and demagogy, holding that the *Führerprinzip* was no substitute for a monarchy.

Acción Española pledged to revive the traditional Spanish ideology, grounded in religion and in strong monarchist institutions. It derived much inspiration from the Primo de Rivera regime, with which nearly all its members had been associated; the critique of the regime's failure was a prime goal.[16] Blame was placed on the lack of elite support and the absence of a clear vision of a modern new authoritarian structure.

The editor of *Acción Española* was Ramiro de Maeztu, formerly a leading *noventayochista* writer who had converted to the principles of authority and religion at the time of World War I. Maeztu was to give the final major historical definition to the traditional Spanish ideology in his *Defensa de la Hispanidad* (1934), a polemic in defense of traditional Hispanic culture and religion, both European and American, as opposed to Soviet socialism and Anglo-American materialistic liberalism.[17]

The group's key political leader was ultimately José Calvo Sotelo, former Young Maurist and finance minister of Primo de Rivera. Forced to flee abroad in 1931, he was converted to right radicalism under the influence of Action Française and French and Italian ideas while in exile in Paris. Calvo Sotelo's return to Spain was made possible first by his election to the new Tribunal de Garantías Constitucionales and finally by his election to the Cortes on the list of the new monarchist Renovación Española party in 1933. The latter, *Acción Española*'s political branch, had been organized after it became clear that the CEDA rejected the group's principles. The CEDA in turn was denounced for being too moderate, compromising, and ambiguous—insufficiently nationalist and authoritarian— whereas Renovación Española proved to be too small and narrow. Later it was badly split between its more conservative and radical wings, and rent by personality clashes.[18]

Calvo Sotelo subsequently tried to form a broader coalition of radical right groups, which took shape as the Bloque Nacional, organized in December 1934 in the wake of the insurrection in Asturias. Calvo and the *Acción Española* writers proposed not the restoration but the "installation" (*instauración*) of an authoritarian monarchy, which would have to be preceded by an indeterminate period of dictatorship. In its founding manifesto, the Bloque called for an "integrating state" to concentrate national energies. The directly elected Cortes was to be replaced by an "organically" organized corporate chamber analogous to those of Italy, Portugal, or Austria, and social and economic problems resolved through state regulation, economic intervention, and reflationary policies. Calvo Sotelo clearly understood that this was not likely to come about through political mobilization but would probably require forcible intervention by the military. The new state would adopt a militantly nationalist policy and foster the development of the armed forces in particular. It would reject laicism and restore the Catholic identity of Spanish government.[19]

The radical right of *Acción Española* and the Bloque Nacional differed from generic fascism not in any squeamishness about violence and dic tatorship, or even in any differences over the goal of empire, but in their distinct socioeconomic strategies and cultural formulae. *Acción Española* invoked traditional rightist elites and feared the emergence of new competitors, even if nationalist in orientation. Both the neomonarchists and Spanish fascists strove for a corporate state, but for the latter this meant the mobilization of labor and a drastic new articulation of national interests behind national syndicalism. In religious and cultural matters, the neomonarchists were clerical and neotraditionalist, and the incipient Spanish fascists were Catholic but nonclerical and zealous to combine traditionalism with modernization.

Unlike many other rightists, however, Calvo Sotelo was not unwilling to be labeled a fascist. His own definition of fascism seems to have been loose, referring rather vaguely to authoritarian nationalism and corporatism. In fact, any analysis of the subsequent Franco regime — especially the "high phase" of the Franquist system from 1937 to 1959 — will reveal that it was built on the ideas and doctrines of Calvo Sotelo and the *Acción Española* group more than on those of the fascist party, Falange Española, which Franco used as the basis of his own *partido único.* The reliance on the military, a corporative Cortes, and the *instauración* of monarchy all corresponded to this doctine. Even the national syndical system functioned primarily as an agency of state control of regulation more or less along lines conceived by Calvo Sotelo. Similarly, the intensely Catholic character of the Franquist system in its heyday corresponded much more to the concepts of *Acción Española* than to those of the Falangists.

More clearly than either the moderate Gil Robles or the radical Falangist leader José Antonio Primo de Rivera, Calvo Sotelo grasped that the most feasible alternative to the Republican system was neither conservative parliamentarianism nor a popular national syndicalism but an integrated mobilization of all the resources of the counterrevolutionary right. The difference, of course, was not a matter of tactics alone but also of values. To the CEDA leader such an extreme of dictatorship was repugnant, while to the Falangist it was inadequate and reactionary. Calvo Sotelo's politics became those of catastrophism. The rightist reaction of the military on which he came to rely could only be achieved in a situation of intense polarization and impending cataclysm. Hence the irony that Calvo Sotelo's own eventual assassination formed an integral part of that very process on which he depended to realize his ideas and achieve his goals.

Authoritarian *alfonsino* monarchism in support of the exiled king and his heir was not the only significant sector of rightist monarchism, however, because traditionalist Carlism revived and took on new life under the Republic. As Spain's classic radical right, indeed the original nineteenth-century prototype of such a force, Carlism had been the only mass movement in the peninsula for much of the preceding century. Defeats in two major civil wars, combined with extensive social and cultural change, had eroded Carlism's following considerably, but just as the emergence of the anticlerical First Republic had reawakened Carlism in 1873, so the anticlericalism and radical mass leftist mobilization of the Second Republic revived Carlism in the early 1930s. A more contemporary and integrated doctrinal base had been provided during the early years of the century by the theorist Juan Vázquez de Mella y Fanjul, who cast Carlist principles fully in the mold of right-wing Catholic corporatism under the leadership of traditionalist but theoretically decentralized monarchy.

During the first phase of the Republic the main branches of Carlism were reunited and given vigorous leadership by a new leader in Seville, Manuel Fal Conde. Popular support was disproportionately concentrated in the historically autonomous northeastern province (formerly kingdom) of Navarre. Some of the Carlists later joined with Renovación Española behind Calvo Sotelo's Bloque Nacional, though the association remained an uneasy one.

The principal new statement of Carlist doctrine was Víctor Pradera's El Estado nuevo (1935). In it he defined Catholic identity and a form of societal corporatism, under monarchy, that would be autonomous from the state though partially regulated by it and also compatible with partial regional decentralization. Though the Carlist youth organization, like the CEDA's Juventudes de Acción Popular, suffered from aspects of the vertigo of fascism and sometimes used fascistlike slogans, the Carlists differentiated their traditionalist, ultra-Catholic, monarchist, and partially decentralized corporatism from the radical, centralized, modern authoritarianism of Italy and Germany.[20]

Emergence of a Spanish Fascism

A categorical fascist movement was slow to emerge in Spain, in considerable measure because of the weakness of nationalism. During the 1920s political space was preempted by the Primo de Rivera dictatorship, sympathetic to Italian Fascism but lacking equivalent fascist political content. Several small imitative efforts to create a new extreme nationalism or protofascism between 1923 and 1931 were stillborn. The first noteworthy figure to propagate fascistic doctrine in Spain was Ernesto Giménez Caballero, editor of La Gaceta Literaria (Spain's leading avant-garde literary review of the late 1920s).[21] Yet he lacked either ability or opportunity to create a political movement and soon found himself shunned by the predominantly liberal and leftist cultural establishment, in his own words a "literary Robinson Crusoe."[22]

The first continuous, organized fascist group was a nucleus formed in Madrid by Ramiro Ledesma Ramos, a young intellectual who began to publish a weekly, *La Conquista del Estado*, its name derived from a widely known Italian Fascist prototype. Ledesma was followed by a mere handful of ten young students, but soon joined forces with a radical right-wing lawyer in Valladolid, Onésimo Redondo Ortega. In October 1931 they formed the first categoric Spanish fascist political organization, the Juntas de Ofensiva Nacional Sindicalista, a typically verbose formulation that produced the acronym JONS and the term *jonsistas* for its few members. Ledesma was possibly the most trenchant intellectual figure in the history of Spanish fascism. He aspired to develop a revolutionary and fascistic nationalism that could compete with the left among the lower classes, but the JONS never attracted more than about two thousand followers in central and north central Spain, failing completely at political mobilization.[23]

A more vigorous, better-financed attempt at a Spanish fascism was essayed by elements of the extreme right in 1933. The triumph of Hitler stimulated interest not so much among potential fascists — of whom there seemed to be few in Spain — but among right radicals or potential right radicals, who were much more numerous. During the summer of 1933 representatives of wealthy financiers and industrialists in Bilbao searched for the possible leader of a counterrevolutionary, demagogic Spanish fascism.

The figure who came to the fore was José Antonio Primo de Rivera, eldest son of the late dictator, who was in the course of his evolution from conservative authoritarian monarchism to a more radical brand of nationalist authoritarianism that at first was not unlike that of Calvo Sotelo. By 1933 the young Primo de Rivera — soon generally known as José Antonio — had become interested in something rather like fascism (Italian-style) as the vehicle for giving form and ideological content to the national authoritarian regime attempted so uncertainly and unsuccessfully by his father. Unlike Ledesma, who initially had greater insight, José Antonio was not at first averse to using the label "fascist," though it was decided to call the new movement that he founded in October 1933 by the more original title of Falange Española (Spanish Phalanx).

The Falange began with much more financial support than did the JONS, prompting the latter to merge with it in early 1934, the resulting organization being called Falange Española de las JONS. During the next two years, the Falange was distinguished primarily by its insignificance. Like the Romanian Iron Guard and several other fascist movements, it relied primarily on a student clientele in the universities, but unlike the Romanian movement completely failed to generate broader support. The depression in Spain generated proportionately less unemployment among lower-middle-class sectors than in central and east-central Europe, thus avoiding serious destabilization of what was often considered the potentially "fascist class" par excellence.

The only advantage of this period in the wilderness was that it gave the movement's leaders some time to reflect on what they were about. After a year or so, José Antonio Primo de Rivera began to move "left," as the national syndicalism of the Falangists took on more radical overtones. Unlike some other fascist movements, the Falangists did develop an official program, the Twenty-Seven Points, before the close of 1934. By that time there was a belated reaction to the danger of mimesis, as Ledesma complained of the earlier "mimicry" shown by Falangists, and before the close of 1934 Falangist leaders were denying that they were fascists. While admitting that they had much in common with, for example, Italian Fascists, Falangists insisted on the Spanishness and singularity of Falangism.

In fact, neither in style, organization, nor doctrine did Falangism differ in any very significant way from Mussolini's party. Falangist rhetoric sometimes followed the productionist line of early Italian Fascism, and José Antonio spoke of converting Spain into a "gigantic syndicate of producers," but the precise articulation of this remained unclear. Falangism supported the concept of significant agrarian reform and realized that the solution to perpetual underemployment lay in industrialization, but its only concrete radical proposal was the nationalization of banking and credit.[24]

Like many fascist leaders, José Antonio projected a distinctive charisma among his few followers. He was in fact probably the most ambivalent of all European fascist party leaders of that period, combining a fastidious estheticism with a genuine if contradictory sense of moral scruple, a cultivated intellectual tone of distance and irony, and, for a Spanish politician of the period, a remarkably limited spirit of sectarianism and group rivalry. Of all European national fascist leaders, he was perhaps the most repelled by the brutality and violence associated with the fascist enterprise, yet however diffident and differential may have been his approach, he never renounced the basic fascist goals.[25]

Up until the spring of 1936, the Falange probably never had more than ten thousand regular members. It tried to develop a nationalist, anti-Marxist trade union movement, the CONS (Confederación Obrera Nacional-Sindicalista), for which it claimed twenty-five thousand members by early 1935, but the figure is doubtful. In August 1934 a pact was signed with Renovación Española in which the Falange pledged to do nothing to hinder the expansion of the monarchists, in return for a monthly subsidy,[26] but this pact was soon discontinued. During the second half of 1935 the Italian government provided a monthly subsidy of 50,000 lire (about 4,500 U.S. dollars) per month, inadequate to carry the party very far. That sum was soon cut in half and then eliminated altogether.[27] In Spain categoric fascism would not be able to challenge the forces of the left in a direct political contest, as in central Europe.[28] That task lay in the hands of the conservative right.

Mobilization of the Economic Interests

The combination of the depression, the Republican labor and regulative reforms, and the increase in strike activity and disorder provoked increasing opposition and mobilization among the organized economic interests. Both a Confederación Gremial Española (Spanish Small Businessmen's Confederation) and a Confederación Patronal Española (Spanish Employers' Confederation) had been organized by the eve of World War I, followed by a Federación de Industrias Nacionales in 1924. There were in addition numerous provincial and regional structures organized both by economic sector and in general associations, as well as a variety of agricultural and stockbreeders' groups. Indeed, the latter were the first to project direct political influence, with the appearance of the Agrarian Party minority in the Constituent Cortes to protect the interests of conservative landowners. In March 1933 the larger landowners came together in a new Confederación Española Patronal Agrícola (Spanish Confederation of Agrarian Employers), and the diverse agricultural and stockmen's groups were active in opposition to the agrarian reform and related legislation.[29]

The main industrial and commercial forces found their existing organizations too divided and weakly structured to form effective lobbies, at least in the majority of cases, leading to the formation of a new Unión Nacional Económica in November 1931. The UNE, however, suffered from the same limitations as the older organizations and never managed to achieve its goal of acting as a single, united, and powerful spokesman for economic interests. A major protest conference was convened at Madrid in July 1933, attended by representatives of what were announced as "more than a thousand" local, provincial, regional, sectoral, and national economic groups. A new effort was made to achieve a strong, cohesive *frente único* with the formation of a new national Bloque Patronal (lit. Employers Bloc) in February 1934.[30]

Most of the major economic interests declared themselves to be independent of specific parties, calling on patriotic forces of the left-center, center, and right to resist costly reforms that raised the price of production and altered the existing property relationships. In practice, they basically supported the center-right and right, from the Radical Party across to Renovación Española. Some small businessmen were, however, left Republicans, so that by no means were all sectors of the employing classes aligned with the political right. The major economic interests sought not merely the reversal of most of the reforms of the first biennium, but also positive reinforcement in the form of further tariff support, credits, and new state contracts for public works. They tended ultimately to seek a special corporative relationship with the Spanish state. The elections of November 1933 offered the most important opportunity to change the course of affairs. Considerable money was invested in the campaign, the main beneficiaries being the CEDA and the Radicals. Yet the economic and employer interests were never able to speak effectively with a single voice. Smaller employers found their own concerns poorly represented by the larger firms that dominated the major associations. Moreover, more liberal employers, particularly in Catalonia, sometimes differed sharply from the rightist positions of the main interest groups. The fragmentation of society and political forces was thus paralleled, though to a lesser degree, by the relative fragmentation of the economic interests.[31]

The Cortes Elections of November 1933

The elections of November 1933 were the second democratic parliamentary contest in Spanish history, but only the first to be fully contested, given the disarray of the right in 1931. The campaign lasted a full month and was generally energetic, even passionate, though there were comparatively few incidents until late in the campaign. Though closely fought, this was not a campaign of total polarization or menace on the part of the major parties, with the exception of two speeches by Gil Robles[32] and an occasional call to revolution by a Socialist speaker.

The electoral system was designed to favor large national parties or alliances, but the effect of this system in 1933 was diametrically opposite from that which occurred two years earlier. Then the various Republican parties and the Socialists had formed winning alliances in most districts, but by 1933 the Republican parties were divided and the alliance with the Socialists had shattered. The Socialist leadership felt betrayed by the outcome of the first biennium and by the veto ultimately exercised against it by many Republicans, including some left Republicans. Thus the Socialists would go it alone, as in most cases would the left Republican parties. The great beneficiary of moderate liberal lower-middle-class votes, cast by those disillusioned with the first two years, would be the Radicals, while the CEDA would capitalize on the large-scale Catholic reaction among northern rural voters and middle-class voters generally. In a considerable number of provinces Radicals and *cedistas* formed a center-right alliance, though the CEDA also reached a general electoral understanding with the other rightist forces (Carlists, Agrarians, Renovación Española) on a broad amnesty, the defense of property, and the priority of revising laic and Socialist legislation. The Socialists and the CEDA both aimed much of their campaigns against each other, the Socialists pointing especially to the uniformed JAP youth and talk of a corporate state as precursors to fascism. The CEDA, meanwhile, expected to be favored by one Republican innovation, the enfranchisement of women, as decreed for the first time in the Constitution.[33]

During the past year an increasing crescendo of criticism of the left Republican government and the Constituent Cortes had been building in much of the press, ranging from moderate liberal to conservative to extreme rightist. A lengthy series of new books contained criticisms and accusations of all sorts, from the reasonable to the most unfair, and from detailed critiques of the perks and emoluments acquired by Cortes deputies of the government parties[34] to categorical ideological diatribes.

The campaign featured many radio broadcasts and some candidate travel by airplane. The CEDA employed the most elaborate schemes, allegedly printing two hundred thousand color photos and preparing short films of Gil Robles's speeches. In the final days, radio spots were run as often as twenty times a day, and even a few neon signs went up. Student disorders meanwhile closed several universities while the continuation of the construction strike in Madrid led to the death of three workers.

Election day was generally calm, though there were a few disorders and altogether six deaths were reported.[35] The Socialists later charged electoral fraud — mainly by the Radicals — in two Galician provinces (Orense and Pontevedra) and in Granada, with some evidence to substantiate their claims, and there was indication of minor leftist fraud in Valencia, but even if all accusations were justified, on balance it still amounted to a free and fair contest.

The big winners were the Radicals and the CEDA, both of whom were able to take advantage of both the electoral system and the moderate and conservative reaction. The Radicals, who had played the game most effectively of all, were in fact somewhat overrepresented, with 104 deputies, while the CEDA emerged with the largest single parliamentary delegation —115 deputies. The Socialists suffered from running alone and dropped to sixty seats, though they had retained most of their popular vote. The big losers were the left Republicans, deprived of coalition support in most provinces and deserted by many of their former voters, who were nearly wiped out. (See table 8.1.)

Clearly there had been some shift of opinion toward the center and center-right, together with a much more intense mobilization of the rightist vote, yet the actual change of opinion was less than the drastically altered composition of parliament made it appear. The overall abstention rate was 32 percent, not far from the average for the three Republican elections. This was well above the west European norm, but not surprising for a country with 25 percent adult illiteracy. Another factor that weakened the left was the alienation of anarchosyndicalists, with an apparently greater rate of abstention among them than in 1931.[36]

The electoral system had created the effect of a broad pendular swing, rather than a mere adjustment.[37] The Socialists and left Republicans, primary authors of the new system, were now a small and impotent minority in the new Cortes, and the more prone to radicalization. The new parliament would be politically and ideologically more balanced, but would contain mutually antagonistic leftist and rightist groups who would almost inevitably promote greater polarization. Moreover, the discontinuity of parliamentary experience that had been so marked in the Constituent Cortes would continue. In 1931 only sixty-four deputies had held seats in the old monarchist parliament, and 55.6 percent of all deputies elected that year never sat in subsequent Republican parliaments. Forty-six percent of the deputies elected in 1933 had not sat in the Constituent Cortes and would not be elected again in 1936, and in those final Republican elections the approximate proportion of newcomers would be the same.[38] Of the large bloc of new CEDA deputies, only ten had previous parliamentary experience.

The only potentially constructive feature of the new Cortes was the increased strength of the democratic center. The Radicals almost equalled

Table 8.1. Electoral Results of 1933

Sector	Estimated Number of Voters	Percentage of Total Voters	Number of Seats	Percentage of Seats
Revolutionary left	190,244	2.24	1	0.2
Socialists	1,685,318	19.84	62	13.1
Left Republicans	1,199,976	14.13	36	7.6
Center Republicans	2,548,939	30.01	176	37.2
Moderate right	2,059,290	24.25	153	32.4
Extreme right	777,254	9.15	45	9.5
Miscellaneous	32,259	0.38	. . .	. . .

Source: Irwin, *1933 Cortes Elections,* 269.

Julián Besteiro voting in Madrid, November 1933

cedistas in number, while the Progressive Republicans of Alcalá Zamora and the Conservative Republicans of Maura had retained the majority of their seats (though dropping from a combined total of twenty-eight to twenty-one), the Liberal Democrats of Melquiades Alvarez rose from a total of two to eight, and the Basque nationalists lost only two seats.

The defeated left reacted with rage and despair, fearing that a rightist or semi-rightist government would undo most of the reforms of the past biennium. They were less disposed than the right in 1931 to accept temporary electoral defeat, even though they had drafted the electoral law and a cabinet of Republicans had administered the elections. "Hence," as Santos Juliá says, "the fact that both left Republicans and Socialists reacted immediately to ask, on the part of some, for the formation of a new government of Republican concentration which, if unable to win a majority in the new Cortes, would dissolve parliament and convene new elections."[39]

Several different proposals to that effect were made in the aftermath of the elections. The first was presented by the Left Radical Socialist justice minister Botella Asensi on the very next day (20 November), urging Alcalá Zamora to sign a decree immediately to annul the electoral outcome. This request was repeated by Gordón Ordás, the otherwise more moderate Radical Socialist minister of industry, who proposed that the president dissolve the new parliament before the second round of runoff elections were held.[40]

Similarly, Largo Caballero declared that the only way out would be a dissolution as soon as possible.[41]

Later, on 4 December, the day after the second round of balloting took
place, Azaña met privately with Martínez Barrio, the caretaker prime
minister. He lamented that the left was severely underrepresented in the
new chamber compared with its combined vote totals, ignoring the fact
that the left had written the electoral law, had conducted its campaign and
alliance policy exactly as it saw fit, and had been defeated in free and fair
elections. Hence he urged that a new Republican coalition government be
formed immediately to conduct new elections. Though the proposal was
rejected by Martínez Barrio, it was repeated on the following day in a letter to the prime minister signed by Azaña, Casares Quiroga, and Marcelino Domingo.[42]

One further proposal was brought to Alcalá Zamora by the Socialist
deputy Juan Negrín on behalf of the Socialist parliamentary delegation,
urging that a new left Republican government be formed, a new electoral
law be written to guarantee victory for the left, that the electoral results
then be canceled and new elections held. When the president asked how a
new parliament could be expected to approve a law for its own extinction,
Negrín replied that the new Cortes would accept a presidential decree temporarily postponing its convocation. In the meantime a new electoral law
could be passed by the reconvened Diputación Permanente (Permanent
Commission) of the old Constituent Cortes.[43] Alcalá Zamora rejected all
these requests to tamper with the constitutional process, but such eagerness on the part of the authors of the new democracy to flout democratic
process did not augur well for the future of the polity.

While the Republican president stood firm against all efforts to manipulate the electoral outcome, the Martínez Barrio caretaker administration
was faced with yet another anarchist-inspired crisis of public order. The
year 1933 had been a time of decline for both the FAI and CNT, but hard-
core *faístas* somehow conceived that the hour had arrived for one last insurrectionary spasm before a new regular government could be formed.
This was yet more anarchist "playing at revolution," the notion being that,
with Barcelona weakening, the initiative might be taken in Zaragoza and
other more peripheral centers of FAI activity, somehow sparking a wider
insurrection. As it turned out, only the Zaragoza sector of the movement
showed real enthusiasm for the newest paroxysm.[44]

On 1 December two large bombs went off in Barcelona, and on the following day, after a request from the Catalan Generalitat itself, the government declared a state of prevention in all Catalonia and two days later
in all Spain. The police began to close down CNT centers and also those

of the Carlists and Falangists, for good measure. The insurrection, last of the *tres ochos*,[45] commenced on 8 December (scheduled date for convening of the new Cortes) with explosions and incidents in eight different cities. By the morning of the ninth a state of alarm had been declared throughout the country. The main fighting took place in Zaragoza and Barcelona, but there were violent incidents in nine other provinces in the north, east, and south. Several trains were derailed; the blowing up of a bridge in Valencia produced a wreck in which between sixteen and twenty passengers were killed, depending on reports. The most spectacular single episode occurred in the town of Villanueva de la Serena (Badajoz), where the local sergeant in charge of an army recruitment center mutinied, taking over the small headquarters with several other troops and some fifteen civilian anarchists. Troops were called in to storm the building the next morning. They killed seven rebels, including the sergeant.

The revolt was strongest in Zaragoza, whence it spread to four neighboring provinces. The FAI-CNT momentarily took over several small towns in Huesca, Alava, and Logroño, and officially declared "libertarian communism," burning records and abolishing money. By 12 December the authorities had largely regained control, and the Ministry of the Interior announced a month later that the insurrection had cost the lives of eleven Civil Guards, three other policemen, and seventy-five civilians, in statistics which were probably incomplete. Hundreds of CNT activists were arrested.[46]

Government by the Center-Right

The search for a stable new government to be formed out of a badly fragmented and polarized new parliament was the most difficult problem yet faced by the Republic. The Constitution left the initiative in the hands of the president, who now came to the forefront of political affairs, a position he would retain for more than two years, until the next elections. He was eager for a more dominant role and, despite the destructive consequences of some of his maneuvers, his often shortsighted initiatives were sincerely intended to stabilize a more moderate liberal democratic regime, equidistant between right and left.

The CEDA now numbered the largest parliamentary delegation, normally the basis of a successful coalition. Yet Gil Robles had already said more than once that the CEDA was not yet prepared to govern, still not being fully unified or mature as a political organization, and might be willing to support a moderate nonleftist government of other forces. Hence, from Alcalá Zamora's perspective, the best option would clearly be the number two party, Lerroux's Radicals, the main force of the center. The Radicals were not without their liabilities. Lerroux was in his seventieth year, and his energies were declining. The Radicals had always been personalistic and opportunist and had recently incorporated many new moderate conservative elements eager to get ahead under the Republic. Their position on many issues was somewhat ambivalent, and they lacked a fully defined program. Some of the old Radical leaders had gained a reputation for corruption in local government in earlier years. Theirs was a very localist party, made up of many diverse provincial groups, held together by Lerroux. The caliber of the Radical leadership was uncertain at best, and they seemed to lack strong, experienced, energetic spokesmen able to confront major problems. One CEDA deputy said, "This Radical minority reminds me of a voyage on a ship: people of all ages and conditions, of the most diverse ideologies, brought together merely to travel."[47] Yet the diversity of the Radicals could also be a source of strength. They had become in some ways the major force in local political life by the end of 1933, numbering in their ranks many mayors and presidents of provincial assemblies, especially in the Levant and the south.[48]

Lerroux presented his new government to the Cortes on 19 December. His cabinet consisted of seven Radicals (including himself), two Republican independents, and one each from Alcalá Zamora's Progressive Republicans, the Liberal Democrats,[49] and the more conservative Agrarians. It promised to sustain the Republican constitution and the positive reforms of the preceding biennium, while providing equal government for all and correction of any abuses. The problem was that the four parties in the new coalition in toto represented scarcely a third of the votes in the chamber and could not survive without the acquiescence of the CEDA. This Gil Robles was willing to provide, despite his occasionally menacing talk during the campaign. That same day he presented to the Cortes the CEDA's legislative program, which included a full amnesty for political prisoners, revision of the religious legislation, and the annulment of certain economic reforms. He attacked *jurados mixtos, laboreo forzoso,* and the legislation on *términos municipales,* and also pressed for a reduction in the amount of land subject to expropriation under the agrarian reform. At the same time Gil Robles declared the need for stronger action against unemployment and an expansion of public works, to be paid for by higher taxes. He differed publicly with the Falangist leader Primo de Rivera on the issue of a national dictatorship, saying that "the divinization of the state and the annulment of individual personality" were against his principles. So long as the Radical government proceeded in a constructive manner according to CEDA norms, it would at least for the moment enjoy the CEDA's voting support, which was also granted to a new bill by the Progressivist minister of agriculture in February, 1934, allowing landless Extremaduran ploughmen (*yunteros*) to remain for the time being on land on which they had been temporarily settled.[50] Gil Robles began to use terms like "deference to," "readiness to work within," and "respect for" the Republic.[51] The Agrarians, now represented in the government, went farther. On 23 January 1934 their minority was officially reorganized as the Partido Agrario Español and declared its willingness "to accept the legally established regime," though this brought the resignation of the group's five most conservative deputies.

Lerroux was pleased. He was convinced that the Radicals were accomplishing a major patriotic service by beginning the domestication of the right within the Republic, something that he saw correctly as necessary to the survival of the regime.[52] The most immediate payoff for the CEDA was that the new administration ignored the Law of Congregations passed six months earlier, allowing Catholic schools to continue to operate normally. In January 1934 the new foreign minister, Pita Romero, was sent to Rome to initiate negotiations for a new Concordat and later, on 4 April, a law was passed with authorized the government to continue to pay the salaries of priests over forty years old in small towns at two-thirds the rate of 1931. That spring Holy Week celebrations were carried out fully for the first time in three years, and old-line anticlerical Radicals were disgusted to see the new Radical interior minister walking in a religious procession in Seville.

The center-right compromise—under the immediate circumstances the only viable option—quickly produced new tensions on both its left and right. Martínez Barrio, the number two figure in the Radical Party and head of the recent caretaker government, showed increasing distress over his party's turn toward the right. It has been speculated that he was also jealous of the eminence achieved by the party's most illustrious new member, Santiago Alba—a major figure in the old monarchist Liberal Party—who had just been elected speaker of the Cortes. Martínez Barrio was also Masonic Grand Master of the Spanish Grand Orient, the top Mason in Spain, and to that extent the leader of Masonic liberalism. The widely read magazine *Blanco y Negro* published an interview with him on 4 February, in which he declared that he was "a man of the left," and said that he could not collaborate with a center-right policy. This was countered with a public manifesto by sixteen of the most conservative Radical deputies that demanded constitutional revision, a more favorable policy toward the Church, and the resignation of any government minister who disagreed. Lerroux tried to smooth all this over, but at the end of the month Martínez Barrio resigned his portfolio of war minister, joined by the Radical finance minister. Two and a half months later he would abandon the party altogether,[53] seconded by a number of the more liberal Radical deputies and a liberal sector of the party in Valencia, one of its strongholds.[54]

This required reorganization of the Lerroux government after only two and a half months, and, as had become his custom, the president took advantage of the circumstance to display pomp and rhetoric, treating this as a major crisis that might require presidential intervention. Within a few days the cabinet was reorganized on much the same basis. Rafael Salazar Alonso, a leader of the most conservative sector of the party, became minister of the interior, and Salvador de Madariaga accepted the portfolio of Education, thus accomplishing, however briefly, Lerroux's goal of bringing at least one of the country's most prestigious intellectuals into his cabinet.[55]

Meanwhile, the CEDA's willingness to support a center-right government had enraged its recent electoral allies of the extreme right, who soon broke with Gil Robles's party, moving quickly to a fully polarized and subversive position. Though the CEDA had won the support of the Vatican, the monarchists sought direct backing from Mussolini's Fascist government, negotiating for Italian support of a violent overthrow of the Republic by the monarchist right. Representatives of Renovación Española and the Carlist Comunión Tradicionalista met in Rome on 31 March with the Italian air minister Italo Balbo and signed a secret agreement that promised the Spanish rebels 1,500,000 pesetas in financial support, 10,000 rifles, 200 machine guns, and other forms of aid, plus the opportunity for training military volunteers in Italian Libya. In addition, the pact agreed that the new Spanish regime would negotiate a treaty of neutrality and friendship with Italy and would coordinate their mutual commercial interests.[56] The first half million pesetas were paid the next day, and soon some fifty Carlist volunteers journeyed to Libya for military training. The entire arrangement was successfully kept secret, but soon became a dead letter because the monarchist groups proved unable to build the strength and unity to take advantage of it. No arms were ever sent to Spain, and the whole project was cancelled by Mussolini a year later after the Spanish monarchists had failed to show many signs of life. The Italian Duce did not wish to complicate his foreign policy as he prepared for an attack on Ethiopia.[57] Nonetheless, Spanish publications of the extreme right now began to discuss openly the doctrine of justified insurrection,[58] and in May the Carlists moved even farther to the right. The existing Junta, which had been willing to cooperate with *alfonsino* monarchists, was dissolved, and a new secretary general, Manuel Fal Conde, appointed. An extremist and exclusivist, Fal Conde sought to promote a Carlist restoration *manu militari* and encouraged the drilling of Carlist militiamen.

Meanwhile the government had fulfilled its pledge to introduce amnesty legislation, presented by the justice minister, Ramón Alvarez Valdés of the Liberal Democrats, on 23 March. Alvarez Valdés soon got into trouble by declaring that he was opposed to all efforts to seize power by force, whether by rightists in 1932 or anarchists in 1933. The crafty Prieto, seeing an opening in which the government might be weakened, demanded to know if Alvarez Valdés also repudiated the Republican rebels of December 1930. To his credit, the justice minister maintained a consistent position, stressing that the Republic had been introduced by the elections of April 1931. His refusal to endorse Galán and García Hernández brought down a firestorm from the left, who claimed that Alvarez Valdés had slandered the sacred martyrs of the Republic. The hapless minister — whose personal position was in fact irreproachable — soon resigned, to be replaced on 17 April by Madariaga, who temporarily occupied two ministries. Madariaga believed that it was necessary to go to considerable lengths to achieve national political reconciliation before the polarization became too extreme. When Socialists objected that the new bill granted amnesty only for acts committed through 3 December 1933, and so would exclude the many hundreds of anarchosyndicalists arrested after the most recent insurrection, the date was soon extended to 14 April 1934, third anniversary of the founding of the Republic. It carried on the twentieth by a vote of 269 to 1.

An impasse quickly developed at the president's level, where Alcalá Zamora opposed the law for weakening the Republic and placing its enemies at liberty. He preferred to return the bill to parliament for reconsideration, as empowered by Article 83 of the Constitution, but Article 84 required the cosignature of at least one government minister for any such act, and none of the current ministers would agree. Lerroux, as was his wont, then proposed a compromise. Two additional decrees would be promulgated with the amnesty, one specifying that none of the land expropriated from *grandes* or any of those convicted of involvement in the *sanjurjada* would be returned, the second that none of the military officers being amnestied would be allowed to return to the active list. The amnesty, dated 20 April, was then officially published on 2 May. The headquarters of *Acción Española* were allowed to be reopened for the first time since August 1932, and Calvo Sotelo returned to Spain two days later.

Alcalá Zamora then deliberately provoked a government crisis, including with his signature of the new bill a pedantic thirty-four-page memorandum in the form of a message to the Cortes detailing all his juridical and political arguments against it.[59] Gil Robles pledged CEDA votes to

Lerroux for a parliamentary vote of confidence, but the latter did not wish to create a new crisis that might threaten the equilibrium of Republican institutions and resigned on the twenty-fifth. By the next day rumors spread rapidly that the Radicals and their friends in the military command were preparing a coup. Though this proved a false alarm, an *estado de alarma* was declared in all Spain, while Azaña and many other left Republicans passed the night on alert,[60] relieved that the president had in effect vetoed Lerroux's continuation as prime minister.

On the following day Alcalá Zamora asked one of Lerroux's lieutenants, Ricardo Samper, to form a government. A bald, homely man with a long face, Samper was a veteran Radical from Valencia and former follower of the novelist Blasco Ibáñez, from the more liberal side of the party. Though the president's veto of Lerroux infuriated many Radicals, they were the party of compromise par excellence and Lerroux advised them to cooperate. Samper's new cabinet was composed of eight Radicals, one member each from the Agrarians, Progressive Republicans, and Liberal Democrats, and one independent, with Madariaga (who had never been a deputy) returning to Geneva. The general impression that this was a cabinet of nonentities manipulated by the president was essentially correct. Azaña observed tongue in cheek that it was such a collection of mediocrities he would prefer to be governed by the monarchy.

The crisis exposed the major problem of Republican government for the next two years: a generalized refusal to allow the constitutional parliamentary system to function normally. The crisis had been a personal and artificial one created by the president himself, who had managed to veto the leaders of both of the two largest parties in parliament as prime minister. In one sense, his interference and manipulation had become more extreme than that imputed to the former king, for, as events would indicate, he personally sought to replace Lerroux — whom he now saw as a personal rival — as leader of the Republican center.[61] In the process he managed to alienate everyone, for he had been unable to block the amnesty bill of the center and right, who were both increasingly angry with him now, while he completely failed to placate the left, who demanded much more. This sort of maneuver would be repeated several times in the two years that followed, on each occasion to the further discredit and weakening of the parliamentary system.

9

The Revolutionary Insurrection
of 1934

SEVERAL historians have argued that the most decisive single development during the history of the Republic prior to July 1936 was the shift in Socialist policy during 1933–34, though there is no agreement concerning the causes of the change. Some ascribe it primarily to the danger from the right, resulting from its defeat in the 1933 elections and the concomitant rise of the CEDA. Others point to the influence of central European affairs after the establishment of the Hitler regime and of a rightist dictatorship in Austria, marking the defeat of the two strongest Socialist movements in Europe. The relative deepening of the depression during 1932–33 is also sometimes cited. Still others point to the beginning of Socialist radicalization in the summer of 1933, a phenomenon not specifically related to the chronology either of foreign affairs or domestic electoral defeat, but which apparently stemmed from the weakening of the Socialist-left Republican coalition, the increasing frustration met by Republican reform initiatives, and the threatened loss of government power.[1]

Santos Juliá has written:

It is perhaps important to remember in this context that the first statements by Socialist leaders about the need to take over power or conquer it by whatever means — which naturally did not exclude the use of violence — bore no relation whatever to a presumed fear of the fascist menace. Socialists began to elaborate the discourse about the conquest of power as soon as they were excluded from the government, facing the prospect of the Radicals assuming the leadership. At that point no one identified Lerroux with fascism and no one, not even Lerroux, thought that within two months he would have to govern with the parliamentary support of the CEDA. It was enough for the Socialists to find themselves excluded from government power to announce their new political intentions: that change, though only incipient, is incomprehensible unless one keeps in mind that they all

189

considered the Republic their own creature and all believed they held the right, prior to any election or popular vote, to govern it.[2]

The possibility of a fundamental change in policy was not, however, merely the result of certain leaders' calculations. It was strongly conditioned by a rising tide of discontent among UGT workers during 1933 and 1934. Deepening of the depression brought steadily increasing unemployment, as indicated in table 9.1, while the momentum had been lost in labor and social reform less than a year after the passage of the poorly conceived agrarian reform bill. Major economic interests — and particularly the larger landowners — went over to the offensive during 1933, as the relatively weak Spanish state demonstrated that it lacked the administrative apparatus to enforce all the new reforms, particularly in the countryside. The new regulations were becoming a dead letter in sections of some rural provinces, and Largo claimed that during his last months as minister of labor he regularly received delegations of provincial workers who had come to Madrid to urge the party to take action.[3] The national committee of the UGT had met as early as 18 June 1933 to face the problem of declining membership. By the end of the year, affiliation in some areas had dropped by as much as a third. The FNTT was claiming that in southern rural provinces wages had dropped as much as 60 percent (probably a considerable exaggeration) and that in some areas work was being offered only to laborers who were willing to drop their membership in the union. The combination of all these factors stimulated a rising tide of militancy among many Socialist workers and, even more, among the Socialist Youth.

It was in this climate that Largo Caballero had hailed the prospect of direct revolution at the Young Socialist summer school in August 1933, sentiments that he repeated, though usually in more discreet or equivocal terms, in a series of speeches during the next year. The Socialist left increased steadily in strength and influence under his de facto leadership, yet it was not clear what new policies or goals would replace collaborationism. The hard-core left had always opposed participation, but Largo Caballero and the other leaders had no alternative strategy to propose.

Table 9.1. Growth in Unemployment

June 1932	446,263
August 1933	588,174
December 1933	618,947
April 1934	703,814

Source: *Boletín del Ministerio de Trabajo*, January, 1935, in Preston, *CSCW*, 219.

When the first Lerroux government had fallen, the party heads gave their support to an abortive effort by the moderate left Republican Felipe Sánchez Román to reorganize the left Republican-Socialist coalition, even on a more moderate basis.

The electoral disaster that soon followed made it clear that no form of leftist coalition was possible and that a more conservative government was inevitable. If, as indicated in chapter 8, the first response was an urgent request of Alcalá Zamora that arrangements be made to change the electoral law, dissolve the new parliament, and then hold new elections under conditions more favorable to the left, the second was to prepare for active measures. Thus in a joint meeting of the executive commissions of the party and the UGT on 25 November 1933 it was agreed that if "reactionary elements" should take power the Socialists "would have to rebel [alzarse] vigorously,"[4] though exactly what that meant was left vague. When the FAI-CNT launched its latest mini-insurrection on 8 December, the executive commission of the party immediately issued a manifesto disclaiming any connection.

Though there was much talk of revolution in some quarters, and increasing nonsense about the similarity to conditions in Russia in 1917, the only strategy that the party leadership could conceive was some sort of undefined semi-defensive action to keep the right from forming a government. Continued deterioration in the terms of industrial relations only exacerbated the mood of militancy among Socialist workers. The first Lerroux government had lifted the *términos municipales* decree in certain provinces, while the second Lerroux government early in 1934 provisionally repealed the law altogether. Even some Socialists might have admitted that the *términos* law was ill-conceived. Much more serious was the change that had begun in the operation of the *jurados mixtos,* no longer particularly inclined to be favorable to the workers. Though all the reform legislation remained on the books, part of it was no longer being enforced, while unemployment maintained its inexorable rise. The response of the leadership remained equivocal. On 3 January *El Socialista* thundered "Class warfare! Hatred to the death of the criminal bourgeoisie!", but five days later a delegation from the FNTT visited the minister of labor to urge him to continue to enforce the existing legislation. Meanwhile the CEDA announced plans to alter drastically the existing norms and also to seek an increase in the Civil Guard to control dissidence.

Aversion mounted even against the Socialists' former allies, and Azaña himself expressed alarm. He noted in his diary for 2 January that "an electoral defeat and its disastrous consequences ought to be repaired in the same manner," lamenting the growing tendency of the Socialists to lump

democratic reformist Republicans under the general category of reactionary bourgeois forces. Though the Lerroux government had clearly rejected
further reforms and was not enforcing all that had been enacted, it was
not a government of stark reaction and did not justify "a violent response."
As Azaña put it succinctly, "The country will not second an insurrection,
because four-fifths of it is not Socialist," accurately proportioning the
amount of the vote that the Socialists had received. A revolutionary Socialist government would have no legitimacy save force: "Its power would
extend as far as the range of its pistols. Such a situation, insupportable
in my political thought and unsustainable in reality, would provide the
pretext for a frightful reaction," an analysis and prophecy that would prove
entirely correct.

Besteiro and the veteran leadership of the UGT still opposed radicalization. Despite or because of his theoretical approach, Besteiro had a much
clearer sense of the general situation than most of his colleagues. He grasped
that Spanish society had entered a danger zone between pure underdevelopment on the one hand and the mature conditions for a prosperous and
peaceful socialism on the other. He had stated in one of his major addresses
the preceding summer that Spanish workers still reflected much of the destructive reaction against early stages of industrialization, discouraging
discipline and moderation, yet at the same time the Spanish economy had
achieved a sufficiently complex level of development that it could not readily
be "conquered" directly by a single revolutionary class. He warned correctly that in somewhat similar circumstances in Italy in 1920 the occupation of the factories by Socialist trade unionists had been a prelude to a
triumphant fascist reaction. Spanish society was not prepared for a creative Socialist hegemony, which in Besteiro's definition would have to be
a democratic one.

By early January there were meetings between the party and UGT leaders
to decide on a course of action. Besteiro attempted delaying tactics, insisting that any drastic initiative should be approved by a full national
congress of the UGT and should be completely clear about its goals. To
meet the latter objection, the party executive commission approved on
13 January a ten-point program drawn up by Prieto. It called for:

1. Nationalization of the land
2. Major priority for irrigation projects
3. Radical reform of education
4. Dissolution of all religious orders, with seizure of their wealth and
   expulsion of those considered dangerous
5. Dissolution of the army, to be replaced by a democratic militia
6. Dissolution of the Civil Guard

7. Reform of the bureaucracy and a purge of anti-Republicans
8. Improvement of the conditions of industrial workers but no nationalization of industry at this time
9. Tax reform, with introduction of an inheritance tax
10. All these changes, initiated by decree, to be ratified by a democrati-
    cally elected new legislature

To this program Largo Caballero added five tactical points of concrete action, with the new government to be composed of all the forces who collaborated in bringing it to power. Besteiro and the executive commission
of the UGT responded with a long program of their own, calling for the
establishment of a special national corporative assembly that would initiate a major program against unemployment and begin a carefully planned,
long-range nationalization of industry.[5]

By this time the elderly official leadership of the UGT was losing touch
with the lower-level heads and much of the rank-and-file, who were increasingly influenced by the new militancy. When the UGT's national committee convened on 27 January it voted by a sizable majority to accept the
more radical party proposal, prompting the immediate resignation of
Besteiro and his fellow moderates in the leadership. The national committee then elected a new executive commission dominated by *caballeristas*,[6]
and Largo felt free to assume actively the post of secretary general of the
UGT, to which he had been elected in 1932 but which he had refused to
accept so long as *besteiristas* were predominant. He had been president
of the party for more than five years and now headed the union organizations as well. *Caballeristas* already led a number of individual UGT federations and on the following day took command of the FNTT, largest
of all, followed by the assumption of leadership in the key Madrid section
of the party.[7] At the beginning of February a revolutionary liaison committee was set up under Largo's personal leadership. Its ten members represented the party, the UGT, and the Socialist Youth organization.

The revolutionary committee had responsibility for the technical organization and financing of a revolutionary insurrection and also for conducting negotiations with possible collaborators. In the time-honored
Spanish tradition, Prieto was to undertake contacts with whatever sympathetic elements might be identified in the military. In this uncertain process, the Socialist Youth, whose representatives held three of the ten seats
on the committee, for the first time came to the fore. They were to play
a leading role in the development of volunteer militias, and they also contributed a more sophisticated "Bolshevik" sense of revolution as a direct
and violent coup. While Largo and the established leaders had been trained
in practical trade unionist and electoral tactics, and had always thought

of revolutionary activity in terms of a general strike by labor, the new activists among the Socialist Youth drew much of their inspiration from
reading about the Russian Revolution. They thought more in terms of organized violence. They were also more attracted to the small but revolutionary Communist groups in Spain, hitherto shunned by the party leaders for their extremism as much as for their insignificance.[8]

In this situation came news of the repression of an attempted revolt by
Austrian Socialists against the new authoritarian regime in Vienna.[9] Hailed
by the Catholic press in Spain, it made a strong negative impression on
the left, particularly on the Socialists, touching off a brief UGT sympathy
strike in Asturias.

Declining membership in the two major national syndical federations
did not so much bring a reduction in strike activity as a feverish concern
to counter the decline and the pressure on labor by an increase in activism. The most intense work stoppage was the CNT's general strike in
Zaragoza, which lasted six weeks and featured the sending of eighteen
thousand children of workers to Barcelona to be fed by comrades there.
Meanwhile a printers' strike in Madrid briefly closed down the major rightist newspapers in the capital. The government declared a state of alarm,
shutting the headquarters of the Socialist Youth, the Communists, and the
CNT. The JAP youth (the CEDA youth organization) in turn saw to it that
El Debate continued to appear, and after ten days or so other conservative
papers were able to resume publication. The strike had been broken, leaving the UGT printers' syndicate to negotiate the best settlement it could.
The long construction strike in Madrid was finally settled on 20 March
through an award by the Ministry of Labor which reduced the work week
to forty-four hours but retained the equivalent of forty-eight hours pay.
A metallurgy strike in Madrid continued until 1 June, and then was settled
on much the same basis — scarcely draconian terms for labor. Yet these had
been bitter disputes attended by more than a little disorder, destruction
of property, and occasional bomb explosions. Moreover, there was an increasing tendency now in some areas for ugetistas and cenetistas to make
common cause in certain of these conflicts.

The initiative in trying to organize a broader united worker left had
already been taken in Barcelona by Joaquín Maurín and his independent
Marxist-Leninist Bloc Obrer i Camperol (BOC, Worker-Peasant Bloc), centered in Catalonia. The BOC was a development of the old Federación
Comunista Catalano-Balear (FCCB), the Catalan section of the original
Spanish Communist Party (PCE), which had been expelled from the party
in 1928 because it had refused to accept the Moscow line. At one point
it had contained nearly half the membership of the PCE and in March

1931, on the eve of the Republic, had merged with the Partit Comunista Català (PCC), a tiny dissident Catalan communist group, to form the BOC. Maurín's position paralleled that of the regular Communist Party in its rejection of the Republic and parliamentary reformism. He was arguably the nearest thing to an original Marxist theorist in Spain and had forcefully argued that the entire political posture of the Socialists had been mistaken, for the Republic had not constituted the beginning of a complete bourgeois democratic revolution. A bourgeois capitalist revolution of sorts had taken place in nineteenth-century Spain under a weak and incompetent bourgeoisie without bringing democracy. By the 1930s the Spanish bourgeoisie was played out, no longer progressive and actively reactionary. The middle classes could neither complete the democratic revolution nor serve as an effective ally in moving toward a socialist revolution, and thus the Socialist policy had been totally misconceived. Spain had, however, developed a sufficiently advanced society to have crystallized around two social forces — the rightist bourgeoisie and the leftist workers. It was up to the latter to complete the democratic revolution but also to move directly toward a socialist revolution, with the dual goals of carrying out a democratic-socialist revolution almost simultaneously. The Socialists were rejected for compromise and reformism, and the tiny Communist group for Stalinism and Soviet domination, but meanwhile the dissident Marxists formed little more than sects.

A new initiative was taken early in 1933, soon after Hitler came to power in Germany, when the BOC joined with the small Catalanist socialist party, the Unió Socialista de Catalunya (USC),[10] to form an Alianza Obrera Antifascista (AOA, Antifascist Worker Alliance), using the terminology of the Alleanza del Lavoro, an antifascist alliance of much of the Italian left in 1922. The goals of the AOA, which later changed its name to Alianza Obrera (AO) *tout court* (probably to avoid sounding primarily negative) were threefold: to defend the gains of the working class, to defeat fascism in Spain, and to prepare the revolution that would create a federal socialist republic. The BOC and the USC were later joined by the Treintistas who had split from the CNT, the Unió de Rabassaires of Catalan sharecroppers, Andreu Nin's tiny Trotskyist Izquierda Comunista (Communist Left), and (by December 1933) the Catalan sections of the Socialist Party and the UGT.[11]

Maurín and the Barcelona leaders of the AO hoped to expand it into an all-Spanish organization. Accompanied by a Barcelona Socialist leader, Maurín met with Largo Caballero and other Socialist figures in Madrid in January 1934, and Largo returned the visit in Barcelona the following month. There was, however, a fundamental divergence between Maurín's goal and that of Largo Caballero. Maurín hoped that the AO might become the vehicle for the creation of a large new revolutionary Marxist-Leninist force; Largo and the Socialist Party leaders conceived it as simply an umbrella organization to instrumentalize a general strike in which the main role would be played by the existing Socialist Party. Meanwhile it was the small Trotskyist Izquierda Comunista that seems to have taken the lead on 21–22 April in expanding a broad strike in Madrid that closed most bars, cafes, and other public places in protest against the large rally of the CEDA in nearby El Escorial.[12]

The customary dilemma for any proposal of united action by the worker left was collaboration between the CNT and UGT. As usual, the CNT decided in the negative at a sizable meeting of regional representatives from all parts of the country at Barcelona on 10 February. They refused to join any revolutionary action not aimed directly at achieving the anarchist goal of libertarian communism. A different situation prevailed only in Asturias, where the severe depression of the mining industry and other problems had helped produce proportionately the highest rate of strikes in all Spain. There Socialists and anarchosyndicalists had first collaborated in the general strike of 1917 and had participated in a number of joint actions under the Republic. Thus the Asturian sections of the CNT and UGT signed an unusual alliance on 31 March which created a joint front called the "Alianza Revolucionaria" for revolutionary action to create "a regime of economic, political, and social equality founded on federalist socialist principles," a unique attempt to synthesize the revolutionary aspirations of Socialists and anarchosyndicalists.[13]

On 5 May *El Socialista* announced formation of the Alianza Obrera in Madrid for "the fight against fascism in all its forms and the preparation of the working class for establishment of the Socialist Federal Republic in Spain." This repeated exactly the formula of the AOA in Barcelona over a year earlier. Under the AO, each member organization was free to carry on its own activity and propaganda independently, but there were to be committees on the regional level in each area for mutual coordination, and these would ultimately choose a national committee. The abstention of the CNT everywhere save in Asturias, however, meant that the AO would basically consist of the Socialists and a number of small allies, whose significance was mostly limited to parts of Catalonia. After a period of time the Catalan USC, original cofounder of the alliance, abandoned it in protest against the domination of the Madrid-based Socialists.

During the spring of 1934 the most active role in labor affairs was taken by the UGT's farmworker federation, the FNTT, centered in Extremadura and Andalusia. While conditions for urban workers had deteriorated only slightly in recent months, there was a growing sense of desperation among rural laborers, who had suffered an increase of more than 50 percent in unemployment during the past two years. The new deal offered by the Republic seemed to be fading away, as landowners became increasingly obdurate and often found all manner of ways of getting around, or in some cases simply ignoring, the reform legislation of 1931–33. With no unemployment benefits or other resources to fall back on, empty-handed laborers were sometimes told to "Comed Republica!" ("Eat Republic"). There was a growing feeling that the government had become the friend of the employer and the enemy of the laborer, even though the facts did not entirely bear this out. Some of the more excessive regulations had been repealed, but the government tried to maintain most of the new regulations and administer the labor *jurados* with an even hand. Workers still won some of the negotiations, and in fact the Radical government was more nearly neutral in such matters than its predecessor. Moreover, during the ten months from December 1933 to September 1934 land was distributed to more rural families than during the last ten months of the Azaña administration. By the spring of 1934 some of the organized economic interests that had backed the Radicals' electoral campaign were claiming to have been betrayed. The decline in wages which farm laborers protested was still comparatively limited,[14] though unemployment continued to spread fairly rapidly and some of the earlier devices to curtail it, such as *laboreo forzoso*, were not being rigorously enforced.

The new *caballerista* leadership of the FNTT headlined its first declaration in *El Obrero de la Tierra* on 3 February: "We Declare Ourselves for the Revolution!" They called for full socialization and praised Soviet collectivization. In fact, however, the FNTT leadership bombarded the Ministry of Labor with practical appeals and frequently petitioned the Ministry of the Interior for greater police intervention to enforce labor regulations and work agreements, and to reverse recent closures of Casas del Pueblo (Socialist centers) in a number of districts. These protests were particularly frequent during the third week of March, culminating in a petition to Alcalá Zamora. The FNTT claimed that hundreds of appeals on nonpayment of wages had gone unanswered (which may well have been true) and that five hundred workers had been imprisoned in the province of Badajoz alone. The Socialist press was full of horror stories about the arbitrary lowering of wages (possibly true in individual instances but not necessarily true of employers as a whole) and of drastic police intervention, including four laborers shot dead during a farm strike.

The new Samper administration, though hand-picked by Alcalá Zamora, seemed to move in some respects farther to the right than the preceding

Lerroux government. A decree of 4 May annulled the original provisions of the agrarian reform for direct confiscation, guaranteeing compensation for all expropriation. On 24 May the Cortes voted 254 to 44 to abolish the *términos municipales* law, at the same time stipulating that there could be no unilateral reduction of wages. The new interior minister, Rafael Salazar Alonso, was a hard-liner. Whereas Azaña's interior minister, Casares Quiroga, had intervened to replace a total of 270 local mayors or municipal councils over a period of two years, Salazar Alonso used the highly centralized Spanish system to suspend a total of 193 within less than seven months, particularly, he claimed, in order to eliminate entrenched Socialist favoritism, especially in the provinces of Badajoz, Cáceres, Alicante, and Jaén.[15]

After a final appeal to the minister of labor on 28 April, the national committee of the FNTT met on 11–12 May to consider a national farmworkers' strike. It got no support from the national UGT leadership, which declared an agrarian strike a bad idea. It would be difficult and somewhat unjust economically because the spring harvest occurred at different times in various regions and would be extremely awkward to coordinate, while a general strike would be even harder on smallholders and sharecroppers, who often needed to hire a few laborers at harvest time, than it would be on largeowners. Under present conditions, such a strike would be considered provocative and would be forcibly repressed. Largo Caballero's revolutionary committee wanted to reserve any general strike for the moment of maximal political crisis. It sent messages to its sections in each province stressing that a national agrarian strike would have nothing to do with their revolutionary movement, while the UGT told the FNTT not to count on urban labor support.

The FNTT's national committee issued a list of ten demands, which were far-reaching but not truly revolutionary. They included the *turno riguroso* (hiring in strict order from the labor list organized by the syndicate), the outlawing of harvest machinery in many areas, creation of local supervisory committees of farmworkers in all districts to guarantee fulfillment of contracts, and other changes to tip the balance of labor relations clearly in favor of workers in the countryside. These far-reaching demands may have been pre-revolutionary but were not revolutionary in the sense of demanding a change in property ownership. The basic goal was a new structure of labor relations rather than the elimination of agrarian capitalism per se.[16]

The official attitude of the Ministry of Agriculture remained largely conciliatory, while the Radical minister of labor, José Estadella, made significant gestures.

On 24 May the government ordered field inspectors of the Ministry of Labor to prevent discrimination in hiring and urged the rural arbitration boards to agree quickly on harvest contracts favorable to the workers. On 2 June the government made further concessions by strengthening the legislation that obliged owners to hire workers only through the local employment offices (though not necessarily in the "rigorous order" the Socialists required) and by authorizing its field inspectors to assign additional workers to each owner in areas where unemployment was severe. Meanwhile the harvest contracts issued by the local arbitration boards established minimum wages that were as high as those that had prevailed during the Azaña era.[17]

Clearly progress was being made, but in the thinking of FNTT this was offset by the rigorous police policy carried out by Salazar Alonso, who treated all talk of the strike as intolerable subversion, outlawing many local strike meetings and arresting a considerable number of local leaders. The government had no intention of meeting the ten demands, and over the vigorous objection of Largo Caballero and the UGT, the FNTT called a national farm strike for 5 June.

While the monthly *Boletín* of the Ministry of Labor listed ninety-eight agrarian strikes for the first five months of 1934, the general strike of the FNTT was declared in a total of 1,563 rural municipalities involving most major parts of the country. It was particularly effective in latifundist areas; approximately half the districts in Córdoba, Málaga, and Ciudad Real were struck, as were about a quarter of those in Badajoz, Huelva, and Jaén. The strike was also supported by the UGT in Seville province, where it lasted longer and involved more sabotage of property and facilities than anywhere else, only ending on 20 June. In general behavior was relatively restrained on both sides, and the government did not declare martial law. A total of thirteen were reported killed, not so much in police affrays as in fights between strikers and antistrikers. The police arrested approximately seven thousand participants in what had been designated an illegal strike, but most of these were released in less than a month. Conversely, emergency courts tried and sentenced a number of FNTT leaders to prison terms of four or more years. The strike had been a total failure, and the UGT's largest affiliate was seriously weakened and dispirited. Many Casas del Pueblo in southern Spain would not reopen till February 1936.[18]

Meanwhile in Madrid and several other parts of the country, a much smaller but proportionately more deadly drama was unfolding between the Socialist Youth (JS) and other leftist activists on one side and the militants of Falange Española, the new fascist organization on the other. The Socialist Youth, particularly, took the formation of a fascist party with grim seriousness and had no intention of suffering the fate of their com-

rades at similar hands in Italy, Germany, and Austria. Thus in Spain it
was the left which seized the initiative. The first young fascist was killed
in November 1933, and seven other Falangist fatalities followed at inter-
vals through the winter and spring of 1934.[19] One open fight between Falangists and Socialists in Don Benito (Badajoz) left eight wounded. On
10 June, while the farm strike still raged in some districts, another skir-
mish took place between members of the two groups in Madrid's Casa del
Campo recreation area across the Manzanares river. In this instance one
young Falangist was shot to death and his corpse allegedly defiled.[20]

Well before this, rightist publicists were ridiculing the Falangists as more
"Franciscan" than "fascist," suggesting that the initials "FE" stood for "Fu-
neraria Española" ("Spanish Funeral") and that its leader should be known
as Juan Simón the Gravedigger rather than as José Antonio.[21] Though the
Falangist press had announced on 1 February that it would not engage
in reprisals, any such resolution was temporary. By early June the Falange
had organized eight *centurias*, or companies, in Madrid, their largest center, and had formed a "Falange de la sangre" for violent reprisals. On the
evening of 10 June, a bus discharging young Socialists in Madrid was
sprayed with bullets by a car of passing Falangists. A young woman, Juanita
Rico, was killed and two others seriously wounded.[22] Rico received a massive funeral and for the next two years was hailed in memory as "the first
victim of fascism" in Spain. This was correct, for the leftist concern about
fascist violence had become a self-fulfilling prophecy, but Rico would not
be the last victim. The running fight between Falangists and Socialists would
continue for two more years, reaching a climax in the spring and early
summer of 1936, when it would provide the final spark that provoked the
outbreak of the Civil War.

Looking back on the events of 1934 years later, Prieto would lament:

> The hands of the Socialist Youth had been intentionally left free, so that, with
> absolute irresponsibility, they were able to commit all kinds of excesses, which under
> emotion or frenzied enthusiasm turned out to be destructive of the goals pursued.
> No one set limits to the outrageous behavior of the Socialist Youth, who, without
> being responsible to anyone, provoked general strikes in Madrid, not realizing that
> they were handicapping the true general strike, the key to the projected movement,
> since a great city cannot be subjected to essays of that nature. Moreover, certain
> deeds which prudence requires me to pass over in silence, committed by members
> of the Socialist Youth, drew no reproach nor any call to responsibility and no ef-
> fort to bring under control.[23]

Nonetheless, after the failure of the agrarian strike, which only strengthened the center-right and right, "the revolutionary ardor of Prieto and even

of Largo began to cool."[24] In Madrid the Alianza Obrera blocked every proposal of the Trotskyist Izquierda Comunista for revolutionary action during the summer of 1934 on the grounds that the UGT must avoid partial actions. On 31 July the national committee of the UGT conducted an inquiry into the FNTT's disaster. Largo stressed that he wanted no repetition of the abortive general strike of 1917 and would not follow Leninist tactics blindly.[25]

The Catalan and Basque Conflicts

For Catalanists, the great achievement of the Republic was autonomy, which brought greater political and administrative freedom and the opportunity to introduce further changes. The down side was social relations, in which left Catalanist leaders at first insisted that the Republic and autonomy would open a completely new chapter. As has been seen, what happened was old rather than new; democracy and autonomy made no impression on the CNT, and social relations soon deteriorated to the terms of 1917–23, the last period in which Catalonia had known partially constitutional government. By 1933 the increase in crime and disorder was frequently blamed by Catalans on the negligence of Madrid-controlled police. There was certainly no enthusiasm among the latter to serve under the autonomous authorities; when the *traspaso* (transfer) of security functions to the Generalitat took place in April 1934, a large part of the regular police personnel resigned or transferred out. A new Catalan constabulary, the Mossos d'Esquadra, whose uniforms featured among other things sandals and gold-braided tunics, was set up to patrol the rural villages and supplement the Guardia Civil (now known in Catalonia as the Guardia Nacional Republicana).

Unlike the situation in the Basque provinces, Catalanism was politically divided between a moderate left and a moderate right. In the national elections of 1933, the conservative Lliga Catalana had taken advantage of the shift in opinion and the new alliance dynamics to best the ruling Esquerra by twenty-five to nineteen seats. However, in the second Catalan regional elections, held in January 1934, the Esquerra won big, the margin in popular votes between a united left and the Lliga being 162,216 to 132,942. This was the only election won by left Republicans during 1933–34 and soon led to the slogan which recognized Catalonia as the "last bastion" of the original leftist Republic.

Internal dissension within Catalanist ranks had nonetheless grown during 1932–33, an extremists rebelled against the eclecticism and increasing moderation of the dominant Esquerra. Extremist separatists from Macià's original Estat Català protested the Generalitat's compromise with the Spanish government and formed several splinter groups. More rightist separatists formed a very small separatist "Partit Nacionalista Català," while leftist separatists adopted an increasingly national socialist and Marxist orientation, forming the pompously titled "Estat Català (Força Separatista d'Extrema Esquerra)" (Catalan State — Separatist Force of the Extreme Left) and also the subsequent Partit Català Proletari (later to merge with the Catalan Communists and several other small Catalan Marxist Groups). The tendency toward splintering of political Catalanism caused the satirical weekly *Bé Negre* to publish the sardonic rhyme: "D'Estats Catalans / N'hi ha mes que dits de les mans" ("There are more Catalan states / Than fingers on the hands").[26]

Yet the most important new force in Catalan nationalism was the Esquerra youth, formed in conjunction with the ruling party in 1932 as the "Joventut d'Esquerra Republicana — Estat Català" (JEREC, "Youth of the Republican Left — Catalan State"). JEREC youth militia took the name of "Escamots", wore olive green shirts, and engaged in strong-arm tactics against the CNT, causing some to term them "Catalan fascists." Escamot leaders, such as the policeman and former army officer Miquel Badía and the physician Josep Dencàs, talked of preparing the way for the Esquerra as a "partit únic" (single party) of the Catalan state, leading a new "national" and "socialist" corporative social order, though some commentators thought that their goals more nearly approximated those of post-revolutionary Mexico or east European regimes than of Fascist Italy.[27]

The elderly Macià died of natural causes on Christmas Day, 1933 and was succeeded by the most salient political leader of left Republican Catalanism, Lluis Companys.[28] The new president of the Generalitat did not enjoy the close relations that Macià had established with Alcalá Zamora, but Catalanists would expect him to complete the *traspasos* of governmental responsibilities that had evolved slowly during the preceding year and to foster an active reform program for the development of the region.

Though Catalonia was the largest industrial center in Spain, it also had a significant agrarian economy. Catalan agriculture was generally more modern and land ownership more broadly distributed than in central and southern Spain, but problems remained. In the countryside the most militant pressure came from the "Unió de Rabassaires" (UR), an organization of sharecroppers who tended much of the land in major wine-producing areas, which Companys had helped form some fifteen years earlier. Though the UR became increasingly radical, the goal of most of its members was to convert the land they worked into their private property.[29] This fit perfectly within the socioeconomic tenets of left Republicanism and the kind of reform that Catalanist leaders intended to achieve under autonomy.

In April 1934 the Generalitat passed its first important socioeconomic reform, the "Llei de Contractes de Conreu" (Law of Cultivation Contracts), designed to give *rabassaire* farmers access to property ownership. Under *rabassa morta* ("dead stock") tenure in the wine-producing regions, share-croppers normally held land for the life of the vine (about fifty years), dividing proceeds fifty-fifty with the owner, and retained sections of land until about three-fourths of the vines were dead. In the early twentieth-century a new problem had arisen because the new kinds of vines introduced after the phylloxera epidemic of the 1890s lasted only about twenty-five years, limiting tenure and in certain respects reducing incomes. The new legislation would enable renters and sharecroppers to buy land that they had cultivated directly for at least fifteen years and in this regard was rather similar to the proposed rental law that had failed to pass the Spanish Cortes in the preceding summer. It also stipulated a six-year minimum for rental contracts, representing an effort to resolve an economic conflict in a key part of the Catalan countryside in favor of what might be called the lowest stratum of the lower-middle class, as opposed to the upper-middle class and the wealthy. Many *rabassaires* and other Catalan renters and sharecroppers were already petty capitalists to the extent that they normally possessed small amounts of capital as well as equipment of their own, while conversely Barcelona big business and the very wealthy did not control large amounts of the countryside. From the inception of the Republic, the *rabassaires* had formed an important part of the Esquerra vote. They had grown in militancy and had increasingly violated or ignored existing contracts, so that by 1934 much legal confusion had accumulated. *Rabassaire* organization was stronger in the provinces of Barcelona and Gerona, where there was a more developed and vocal lower-middle-class rural society, albeit in some cases technically landless, than in the less developed provinces of Tarragona and Lérida.

The Catalan Statute gave the Generalitat certain powers to legislate in civil matters, but the Constitution reserved social legislation for the jurisdiction of the central government, while the Agrarian Reform Law reserved for the Spanish parliament jurisdiction over all cultivation contracts. The Lliga and other conservative Catalan groups protested the new legislation as radical, unfair to owners, and also unconstitutional. They asked for an appeal to the Tribunal de Garantías Constitucionales. This was approved by the cabinet in Madrid on 4 May, and on 10 June the Tribunal ruled thirteen to ten that the Law of Cultivation Contracts was unconstitutional.[30]

The ruling sparked major protests in Barcelona and some other parts of Catalonia. When the Generalitat met two days later, it passed identical legislation in defiance of the Tribunal, with a clause making the law's application retroactive to the original date, while the Esquerra and the miniscule Unió Socialista de Catalunya announced their withdrawal from the Cortes. Shocked, Prime Minister Samper asked why they had taken such abrupt action without any attempt to negotiate and indicated his willingness to discuss the problem in an effort to reach some compromise.

For the rest of the summer of 1934, the Catalan dispute remained the main focus of attention. All the left, as well as the Basque nationalists, stood behind the Esquerra. In a Cortes address of 21 June, Azaña hailed Catalonia as "the last bastion remaining to the Republic," stressing that "the autonomous power of Catalonia is the last Republican power that still stands in Spain."[31] This was dangerous nonsense of the worst kind; rumor had it that Azaña and his followers were talking of withdrawing to Barcelona to set up a new ad hoc provisional government of the Republic. The Lliga leader Cambó pointed out that it was irrational for the autonomous government to ignore the terms of the Autonomy Statute and Republican Constitution as soon as the first problem arose, especially since it was Azaña and the left who were primarily responsible for the terms of the Constitution, "so that if the honorable gentlemen have anything to protest it is their own acts."[32] He also decried talk of Catalonia as simply the bulwark of leftism, since a democratic Catalonia would have to include and represent all the citizenry. Dr. Josep Dencàs, the main leader of the JEREC and the green-shirted Escamots, was meanwhile appointed the new councillor of security in the Catalan government, and set to work (as it turned out, quite ineffectively) to develop the means of armed resistance in Barcelona.[33]

On 26 June the cabinet in Madrid voted to consider the latest Catalan cultivation law null and void, since it merely repeated the earlier legislation that had been ruled unconstitutional. It then announced on the following day that it planned to seek authorization to rule by decree in order to work things out directly with the Generalitat. This was denounced both by rightists and by Azaña, who termed it "a real coup d'état." When the Cortes made clear its disapproval, the Samper government gave up its effort to assume plenary power and, on 4 July, announced that the government would simply ask for a vote of confidence to solve the matter legally and then obtain presidential authorization to suspend the current session of parliament, on the grounds that the deputies were nearing exhaustion and the government needed to concentrate on complicated economic issues. A raucous debate took place that day in the Cortes as Gil Robles charged that the rebellion of the Generalitat had accomplices within the parliament

itself. A Socialist deputy who tried to shout him down was physically assaulted while, according to reports, Prieto and several others brandished
pistols. Santiago Alba, the speaker, abandoned the chamber for ten minutes
in protest.[34] The government then won the vote of confidence 192 to 62,
though less than half the deputies actually voted for it.

The Generalitat then passed thirty regulations on 10 July to enable it
to carry out the terms of the controversial legislation, but at the same time
various efforts were being made to find a solution. Companys was handicapped by the absence of the close personal relations that Macià had developed with Alcalá Zamora, but he was no extremist. On the day before
the approval of the new regulations, La Publicitat, one of the leading Esquerra newspapers, declared that if the dispute involved "some error that
might be corrected with dignity," the matter should be solved through negotiation. Soon afterward the Generalitat's councillor of justice met with
Samper, while the Catalan government officially stated that it sought to
have the legislation adapted to the "basic laws" of the Republic. Though
two Catalan newspaper editors had been sentenced to prison terms by the
Republican courts in the past two months for slandering the Republic and
its justice system, the central government continued to cooperate in the
delegation of administrative and fiscal authority to Barcelona, handing over
further powers of taxation on 12 July.

Just as a solution to the Catalan conflict seemed possible, a new controversy began to develop with the Basque provinces, where yet a third
proposed autonomy statute had failed late in the preceding year, due to
the opposition of the province of Alava. The new conflict was touched
off by new tax regulations on wine originated by the national government
in Madrid, which leaders of city councils in the Basque provinces impugned
as a violation of the special tax arrangement (concierto económico) the
provinces had always enjoyed and a serious blow to local government
finance. Numerous visits to Madrid failed to produce agreement. Basque
spokesmen began to call for provincial elections as soon as possible, since
none had been held under the Republic, and laid plans for special elections of their own in mid-August to choose a new all-Basque executive
commission to defend their rights.

On 10 August, the eve of the new Basque initiative, the Samper government promised to hold elections for provincial chambers in all Spain within
three months and also pledged to respect the terms of the existing concierto económico. It also took the position that the special election of a Basque
executive commission by the municipal councils would be illegal and proceeded within the next week or so to arrest twenty-five mayors and thirty
municipal councillors in Vizcaya, and fifteen mayors and twenty-three coun-

cillors in Guipuzcoa. Nonetheless on 21 August the Basque Interim Commission created by the nationalists to supervise special elections announced that the elections had been held. A major incident that day in San Sebastián led to the arrest of eighty-seven nationalists, including ten more mayors. On 26 August José Antonio de Aguirre, the nationalist leader, met with Samper, who repeated the government's promise to find a workable solution. This was reiterated in a government note several days later, which pledged to respect fully Basque tax privileges, suspend any collection of income tax in the Basque provinces, and do all in its power to arrange for Basque representation in Madrid to negotiate these matters directly as soon as the Cortes reopened. As it plaintively asked, "What more can the government do?"[35]

Meanwhile Basque nationalists, implementing a proposal by the Bilbao Socialist Prieto, went ahead with plans to hold a special assembly of their newly selected representatives together with sympathetic Cortes deputies from the three provinces in Zumárraga on 2 September. The town was cordoned by police, who allowed only Cortes representatives to enter. Some fifteen deputies of the Catalan Esquerra (there to show solidarity), five Basque deputies each from Vizcaya and Guipuzcoa, and one deputy from Alava met briefly, and soon afterward it was decided that all remaining members of Basque city governments should resign on the seventh. This brought a wave of resignations in the two northern Basque provinces, but in Alava resignations occurred in only five of that province's seventy-seven municipalities. This was followed by a meeting of representatives of the Basque nationalists, Socialists, UGT, Communists, and Republican left in San Sebastián. The leftist parties sought a common front with Basque nationalists against the center-right and right, but the Basque Nationalist Party would promise no more than to oppose "with all its strength" a monarchist restoration or a new dictatorship, refusing to join forces generally with the left.

Toward Red October

The political crisis of the summer and early autumn of 1934 was played against a background of relative economic recovery. The year's harvest was one of the two best in Spanish history to date, and industrial production was recovering from the low of 1932–33, though the increase in unemployment was only temporarily halted. This proportionate improvement was not transmitted into any significant improvement in the workers' immediate economic condition but it does underscore the extent to which the events of September–October 1934 were primarily political, even though conditioned by a general context of depression.

At the beginning of autumn Alcalá Zamora delivered one of his typically florid speeches at a ceremony in Valladolid, in which he intoned that the Republic would soon have:

. . . a sound economy, a balanced budget, little foreign debt, and a political transformation with peace and order to make up for the destruction of our earlier civil wars. With all this within its grasp, Spain in our days sees unfolding a future of greatness and wellbeing never dreamed of before. . . . In 1935, and even in the remainder of 1934, the horizon of Spain's greatness appears clear and cloudless, so that if we seek it Spain may become one of the relative paradises of the earth. Impatience and agitation have no justification.[36]

The impending political crisis was, of course, more a matter of emotion, of pent-up grievances and of political sectarianism than of rational calculation. Three days later, as he was about to attend army maneuvers in León, Alcalá Zamora was warned by Martínez Barrio that there were serious rumors he was about to be kidnapped by either the police or the military. As the president noted in his diary, "I thought I was dreaming or had suddenly landed in an insane asylum."[37]

The Socialist revolutionary committee under Largo Caballero continued to make preparations for a possible revolt, but implementation was quite limited.[38] The question of timing or triggering was highly important, and Largo's position was that the event which would set off revolt would be the entry of the CEDA into the Republican government. Paradoxically there is abundant testimony that Largo was convinced that Alcalá Zamora would never permit the CEDA's admission. Thus Paul Preston has written that "the Socialists tried to preserve the progressive character of the Republican regime by threats of revolution, which they hoped never to fulfill."[39]

The principal publicist of revolutionary Socialism was the journalist and essayist Luis Araquistain. His monthly *Leviatán* (*Leviathan*) declared in its first number of May 1934 that "the Republic is an accident" and that "reformist socialism has failed," concluding that "we must not trust only in parliamentary democracy, even if sometimes socialism wins a majority: if socialism does not employ violence, capitalism will defeat it on other levels with its formidable economic weapons."[40] Only a few weeks earlier he had correctly written in the American journal *Foreign Affairs* (April, 1934) that true fascism, Italian or German style, was impossible in Spain because of the absence of large numbers of unemployed veterans or university youth without a future, that—compared with Germany—there was no huge population of unemployed and virtually no support for Spanish nationalism or imperialism, as well as no effective leaders. All this was true. Yet for the left in Spain, the functional equivalent of fascism was simply the right, in general, and most especially its primary force, the CEDA, because of CEDA's opposition to Republican reformism and in large measure to Republican democracy. The CEDA hardly introduced mass politics and mass rallies to the Republic, but its broad mobilization tended to escalate this phenomenon. The concentration of fifty thousand young *japistas* at El Escorial on 22 April had much of the look of a fascist meeting, replete with slogans like "antiparliamentarianism" and "the chief [Gil Robles] is never wrong," as did a smaller rally at Covadonga, nominal birthplace of the Spanish nation, on 6 September.

Meanwhile the main forces of the Republican left underwent reorganization and assumed a more advanced position. At a meeting held on 1–2 April, Azaña's Partido de Acción Republicana, the splinter Partido Radical Socialista Independiente, and most of the left Galicianist Partido Republicano Gallego joined together to form a new united Partido de Izquierda Republicana (Party of the Republican Left). Most notable was its new economic program, already heralded by a speech of Azaña on 11 February. This called for greater state regulation of credit and finance, control of certain industries by state agencies or even possible nationalization, expansion of public works, prosecution of the agrarian reform though with clearer exemption of small and medium owners, creation of a National Bank of Agricultural Credit, tariff revision, progressive tax reform, expansion of social security, and creation of a central government economic council.[41] In this way the middle-class Republican left sought to move nearer the Socialists and mobilize greater support among increasingly radicalized leftist opinion. Later, at the close of June, a newly constituted "Juventudes de Izquierda Republicana" (Republican Left Youth) held its first congress, proclaiming its members "leftists, democrats and parliamentarians, in that order." Even more stridently than the parent party, the Republican Left Youth made it clear that, if necessary, leftist goals were predominant over technical, legalitarian democracy, depending on circumstances.[42]

In May Martínez Barrio, who had earlier resigned from the Radical government, left the Radical Party altogether, forming a splinter "Partido Radical Demócrata" distinctly to the left of his old party. As Grand Master of the Spanish Grand Orient, he was able to take approximately one-third of the Masons in the Radical Party with him.[43] The position of Martínez Barrio's group as the most moderate sector of broader middle-class left Republicanism was very close to what remained of the original Radical

Socialist Party, now led by Gordón Ordás, which shared an equal antipathy toward the Socialists. In a speech on 25 July Gordón lamented:

> The tragic situation of Spain today is the powerful presence of two great forces that are acting outside the Republic, one a force of the extreme right which, whether due to internal influences or procedures imported from Italy or Germany, wants to establish a totalitarian state here under capitalist domination, and the other of the extreme left which, through procedures similar to those of Lenin, wants to establish here the proletarian form of the totalitarian state.[44]

Martínez Barrio and Gordón Ordás urged Felipe Sánchez Román, the other major moderate Republican center-leftist, to join with them, but the latter organized a separate "Partido Nacional Republicano." The followers of Martínez Barrio and Gordón Ordás then met at the close of September to form a new "Partido de Unión Republicana." Its key leadership posts were held by the relatively pragmatic Martínez Barrio and his former Radical colleagues, who adopted a minimum program that was moderate but firm. They called for greater attention to public works and the agrarian reform but also for a balanced budget, with the restoration of state authority and dissolution of all parties or groups which sought to subvert the state, together with the outlawing of all paramilitary political organizations.[45]

From April on, the left Republican leaders had become increasingly alarmed over the possibility of a rightist coup or entry of the CEDA into the government. Following further meetings of Azaña, Miguel Maura, Sánchez Román, and Martínez Barrio, the latter had visited Alcalá Zamora on 7 July to urge the appointment of a new all-Republican government that would prepare for new elections which could reverse the results of the preceding year.[46] Equally important for Azaña was restoration of the alliance with the Socialists, and a meeting was held a week later, attended by Largo Caballero and others, to consider the matter, but *caballerista* Socialists were not impressed by the highly interventionist new economic program of Izquierda Republicana and spurned any resumption of the alliance.

Socialist preparations for some sort of direct action were scarcely a secret. On 6 June Madrid police discovered a cache of 616 pistols and 80,000 cartridges, whose custodians claimed that it was destined for a Socialist deputy in parliament, while in the latter's home another 54 pistols were found. After the failure of the agrarian strike, however, the government's only direct measure against the Socialists was more frequent censorship of the increasingly incendiary Socialist press. It tried to maintain an even hand in the escalating violence between Socialists and Falangists. Eighty of the latter were arrested at the Falange's Madrid headquarters on 11 July, followed by a decree of the Ministry of the Interior outlawing any meeting at which either fascist raised-arm or revolutionary clenched-fist salutes were given. Mid-summer brought more public marches by the Socialist Youth, while a statement by the national committee of the UGT on 1 August denounced the Samper administration with grotesque hyberbole as "a regime of the white terror." More accurately, it pointed out that of the 415 days of "Lerrouxist government," 222 had been passed under the state of either prevention or alarm, and that only 93 were days of full constitutional normalcy and civil rights (60 of the latter pertaining to the electoral period).[47]

The principal scandal concerning arms discoveries prior to the insurrection took place on the Asturian coast on 10 September. This involved a shipload of arms which the Azaña government had originally procured for Portuguese rebels two years earlier and which the Socialists finally managed to purchase through middlemen from the state Consortium of Military Industries. The arms were transmitted from a warehouse in the south aboard a ship named *La Turquesa*, which began to unload them by night off the Asturian coast, only to be quickly discovered by *carabineros* (border guards). *La Turquesa* immediately put out to sea again with most of the arms still on board and steamed to Bordeaux where the boat and its cargo were impounded by the Spanish consul. Indalecio Prieto, in overall direction of the operation, was near the site but managed to talk his way past police and soon fled to France, where he would remain for the next seventeen months.[48] The Madrid Casa del Pueblo was searched by police on the eleventh. The search revealed a sizable number of guns, 107 small boxes of ammunition, and 37 packets of hand grenades. Several other small caches of arms in possession of the Socialists were uncovered in the capital and elsewhere, while in a search for arms on the Madrid-León highway a few days later, the Civil Guard mistakenly killed an innocent driver.[49]

The volume of strike activity remained high throughout the summer. There were numerous minor clashes involving gunfire as well as frequent cases of arson in widely scattered parts of Spain. Four moderates and conservatives were killed, as were a number of workers. The most publicized deaths were the murder of the Falangist provincial chief of Guipuzcoa in San Sebastián, followed by the retaliatory killing the same day of Manuel Andrés Casaus, minister of the interior in the last left Republican government.

The biggest of the summer work stoppages was a general strike called by the UGT in Madrid when a major protest meeting of all the principal landowners' associations was held in the capital. Altogether six people were killed in Madrid on this occasion. *El Sol* editorialized on the morrow:

An arm which is too often employed in inappropriate situations ends up weakening itself to the point where it can no longer be used when the propitious moment arrives, not only because it tires and the edge is dulled, but also because the appropriate reaction grows, perfecting contrary arms, to counteract it.

. . . By using all revolutionary means with ill-measured frequency to fight against a fascism which does not exist, except as a pallid imitation, what definitely might happen is the production of the necessary conditions, the soil, the climate, for the real growth of fascism. Not the gentleman's fascism which we have [in Spain] by reason of style, but the true and fearful one, against which the arms raised by the liberal state are no good. In a not dissimilar manner fascism was engendered in other countries.

Thinking to follow the lessons of history, the Socialists in fact grew more confused by the month and ended by completely ignoring the real lessons of history.

Heretofore the Socialists had been unsuccessful in broadening the scope of the Alianza Obrera. The CNT, with the exception of its Asturian branch, still refused to participate. On the other hand, relations were becoming ever closer between the Socialist Youth and the small Communist Party (PCE), especially in Madrid, where the funeral of a Communist central committeeman killed by Falangists on 29 August turned into a major occasion for fraternization between the two groups. The Socialist and Communist Youth held their first official joint rally at a stadium in Madrid early in September to protest the Interior Ministry's new decree banning participation of minors in political groups. A major goal of Communist policy had always been Socialist inclusion in a two-party *frente único* that might give them increased leverage over the much larger and looser, much less unified Socialist organization. This the Socialists had always refused, while outflanking the Communists with the militant new Alianza Obrera that included all the socialist and Marxist organizations in Spain, except for the Communists themselves. Joining the latter was clearly preferable to continued isolation, and the Moscow headquarters of the Third International, following a recent precedent in France, finally gave the Spanish Communist leaders the green light. On 12 September the PCE officially joined the Alianza Obrera.

The major events of September concerned a new series of minor legal crises between Barcelona and Madrid, climaxed nonetheless by fundamental resolution of the Catalan agrarian reform dispute. On 9 September a Catalan lawyer being tried for contempt of court was forcibly "rescued" by a mob, and when the state prosecutor in Barcelona tried to stop this interference, the head of the Catalan police, Miquel Badía, simply had him arrested. Outraged, the Madrid government initiated constitutional measures on 10 September to intervene directly and restore the integrity of the court (since this was but one of a series of courtroom and jail abuses in Barcelona). The Generalitat responded appropriately by forcing Badía to resign on the twelfth. A series of mass meetings were being held by left Catalanist groups, but after Catalan Carlists received permission to hold one of their own, ninety-nine of their members were arrested all the same. To curb further abuse of judicial procedure, the government then issued a new ruling delimiting the power of the Generalitat over court personnel. Companys's response on the twenty-fifth was so intemperate that the government presented a suit against the Catalan government before the Tribunal de Garantías Constitucionales, charging injury and disrespect. This sequence of operetta-style vendettas was nonetheless concluded by a workable compromise on the original agrarian conflict. On 13 September the Generalitat had published a series of new regulations slightly modifying the original terms along lines sought by Madrid, and when the Cortes opened for the fall session on 1 October the prime minister announced that this modification amounted to a *refundición* (revision) of the Law of Cultivation Contracts that had the "character and force of law," so that he now judged the legislation to be constitutional, finally resolving the lingering dispute.[50]

Unfortunately the resolution of the Law of Cultivation Contracts was not the prime order of business at the opening of the Cortes, for the Samper government resigned immediately. Four days earlier the CEDA had announced that it would no longer support an ineffective minority government, but would require participation in any new coalition. Similarly, leaders of the Radical Party had met on 29 September and agreed not to give in to any further pressure from the president or the left to keep Lerroux out of the premiership. Thus when Samper opened the new Cortes session on 1 October, the only spokesman to reply to his speech was Gil Robles, who simply said there must be a change in government, leading to the immediate resignation of the cabinet.

It was widely expected that entry of the CEDA into the government might trigger a Socialist revolt, but the CEDA and the Radical leadership were willing to chance that, and indeed some of them preferred to face an insurrection at a time when the left remained divided and the center-right united and strong.[51] Alcalá Zamora no longer had much choice, since a coalition led by Lerroux and including, as it turned out, three *cedistas* was the only formula that could produce a parliamentary majority. The alternative was dissolution, which the president was reluctant to undertake because he might be subject to parliamentary review and impeachment for calling two elections within a year. The three cedista ministers would be Rafael Aizpún (Justice), José Oriol Anguera de Sojo (Labor), and Manuel Giménez Fernández (Agriculture). All three had reputations as moderates, while Giménez Fernández was probably the most liberal of all the CEDA leaders. The other major change in the new government stemmed from Alcalá Zamora's insistence on replacing the hard-line Salazar Alonso as minister of the interior, a post taken over by the more liberal Eloy Vaquero, an autodidact, teacher, and lawyer from Córdoba and a crony of Lerroux's.[52]

Though Largo Caballero had doubted that the day would ever come, this was the "provocation" awaited by the Socialists. *El Socialista* had declared menacingly on 27 September:

> The skies are darkly overcast en route to October. We repeat what we have been saying for months: watch for the red flare! Next month may be our October. Hard tasks and days of challenge await us. The Spanish proletariat and its leaders face enormous responsibility. We have an army waiting to be mobilized. And our international policy. And our plans of socialization.

The left Republican *Heraldo de Madrid* concluded on the morning of 4 October: "The Republic of the 14th of April has been lost perhaps forever. That which will begin its life today is of no concern to us. Our Republic we find moribund."

When news of the new coalition leaked out on 4 October, the middle-class left Republican leaders tried to reach a common formula of protest but failed. They were at least to some extent hampered by the fact that formation of the new government was not the result of any extraparliamentary direct action, as in Italy, nor of a backstairs deal, as in Germany, but was a scrupulously legal and constitutional coalition of the two major parties elected less than a year earlier by democratic suffrage in free elections. On the evening of 5 October Azaña's Izquierda Republicana issued the following manifesto: "Izquierda Republicana declares that the monstrous act of handing the government of the Republic over to its enemies is treason. It breaks all solidarity with the present institutions of the regime and affirms its decision to make use of all means of defending the Republic." Somewhat similar statements, which might readily be interpreted as aligning the left Republicans with the Alianza Obrera insurrection now beginning, were delivered by Martínez Barrio's Unión Republicana, Sánchez Román's Partido Nacional Republicano, Miguel Maura's Partido Republicano Conservador (which said the new government was "engendering civil war"), the Izquierda Radical Socialista, and the Partido Federal Autónomo. The problem, of course, stemmed from the left Republicans' insistence on identifying the Republic not with democracy or constitutional law but with a specific set of policies and politicians, any change of which was held to be treasonous.

The initiative of the Alianza Obrera began to go into action on the night of 4 October, but it was highly compartmentalized and decentralized, so poorly coordinated that it could scarcely be called a true plan. Nor was any program or set of goals announced; the program agreed upon in January 1934 was not published for the first time until January 1936.[53] On the national level, the initiative relied above all on the traditional weapon of the general strike, which began in Madrid, Barcelona, and all areas in which Socialists were strong on 5 October. Preparations for revolutionary insurrection, however, ranged from feeble to nonexistent. In Madrid, for example, armed power was to be provided by the nominally organized militia of the Socialist Youth,[54] by proleftist elements within the military barracks supposedly being won over, and by ploys to attract sympathetic elements in the police, especially the Assault Guards. In fact, the Socialist Youth simply were not prepared for serious military activity, and all the devices for winning over sectors of the military and police failed. There was no remote comparison between the Russian army of 1917 — demoralized by three years of defeat, bad leadership, and millions of casualties — and the modest but effective Spanish army of 1934 — well-rested, relatively united, and with morale fully intact. Plans to seize major public centers in Madrid quickly broke down into feeble and unsuccessful skirmishes. The strike itself was reasonably effective, but both the workers and their leaders simply remained at home, further discouraged by the street sniping which the armed sectors of the Socialist Youth carried on for some forty-eight hours. A few barricades were put up in worker districts, but in general revolutionary masses in the streets were nowhere to be found.

The government was initially almost as slow to respond as the offensive itself in most areas was lethargic. If Largo Caballero had never thought Alcalá Zamora would allow CEDA ministers into the government, Lerroux had never believed that the Socialists would actually launch an insurrection.[55] Martial law was not declared throughout Spain for more than twenty-four hours, finally being imposed by the morning of 6 October. The Radical minister of war in the new government was Diego Hidalgo, who had held that office since December 1933. Hidalgo was from one of the more liberal sectors of the Radical Party and had been the strongest Radical supporter of the agrarian reform, but he distrusted the army chief of staff, General Masquelet, as too liberal and possibly sympathetic to the rebels. Hidalgo had therefore already selected a special advisor in General Francisco Franco, who seven years earlier had been the youngest general in any European army, and who was a major hero of the Moroccan cam-

Assault Guards frisking citizens during the revolutionary strike in Madrid, October 1934

paigns and one of the most prestigious figures in the Spanish military. Hidalgo had awarded him the first promotion to major general that became available under the center-right government. Franco had been invited to assist Hidalgo during the recent army maneuvers in León and then return with him to Madrid. Soon after the revolt began Hidalgo turned over coordination of the repression to Franco, who slept in a room at the War Ministry for the next two weeks.[56]

In Barcelona the Alianza Obrera found an ally in the Generalitat government, which had been making rather lukewarm plans for armed resistance against Madrid depending on the outcome of the summer autonomy crisis and the struggle for power in Madrid. The Alianza Obrera began its general strike in the Catalan capital on 5 October with some success, in view of the fact that most organized labor was dominated by the CNT. On the following day an effort was made to extend the strike throughout Catalonia, with the assistance of the green-shirted Escamots of the Esquerra. At the same time the Catalan police arrested some of the main anarchist leaders, for fear they might sabotage the operation. At 8:00 P.M. on the sixth Companys announced from a balcony at Generalitat headquarters: "Catalans: Monarchists and fascists have assaulted the government. . . . The democratic Republic is now in grave peril."[57] He declared that all authentic Republicans were in revolt and that the Generalitat was seizing all power in Catalonia. He announced formation of the "Catalan state in the Spanish Federal Republic" and invited other left Republicans to establish a new provisional government of the Republic in Barcelona. The Generalitat had the backing of all the *catalanista* left Republican groups and the small worker parties of the Alianza Obrera.

Companys was a basically reasonable man who had been under extreme pressure from Catalanist radicals for months. All preparations for revolt had been left in the hands of the councillor of security, the extremist adventurer Dencàs. On paper he had organized seven thousand Escamot volunteers and was able to distribute arms to some of them, but like the Socialists in Madrid, they were not prepared for real fighting. The popular response in the Catalan capital was not so much like the active enthusiasm of Madrid and Barcelona in April 1931 as like the passive anxiety of Berlin in September 1938: relative silence, no crowds filling the streets, people hurrying home. The Catalan revolt briefly took the form of a sort of civilian pronunciamiento, in the hope not of conquering Madrid but of having enough other leftists rally round.

The commander of the military garrisons in the Barcelona district was General Domingo Batet. His Catalan ancestry had led some of the leaders of the revolt to assume or hope that he might remain a passive spectator, but in fact Batet was energetic and absolutely decisive. He declared martial law throughout Catalonia at 9:00 P.M., only an hour after Companys's announcement, and by 11:30 that night a small army detachment had moved light artillery into place to begin bombardment of the Generalitat building. Even before that, two rounds into the headquarters of the CADCI, the ultra-Catalanist white-collar union, had killed its leader, Jaume Compte, and brought surrender, while the Comandancia General de Somatenes (headquarters of the Catalan militia) surrendered equally rapidly. Bombardment of the Barcelona Ayuntamiento (city hall), the other remaining rebel center, began just before dawn, quickly producing another white flag. Dencàs had evidently promised Companys that there was no immediate danger from the army garrison and that reinforcements would begin to arrive by morning. Since neither was correct, Companys surrendered the Generalitat at 6:00 A.M. Batet then read him a little lecture on the ills of resorting to force and required him to announce the surrender over public radio. Dencàs had hoped for the support of Catalanist militia from the rural areas, but many of his police deserted instead. He fled through an escape hatch into the sewer system, an arrangement obviously prepared in advance that gave rise to much mirth. Altogether in the abortive Barcelona revolt, forty-six were killed, eight soldiers and thirty-eight civilians.[58]

There was minor skirmishing in several parts of Catalonia on 6 and 7 October, as local Alianza Obrera groups took over several towns, including for a very brief time part of Gerona and Lérida. They were quickly and easily put down by the army and police,[59] though not before they had committed several killings, including the slaying of at least one priest.

Azaña was in Barcelona at the time of the revolt, his intentions ambiguous. He obviously was not trying to play the role of loyal opposition to Alcalá Zamora and Lerroux. He made no effort to warn the government, and his party's announcement could easily be interpreted as supporting the revolt. Azaña had left Madrid on 27 September carrying only one suitcase, to attend the funeral of his former cabinet minister Jaume Carner. He later spent 3 and 4 October in a series of interviews with leaders of left Catalanism. It has been conjectured that one goal of these talks was to dissuade Companys from declaring separatism. Very likely Azaña remained in Barcelona because its heavily leftist atmosphere made it the safest place in a crisis. At 8:00 P.M. on the sixth he left his room at the Hotel Colón for the home of a Catalan friend, where he was arrested three days later and subsequently placed on a prison warship.[60]

Largo Caballero's revolutionary committee had in theory named rebel commissions for all provincial capitals in Spain, but most cities remained quiet, while Socialists in the southern countryside were still exhausted from the failed agrarian strike. There were various strikes and disorders in scattered spots of the south, and several people were killed, but no general insurrection took place there.[61] In Aragon some anarchist groups did engage in outbursts of their own. A general strike in Zaragoza lasted from 6 to 9 October, and libertarian communism was briefly declared by anarchosyndicalists in a few small towns.

After Asturias, the only serious Socialist revolts occurred in the two industrialized Basque provinces of Vizcaya and Guipuzcoa, and in Palencia and León. The general strike was for several days effective in the industrial regions of Vizcaya, while in Guipuzcoa the Socialists temporarily took control of the cities of Mondragón and Eibar, officially proclaiming the social revolution and killing two hostages in the former. Troops were moved in from other regions, and there was some fighting before the area could be pacified.[62] In Palencia, a Socialist miners' insurrection began on the fifth and held parts of the province for several days. The revolt broke out the following day in León (part of whose garrison had already been dispatched elsewhere), and about three-fourths of the province was held for several days until military detachments regained control.

The great drama of the 1934 insurrection took place in Asturias, where a united revolutionary Alianza Obrera, based especially on the mining districts, set up the first revolutionary commune in western Europe since Paris in 1871. Given the ineptitude and halfheartedness of Socialist preparation in most other regions, why was the Asturian rebellion so fierce and determined? The first answer lay in the unity of the worker left in a region where nearly 70 percent of all workers were unionized. Though it was far from enjoying a monopoly, the UGT's Sindicato Minero Asturiano had built a strong position in the years around World War I, only to see both the union and jobs decline precipitously in the face of foreign competition during the 1920s. The Republic had provided a great opportunity for organized labor to make a comeback, but the lack of basic solutions for mining and metallurgy during the depression meant that renewed mobilization had only heightened frustration and militancy, with the attitudes of younger workers particularly inflamed. The fact that the labor force still remained partly rural, with some workers employed in the countryside part of the year, underscored the limits of industrialization but apparently did not retard radicalization.[63] Thus Asturias had proportionately led all Spain in strike activity under the Republic, with the UGT and CNT increasingly making common cause, the fruit of which had been the 31 March "Alianza Revolucionaria," the only worker alliance joined by the CNT. Moreover, this militant unity meant that Asturian labor developed its own goals of a "federal socialist" regime for the insurrection.[64]

The revolt in Asturias began on the night of 4–5 October. The mining areas were quickly seized, with only three larger police stations holding out until the second day. The defensive plan of the local authorities was passive, expecting that the police would hold out in their district posts as they had elsewhere during anarchist mini-insurrections. The force and combativeness of the Asturian insurrection was much greater. More than twenty thousand worker militia were soon mobilized. Though many lacked weapons, they successively gained more arms from each police post overrun, eventually acquiring the Trubia artillery works and twenty-nine cannon as well. Moreover, in these first days the miner militia developed an innovation in weaponry: the use of lighted sticks of dynamite as hand grenades, a device initially frightening to their enemies. On the sixth they moved into the provincial capital Oviedo, a city of eighty thousand, garrisoned by nine hundred troops and three hundred armed police. Since these seemed inadequate to hold the entire area, the local military and police commanders, somewhat weak and divided, undertook another system of passive defense organized exclusively around nine strong points in the city. Most of Oviedo, including the center of town, was then occupied by eight thousand revolutionary militiamen. In the "liberated area," they officially declared the proletarian revolution, abolished regular money, and also instituted a revolutionary terror that took more than a score of lives, mostly of clergy. As the struggle continued, portions of the city were blasted apart by shelling, bombing, and dynamite. Though lack of coordination deprived the revolutionaries of support from other UGT contingents in León and Palencia, the government was similarly unable to provide immediate reinforcements. In the first days, the only succor for defenders came from two squadrons of the Spanish air force that attempted to bomb and strafe rebel positions, killing ten people with a bomb dropped on the central plaza on the tenth.

Army reinforcements were soon being rushed toward the region, for which a new field commander had to be named. Franco may have wanted the post himself, but the new prime minister, Lerroux, preferred to have one of the liberal minority in the army command in charge and appointed the inspector general of the army, Eduardo López Ochoa, to head the main relief column. López Ochoa was a Republican liberal and a Mason and had been a leader in the pro-Republican military conspiracy of 1930. He was flown to Galicia on the afternoon of the sixth. The next day he began to make his way eastward with a modest force of some 360 troops in trucks, half of whom had to be detached on the way to hold the route open. Meanwhile a garrison of 460 soldiers and police had held out in the main Asturian coastal city of Gijón, where reinforcements first arrived by sea on the seventh, followed by larger units from the Moroccan Protectorate on the tenth,[65] so that the main relief for Oviedo came due south from the direction of Gijón on the eleventh. This also involved the first historical military use of a helicopter (at least in part a Spanish invention) as reconnaissance for the column. The city proper was reoccupied on 12 and 13 October, the revolutionary committee at Oviedo being momentarily succeeded on the twelfth by an all-Communist committee as the main militia groups began to retreat. The hardest fighting probably took place between the fourteenth and seventeenth for control of the southern and eastern out-lying districts that controlled access to the mining basin. By this time yet another relief column had come in from the east and López Ochoa had a total of fifteen thousand troops and three thousand police concentrated in the area, outnumbering the miner militia. After a parley on the eigh-teenth, the revolutionaries surrendered, and the mining district began to be occupied relatively peacefully on the following day.

Sharp internal tension developed between the moderate López Ochoa and his chief subordinate, the hard-line Lt. Col. Juan Yagüe, who com-manded the elite Legionnaire and Moroccan Regulares units from the Pro-tectorate. Yagüe, a close colleague of Franco, complained that López Ochoa's orders had exposed his troops to unnecessary risks during the advance and that López Ochoa had agreed to the revolutionary committee's demands that they not be allowed to enter the main mining areas.[66] There was fur-ther allegation that the commander in chief was too soft on the revolu-tionaries, who were not being required to give up all their arms. On the twentieth, a truck full of soldiers was blown up, the army reporting twenty-five fatalities. This provoked an immediate decree from López Ochoa that anyone found with arms on his person or in his home would be tried by summary court-martial and, if found guilty, immediately executed. He also seems to have approved a number of summary executions under martial law. Some sniping at troops and the police continued and not all arms were recovered, petty guerrilla actions continuing into the first part of 1935. The exact loss of life in the insurrection can never be precisely determined. The best estimates suggest 1,200 fatalities for the rebels, 1,100 of these in Asturias.[67] Deaths among the army and police apparently totaled approxi-mately 450, again concentrated primarily in Asturias.[68]

After the military occupation, a thorough police sweep of the mining regions took place, producing thousands of arrests. Hundreds of prisoners were subjected to systematic beatings and torture, especially under the spe-cial police repression in Asturias conducted by Maj. Lisardo Doval of the Civil Guard.[69] Several prisoners were literally beaten or tortured to death. In all Spain, more than fifteen thousand arrests were made, with the left claiming that the total was at least twice that high.[70]

For the next eighteen months, Spain was filled with atrocity stories. The right emphasized the violence of the revolutionaries and the murders of priests and other civilians (apparently about forty altogether, including thirty-four clergy and seminarians, and one conservative Cortes deputy — Marcelino Oreja in Mondragón).[71] The left stressed the scores of execu-tions with or without court-martial, alleged military atrocities against

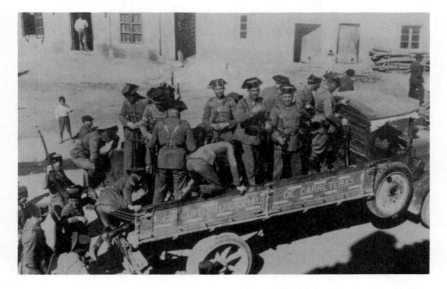

A truckload of Civil Guards involved in repressing the insurrection in Asturias, October 1934

miners' families, and the continued brutal mistreatment of some of the prisoners.[72] As Gabriel Jackson wrote thirty years later: "In point of fact, every form of fanaticism and cruelty which was to characterize the Civil War occurred during the October revolution and its aftermath: utopian revolution marred by sporadic red terror; systematically bloody repression by the 'forces of order'; confusion and demoralization of the moderate left; fanatical vengefulness on the part of the right."[73]

There were also numerous arrests and prosecutions within the armed forces, beginning with six senior commanders of the army and Civil Guard garrisons in Oviedo, all of whom were sentenced to prison. In addition, one army lieutenant and one regular soldier received severe sentences for having joined the revolutionaries. Within the lower ranks of the Civil Guard, nine men were condemned to prison, including one junior officer and four noncommissioned officers. They, like the senior commanders, were mostly charged with neglect of duty, save for one guard indicted for having joined the revolutionaries. Cases of desertion or mutiny among troops were rare, but with sailors it was a different story. There were more than a few organized leftist cells among the seamen, who had a closer common identity due to the circumscribed character of navy life. Though none of several alleged plots of shipboard mutiny actually came to fruition, seventy-two sailors were arrested and prosecuted. Conversely, the only military directly punished for excesses in the repression were four Moroccan Regulares summarily executed by López Ochoa.

For the left the result was disaster, with extensive loss of life and many thousands of militants arrested on top of those already in jail, the detention or flight of most of their leaders, the closing of many (though not all) Socialist Party and UGT local headquarters, and the general elimination of the left as a parliamentary and political force for the next sixteen months. The entire fiasco had been justified on the grounds of the sinister, fascistic intentions of the CEDA. If those intentions were as strong as the left insisted, the CEDA would now have an easier opportunity to strike than ever. In fact, the genuinely fascist intellectual Ledesma Ramos would write some months later that much of the Spanish right was *apparently fascist but, in many instances, essentially antifascist*" because of their legalism and squeamishness about violence, whereas much of the Spanish left was "*apparently antifascist, but in many characteristics and aims, essentially fascist,*" because of their readiness to employ violence and rejection of democratic legalism.[74]

Historians have been nearly unanimous in viewing the revolutionary insurrection as the beginning of the decline of the Second Republic and of constitutional government and constitutional consensus in Spain. Historians as diverse as Gerald Brenan, Salvador de Madariaga, Raymond Carr, Gabriel Jackson, Richard Robinson, Carlos M. Rama, Carlos Seco Serrano, and Ricardo de la Cierva have described it either as "the prelude to" or "the first battle of" the Civil War. The most widely quoted evaluation has been that of Madariaga:

> The revolt of 1934 is unpardonable. The decision of the president in calling the CEDA to share in the government was not only unimpeachable, not only unavoidable, but long overdue. The argument that Señor Gil Robles intended to bring in Fascism was both hypocritical and demonstrably untrue. . . . As for the Asturian miners, their revolt was entirely due to doctrinairian and theoretical prepossessions. Had the hungry Andalusian peasants risen in revolt, what could one do but sympathize with their despair? But the Asturian miners were well paid, and, in fact, the whole industry, by a collusion between employers and workers, was kept working at an artificial level by state subsidies beyond what many of the seams deserved in a sound economy. Lastly the Catalan case was no more justified.[75]

Edward Malefakis has written: "The tragedy of the Spanish left, and ultimately of Spain itself, was that in 1934 it lacked the self-confidence to ride out that crisis through which it was passing as the right had ridden out its own crisis in 1931–33."[76] Raymond Carr observes:

Socialists might have reflected that they, like the CEDA, had their own form of accidentalism. They were a party in theory committed to major social changes which must destroy bourgeois society, but they had been willing to cooperate in a bourgeois parliamentary government.

The revolution of October is the immediate origin of the Civil War. The left, above all the Socialists, had rejected legal processes of government; the government against which they revolted was electorally justified. The left was later to make great play of the "legality" argument to condemn the generals' revolt in July 1936 against an elected government.[77]

Of the top Socialist leaders — aside from Besteiro, who had always recognized the disaster an insurrection would bring — the one who most quickly grasped the magnitude of the mistake and repented of it, determined never to repeat it again, was Indalecio Prieto. Years later, he confessed in a speech in Mexico City on May Day, 1942:

I declare myself guilty before my conscience, before the Socialist Party and before all Spain, of my participation in the revolutionary movement of 1934. I declare it as guilt, as a sin, not as a glory. I share no responsibility for the genesis of that movement, but I share fully responsibility for its preparation and development. . . . And I accepted tasks that others avoided, because behind them lay the danger not only of losing liberty, but the deeper danger of losing honor. Nonetheless, I accepted them. . . .[78]

Henceforth the goal of the Republican left and the moderate wing of the Socialists would be to restore unified political, not revolutionary, action to overcome the twin disasters of 1933–34.

10

Government by the Center-Right, 1934–1935

LERROUX'S radio address to the nation on 7 October called for calm and respect for the Constitution. The prime minister expressed his confidence that most Catalans would support the legally established order and promised that the government would "conserve the liberties recognized by the Republic," while pledging that "the rule of law" would triumph. With occasional sniper shots still being heard in Madrid, the Cortes reopened on the ninth to applause for Lerroux, who would face the task of completing the defeat of the insurrection and presiding over the resulting repression as fairly as possible. The latter would prove difficult, for just as the *sanjurjada* had strengthened the left Republican coalition, so the failed insurrection energized the right and even led some moderate liberals to urge a policy of extreme rigor. The rightist press was full of lurid atrocity stories and assured its readers that the revolutionaries guilty of such deeds could not be human beings. On 19 October 1934, even *El Sol* intoned; "For wild beasts capable of such monstrous deeds that even a degenerate would not be capable of imagining, we ask for severe, implacable, definitive punishment. For men, as men; for wild beasts, as wild beasts."

Well over fifteen thousand people were arrested in the weeks that followed, including approximately three thousand each in Madrid and Barcelona, about fifteen hundred in Vizcaya and Guipuzcoa, and most of the rest in Asturias. As provided for in the Republican security legislation, military tribunals quickly set to work in *sumarísimo* courtmartial proceedings to prosecute the leading figures. A tribunal in Barcelona soon delivered six death sentences, beginning with Major Pérez Farrás and two other former army officers who had been commanders of the new Catalan constabulary (Mossos d'Esquadra) and militia (Somatén) involved in the insurrection.

The terms of the repression became the central political drama of the next three months. The Cortes, which had earlier refused to restore the death penalty after the last anarchist insurrection, now voted to reintroduce the maximum sentence. All the right demanded severity, but the president, Cardinal Vidal i Barraquer, Cambó, the leaders of the Lliga Catalana, and various other moderates urged leniency, with commutation of death sentences. Though its position was at first unanimously opposed to commutation (with the exception of the case of Capt. Federico Escofet, whose involvement was limited[1]), the new government soon found itself holding a series of lengthy meetings. Alcalá Zamora, in what had become a habitual extension of the presidential prerogative, made one of his lengthy presentations to the cabinet on 18 October, citing Article 102 of the Constitution, which stated that, "The President of the Republic has the power to commute penalties in crimes of extreme gravity, after a report from the Supreme Court and a recommendation from the government." He made it clear that he would seek to use this authority even if the government refused to appeal cases to him.[2] The resulting tension led to a rumor repeated by Radio Toulouse that the president would be forced to resign and replaced by a military government led by General Franco, though there is no indication of a military conspiracy at that point. Though his pressure and the procedure which he threatened were basically unconstitutional, Alcalá Zamora apparently had no intention of giving in.[3] Two cabinet meetings were held on 31 October and two more on the first, with the president directly threatening to withdraw confidence and force a governmental reorganization or new elections. Though the report of the Supreme Court did not recommend commutation, Lerroux finally decided to capitulate in order to make peace with the president and appease the moderates. After another cabinet meeting on 5 November, Lerroux announced that of the first twenty-three death sentences, twenty-one would be commuted.

The regular Cortes session also opened on 5 November, and Lerroux expressed his satisfaction to the right:

I will die satisfied for having contributed to my fatherland the service of having brought over from you, the monarchists, all those elements that now constitute the right wing of the Republic. . . . We are accused of being fascists and of having altered the spirit of the Republic. What projects have been approved contrary to the letter and spirit of the Constitution? . . . And there will be no modification of the fundamental laws, save by following the course prescribed in the Constitution itself.

Melquiades Alvarez, the veteran Republican and leader of the Liberal Democrats, observed that he had been a leader in the popular movement of pro-

Alejandro Lerroux delivering a public address

test in 1917 but that he and his associates had avoided political murders and common crimes. He invoked the example of the founders of the French Third Republic who executed Communards en masse, concluding that "with those executions they saved the Republic and its institutions and maintained order." Calvo Sotelo made a stronger speech yet, pointing out that the Spanish Socialists' "tactics differ from those of all the responsible socialist parties of Europe, since none of the latter advocate violent class struggle." In such a situation, the army was now the "spinal column" of Spain. The government easily won a vote of confidence of 233 to zero, with the extreme right abstaining. Though none of the left and left-center deputies initially returned to parliament, Martínez Barrio and Miguel Maura came back on the ninth, followed six days later by the left Catalanist deputies. After the government ended temporary censorship on parliamentary debate early in November, others began to take their seats. Meanwhile, the CEDA carried by a vote of 161 to 13 a motion that declared all deputies personally involved in the insurrection to have forfeited their seats and mandated an investigation of all trade unions, providing for the dissolution of those found to have been implicated and the confiscation of their assets to pay for damaged property.

The first conflict of the new session was an attack on two cabinet members, Samper and Hidalgo, for their alleged irresponsibility during the former government in failing to prevent the preparation of the insurrection. Without the support of the CEDA, they resigned on 16 November, Lerroux doubling as minister of war in place of Hidalgo and the veteran Radical Juan José Rocha replacing Samper as foreign minister, which was regarded as a secondary post. Rocha, who had been minister of war in the first Lerroux government and minister of the navy in the past three administrations, was becoming known as "Miss Ministry" for always turning up with some position in successive governments.

During this mini-crisis, rumors of military conspiracy that had swirled for several weeks took more concrete form when two hard-line generals, Goded and Fanjul, urged Gil Robles to adopt a firmer policy on the repression, pledging the support of the military. Yet they had spoken too soon; after two days canvasing military opinion, they came back to advise the CEDA leader to continue to cooperate with the coalition government, for the army leaders were generally unwilling to take any political responsibility and a sudden new election might return the left to power.[4]

A commission of four cabinet ministers was appointed to make a recommendation on how to proceed vis-à-vis Catalan autonomy. It presented a bill on 28 November which temporarily suspended autonomy but provided that all rights and guarantees be restored no more than three months after full constitutional guarantees were returned to Spain as a whole. An interim governor general would be appointed in Barcelona while a new committee would determine how much autonomy was to be enjoyed by Catalan administration in the interim. During the next ten days a bill by the extreme right to replace the Catalan autonomy statute with completely new legislation was defeated, but the CEDA added amendments to the main bill that would suspend autonomy indefinitely until such time as the government and Cortes saw fit to reinstate it gradually, step by step. This amended version then carried on 14 December. Thirteen days later the government appointed Manuel Portela Valladares as governor general. An elderly veteran of the old monarchist Liberal Party, Portela had earned a positive reputation as the last constitutional provincial governor of Barcelona in 1923. He appointed José Pich y Pon, a veteran Radical politician, as mayor of Barcelona and turned the city council over to the Radicals. Meanwhile the government found it impossible to prepare an adequate new budget for the coming year, and so on 14 December the existing budget was simply prorogued for three more months.

The controversy over the repression continued without abatement. While the extreme right condemned the government's "appeasement" in commuting most death sentences, protest from the left mounted over brutal police procedures in Asturias. While in Catalonia and the rest of Spain the terms of repression appear to have been relatively moderate, the Civil Guard's jurisdiction in Asturias, where the brutal Major Lisardo Doval was in charge of investigations, seems to have been a law unto itself. Savage beatings and torture remained commonplace, and several more prisoners died. In the most subsequently publicized atrocity, a liberal investigative journalist who went by the pseudonym of Luis Sirval was arbitrarily arrested, then abruptly shot dead in prison by a sadistic Bulgarian Legionnaire officer named Ivanov. Continued censorship under martial law made independent reporting almost impossible, so a special commission of Socialist and left Republican deputies carried out an investigative mission of their own. Their report was able to dismiss the most extreme atrocity stories of both sides, but provided evidence of continued beatings and torture in Asturian jails. After more protests and an attempt by Doval to appeal to monarchist deputies for special protection, Lerroux reassigned the infamous major on 7 December, but even then police practice in Asturias was not fully moderated. In January 564 prisoners signed a collective letter protesting use of torture in Oviedo prison. This was followed by another collective letter of protest to Alcalá Zamora, which included the signatures of moderate and conservative luminaries such as Unamuno and Valle Inclán. By that time the protest had become international, a depression-era equivalent of the Ferrer campaign of 1909, with the left lending it major attention throughout western Europe and the Comintern also investing considerable resources. A commission of British Labourite deputies was allowed to visit Asturias, while in February 1935 the French Socialist Vincent Auriol talked with Lerroux as his party collected thousands of signatures on amnesty petitions in France. The consejos de guerra continued, but all death sentences were commuted save for two prisoners executed in February, the army sergeant and deserter Diego Vázquez who had fought with the revolutionaries and a worker known as "El Pichilatu," who was accused of several killings.

Though the government had intended to be reasonable, and was in fact reasonable in most cases, there was no doubt that the repression was badly handled. Justice was uneven, and in Asturias the police administration was allowed to run wild. Though only four executions took place—all of men convicted of murderous crimes—there was much mistreatment of prisoners in Asturias, leading to a number of further deaths. Moreover, the revolt of the Esquerra government was not adequate constitutional ground to suspend Catalan autonomy, with no distinction made between the excesses of one political group and the constitutional rights of the region.[5] More than one-eighth of all the mayors in Spain were replaced by the government in the weeks after the revolt.[6] Continuation of the censorship was counterproductive, and eventually even the monarchist deputies initiated a Cortes debate over its unnecessary prolongation. Martial law was finally lifted for most of Spain on 23 January 1935 but was retained for the provinces of Madrid, Barcelona, and six others in the north which had been prominent either in the October revolt or in the last anarchist insurrection. Three weeks later, Calvo Sotelo observed that, in the nearly four years since the beginning of the Republic, Spain had enjoyed only twenty-three days of *plenitud constitucional* (full constitutional rights) for the entire country. The excesses in Asturias, and also the widespread rightist propaganda about atrocities, were even more counterproductive, building sympathy for the left among more moderate sectors of the left-center and center. The same may be said of the government's refusal to free leftist leaders who bore little or no responsibility. The lengthy imprisonment of Azaña and the effort to prosecute him would also backfire, earning him new sympathy and prestige among the left and even part of the center. A further example was the policy of taking advantage of the situation to close many CNT centers and arrest hundreds of anarchosyndicalists outside of Asturias who had nothing to do with the revolt, a practice that created greater mutual sympathy between anarchists and Socialists and better prospects for leftist unity than had existed before the revolt. The insurrection had been a disaster for the Socialists, but the miscalculations and excesses of the repression had the effect of restoring much of the left's strength. Moreover, the controversy tended to weaken the government itself, dividing the center and the right.

Probably the clearest voice of reason in the Cortes of 1935 was that of the Catalan centrist Francesc Cambó. He answered Calvo Sotelo's speech of 13 February two days later with the firm denial that democracy itself was responsible for the ills of contemporary Spanish society or incapable of producing progress and concord. The worst horrors at the present time, he stated, were not occurring in democratic western Europe but in the new dictatorships of eastern and central Europe. He pointed to another source of Spain's deteriorating condition:

> We live in a period of weakening public power, such as we have never before experienced, and this weakness . . . is reflected in parliament, where I must say that I have never previously sat in a parliamentary chamber so insensitive to the wounds being inflicted on the public interests as in the present Cortes.

Cambó also stood as the chief defender of Catalan interests and the constitutional principle of autonomy.

Prosecution of those involved in the repression continued, and would go on until the beginning of 1936. Of all those indicted, the best known was Azaña, who had been placed at liberty by a decision of the Tribunal Supremo on 28 December 1934. The results of the judicial investigation into his role, together with the facts on the initial arms deal with Portuguese exiles and the *Turquesa* affair, were presented to the Cortes on 15 February 1935, though the debate on the latter did not begin until 20 March. It was clear that there was no evidence to connect Azaña with either the planning or the outbreak of the insurrection itself, and that the dredging up of facts on the Portuguese arms deal threatened a delicate area of foreign relations. Azaña was publicly cheered by a large crowd as he left the Cortes following the conclusion of the fruitless debate on 21 March, and he was fully absolved of any charges connected with the insurrection itself by the Tribunal Supremo on 6 April.

The final round of Azaña's prosecution involved the report of a special parliamentary commission of twenty-one deputies concerning his responsibility in providing arms through the *Turquesa* affair. The commission was very slow to issue its report. Despite this delay, the result of foot-dragging by the commission's Radical members, who were reluctant to indict the former prime minister, the eventual recommendation to the Cortes on 20 July was that Azaña should be tried for his actions in this matter by the Tribunal de Garantías Constitucionales, since it involved foreign affairs. The Radicals avoided this session, which produced 189 black balls from the right versus 68 white balls from the left and center. An absolute majority (222) was required to proceed to his prosecution, and thus Azaña was freed from any further indictment.

Meanwhile the latest round of court-martials produced death sentences for some of the main Socialist leaders in Asturias, including Ramón González Peña — arguably the most important single leader — and the moderate Teodomiro Menéndez, who had in fact always opposed the revolt.[7] In this case the Supreme Court did recommend commutation for González Peña and a number of others. The matter was discussed in a cabinet meeting on 29 March, with Lerroux proposing commutation for González Peña and twenty others, including Menéndez. The cabinet split down the middle, with Lerroux and the six other Radicals voting in favor, the three *cedistas*, the Agrarian, and the Liberal Democrat voting against.[8] This vote was sufficient to decide the issue but also broke up the government, with Alcalá Zamora initiating consultations for a new coalition on the following day.

Reconstitution of the coalition was not viable because both the CEDA and the Agrarians demanded increased representation and competed for key ministries. Alcalá Zamora remained determined to exclude the CEDA from any position of power proportionate to its parliamentary strength. He hit upon the makeshift solution of invoking Article 81 of the Constitution, which empowered him to suspend parliament for thirty days and to appoint an interim administration under Lerroux, composed mainly of Radicals but with two representatives of Alcalá Zamora's own Progressive Republican Party and with the independent Portela Valladares (not a parliamentary deputy) in Interior as recognition of his recent labors as governor general of Catalonia. Though Alcalá Zamora hyperbolically called it "the best government of the Republic," it was mostly made up of cronies of the president and prime minister. A surprising number of its ministers had been members of the old García Prieto faction of the monarchist Liberal Party, and for the first time under the Republic a general and an admiral held the portfolios of War and Navy. This government was finally able to put an end to martial law in all Spain on 9 April and presided over a rather dreary anniversary of the Republic (compared with which Holy Week that year was quite festive), but its days were obviously numbered. Seeking a positive note and to identify itself with prestigious luminaries, the government awarded the new decoration of the "Banda de la República" to Ortega y Gasset. He refused to accept it, saying that he no longer had anything to do with politics. In doing so, he expressed the disenchantment of many moderates.

The most positive accomplishment of the interim government was to restore the functions of autonomy, except for public order, to a reconstituted Generalitat in mid-April. The new president was Pich y Pon, the top Radical politician of the region, functioning in cooperation with the Lliga. During the course of the spring, conditions deteriorated. On the one hand Pich y Pon handed over many top jobs to cronies, which did not improve efficiency or honesty. On the other, with martial law ended, the FAI-CNT became more active. Petty disorders, such as the periodic burning of municipal streetcars, increased in frequency, as did violence against persons. On 29 June martial law was reimposed on Barcelona province, both the ministers of war and of interior flying there to restore order.[9]

During the course of April the four party leaders of the preceding coalition (Lerroux, Gil Robles, Melquiades Alvarez, and Martínez de Velasco) began to reach a new agreement on the obvious ground that the only viable government was a restoration of the coalition, particularly between the Radicals and the CEDA. Gil Robles now required greater representation for his party, which Lerroux conceded. Alcalá Zamora was out of alternatives, and therefore a new coalition under Lerroux was installed on 6 May. Gil Robles, the first of five CEDA ministers, took over the key Ministry of War. Federico Salmón, one of the more progressive CEDA leaders, became minister of labor. However, the liberal Manuel Giménez Fernández, who had pursued a further reformist policy as minister of agriculture in the autumn-winter coalition, was for that reason vetoed by the conservative majority of his own party. Giménez Fernández was replaced by the ultra-conservative Nicasio Velayos of the Agrarian Party. The "inevitable" Rocha ("Miss Ministry") remained foreign minister, as in the two preceding governments. Altogether the new cabinet contained five cedistas, four Radicals (including the prime minister), two Agrarians, one Liberal Democrat, and one independent, Portela Valladares, who remained in Interior. Alcalá Zamora's main achievement in the new arrangement was the continued exclusion of the leader of the largest party from the premiership, an office which Gil Robles had decided not to insist on attaining.

Though martial law had ended in most of Spain, a state of either alarm or prevention was in effect in sixteen provinces. On 6 June the government gained approval for prorogation of this condition for another thirty days, the eighth prorogation of a state of constitutional exception under the Republic. This provided the opportunity for Calvo Sotelo to declare on that day in the Cortes that this situation manifestly demonstrated "that the Constitution is not viable." The Lerroux governments of early 1935 had been making intermittent efforts to come to grips with the dilemma of continuing censorship and had introduced two new bills for new laws regulating the press (in February and in May), but finally gave up, unable to achieve an effective balance between civil rights and the need to control incendiary and subversive agitation.

In the continuing repression, the principle of commutation was now well established. No more executions would take place, and the new government began with a round of *indultos* (commutations), even including common criminals. The most important new prosecution was of Companys and the other councillors (ministers) of the rebel Generalitat. There had been uncertainty as to which tribunal in the somewhat confusing and not fully consolidated Republican judicial system was appropriate to hear their case and, because of the relationship with an autonomous regional government, the Tribunal de Garantías Constitucionales had been agreed upon. On 6 June it handed down the verdict that all were guilty of "military rebellion" and were sentenced to thirty years each.[10]

Military courts continued to try cases involving violence during the insurrection. During the balance of June, nine more death sentences were handed down, though it seemed unlikely they would be carried out, and many long prison terms were imposed. By this point, however, with martial law ended, there was now much more reaction from the left. Asturian miners declared their first new sympathy strike in solidarity with the condemned, and several judges received anonymous death threats in the mail.[11]

May and June were a time of big new political rallies. Azaña began his political comeback with a huge rally that filled Valencia's Mestalla stadium in May. The CEDA was the most active party in promoting large meetings, and Gil Robles addressed an audience approximately equal to Azaña's in Mestalla stadium on 30 June. Not to be outdone, Lerroux addressed a Radical rally in the same spot a week later, announcing: "Who are the ones who have evolved? They [the right] have, and similarly in other ways. . . . I prophesy to you that the Republic has been definitively established in Spain."[12]

Monarchist leaders, keenly resentful of the CEDA's "opportunism," at that point tended to agree with Lerroux. Though considerable tension continued to exist between the Radicals and the CEDA, the prime minister was now convinced that he had saved the Republic by domesticating the strongest force on the right. He seems to have thought that if the left Republicans would now settle down and coalesce into one large but responsible opposition party, the function of the Radicals would be to hold the balance of power between a Republican left and right, and he could soon look forward to an honored retirement.[13]

Republican Reform "Rectified"

Cedorradical coalition government was possible because, in addition to their common opposition to the left, both parties recognized a need to "rectify" the reforms of the first biennium. Yet they differed profoundly in terms of the character and extent of that rectification. The Radicals sought only a genuine rectification in the sense of moderation, while in key respects the CEDA sought a counterreform, especially in religious and socioeconomic policy, and in the basic alteration of the Constitution.

The terms of industrial relations had already begun to change somewhat under the first Lerroux governments of 1933–34, and this was a factor in further labor radicalization. The *jurados* had become more neutral, less prolabor, while some of the new regulations had simply not been enforced. Nonetheless, prior to the October insurrection there had been no legal reversal of the basic reforms, nor had the syndicates by any means lost all of the contract settlements of 1934.

The situation changed much more in the aftermath of the insurrection. Though UGT syndicates were not generally dissolved (the government being unable to prove their responsibility for the revolt), hundreds of *jurados mixtos* were closed down, particularly in the industrial areas, and they had already been weakened in the countryside. A government decree of 1 November 1934 established the legal category of *huelga abusiva* (roughly, illegal strike), which would henceforth apply to all strikes not undertaken over specific labor issues or which failed to follow all legal regulations. In such a situation, employers would henceforth be free to rescind contracts and fire workers.

Federico Salmón, new CEDA labor minister in May 1935, was a representative of the "social Catholic" wing of his party. He sought to make the *jurados* more neutral and effective by introducing civil servants as their presidents, but neither the UGT nor the CNT would participate, and Salmón virtually admitted that at the present time labor was not being fairly represented. In many areas the *jurados* virtually ceased to operate, while some concrete gains were officially rolled back. The forty-eight-hour week, for example, returned to the construction and metallurgical industries. Unemployment continued to rise. Thousands of workers had been fired by employers for having participated in political or other strikes, even though employers were officially urged not to retaliate. The improvement in industrial production in 1934–35 and increased business confidence and investment under the center-right may have reduced the rate of growth in unemployment during 1935 but certainly failed to reverse it, as employers sought to limit and streamline employment of workers who were in general still enjoying higher wages than in 1931. The unemployment statistics for 1935 (table 10.1) showed a significant drop in mid-year because of the great seasonal increase in agricultural employment, but overall the problem continued to worsen.

Salmón thus gave priority to reducing unemployment. He immediately introduced a new plan to spend 200 million pesetas for new construction and public works, with subsidies and insurance incentives designed to trigger a total volume of new private investment at least four times greater. This plan was aimed in considerable measure, though not exclusively, at the private sector and also at the local level. It was approved in June 1935 and marked the first direct new employment scheme from the government. In fact, the money was spent bit by bit in small proportions and never triggered the volume of new construction and employment anticipated. Subsequently, Luis Lucia, one of the two most important Christian democrat leaders in the CEDA, became minister of public works in September and laid the groundwork for a new public works program that was presented to the Cortes on the eve of the coalition's collapse. These well-meaning initiatives, the second of which came too late to be approved, were a matter of too little too late and failed to reduce the rise in unemployment.

More controversial was the revision of the agrarian reform. Minister of agriculture for much of 1934 had been the Progressive Republican Cirilo del Río, who sought to continue the basic program of the agrarian reform

Table 10.1. Unemployment, 1934–1936

	1934
January	625,097
April	703,814
July	520,847
October	629,730
	1935
January	711,184
April	732,034
July	578,833
December	780,242
	1936
January	748,810
February	843,872

Source: *Boletín Informativo de la Oficina Central de colocación obrera y defensa contra el paro*, in J. Tusell, *La Segunda República en Madrid* (Madrid, 1970), 84, 128.

while correcting other abuses. Thus the sharecroppers placed on uncultivated land in 1931–32 were evicted, the *términos municipales* law was annulled, rent revisions were suspended and procedures for evicting insolvent renters expedited, but the regular agrarian reform proceeded undisturbed, more landless families being settled in 1934 than during 1932–33.

Agriculture minister in the first *cedorradical* government of October 1934 was the advanced social Catholic and Christian democrat Giménez Fernández. His first major act had been to extend for one more year (until 31 July 1935) the continued occupation of formerly untilled land worked by *yunteros* (plowmen) in Extremadura since 1932–33. Though the issue split the CEDA (Gil Robles supporting it), the measure was passed on 20 December 1934. Giménez Fernández's second major act was a decree of 2 January 1935 that altered somewhat the terms of the administration of the agrarian reform. During the rest of the year there would be no more forcible expropriations, preference would be given to landless families with their own instruments of cultivation, and a target of ten thousand landless farmers to be settled on new land was set for the year. This was not, as the left insisted, an attempt to destroy the reform but simply an effort to make it less costly and more efficient. The total number of landless to be settled was exactly the same as that which had been proposed by Azaña for 1933, while the end to forced expropriations was designed at least in part to save money until a more flexible compensation system could be worked out. In fact, resettlement under the agrarian reform continued at a normal rate until May 1935.

Giménez Fernández encountered the most severe opposition against his proposals to benefit agrarian renters. He held to the social Catholic position that private property was a basic right but not an absolute one, its usufruct subject to regulation by objective community needs. Expanding an earlier plan by Del Río, he proposed that renters be allowed to purchase farmland which they had worked for a minimum of twelve years at prices mutually agreed upon with owners or set by independent arbitration. Otherwise, they would be guaranteed six-year leases, receive compensation for improvements made, enjoy the opportunity to have their rents set by arbitration tribunals, and be subject to eviction only for non-payment of rent. Giménez Fernández argued that the government simply lacked funds to compensate owners for legal expropriation other than at the present slow rate, and therefore the most appropriate alternative was to make it possible for productive long-term renters to purchase their farms on the private market. This constructive proposal met a firestorm of criticism as the subversion of private property: Giménez Fernández was viciously denounced as a *bolchevique blanco* (white Bolshevik). Its main terms had to be given up. Legislation finally approved by parliament in February–March 1935 only granted renters minimum leases for four years and some compensation for improvements, while leaving arbitration to the regular courts.[14]

When the CEDA reentered the government in May 1935, the arch-conservative Nicasio Velayos of the Agrarians took over the ministry. During the months that followed, many owners — possibly as many as "several thousand"[15] — took advantage of a provision in the recent legislation allowing owners to evict tenants in order to farm the land directly, in many cases fraudulently, without any effort at direct cultivation. The number of farmers illegally evicted may have run into the tens of thousands, but Velayos refused to intervene to see that rules were followed.

His proposal for a new "Law for the Reform of the Agrarian Reform" was introduced to the Cortes in July. It introduced the principle that there would be no expropriation of any kind without full compensation, while terms for calculating the latter were substantially altered in the landowners' favor. It annulled the inventory of properties technically subject to expropriation, making it possible for owners of eight-ninths of the lands in that category to sell off properties to third parties, grant them to children or take a variety of other measures to gain exemption. Certain kinds of land were now totally excluded, and all collective experiments were forbidden. The bill also repealed the *ruedo* provisions (one of the most dubious aspects of the first bill) and arrangements for expropriation of rented properties. The increase in costs of administering the reform would drastically reduce the number of new farmers settled, while eligibility requirements were steeply raised. Finally, as a sop to moderates and Christian democrats, the bill did give the state the right to seize any land for reasons of "social utility," though without the slightest plan for doing so.

Velayos's new bill was vehemently denounced by the left and also by part of the center. The Falangist leader José Antonio Primo de Rivera calculated publicly that at this rate the agrarian reform would take more than 160 years to complete and warned that the amended project would last only "until the next round of reprisals." When the measure was passed on 25 July, the left Republicans temporarily withdrew from parliament once more.

In general, 1935 was a year of severe reprisals in the central and southern countryside, with numerous expulsions and firings, lowering of wages, and arbitrary changes in working conditions. The leading conservative historian of this period judges that landowners' tactics in the south "were genuinely ferocious," involving violence as well as the deaths of a number of Socialists and farmworkers. He concludes that "the behavior of the right in the countryside in the second half of 1935 was one of the principal causes of hatred in the Civil War, and probably of the Civil War itself."[16]

Another basic area of reform for *cedorradical* government was military policy, though there was a divergence of interest and intention between the two coalition partners. Altogether between September 1933 and December 1935, there were seven different ministers of war, but the two whose leadership was important were the Radical Diego Hidalgo (minister from January to November 1934) and Gil Robles (minister from May to December 1935). The goal of the Radicals was to pacify the military—whom Lerroux still considered relatively liberal at heart—after the alleged *trituración* by Azaña, in order to make them feel happier with the Republic, without further changes or spending much more money. Of those previously prosecuted and then amnestied by the legislation of April 1934, all save the ringleaders of the *sanjurjada* were offered the option of retiring, going on the reserve with full pay, or returning to active duty. Most took the first two options, but some key figures such as Gen. Emilio Mola (last police chief of the monarchy), Gen. Andrés Saliquet, Col. José Millán Astray, and a number of others chose to return to active duty. Franco was given the first new promotion to major general, while on 19 July 1934 Hidalgo published a new decree prohibiting all political activities by the military. Lerroux took over the ministry when Hidalgo was forced out and tried to be even-handed in constructing a personnel policy that balanced the concerns of both conservative hardliners and pro-Republican senior commanders.

When Gil Robles entered the ministry in May 1935, leftists prophesied the worst, fearing preparation of a CEDA coup d'état. Calvo Sotelo and his Bloque Nacional, having little civilian support, publicly sought military backing, with Calvo hailing the army as "the spinal column of the fatherland." Gil Robles scoffed at the idea of a coup, saying that, on the one hand, dictatorship could never solve the country's political problems and, on the other, that the CEDA had adequate legal political support to triumph. "The people," not the army, were the "spinal column," while the army was the *brazo armado,* the "weaponed arm" of the state for the entire citizenry and should not be involved in politics.[17] He did propose, however, to reconservatize the officer corps and army command and to improve its combat readiness to face any future subversion.

Gil Robles's command appointments were very rightist. The sometime Agrarian deputy and extreme rightist Gen. Joaquín Fanjul became his undersecretary in the ministry, and Franco was named chief of the general staff. Gil Robles publicly complained of "Masonic influence" in the army command, and some forty top *azañista* appointees, liberal senior commanders, were removed and in certain cases placed on reserve. Old regimental names and religious services were restored and the Code of Military Justice partially revised, as were the combat promotions (*méritos de guerra*) which in some cases had been annulled by Azaña. A project to lower by two years the age for passage to the reserve was blocked by the intense opposition of the president and senior pro-Republican generals, some of whom would have been eliminated by it.

There was no money to increase salaries, but in December the Cortes approved a law promoting all the *subtenientes* created by Azaña to lieutenant, expanding the officer corps by 3,500, so that the total size of the officer corps rebounded to about 14,000. The proportion of volunteers was raised to 8 percent of all new recruits, and in July a new law required all candidates for any of the police or constabulary corps to first acquire three years of active military service.

Despite the shortage of money, a three-year rearmament plan was drawn up, projecting a new extraordinary budget to be paid for out of savings and more progressive taxation, but the latter was killed by the government. Two new brigades were created, and plans were drawn up for new warplanes, tanks, artillery, and machineguns, though very little could actually be purchased.[18] The murkiest aspect of all these plans was a proposal by Cándido Casanueva, the CEDA minister of justice, to arrange for German suppliers for the military buildup, with a rake-off to go into party campaign coffers.[19] Nothing came of this.

Since the end of 1933 a new army officers' semi-clandestine association had been developing in Spanish garrisons. Called the Unión Militar Española (UME), it was a sort of more rightist variant of the Juntas Militares movement that had flourished during 1917–19. The UME was scorned by Gil Robles, who wanted nothing to do with sectarian army politics as distinct from a stronger, more conservative professional military. Its main goal was the complete reversal of all the Azaña personnel and political reforms. The UME was organized and led by monarchists, particularly the staff officers Capt. Bartolomé Barba Hernández and Lt. Col. Valentín Galarza, but it was a loose organization that appealed to garrison officers primarily with regard to professional concerns rather than a political program. It may have been encouraged and protected by Fanjul and several other appointees of Gil Robles.

Educational policy also changed. The most positive accomplishments were made under the Liberal Democrat Filiberto Villalobos, who served as minister of public instruction for eight months between April and December, 1934, before being forced out by the CEDA.[20] Between 29 December 1934 and 30 December 1935, the ministerial portfolio became a football, changing hands seven times among six different ministers, including the ubiquitous and persistent Rocha for a month, and ending with a brief return by Villalobos. The initial Radical governments did not cut educational expenditures but increased them to an all-time high of 7.08 percent of total state expenditures, dropping to 6.6 percent in 1935. The number of new schools constructed declined to only thirteen hundred in 1934, but with Catholic schools no longer being closed the deficit was much less. In July 1934 requirements and examinations for all levels of secondary education were standardized and in August the *bachillerato* curriculum was reorganized into successive cycles, a reform generally well received. At the same time, coeducation was ended in primary schools, and during 1935 the national school inspection apparatus that had been developed under the left was largely eliminated. Policy under the center-right became steadily more conservative, especially in 1935. After the October insurrection student representation in the university was abolished, while Catholic educational groups became increasingly active.[21]

Of all changes, the ultimate for the CEDA was constitutional reform. *La táctica* was basically to counter the anti-Catholic legislation, introduce aspects of the CEDA's social program, strengthen conservative institutions (such as the military), and to prepare fundamental constitutional reform. Yet though this goal was ultimately crucial, the party leadership was not in an immediate hurry, for any constitutional amendment adopted prior to 9 December 1935 (fourth anniversary of the Constitution) would require a two-thirds majority, whereas after that date a simple parliamentary majority would suffice. Moreover, the law required that after parliament passed an amendment it must be dissolved. Otherwise there was no need for the CEDA plurality to face new elections until November 1937, and thus in this most critical area the leadership proceeded slowly.

Alcalá Zamora concurred in the goal of constitutional reform, yet his own objectives differed fundamentally, for he wished the Republican charter to be altered into a more moderate and efficient, yet still essentially liberal democratic, constitution. He had made a long exposition to the first *cedorradical* cabinet in January 1935, proposing reform of all four of the articles pertaining to regional statutes, Articles 26 and 27 on religion, and Article 51 on the *cámara única* in order to create a bicameral legislature. He also proposed to change the statement on the socialization of property and make changes in twenty-seven other articles, amounting virtually to a new Constitution.[22] The government appointed a parliamentary commission under the Liberal Democrat Joaquín Dualde to prepare a formal set of draft proposals. This, however, moved slowly, at least in part because the CEDA and others saw no need to proceed until December.

Meanwhile there was serious consideration of electoral law reform. A first meeting of party representatives was held on 16 June, followed by a second not long afterward. The CEDA came out for proportional representation, while the Radicals and most other republican parties urged the elimination of the 40 percent quorum and called for cutting in half the largest electoral districts. Lerroux announced that he would take responsibility for a new electoral law that would "satisfy all," based on a majority system for the smaller districts and proportionality only in the four or five largest ones. His energy, however, was in serious decline, and no such proposal ever appeared.[23]

On 5 July Lerroux presented to parliament the proposals of the Dualde commission. Its preamble proudly stated:

> For the first time in the political history of Spain, a constitutional revision is being carried out by making use of the juridical possibilities provided by the existing constitution. Previous preconstitutional regimes and constitutions have tended toward immutability, with the result that every change could come only through violence.

The proposal contained general guidelines for revising no less than 41 of the 125 articles in the Constitution. Principal would be the revision of provisions for regional autonomy to safeguard public order and unity, democratization of the religious articles, with provision for negotiation of a concordat, revision of Article 44 that permitted expropriation without compensation, creation of a senate, and revision of the presidential prerogatives to give the president greater freedom to dissolve parliament but to reduce his authority over the ordinary conduct of government. The proposal gained the backing of the government coalition but was vehemently rejected by all the left. A commission of twenty-one deputies was immediately appointed to study it and make further detailed recommendations that could be discussed in Cortes during the final months of the year.

These proposals were more moderate than the goals earlier set by the CEDA and particularly by the JAP, their youth group. It is doubtful that these changes would have completed the constitutional reform sought by the Catholic movement. JAP publications had been calling for a stronger executive, with limitations on the power of the legislature.[24] At various times during 1935 Gil Robles sought to dissociate himself from the extreme authoritarian, nationalist rhetoric of the JAP—sometimes closer to Calvo Sotelo's Bloque Nacional than to the CEDA—though he took no decisive action to silence it. The CEDA leader gave some indication that he appreciated the importance of a parliament, though he did believe that its powers and functions should be somewhat reduced.[25]

A more immediate problem than constitutional reform was the budget. Republican governments encountered increasing difficulty in preparing a budget, not because they were teetering on the verge of bankruptcy—almost the opposite was the case—but because of political fragmentation. Agreement was handicapped by steady (though scarcely overwhelming) growth of the deficit, continued relative depression, and above all by government instability.[26] Under the *cedorradical* government of mid-1935, this problem was placed in the experienced hands of Joaquín Chapaprieta, wealthy lawyer and businessman, a member of the Alba wing of the old Liberal Party, and last minister of labor before the dictatorship. Elected as a Republican independent in 1933, Chapaprieta had some reputation as an expert in administration and finance. His initial proposals, presented on 29 May, foresaw the reduction of the past year's 750 million peseta deficit by one-third during the current year, with the full balance to be achieved by 1937 or in the final months of 1936 through a combination of budget reductions in certain categories, modest tax increases and revisions, and improved collection. His reductions aimed at trimming government administration and personnel costs while retaining necessary public works and social programs. He observed: "In economic policy I don't see that the governments of the left have had a different policy from those of the center and right,"[27] and he believed that with sounder management the Spanish economy might soon enjoy considerable investment from both domestic and foreign sources. Chapaprieta refloated a significant part of the public debt, but his key proposals drew strong opposition from the left, the civil service, and certain economic interest groups. One major feature of his administrative reorganization and budget reduction plan was the elimination of three government ministries, their activities to be reconsolidated among the remaining ministries.[28]

As soon as this reform was decided on 19 September, the two Agrarian ministers abruptly resigned, primarily because of opposition to the restoration of further areas of administration (in this case, public works) to the reconstituted Catalan Generalitat, and also in part because of the impact of the reform on their ministries. There was no reason for their resignations to precipitate a major crisis, since neither of the main coalition parties was involved and each was fully prepared to continue the existing coalition on the same basis, but on the following day, to conform scrupulously to political precedent, the entire cabinet formally resigned, as a preliminary to reorganizing the coalition.

The Collapse of the Radicals and Frustration of the Parliamentary System

The governmental crisis provided Alcalá Zamora with a golden opportunity to weaken the Radicals and the CEDA and try to shift the government more decisively toward the center. Rather than immediately authorizing reconstitution of the coalition by the two largest parliamentary parties, he opened another full round of consultations, bringing the Radical Guerra del Río to the observation that "we are in a lunatic asylum." Alcalá Zamora's initial plan was to ask the distinguished speaker of the Cortes, the former Liberal Party leader and now Radical convert Santiago Alba, to form a new coalition that would include all the center-left, including the left Republicans and the most moderate wing of the Socialists, the Besteiro group (despite their notorious opposition to government participation). Alba undertook the responsibility but found that Gil Robles would not accept coalition with any elements beyond the center and quickly gave up.[29]

Refusing to call on the leaders of either of the two largest parliamentary parties to lead the next government, Alcalá Zamora turned instead to the independent, nonparty finance minister and asked him to reorganize the coalition, a decision guaranteed to make the next government as weak as possible. Once more, Lerroux and Gil Robles gave in, and Chapaprieta quickly formed a new government, extending it slightly toward the center by including a member of the Lliga Catalana as minister of the navy. A tiny man, scarcely more than five feet tall, Chapaprieta was intelligent, strong-willed, and energetic. In line with the planned budgetary austerity, he reduced the number of ministries from thirteen to nine by combining a number of ministerial assignments. The CEDA still held three portfolios: Gil Robles in War, Lucia in Public Works and Communications, and Salmón in Labor and Justice. The heavy-handed role of the president, entitled by the Constitution to designate each new prime minister (with the latter empowered to select his own cabinet ministers), was painfully obvious.

The new government was presented to the Cortes on 1 October, where it immediately faced a blast from Calvo Sotelo. The monarchist leader defined it as a "pathological crisis," the thirteenth or fourteenth in the four and a half years of the Republic, in which the government had endured seventy different ministers, individual ministries that had known ten different ministers, ministers who had held at least four different portfolios, and governments of such scant duration as thirty days, all this to the accompaniment of long-winded presidential declarations that were both "diffuse and profuse, full of gerunds and gongorine prose." The way in which

Alcalá Zamora manipulated governments "ignores and darkens the so-called proud sovereignty of parliament." Calvo charged that Alcalá Zamora not only personally determined in almost every case who would be prime minister but also interfered in the selection of individual ministers, which was technically unconstitutional. Thus, "the chief of state currently directs Spanish politics. In my judgment it is not wrong for the chief of state to enjoy strong authority; quite the opposite. If Spain had to live permanently under a Republican regime, I would rather a hundred times vote for a presidentialist than for a parliamentary Republic." In Calvo's judgment, the failure lay first in the fact that the Republican system was hopelessly divided against itself and second in that "the chief of state does not support the counterrevolution" at a time when the "revolution" was more "alive than a year ago."

The main tasks of the new administration were financial, with Chapaprieta planning to complete his fiscal and administrative reform as soon as possible. The new CEDA minister of public works, the Christian democrat Luis Lucia, was at the same time drawing up a new program of public works to benefit small rural communities with improved roads, communications, and railroad service, while maintaining the existing dam construction program. In addition to beginning the balancing of the budget, the new government hoped also to prepare an electoral reform that would introduce some proportionality, reduce the 40 percent quorum, and break up at least the largest districts. It readily won a vote of confidence, 211 to 15, obviously with very many abstentions. Chapaprieta's seventeen basic budget reduction decrees had already appeared in the *Gaceta* on 30 September. They eliminated five administrative sections (*Direcciones generales*) in the Ministry of Agriculture, three in Justice, and so on down the line. Government salaries and fees (*gratificaciones*) over one thousand pesetas would be automatically reduced 10 percent. Half of all vacancies in government employment would henceforth be eliminated, as would 597 doormen in the ministries and three hundred official automobiles. Chapaprieta presented a fuller explanation of his budget to the Cortes on 15 October, explaining that he had already reconverted much of the debt from 5 to 4 percent and had reduced the total budget by 400 million pesetas, while taxes were being raised by an approximately equivalent amount and improved collection during the past five months had added another 172 million pesetas in revenue. Thus, though the government planned to spend 400 million more than previously on public works and 250 million more on national defense, the deficit anticipated for 1936 would decline to only 148 million and would be eliminated altogether by the end of the year. It seemed an impressive feat that astonished the Cortes. In general, industrial production had been increasing somewhat while the 1935 harvest was excellent, creating a problem over how to withdraw excess grain from the market in order to maintain reasonable prices.

Chapaprieta recognized the special role in his cabinet of Gil Robles, who often came to cabinet meetings half an hour early to discuss important matters with the prime minister. In turn Chapaprieta sometimes visited the Ministry of War daily and gave it special consideration in his stream-lined budget.

A final goal of the new government was to normalize political life, and thus all political centers in Barcelona were allowed to reopen with the exception of the extremist Estat Català. Mass meetings continued, Azaña setting a record with a huge turnout (two hundred thousand or more) to hear him talk for more than three hours at the south edge of Madrid. The CEDA announced plans for a rally of "half a million," and the Socialists were authorized to hold one of their own as well as a new national congress.

Political violence had by no means disappeared, but the pace of 1935 was slower than the two preceding years. The government curiously announced that only 140 people had been killed in political violence since the start of the Republic, when the true figure was much higher. All the while *consejos de guerra* continued their work in repression, handing down numerous convictions for long prison terms, as well as more of the ritualistic death sentences that would not be carried out. On 6 October the only conviction for excesses in the repression itself took place, when one of the defendants in the Sirval murder case — Lt. Dmitri Ivanov, who had pulled the trigger — was given the modest sentence of six months imprisonment and an indemnity of fifteen thousand pesetas to the family of the victim, having been found guilty of *homicidio por imprudencia* (homicide by negligence). The last big round of *consejos de guerra* took place in the first days of 1936, when thirty-four leaders of the Socialist militia, including the most active Socialist militants formerly in the Civil Guard and Assault Guard, were sentenced to terms of varying lengths.

It was in this ambience of partial economic improvement, prospects for some constructive reform, and delicate political balance that the principal corruption scandals of the Republic suddenly broke. The first concerned a new electronic roulette-type gambling device, known as the "Straperlo,"[30] whose owners had hoped to legalize in Spain through personal negotiations with various politicians, mainly Radicals. A number of bribes were apparently requested and offered, but legalization never effectively took place and the frustrated owners finally sought compensation or revenge. David Strauss, a Dutch businessman who was the principal promoter, had eventually been placed in touch with the exiled Prieto (who temporarily moved to Holland) and with Azaña, who urged Strauss to write to the president of the Republic, which he soon did.[31]

Rather than turn this material over to the courts for investigation, Alcalá Zamora retained the correspondence, first bringing it to the attention of Lerroux just before the September crisis. The Radical leader brushed it aside as an unjustified triviality (which in some respects it was). For Alcalá Zamora, however, it provided further opportunity for manipulating and discrediting the major center party, his chief personal competitor for political space. The old Radicals in Barcelona municipal politics had gained a reputation for corruption during the early years of the century, a reputation that the expanded catchall party of the Republican years had never been able entirely to shake off. Even though it was the president and the right who had been responsible for the continuing crises since the end of 1933, the spectacle of numerous Radical ministers — led by the indefatigable Rocha — playing musical chairs with Republican ministries, produced the cynical conviction among some that the principal motivation for frequent crises was to permit as many senior Radicals as possible to qualify for the ministerial pension.[32] The party had expanded greatly during 1931–33 as a kind of moderate Republican umbrella organization without a distinct ideology, at least compared to leftist and rightist groups, who argued political affairs in terms of eschatological damnation and salvation. Lerroux continued to rely especially on his veteran cronies in the party leadership, men loyal to him personally but in most cases not especially competent, who often gave the impression of being a group of party hacks (as indeed some were).[33]

Alcalá Zamora informed the new prime minister of the correspondence only after the first of October, and Chapaprieta was alarmed at the potential complications. He advised Alcalá Zamora not to respond to Strauss but to let him take the matter to court if he chose, surely the most sound and appropriate advice. Indeed, Alcalá Zamora might have followed the path of discretion had it not been for a petty incident a few days later. The Radicals had organized several large banquets "de desagravio" (meaning compensatory respect and recognition) for Lerroux after the dubious manner in which the president had just eased him out of the prime ministership. A banquet took place in Barcelona's luxurious Hotel Ritz on 9 October, with Gil Robles in conspicuous attendance, fulsome in his praise of Lerroux. The Radical leader in response added words approximately to the effect that one must always respect the office of chief of state, whatever opinion one might have of any individual occupant.[34] This incident deeply offended the sickly, egregious vanity of the president, and before the next day was out he informed the prime minister that he was handing all the Straperlo correspondence over to the government, which he did on 15 October. The council of ministers took the matter up immediately, having received word that Azaña was about to make public reference to it in an imminent mass meeting. It was decided to announce that a complaint had been received from a foreign source alleging irregularities by certain Spanish officials and was being handed over to the prosecutor of the Supreme Court for investigation.

As soon as the announcement appeared (19 October), the opposition deputies, sniffing blood, insisted on a full parliamentary investigation, and the usual commission was quickly appointed. After the parliamentary foot-dragging of the past two and a half years, the "Straperlo commission" moved with unaccustomed speed, reporting back to the Cortes in four days. According to the available data, David Strauss had first attempted to gain authorization for his gambling device in Barcelona at the end of 1933 and had been rebuffed. He returned to the Catalan capital in May 1934 and was introduced to the local Radical leader Pich y Pon (then undersecretary of the navy) and to Aurelio Lerroux, nephew and adopted son of the party chief. They convinced Strauss to form a new corporation in which Pich y Pon and Aurelio Lerroux[35] received 50 percent of the stock in return for gaining authorization from the government. They won the approval of the minister of the interior, then Salazar Alonso, and his undersecretary (Eduardo Benzo), though apparently no bribes were actually paid to these officials, and approval was also necessary from the prime minister, Samper. The latter's close associate, Sigfrido Blasco Ibáñez, son of the famous Radical novelist, allegedly promised to arrange matters in return for a 400,000 peseta bribe for the prime minister and a lesser amount for the minister of the interior. Authorization was obtained and in August 1934 Strauss presented Alejandro Lerroux and Salazar Alonso with expensive gold watches valued at 4,600 pesetas each, the only money or objects of value known to have changed hands. The Straperlo casino opened in San Sebastián on 12 September 1934, but within three hours was closed by police, allegedly because of Strauss's failure to come up with bribes. An irate Strauss then demanded of Aurelio Lerroux that he obtain the return of all that had been invested, but the latter allegedly convinced him that it would be possible to mount the operation successfully on the Balearic island of Formentera, provided that modest bribes were paid to Juan José Rocha, now minister of the navy, to Pich y Pon, Benzo, and a few others. Strauss then invested in opening the new casino in Formentera, only to have it closed within eight days due to the pressure of local Balearic business interests. Strauss next attempted to salvage whatever he could from his investments — demanding the return of 50,000 pesetas allegedly paid to Aurelio Lerroux and 25,000 to Benzo. The corporation was dissolved, Strauss recognizing the return of some 75,000 pesetas as against 450,000 allegedly lost.[36]

The main document presented by Strauss and his lawyer was written correctly in Spanish but was unsigned and was accompanied by no material evidence of any bribes paid. The truth of all the allegations might be almost impossible to ascertain, the only valuables known to have changed hands being the two gold watches. The Straperlo device was not something forbidden by existing Spanish legislation, and when the report was debated by the Cortes on 28 October, Arranz, the independent head of the parliamentary commission, declared "I would not go so far as to conclude from the material investigated that a crime has been committed." The commission's report nonetheless recommended that all the principals who were the object of major allegations—Salazar Alonso, then mayor of Madrid, Pich y Pon, the governor general of Catalonia, Aurelio Lerroux, government representative in the national telephone company, the Cortes deputy Blasco Ibáñez, undersecretary of the interior Benzo, and two more minor figures—all resign their positions. They immediately did so.

The report caused a sensation, most eloquently symbolized in the words of the Falangist leader Primo de Rivera, who declared in parliament, "Here we simply have the case of the disqualification of an entire political party: the Radical Party." Some days later he shouted down from the Cortes galleries to the deputies: "Viva el Estraperlo!" This became a perfect symbol for the extremists of left and right to satirize the alleged corruption of the parliamentary system. More moderate deputies also severely censured the Radicals, and their allies of the CEDA became increasingly zealous for prosecution. A close parliamentary vote spared Salazar Alonso but all the others named in the report were ordered by the same vote to be prosecuted, despite the lack of clear-cut evidence.

On the following day the two leading Radicals in the government, Lerroux and Rocha, resigned, but this did not become another "presidential crisis" since Alcalá Zamora had no alternative to Chapaprieta. The prime minister reorganized his cabinet with the Agrarian chief Martínez de Velasco replacing Lerroux as foreign minister and two minor Radicals taking the two ministries that had been held jointly by the ubiquitous Rocha. Later, on 19 November, the *cedista* Ignacio Villalonga was named to replace Pich y Pon in Barcelona, where he worked closely with the leaders of the Lliga.

The impact on the Radicals was profound. A lengthy round of meetings was held, but the seventy-one-year-old Lerroux was increasingly listless and had lost all spark. He did not know what to do and offered little defense or leadership. Though still in the coalition, the Radicals abstained in the initial vote of confidence for the new government but seemed incapable of a counterattack or forceful measures to clear their reputation. The general opinion in parliament was that the charges were basically true, even though almost nothing had yet been proven. The Radicals in turn had become extremely hostile to the prime minister, even though the hapless Chapaprieta had sought to dissuade Alcalá Zamora from allowing the scandal to become a political issue and had functioned as no more than an honest broker.[37]

Parliamentary attendance was once more in decline, with the limited appearances of the left and the disorientation of the Radicals. Only an occasional personal attack by a member of the opposition — or on 12 November that of the Radical Pérez de Madrigal against the prime minister — was capable of arousing momentary interest, sometimes to the extent of a verbal free-for-all or tumult, denounced by the speaker of the Cortes on one occasion in mid-November as "a shameful spectacle."

Another scandal broke on 28 November, when the former inspector general of colonial administration, a former army officer named Nombela, made a public protest to the Cortes over improper payment of state funds by Lerroux when prime minister, which had resulted in the firing of Nombela following his initial protests. This murky affair stemmed from cancellation of a colonial shipping contract some years earlier due to nonperformance of services. In April 1935 the Supreme Court had found in favor of the claimant, an elderly Catalan shipping merchant named Tayá, who demanded 3 million pesetas in settlement. The court had directed that a commission of experts determine the final sum, but Tayá, who had had financial dealings with Lerroux in earlier years, managed to make arrangements for direct payment from colonial administration funds through Lerroux's undersecretary of the prime minister, Moreno Calvo. Nombela had protested, and a subcommittee of cabinet ministers had reviewed the matter but routinely approved payment on 11 July. Once more Nombela protested, this time directly to Gil Robles, and on 17 July the council of ministers cancelled the payment, but at the same time Nombela was dismissed. He now demanded justice and the clearing of his name.

There was little doubt that some irregularity had occurred. Such problems, however, are not normally resolved by being referred to parliament where they readily become a political football. Nombela had taken the issue directly to Alcalá Zamora,[38] and Chapaprieta saw the hand of the president, determined to break Lerroux and the remaining power of the Radical Party, behind the appeal to parliament.[39] The Cortes immediately voted to appoint an investigating commission, chaired, as in the Straperlo case, by the independent conservative Arranz. It found that the only person at fault was the undersecretary Moreno Calvo, but this time Arranza resigned from the commission because of the bland language of the report. He was replaced in the final phase by a Liberal Democrat.

The report was discussed at an all-night Cortes session on 7–8 December and was approved 105 to 7, with the CEDA voting to accept and most deputies abstaining. The monarchist minority then introduced a *voto particular* against Lerroux for prevarication and falsification, but he was technically absolved by a vote of 119 to 60. A similar vote against Moreno Calvo, however, carried 116 to 48.

This second scandal — even though no incorrect payment had ultimately been made — completed the discrediting of Lerroux and the Radicals, with yet more complaints about Radical corruption waiting in the wings. The Straperlo-Nombela scandals have been compared with the Stavisky affair in France during 1933–34, when French Radical politicians had been involved in a bribery scandal. Though French politics were rocked by the Stavisky affair, their ultimate balance was not greatly affected and in the long run the strongly institutionalized French Radical Party suffered comparatively minor damage. But in a much more fragmented and weakly institutionalized Spanish system, the combined effect of the Straperlo-Nombela scandals — small potatoes though they were in themselves — was devastating.

There were arguably two reasons for this. One was that in Spain, unlike other countries in parts of eastern Europe or Latin America also trying to establish democracies, governmental officials were generally honest and above-board in financial dealings. When cases of public corruption were uncovered, the resulting outcry was consequently that much stronger.

A second reason was that many Spanish political groups argued in chiliastic terms of absolute morality and doctrinaire ideology. In so supercharged an atmosphere, the spectacle of the Radicals as a normal, democratic catch-all party, given to the ordinary gamut of wheeling and dealing and involved in more than a little small-scale corruption, brought universal censure and the rapid decomposition of the party. The Radicals had limited internal structure and cohesion: they were strongest on the local level of politics, dealing with grassroots issues. They had elected more mayors, city councilmen, and provincial deputies than any other single force, yet these petty local notables were in no position to provide national leadership. Most members were recent affiliates of pragmatic motivation. As the national organization foundered and the bitter, exhausted Lerroux showed that he had lost the capacity for leadership, many ordinary Radicals began to seek new political homes.[40]

Throughout this dreary spectacle the tiny, beleaguered prime minister struggled to carry through his budgetary and financial reform. On one public occasion he took the Cortes to task for the sectarian, partisan concerns of most deputies and their lack of interest in pressing economic issues,[41] and in this he was largely correct. With the Radicals in disarray, Chapaprieta's majority depended on the CEDA, most of whose deputies were opposed to key aspects of the budgetary and tax reforms. When the council of ministers met on 9 December, Gil Robles repeated to the prime minister that the CEDA would accept the modest increase proposed for corporation taxes but would have to vote against other features, especially a small rise in inheritance taxes. For Chapaprieta, lacking any party or majority of his own and buffeted by all manner of partisan pressures, this was the last straw. As foreseen by the CEDA, the prime minister resigned, pointing out in his note to the press that the government's failure was tantamount to "a confession by the present Cortes that they lack the capacity to complete a single regular budget."[42]

The ball was now back in the court of a president who had refused to allow the leaders of either of the two largest parliamentary parties to preside normally over a government, and in Gil Robles's case resolutely denied him the prime ministership altogether. There seem to have been several elements to Alcalá Zamora's grand design. One was to prevent the CEDA from dominating the government, and the second was to drive Lerroux from power, both of which had been largely achieved. Like the left, the president preferred to have new elections that would weaken the right but found himself in an ambiguous constitutional position. Having already dissolved one parliament, albeit a constituent one, a second dissolution might provide grounds for subsequent impeachment. Alcalá Zamora's positive goal, on the other hand, was constructive reform of the Constitution, badly in need of amendment. He had hoped to keep the present government going under his arbitration and manipulation until the constitutional reforms, scheduled for discussion in the last weeks of the year, might be approved, possibly together with an electoral reform law. Even very limited constitutional amendment, or simply a change in the rules for constitutional reform, might itself suffice to trigger automatic self-dissolution of the Cortes that voted it. Thus at one and the same time might be achieved some sort of constitutional reform and the liquidation of the — from the viewpoint of the president and the left — hated center-right parliament, without having the dissolution charged to the president himself. The great unknown, however, was how the Cortes might be kept functioning to achieve reform, in view of the mounting hostility of the CEDA and the incipient collapse of the Radicals.

Gil Robles's calculations were of course different. Though he recognized the constructive character of Chapaprieta's financial reforms, Gil Robles did not make a maximum effort to overcome opposition to them inside his own party. With the Radicals in serious decline, downfall of the present government would leave little alternative to the desired goal of a CEDA-dominated cabinet, with Gil Robles prime minister. Such a government would continue the conservative counter-reforms of 1935 and could at least begin the process of constitutional reform, though it might not be able to summon the 51 percent Cortes majority needed after 9 December. The goal would be a much more rightist reform than Alcalá Zamora desired, with a more powerful executive and an at least partially corporative structure, but the president would have scant alternative other than to dissolve the Cortes on his own initiative. That conclusion was correct, though it did not fully take into account the president's endless capacity for manipulation.

Alcalá Zamora began consultations on 10 December. His first attempt was to convince the honest, well-liked Agrarian leader Martínez de Velasco to form a new center-right coalition as a delaying action, with the Cortes suspended for thirty days. Strong opposition from the CEDA and others, however, revealed this to be impossible.

By the afternoon of 11 December, it was becoming clear that Alcalá Zamora had no more intention than ever of appointing a CEDA government, even if that meant a direct dissolution and all the uncertainties involved. Gil Robles went directly to the president to protest angrily and vehemently such a leap in the dark. He promised that a CEDA-led government could balance the budget with more funding for public works and measures to alleviate unemployment, could complete the prosecutions stemming from the insurrection, strengthen both the economy and the armed forces simultaneously, and also begin constitutional reform, but Alcalá Zamora remained unmoved.[43]

New rumors of a military coup had begun to circulate, and the War Ministry was already under armed surveillance by detachments of the Civil Guard. At the ministry, two senior commanders (Fanjul and Varela) talked rapidly to convince the angry, indignant CEDA leader that the time had come to use military force. Now for the first time he wavered. Another partial pronunciamiento would be a disaster, but if the army commanders were united behind such a move to prevent the violation of constitutional law and an "illegal" dissolution of parliament, Gil Robles would be willing to "decree martial law and transmit the orders."[44] The key figure now was Chief of the General Staff Franco, who could most effectively unite the military. Immediately consulted, Franco was categorical: the present crisis, while destructive, was not of such mortal character as to justify military intervention. Much of the army would not support such a step, which at the present time could only end in disaster.[45]

Alcalá Zamora then asked Miguel Maura to try to form a new center-right coalition, but this move quickly encountered the veto of Gil Robles, while Chapaprieta refused repeated requests to try again. There was now no alternative to preparing for dissolution, but the president sought to arrange a *gobierno de gestión* (interim government) of centrist elements strong enough to build a center coalition that could win the balance of power. His choice fell on Maura and on the elderly former Liberal politician Manuel Portela Valladares, who had shown tact and firmness as minister of the interior early in the year. That Portela was not a member of parliament and had no party backing was not a weakness in the president's eyes, for it would make him the more dependent on Alcalá Zamora and loyal to a new centrist coalition led indirectly by the president himself. Maura, however, indignantly refused to participate in this most ambitious and outrageous of the president's manipulations, announcing to reporters on 13 December that Alcalá Zamora was planning a government "of the worst kind of old-fashioned politics."

A cabinet was thus formed under Portela on 14 December, with the clear (though as yet unannounced) plan of new elections, in which it might be possible to (in the President's phrase) "center the Republic" by electing 140 to 150 deputies from a new centrist bloc. Alcalá Zamora calculated that Portela, who was nearly seventy years old, would require several months to carry out the scheme, and so the government was presented as a new centrist coalition which would begin with the closing of parliament for thirty days, under the president's prerogative. It was composed of two independents (Portela himself and Chapaprieta in Finance), two Radicals (immediately disavowed by Lerroux), two military men (a general and an admiral in charge of the War and Navy Ministries), one Agrarian, one Liberal Democrat, one Progressive Republican, and one minister from the Lliga Catalana.

Gil Robles released a long note to the press on 16 December, declaring that the outcome of the crisis eliminated any possibility of accomplishing the CEDA's economic goals, such as a major new program of public works, government credit to combat unemployment and sustain grain prices, or the strengthening of the armed forces. CEDA representatives in municipal and provincial governments throughout the country resigned, and the party's media launched a massive propaganda campaign against the new government and, by implication, against the president, whom Gil Robles was now determined to oust. The left, conversely, was jubilant, correctly reading the appointment of the new government as the prelude to new elections.

Manuel Portela Valladares when he was the governor general of Catalonia in 1935

The left would immediately dub the work of the center-right in 1934–35 as the *bienio negro* — a "black biennium" of the destruction of Republican reformism, but this propaganda approach is too simplistic. None of the major Republican reforms were annulled by law, except for the drastic reduction of what had never been a very extensive agrarian reform. Much of the labor reform had been allowed to lapse in practice, as was the case with the program of discrimination against the Church, while negotiations had begun with the Vatican for a new concordat. With these notable exceptions, the reformist legislation still survived, and the parliaments of 1934–35 in toto had passed 180 items of new legislation that in several respects complemented the original reforms. What seemed decisive at the time, however, was the veto of further reformism and the general determination to limit what had been accomplished. Temporary outcomes of that sort are normal in representative systems, but to the left it all amounted to two years of reaction and sterility.

The biennium had certainly been a time of sterility, for neither the CEDA nor the Radicals had been able to accomplish their main goals, and all the political forces, with the partial exceptions of the center parties themselves, shared responsibility for this failure. The concept of loyal opposition was totally alien to the left, the left Republicans identifying the regime exclusively with their own goals and projects, denying effective representation or a share in power to their rivals. The anarchists and Socialists were worse yet, while the stance and rhetoric of the CEDA were often provocative and threatening. The monarchists' activity was primarily obstructionist.

There were numerous negative influences at work, among them the destructive power of the large, partisan party press, the influence of pressure groups, and the effect of the financial scandals. The repression was handled very badly and was ultimately counterproductive, winning sympathy for the left among moderate elements of the center. The social and economic policies of increasingly short-lived governments were inept, and even Chapaprieta's reform was inadequate and restrictive. For the workers, trade union organization was highly politicized, and the weak Catholic trade union movement, with scarcely a quarter-million members, failed to provide a viable nonleftist alternative.

Alcalá Zamora was motivated by the laudable goal of defending a centrist and liberal democratic regime, but his vanity and ego were too great to permit him to be a fully functional president. Constant interference made it impossible for the parliament and Constitution to function normally. Nothing was gained by persistent manipulation and the denial of greater access to the CEDA. Even the possibility of Gil Robles's domination of the government and introduction of more conservative and authoritarian features to the Republic would have been preferable to the absolute breakdown which occurred in 1936.

Only the center parties were truly willing to break with the undemocratic forces and hew to the line of constitutional democracy. More effort to broaden the center would thus have been helpful, perhaps in the direction of the Basque nationalists or the Lliga Catalana earlier than September 1935. A more broad-minded policy might also have taken advantage of the split in the CNT. All responsible leaders save the president recognized the importance of maintaining a viable coalition, prosecuting the work of government, and avoiding premature elections that might result in another pendular swing, inherently destructive. If elections would have been delayed until the end of the constitutional mandate, in November 1937, there was at least some reason to believe that polarization might decline, the center might grow slightly stronger, and the economy might continue to improve, while the increase in international tension might actually have encouraged domestic moderation. An amnesty for political prisoners in 1936 (though admittedly unlikely under the CEDA) would have taken much of the steam and bitterness out of the left, and in any case a CEDA-led coalition could definitely have governed until 1937. Moreover, some degree of electoral reform (along the lines of greater proportionality, as strongly favored by the CEDA and the Lliga) would have moderated electoral polarization.[46]

The only large party that supported liberal democracy was the Radicals. Their very lack of doctrinairism and their willingness to compromise made them quintessentially suspect in the eyes of the doctrinaire and extremist groups, yet they were the only sizable force that always played by the constitutional and democratic book, no matter how unfairly treated. The extremist groups of left and right that decried Radical "immorality" would soon be setting to work to murder each other on a massive scale, while the way they would handle state and other finances only a year later during the Civil War would make the peccadillos of the hapless Radicals look like a church picnic. Thus we see that concepts of political morality vary greatly. It is to the lasting credit of the Radicals that for better or ill they stood as the principal defenders and practitioners of a democratic Republic for all, and that must merit them some place in the history of Spain.[47]

The political failure of 1935 was the more striking compared with the contemporary Spanish success in the arts and (very modestly) even in science. The Republic coincided with a general publication boom, producing many series of books and foreign translations. The theater was strong with older playwrights like Jacinto Benavente and new ones such as Alejandro Casona, while the poet Federico García Lorca, brightest young star in an impressive literary firmament, saw three different plays of his premier in little more than twelve months between late 1934 and the close of 1935. Other major new poets such as Vicente Aleixandre, Rafael Alberti, and Jorge Guillén were making names for themselves, while Spanish painters — Picasso, Gris, and Miró — stood atop the international art world. The cellist Pau Casals was already internationally renowned, and new Spanish filmmakers such as Luis Buñuel were beginning to draw attention. Ramón Menéndez Pidal was at the height of his powers and already the dean of Spanish historians; he had just begun the forty-volume *Historia de España* series. In 1935 a world-famous Spanish entomologist hosted the International Congress of Entomology in Madrid, and Spain triumphed in beauty contests, as Alicia Navarro, "Miss Spain" of 1935, won the "Miss Europe" title in London. The country could even boast its first twentieth-century international sports celebrity, as the Basque boxer Pablo Uzcudún had recently fought (unsuccessfully) for the heavyweight championship of the world.

11

The Elections of 1936

IT was widely anticipated that so irregular a government as that of Portela Valladres could only be the prelude to dissolution of parliament and new elections. There were two basic questions: one was the timing of the new contest; and the second, the structure of alliances that would wage it. According to Portela's memoirs,[1] his original agreement with Alcalá Zamora was that his government would continue for at least two months, giving him time to gain firm control over the levers of administration and to construct an effective new center grouping. Only in mid-February 1936 would new elections be announced, to be held at the beginning of April, yet various pressures accelerated this timetable and narrowed the project considerably.

The tall and elderly Portela, his head crowned with a full mane of snow white hair, looked to some observers like a sort of aging magician or warlock appointed to cast a new spell that might somehow overcome civic fragmentation. During the second half of December he busied himself with the usual changes in personnel and replacements of civil governors, in an effort to build a loyal new apparatus of political power as rapidly as possible.

The most notable innovation of the new extra-parliamentary coalition government was the complete restoration of civil guarantees, for one of the few times in the history of the Republic. The leftist press reemerged in full panoply, featuring on the one hand attacks on the military and on the governments of the *bienio negro* ("black biennium" becoming their standard term for the past two years), and on the other praise for the self-sacrifice and supposed achievements of the rebels of 1934. The left Socialists now held that the insurrection, though apparently a disaster, had in fact been a defensive victory, for it showed the forces of reaction and fascism that they would not be tolerated and kept the Republic from swinging completely to the right.

Aside from the prime minister himself, the most active member of the coalition was Chapaprieta, not with financial reforms (which had to be postponed for the time being) but with the attempted negotiation of a broad new center-right electoral alliance that could include the CEDA. Since the left (as discussed below) was known to have been successful in recent months in reconstituting the left Republican-Socialist alliance, it was clear to Chapaprieta that a broad new leftist front could be defeated only by an equally broad alliance of all the constitutionalist, parliamentary forces of the center and moderate right. Though the CEDA had launched a furious press campaign against the president and against the Portela government, Chapaprieta continued his negotiations and had an encouraging interview with Gil Robles on 19 December.[2]

A major stumbling block was the new government's announced plan to prorogue the existing budget by decree for another three months. Something of the sort was necessary, since no budget had been voted, but the Constitution indicated that it was the Cortes which held the power of the purse and of any prorogation. Alcalá Zamora and Portela took the facilely ingenuous position that since the preceding budget had been voted by the Cortes, it was legal for the government temporarily to prorogue the same budget while the Cortes was not in session, ignoring the fact that they were intentionally keeping the parliament closed. Gil Robles protested vehemently in a public letter to the speaker of the Cortes on 17 December, and there was a meeting of the leaders of the various parliamentary minorities on the twenty-third to discuss the problem.[3]

The CEDA leader became increasingly impatient. He judged (correctly) that Portela's fundamental goals were as much antirightist as antileftist, and on 27 December the CEDA announced that it was planning to form "a very broad counter-revolutionary front" but would not negotiate to include any party that continued to form part of Portela's government. When the cabinet met on 30 December, Portela Valladares denounced the activities of various cabinet members who were negotiating outside the existing government, even though he had earlier given nominal approval to Chapaprieta's efforts to deal with the CEDA. The entire cabinet resigned, whereupon Alcalá Zamora immediately authorized Portela to replace all the former ministers, which in fact he managed to do by 7:00 P.M. that day. The new cabinet was composed of two dissident Radicals, one Progressive Republican, one Liberal Democrat, and a number of independents. The note released to the press on the following day justified the new cabinet as a necessary effort to create a Republican center that could overcome the polarization between left and right before it was too late. On 31 December the budget was prorogued by decree, despite the dubious constitutionality of the procedure, and on 2 January the *Gaceta* carried a presidential decree suspending the Cortes for another thirty days. The object, of course, was to allow the new cabinet time to gain control of political and administrative procedures prior to the holding of new elections.

By this point the governmental practices of the Spanish Republic had begun to parallel some of the negative aspects of the Weimar Republic during its last years in Germany. In both cases presidential authority had superseded the normal functioning of parliament. Though this tendency had not gone nearly as far in Spain as in Germany between 1930 and 1933, Alcalá Zamora's intermittent practice of appointing short-term governments without parliamentary support was leading to a similar vacuum of authority and facilitated, rather than restrained, irresponsible behavior by political parties.

On 2 January forty-six deputies of the CEDA, in conjunction with a number of Radical and monarchist deputies, petitioned the speaker of the Cortes for an immediate meeting of the Diputación Permanente of the Cortes — the small standing body that could be convened when parliament was not in session — to indict the prime minister and his cabinet for criminal responsibilities involved in the illegal proroguing of the budget and the "unconstitutional" suspension of parliament. Portela agreed to appear before the Diputación Permanente, whose meeting was scheduled for 7 January. On the preceding day, however, Portela called upon the president and immediately published a decree from the latter dissolving parliament, with elections scheduled for 16 February, and announced that he would be represented at the meeting of the Diputación Permanente by his minister of agriculture.

When it met the following day, Miguel Maura denounced Portela's government in the following terms:

Charges against the government were pending that had met all constitutional requirements for being pursued. And when these justified charges were pending, the President of the Republic, in agreement with the prime minister, dissolves parliament and fails to appear before the Diputación. And this is done through a government which has no identity other than presidential favoritism, and is led by an electoral manipulator certified as such many years ago, composed of six ministers who are not deputies and four others who represent no one. That is twenty times worse than the behavior of the monarchy and has nothing to do one way or the other with the Republic.[4]

Portela would now set to work to concoct his new Partido del Centro Democrático (a sort of updating of Alcalá Zamora's Partido Republicano Progresista), while the CEDA prepared to wage a massive new electoral operation of its own.

Formation of the Popular Front

All the left Republicans, together with many of the Socialists, recognized that the reason for the electoral disaster of 1933 had been the breakdown of the alliance. For the left Republicans, its replacement became a fundamental goal. In April 1935 a unity of action agreement was reached first among three left Republican parties — Azaña's Izquierda Republicana, Martínez Barrio's more moderate Unión Republicana, and the tiny Partido Nacional Republicano. On 12 April, fourth anniversary of the defeat of the monarchy, they issued a joint declaration specifying the minimum requirements for restoration of Republican democracy as they defined it: the reestablishment of constitutional guarantees, release of those imprisoned in October, abolition of police torture, an end to all discrimination against liberals and leftists in state employment, freedom for all trade unions, readmission of all those fired for political reasons since October, and the restoration of all municipal councils ousted by the government since October.[5]

Since November 1934 Azaña and Indalecio Prieto had been in correspondence about the need to restore the alliance, Prieto making use of his freedom in exile to become the most active figure in the Socialist leadership. The line that he adopted from November 1934 on was that the insurrection had been fought to defend Republican democracy rather than to impose revolution, and that the full restoration of Republican democracy must be the basic goal. As early as January 1935 he came to a basic meeting of minds with Azaña. The Socialists and left Republicans must reestablish their alliance in new elections, adopting an essentially moderate program within the bounds of Republican constitutionalism and arranging for a sizable number of left Republican candidacies within the electoral coalition so that the latter would have a strong parliamentary base for a new government made up exclusively of left Republicans.[6] On 23 March 1935 Prieto wrote to the executive commission of the party, outlining some initial plans, emphasizing the importance of alliance with the left Republicans, and also mentioning the need to discipline the Socialist Youth.[7] By the end of the month Prieto's ally Juan-Simeón Vidarte, secretary of the executive commission and de facto head of the party apparatus, had issued a party circular that stressed the importance of Republican liberties, the defensive nature of the October insurrection, and the moderate, responsible character of the party.[8] On 14 April, fourth anniversary of the founding of the Republic, Prieto and the moderate left-center Republican Sánchez Román both published articles in Prieto's *El Liberal* on the need for unity of the left.

Largo Caballero strongly protested any alliance in a letter to the executive commission on 29 April. Juliá has termed this the beginning of *caballerismo* as a separate faction within the party. It insisted on the proletarian, revolutionary, and class nature of the party and the UGT, and protested any movement or gesture toward alliance with the left Republicans.[9] By this time the Socialists were effectively divided into three sectors — the small and impotent self-styled "orthodox" Marxists of the *besteirista* "right," the social democratic *prietista* "center," and the *caballerista* "left". From April 1935 down to the start of the Civil War, the Socialist press would be filled with bitter polemics between the three sectors. On 28 April, the day before Largo's formal letter of protest, Besteiro delivered his speech of admission to the Academy of Political and Moral Sciences on "Marxism and Anti-Marxism," claiming that Marx had not propounded the dictatorship of the proletariat as a desirable or necessary goal in itself and that true Marxism led to democratic socialism.[10]

Prieto's main forum in 1935 was his Bilbao newspaper *El Liberal*, in which he published a series of five articles late in May, reprinted in at least eight other newspapers, on the need for a practical program of broader unity. He pointed out that when the incendiary spokesmen of the Socialist Youth talked about the undermining of socialism, their words ought first of all to be directed toward the extremist and sectarian actions of the Socialist Youth themselves. Collected as the booklet *Posiciones socialistas del momento*, they were immediately countered by Carlos de Baráibar's *Las falsas 'posiciones socialistas' de Indalecio Prieto*, which argued among other things that a new electoral coalition would be futile because, by the time that elections were next held, the *cedorradical* government would have totally changed the electoral law, whereas in fact the entire system should be destroyed.

The new wave of *caballerista* radicalism proclaimed the goal of "bolshevization," of converting Spanish Socialism into the same sort of "revolutionary instrument" as Russian Bolshevism in 1917. Its chief spokesmen were Araquistain's theoretical monthly *Leviatán* and the new *caballerista* weekly *Claridad*, which began publication in July. Araquistain declared that month in *Leviatán* that "today the CEDA is nearer Azaña's Izquierda Republicana than to the monarchists of Renovación Española, and Izquierda Republicana is nearer the CEDA — in terms of ultimate ideals for the Republic — than it is to the Socialist Party." He prophesied that the CEDA would join moderate Republicans and go into the next elections "under a frankly Republican banner." Araquistain concluded that Azaña "and a few others like him" posited a "utopian" democracy above social classes, but assured his readers that such a project would be destroyed by inevitable historical processes. The most extreme statement of "Bolshevization" was probably the booklet *Octubre — segunda etapa* (*October—The Second Stage*), written by Carlos Hernández Zancajo, president of the executive commission of the Madrid section of the Socialist Youth, and several colleagues. It urged expulsion of the *besteiristas* and the complete bolshevization of the party, calling for completion of Spain's October Revolution by a second stage that would construct a centralized Leninist organization with a secret apparatus, a revolutionary red army, and the eventual establishment of the dictatorship of the proletariat throughout the world.[11]

The Socialist organizations had to deal with alliance questions not merely with the left Republicans on their right but also with the small but growing Communist Party on their left. The October insurrection, which the Communists had been able to join only at the last minute after a change in Moscow's line, marked a breakthrough for them. For the first time they participated as a full ally with the other major worker movements in a revolutionary undertaking. Moreover, while the Socialist line afterward was muted — Largo Caballero cynically denying all responsibility in order to avoid a major jail term — the Communists wrapped themselves in the flag of the insurrection and fully identified themselves with it, in the process greatly exaggerating the importance of their own role and winning sympathy among some of the most incendiary sectors of the other worker movements. Their goal was a united front with the Socialists, placing them in a position to begin to take over the larger organization, and from November 1934 through the first half of 1935 they made persistent proposals to the Socialists for broad liaison committees (*comités de enlace*) to coordinate the various organizations of the two movements and even to begin the fusion of the UGT and the CGTU, the Communist trade union. Despite the pro-Communist stance of many of the *bolchevizantes*, the leadership of the party (including Largo and his closest colleagues) persistently rejected these overtures, forming a joint committee only to administer relief for the victims of the repression.[12] The Alianza Obrera virtually died away, and by mid-1935 the Socialists found themselves in de facto isolation.

The summer of 1935 was a time of major leftist mass meetings. The largest Communist rally ever held in Spain was convened at Madrid on 2 June, and there was no doubt that the party was growing. The largest crowds, however, were generated by Azaña, particularly at his huge open-air rallies in Valencia on 26 May and at Baracaldo on 14 July. The size of Azaña's crowds was noted even by the Socialist left. *Prietista* sectors also held a few joint meetings with the left Republicans, and various of the leftist rallies were conducted under the banner of Alianza Obrera or Frente Antifascista, maintaining the idea of some sort of broader union.

At first the *caballeristas* were not impressed. They maintained that nothing more would be needed than the revival of the loose Alianza Obrera. Communist calls for joint action were put down (in large part correctly) to the exigencies of Soviet foreign policy, while Azaña's huge crowds were at first explained as mere petit-bourgeois sentimentality. Araquistain pontificated that Azaña should not forget what his role really was, implying that it was essentially that of Kerensky on behalf of the Bolshevists/ caballeristas.

The initiative in leftist union had been taken by the Communist and Socialist organizations in France in 1934 and produced the huge anti-fascist "rassemblement populaire" of leftists and middle-class liberals (mainly the French Radicals) in Paris on Bastille Day, 14 July 1935. This trend in Communist policy was climaxed by the decision of the Seventh Congress of the Comintern meeting in Moscow the next month to adopt the policy of a political Popular Front with other leftist groups and with bourgeois liberals to close the door to fascism and prepare the way for the triumph of socialism. As usual, Communist policy was to function on several different levels, according to circumstances. In a country where there was a real chance for domination by a worker frente único, that would be preferable, while, conversely, the function of a popular front was not to cancel the possibility of revolution, but to strengthen the left so as to hasten the day in situations where the menace from fascism or the right was strong.[13] But whereas the initiative for the Popular Front in France came in large measure from the Communists, their limited numbers in Spain gave them little opportunity to stimulate such a pact there.

The primary factors in Spain continued to be first the union of the left Republicans and second the negotiations between the latter and the Socialists. During the summer of 1935 the left Republican leaders began work on the definition of a common electoral program, but for some time no headway was made in negotiations with the Socialists because of caballerista opposition. Azaña addressed the largest of all the mass meetings that year in the Campo de Comillas outside Madrid on 20 October. At least two hundred thousand people attended (organizers claimed many more), and this may have been the largest single political rally in Spanish history to that time, with many Socialists and Communists in the audience. Azaña's own speech was reasonably moderate, and he pointedly failed to respond to the clenched-fist salutes of the many young revolutionaries.[14] It was clear that there was occurring something of a movement of moderate opinion back toward the left-center, in revulsion against the excesses of the repression and the political frustrations of the moment. This phenomenon of mass mobilization even impressed the caballeristas, and on 2 November their organ Claridad spoke for the first time of the possibility of a temporary electoral alliance with the left Republicans, provided that the most moderate elements of the latter were not included.

On 14 November Azaña dispatched a formal letter to the Socialist Party leadership, proposing a new electoral alliance with a common program and received a surprisingly rapid and positive response. Largo Caballero by that point was doing another of the flip-flops that had characterized his leadership, if it could be called that, during the past eleven years. He immediately convened the executive commissions of all the main Socialist groups (the Party, the UGT, and the Socialist Youth), who accepted Azaña's proposal, provided that the Communist Party and its union, the CGTU, be included. That was most distinctly not part of the proposal made by Azaña, who had no intention of forming a French- or Comintern-style Popular Front.

Largo Caballero, however, had now decided on another of his *Flucht nach vorn* convulsions. He arranged that the UGT propose to the CGTU to initiate a process of fusion of the two trade union organizations and also adopted the stance that the Communist Party and the CGTU must have the right to participate in approving the new electoral alliance's program. The about-face surprised and angered Prieto and the Socialist "center," for the new *caballerista* tack would shift the weight of the alliance more toward the left and leave the three left Republican parties outnumbered by the four worker organizations. The Communists eagerly accepted the UGT's offer, and the fusion of the two Marxist trade union organizations began on 30 November.

These differences were faced at a meeting of the national committee of the party on 16 December. Largo insisted on the participation of the Communists in preparing the program of the new electoral alliance, even though that had initially been rejected by the left Republican leaders. At this point — obviously to provoke and weaken Largo Caballero — Prieto reintroduced an old issue that had divided the leadership on the eve of the October insurrection. He moved that the Socialist parliamentary minority be bound in its actions by the decisions of the executive commission and national committee. Largo was vehemently opposed to this proposal for his usual not very good reasons, and earlier he had temporarily resigned the presidency of the party over it. He viewed the proposal as an attempt by the moderates to gain political leverage and took the position that in a revolutionary organization all decisions should be taken unanimously (which would doubtless have guaranteed that there would never be a revolution). When the national committee carried Prieto's proposal by a vote of nine to five, with two abstentions, Largo resigned definitively, and was quickly joined in resignation by his three closest supporters on the executive com-

mission. The increasing antipathy, now amounting to outright hatred, between Prieto and Largo Caballero had broken into the open and had helped
split the party. Henceforth the executive commission and the national committee of the party would be dominated by the *prietista* center and the
UGT by the *caballerista* left (even though two of the latter's most important regional groupings in Asturias and the Basque provinces were largely
pro-*prietista*). The UGT had in effect split from the party and henceforth
would function almost as its own separate Socialist movement.

Negotiations between the Socialists and the left Republicans were quickly
accelerated in the week after Portela officially announced elections, though
the official pact of what soon became known as the Popular Front (to
Azaña's distaste) was not announced until 15 January. Largo and the UGT
did not participate directly but managed to establish certain basic conditions.[15] First, the alliance would be strictly for electoral purposes (as distinct from Prieto's plan of maintaining close collaboration with a post-
electoral left Republican government); second, though the new program
would be a Republican, not a revolutionary, program, the Socialists and
other members would make clear the differences between the temporary
electoral program and their own long-range goals; and third, all other
worker groups and parties who wished to participate might join the new
electoral alliance. Thus, though the Popular Front program was negotiated by the leaders of the left Republicans and the Socialist Party, the resulting electoral alliance was joined by the Communist Party, the CGTU,
the small dissident Partido Sindicalista of Angel Pestaña, and the new Partido Obrero de Unificación Marxista (POUM), which had brought together
the Trotskyist Izquierda Comunista and the Marxist-Leninist BOC in September 1935.[16]

If Prieto initially had faced considerable difficulty in gaining the agreement of the Socialist left, Azaña had continuing difficulty with the two
more moderate left Republican parties. Initially, Martínez Barrio had sought
a union of the left Republican groups alone but was convinced by Azaña
that the support of the Socialists was indispensable. Having agreed to that,
the pliable Martínez Barrio did not balk at eventual inclusion of the Communists and other elements of the extreme left. Conversely, Felipe Sánchez Román, leader of the tiny Partido Nacional Republicano (made up
largely of progressivist professional men and a few of the more progressive small industrialists), had always recognized the indispensability of the
Socialists. He was active in negotiating the final terms of the alliance's program, much of which he wrote himself. At the last minute, however, he
withdrew from the alliance which he had done so much to promote, in
protest over the inclusion of the Stalinistic Communist Party.

The manifesto of the Popular Front was quite lengthy. It called for a "full amnesty" for political crimes committed after November 1933 and the rehiring of state employees suspended, transferred, or fired "without due process or for reasons of political persecution." It proposed reform of the Tribunal de Garantías Constitucionales "in order to prevent having the defense of the Constitution entrusted to those whose thinking has been formed by convictions or interests contrary to the health of the reform." Other goals included the reform of Cortes rules to expedite the work of parliamentary commissions, establishing the independence of the judiciary, and investigating and prosecuting acts of unwarranted violence by the police, as well as revision of the Law of Public Order (written by the left Republicans themselves), "so that, without losing any of its defensive efficacy, it provides a better guarantee for the citizen against arbitrary power."

In economic matters, "the Republicans do not accept the principle of the nationalization of land and its free distribution among peasants, as sought by the delegates of the Socialist Party." The manifesto proposed instead economic assistance to agriculture, a new and more progressive tenancy law, and stimulation of collective forms of production. References to industry were more vague, stressing the need for "a strict criterion of subordination of the interests of the economy [as a whole]." The manifesto pledged protection of national industry and encouragement of state research for its benefit, together with new measures for the protection of small business. Major expansion of public works received high priority, although there was no indication of how it was to be paid for. The manifesto called for more progressive tax reform but failed to provide details, while urging more efficient collection and administration.

"The Republic conceived of by the Republican parties is not a Republic dominated by social or economic class interests, but a regime of democratic liberty. . . ." Therefore "the Republican parties do not accept the worker control sought by the representatives of the Socialist Party," but pledged full restoration of the social legislation of 1931–33 and above all support for the wages of farmworkers, together with the full reestablishment of legislation on regional autonomy.[17]

This was strictly an electoral program, not a program for a coalition government. No effort was made, nor could have been carried out, to remove the contradictions between the revolutionaries and the Republicans, whose role the former conceived as basically Kerenskyist. Two days before the announcement of the manifesto, El Socialista, which was not the organ of the bolchevizantes, declared, "Therefore we must say clearly: 1936 will be a revolutionary year. Once the left are victorious, nothing can prevent 1936 from marking the beginning of the revolution that did not occur when the monarchist regime crumbled and the Republic appeared."

The relative moderation of the Popular Front program in Spain has frequently been stressed, but its character can be better understood by comparing it with that of its nearest counterpart, the contemporary Popular Front in France. The latter also represented a heterogenous coalition linking Socialists, Communists, and middle-class liberals (mainly the French Radicals). The goal of the French Popular Front, however, was primarily to defend the existing French democracy against the menace of fascism. It did propose certain social reforms, though these were proportionately more modest than those of its Spanish counterpart, and it included no sizable groups which insisted on a rapid transformation into revolutionary collectivism and the dictatorship of the proletariat, as in the Spanish case. The French Popular Front did not propose major institutional changes to insure the future political predominance of the left, but made of democracy a value in its own right. The Radicals even managed to impose the formal title "Rassemblement Populaire," since "Popular Front" was identified too closely with the Comintern. Finally the French Popular Front provided a positive basis for government, for Socialists and Radicals would collaborate in forming a democratic, parliamentary, and law-abiding coalition. Thus the French Popular Front reflected a democratic consensus (even though of recent origin) and lacked the same degree of radical reformist overtones as its Spanish counterpart. Both Popular Fronts comprised inherently contradictory liberal and leftist forces, so that the French coalition began to break down within only a year, and the same thing would doubtless have occurred in Spain had not the Civil War intervened, despite the radical liberal position of Azaña's Izquierda Republicana. The Spanish Popular Front stood somewhat to the left of its French counterpart, nonetheless, and thus was able — when combined with the hard rightist position of its main adversaries — to contribute to a decisive national political polarization which never took place in France.

The only worker/revolutionary party represented in the Popular Front central committee was the Socialist Party. The Communists were denied a seat by the left Republicans, who in turn offered to admit a UGT representative, but this was spurned. The original Azaña-Prieto plan was carried out to the extent that the left Republican parties gained the lion's share of electoral candidacies, even though it was doubtful that they would provide the lion's share of the vote. Altogether 193 left Republican candidates held places on the Popular Front ticket, compared to 125 Socialists. The other small worker parties were given only twenty-five candidacies, nineteen of which went to the Communists, potentially the only party

other than the left Republicans which was overrepresented in the appor-
tionment of seats.[18] The FAI-CNT officially rejected electoral participation, with the declared intention of campaigning against it. In fact, however, anarchosyndicalist propaganda was weak and vacillating, so that
most observers came to conclude that many, perhaps most, members of
the CNT would vote for the Popular Front, even though such a position
was taken only by the CNT in Asturias, and even there unofficially.[19]

The Socialist electoral campaign was led by Largo Caballero, since Prieto
remained in exile (having never been cleared for his complicity in the insurrection) and could participate only through newspaper articles. On
12 January, just before the official formation of the Popular Front, Largo
emphasized that electoral arrangements did not mean a return to mere social democratic reformism, stressing that the Republic must be turned into
a "Socialist republic." "Let it be quite clear that we are not mortgaging
our ideology or our freedom of action in the future."[21] *Claridad* essentially came to accept the "two-class" theory of the POUM, declaring that
though the left Republican petite bourgeoisie might survive for the time
being with electoral support from the workers, ultimately it would have
to merge with the latter in a worker revolution or return to the bourgeoisie
proper. On 9 February Martínez Barrio—the arch-representative of the
petite bourgeoisie within the Popular Front—repeated his standard maxim
that the task at hand was essentially a "conservative task," but that same
day *El Socialista* trumpeted: "We are determined to do in Spain what has
been done in Russia. The plan of Spanish Socialism and Russian Communism is the same. Certain details may change, but not the fundamental
decrees. . . ."

Despite the continued antipathy of the left Republicans, the Popular
Front was a great boon to the Communists, who urged formation of Popular Front committees at all levels. The Communists strongly encouraged
the unity of the left, much more than did *caballeristas*, and the common
jail experiences of militants from diverse organizations during 1934–35 made
this goal seem more tangible. Relations between Communists and the Socialist Youth, particularly, drew ever closer. To the latter, the Communists
represented a genuine revolution, a categorical and victorious Marxism-
Leninism, and one that preached the unity of the left without giving up
revolutionary goals.

The propaganda of the worker parties, like that of the right, was often
virulent, laden with atrocity stories of the repression. Much was made of
the supposed thirty thousand leftist prisoners still in jail, when the true
figure was scarcely more than half that.[21] Whatever the precise number,
the repression and the lack of amnesty for the thousands of prisoners was

the strongest single weapon in the Popular Front's campaign arsenal, rallying the support of moderates and of anarchists who otherwise might not
have voted for the left. Yet, in view of the massive campaign being developed by the right, there was no overconfidence. Though, logically, the
Popular Front was expected to do better than the disunited left in 1933,
there was no mere assumption of a decisive victory. During a well-publicized
interview on the eve of elections, Largo Caballero gave voice to pessimism
and virtually prophesied defeat.

The Campaigns of the Center and Right

Portela was proud of the fact that the electoral campaign period restored
full civil guarantees for one of the few occasions in the history of the Republic, but he found it more difficult to make headway with his new Center Democratic Party than he had supposed. A large part of society was
politically mobilized and fully civic-minded, so that old-style administrative and electoral manipulations could in most cases no longer be carried
out. In so tense a situation, with nearly all political space already occupied, creation of a new political force ex nihilo was almost impossible.
Portela had hoped to have at least one more month before announcing
elections, but the opposition of the right had made that delay impossible.
About the first of February he tried to gain time by proposing to Alcalá
Zamora that the actual date of elections be postponed until around the
tenth of March (according to the forty-day delay which the Constitution
permitted the president to decree), but the latter demurred, replying that
it would create too many complications.[22]

Portela has claimed that the president's bottom-line request was to do
all he could to see to it that the left gained increased representation, even
as many as 180 seats, while Portela was hoping that the centrist forces might
win at least 100 seats, to mediate between a weaker right and stronger left.
He calculated that the Lliga would win the majority in Catalonia, gaining
at least twenty seats, and that the centrists would win forty more between
the south and the Valencian region, with twenty to be added in Portela's
native Galicia and at least twenty more from all the rest of Spain.[23] Little
of this, however, proved to be within his grasp.

The manifesto of the Center Democratic Party on 28 January rejected
both "civil war" and "red revolution," stressing constitutional process, national unity, and progress. Yet the manifesto itself was vague and full of
liberal platitudes so that, however more desirable the latter than the ex-
tremisms of left and right, the new formation failed to present a clear image. In general, Portela's effort looked more toward alliance with the left

than with the right, but, though the Popular Front seemed somewhat more friendly at first, a regular left-center alliance was completed only in Lugo province, where the prime minister dominated all the political machinery.[24] A major goal was to complete the break-up of the Radicals, winning over as many as possible, but this too brought only limited benefits. Portela enjoyed significant strength in only a few provinces of Galicia and in the southeast, and on 7 February he announced that his party would be willing to ally with the right in districts where entente was not possible with the left. The consequence was that center-right alliances were eventually formed in various provinces of the south where the right was willing to ally because of relative weakness.[25] In Alicante province Portela first tried to reach understanding with the right; when that proved impossible, he dealt with the left, placing the provincial government and most municipal councils in the hands of left Republicans and Socialists. To this the right responded by offering more favorable terms, whereupon the new leftist local government figures were replaced by decree with rightists.[26] The final result was that Portela was able to present candidacies in only about half the country's electoral districts and, when alliances were formed, they usually had to be made with the weaker side.

The most vigorous campaign waged by moderate parties occurred in the Basque country and in Catalonia. Both the Basque Nationalists and the Catalan Lliga mobilized major efforts. The remnants of the Radicals struggled as best they could and made their strongest campaign in Catalonia. Due to numerous defections, however, they were able to field only seventy-eight candidates, and of these only twenty-three were able to gain places on broader center-right coalition tickets.[27]

The right was much stronger than the center but never so united as the Popular Front. The monarchist groups demanded of Gil Robles a broad national alliance of the right on a maximalist program, but this the CEDA wisely rejected. The rightist coalitions were sometimes referred to in the electoral campaign as the "Bloque Nacional," but no such bloc existed, all CEDA alliances being made on a provincial basis. Where the left was strong, as in the south and in Asturias, the CEDA formed center-right alliances. In more conservative Salamanca, it allied with the Carlists and Agrarians, and in Carlist Navarre with the Carlists only. In Catalonia a broad Frente Català de l'Ordre (Catalan Front of Order) was formed by the CEDA, Lliga, Radicals, and Carlists. In the long run, the CEDA electoral strategy was excessively ambiguous and opportunistic, for a broad and more categorical alliance with the center would have probably benefitted both the center and the moderate right, as Chapaprieta had always argued.

The CEDA campaign was in technical terms the most elaborate seen in

Spain prior to 1977. No avenue or medium of expression was overlooked. The electoral message was carried by neon lights, telephones, radio broadcasts, specially prepared short movies, and big mural signs, with 50 million leaflets and 10,000 posters printed. Gil Robles and other party leaders were in constant motion, sometimes traveling by airplane, à la Hitler in 1932. A half million leaflets were said to have been mailed to voters in Madrid alone, and the huge sign in the Puerta del Sol, the center of the city, was three stories high.

The basic theme of the CEDA's campaign was proclaimed in the slogan "Contra la revolución y sus cómplices!" ("Against the revolution and its accomplices"). Propaganda harped on the insurrection, the atrocities of the revolutionaries, and the marked increase in crime under the Republic, not eschewing various extravagances about the collectivization of the family and children that allegedly occurred in the Soviet Union. At times, however, the CEDA seemed to be campaigning against Alcalá Zamora as much as against the left, for the president was repeatedly denounced for having blocked government access and being in complicity with the left, the first charge being valid and the second largely invalid. Moreover, the CEDA publicly denounced quite a few of the manipulative abuses being committed by Portela Valladares in his effort to create a new government-led center.

As usual, JAP spokesmen were more extreme than the main CEDA leaders. JAP crowds acclaimed Gil Robles fascist-style as "Jefe, jefe, jefe" (echoing "Duce, duce, duce!"). JAP leaders proposed to depose the president and give full power to a new rightist executive, dissolving the Socialist Party and writing a new constitution. Gil Robles and the main leadership tried to maintain the party's basic ambiguity, cautiously refusing to commit themselves to a precise blueprint for all the changes to be wrought if the CEDA won the absolute majority for which it aimed. Finally, however, pressure from the JAP forced Gil Robles to announce during the final week of the campaign that the goal of the next Cortes would be revision of the constitution.

The main *tremendismos* on the right came not from Gil Robles but from Calvo Sotelo and the monarchists, who held a clear and unambiguous position. Calvo Sotelo insisted that in 1934 the left Republicans had killed their own constitution and that a democratic Republic was already dead because the majority of politically active Spaniards by the winter of 1936 no longer recognized it as legally or morally binding nor planned to respect it in the future. He reiterated that Spain needed an authoritarian, corporative, unitary, Catholic, and nationalist state. Calvo Sotelo continued to hail the military as the country's "vertebral column" and voluntarily accepted the appellation of "militarist" and "pretorian" (as he did that of "fascist") since only the military could save Spain from the revolutionary outburst and civil war that were looming. He was categorical that these elections would be "the last for a long time,"[28] as unfortunately proved to be the case.

At the same time, there were many voices of reason and moderation. In the provincial *La Publicidad* of Granada, a moderate pro-Republican newspaper, one writer lamented that

Listening to the speeches of the party leaders or reading their writings and manifestos one reaches the conclusion that at the present time none of them has a clear and sure vision nor made a conscientious study of the social, economic and psychological situation of our country in the light of its history and the evolution of ideas and systems in the world. We live amid wildly gesticulating political epilepsy. This seems to be a land of the possessed or of simians.[29]

A significant minority of Spaniards sought a rational middle ground but found most political space already occupied by left and right.

Though both sides constantly emphasized the plebiscitary and decisive, even eschatological, character of the contest, there were comparatively few incidents during the campaign and only a few people killed. The principal complaints had to do with constraints employed by conservative forces in the countryside of Granada, a province in which four thousand gun licenses had been issued in a comparatively short time. The stock market actually rose during the campaign, due in considerable measure to what was often anticipated as some sort of rightist victory, even if not an absolute majority.

The Electoral Results

Conditions for the balloting on 16 February were good, and the elections were generally free and fair. The only areas where there were noteworthy evidences of corruption or coercion were parts of Galicia (subject to manipulation by the government and in La Coruña by left Republicans) and in Granada, where balloting in some rural districts was forceably dominated by the right.[30] Early returns from urban districts indicated a stronger showing by the left than many had anticipated, due in some measure to the electoral support of anarchosyndicalists, and by the late evening it was clear that the Popular Front was winning, though the dimensions of the victory were not yet clear. The official recording (*escrutinio*) of electoral results would not take place until four days later, on 20 February.

It was clear by 17 February that the Popular Front had not merely won

Crowd in center of Madrid celebrating the triumph of the Popular Front, 17 February 1936

but would hold a parliamentary majority. That fact was not contested at the time, but subsequently there was much confusion and controversy about the overall totals in the popular vote, made the more confusing by the irregular functioning of the alliance system. The government never published exact overall figures, and the Catholic *El Debate* was the only national-level newspaper to publish relatively full and precise reports for all provinces and major districts. The results later sparked polemics, and historians would subsequently employ guesstimates strongly influenced by political preferences.[31] These might suggest such broad disparities in the popular vote as nearly five million for the left and less than four million for the right, a figure apparently arrived at by adding for the Popular Front the results of the second round of balloting in several provinces on 1 March, while subtracting from the right all the votes annulled by the highly partisan new Cortes, as well as those from districts from which the right withdrew in the second round. Ultimately the only way to reconstruct the outcome accurately was to compile the original vote totals for each district as reported in the press, a task carried out thirty-five years later by the historian Javier Tusell and a group of colleagues. The resulting totals are presented in Table 11.1.[32]

It is clear from the cumulative totals that the Popular Front won the popular vote, but its margin over the right may be judged either large or

Table 11.1. Results of the Elections of 16 February 1936

Category	Total Number	Percentage of Electorate
Eligible voters	13,553,710	. . .
Votes cast	9,864,783	72.0
Popular Front	4,555,401	. . .
Popular Front with Center (Lugo)	98,715	34.3
Center	400,901	5.4
Basque Nationalists	125,714	. . .
Right	1,866,981	. . .
Right with Center	2,636,524	32.2

Source: Javier Tusell, et al., *Las elecciones del Frente Popular* (Madrid, 1971), 2:13.

small depending on the categorization of the remaining votes of the center and right, which together exceeded the total for the left. Of nearly
ten million voters, 47.2 percent voted for the Popular Front and its allies,
while 45.7 percent voted for the right and its allies. If all the latter vote
is categorized as rightist, then the right is calculated to have trailed by
only 1.5 percent among the total eligible voters, while the votes cast exclusively for the center amount only to 4.1 percent for Portela's Democratic Center, or to 5.4 percent, if the Basque nationalist vote is added.

If, however, the vote is broken down by tickets for each district, a somewhat different pattern emerges. This, admittedly, is difficult to do with absolute precision because of the complexity of the alliance system and the
existence of several minor or incomplete tickets. The nearest approxima-
tion has been made by Juan Linz and Jesús de Miguel, who have made
an effort to separate out individual party totals, particularly with regard
to the right-center coalition tickets. (See table 11.2.) Their results are less
definitive than the broad totals given above but suggest that the Popular
Front directly received about 43 percent of the votes cast, that the right
directly received only 30.4 percent, and the various center and right-center
groups a collective total of 21 percent, with 5.6 percent of the votes going
to unclassifiable candidates.[33]

The abstention rate of 28 percent — compared with 32.6 percent in 1933
— indicated that, despite the frenzy in many quarters, Spanish society as
a whole was not as hyperpoliticized as it may have seemed. It is doubtful
that more than 1 to 2 percent of the abstention could be directly attributed to rightist coercion in the provinces, though a small part of it was
undoubtedly attributable to those anarchosyndicalists who still refused

Table 11.2. Deputies Elected in the *Primera vuelta* of 16 February 1936

Popular Front		Bloque Nacional		Center	
Socialists	88	CEDA	101	Centrist Party	21
Izquierda Republicana	79	Traditionalists	15	Lliga Catalana	12
Unión Republicana	34	Renovación Española	13	Radicals	9
Esquerra Catalana	22	Agrarians	11	Progressives	6
Communists	14	Rightist independents	10	Basque Nationalists	5
Acció Catalana	5	Conservatives	2	Liberal Democrats	1
Leftist independents	4	Independent		Total	54
Unió Socialista de Catalunya	3	monarchists	2		
Galicianists	3	Spanish Nationalist			
Federal Republicans	2	Party	1		
Unió de Rabassaires	2	Catholic	1		
POUM	1	Total	156		
Partit Català Proletari	1				
Estat Català	1				
Revolutionary Catalan					
nationalist	1				
Partido Sindicalista	1				
Independent syndicalist	1				
Esquerra Valenciana	1				
Total	263				

Source: Tusell, et al., *Las elecciones*, 2:82–83.

to participate in elections. The rate of abstention was highest in Cádiz, Málaga, and Seville, where illiteracy and poverty coincided with considerable support for anarchosyndicalism.

The leftist vote was strongest in the south and southwest—the agrarian regions of poverty and of UGT and CNT strength—and also in the east, where the left was well organized and there was an historical tradition of opposition, as well as in much of the northern littoral and in Madrid. It was stronger particularly in most of the main cities where masses were more readily mobilized. Anarchist participation was a real help in some areas, while in certain districts the Popular Front drew moderate or middle-class votes that had gone to the center-right in 1933 but had been alienated by the repression and frustrations of 1935.

The right, by contrast, had done best in the typical strongholds of Catholic and smallholder society in the north and north center, though it had significant elements of strength in various parts of the country. The CEDA remained the largest single party in Spain, drawing at least 23.2 percent of all votes cast, whereas the Socialists drew 16.4 percent and the two left Republican national parties a combined total of 19.6 percent (though admittedly it is difficult to sort out accurately the Socialist and left Republican vote). The CEDA's allies, however, added fewer votes, so that the CEDA gained only 19 percent of the seats with 23.2 percent of the votes, whereas the Socialists gained 21.4 percent of the seats with 16.4 percent of the votes, and the two main left Republican parties 27.2 percent of the seats with 19.6 percent of the vote.[34]

The elections were a disaster for the center, due not so much to the decline in the absolute number of voters as to the consequences of Alcalá Zamora's manipulation and the character of the alliances that the center was able to form. Altogether, the various center and right-center candidates drew about 21 percent of the vote, down from 26.3 percent in 1931 and 22.3 percent in 1933, but in the first elections the center had often been allied with a victorious left and in the second with a victorious right. In 1936 the small center groups had either to run independently or in some cases ally with a weaker right in provinces where the latter had less strength. The machinations of Alcalá Zamora had helped to destroy the only sizable center party, while the effort to substitute a novel ad hoc formation conjured by a strictly caretaker government failed completely. In half the provinces Portela was not even able to present candidates, while the Radicals were deserted by their former voters en masse. The tiny center liberal parties of Miguel Maura and Sánchez Román lacked allies, while the Liberal Democrats of Melquiades Alvarez were scarcely any better off. Only eight of the seventy-eight Radical candidates were elected, six as allies of the right, two as independents. Of these, three were later denied seats by the Popular Front parliament, and one of the remaining five became an independent, leaving only four Radicals under the leadership of Santiago Alba in the final Republican Cortes. Of all the changes in the 1936 elections, one of the biggest was probably made by a large number of moderates who had previously voted for the Radicals and now made up the most conservative wing of those voting for the Popular Front. Radical voters were often more liberal than the party leaders and in the second round two weeks later, apparently even more former Radical votes went to the left.[35] The center won a few seats in alliance with the Popular Front in La Coruña and Lugo provinces in Galicia, probably two of the most corrupt and manipulated contests. Though the Basque Nationalists, who refused to band with either left or right, maintained most of their ground, their vote declined from 1933. In a generally polarized contest, none of the autonomist movements did particularly well in and of themselves.

The absolute majority of seats won by the Popular Front represented a breathtaking pendular swing compared with the 1933 results, yet this was the effect of bloc voting for alliance systems, the Spanish voting pattern in fact being considerably more stable than the outcome in parliamentary seats made it appear. The great majority of votes were cast in much the same way as in 1933, the main differences being the shift by Radical voters and the partial participation of the CNT membership. The main change was thus not toward the extremes of right and left but a shift from the center or right-center to left-center, together with the achievement of leftist unity. Though impossible to measure, there was also the phenomenon of the *voto útil*, the "useful vote" cast by an undetermined number of moderates who figured that either left or right would win and did not want to waste their vote, casting it for the side they opposed less.

Moreover, despite the massive representation of left and right and the virtual disappearance of the center, the tendency of the vote was not quite so extreme as it appeared. The left Republicans led the Popular Front list, drawing the highest number of leftist votes in thirty-six provinces, compared with only eight for the Socialists. In Madrid, Azaña and Julián Besteiro, not the *caballeristas*, drew the largest number of votes, and altogether the left Republicans held 151 of the 263 Popular Front seats. Communist candidates invariably came in last and in fact may have been overrepresented due to their success in winning a considerable number of places on the Popular Front ticket. The fascistic Falange drew only 46,466 votes, or scarcely more than one-half of one percent of the total, possibly the lowest voting percentage for a fascist party in all Europe.

Caballerista Socialists nonetheless argued, with the support of considerable evidence, that in fact the left Republicans had been deliberately overrepresented in the composition of the electoral lists to give them the parliamentary strength to form their own government. The consequence was somewhat to underrepresent the Socialists,[36] while the CNT was not directly represented at all.

The relative authenticity of the electoral map produced by the elections was confirmed five months later, when the Civil War began. The division of Spain into two armed camps roughly conformed to the electoral results.[37]

The Precipitous Resignation of Portela Valladares

The electoral result at first stupefied the right, which had been fairly confident of victory, though none of the rightist spokesmen in the first days impugned the validity of the Popular Front triumph. The electoral process had generally been orderly, but a total of six people were killed in various parts of the country that day, and approximately thirty were injured. By the evening of 16 February crowds were demonstrating on behalf of the Popular Front in a number of cities. Several churches and other religious buildings were torched, with more serious disorders spreading on the day following. There is no indication that this agitation, however, significantly interfered with the counting and registration of the vote.

The first tactical reaction of the CEDA was very similar to that of the left Republicans in November 1933. As soon as the left found that they had lost disastrously on that occasion, they had begun to importune the president to cancel the elections and to form an extraordinary government that would look toward new contests more favorable to the left. Similarly, in the early hours of 17 February Gil Robles visited Portela Valladares to urge him not to resign but to declare martial law and remain in power as a sort of temporary dictator, pledging full support on almost any terms. The difference between Gil Robles's proposal in 1936 and that of Azaña in 1933 was that the former did not propose holding any more elections — at least for the time being — but simply to govern by decree. Portela replied that he was profoundly disappointed and apprehensive, fearing that such polarized elections were the prelude to civil war, but that he could not function as dictator for fundamental reasons. He had presided over the electoral process and was reluctant to invalidate his own efforts, however disappointing the results. Second, he was too old and had no ambition to be dictator. Third and probably most important, he had no political party or organized force on which to rely, nor any appropriate ideology, having been a lifelong liberal. Finally, though he expected the situation to deteriorate rapidly, the full effects would not be felt for some weeks or months, and in the immediate aftermath of the elections there would have been little support for a dictatorship.[38] Portela knew well that worse was soon to come, but he was not the stuff of which dictators are made and therefore planned to resign as soon as possible after the registering of the electoral results on 20 February. When it was objected that this was too precipitous and that Martínez Barrio had remained in office for a month after administering the elections of 1933, Portela insisted that was entirely different, since Martínez Barrio had then been a leader of one of the major winners in those elections and thus had the support of the second largest party in the new Cortes. The steady expansion of disorder only strengthened his resolve to resign as soon as possible.

Army Chief of Staff, General Franco, became increasingly alarmed. Late on the night of 16 February he telephoned Inspector of the Civil Guard, General Pozas, urging the need to quell all disturbances, but, according to Franco's later testimony, Pozas refused to adopt any special measures. Later still, General Fanjul came to the War Ministry to report that disorders were becoming extreme in some districts, after which Franco awoke the minister, General Molero, who allegedly agreed that he would urge the prime minister to declare martial law.[39]

Alcalá Zamora presided over a special council of ministers meeting about noon on the seventeenth, immediately after a violent disturbance had been ended in Madrid. Afterward Portela announced the imposition of a state of alarm, including prior censorship, for eight days, and added in his press release that the president had already given him a signed authorization to impose martial law whenever he might deem it necessary.[40] During the course of the day civil governors resigned in three of the provinces in which disorders were most extensive, and military units were ordered into the streets of several cities to maintain order. According to the prime minister, Franco visited him around 7:00 P.M. to urge him "courteously and respect-fully" not to resign but to remain in office indefinitely, making use of the martial law decree if need be. He promised the support of the army, but again Portela demurred.[41] Franco's version differs from that of Portela in that he has testified that he visited the prime minister about 2:00 P.M. on the eighteenth to insist that the situation was getting out of hand and that martial law must be imposed but that the prime minister simply replied that he must "sleep on it" ("consultar con mi almohada"). He adds that later that afternoon several other senior commanders came to tell him that the army must act on its own, if necessary, but that he replied they must first consult their regimental commanders to determine the degree of support. Since many of the replies received were negative, Franco refused to act on his own.[42]

Portela has stated that at Gil Robles's insistence, he met the latter once more at a secluded spot on the highway at the northern edge of Madrid, again resisting his urging to remain in power and ignore the electoral re-sults.[43] The morning's news from around the country was even more dis-couraging, however. Portela became convinced that it would be very diffi-cult to resist further the left's vehement, almost violent, insistence that all prisoners be released immediately and that the local government offi-cials removed from office in 1934 be reinstated. Therefore he arranged for Martínez Barrio to meet with him that evening in order to inform Azaña that Portela planned to resign within less than forty-eight hours. The news caused visible displeasure to the Republican Union leader, for he and his colleagues were not eager to have to assume immediate governmental re-sponsibility for quieting the leftist masses.[44]

By the morning of the nineteenth, the national press had picked up rumors of military conspiracy and a possible coup that had first begun to circulate during the electoral campaign. When the cabinet met at mid-morning, reports of demonstrations, riots, church burnings, and prisoner takeovers or liberation in several jails were even more numerous than the day before, and the ministers agreed unanimously to resign immediately.

Portela was of the opinion that even the left Republicans were encouraging the rioting, and that they should take responsibility for government as soon as possible. Passing by the Ministry of the Interior en route to the presidential palace, he found Franco waiting to see him. Franco again insisted that Portela must not resign but impose martial law immediately. When Portela objected that parts of the army might not cooperate, Franco replied that units of the Legion and Moroccan Regulares could be moved in from Africa to stiffen discipline. Yet, though Portela agreed with much of what Franco told him,[45] his mind was made up.

He then went directly to Alcalá Zamora to present the resignation of the entire cabinet effective immediately. The president resisted the impropriety of such a maneuver, insisting that the present government continue until the new parliament opened, if necessary imposing the state of martial law for which a decree had already been signed. In the face of Portela's refusal, Alcalá Zamora insisted on calling the entire cabinet to the presidential palace, but he found that the only incumbent ministers willing to face the explosive situation were the two armed forces commanders in charge of the Ministries of War and Navy, excluded by the Constitution from holding the position of prime minister. The caretaker government thus resigned en masse on the nineteenth, not even waiting for the official recording of the electoral results to take place on the morrow, bringing with it the mass exodus of many provincial governors and other local government officials, who resigned in a panic without waiting for adequate replacements.[46]

12

The Left Returns to Power, February to May 1936

THE new left Republican government under Azaña was quickly assembled and took over before the close of 19 February. Azaña was displeased with the unseemly haste of his predecessor in resigning, for it required the new administration to assume office well before the responsibilities of its predecessor had ended.[1] Since the government was to be composed exclusively of left Republicans, he hoped to assemble as broad a representation as possible, reaching as far to the left-center as Martínez Barrio's Unión Republicana (which he partly distrusted as being composed of ex-Radicals) and to Felipe Sánchez Román, whom he respected highly even though the latter had withdrawn from the Popular Front. Prudent liberal that he was, Sánchez Román rejected Azaña's offer, fearing correctly that under the present circumstances the new government would be subject to intolerable pressure from the worker left.

Of the thirteen members (including the prime minister), ten were from Izquierda Republicana and its affiliates, two from Unión Republicana, and one a left-liberal Republican independent. Nearly all were professional men (mainly lawyers and professors), and several were of wealthy backgrounds. Azaña followed Portela's precedent in naming a general to the War Ministry in the person of the elderly Carlos Masquelet, a liberal and pro-Republican general who had been one of his advisers during 1931–33. Masquelet also replaced Franco as chief of the general staff.

Azaña addressed the nation by radio on the following afternoon (20 February). His message was perhaps the most conciliatory since he had first become prime minister in 1931, declaring that

> The government speaks with words of peace. Its hope is that all the nation may share its goals of pacification and reestablishment of justice and peace. . . . So long

as all limit themselves to the constitutional rights guaranteed each of us no one need fear the pressure of the government. Only he who is not at peace with the rule of law and public authority need fear the rigor of the government, which in no circumstance will depart from its duties and the law. . . . The people can rely on our careful fulfillment of what we have promised. . . . Let us all unite under our national flag where there is room for both Republicans and non-Republicans, and for all who are inspired by love for the fatherland, for discipline and for respect for constituted authority.[2]

Public order was a major problem from the moment the government first drew breath. Arson, vandalism, and demonstrations tinged with violence were reported in at least eleven provinces, and probably a good many more, with numerous attacks on local offices of rightist groups and even in some instances on those of the Radical Party. Azaña noted on the twentieth that "people are going to take out anger against churches and convents, and the result is that as in 1931 the government is born with scorching [con chamusquinas]. The result is deplorable. They are behaving just as though they had been paid by our enemies."[3] His choice for minister of the interior fell on the amiable and honest Amós Salvador of Izquierda Republicana, a well-liked architect and landowner of some wealth who lacked the energy and ability for so difficult a task.[4] For the key post of director general of security, the new government appointed José Alonso Mallol, a middle-aged former Radical Socialist who had served as civil governor of two different provinces during the first biennium. Mallol would subsequently acquiesce in the policy of restoring to their commissions various revolutionary leftist Civil Guard and Assault Guard officers convicted of armed rebellion in 1934.

Even more pressing, however, was the need to fulfill the campaign pledge of a general amnesty for imprisoned revolutionaries as soon as possible, for hundreds of leftists were already taking the law into their hands in provincial jails.[5] The Diputación Permanente of the Cortes was hastily convened on 21 February and, with the cooperation of the right, quickly agreed to general amnesty for all convicted of or imprisoned for delitos políticos y sociales since the elections of 1933, conditions that also included the freeing of a number of Falangists amid the approximately fifteen thousand officially released on the following day.

The government proceeded to dissolve approximately half the municipal councils in Spain, in most instances reappointing members of the left who had been sacked in 1934 on the grounds that since the latter had in most cases been legally elected they should serve out the remainder of their term of office regardless of whether or not they had been involved in violent insurrection. Similarly, new comisiones gestoras were appointed for all those (largely rightist) provincial governments where the first leftist government had installed them during 1931–33.[6]

Upon his release from prison, Lluis Companys, former president of the Catalan Generalitat, made a radio speech to his Catalan constituency that praised the effort of October and refused to return to Barcelona until autonomy had been officially restored. After two long sessions, language was finally agreed to by the Diputación Permanente on 26 February authorizing the Catalan parliament to resume its functions and elect a new president, which it did immediately by once more selecting Companys on that same day. The full legal and political system of Catalan autonomy was quickly restored. While still in Madrid, Companys attended a large Socialist-Communist rally in the Plaza de Toros on 26 February, where he gave the clenched fist salute amid red flags and portraits of Lenin and Stalin.

He returned to Barcelona on 2 March to a euphoric mass greeting. Once more he hailed the achievements of October and then restored nearly all the cabinet members who had gone down to defeat. Notable exceptions were the protofascist Catalan military leaders of that affair, the interior councillor Dencàs and the police chief Badía, who did not return. (The latter, together with his brother, would shortly be shot down by anarchist gunmen in one of the few political killings in Barcelona during the spring of 1936). Henceforth Companys would look toward conciliation with Republican Madrid and with the left inside Catalonia.[7] On 3 March, the Tribunal de Garantías Constitucionales in Madrid declared unconstitutional the legislation of 2 January 1935 that had annulled Catalan autonomy.

The Popular Front victory march in Madrid on 1 March was estimated to involve about 250,000 people. The Socialist and Communist components stood out with their thousands of uniformed youth, revolutionary emblems, and party anthems. More important, however, was the government's decree that day requiring all Spanish employers to rehire all workers fired for political reasons or for political strikes since the beginning of 1934, and to reimburse them for wages lost to the extent of not less than thirty-nine days wages nor more than six months, depending on individual cases. On the following day civil governors and district labor boards began to put the new law into effect. The Madrid Chamber of Industry and other employer organizations protested that whatever had been done by employers had been legal under the prevailing legislation of 1934 and that the new edict would produce chaos and crushing costs. Rightists would later claim that in at least one instance a widow left in charge of a business was forced to reemploy a worker responsible for her husband's death in a political altercation.

Second round elections were held on 2 March. These were required wherever the leading ticket received less than 40 percent of the vote, but thanks to the alliance system this occurred in fewer provinces than in 1933, being required only in Castellón, Soria, and the Basque provinces. The right largely withdrew, so that the left did better than ever, though these were generally moderate districts. The right threw their support in the Basque country to the nationalists, who then won in Vizcaya and Guipuzcoa, while the two seats in Alava were divided. Altogether the Popular Front, which in the first round had led for only five seats in these five provinces, gained eight seats, the right (which had led for eleven) added only three, while the center (mainly Basque nationalists), gained nine, including a seat in Soria for Miguel Maura.

The initial response of the CEDA was conciliatory. Party leadership was temporarily left in the hands of the Christian democrat Giménez Fernández,[8] who told *El Adelanto* of Segovia on 22 February that the CEDA was simply "the right wing of the Republic" and would always act "within legality and within the Republic." When the CEDA national council met on 4 March, it declared that the vote totals had shown the party to be stronger than ever, though with fewer deputies because of the way the alliance system had functioned. It promised to continue the "legal struggle" and would support the government "in everything that affects public order and the national interest," while opposing "everything revolutionary."[9] Subsequently, at the first meeting of the new CEDA parliamentary delegation on 19 March, Giménez Fernández dramatically raised the question of whether the party would support "democracy or fascism," and the CEDA delegation opted for democracy, though with the proviso that if democracy became impossible the party would be dissolved so that the members could go their own way.[10] Already the youth group of one of the more advanced sectors of the party, the Derecha Regional Valenciana, was indeed going its own way, having begun secret talks with army officers and others about the possibility of armed rebellion. Though the official position of the party was clear, its more volatile youth were beginning to cross other boundaries.

The level of disorder and violence remained high and would not diminish until the latter part of March. Numerous church-burning incidents continued, and someone was killed in a political altercation almost every day. The biggest disturbance took place in Granada where, allegedly in response to a violent incident by the right, a general strike and mass riot occurred on 10 March, including the burning of the press and offices of the conservative newspaper *El Ideal*, as well as of rightist political centers and a number of churches, and of at least two private homes. Two people were killed and at least seven injured.[11] Even in Pamplona, a Communist flag was placed on the balcony of the provincial government, and twelve leftists were injured in a clash with police.

Most of those killed in political assaults were rightists or nonleftists slain by leftists, though some leftists were also killed by rightists and Falangists. Most of the casualties suffered by the left, however, were inflicted by the police trying to put down demonstrations and riots.[12] In a grotesque gesture, Salvador feebly tried to reassure public opinion that the situation was not as grave as it appeared, the worst incidents being perpetrated by "bands of youths" who were not members of political parties, which in some cases was technically true, though their political allegiance was often clear enough. The standard response of leftist leaders was that the violence stemmed from provocations by the Falangists and the right, and that any actions by the left were simply in response to such provocations. The main leftist leaders occasionally issued statements discouraging violence by their supporters, but the extremist youth groups were largely left free to act on their own.

Though rightists sometimes took the initiative in violence in the provinces, the main affrays in the larger cities were fought by the Socialist and Communist Youth and the Falangists. On 27 February the Falangist center in Madrid was closed down by police for illicit possession of arms by its members. No effort, of course, was made to check leftist centers. The government later recognized that "some fascists" (*unos fascistas*) had been killed in Almoradiel. On 6 March four members of the Falangist trade union, CONS, who failed to support a leftist strike and were employed in the demolition of the old Plaza de Toros in Madrid were shot to death with automatic weapons. On the following day, a member of the Falangist student syndicate, SEU, earlier shot in an attack on a SEU meeting in Palencia, died of wounds. Four days later, 11 March, two young law students, one Falangist and the other Carlist, were shot to death in Madrid, allegedly by members of the Socialist Youth. Since this amounted to the sixth Falangist-affiliated fatality in Madrid in five days, Falangists quickly retaliated. On the morning of 13 March, several gunmen fired on the well-known Socialist leader and law professor, Luis Jiménez de Asúa, one of the authors of the Republican Constitution. He managed to flee unharmed, but his police escort soon died of wounds. Since this was no longer a case of the right being attacked by the left, but vice versa, the police made some effort to carry out arrests, jailing several Falangist students, though the real gunmen escaped by air to France.[13] Burial of the slain police escort then became the occasion for another demonstration and riot. A rightist newspaper office was set ablaze and never resumed publication, while two major churches in downtown Madrid were torched, one being completely gutted. However, the subsequent official statement by the Dirección General de Seguridad placed the matter in clearer perspective than have subsequent writers, relating the *atentado* on Asúa to the preceding deaths of "fascists" in Almoradiel, the killing of the workers on the sixth, and the students on the eleventh.[14] There was one fatality in the disorders attending the funeral of the police escort, and two Communists were said later to have been killed in a bar in a second Falangist attack.[15]

The attempt on the life of Asúa represented something of an escalation, for amid all the violence of the Republican years the major party leaders, though frequently accompanied by armed escort (since 1934), had scarcely ever been the targets of direct assassination attempts. Azaña held a long meeting of the council of ministers, followed by an official statement urging calm and order. What was clear was that the *atentado* came from Falangists, the only categorical fascist movement in the country, a movement to that point generally isolated and frozen out of any electoral alliance by the CEDA in the recent contest. Though the bulk of the violence under the Republic had always come from the left, the Azaña government reasoned that the abolition of the Falange would only improve public order and reduce the provocation and excuses of the revolutionaries. On 14 March the entire Junta Política and national leadership of the party were arrested, including José Antonio Primo de Rivera, and a sweep was made of many of the leaders in the provinces as well. Three days later a Madrid court ruled the party an illicit organization for illegal possession of arms and violent activities and suspended all its activities. In this manner "fascism" would simply be abolished, though in fact the matter was not so simple. The Falange could no longer operate as a regular political movement, but Republican Spain was not a police state. Though the party was driven underground, new recruits to Falangism far exceeded those arrested. With *cedista* moderation discredited, thousands of members of the JAP began to join, while many others made common cause with Falangists. The outlawing of the party did help to effect a momentary decline in violence during the latter part of March, but the rate picked up again by mid-April and then continued at a high level.

The government could not take the same approach to the revolutionaries as to the fascists, since it depended on revolutionary votes. Though leftists might (with some reason) grumble about conservative judges who were too lenient with imprisoned Falangists, the police were in fact more rigorous with the latter, while more often than not overlooking leftists who attacked Falangists.[16] The left Republicans were increasingly bewildered by the inability or unconcern of the leftist leaders to control their activists. *Política*, the organ of Azaña's party, declared on 27 March that

It becomes almost anodyne to repeat that fascism is not fearsome for its numbers but because it can grow through demagogy and sterile agitation. Therefore any tactic founded on a theory of "permanent revolution" has been discredited by its catastrophic results in Germany and other countries affected by fascism. . . . It is incomprehensible how forces that never stood for worker extremism [the Socialists] can repeat methods defeated elsewhere and undergo the illusion of a revolution that is bereft of the process described by Marx.

Luis Romero has presented perhaps the best analytic summary of the dialectic of violence which unfolded during the spring of 1936:

The government proved incapable of maintaining order, and bloody incidents — including deaths and severe wounds — stained all of Spain. Churches, monasteries, rightist centers, all manner of religious art of greater or lesser value were burned or sacked in widely scattered areas. In mid-March a furious iconoclastic assault in Yecla set fire to churches and particularly destroyed a large number of images. On the 22nd the Liberal Democrat Alfredo Martínez, briefly a Minister of Labor in the first Portela government, was killed in Oviedo. On the morning of the 31st a 19-year old medical student, Antonio Luna, described as being of "fascist" ideology, was shot at by three or four gunmen on leaving his home in the center of Madrid. That same day four individuals in Seville shot down Manuel Giráldez Mora, described as *afiliado al fascio* and who had worked as a dock foreman. . . .

Some authors, including José Pla, have published long lists of bloody incidents. Not all of these appeared in the censored press, but even a brief review of newspapers makes clear the large amount of politico-social violence. The limited importance attributed to them, except in the most important cases, indicates that they made little impression on public opinion, unless they occurred in one's own city or region. Pla comments: "Did the existing political formula permit any hope of pacification? This was, in my belief, impossible. In the first place, the political formula called the Popular Front was revolution itself. It meant the possibility of carrying out the revolution with impunity. It was after all the members of the Popular Front itself, the allies of the government who provided their parliamentary majority, who directed, covered and sustained the subversion. . . . " This text perhaps . . . generalizes too much. What happened was the Republicans were required to pay for the victory which the Popular Front had given them. Only very few times did the disorders stem from members of Izquierda Republicana or Unión Republicana; the authors of the attentats as of the arson and other acts of destruction were usually Socialists or Communists, and on occasion anarchists. And although it has been customary to blame the extremism on the followers of Largo Caballero, in moments of direct action those of Prieto did not remain behind.

The rightists also showed themselves capable of direct action, though in this period they usually acted . . . on the defensive. Primarily in the smaller towns supporters of the CEDA frequently took up weapons; depending on whoever drew up the report they might be given the label of "fascist" pure and simple (whether as killer or victim) and there was no more to it. Rightist publicity drew attention to burnings, destruction of property or other horrors without explaining how they began; in some cases it could be verified that they were the consequence of the "death of a Socialist," or even two. . . . Falangists were also active, and from this time forward, even more so; in their cases they boasted of it then and afterwards, which permitted other elements, who exercised greater discretion, to place all the blame on the Falange.

There has been so much exaggeration in books published during the Civil War and afterward that to accuse Falangists became a meaningless cliche. Some deliberately employed exaggeration as a political weapon, but others did so because they really believed. Later they simply copied each other. . . [17]

Romero notes that rightists were particularly outraged by anticlerical violence and destruction and used the issue to attract moderates and people of modest means:

The tolerance of the government, which reacted to the disorders only slowly and feebly, attracted to the right many Spaniards who, because of their weak economic position, precarious incomes or meager socio-cultural circumstances, had no reasons other than religious ones to join those who were their natural "enemies." The bourgeois left which governed at that time — rabidly anticlerical and with a high percentage of Masons among its leaders — thought it found an escape valve for the the left in attacks on the Church. It might even be said that they took satisfaction in them, considering them a just historical revenge.[18]

Some sectors of the Republican left nonetheless reacted with greater alarm than did the government. In mid-March governors of five different provinces resigned due to inability to deal with these problems, and in some cases because they felt that the government was not making a serious effort to maintain order. Ultimately, this raised the question of the future of the Popular Front, which still existed on the political, though not the governmental, level. The distinguished historian and moderate Izquierda Republicana leader Claudio Sánchez Albornoz was one of the first to raise the issue of the decomposition of the alliance with the worker left, and before the end of March he talked with Azaña about the need to prepare for a new and more responsible parliamentary majority, even if without the support of the Socialists.[19]

The Military

The perennial "problem of the military" had supposedly been solved by the Azaña reforms of 1931–33, but the left soon found that this was not the case. The old issue of "responsibilities" that had dominated much of political life during 1921–23 and 1931 was thus resurrected by the Popular Front in 1936. Its demand of amnesty for political prisoners responsible for killings during the October insurrection did not include military personnel who had killed people in the repression. According to the logic of the left, the former were "political" deeds, the latter "criminal" ones. Most outspoken demagogue on this issue was the vitriolic Dolores Ibárruri ("La Pasionaria"), a principal leader of the Communist party, who declared in a speech on 1 March:

> We live in a revolutionary situation and cannot be delayed by legal obstacles, of which we have had too many since 14 April. The people impose their own legality and on 16 February asked for the execution of their murderers. The Republic must satisfy the needs of the people. If it does not, the people will throw it out and impose their will.[20]

The Azaña government found that it could not resist these demands, echoed by almost every sector of the worker left, and on 10 March arrested General López Ochoa, the former inspector general of the army who had been field commander of the Asturian campaign (where, paradoxically, he had been criticized by military hardliners as too lenient toward the rebels). A Civil Guard captain and several other officers were also arrested.

Military pressures for a coup were not entirely a secret to government leaders, who responded by reassigning all the top commands, placing nearly all of them in the hands of pro-Republican or at worst politically neutral senior commanders. Franco was removed as chief of staff and given the command of the Canary Islands hundreds of miles out in the Atlantic, where he would find it impossible to conspire directly with other generals. Fanjul, former undersecretary, was left without assignment. General Goded, the director general of aeronautics, was moved to the Balearic islands, General Mola from a major command in Morocco to the twelfth brigade in Pamplona, and so on down the line. When the musical chairs had been completed by mid-March, one estimate calculated that of the twenty-two top commands in the army, fourteen were held by loyal Republicans, four by conservatives, and only three by potentially active conspirators. Subsequently, much the same policy was followed with regard to Civil Guard officers. A special decree of 21 March opened the category of *disponible forzoso* (without assignment) for officers under suspicion, and during the five months down to 18 July the government shifted 206 of the corps' 318 captains, 99 of the 124 majors, 68 of the 74 lieutenant colonels, and all 26 colonels.[21] All leftists earlier expelled from the army and police units for complicity in the events of 1934 were restored by decrees of 22 February and 2 March.

Hatred of the military was so intense among the left that there were frequent cases of public insult to army officers and even a few instances of physical assault. Azaña noted in his diary that a young aide to the new minister of war, a junior officer of irreproachable conduct, had been shoved around by a leftist crowd, and on 13 March the Ministry of War issued a note expressing "indignation over the unjust attacks" on officers and urging the latter not to allow themselves to be provoked. The ministry also denied publicly that there was any danger from the "military plots" being rumored and declared that the military deserved the respect and support of all, being "the firmest support of the Republican state."[22]

The government had indeed ensured the loyalty of most of the top commanders. The eventual rebellion of 18 July would be supported at the active command level only by the director general of the border constabulary Carabineros (Queipo de Llano), two of the major generals (Cabanellas and Franco), and two of the brigadiers (Goded and Mola). Yet the shift in assignments was hardly enough to avert conspiracy, which had begun among the hard-core right in the military on the evening of 16 February and never ceased thereafter.

A semi-secret organization did exist, the Unión Militar Española (UME), and by the spring of 1936 it claimed 3,436 members or about one-fourth of the active officer corps, together with the support of 1,843 retired officers and 2,131 NCOs.[23] The political coloration of the UME was antileftist, but beyond that its program was vague. It was an almost trade-union-like professional officers' organization, lacking tight structure and leadership, and was not an effective instrument of conspiracy.

A more directly political leftist counterpart, the Unión Militar Republicana Antifascista (UMRA) had been created in 1935 by the fusion of the Unión Militar Republicana (created in Morocco the preceding year) and the very small, clandestine Communist-led Unión Militar Antifascista. The UMRA had no more than a few hundred members, but among them were two generals, including the new director general of aeronautics, Miguel Núñez de Prado. Masonic membership was also important in the UMRA, whose two main branches were in Madrid and Barcelona.[24]

On 8 March some of the leading antileftist commanders held a meeting in Madrid at the home of a CEDA leader who was a reserve officer.[25] Five hours of talk failed to produce full accord or a detailed plan of action, though they agreed to be ready to rebel if the revolutionary sector of the Socialists took power or there was a grave emergency threatening complete breakdown. The retired Gen. Rodríguez del Barrio was left to serve as a kind of liaison and organizer in Madrid, but his efforts during the next month only led to the imprisonment of two commanders and produced no results. A vague deadline of 20 April came and went without consequence. General Sanjurjo was conceded a certain seniority among rebels, but he lived in Portugal and made little effort to organize a conspiracy directly.[26]

Thus by the early spring there existed multiple strands but no effective plot. Until he fell ill, Rodríguez del Barrio tried to coordinate schemes in Madrid with several other generals, Sanjurjo vegetated in semi-isolation abroad, Franco took a command out in the Atlantic Ocean, and the various UME groups were uncertain and lacking organization. The Carlists semi-secretly trained their own militia but were noteworthy only in the province of Navarre. The Falange had been dissolved and its members driven underground. Even so, they rapidly increased in numbers. Part of the JAP were now turning toward the Falange or in a few areas making their own paramilitary plans, but after 19 February the CEDA leaders had quickly returned to legality. Calvo Sotelo and the more extreme monarchists preached a corporative dictatorship sponsored by the military but lacked direct support, either civilian or military.

The prime minister and minister of war were aware that plotting was afoot but feared to purge the military directly, for several reasons. On the one hand, they held army officers in low esteem and doubted their ability to organize an effective revolt. On the other, they could not abandon altogether efforts at coexistence with the right. There existed the further paradox that the army was ultimately the only protection of the Azaña government from the revolutionary left, should the Popular Front break down. Thus the government hesitated to go beyond tepid gestures such as a decree of 18 April which allowed the government to suspend the pension of any retired officer found to belong to an illicit political organization, such as the Falange. The government was playing with fire, or more precisely, was playing with two different fires, and feared to try to extinguish either one altogether for fear that the other would get out of control. This policy, such as it was, continued for five months until it ended in disaster.

The Socialist Split Deepens

The electoral victory did not resolve the divisions within the Socialists' ranks, but only deepened them, for it immediately raised the question of how the victory was to be used. The *prietistas* continued to maneuver for a relatively moderate course in alliance with left Republicans, while *caballeristas* steadfastly vetoed participation in the government, and even, in some cases, cooperation with it. They insisted on a radical policy that would seek alliance with the Communists and even the CNT.

The main internal issue facing the Socialists was national leadership, since Largo had resigned his position in December and the present executive commission was more than three years old, having been chosen after the XIII Party Congress of October 1932. On 8 March new elections were held for the leadership of the Madrid section of the party and these were won by the *caballeristas*—who usually referred to themselves as "de izquierdas" (leftist) or "revolucionarios marxistas"—by a margin of three to one. The left Socialists thus held control of the Madrid section of the party and of most of the UGT, their main base of support. The *prietistas*—otherwise called "centrista" or "moderates"—held control of the national party apparatus, the direction of the party daily *El Socialista*, the strong Basque section of the UGT,[27] and also much of the Asturian section of the UGT. Yet, after the resignation of Largo and three supporters from the executive commission, the withdrawal of two other members meant that the present executive commission consisted of Prieto and four supporters, altogether less than half the nominal membership. A new party congress would be crucial. The *caballeristas* insisted it be held in their Madrid stronghold, while the *prietistas* opted for delay and a possible autumn congress in Asturias, where they were stronger. The result was stalemate, with neither leftists nor moderates able to impose their policy on each other.

The basic strategy of the left Socialists was to arrange for the Azaña government, after swiftly completing its putatively Kerenskyist task, to give way to a Socialist government, presumably (though never clearly) by legal means. Since the party held only a fifth of the votes in parliament, a Socialist-led revolutionary government would have to be a coalition supported by the Communists and others; in its initial stages it would require the voting support of the left Republicans, as well. In other words, the present relationship of the Socialists and left Republicans would have to be reversed. There was no plan or preparation for a direct revolutionary takeover, despite much rhetoric about the "dictatorship of the proletariat." The only other alternative considered was the necessary response to a military or rightist coup attempt, which would take the form of a revolutionary general strike, presumably followed by the transfer of power to a Socialist-led regime, though possibly not immediately.

In this situation the Communist Party was able to play a role of some modest significance for the first time. Sixteen Communist deputies made the party a minor parliamentary force (thanks also in part to the *caballeristas*), and Communist influence was bolstered by close relations with the Socialist Youth, the assistance provided to victims of the repression by the Socorro Rojo Internacional (International Red Relief), and by a multitude of front and auxiliary organizations, from women's cultural and sport groups to the formal Amigos de la URSS (Friends of the USSR). The party was a strong defender of both the Popular Front in general and the Azaña administration in particular, even though only for the short term. Communist demands of the government included not merely completion of the Popular Front platform, but also land expropriation on a large scale without compensation and the effective elimination of the rightist parties through either judicial, legislative, or government action, as in the outlawing of the Falange. After this was done, the Azaña administration was expected to give way to a revolutionary leftist coalition which would be termed a "Worker-Peasant Government." Even this, however, was still to be a preliminary stage, and at a joint Communist-Socialist meeting in Madrid just before the elections, the secretary of the Communist Party, José Díaz, had stressed that a "Worker-Peasant Government does not mean either the dictatorship of the proletariat or the construction of socialism,"[28] which would be the third, not the second, phase in a three-phase process. Communist leaders subsequently chided *caballeristas* for loose talk about the dictatorship of the proletariat.

The Communist leadership urged creation of "Bloques Populares" representing the Popular Front groups at the local and provincial levels throughout Spain, separate "Worker Alliances" of all the worker groups, and organic unity with the Socialists. Fusion of the small Communist CGTU with the UGT was carried out during the first months of 1936. On 4 March the Communist central committee dispatched a long letter to the Socialist executive commission, proposing formation of a permanent liaison committee that would lead to creation of a united Marxist-Leninist party. Its basis would be:

Complete independence vis-à-vis the bourgeoisie and a complete break of the social democratic bloc with the bourgeoisie; prior achievement of unity of action; recognition of the need for the revolutionary overthrow of the domination of the bourgeoisie and the installation of the dictatorship of the proletariat in the form of Soviets; renunciation of support for the national bourgeoisie in the event of an imperialist war; construction of the unified party on the basis of democratic centralism, assuring unity of will and of action, tempered by the experience of the Russian Bolsheviks.

The unified party would lead a broader Worker-Peasant Alliance into a Worker-Peasant Government that would eventually supplant the Azaña administration. Such a regime would prepare the way for socialism by confiscating all large estates, nationalizing large industry, and replacing the armed forces with a revolutionary Red Guard.[29] At that time the only more extreme proposal came from the POUM, which urged an alliance of all the revolutionary groups to proceed directly to a revolutionary socialist regime.

During the electoral campaign the sixty-six-year-old Largo had stressed that the left Socialists were not separated from the PCE by "any great difference. What am I saying! By any difference at all!" He added, "the fundamental point: the conquest of power cannot be made through bourgeois democracy." Largo had lamented that "there were even Socialists" who failed to perceive the beauty of a Socialist-Communist dictatorship and still "speak against all dictatorships."[30]

On 5 March the executive commission of the UGT proposed to the party executive that a new joint committee be formed of two representatives from each of the worker parties to unite energies for completion of the Popular Front program. Two weeks later, the *caballerista* leadership of the Madrid section of the party announced that it would urge the next party congress to give priority to creation of a united party with the Communists.

It was in this climate that the *besteirista* Gabriel Mario de Coca published a brief book criticizing the "bolshevization of the party." He concluded:

> I close my work with the impression of Bolshevist victory in every sector of the party. The Socialist parliamentary minority in the Cortes will be impregnated with a strong Leninist tone. Prieto will have few deputies on his side while Besteiro will be completely isolated as a Marxist dissenter. . . .
>
> The outlook that all this leaves for the future of the working class and of the nation could not be more pessimistic. The Bolshevik centipede dominates the proletariat's horizon, and Marxist analysis indicates that it is on its way to another of its resounding victories. So that if in October 1934 it only achieved a short-lived Gil Robles government accompanied by the suspension of the constitution and the most horrible, sterile shedding of working class blood, it can now be expected to complete its definitive work in the future.[31]

This prophecy, accurate as a long-term prognosis, nonetheless exaggerated the situation as of March 1936. The *prietista* domination of the Socialist Party apparatus meant that all direct Communist proposals would be completely stonewalled so long as the centrists remained in control, and no process of party fusion in fact ever began, while the internal chasm between Socialist left and center continued to broaden. *Claridad* published on 19 March the goals of the Socialist left: a worker regime, collectivization of property, "confederation" of the "Iberian nationalities," and dissolution of the regular army, but none of this was accepted as an immediate working goal by the *prietista* leadership.

Communist fusion tactics were successful only with the Socialist Youth. On 5 April the United Socialist Youth (JSU) was officially created, merging the forty thousand or more members of the Socialist Youth with their three-thousand-member Communist counterparts on terms which amounted to a takeover by the Communist leadership.[32] Communist orators made the most extreme speeches of any group of party leaders during the spring of 1936, and on 1 April *Mundo Obrero* urged, "All power for the Worker-Peasant Alliances, which on the national level will be the organs charged with exercising the dictatorship of the proletariat, superseding the bourgeois democratic phase rapidly, transforming it into the socialist revolution."

For the moment, however, the Communists supported the Azaña administration more fully than did the Socialist left. More than the latter, the Communists opposed the massive strike wave that was beginning, calling it premature and counterproductive, which of course it was. For the moment, they proposed only a radical extension of the agrarian reform, to be paid for with government bonds. During these months the party came up with the concept of the "pueblo laborioso" — the "working people," not in the sense of the working class but of all who were productive, including smallholders, the lower middle class, and even the "nonfascist" sector of the bourgeoisie. Communist strategists grasped that no simple jump could be made into a revolutionary regime and that temporary maintenance of the Popular Front was important. Party membership was expanding rapidly, and the PCE became a genuine mass party for the first time with a fully developed structure, though whether it really had the 100,000 members it claimed by June is open to some doubt.[33]

Apart from the Communists, the other concern of Largo and the UGT leadership was some form of joint action with the CNT. The latter was wary and rebuffed UGT overtures, which sometimes aimed at alliance and even spoke vaguely of fusion. CNT spokesmen lamented that "no one ever knows how this would be organized, but it frequently seems directed toward absorption"[34] of the CNT, and always concluded that "the Spanish revolution will be of a libertarian type"[35] and not Marxist-Leninist. Nonetheless, by the spring of 1936, there was more fraternal feeling between CNT and UGT members than for many years. The common experience of the repression had brought them closer together, as did the common expectation of decisive new victories. There would be many joint UGT-CNT strikes that spring, even though strong rivalry would remain, as well.

In this situation of spreading violence, mushrooming strikes, and more and more bluster about revolution, yet a new symptom appeared soon after the beginning of April: the distribution of false leaflets, apparently concocted by rightist agent provocateurs, containing detailed plans for violent revolution, with blacklists of rightists to be eliminated.[36] The extreme right was eager to bring all this prerevolutionary agitation to a close, yet realized that the opportunity would not present itself unless provocation and polarization were carried at least one step further.

The *Comisión de Actas*

The Cortes opened on 15 March with a pro forma session presided over by the "presidente de edad" (oldest member), a well-known rightist from Cádiz. His refusal to close the session with "Viva la República" led to tumult, and the Communist deputies sang the "International" in the Spanish parliament for the first time. Thirty-three political parties were represented. There had been a large turnover of deputies, with a host of new faces. Even among the Socialists, who with the CEDA enjoyed the greatest continuity in size of delegation between 1933 and 1936, nearly half the party's deputies were new to parliament. The Cortes approved continuation of the existing "state of alarm" for another thirty days (it would in fact remain permanent until the beginning of the Civil War), and on the following day Martínez Barrio was elected president (speaker). More incidents soon followed. On 20 March several leftist deputies were physically restrained from an assault on a conservative member.[37]

Under the Republican system, the first major task of a new parliament was to elect a *comisión de actas* to review the electoral results and determine if they should be cancelled or reversed in any district, due to fraud or other improprieties. This meant in effect that the victors in each election had the power to sit in judgment on the losers and determine if their parliamentary representation should be reduced still further. This power was exercised with moderation by the center-right in 1933, but the Popular Front intended to conduct a sweeping review of all the districts won by the center and right in 1936. The extreme left demanded cancellation of nearly all rightist victories,[38] judging, as *El Socialista* put it on 20 March, that "not a single rightist deputy can be said to have won his seat honestly." Membership of the *comisión* was voted on 17 March with a heavy leftist majority.

As Carlos Seco Serrano has explained it: "The leftist majority was not so absolute as to provide the complete quorum required for the automatic approval of legislation. The Comisión de Actas would soon act to correct this, reassigning a sufficient number to beat all the records of the old monarchist regime in manipulation."[39] Or, in the words of Madariaga:

Diego Martínez Barrio, speaker of the Cortes in 1936

With a majority won, it was easy to make it overwhelming. . . . The Popular Front elected a Comisión de Actas that proceeded in an arbitrary manner. All the results were annulled in certain provinces where the opposition had won, while friendly candidates who had lost were declared elected. Thus various deputies from the minority were evicted from parliament. This was not merely the result of blind and sectarian passion, but the execution of a deliberate plan of broad scope. Two results were sought: to make of parliament a convention, smash the opposition and guarantee the strength of the most moderate sectors of the Popular Front.[40]

The decisive votes on the Comisión de Actas were those of the left Republicans, although they were constantly pressured by the worker parties. It was decided not to challenge the results in a number of provinces impugned by the extreme left, where though there was held to be a "moral certainty" of rightist fraud or coercion, the evidence was weaker. The Comisión began on 24 March by annulling the election of two conservative candidates in Burgos and Salamanca. When the rightist deputies asked for investigation of the close leftist victory in Valencia and the Popular Front triumph in Cáceres, their request was ignored, and on 31 March the rightist deputies temporarily withdrew from parliament.

The nearest thing to a clear example of fraud and coercion may have been the election in Granada. Seventy affidavits were obtained from citizens there attesting to threats of force, economic pressure, and vote fraud.

In a number of poor pueblos no votes were recorded for the left, while in one mountain town (Huéscar) all two thousand votes were recorded for the right.[41] Since the elections, a total of 10,298 firearms had been confiscated in the province, mainly from the right. Though a full and careful presentation of all evidence was not completed, the results were annulled and new elections mandated.[42] A somewhat similar verdict was rendered for Cuenca province, where it was judged that if all fraudulent votes were thrown out, the victorious right would hold less than the required 40 percent, though in this case the evidence was more dubious and the Basque nationalists refused to vote with the majority, as they had done previously.

The region of Galicia had the worst record for electoral manipulation, but the Radical minority was unsuccessful in obtaining any reexamination of the Popular Front vote in Pontevedra. The leftist triumph in La Coruña, though procedurally somewhat dubious, was similarly allowed to stand. There was much more interest in annulling the rightist vote in Orense, for that would deprive Calvo Sotelo of a seat. Ibárruri's extremely incendiary and scurrilous speech encouraging the Comisión to throw out this vote proved too overheated, however, and somewhat counterproductive. Calvo Sotelo was himself allowed to speak and made a telling address. He pointed out the unlikelihood of there having been as many as 106,000 fraudulent votes, as alleged by the Communists, and dwelled on the contradictions in the review process. If Spain were to have a Marxist or totalitarian dictatorship, elections would be of no consequence, but if a democratic Republic were to continue, it could only be on the basis of respecting electoral results. He concluded by comparing the current purge with Hitler's elimination of Communist deputies as soon as he became chancellor, and this seemed to give the left Republicans some pause. The majority reconsidered, much to the anger of the extreme left, and Calvo Sotelo was permitted to keep his seat.

The final result was the complete annulment of the elections in Cuenca and Granada, both of which the right had won, and partial annulments affecting one or more seats in Albacete, Burgos, Ciudad Real, Jaén, Orense, Oviedo, Salamanca, and Tenerife. New elections would be held in the first two provinces, and elsewhere seats were simply reassigned to the Popular Front majority, though the center also gained a few seats and in Jaén a seat taken from the Radicals was awarded to the CEDA so as not to appear totally partisan. No evidence was produced to demonstrate clear, overt fraud except in Granada and perhaps in parts of Galicia.[43] Irregularities in Galicia were mostly ignored, since there they had benefitted the Popular Front more than the right. In no case, needless to say, was a seat taken

Dolores Ibárruri, "La Pasionaria"

from the left. The right charged that the elections had been stolen by the left in four or five provinces where the disorders of 17–20 February had made it possible to falsify the electoral results. This was categorically denied by the Popular Front deputies on the Comisión, and the charges were never investigated. Altogether thirty-two seats changed hands, mostly to the Popu-

lar Front, Martínez Barrio's relatively small Unión Republicana benefitting more than any other single party. After all these reassignments of
seats, the final composition of the Cortes was 277 seats for the left, 60 for
the center, and 131 for the right.

During the course of this reorganization of electoral results, the chairman of the Comisión, Indalecio Prieto, resigned. His decision was prompted
not because he objected to invalidating fraudulent rightist votes in principle, but because he felt that the Popular Front majority was going too
far. He also would have preferred to see a more nonpartisan investigation
of the electoral process in Galicia, though there Alcalá Zamora seemed
at first as concerned to protect the machinations of the Portela administration as the Popular Front was those of the left.[44]

The final judgment by the most thorough study of the electoral process
concludes:

> If irregularities did not alter the proportionate total votes gained by each side,
> the number of seats, quite aside from the effects produced by the electoral law,
> was gravely affected by the work of the Comisión de Actas, which can accurately
> be called distressing. If it is appropriate to accuse the right at that time of hav-
> ing a mentality more reactionary than conservative and of having exploited the
> most politically ignorant sector of the electorate, it is also appropriate to charge
> the left with looking more toward momentary benefits than the long term and of
> having acted in a totally partisan manner in determining the validity or invalidity
> of the voting. The left should have understood that, in the long run, they would
> have benefitted more from the consolidation of the democratic system than by
> creating a momentarily larger majority, encouraging the right to adopt the path
> of subversion. Moreover, this was especially the responsibility of the Republican
> left, since the Communists and a large number of Socialists had already placed
> themselves outside the democratic system. It was the Republican left, which theo-
> retically constituted the firmest support of the Republic, which benefitted most
> from the redistribution of seats and which, even so, was subsequently incapable
> of facing up to extremism in the new Cortes directly. Finally, it was the Republi-
> can left which, after the personal intervention of Azaña to prevent the exclusion
> of Calvo Sotelo, made reference, in the words of one of its deputies, to the "need
> to sacrifice." That phrase is sufficiently expressive of its abandonment of demo-
> cratic practice.[45]

Alcalá Zamora this time agreed with the right:

> . . . Though the Popular Front's parliamentary delegation was near an absolute
> majority, certainly with more than 200 seats, it still failed to achieve the majority
> in the voting. It achieved an absolute majority, and even an overwhelming one,
> in the post-electoral administration, full of violence and manifest illegality. . . .
> The flight of civil governors and their tumultuous replacement with anonymous

and even irresponsible replacements permitted the registration of votes to be made by amateurs, mailmen, wandering workers or simply by crooks with whom anything was possible. . . . And in the second-round elections on 1 March, even though few seats were involved, fraud was employed and the government got what it wanted. How many results were falsified? . . . Cáceres could not be denied . . . and with regard to . . . all Galicia, as was also the case unfortunately with Almería, all the results should have been nullified even though they appeared to be properly registered. The most general calculation of the number of post-electoral changes would be eighty seats, though of that approximate number . . . not all were done for the benefit of the Popular Front, since the price of complicity was to give some to the opposition. . . .

The worst and most audacious frauds were carried out by the Comisión de Actas. . . . In the parliamentary history of Spain, never very scrupulous, there is no memory of anything comparable to what the Comisión de Actas did in 1936.[46]

The Resumption of Radical Reform

The policy of the new Azaña administration would be more directly interventionist and more radical than that of 1931–33, for several reasons. The most important was doubtless the pressure of the worker parties, but this theoretically suited the leftward turn taken by Izquierda Republicana on its official formation in 1934, much more statist and interventionist than its predecessor, Acción Republicana. Though there had been some recovery from the depression during 1934–35, this improvement had not affected unemployment, which continued to worsen, totalling 843,872 by the end of February 1936.[47] This figure included the only partially unemployed but amounted to nearly 9 percent of the active population.

As usual, the keenest tensions were in the countryside. The winter of the Popular Front victory was extremely rainy, the wettest of the century to that point, resulting in heavy farm losses and increased rural unemployment. Whereas urban unemployment had risen only 5 percent, rural unemployment in some areas increased by more than 20 percent. The coincidence of increased privation and the electoral triumph of the left produced rapid expansion of rural syndicates once more, as they regained their 1933 level of membership and increased further.[48] The radicalization of the mood of farmworkers was extreme. On 3 March villagers in Cenicientos, a small hill town in Madrid province, occupied grazing land which they claimed had earlier been part of village common lands and were now largely abandoned. This was the first in a lengthy series of illegal direct occupations of land involving scores of villages and tens of thousands of farmworkers and smallholders first in Madrid, Toledo, Salamanca, and Murcia, and then in other provinces of the center and south.

The government intended to respond much more rapidly and sweep-ingly than before. The new director of the Institute of Agrarian Reform declared before the end of February: "The concept of private property, with all its privileges and prerogatives, is, as far as the land is now concerned, obsolete in fact as well as in theory."[49] Mariano Ruiz Funes, the minister of agriculture, published a decree on 3 March encouraging yunteros who had been evicted in Extremadura during the preceding year to petition for restoration. These terms were rapidly expanded and by 20 March, "he elimi-nated all other exemptions and authorized the Institute of Agrarian Reform to occupy immediately any farm anywhere in Spain if it seemed socially necessary."[50] This measure was an effort (ironically made possible by a clause in the revised legislation of 1935) to head off direct action by the landless, but soon failed altogether in that regard.

Despite Ruiz Funes's efforts to expedite the process, settlement of yunteros moved at a measured rhythm for two weeks, some three thousand gain-ing authorization to occupy land. The Socialist FNTT decided this was too slow, and at dawn on 25 March they launched a mass occupation of land in Badajoz province, with about sixty thousand farmworkers and renters participating. Though troops were ordered in by Azaña and some activists arrested, the government soon gave in, withdrawing the troops and releasing prisoners on the thirtieth. The mass occupation was resumed, then legalized ex post facto by the government.

A lull set in with the spring season. For the spring grain harvest, the government reestablished the *turno rigoroso* (though not *términos munici-pales*), replaced the presidents of *jurados mixtos*, and began to impose heavy fines on landowners who violated the new labor contracts. These measures, though more extensive than those taken during 1931–33, were unsuccess-ful in preventing a massive outbreak of rural strikes. The Ministry of Agri-culture recorded 192 between 1 May and 18 July, approximately equaling the total for all 1932 and nearly half as many as during the preceding peak twelve-month period (1933). Socialists and anarchists now often cooper-ated, producing broad district stoppages. During some weeks in late spring, at least 100,000 farmworkers were on strike at a time.

Rural labor costs increased enormously, at a much higher rate than dur-ing 1931–33. In many provinces harvest wages were set at eleven to thir-teen pesetas a day, approximately twice the rates for 1935, and at least 20 percent more than in 1933. Moreover, rural unions often imposed agree-ments on limiting machinery and other structural reforms. *Turno rigoroso* meant taking on many inexperienced local registered workers, while the policy of labor *alojamiento* (direct assignment or "lodging" of workers on a specific piece of land) was frequently imposed, in some cases workers directly taking over land to work or requiring more workers to be hired than there was work for. Though by June even the government was publicly insisting that wages should be based on achievement of a specified production norm, the syndicates seem to have agreed on a slowdown. The most thorough study has thus concluded that, compared even with the highest preceding levels (1933), by June and July rural labor costs had in toto risen by 50 to 60 percent.[51] The goal of the FNTT and CNT was not at this point revolutionary seizure so much as a drastic alteration in the terms of labor and a new syndical domination of the present agrarian economy.

The government tried to gain control of agrarian reform and expedite it through new legislation which Ruiz Funes presented to the Cortes on 19 April. This reduced considerably the maximum property limits exempt from reform (from 16.6 to 62.5 percent, depending on category), restored the original compensation levels of 1932–33, and gave the government complete authority to seize any piece of land "for reasons of social utility." Another bill two weeks later proposed to initiate expropriation through taxation, levying a surtax of more than 100 percent on landowners with agrarian incomes of more than twenty thousand pesetas a year. Moreover, the government moved much more rapidly than during the first biennium. On 2 June the Cortes voted to restore all land taken from new tenants during the conservative biennium, and a more drastic version of the original 1932 Agrarian Reform Law was passed on 11 June. As indicated in table 12.1, much more land was redistributed in the five months between March and July 1936 than in the five preceding years of the Republic.

It is the consensus of specialists that these figures are incomplete, since the IRA was slow in recording actual transfers. During June and July the press reported land transfers that did not appear in IRA statistics, while Ruiz Funes himself declared publicly that as of 19 June 193,183 *campesinos*

Table 12.1. Land Distribution under the Popular Front, 1936

Month	Farmers Settled	Area Occupied (hectares)
March	72,428	249,616
April	21,789	150,490
May	5,940	41,921
June	3,855	55,282
July	6,909	74,746
Total	110,921	572,055

Source: *Boletín del Instituto de la Reforma Agraria* (March–July, 1936), in Malefakis, *Agrarian Reform*, 377.

and their families had been settled on 755,888 hectares,[52] probably a more nearly accurate statistic. The IRA seems to have gained some control over the process during the spring. Though the terms were radicalized to hit wealthy landowners harder and subject more land to potential expropriation, the *ruedo* clause of 1932 which affected modest owners was not revived. Though land was virtually being confiscated from the wealthiest, medium owners who lost land were in the process of being paid something approaching market value, while the new tenants could take advantage of arrangements for the full purchase of their land. Even so, this was not enough in the conditions of 1936 to restore peace to the southern countryside.

Rapid and sweeping prosecution of the land reform was the only clear economic policy of the new government. It was slow to take concrete steps to combat unemployment or the depression, and the most incisive statements about economic problems in the Cortes came from centrist and rightist spokesmen. The Azaña government never completed a full budget, but it did increase spending in most categories. The Chapaprieta reforms were categorically rejected, and the state payroll expanded, with considerable new hiring, needless to say always of bona fide leftists.[53]

An obvious goal in labor policy was full restoration of the *jurados mixtos*, as they had been in 1931–33, but this was approached piecemeal and action was not categorically taken on a national scale until 28 May.[54] As indicated earlier, on 3 March the government had decreed blanket reinstatement and compensation for workers fired for political reasons, though it resisted demands from Communists and Socialists that employers who had previously violated labor regulations be jailed. The government obviously faced an avalanche of labor demands, particularly after the beginning of the massive new strike wave in April, whose goals were not simply better wages and working conditions, but categorical changes in labor relations, such as the thirty-six-hour week and retirement with pension at age sixty. The forty-four-hour week was soon restored in metallurgy and construction, but Spanish employers lacked resources to meet many of the new demands. Labor costs increased precipitously, and during the spring the rate of bankruptcies rose. Trade unions sometimes opposed the closing of businesses and demanded to be allowed to take them over. Eventually, in May, the government announced plans for major spending increases to combat unemployment and also to introduce more progressive tax legislation, but these were never completed before the start of the Civil War.

The other major area of goverment activism was education, where Marcelino Domingo returned as minister. He immediately announced plans to close schools still taught by religious personnel no later than the middle of 1936. A decree of 29 February announced the creation of 5,300 new state teaching positions. Domingo claimed that in 1931 Spain had needed 27,151 new "schools" (classrooms) and that 16,409 had been constructed, 12,988 of these during 1931–33. Of the remaining shortage of 10,472, half (5,300) would be built in the remaining ten months of 1936, and the remainder completed no later than 1 May 1938.[55]

Domingo later issued another decree on 6 May authorizing district educational inspectors to make temporary arrangements in areas where new classrooms were badly needed but for various reasons could not be constructed. This led to a series of takeovers of private schools and certain other facilities, which even Izquierda Republicana's official organ *Política* recognized on 29 May were sometimes "of doubtful legality." Five days later the Lliga protested in parliament there had been many arbitrary seizures of private schools. In some cases the schools were closed simply on the grounds of having given confessional instruction. On 4 June a CEDA deputy claimed that in the twenty-five days prior to 15 May a total of 79 private schools with 5,095 students had either been closed, taken over, or set afire.

The Azaña government, as might be expected, was totally absorbed in domestic affairs and paid little attention to the dramatic events that were currently breaking in Europe and Africa. Despite the intense antifascism of the Popular Front, Azaña had no interest in participating further in economic sanctions against Italy for the invasion of Ethiopia — an attitude in sharp contrast to that of the last parliamentary government headed by Chapaprieta. Azaña feared diplomatic, economic, and military complications that Spain was simply in no condition to face. According to Madariaga, the Republic's spokesman in Geneva, "The first thing Azaña said to me was: 'You must get me rid of Article 16 [on sanctions]. I will have nothing to do with it.' This was his official language. His unofficial language was: 'What do I care for the Negus [the deposed Haile Selassie]?'"[56] The left Republican leaders did not regard themselves as involved in any great international struggle between democracy and fascism. After the Civil War began, this attitude would change.

The Spread of Violence and Disorder

During April disorders continued and increased, assuming four different forms: arson of and attacks on religious buildings, strikes and demonstrations in the towns that often took a violent turn (and sometimes involved more arson), the direct occupation of farmland in the central and southern provinces either as a permanent takeover or to impose new worker-controlled labor conditions, and the direct clashes between political groups, often carried out by small hit squads of the left (mostly Socialist and Communist, and occasionally anarchist) and of the Falangists.

In the words of Madariaga:

> The country had entered into a plainly revolutionary phase. Neither life nor property was safe anywhere. It is sheer prejudice to explain matters with parrot cries on variations of the word "feudal." It was not only the owner of thousands of acres granted his ancestors by King So-and-So whose house was invaded and whose cattle were left bleeding with broken legs on the smoking fields of his lands. It was the modest Madrid doctor or lawyer who held a villa of four rooms and bath and a garden as big as three handkerchiefs, who saw his house occupied by land-workers, by no means houseless and by no means hungry, who came to harvest his crop: ten men to do the work of one, and to stay in his house till they finished. It was the secretary of the local gardeners' union who came to threaten the young girl watering her roses that all watering had to be done by union men; it was a movement to prohibit owner-drivers from driving their own cars and to force them to accept a union driver.[57]

In the countryside farmworkers sometimes ran into either armed police or armed landowners. During 1934–35 the government had granted 270,000 private licenses for firearms, mostly to rightists, and in many provinces conservatives were far from defenseless,[58] though some of these licenses were rescinded and weapons confiscated under the new administration. In the provinces of Málaga and Seville six farmworkers were killed on the first of April, allegedly in the "invasion of estates." Later that month four workers were shot and killed by the Civil Guard in Huelva, apparently after a demonstration got out of control. The police or Civil Guard also suffered one or more deaths each week, sometimes in direct clashes, sometimes due to sniping attacks. The most notorious political murder during the first half of April was the killing by Falangists on 13 April of Manuel Pedregal, a Madrid judge who had sentenced the accomplices in the Asúa *atentado.* In Barcelona April was the most violent month of the spring, with numerous cases of arson and bomb explosions, some of them in connection with a major CNT metallurgical strike. The CNT also committed four political murders that month, killing the Badía brothers of Estat Català as well as two nonleftist workers, but then disorders subsided somewhat and deadly violence became more rare in the Catalan capital.

The most notorious incidents occurred in Madrid in mid-April. During the Republic Day parade on 14 April, a Falangist threw a smoke bomb at the presidential reviewing stand, and when the Civil Guard paraded, insults were shouted by part of the crowd. Several Guard officers, off duty and in civilian clothing, reproved those jeering near the presidential stand. At that a number of leftists opened fire, killing a fifty-five-year-old Guard officer in the crowd, and wounding two other off-duty Guardsmen as well as a woman and a child. The burial of the Civil Guard, Lt. Anastasio de los Reyes, two days later was turned into a major rightist demonstration and a pitched battle in the streets of Madrid. Though the funeral procession had been prohibited from marching directly through the city, its leaders insisted on doing so, and it was fired at by leftists on numerous occasions. Altogether, six people were killed — apparently all members of the funeral procession — and many were wounded.[59] That same day there was also a major leftist riot in Jerez, something of a copy of the events in Granada on 9–10 March, with the burning of two newspaper offices and the temporary arrest of "class enemies." It produced numerous injuries but no reported fatalities.

Azaña was increasingly embarrassed and even frightened by the disorder,[60] but he took the usual line on 17 April, declaring that it had been due to a fascist provocation. That was the day on which the government introduced the new legislation stipulating that retired officers who joined illegal political groups would automatically lose their pensions, while one retired monarchist general engaged in conspiracy was exiled to the Canaries and numerous Civil Guard officers were reassigned. The courts were also beginning prosecution of those charged with crimes during the 1934 repression, bringing the conviction of a Civil Guard sergeant for the killing of a Socialist mayor. His sentence of twelve years imprisonment and fifteen-thousand-peseta fine was said to have been the first of this sort in the history of the Civil Guard.[61]

Conditions varied greatly from province to province. Several were relatively unaffected, and in some the authorities made more of an effort to maintain order than in others. Near the bottom was Fernando Bosque, civil governor of Oviedo, who was quoted by *Mundo Obrero* on 20 April as saying:

I have appointed Popular Front delegates throughout Asturias, who have been carrying out antifascist sweeps [*batidas*] with very good results: they have jailed priests, doctors, municipal secretaries and whomever it may be. They fulfill their tasks admirably. Some of the delegates are Communists, and even like Fermín López Irún, who was sentenced to death for his participation in the events of October. . . . the one in Taverga has jailed the local telegrapher and court secretary; the former is let out during the day to do his work and locked up at night. Among those in prison are two canons from Covadonga.

This frank statement made it perfectly clear why there would not be public order under the left Republican administration. It raised a scandal in Madrid and eventually Bosque, who had been moved from civil governor of Huesca to Oviedo on 11 March, was forced to resign, as the interior minister finally announced on 18 June.[62]

The threat of violence was present even in the Cortes. In the words of a Socialist historian:

> The parliament, as soon as it began to function, asphyxiated the government. It acted as a sounding board for civil war, reflecting and aggravating the nation's own turbulence. The deputies insulted and attacked each other by design; each session was in continuous tumult; and since all the representatives — true representatives of the nation — went armed, a catastrophe could have been expected any afternoon. In view of the frequency with which firearms were exhibited or referred to, it was necessary to resort to the humiliating precaution of frisking the legislators as they entered.[63]

The Destitution of Alcalá Zamora

Both the left and right had campaigned against the president during the elections. The CEDA in particular, convinced that he had robbed the party of its earlier mandate, made little secret of the fact that if it won it would ask the new Cortes to review the last parliamentary dissolution, with the aim of deposing Alcalá Zamora according to the Constitution.

Yet his aim never had been to hand all power to the left, and after the complete failure of his strategy in the elections, Alcalá Zamora directed his animus against the left and the new government, whose extremism and general behavior he found even more intolerable than he did the CEDA. There is little doubt that Alcalá Zamora sought the ultimate good of the Republic, but his vain, pompous, and personalistic style, with its constant manipulations, had placed him at odds with nearly all the leading politicians of the left and right, and even of the center. During the first weeks of the new Azaña government, Alcalá Zamora met several times with the council of ministers and tried vainly to encourage a course of greater moderation. In his view, the new administration was using the state of alarm and the partial suspension of constitutional guarantees not to maintain law and order but to give free hand to the forces of disorder.[64] Relations grew ever more tense, and Azaña claimed that he forced the president to back off on more than one occasion by speaking to him in harsh and aggressive language.[65]

In one instance, a rural property in Jaén province of which Alcalá Zamora was co-owner was occupied by farmworkers on 20 February. When

a truckload of Assault Guards arrived, they arrested the president's rela-
tives but did little or nothing to end the illegal occupation, finally releasing the latter but warning them not to return to their homes.[66] As Alcalá
Zamora complained to the government, the police did not use the authority created by the suspension of guarantees to restore order, but "practi-
cally placed it in the hands of the lawless; they ordered local authorities
to follow the dictates of the latter."[67]

He urged Azaña to announce a detailed legislative program as soon as
possible and to proceed through legal channels with positive remedies, but
on most issues the government seemed in no hurry. Conversely, Alcalá
Zamora protested one of the government's first decrees, the blanket terms
for reinstatement and compensation of workers fired in 1934, since in some
cases "the owners of small family businesses were now required to rehire
the murderers of a father or a brother. . . . According to a former governor of the Banco de España, the latter was required to take back an
employee who had fired seven gunshots at an administrator."[68] Alcalá Zamora did manage firmly to veto one proposal,

which was absolutely illegal . . . and in violation of the Constitution. It would
have created special ad hoc municipal committees to fix arbitrarily the production
expenses of each landowner and would also have had the power to confiscate totally without indemnity any agrarian goods to reassign to whatever individual or
collective they saw fit. Moreover, all legal appeal was denied and any administrative appeal was also denied if the local committee ruled unanimously.[69]

He adds:

There was a moment when I had some hope that this toleration of anarchy would
be ended. That was after we had received word from leading diplomats like Buylla,
Barcia and Madariaga of the alarm this created abroad, reflected even in the sar-
castic jokes of Soviet diplomats. Then the government brought for me to sign the
termination of several provincial governors, but in such honorific terms that it was
like voluntary resignation. I signed this formula of unmerited benevolence with
regard to the governor of Jaén, responsible for outrageous acts against my family
and myself, which required the utmost delicacy on my part, but I sent back the
decrees referring to those of Cádiz, Granada, Murcia and Logroño, advising the
government that at the very least it could officially fire them if it was unwilling
to prosecute them for dereliction of duty. The ministers admitted that I was right
but still asked for me to sign lenient terms in order not to provoke the Popular
Front. And these were extreme cases that had even created humiliating international complications: arson against the homes and factories of political enemies;
guards murdered with their own weapons; and a bloody clash with a barracks
in which several people were killed.

    . . . The government often tried to hide from me what was going on . . . , but in one meeting of the council I was informed of the burning of two churches in Alcoy carried out by the city council as a whole. I invited the minister of justice to rectify the situation but he said it was under the jurisdiction of the minister of the interior, who silently exhibited his usual disdainful indifference, encouraged and directly protected by Azaña. . . . But the minister did have to call me about midnight on one occasion after a day of severe disorder and said:

"I'm calling to tell you that the sport is still going on."

"Do you call this shameful arson sport?"

"Yes, because the demonstrations don't go beyond that and otherwise are peaceful."

"But the one today was presided over by you yourself and by the minister of war and ended with the burning of the church of San Luis, a few steps away from and in full view of the ministry full of guards and right in front of your own office. How could you not have prevented that?"

"The guards couldn't manage it because the people there prevented them, though there was no fight. They almost burned the convent of the Trinitarians too."

. . .

"But don't you know who is buried there? Its profanation was an ignominy before the world."

"I don't know, but it was saved by chance."

"Cervantes is buried there. Didn't you know that?"

He didn't know and he didn't care.[70]

By the end of March the major new issue, aside from the partisan deliberations of the Comisión de Actas, was the municipal elections, which the government had scheduled to be held in all of Spain save Catalonia in the following month. There had been no municipal elections since the start of the Republic, except for those held in a minority of districts in 1933. Though the Constitution stated that half the seats were to be placed up for election every three years, the government now planned total plebiscitary municipal elections. The CEDA protested that this was unconstitutional, and that moreover under the present climate of violence, disorder, and censorship, fair campaigning and elections would be impossible. Alcalá Zamora agreed and warned moreover that the inevitable leftist victory would generate a revolutionary demand for a new leftist system, analogous to that stemming from the Republican triumph of 12 April 1931.[71]

The president still possessed the constitutional power to dismiss the government, even with its parliamentary majority, as he had done in September 1933 and December 1935, and replace it with a minority government that could hold new elections. On 31 March Chapaprieta spoke with him and urged him to do so, adding that he believed the president could count on the support of the army in a crisis.[72] This the latter was reluctant to do because it would bring the country close to civil war. The government, for its part, was very near a decision to depose the president but, on the issue of the municipal elections, decided that discretion was the better part of valor. Some of the left Republicans agreed that the most appropriate thing would be to postpone the elections, and all the more if a constitutional crisis were looming. On 3 April, hours before the opening of the first regular session of the new Cortes, the government announced postponement.[73]

That afternoon Azaña addressed the new parliament for the first time, stressing especially the more radical economic policy that would be necessary. He promised to govern within the law and the Constitution but warned:

> There is another kind of obstacle: the reactions and aggressions of the economic interests affected by government policy. Yes, it is correct that we are going to infringe [lastimar] interests whose historical legitimacy I am not going to question, but which now constitute the main part of the disequilibrium from which Spanish society suffers. Now those who accuse us of destroying the Spanish economy wish that our earlier program [of 1933] had not been interrupted, because now the sacrifice will have to be much greater! We come to break the abusive concentration of wealth wherever it may be, to harmonize social burdens and to recognize only two types of citizens: those who participate in production and those who live off the labor and effort of others. The privileged elements of Spain will face the option of accepting the sacrifice or facing desperation. If the offensive reaction of the interests affected repeats the same assault that it launched against the Constituent Cortes, we shall have lost the last legal, parliamentary and Republican opportunity to attack the problem head-on and resolve it justly.

There were no details and no discussion of basic economic problems, other than to refer to "the growing interventionist role of the state in regulating the problems of labor and of production."[74]

The CEDA returned for the opening of the Cortes, and at a meeting of its parliamentary group the great majority voted to continue to cooperate with the government.[75] El Debate had earlier suggested that an understanding might be possible on the basis of disarming all the political militias and undertaking a broad national program to overcome unemployment and the depression. The government had made it clear, however, that it proposed to disarm only the Falange and to impose its own economic program, vague and slow though it was in developing one.

Even before Azaña's speech, a petition had been presented to the speaker of the Cortes asking that Article 81 be invoked, which granted a new parliament produced by a second dissolution during a single presidential term the right to review such action, and, if it found this action unjustified, to vote to depose the president. The petition had been organized by Prieto and was signed by seventeen deputies from the worker parties, mainly Socialists. The initial argument was that the dissolution of 1933 should count as a regular dissolution, not the pro forma ending of a short-term Constituent Cortes, for the first parliament continued nearly two years after the constitution had been completed. Spokesmen for the center and right held that the matter was so complicated it should go before the Tribunal de Garantías Constitucionales. There was also the question of Article 82, dealing with impeachment pure and simple, which stipulated that a motion to depose a president must be backed by a hundred deputies, with three days notice given of the debate, and that the motion then must be carried by three-fifths of the chamber. Prieto preferred to avoid Article 82, for fear of not having enough votes. The initial proposal carried 181 to 88, with many abstaining, and the crucial debate was scheduled for 7 April.[76]

Azaña himself remained uncertain for three days. In December 1931 he had taken the position that dissolution of the Constituent Cortes should not count against the president, and more than a few left Republicans hesitated both to undergo the hypocrisy of deposing the president for doing what they had beseeched him to do for two years and also to make the presidency the merest football of partisan passion. Finally, as was ever the case with Azaña, sectarianism won out. In typically hyperbolic language, Azaña said: "I told myself that I could not accept the responsibility of leaving its worst enemy as President of the Republic."[77] His decision to commit the government, and hence all the Popular Front parties, to impeachment predetermined the outcome.

The argument employed on 7 April was Byzantine, to say the least. It justified deposition on the grounds that the recent dissolution was "not necessary" because (1) it should have been done much earlier and (2) when it was done, it was done improperly, with an attempt to manipulate the outcome. There was of course some truth in the latter charge. Moreover, Prieto read aloud excerpts from Gil Robles's campaign speeches declaring the January dissolution to have been unjustified. Alcalá Zamora had alienated almost all the major political personalities. No one spoke in his favor, though some leaders of the center and right urged a more careful and deliberate procedure, either by invoking Article 82 or by referring the matter to the Tribunal de Garantías Constitucionales. Miguel Maura warned, "Why must you stain the honor of parliament by making people think you are motivated solely by political passion? Listen well! What is being decided this afternoon is more than a mere personal or political case: it is the essence of the Republic itself." The Popular Front deputies understood that well enough and intended to conform the "essence of the Republic" completely to their own domination by removing the last obstacle to full power. The vote to depose was 238, while only five of Portela's deputies voted against it, the right and the rest of the center abstaining.

Again, to quote Madariaga,

Now this parliament which owed its existence to the presidential decree, a decree which turned a majority of the Right into a majority of the Left and which therefore proved, at any rate to the satisfaction of the Left, that the nation had changed its opinion radically and that therefore the previous Parliament no longer represented the will of the nation at the time when it was dissolved, this Parliament officially declared by 238 votes to 5 (the Right abstaining) that the dissolution had not been necessary. That is, it did not hesitate to show the world that the Spanish Republic was incapable of keeping its first president in office for more than half his term, and in order to satisfy its vindictiveness (though it is not easy to find out for what) it committed itself to the most glaring denial of logic the history of a free nation can show.[78]

The Constitution provided that the speaker of the Cortes succeed to a vacant presidency until a special election could choose new delegates (*compromisarios*) to select the next president, and Martínez Barrio was thus sworn in as interim president that night. Then the Cortes, apparently feeling that it had no serious matters to deal with amid the national crisis, took eight days off.

Intensely outraged, Alcalá Zamora made no gesture of rebellion. He knew that he might have been able to rally military support for a kind of coup to keep himself in office (and indeed a general staff colonel, possibly Valentín Galarza, urged him to do just that), but he wished to take no personal responsibility for unleashing the grave conflict that he saw ahead.[79] As he later wrote:

It is possible that if I had resisted what became a three-year civil war might have lasted only three months, weeks or days, but even if that—which was then so uncertain—had been so, it would then have been *my* war, *mine* with its deaths, horrors, iniquities and crimes against the conscience. As it was, it became their war of one side and the other, as they boasted of false and execrable glories, of popular and national epics and triumphal years: such deceitful glories, with their terrible responsibilities, are for them instead.[80]

The Parliamentary Duel of 15–16 April

The new Cortes only began its regular work on 15 April, when Azaña first presented his legislative program. This included reparations for political persecution, the full restoration of Catalan autonomy, reform of the rules of Cortes to expedite the legislative process, and reform of the rules for electing members of the Tribunal de Garantías Constitucionales and of selecting the president of the Tribunal Supremo, to assure leftist domination of the two highest courts. All this had been part of the Popular Front program, and the first two items had already been carried out by decree. In toto, this program could hardly be considered an adequate response to the proto-revolutionary ferment gripping much of the country.

Azaña therefore also emphasized that "the phenomenon we are witnessing in Spain is the access to political power of new social classes, a phenomenon that we can locate in the first third of this century." "For the moment," the government was especially concerned with unemployment and with labor problems in the countryside, though persistent deficits, weak government finance, and a negative balance of payments severely limited state resources. Azaña thus admitted that the state of the economy was serious, declaring that it was important to stabilize foreign debt so as not to risk vital imports. He declared that it would be necessary to reduce expenses in certain unspecified areas while redistributing more income through progressive taxation, expanding public works, and accelerating agrarian reform. Wages must be maintained and yet sufficiently controlled to prevent inflation. Azaña concluded that major reforms had to be undertaken on a virtually self-sustaining financial basis, a task so difficult that he was unable to provide specifics. Violence and disorder he discussed partly from the role of spectator: "Knowing as I do how deeply rooted violence is in the Spanish character, this cannot be proscribed by decree, yet we still hope that the time has come when Spaniards will stop shooting each other," mentioning also that out of "pity and mercy" certain excesses had not been repressed by the government.

Calvo Sotelo and Gil Robles replied for the right, with the difference that the former, speaking for the radical right, denounced the present situation altogether and sought a drastic alternative to it, while the CEDA leader still sought to influence the government to moderate its policy even while it remained in power. In a speech whose text and appendices filled eleven long pages of the *Diario de las Sesiones*, Calvo Sotelo presented the first of what would become a series of statistical reports on alleged acts of violence, declaring that between 16 February and 1 April a total of 74 people had been killed and 345 wounded in political incidents, and 106 churches burned, including 56 completely destroyed. He then cited speeches by revolutionary leaders which indicated this was just the beginning of the destruction. He warned that, as opposed to the dictatorship of the proletariat, "Spain will be able to save itself through the formula of the authoritarian corporate state."

Gil Robles then spoke among shouts and tumult, saying that necessary social reforms would have the CEDA's votes, but that rightists were being assaulted all over Spain and legal social reform no longer seemed to be the main concern. Gil Robles warned against the sectarian concept of trying to govern for only half of Spain: "A considerable mass of Spanish opinion which is at least half the nation will not resign itself to die." Turning to Azaña, he added:

There I think that you will suffer a sadder political fate, which is to preside over the liquidation of the democratic Republic. . . . When civil war breaks out in Spain, let it be known that the weapons have been loaded by the irresponsibility of a government that failed to fulfill its duty toward groups that have kept within the strictest legality.

This session was also the occasion on which José Díaz, secretary of the Communist Party, in a subsequent speech declared that Gil Robles "will die with his shoes on." Martínez Barrio, speaker of the Cortes, called Díaz to order and had the remark stricken from the record. Benito Pabón of the tiny Syndicalist Party, the most moderate of the worker groups, later urged the worker parties to support the government more loyally because "Azaña has not used violence against the excesses of the workers."

Parliament met the following day in a supercharged atmosphere created by the De los Reyes funeral procession, which at one point threatened to march on the Cortes. Azaña began with his customary bluff and braggadocio, claiming once more that disorder was inspired by the right and its "prophecies": "I don't intend to serve as anyone's guardian angel. The honorable gentlemen should show less fear and not ask me to extend them my hand. . . . Did not you want violence, were you not disturbed by the social institutions of the Republic? Then take to violence. Be prepared for the consequences. . . ." Despite this incendiary language from a parliamentary prime minister, he would be totally dismayed when the right took him up on his invitation.

Azaña underlined the importance of maintaining the unity of the left. "We must not permit a single break in our coalition. I will not be the one to open it." Then he withdrew from the provocative position just adopted. Turning to Gil Robles, he demanded:

With what authority do the honorable gentlemen challenge those who once either due to vengeance or confusion launched a revolution? Vengeance is an instinct that ought not to enter personal life and even less public affairs. At no time does anyone have a right to take justice into his own hands. . . . No one can describe with sufficient vividness and vigor not merely the opposition but the repugnance felt by the government for certain events that are sporadically occurring. No one can doubt the exertions of the government to prevent or repress them. I am convinced that flames are an endemic malady in Spain; once heretics were burned, and now saints are consumed, at least as images.

This feeble resort to invoking the ills of an alleged "Spanish character" showed how reluctant Azaña was to come to grips with reality. He then went on to criticize the foreign press for making things sound worse than they were, blaming them for discouraging the spring tourist trade.
    Juan Ventosa of the Lliga concluded:

Simply listening to this debate, simply hearing the declarations made yesterday and today—repeated insults, incitement to personal assassination, invocations of that barbarous and primitive form of justice called the law of revenge [Talión], the strange and absurd demand that only the right be disarmed, but not every-body—simply attending and observing the zeal for persecution and oppression revealed by some sectors of the chamber, you can clearly see the genesis of all the violence occurring in the country.

Special Elections in Cuenca and Granada

On 9 April the government announced that, pursuant to the verdict of the *Comisión de Actas*, the rightist electoral triumphs in the provinces of Cuenca and Granada had been completely annulled, and new elections were scheduled for 5 May. Both sides geared up for a maximum effort. The CEDA prepared a *candidatura de batalla* (combat candidacy) for Granada, made up of five young and determined CEDA candidates, four Falangists, and one "independent" (in fact, Carlist), Col. José Enrique Varela (already active in military conspiracy). The union with the Falange created something of a sensation, for in the regular elections the CEDA had resolutely cold-shouldered the fascist party. As a result Primo de Rivera had lost his seat in parliament and now, like nearly all the other top leaders of his party, was in jail. This was a measure of the extent to which things had changed in only two months. The Popular Front candidacy was composed entirely of representatives of the worker left, with no left Republicans, a further indication of the new state of affairs.
    The simplest description of the campaign for the new election in Granada is to say that the terms of the original campaign were reversed and possibly exceeded. In January and February there had been rightist coercion against the left, and in April and May the opposite held true. Gil Robles claimed that at one point the right was offered a deal which would have allowed them the three minority seats. He denounced this pressure in a letter to the minister of the interior, which he had read into the Cortes record.[81] Failing that, the obstruction to which the right was subjected be-

came so great that they withdrew from the Granada election altogether.

For Cuenca the original rightist ticket was reorganized on 23 April to include the names of the monarchist leader Antonio Goicoechea, José Antonio Primo de Rivera, and General Franco. It was Primo de Rivera who privately insisted from prison that Franco's candidacy be withdrawn, for it gave the rightist ticket too military a look and would only increase government pressure. Franco quickly agreed,[82] but on 27 April the Junta Provincial del Censo ruled in favor of a petition from Prieto that no new candidates be allowed to stand who had not received at least 8 percent of the disputed vote in the original election. In 1933 there had been a complete rightist victory in Cuenca and in the original voting of 16 February 1936 the left had failed to gain a single seat. The left was determined to reverse that completely; to give the proper tone to the campaign, a considerable number of the Socialist militia group known as "La Motorizada" were given official deputy police status for the campaign as *delegados gubernativos.*[83] This was part of the process by which the left Republican government mixed activists of the worker parties into the regular police structures, a process which later helped make possible the bizarre assassination of Calvo Sotelo on 13 July.

On May Day, there was a large joint Socialist-Communist parade down the Castellana involving as many as 300,000 people, with the chant of "Hijos sí, maridos no" ("Children yes, husbands no") by some of the young women activists particularly scandalizing middle-class Catholic citizens. This mass demonstration was peaceful, but those in other parts of the country led to the usual skirmishes, with several killed and many injured.

Two days later occurred the notorious *bulo de caramelos* ("candy scare") in the capital when a rumor swept through one worker district that nuns in one of the few remaining Catholic schools were distributing poisoned caramels to their pupils — an indication of the state of hysteria at that point. One church was soon torched and religious personnel attacked, and on the following day six Catholic churches and schools were ablaze, some forty religious personnel and Catholic laymen attacked, and at least one killed.[84] On the night of the fourth the government felt the need to announce publicly that no poisonings had in fact taken place, the whole matter being put down by leftist leaders to more "provocations" by the right.[85]

In the city of Cuenca, the local CEDA center and several other rightist offices, together with at least one church, were burned on 1–2 May. The new delegados gubernativos arrived on the evening of the first and for the next three days ruled with an iron hand, making campaigning for the right difficult. Prieto also drove in late on the first to deliver the principal leftist campaign address. He later wrote: "When I arrived at the theater,

there smoldered nearby the ashes of the fire which had consumed the furnishings of a rightist center that had just been attacked by the masses. A
number of important monarchist personages were holed up in a hotel in
the center of town since the night before. The atmosphere was frenzied."[86]
The Socialist leader then went on to give one of his most important and
complicated speeches of the year, in which he endeavored on the one hand
to stimulate the left to electoral victory while trying on the other to discourage the sort of disorder and violence still going on at that moment
outside the theater.

Prieto soon indicated his satisfaction with Franco's withdrawal. While
praising the general's professional skills, he showed his customary prescience by observing that the latter made Franco precisely the sort of
figure who might most effectively lead a potential military revolt, diplomatically adding that "I would not dare attribute any such intentions to
General Franco."

With equal prescience Prieto dedicated a major part of the speech to
the problem of public order. While carefully stressing that the real cause
for most of the current excesses stemmed from the reaction to the unjustified severity of the repression following the October insurrection, he insisted that the time had come to call a halt and show greater discipline.

It's time to stop! Enough, enough! Do you know why? Because in these disorders whose cause I have just defined I can find no trace of revolutionary strength.
If I could, I might praise them. No, a country can stand the convulsion of a true
revolution. . . . What it cannot stand is the constant drain of public disorder with
no immediate revolutionary goal; what a nation cannot stand is the drain of public authority and its own economic strength, with constant unrest, tumult and alarm.
Simple souls may say that this unrest is produced solely by the dominant classes.
That, in my judgment, is erroneous. The pernicious effects of that unrest will soon
be suffered by the working class itself due to the upset and possible collapse of
the national economy. . . . Abroad people consider Spain an insolvent country.

If disorder and tumult become a permanent system, . . . the result will not be
the consolidation of revolution, or the building of socialism or communism. The
result will be desperate anarchy of a kind that is not found within the creed of
libertarian anarchism itself; the result will be economic disorder that can destroy
the country.

His final warning, once more completely accurate, was that continuation
of the disorder would only increase the possibility of a "fascist" reaction.[87]

The next four days which concluded the campaign in Cuenca gave no
evidence that Prieto's words had the slightest effect. Several companies of
Assault Guards had been assigned to patrol the province, and the civil governor ordered the preventive arrest of scores of rightists, so numerous that

special emergency jails had to be set up to hold them until the balloting was over. A sweeping victory for the Popular Front was recorded amid armed coercion and blatant electoral fraud, with the *prietista* delegados playing a leading role, despite the remarkably frank speech their leader had given on 1 May, all of which made a mockery of his call to moderation. On the one hand, he wanted greater responsibility and restraint, but on the other he was equally determined that the left sweep the special election.

Romero has penned the best epitaph:

> The May elections in Cuenca were an episode that can be properly described as shameful, in which Prieto played a leading role, taking much of the responsibility. Every kind of outrage and abuse was committed, with extreme coercion and bold-faced illegalities. The civil governor, the electoral board [Junta del Censo] and, as a fitting climax, the young men of the "Motorizada," pistols in hand, won those elections without glory. Primo de Rivera was deprived of a seat that he had won in popular votes, after the governor announced that his votes simply would not be counted, as occurred in various districts, and that announcement by the leading authority in the province intimidated others.[88]

It was not merely Largo Caballero, but, on occasion, Prieto as well, who expressed the almost schizophrenic duality of Spanish Socialism.

On the following day Calvo Sotelo arose in the Cortes to read his latest data on violence, claiming that forty-seven people had been killed in political affrays between 1 April and 5 May. Another of Azaña's *incondicionales*, Santiago Casares Quiroga, now minister of the interior, replied that the government "is the first to condemn and execrate the lamentable events that have occurred," but that nonetheless the only real problem came from the right. "Only the right worries me while the social revolution does not worry me at all. In the proletarian masses I have found loyalty and aid in getting out of this situation." A major goal of government policy, he said, was to disarm the right, from whom thirteen thousand weapons had been confiscated in Granada province and seven thousand in Jaén province. Nothing was said about disarming the left. Calvo Sotelo replied that it was irrational to suppose that the current violence stemmed merely from rumors that the right launched in order to injure itself, adding that the right did not want a civil war, but that violence must cease on both sides, not just one. Fascism "here and abroad is not a primary initiative, but a secondary response. It is not an action, but a reaction."

Two days earlier, José Antonio Primo de Rivera had decided on a fundamental change in Falangist tactaics. He had previously sought to avoid being involved with military conspirators, whose aims and style he considered reactionary and exploitative. He had given up hope of any normal political relations or due process under the left Republican regime. Consequently he drafted a *Carta a los militares de España* (*Letter to the Spanish Military*), subsequently distributed as a clandestine leaflet, urging the military to prepare rapidly for decisive political intervention.[89] Since the end of April the pluriform strands of military conspiracy had begun to come together in clearer form for the first time, though this was known only to a small minority within the military themselves.

13

Breakdown, May to July 1936

No other candidate was in a position to contest the presidency with Azaña. He himself would evidently have preferred to see the office of chief of state in the hands of Felipe Sánchez Román, whose stature in Azaña's eyes was inversely proportionate to the minute size of his party and parliamentary strength. Since Sánchez Román was not a member of the Popular Front, this was impossible. Largo Caballero preferred the candidacy of the meteoric Alvaro de Albornoz, who stood clearly to the left of Azaña, but Albornoz tended toward the irresponsible and had little support. Thus the Unión Republicana quickly nominated Azaña and, after overcoming the nominal resistance of Azaña's own Izquierda Republicana — which at first was reluctant to lose his leadership to the more distant office of chief of state — Prieto helped swing Socialist votes in line, and the matter was quickly settled.

Voting for electors (*compromisarios*) for a new presidential election took place on 26 April. With much of the right abstaining, these elections were swept by the left, the Popular Front electing 358 *compromisarios* to 63 for the opposition, and Azaña was overwhelmingly chosen by a special assembly of electors in the Crystal Palace of Madrid's Retiro Park on 10 May. The formal ceremony for the oath of office took place on the following day, when Gil Robles claims to have been impressed by the extreme pallor and seeming numbness which the new president exhibited.[1]

The motives of the main leftist leaders in elevating Azaña to the presidency were subsequently a matter of controversy and one which has never been totally resolved. Though it seemed clear enough that among the Socialists the initiative throughout was exercised by Prieto, the left Socialist Araquistain would later insist that the whole affair was a Machiavellian plot to deprive the government of its top leader, sweeping Azaña aside into the presidency and leaving the administration in the hands of a weaker figure who would be totally unable to restrain the revolutionaries, thus extending the Trojan horse tactic of the Popular Front to its maximum.[2] This, however, is contradicted by the evident initiative of Prieto, not Largo Caballero, and the latter's pique at Prieto's arranging for a rapid endorsement of Azaña's candidacy by the executive commission of the party.[3]

With regard to Azaña, it has been speculated that he really hoped to be more effective in stabilizing the regime from the presidency — that he took the new office for positive reasons — as opposed to the interpretation that he accepted the presidency largely from the negative considerations that he could no longer control events and that it was better to make his escape into a more withdrawn and ceremonial office. There is inadequate evidence available to resolve this problem, and an either/or conclusion is perhaps unrealistic. There is little doubt that at some level Azaña wished to escape, as he had earlier indicated on various occasions, but as several of his friends have testified, he also expressed the rationalization that with the powers of the presidency he might somehow be able to protect the Republic more effectively.

The main political actor in this drama was, however, neither Azaña nor Largo Caballero but Prieto. It is clear that his long-range plan was to realign the government so as to cement the power of a left Republican-Socialist regime. For that, Alcalá Zamora had had to be deposed and Azaña removed from active politics to the office of president. With the only truly dominant political personality out of the running, the way would be open for a stronger coalition led by Prieto, one which could govern more firmly and effectively, and with a broader basis.

Even Azaña seemed to be aware that the existing left Republican (technically minority) government was not able to govern effectively, and since early the preceding month (April) there had been a number of private talks and meetings among the more moderate and practical leaders of the center-left aimed at building support for a stronger majoritarian government that would be able to restore authority and order, while pressing forward with basic reforms. Prieto was a key figure in these somewhat desultory conversations, which also at times included the two most progressive leaders of the CEDA, Giménez Fernández and Luis Lucia, Miguel Maura of the Republican center, as well as the sensible and pragmatic Claudio Sánchez Albornoz and occasionally even Besteiro. Sánchez Albornoz has related that at the beginning of May a meeting of the Izquierda Republicana elite (ministers and ex-ministers) concluded that only a short-term Republican legalitarian dictatorship could restore order and save the regime.[4]

The problem lay in how to construct a progressive majority of the center or left-center. This was always the basic dilemma of Alcalá Zamora, and his elimination altered the terms of the equation only a little. A true Republican center coalition would probably have required splitting either the CEDA or the Socialists, or possibly both. The CEDA could only have been included to the extent that Lucia and Giménez Fernández could have attracted a significant minority of the CEDA deputies by splitting off the more liberal, but the prospects for such a maneuver were highly dubious. The main fulcrum still remained restoration of the left Republican-Socialist alliance that had led the government during the first biennium.

Though Prieto would later allege that Azaña's intentions were not altogether serious,[5] the new president moved immediately on the day of his inauguration to ask Prieto to form the next government. There is little doubt that he was seriously interested, or even that he was the best possible choice. The Bilbao Socialist was no miracle-man, but his good sense and patriotism had attracted the attention of other leaders in the center and even in the moderate right. All the left Republican groups, and even Portela Valladares, seemed willing to support a Prieto-led coalition. Giménez Fernández was personally eager to collaborate, while on one occasion José Antonio Primo de Rivera had half seriously proposed that, if Prieto would espouse a socialistic nationalism, the Falange would join his branch of the Socialist Party, with Primo de Rivera becoming a subordinate.[6]

The kind of government which Prieto apparently proposed was not a grand "national coalition" but simply a genuine Popular Front coalition (probably minus the Communists and the POUM) that would carry out accelerated economic reforms, crush the latent military conspiracy with a limited but decisive purge of the army, and restore order through a more energetic and responsible police policy to achieve the *despistolización* (disarming) of Spain. He proposed priority attention to agrarian reform and to new irrigation projects and new housing construction, the latter intended especially to reduce unemployment. He also intended to expand the largely pro-Republican Assault Guards while reducing the strength of the Civil Guard.

The main obstacle, however, was the Socialist left, who refused to abandon their position, held tenaciously since the autumn of 1933, that the party should never enter another government coalition with the left Republicans. As Paul Preston has said, "In a very real sense, the ambiguity of the Socialist attitude to the Republic was to be the crucial factor of 1936."[7] As the left Socialists saw it, the presidency of Azaña, which most of them had not encouraged, should merely expedite the left Republicans' task of prosecuting and liquidating the "bourgeois" phase of the Republic. On 9 May, *Claridad* emphasized that the Spain of Azaña's presidency would be totally different from that of his first government in 1931: "Azaña himself realizes it and that is the source of his internal drama. Azaña is not

capable of violently confronting the ascending and inevitable march of
the proletariat. He cannot be either a Kerensky or a Hitler. . . . Hopefully
he will be a good midwife of history. Let us expect so."[8] Largo Caballero
would later lament that "according to Prieto the Socialist Party had no
other role in Spanish political life than to be Azaña's hodcarrier,"[9] and
the left was determined to prevent that, fearing to see Prieto become the
"Spanish Noske." Therefore in a quick poll of most of the Socialist parliamentary delegation on 12 May the vote was 49 to 19 against government participation.

This was a bitter blow to Prieto but was a foreseeable outcome. The
Socialist left was being consistent, and the split within Socialist ranks widened further. Yet Prieto did not put up much of a fight. He may simply
have been hoping against hope that, faced with a new political equation
after the elevation of Azaña, the left would change their minds. Failing
that, the only practical recourse would have been officially to split the party,
which in many ways would have been desirable and would have recognized a virtual fait accompli. Yet party identity and loyalty was deeply
developed among Socialists, while the basic polarization of Spanish political life had opened a gulf deeper even than the split among the Socialists,
so that Prieto shrank from officially sundering the party. When his Socialist friend and ally Juan Simeón Vidarte urged him to go ahead and form
a coalition, reasoning that once Prieto was prime minister the *caballeristas*
would shrink from actually voting against him, Prieto refused, adding bit-
terly "Let Caballero go to hell." According to Vidarte, Prieto feared to play
the role of a "Spanish Briand" and to leave much of the party behind amid
the existing polarization.[10] Moreover, as a practical politician, he may have
judged a party split not viable unless he could carry at least a bare majority of the parliamentary delegation, which was not possible at that point.
Though some conversations were continued with the more liberal elements
of the CEDA,[11] the possibility of a Prieto government or any sort of broader
Popular Front government was over for the time being. Azaña turned next
to Martínez Barrio, whose party had gained a not insignificant number
of seats from the Comisión de Actas, but the latter quickly declined because of the formidable obstacles involved.

Azaña thus found himself painted into a corner. Unless he wanted to
break the Popular Front, which he had no intention of doing, the only
alternative was some sort of Azaña government without Azaña, led by
one of his Izquierda Republicana colleagues. He himself recognized that
his party was thin in leadership ability,[12] but he found no better alternative than to turn to one of his closest collaborators, Santiago Casares
Quiroga, who had been — absolutely ineffectually — minister of the interior

for the past month. Casares was totally loyal to Azaña, and their wives were close friends. He had once shown energy as minister of the interior during 1931–33 and earlier enjoyed some reputation for vigor and determination, though this was perhaps due more to emotionality and partisan rhetoric than achievement. He now suffered from tuberculosis, and his most notable action during the past month had been simply to reassign many Civil Guard officers. According to Martínez Barrio, when his appointment as prime minister was announced "public opinion and even the Popular Front parties did not hide their surprise and disgust,"[13] for it was clear that Azaña had made a dubious appointment from among his personal clique. According to his brother-in-law, Rivas Cherif, Azaña himself had misgivings but could find no alternative.[14] In the new cabinet, Casares would also hold the Ministry of War to avoid the need for a military member and supposedly the better to control the army. Gabriel Franco, the minister of finance, refused to continue because of the government's contradictory and chaotic fiscal policy and was replaced by a member of Izquierda Republicana. The cabinet was broadened to include one representative of the Catalan Esquerra, Juan Lluhí Vallescà, as minister of labor, a position in which he was soon to prove incompetent. Altogether the last regular government of the Republic included seven ministers from Izquierda Republicana, three from Unión Republicana, one from the Esquerra, and one Republican independent, Juan Moles, in the crucial Ministry of the Interior.

This feeble effort was Azaña's last direct political initiative before the Civil War began. Henceforth he would withdraw into the presidency, preoccupied, it would seem, with esthetics, arguably his main interest. He initiated a major redecoration of the Palacio de Oriente, temporarily residing in the Casita at the Pardo palace (near the building which would later be Franco's personal residence for thirty-six years). He increased the presidential budget, drastically expanding the fleet of limousines,[15] and lent his attention to preparing new legislation that would establish severe penalties for attacks on the presidential family. On only one further occasion, the night of 18–19 July, would he make a belated effort to establish a broader and more effective coalition government, and then it would come at least six or seven days too late.

Casares Quiroga presented the new cabinet to the Cortes on 19 May in belligerent terms:

> After five years the Republic still needs to defend itself from its enemies. How long will this go on? So long as I am leading the government, I promise you that it will continue just as little as possible. Simple defensive tactics are inadequate. A direct attack is more effective. . . .

Santiago Casares Quiroga

Declared enemies will be smashed and hidden enemies will be searched out to be smashed as well. The government cannot be an idle spectator when enemies rebel against the Republic and are brought to trial but are sometimes absolved by the courts. We must prepare new legislation to radically eliminate this abuse. . . . And I say when it has to do with fascism, I will be unable to remain impartial. I declare to you that this government is belligerent against fascism.

Casares's appointment had pleased *Claridad,* which on 13 May had hailed it as one of the best possible because of the new prime minister's outspoken partisanship. Nonetheless, not merely moderates but also some left Republicans were critical of his "belligerency" speech, for its partisanship and ambiguity,[16] since leftist propaganda routinely called all rightists "fascists." Casares did add in his remarks that the left must also obey the law and must renounce "political strikes outside the law, illegal takeovers and acts of violence."

The parliamentary session that day was one of the most tumultous, with much shouting, interruption, and verbal abuse. Gil Robles once more warned of the danger of civil war unless the law were firmly applied to all, while Calvo Sotelo became engaged in an exchange of insults with a Socialist deputy. Ventosa found Calvo Sotelo's remarks too partisan but pointed out:

I think that the "enemies of the Republic" are the people who daily provoke public disorders and create the state of anarchy which is consuming the Republic. In every country where fascism has been installed it was preceded by disorders and persecution like those occurring in Spain today. . . . I call your attention to the evident similarity that exists between the political situation of Italy in 1920–21 and of Germany in later years.

It was clear from the beginning that the Casares Quiroga administration would not provide the answer to Spain's problems, and conversations continued among moderate leaders of the left center and right center about the formation of a strong new practical coalition. The same personalities who had been active in April and early May were still involved, and the designated leader continued to be, for want of any real alternative, Indalecio Prieto. The well-known journalist Manuel Aznar wrote in *El Heraldo de Aragón* on 29 May that "every day there is more talk about a Prieto government and its members are being mentioned." Yet the fulcrum continued to rest on his willingness (or not) to split the Socialist Party, now going through further internal turmoil. One scenario had the executive commission of the party approving government participation (even though this would still be rejected by the UGT), with Ricardo Zabalza of the FNTT, a UGT dissident, taking over the Ministry of Agriculture, Miguel Maura

the Foreign Ministry, and Lucia of the CEDA the Ministry of Communications (apparently for purposes of national unity). Yet, amid the growing
internal strife, Prieto could not bring himself to take the plunge, while on
the right Gil Robles had always been skeptical of any such scheme. Under
certain conditions he might have supported a more broadly based coalition with CEDA votes, but there is no indication that he was ready to approve CEDA participation in a Prieto government. He reports that he vetoed
any further participation by CEDA representatives in such negotiations
on 2 June, and some time afterward the project was evidently shelved altogether.[17]

The Casares Quiroga government pressed ahead with its predecessor's
labor and economic policies, as well as in educational change and judicial
reform. The new minister of public instruction, Francisco J. Barnés, was
even more radical than Domingo.

Azaña's government had on February 28 ordered inspectors to visit schools run
by religious congregations. Apparently these inspectors often closed down schools
on their own initiatives. With the appointment of Barnés, however, it would seem
that closure of schools run by the congregations and the illegal confiscation of private schools became, in effect, official policy. Cedista spokesmen asked that no
schools be closed unless there were places for the pupils in State schools. The minister replied that Catholics must now suffer for their sins of omission in failing
to develop sufficiently the State system since 1933. On June 4, the CEDA temporarily
withdrew from the Cortes because the minister's insulting language as much as
his policy gave "intolerable offense to the Catholic conscience of the country." Cedistas continued to complain of religious persecution, while the government went
ahead with its laicizing policies.[18]

The government was "belligerent" not merely against "fascism," private
schools, and the property structure, but also against the existing judiciary,
deemed inadequately leftist. On 3 June new legislation was introduced to
create a special jury, as provided for in Article 99 of the Constitution, to
bring charges against judges and prosecutors who failed to fulfill their functions or engaged in misdeeds. Over the protest of the right, this bill was
approved on 10 June. It was followed by another measure, approved by
the Cortes on 9 July, providing for the forced retirement of judges and prosecutors, which the right charged was simply a political weapon to use against
conservatives.

After public order, the most serious problem facing the new government
was economics. Prices were increasing rapidly, the peseta was in serious
decline, and stock prices had naturally fallen. The Azaña government had
taken the position that all economic problems had basically been caused

by the right, yet it had pursued a contradictory policy of expanding major budget categories and pursuing a more interventionist tack while hoping to stabilize the peseta and reduce both the trade imbalance and national debt. The progressive tax reform proposed by Gabriel Franco, Azaña's finance minister, had never even been discussed in the Cortes, where the deputies were too busy denouncing each other. On 14 May the Bloque Patronal demanded to know whether the government was taking the position that capitalist employment was to be abolished and private industry eliminated.[19]

It was clear from Casares Quiroga's introductory speech of 19 May that the government still lacked a coherent policy. He referred only to maintaining the acceleration of the agrarian reform, restoring all the labor regulations of 1931–33, and adding another 100 million pesetas to the 90 million already allocated to public works to combat unemployment. No reply was possible to criticism from both the center and right that the left Republican administration was the only new leftist government in Europe without a serious fiscal strategy, neither clearly deflationary nor clearly reflationary (though in practice somewhat nearer the latter). The government was obviously not adhering to the relative moderation of the original Popular Front program, but neither had it substituted any systematic alternative. Instead it instituted piecemeal measures, such as limiting the amount of money that could be taken out of the country, but never managed to prepare a budget. Finally, on 30 June, the government asked the Cortes to prorogue the preceding budget for the third quarter of the year. The only lucid remarks about the economy in the Cortes came from the center and right; Popular Front deputies were preoccupied by other issues.

The worst economic dislocation took place in parts of the central and southern countryside, while urban industry was affected somewhat less. Nonetheless the major increases in production costs, due particularly to boosts in wages and expanded fringe benefits, coupled with the loss of investment, became increasing handicaps. The activity of Catalan industry apparently declined, in the face of declining demand at home and abroad and flight of capital.[20] By mid-June rightist spokesmen were even praising Léon Blum, leader of the Popular Front government in France, for having developed a coherent plan of national reconstruction for both capital and labor, and Calvo Sotelo had positive words for the Rooseveltian New Deal for the same reason. Later Fernando Valera of Unión Republicana admitted that the government could never deal with unemployment when it could not even draw up a budget, was suffering both a fiscal and balance of payments deficit, and was dealing with an industrial structure that was not strong enough to absorb all the labor reinstatements mandated by the February decree.[21]

On 11 June the Cortes finally voted to restore the original agrarian reform law of 15 September 1932, but the right protested that the more radical new decrees had gone far beyond the original legislation, which was technically correct. Much more serious than any confiscation of larger estates were the labor problems and great cost increases resulting from new wage settlements and *alojamientos* (assigning workers to properties). On 15 May the Confederación Española Patronal Agrícola formally petitioned that all existing labor relations be enforced—a novel position for them—but asked that the line be held there.[22] Twelve days later the governor of Badajoz province reported that some farmworkers would not even accept wages of twelve pesetas a day, more than double what they had received the preceding year.[23] Sometimes even smallholders and renters had to make payoffs to avoid ruinous *alojamientos*.[24] Moreover, the practical effect of the acceleration of agrarian reform was increasingly disorderly and uncertain. Some of the small number of families who had received land in 1935 were now forced to give it up simply because it had been received under the preceding legislation, while the average size of allotment was only 5.5 hectares (about 11 acres), and Ruiz Funes admitted in the Cortes on 27 May that in fact it could not be expected that the economic success rate for such small holdings without capital would be more than 40 percent, so that in effect the government was admitting that for the most part its agrarian reform was not likely to work. Employers began to demand that all wage settlements include production standards, specifying how much effective work was being purchased by the greatly increased wages. Production standards were rejected by the Socialists and Communists, of course, but the inept labor minister Lluhí admitted on 1 July that production standards were probably desirable. In Cortes interpellation, the opposition charged that, on the basis of the Ministry of Labor's own official statistics, the cost of the total harvest would exceed its market value, to which Lluhí had difficulty replying.

The Socialist—or at least the UGT—position was that the time had come for the socialization of industry, though no firm plan was presented. On 9 June the government introduced legislation aimed at the mining industry in Asturias and León, providing for mine shafts and deposits no longer being actively mined to be taken over as worker cooperatives. By the end of the month Socialist and Communist deputies claimed that the extent of obstruction by landowners was so great that in some areas the harvest process should either be taken over by the local government authorities or handed to the farmworker syndicates.

The Drive for Regional Autonomies

The tidal wave of change unleashed by the Popular Front victory quick-
ened all the regionalist movements. Restoration of Catalan autonomy was
quickly followed by a new initiative from Basque nationalists. The demonstration effect which these provided, together with the obvious examples
of new worker initiatives on every hand and the encouragement, or at least
support, by the left Republican administration energized the autonomist
forces in all the major regions.

Most basic functions of Catalan autonomy were quickly reestablished.
The Esquerra had learned much more from the 1934 fiasco than had, for
example, left Socialists elsewhere, while in Catalonia the moderate Lliga
was ready and willing to play the role of a loyal conservative opposition.
Thus, unlike in the rest of Spain, the two polarities of Catalanist politics
proved mutually cooperative. Though there were many strikes and some
disorder by the CNT, fatalities were few. Compared with Madrid or Seville, Barcelona (and certainly Bilbao) remained relatively calm. The Junta
de Seguridad Catalana was restored on 10 May, with terms established
for the transfer of other autonomist functions, and on 2 June the crucial
administration of public order was returned to Barcelona by decree.

By this point Indalecio Prieto, certainly the most influential non-nation-
alist leader in Bilbao, understood that further delay in arranging Basque
autonomy would only strengthen the more extreme nationalists, while
the Basque Nationalist Party fully grasped that autonomy would only
come from democracy and not from or in conjunction with the right. A
special Cortes committee was established, composed of Aguirre (the PNV
leader), a Basque Socialist, and a Basque left Republican who were to
work out the terms of Basque autonomy, and on 24 May Prieto declared
in Bilbao that he was determined to achieve Basque autonomy as soon as
possible, even if it were his last political achievement. A new statute proposal was given to this committee in April, and approval was nearly ready
by mid-July.

At the beginning of May representatives of the three Aragonese provinces met in Caspe to begin work on a statute for Aragón, closely modeled on that of Catalonia.[25] Delegates of the Agrarians and the CEDA
commenced work on a statute for Castile and León on 20 May, though
dissidents wanted to include only Old Castile and León, while on 9 June
the city government of Burgos voted in favor of a statute for Old Castile
alone. A campaign was launched in Gijón on 29 May to rally support for
an Asturian statute, while broader efforts were already under way in the
Valencian region. On 6 July a body of delegates met in Seville to begin

drafting a statute for Andalusia, while on the fifteenth a similar body met in Santa Cruz de Tenerife to prepare a document for the Canary Islands.

The process was farthest advanced in Galicia, where the autonomist campaign was actively promoted by the Popular Front. A plebiscite to vote on a newly prepared statute was held on 28 June, with official electoral participation of 74.52 percent, of whom 74 percent were registered as voting in favor. The results surprised all objective observers, since Galicia traditionally had the highest abstention rate in Spain, and the turnout recorded for the general elections of February had been considerably lower. In fact, prior to the plebiscite, Galicianists had struggled to gain an exception to the constitutional requirement that an absolute majority of the electorate vote in favor of a proposed statute. It was generally concluded that there had been massive manipulation, particularly after it was found that in some rural, typically abstentionist, districts 100 percent of the local electorate had been recorded as voting in favor. The new statute was officially submitted to the Cortes on 15 July for final ratification.[26]

With autonomist campaigns developing all over Spain, there were demands on both the radical right and revolutionary left for complete standardization of the process. Calvo Sotelo declared in *ABC* on 20 May that there should be autonomy statutes for all regions or none, while the Marxist-Leninist POUM touted creation of an "Unión de Repúblicas Socialistas de Iberia," a sort of Iberian Soviet Union, one of the few points on which it coincided with the Stalinist Spanish Communist Party.

Reunification of the CNT

The CNT had long been enervated by its disastrous round of mini-insurrections in 1931–33 and the repression which these provoked. The second extraordinary congress in the history of the organization met in Zaragoza during the first ten days of May to reunify the CNT and to forge a united policy. The delegates in Zaragoza officially represented syndicates numbering a total of 550,595 members. This number marked a decline of 40–50 percent from the organizational highpoint in 1931–32, though the decline was now being rapidly made good by an active campaign of expansion in which the new strike offensive and competition with the UGT played major roles. The report of the CNT Secretariat ridiculed the revolutionary pretensions of the *caballerista* Socialists, declaring that the rhetoric of the "Spanish Lenin" reminded it of the fable about the frog that wanted to become an ox. It further stressed that the internal division and "indecision" of the anarchosyndicalist movement in the past two years had permitted the Communists and other Marxist parties to grow at their expense and had allowed the bourgeois left to take over the government once more with a policy "exactly the same as at the time of Casas Viejas."[27]

The committee charged with investigating the role of the CNT in the October insurrection attributed both the initiative and the fiasco in that enterprise to the Socialists' "anger at having been thrown out of power." An equal share of blame was also allotted to Azaña, "the leader of socializing radicalism, the most cynical and coldly cruel politician ever known to Spain." The feeble effort by Catalanists and by Socialists beyond Asturias was ridiculed, and the nonparticipation by the CNT elsewhere was justified by its "refusal to become the sacrificial vanguard for other factions that would have coldly liquidated those of us who survived the struggle against the government." Union with the UGT was declared possible only on the basis of the latter's complete renunciation of any collaboration with a Republican government, agreement on "the complete destruction of the political and social system," and the support of 75 percent of the membership in a referendum.[28]

The congress endorsed once more "the insurrectional method for the conquest of social wealth." A report on the installation of libertarian communism declared that its goal was to abolish private property and reorganize society on the basis of syndicates and autonomous communes to form the "Confederación Ibérica de Comunas Autónomas Libertarias." The army and police would be abolished, all weapons handed over to the communes, and the theory of the nonexistence of God taught in schools.[29]

Though relations with the UGT remained difficult, there was more cooperation at the local level than ever before, as a growing number of the multitudinous new strikes became joint UGT-CNT initiatives. On 24 May Largo Caballero publicly embraced a CNT leader at a meeting in Cádiz, yet most of the differences persisted. In some major strikes the CNT seized the initiative in opposition to the UGT, whose leaders sometimes tried to follow a more prudent course than indicated by revolutionary rhetoric.

"Competitive radicalization" between the two movements reached its climax in Málaga, where a strike by CNT fish salters was not seconded by the local UGT fishermen's syndicate. In retaliation on 10 June CNT gunmen killed a Communist city councilman who had supported the UGT. The local UGT then did go on strike, but against their "proletarian brothers" of the CNT, attacking several local CNT centers, with a number of people injured on both sides. After the Socialist president of the provincial assembly was murdered on 11 June, apparently by cenetistas, the government closed all CNT centers in the province, but violence contin-

ued. Police reinforcements were rushed in from Madrid; many *cenetistas*
were arrested and one killed, while Socialists and Communists distributed
leaflets accusing the CNT of serving "el fascio."

The Socialist Schism Deepens

Growing national political polarization did not have the effect of narrowing the split between the Socialist "left" and "center," which only deepened.
This made impossible any coherent response by the Socialist Party and
UGT to the crisis of the Republic. The left was determined to prevent any
new coalition to strengthen the left Republican government and constantly
labeled all who supported such a tactic as "traitors" who merited expulsion
from the party, while the *prietista* center — lacking any real majority in the
party but controlling the executive commission — always saw its efforts
stymied.

Though the policy of the left was exclusively negative and destructive,
aimed at the deterioration of the economic structure and ultimately of the
left Republican government, it had no revolutionary plan of its own. The
left was not a united group but, as Santos Juliá has pointed out, consisted
of four distinct nuclei:

1. The majority of the UGT, led by Largo, constituted the main force.
Despite their radical stance, UGT leaders eventually became somewhat
frightened by the massive new strike wave. Despite their vituperation of
Prieto and Besteiro, they wanted to avoid an official split in either the party
or the UGT, and, despite all their pro-Communist talk, they shied away
from further mergers with the Communists.

2. A second group was the revolutionary rhetoricians grouped around
Araquistain and the editorial staff of *Claridad.* Though they were the principal providers of revolutionary rhetoric, they were nonetheless much more
interested than Largo in supporting the Casares Quiroga government, which
Araquistain saw as essential.

3. A third sector was the United Socialist Youth (JSU), since March essentially taken over by the Communists. Earlier receptive to the POUM argument of moving directly to revolution, they now adhered to the Communist
line of temporary loyalty to the broader Popular Front formula.

4. There was also a small number of crypto-Communists, such as Araquistain's brother-in-law Julio Alvarez del Vayo, who had some limited influence but did not form an organized group. Only the crypto-Communists
were really interested in officially splitting the party and joining the Socialist left with the Communists.[30]

Despite Araquistain's boast to an American reporter that "we Spanish

Socialists are now more advanced, more communistic, than the Communist Party,"[31] the left was based on the trade-unionism of the UGT, and in general showed little sense of or interest in the Leninist tactic of the "vanguard party." Araquistain tried to compensate by prattling on — in a kind of "Latin American" style — about the role of a revolutionary "caudillo" with regard to the masses, so that *El Socialista* complained on 13 May that *Claridad* "is forging the universal authority of the future dictator."

On 25 May the *prietista* executive commission convened a meeting of the party's national committee, which decided that the next party congress would meet in Asturias in October. Special elections were declared to fill the vacant positions on the executive commission, and the center nominated a moderate slate headed by Ramón González Peña, while warning through the national committee that local party sections which failed to follow party regulations and instructions would be dissolved. The *caballeristas* who controlled the Madrid section of the party countered with their own slate, led by Largo, and made plans to convene their own party congress in Madrid at the end of July, though the center warned that this would be a schismatic meeting which would only make the party split official.

The intraparty conflict reached a high point at a Socialist meeting on 31 May in the southern town of Ecija, where Prieto and González Peña tried to address an increasingly hostile Socialist audience that included many *caballeristas*. Shouted insults and the hurling of rocks and bottles were climaxed by gunshots, with the centrist leaders beating a hasty retreat to their waiting cars. They fled town at breakneck speed, pursued by local leftists in other vehicles. There were several injuries, and Prieto's secretary was temporarily captured on the highway by the pursuers and carried back to town before being freed by the Civil Guard.

The war of words became even more bitter as Prieto charged Largo with having betrayed the party in October 1934. Prieto now began to consider a formal split inevitable and sounded increasingly pessimistic. *La Petite Gironde* of Bordeaux quoted him on 15 June as saying: "It is unjust to consider all rightists as fascists. The fascist danger doesn't exist unless it is generated by the left. The next congress of the Socialist Party will produce a split." Two days later, he declared in his own newspaper, *El Liberal*, "In view of the dangerous turn being taken by events let us consider if our critics [of the right] may not be partially correct." And after Jiménez de Asúa introduced a petition in parliament for the construction of a special prison for political detainees, Prieto remarked: "Let them prepare the jail for us as comfortably as possible, if we are not lucky enough to get across the frontier next time. If the future once more holds for us imprisonment or expatriation, we shall deserve it. For senselessness [*insensatos*]."

When the results of the special election to the executive commission were announced by the *prietista* secretariat at the end of the month, the González Peña slate was declared the winner, 10,933 to 2,876. This seemed like a very low vote in view of the 59,000 names on the party membership rolls, but the administration had systematically invalidated votes from local *caballerista* groups who had not maintained their dues or were guilty of other infractions, while ignoring ballots from members of the JSU who had no proper claim to party membership.[32]

On 2 July *Claridad* replied that in fact nearly 22,000 votes had been cast for Largo and claimed further that at a recent congress in Jaén the revolutionary platform, including the building of a broad Worker-Peasant Alliance and a unified Socialist-Communist party, had carried by 1,438 votes to 523. It suggested that a special investigative committee, selected half by the executive commission and half by the Madrid section of the party, be chosen to scrutinize the electoral results, but the executive commission quickly decided to have none of that.

During the second week of July, Largo was in London to represent the UGT at the international trade union congress. There, once more, he struck down the line assiduously cultivated by moderates which tried to present the 1934 insurrection as an effort to "save Republican democracy," stressing instead that the insurrection had been strictly a "class movement."[33] On 10 July another Andalusian provincial Socialist congress, this time in Cádiz, supported the left position by a vote of eighty-eight to two.[34]

Aside from the Communist-dominated JSU, the only unity during June was to be found in Catalonia, where the Catalan sections of the Socialist and Communist parties, together with the small regional Unió Socialista de Catalunya and Partit Català Proletari, reached agreement on the formation of a new united Partit Socialist Unificat de Catalunya (PSUC), which would prove to be increasingly Communist-dominated.[35]

The "Catalan Oasis"

Catalonia, in fact, proved a partial exception to the jagged pattern of misgovernment, extreme polarization, and violence during the spring of 1936. Though the CNT sustained a high volume of strike activity and there were numerous strike-related incidents as well as nonlethal bomb explosions, only three political killings were recorded in Barcelona (two of them the Badía murders in April). The Catalan economy suffered as did that of the rest of Spain, but extreme disorder and major arson were rarer. The Catalan government pushed through a new version of the "Law of Cultivation

Contracts" that was largely accepted by the Lliga, resolving the original controversy of 1934.

Lluis Companys, once again president of the Generalitat, had learned much more than the *caballeristas*. He made a more serious effort than Azaña and Casares Quiroga to maintain order and Catalonia was spared at least the worst effects of the new round of churchburnings and religious persecution. Companys also tried to encourage a broad labor settlement to shore up the economy, though in this he was less successful. He did not promote the politics of polarization, and in May the more extreme Estat Català separated from the Esquerra, though it continued to participate in the Catalan government. Though sharp tension between left and right also existed in Catalonia, both the Companys government and the center-right made an effort to work toward understanding. A number of local centers of the Lliga were closed by the authorities, but the Lliga leaders tried to meet the responsibilities of a loyal opposition, and by early July Companys had begun negotiations to achieve a new agreement with Catalan conservatives.[36]

The Strike Wave and Disturbances of May and June

Major strike activity had not been a primary feature of the first weeks after the Popular Front victory. Negative measures taken by some business interests — the abandonment of a number of enterprises, various lockouts, and above all the flight of capital — had been responses to the election results but not at first the result of major new trade union pressure. The Azaña administration, as mentioned earlier, had moved quickly to begin to restore the structure and authority of the *jurados mixtos,* even though new legislation that totally reestablished their original character was not approved by the Cortes until 20–21 June. Massive strikes only appeared with warm weather in mid-spring, with a great increase in May that continued at an even more intense rate desiring June. During those two months alone, strike activity was approximately as great as in all of 1932 or 1934 (minus October), and for the first six and a half months of 1936 was greater than for 1933 (the previous high in Spanish history), if the total number of strikers is considered as well. (see table 13.1.) The absolute volume, which may have involved as many as one million workers at the same time by late June, was proportionately no greater than that of the strike wave in France that developed following the Popular Front electoral victory there in May. The French strike wave of late May and June is thought to have involved possibly as many as two million workers at its height, roughly the same proportion of the labor force, mu-

Table 13.1. Strike Activity under the Republic

Strikes by Year	
1931	734
1932	681
1933	1127
1934	594
1935	181
1936	1108
Strikes by Month 1936	
January	26
February	19
March	47
April	105
May	242
June	444
July	225

Source: *Boletín del Ministerio de Trabajo 1936.*

tatis mutandis, as in Spain. The main difference was that in France the government quickly channeled the strikes into pragmatic economic settlements, while the massive work stoppages in Spain took on more of a pre-revolutionary tone. This was not because the CNT and UGT were demanding immediate collectivization of industry or the land, but because economic terms in Spain were so extravagant that in many cases they were simply beyond the ability of employers to pay or, if fully granted, would have amounted to de facto worker control. They were also frequently successful in imposing the closed shop, resulting in the firing of a considerable number of Catholic trade union members and precipitating a rapid decline of the smaller Catholic syndicates.[37] A remarkable feature was that all this occurred while the official unemployment rate remained at about 800,000 (approximately the same total as in France, indicating that registered unemployment was proportionately nearly twice as much in Spain — though again Spanish statistics included the only partially unemployed). This underscores the essentially political character of many of the strikes, a feature stressed by many commentators.

The large seamen's strike in May had international repercussions, tying up Spanish shipping in some foreign ports as well. By early June the dockers and crewmen had won total victory with a large wage increase, reduction in hours, and major fringe benefits. The terms of settlement would nominally require such an increase in manpower that there were neither enough crewmen nor enough space in the crewmen's quarters of Spanish merchant ships to hold them, leaving some vessels to idle in port and Spanish commerce facing catastrophic costs. Prieto warned on 25 May that the terms impending would provoke "a crisis infinitely greater"[38] than the preceding exploitation of dockers and crewmen.

In Barcelona the demands of hotel employees would have wrecked the hotel industry. When owners offered to cede part of their property to workers as shares in return for a more cooperative settlement, the CNT refused. In similar actions, the Valencia streetcar company and an Andalusian rail line were forced into dissolution, their services taken over by local government. Less spectacularly, hundreds of small businessmen were being ruined. After the contractors' association gave in to exorbitant demands by striking CNT construction workers in Seville, the secretary of the CNT national committee, Horacio Prieto, urged his comrades to moderate demands before desperate employers, now willing to concede anything reasonable, were pushed into the arms of a protofascist reaction.

In some categories unemployment inevitably increased, general production declined, tax receipts dropped, and more and more capital fled the country. It became increasingly difficult to fund the debt and float government bonds. Business leaders pleaded with the government to take decisive measures to stabilize the economy and reach some sort of agreement with the trade unions. On 7 June *La Veu de Catalunya* published a "Manifesto" signed by 126 local and regional employers' associations. It expressed their willingness to accept most of the Popular Front's economic program but urged the government to take immediate measures to control economic anarchy, suggesting a temporary end to wage increases, reform of labor tribunals to achieve fair arbitration, and a national "Labor Conference" to try to straighten things out. Resolutions of the extraordinary assembly of the national chambers of commerce and industry in Madrid, as reported in *El Sol* on 26 June and 5 July, expressed the same concern. These urgent pleas were virtually ignored.

Perhaps the most conspicuous and conflictive single strike was the one initiated by the CNT in Madrid construction on 1 June. As mentioned earlier, the CNT's "Sindicato Unico de la Construcción" (SUC) in Madrid had grown greatly, particularly by championing unskilled workers. On 19 April it had voted to demand a thirty-six-hour work week, a pay increase of 15 to 17 percent for skilled and semi-skilled workers, and a 50 percent increase for the unskilled (*peones*). These demands were also assumed in toto by the UGT the following month to avoid being outflanked. The employers, facing ruinous cost increases, took a hard line, and soon after the strike began it involved 110,000 workers, the construction workers having been joined by other allied trades. As usual, the CNT refused to cooperate with the *jurado mixto*, though the UGT was willing to do so, so the Ministry of Labor unilaterally presented its own *laudo* or settlement on 3 July on the basis of a forty-hour week and salary increases ranging from 5 to 12 percent—very generous under the circumstances, but not ruinous for employers. UGT strikers voted three to one to accept these terms, which were rejected by the SUC. Even *ugetistas* were slow to return to work, and the strike was still continuing when the Civil War began.[39]

Major strikes such as this one involved large-scale demonstrations and sometimes violence, the CNT particularly not being reluctant to use force to keep strikes going. In late spring, sixty thousand shop clerks were on strike in Barcelona, and it was claimed that approximately half the workers in Madrid were off the job by July, though conditions, as usual, varied greatly in different parts of the country.[40]

Even leaders of the Socialist left became somewhat concerned about the proliferation and radicalization of strikes. On 22 May the executive commission of the UGT ruled that there should be no further UGT strikes without direct authorization from the pertinent national federation, but this was sometimes ignored. From about the second half of May the pro-Republican press registered increasing alarm and *Política*, the main organ of Izquierda Republicana, called with mounting frequency for law and order. On 23 June the editors of *Solidaridad Obrera* also admitted that the strike wave had gotten out of hand and recommended that the CNT as a whole might want to push for lower prices, rather than ever higher and more unrealistic wage settlements. Alternately, CNT leaders suggested that the syndicates might wish to save their strength for the great revolutionary general strike at some unspecified point in the future. The leadership of the Communist Party also began to work to moderate the strike wave, though it had only limited influence among organized labor.

The greatest labor disorder was to be found not in the cities but in the countryside of the south-center and south. The FNTT resolutely rejected any minimal work or productivity standards and also rejected as inadequate the government's proposal to give land to 100,000 new settlers per year. The CNT also added members rapidly in the southern countryside and set even more radical terms. Forced *alojamientos* and *siegas por asalto* (arbitrary entry to harvest on the workers' terms) drove smaller landowners to the brink of ruin, yet did not meet all workers' needs either. New labor contracts in the countryside imposed severe terms to maximize the employment of adult male labor. The increased labor costs under the Republic had encouraged many large landowners to move more rapidly toward mechanization, yet new labor contracts in the southern countryside placed specific restrictions on the use of machinery.[41] Continued bad weather, late planting and harvesting, and lack of credit for small farmers and new settlers all compounded the problems, leading the Ministry of Agriculture to forecast a 27 percent decline in the wheat harvest.[42] Some farmland was simply abandoned, and smaller owners sought to hire only the most minimal outside labor. The most extreme conditions probably prevailed in Badajoz province, where over one-third of all adult male landless laborers had already received some land. This only whetted the appetite for further economic relief, producing arbitrary actions on a large scale, as "thousands of workers wandered around . . . in a futile search for jobs" in a province "which seems to have been in complete chaos on the eve of the Civil War."[43] By the end of June the UGT had begun a national campaign for the immediate uncompensated expropriation of all land not being cultivated, and illegal takeovers of one form or another were apparently still continuing in certain provinces.

A precise census of all the land that changed hands in these months will probably never be possible. A leading social historian concludes:

> Our hypothesis, though it is not certain and needs to be tested further, is that the de facto occupation of land, whether by *yunteros*, by legal beneficiaries of the agrarian reform, new settlers on confiscated land already in process of reclassification, or simply de facto occupation — sometimes in the form of *alojamientos* — registered by the rural police commission with the Junta Provincial Agraria, may have amounted to about one million hectares by the time the Civil War began.[44]

This calculation, the best that can be made without much more research, would amount to about 2.5 percent of the 40 million hectares of agrarian property in Spain, but 5 percent of the approximately 20 million hectares of cropland. This was not yet a revolution, though it could be seen as the beginning of one. The shift in land ownership had already provoked massive consequences in some of the southern provinces where the proportion of cropland which had changed hands was much higher than 5 percent.[45]

Yet the great majority of the farmworkers in the UGT and CNT seem to have had little notion of a thoroughgoing economic revolution. Most evidently wanted much higher wages or land of their own to work on easy terms. As Julián Besteiro warned in the Cortes and as an agrarian expert pointed out in *El Sol* (15 and 17 July), the real effect of all the strikes and rural harassment, especially in the southwest, was not to effect a positive revolution in ownership and production but to divert as much as possible of the short-term income to farmworkers and some smallholders. Mechanization was thwarted, and medium and sometimes even smallholders were being ruined without any real attempt to build the basis for a more modern and efficient rural economy. The economic consequences of the agrarian prerevolution in the south were primarily destructive.

Many strikes were accompanied by violence, the rate of which had begun to increase in mid-April. The incidence of violence mounted steadily with warmer weather, hitting a high point around 25 May, and remaining very near that level for the next seven weeks. Falangists and rightists were killed by the left, leftists in turn were slain mainly by Falangists, striking (usually demonstrating) workers were shot at and killed by police, and sometimes policemen were killed in return. After Falangists killed a Socialist newspaper editor in Santander on 3 June, four Falangists or suspected Falangists were slain in that city during the next forty-eight hours.

One of the more bizarre set of incidents, which caused no fatalities, started in Alcalá de Henares on 15 May, when several officers of the local garrison were assaulted by leftists, who then set fire to the home of one of the officers. The Socialists of Alcalá then petitioned the government to transfer the two regiments of the local garrison, alleging fascist and conspiratorial proclivities among its officers. Casares Quiroga agreed, and the units were ordered to be ready to move within forty-eight hours. When the officers protested, a number were arrested, court-martialed, and sentenced to varying prison terms, heightening the sense of outrage among the military. Rather similarly, after an affray between workers and the Civil Guard in Oviedo on 23 May, protests against the use of force by the latter led to the arrest and prosecution of five Civil Guard officers.

The heaviest mortality from any of the explosions of violence that spring took place near the small town of Yeste in Albacete province, southeast of Madrid, on 29 May. The inhabitants of a neighboring hill pueblo called La Graya had lost much of their livelihood following inauguration during the previous year of a new dam in the valley below, one of the accomplishments of the Republic's public works program. Approximately a thousand families had drawn their living from logging and other activities in the area now under water, while the remaining forest in the hills above could not be exploited economically for the opposite reason — there would be too great a distance between the felled logs and the water needed to transport them. The new provincial government appointed by the Azaña administration had opened some small public lands for private timbering by local workers, but with the coming of warm weather many began to take the law into their own hands, illegally cutting timber on private property, though it could not be marketed in large quantities. After complaints from landowners, the local workers were ordered to cease this activity and nineteen Civil Guards were dispatched to La Graya, where six workers were arrested on 27 May. Their arrest brought out a large concentration of workers and their families from surrounding villages, who blocked the road on the twenty-ninth when the Civil Guards attempted to take their prisoners to Yeste. Local authorities decided to pacify the crowd by freeing the prisoners.

When, however, the Guard detachment resumed its journey to Yeste, it was surrounded and almost overwhelmed on the road by a crowd of perhaps as many as two thousand. One guard was killed, struck in the head with a logging hook (*gancho pinero*), and all the rest suffered some sort of injuries, ranging from minor bruises to serious wounds. Three managed to hold onto their weapons, drawing off from the crowd just enough to begin to pour volley after volley into them at point-blank range. The gunfire immediately sent the crowd into a panicked flight, and as other guards picked themselves up and recovered their weapons, they joined in the shooting. By the time that the crowd had gotten out of range, seventeen lay dead and more than thirty had been wounded.[46]

This bloody incident reflected the sense of desperation among poor workers, as well as their extreme hostility and aggressiveness, and also the oft-demonstrated inadequacy of the Civil Guard—in both training and equipment—to handle crowd control humanely. It drew a storm of protest from the extreme left, which alleged another Arnedo or Casas Viejas, though the circumstances were quite different. The matter was aired in the Cortes on 5 June, though it was then agreed to leave it in the hands of an investigative judge.

The government's only response to these incidents was to arrest more Falangists and also sometimes to close the local centers of sections of the CNT who prosecuted strikes by illegal or violent means, ignoring the *jurados mixtos*. Neither of these policies had much effect, for both the fascist and anarchosyndicalist organizations were growing rapidly. It is no exaggeration to say that for every Falangist arrested—and there were eventually several thousand in jail—ten young rightists joined the movement in order to participate in direct action against the left.[47]

Nor did the partial press censorship, which continued to the very end, have any effect in dampening passions. As one American scholar put it:

Government censorship tried to suppress the news of strikes and assassinations because the ministers feared the contagion of violence. Copy for daily newspapers had to be rushed to the official press bureau for examination; the deleted sections appeared as blank space or with broken type. The Paris *Temps*, arriving a few days late in Madrid, was often more informative than the newspapers of the Spanish capital. Only when one gathered a batch of provincial papers and turned to the pages entitled Social Conflicts could one fully realize the scope of labor discontent for which there were no official statistics.[48]

The national council of Izquierda Republicana issued a public statement on 30 May that lamented: "Spain has been viewed abroad as a country in permanent civil war, incapable of democratic coexistence. The Republic is considered an unstable, interim regime, whose consolidation is made difficult by the Republicans themselves."[49] It urged all the local sections of the party to do everything possible to calm passions and maintain legality. The party newspaper *Política* made frequent calls for moderation, while also lamenting that convicted Falangists and rightists often received mild sentences. The parliamentary delegations of Izquierda Republicana and Unión Republicana approved a joint resolution on 11 June, asking the government to undertake stronger measures to restore order. In the days that followed *Política* praised the French CGT for having just signed a sweeping new national labor agreement dampening the strike wave in France, while it continued to denounce the CNT for flaunting the arbitration of jurados and seeking to ruin the UGT. At the same time it championed the position of the petite bourgeoisie and underscored the importance of the alliance between petit-bourgeois left Republicanism and organized labor, assigning major responsibility for social and economic turmoil to the larger employers. The only real polemic between *Política* and *Claridad* took place during the second half of June, when the former blamed the Socialist left for the bizarre incident in Ecija and for subverting the Socialist Party and the unity of the Popular Front.

On 11 June the government, as usual, asked the Cortes to extend the *estado de alarma* for thirty days more, and on the morrow issued new orders for the disarming of those who possessed weapons illegally (though scarcely any Socialists were ever arrested), together with new sanctions against employers who flouted official labor regulations and new measures to end strikes conducted by illicit means. This was accompanied by further reassignments in military and Civil Guard posts, but there is no evidence that anything was achieved by any of these measures. The government was now acutely aware that it was conducting—with the utmost confusion, uncertainty, and incoherence—a battle on two fronts. One indication was that by mid-June Casares Quiroga was making positive remarks about the Civil Guard.

Confrontation in the Cortes

Some moderate Republicans lost hope for the Casares Quiroga government within a matter of days, and soon a few proposed more drastic alternatives. Felipe Sánchez Román had actively participated in conversations for some six weeks concerning the formation of a larger and stronger majority coalition, yet the proposed leader, Prieto, had refused to take the plunge, due to the veto of the left Socialists. A meeting of the leaders of Sánchez Román's tiny Partido Nacional Republicano (PNR) therefore approved the following declaration on 25 May:

At the present time the PNR, its authority increased by having foreseen the difficulties that the Popular Front would face and enjoying the freedom of movement provided by its absence from the government, has the responsibility of uniting other Republicans in an understanding of the seriousness of the situation, recognizing the failure of the so-called Popular Front in its present form and the need to take measures to save the country and the Republic.

Political agreement should be based on the following measures:

Immediate execution of the program of defense of the Republican state, vigorously reestablishing the principle of authority together with a program of social reform and economic development agreed upon by the Republican Left, Republican Union and National Republican Parties.

Fulfillment of the reforms benefitting the working class that were included in the Popular Front electoral program.

The taking of necessary measures to prevent those social and political forces that are actually most interested in the execution of this program from being the greatest obstacle to its accomplishment.

The following steps should be taken:

a. Severe repression of incitement to revolutionary violence.

b. General disarmament.

c. Dissolution of all political, professional, economic or religious organizations whose activity gravely threatens the independence, constitutional unity, democratic-republican form or security of the Spanish Republic.

d. Prohibition of uniformed or paramilitary societies.

e. A law establishing the legal responsibility of leaders of political organizations for the crimes provoked by the latter's propaganda.

f. Prosecution of local government authorities for the infractions of law which they may commit in exercising their functions. Where circumstance requires, mayors may be relieved of supervision of public order and this function transferred to other authorities.

g. The rules of parliament will be reformed to improve the structure and functioning of parliamentary committees, so that with the assistance of technical agencies new legislation can be completed more quickly.

Señor Sánchez Román will present our request to the leaders of the Republican Union and Republican Left Parties. Once an agreement has been reached, the Socialist Party will be publicly invited to participate in a new government to carry out this program.

Should the Socialists refuse to collaborate, the [left] Republicans will urge the President to form a government of representatives of all the Republican forces [presumably referring to the center parties] willing to support the program approved by the left Republican parties. A team of Republican ministers recognized for their authority, competence and prestige will be appointed. They will govern above the level of party politics, rejecting any kind of demagogic appeal.

If the government does not receive parliamentary support, Cortes sessions will be suspended in conformity with constitutional statutes.

Alternately, parliament might be presented with a bill authorizing the government to legislate by decree, under the powers granted by Article 81 of the constitution, regarding concrete matters that demand urgent attention.[50]

Not for nothing was Sánchez Román the political figure whom Azaña perhaps most admired for measure, wisdom, and judgment, but the president showed no inclination to take this sage, if drastic, advice from his good friend. It would have required him to abandon the basically leftist strategy to which he had always clung and would officially have broken the Popular Front, though the latter had no official existence on the national level since the elections.

Nonetheless, the proposal of the PNR, in some ways a logical alternative to the earlier project of a Prieto majority coalition, found support among some of the most moderate and sensible left Republicans, as well as among sectors of the center, and perhaps Prieto itself. It was apparently discussed at the meeting of the Izquierda Republicana and Unión Republicana parliamentary groups, who may have passed the proposal on to the Casares Quiroga government, which rejected it.[51] Casares declared that there was no need for a special coalition or a government with extraordinary powers, declaring in the next Cortes session on 16 June that this would "open the path to dictatorship."

During the final two months of the Republic the Cortes served as the only political sounding board not subject to censorship, and during this last phase the principal spokesmen for the two sides were the prime minister on the one hand and Calvo Sotelo on the other. Though Gil Robles and spokesmen for the center still held the podium from time to time, Calvo Sotelo, more clear and uncompromising, had become more and more the voice of the right. Casares Quiroga and Calvo Sotelo were both Galicians, yet totally different in physique, style, and political loyalties, and cordially detested each other. Casares was slender, intense, emotional, and physically ill with a consumption that was controlled but never quite cured. Calvo Sotelo was broad-shouldered, corpulent, a bull of a man, vigorous, analytical, and with greater emotional control, yet categorically outspoken.

The session of 16 June was possibly the most dramatic and oft-quoted in the history of the Republic. Gil Robles read another of his periodic statistical summaries of disorder, alleging that from 15 February to 15 June 269 people had been killed and 1,287 injured in political violence, 160 churches totally destroyed, and 251 churches and other religious buildings damaged. During the month since Casares Quiroga's appointment, there had been sixty-nine deaths and thirty-six churches had been destroyed. All these indictments by the right were simply the reverse image of those by the left; whereas the latter insisted the right was to blame for everything, rightist spokesmen categorically blamed all violence on the government and the left. Gil Robles concluded with a final list of disorders which he said had been committed during the past twenty-four hours, reporting that the British Auto Club had informed its members that it was unsafe to drive in Spain because of random violence and money extorted by leftists from motorists on the highways.

Calvo Sotelo then rose, declaring that this was the fourth time in three months that he had addressed in parliament the problem of public order. By this point the session had grown stormy, with frequent interruptions and name-calling, a tactic that Calvo could not resist using against the prime minister himself when the latter interrupted his speech with a remark. Calvo insisted that the situation in Spain could only be rectified by an "integral state" of authority, and that if such a state need be called "a fascist state," then "I declare myself to be a fascist." Casares then took the floor to denounce the preceding speaker, declaring that "after what the honorable gentleman has said in parliament, I shall hold him responsible before the country for whatever may or may not occur." Casares also denied that International Red Aid was practicing extortion on the highways — a blatant untruth, Alcalá Zamora having been one of the victims.[52]

As usual, Juan Ventosa of the Lliga provided the most objective and telling analysis:

> What most alarms me in today's session is the optimism of the president of the council of ministers, who finds the situation acceptable enough and even agreeable. I leave for him the responsibility for that statement before Spain and the world abroad, since the events occuring here are well known everywhere. And the gravest aspect is his argument that what is happening today is justified because of what happened two years ago. But can the excesses and injustices of some justify the outrages, injustices and violence of others? Are we perpetually condemned in Spain to live in a regime of successive conflicts, in which the rise to power or triumph in elections initiates the hunting down, persecution or liquidation of adversaries? If that were so, we would have to renounce being Spaniards, because civilized life would be incompatible with our country.

Ventosa denounced the new legislation to "republicanize the judiciary," terming it correctly a project to "destroy the independence of the judicial branch" and concluded:

José Calvo Sotelo

Maintain the Popular Front or break it; do whatever you please, but if the government is not prepared to cease to be a belligerent on one side and to impose on all equally the respect for law, it is better that it resign, for above the parties and political combinations is the supreme interest of Spain, now threatened with catastrophe.

Joaquín Maurín of the POUM rose to make exactly the opposite point, that "the government has not even carried out the hundredth part of the Popular Front program," asserting that what was needed was rule of the revolutionary parties, the nationalization of much of the economy, and the elimination of fascism, "today a real threat."

After Gil Robles spoke the second time, Calvo Sotelo rose to utter the most famous paragraph of his life, often quoted subsequently as a kind of epitaph:

I have, Señor Casares Quiroga, broad shoulders. The honorable gentleman is quick and facile in threatening gestures and words of menace. I have heard three or four of his speeches as prime minister, and in all of them were words of threats. Very well, Señor Casares Quiroga. I am fully notified of your threats. . . . I accept with pleasure and shirk none of the responsibilities that may be derived from acts that I perform, and I also accept those of others if they are for the good of my country and the glory of Spain. . . . Let the honorable gentleman measure his own responsibilities, review the history of the past twenty-five years and observe the sad and bloody tones that envelop two figures who played premier roles in the tragedy of two peoples: Russia and Hungary. They were Kerensky and Karolyi. Kerensky represented ignorance; Karolyi, the betrayal of a whole millenary civilization. The honorable gentleman will not be Kerensky, because he is not witless, he is fully aware of what he says, what he keeps silent and what he thinks. May God grant that the honorable gentleman may never be able to compare himself with Karolyi.

The debate eventually ended with the government winning a vote of confidence by a wide margin.

Julián Zugazagoitia, the editor of *El Socialista*, later wrote that this session

was one of the days when I saw Prieto most worried. His concern was deepened by great irritation: "This chamber has no sense of responsibility. I don't know if we are really deaf or merely pretend to be. The speech that Gil Robles delivered this afternoon was extremely grave. When I heard behind me bursts of laughter and stupid interruptions, I couldn't help feeling shamed. Gil Robles, who was fully conscious of that he was saying, must feel for us a mixture of pity and scorn. I remember that the chief of the CEDA told us that his party, after a careful examination, had developed its activity within the orbit of the Republic but that he, personally, was not sure if he had made a mistake by so advising his colleagues, and that in any event his authority and influence to keep them from breaking with the Republic was less every day. 'This decline of my authority,' he said, 'stems from the conduct of the Republic and the decline of my own faith that it can become a legal channel of the national will.' And he even added: 'I condemn violence, which promises no good result, and deplore that many and dear friends accept that hope as the only solution.' The meaning of those words could not be clearer. The CEDA itself is being absorbed by the movement that the military are preparing together with the monarchists." With a gesture of fatalistic despair, Prieto added: "Only one thing is clear: that we are going to deserve a catastrophe because of our stupidity."[53]

With all hope for a broader left-center/center majority coalition apparently at an end, the increasingly desperate situation was analyzed by Miguel Maura, one of the founders of the Republic, in a series of six widely read articles in *El Sol* between 18 and 27 June. He observed that

In rural and provincial affairs the anonymous, radicalized masses rule through the governors controlled by the Jacobin committees of the Popular Front, whose disorders and excesses are legalized by the mayors and *gestora*[54] presidents, a veritable Bolshevist plague that is devastating the country. Peaceful citizens live with the sensation that laws are a dead letter and that arson, assaults, destruction of property, insults, murders and aggression against the armed forces no longer count in the penal code for those who wear a red and blue shirt[55] or the insignia of the hammer and sickle. The clenched fist is safe conduct and talisman for the greatest excesses.

There could not fail to be a reaction. This has taken shape in the alarming form of what is called "fascism." People have joined that movement en masse . . . , though of authentic Italian Fascism it has only the name and a few doctrinal postulates of which the majority of its affiliates are ignorant.

Today the Republic is no more — though I would like to believe unconsciously — than the tool of the violent, revolutionary sector of the working classes, which, shielded by the liberal democratic system and the blindness of certain leaders of the Republican parties, is preparing in minute detail an assault on the government and the extermination of capitalist and middle-class society. . . . They tell us this themselves in their newspapers and public meetings.

. . . If the Republic is to be this, it is inexorably condemned to swift extinction at the hands of those who claim to be its defenders, or, which is more probable, at the hands of a reaction from the opposite direction.

Maura called for a multiparty "national Republican dictatorship"[56] to save the country, but added, "I do not harbor the slightest hope that my reasoning could convince those who currently bear responsibility for government." This dismal conclusion was absolutely correct, for Maura's telling analysis, accurate both in perspective and detail, merely drew the standard denunciations from the left Republican, *caballerista*, Communist, and anarchist press. *Política* blustered on 28 June that the proposal was "as reactionary as anything that could have been thought up by a leader of the extreme right." Four days earlier it had assured its readers that if the CEDA ever got back into government "it would establish a fascism as ferocious and inhuman as that of the Nazis."

Of the Popular Front groups, the one which showed the most concern was Unión Republicana, the most moderate. It held a national congress from 27 to 29 June in Madrid, where Martínez Barrio warned that "what the Spanish people cannot stand is to live in a state of constant insurrection" and proposed as a possible solution "governmental collaboration with the Socialists, even giving them the leadership." Though, in the closing address, he said that the Casares Quiroga government would not soon come to an end, Martínez Barrio repeated that in the long run they must look toward Socialist collaboration, and possible leadership. References to a possible Prieto government could still be found from time to time in the left Republican press,[57] and Prieto was quoted by a French newspaper on 2 July as saying that what the Republic needed was a government that was "not dictatorial, but authoritarian. Authority must reside, more than in persons, in institutions."[58] As Ossorio y Gallardo had written a few days earlier:

No one is happy with the present situation. I talk with representatives of all sectors of the Popular Front and in private conversations all reveal themselves to be as worried, preoccupied and anguished as the conservative forces. This is the truth, the pure truth, though it is always covered up in the service of party politics.[59]

The final long, conflictive Cortes debate began at 7:00 P.M. on 1 July and lasted twelve hours, marred by frequent shouts and incidents. Deputies were involved in pushing and punching each other on at least two occasions, one CEDA deputy was expelled from the chamber, and Martínez Barrio, the president of the Cortes, even threatened to walk out in protest. This was also the session in which the Socialist Angel Galarza replied to Calvo Sotelo with the remark that against the latter "anything was justified, even personal assassination," words that Martínez Barrio ordered stricken from the record but that were picked up by several journalists.[60]

The main business was the right's interpellation of Ruiz Funes, the agriculture minister, which the Socialists attempted to guillotine but failed for a lack of votes. Jose María Cid spoke for the Agrarian Party, reciting a long catalogue of abuses in the countryside, concluding "Does the government wish to convert the capitalist system into a Marxist one? Let it say so with all clarity!" Ruiz Funes replied that the government had to wrestle with grave problems, including no less than eight thousand claims for damages still facing the Agriculture Ministry over lost jobs and illegal wage reductions in the past two years. He insisted that "in all the labor problems with which I deal I respect the limits of economic profitability. I will not tolerate anyone insinuating that the government is going along with a movement toward socialization."

In this final stage, the leftist group with the most clearly defined policy was the relatively insignificant Communist Party. Two of its priorities for the present Popular Front phase — confiscation of sizable amounts of land and beginning of direct elimination of the rightist political groups — had already been initiated piecemeal by the government, even though the latter did not at all define these in the same terms. On 1 July the Communist delegation in the Cortes submitted to other Popular Front delegations a legislative proposal to order the arrest of everyone in any position of responsibility at the time of the Asturian insurrection from Lerroux on down, subjecting them to plenary prosecution and confiscation of property.[61] This was of dubious constitutionality and was not accepted by the left Republicans, but on 9 July the Communists won a pledge from the other Popular Front groups to delay the summer recess until the question of "responsibilities" for the repression had been settled.[62]

The last eight regular sessions of the Cortes in early July were devoted primarily to discussing the restoration of traditional common lands to municipalities and a possible drastic surtax on the wealthiest landowners. As the summer heat increased, interest waned and attendance declined. Parliament also took up the issue of extending further amnesty legislation, with center and rightist deputies saying that any such move would be unjust unless it included amnesty for those who had defended the legally established order in 1934.

There were a few signs of moderation. After a special caucus of the Popular Front deputies and visits by the Socialist executive commission to the prime minister on 9 and 10 July, there was renewed speculation about a possible change in government. Rumors conjectured that the left might have lost control of the Socialist parliamentary delegation, which might now be willing to support a more broadly based coalition, though there has never been any evidence to support such a speculation. In an interview with an Argentine reporter on 11 July, Calvo Sotelo opined that despite the increase in strikes he believed that there was less danger of another leftist insurrection than there had been in February.

The rumors and conversations of 9–11 July proved a brief lull before the final storm. Calvo Sotelo and key leaders of the CEDA had already been informed that a military revolt was imminent and had pledged their support.

The Assassination of Calvo Sotelo

The extreme tension of the summer of 1936 has obscured the fact that the vast majority of Spaniards were leading normal lives and spending an unusually large amount on entertainment. Movie theaters were full, and there were numerous summer festivals and special athletic events, the most unique of which was the international "People's Olympics" scheduled to open in Barcelona on 19 July, in antithesis to the regular Olympics held in Hitler's Berlin that summer.[63] The "People's Olympics" had strong political overtones, but elsewhere many millions were simply trying to enjoy themselves and forget social and political strife.

Yet violence continued with little abatement, as did church burnings and the confiscation of religious property. A group of CEDA members from the east petitioned the Ministry of Justice that in a district in Valencia province comprising forty-one towns, with a combined population of about 100,000, all churches had been closed and eighty-eight priests expelled. A major incident occurred in Valencia on the evening of Saturday, 11 July, when four armed Falangists briefly seized the microphone of Radio Valencia to announce the imminent outbreak of the Falangist "national syndicalist revolution." This provoked a leftist riot in Spain's fourth-largest city that put rightist centers to the torch and was quelled only after a regiment of cavalry was ordered into the streets.

Four days earlier *El Socialista* had lamented that "the system of violence as party politics is expanding in menacing proportions, though every civilized value is outraged by the shameful murder of citizens. A psychological regression has reduced us to political 'gangsterism'." By this time the pessimistic Prieto had finally given up hope of redeeming the immediate political situation and accepted some sort of breakdown, blowup, or armed revolt from the right as inevitable and not long to be delayed. He no longer continued his persistent but unheeded calls to moderation and now began to emphasize the importance of the unity of the left, urging the government to be more vigilant and vigorous, writing in *El Liberal* on 9 July that "a man well prepared is worth two and a government already prepared is worth forty."

The final and conclusive round of violence began in Madrid on 2 July, when a group of JSU gunmen fired on a bar frequented by Falangists, killing two Falangist students plus a third customer. On the following night, Falangist gunmen sprayed with gunfire a group of workers leaving a neighborhood Casa del Pueblo, killing two UGT workers and seriously wounding others. On the following day, two corpses were discovered outside

Madrid. One was identified as that of an eighteen-year-old student and son of a local businessman, not a Falangist officially but a friend of Falangists, who had evidently been held prisoner for several days and then shot to death. The other was that of a thirty-year-old retired infantry officer, either a member or sympathizer of the Falange, who had been kidnapped and stabbed thirty-three times. The government responded with further arrests of Falangists; during the next three days it announced the arrest of three hundred Falangists and rightists in Madrid province alone, though as usual no Socialists were arrested.[64]

The climactic acts took place the following weekend. About 10:00 P.M. on Sunday, 12 July the Assault Guard officer José del Castillo was shot and killed on a street in central Madrid as he was en route to reporting for duty on the night shift. Castillo was a former army officer and an ardent Socialist who had transferred to the Assault Guard and was arrested in 1934 for refusal to obey orders during the repression. The Azaña government had reassigned him to active service once more, and in recent months he had distinguished himself for his zeal in repressing the right, having severely wounded a young Carlist student during the mayhem of 16 April, as well as having engaged in various actions against Falangists. A militant of the UMRA and a leader in the Socialist militia, he had long been a marked man.[65]

His killing immediately provoked intense reactions among his comrades in the UMRA, Assault Guards, and Socialist militia. Two months earlier on 8 May Falangists had murdered in Madrid Capt. Carlos Faraudo, an army officer on active duty and also a leading figure in the UMRA and instructor for the Socialist militia. Though two Falangists had soon been arrested for Faraudo's killing, his UMRA comrades had vowed to exact vengeance if another of their number were killed. Soon after learning of Castillo's death, a group of Assault Guard officers went directly to the Ministry of the Interior to demand action, where they were received by the Left Republican undersecretary Bibiano Ossorio Tafall, who was being assiduously courted by the Communists and would later reveal himself to be a fellow traveler.[66] He quickly took them to see Juan Moles, the minister, who approved their demand that leading rightists be arrested in retaliation, ordering that the Dirección General de Seguridad rapidly prepare lists of suspicious rightists to be arrested that night. After the lists were made out, the Assault Guard officers returned directly to their central Pontejos barracks, less than a block from the ministry, where arrest orders were prepared and given to various squads of Assault Guards.[67]

The busy Pontejos barracks was frequented that night by a good many others, including Socialist and Communist activitists and militiamen, in

Lt. José Castillo

addition to authorized personnel. It had generally been the policy of the government to reinstate leftist personnel irrespective of charges against them and to permit increasing politicization of police functions, including the intermittent inclusion of civilian leftist activists, such as the Socialist militia "deputized" for the Cuenca elections. Thus the Assault Guard squads which arrested dozens of rightists in Madrid that night were sometimes also accompanied by civilian leftists.[68]

Since not all the names on the lists could be apprehended in one night, a selection was sometimes made of the most important rightists. It is not clear that the original lists prepared by the Dirección General included the names of major parliamentary leaders such as Calvo Sotelo and Gil Robles, who possessed immunity and against whom no charges were pending, but their names and those of a few other rightist leaders were apparently added in the Pontejos barracks, with the aim, it would seem, of holding them at least temporarily as hostages to avert further killings by the right or even to find incriminating evidence that might strip them of immunity.

The unit assigned to arrest Calvo Sotelo was not led by an Assault Guard officer but by a Civil Guard captain named Fernando Condés. Like the slain Castillo, Condés was a former army officer (decorated in the final Moroccan campaign) who had passed to the Civil Guard, where he was one of the few leftist officers. He had played a direct role in the abortive insurrection of October 1934 in Madrid, for which he had been sentenced to life imprisonment and then reprieved by the Popular Front victory. Yet because he had betrayed the Civil Guard in 1934 even the Azaña–Casares Quiroga administrations hesitated to restore him to duty immediately. He had finally been returned to duty on 1 July, with promotion to captain as a reward for his earlier subversion. Even so, he still had not actively returned to service and was dressed in civilian clothes when he led an Assault Guard troop truck in the early hours of 13 July. Condés was accompanied by ten to twelve regular Assault Guards (the exact number has never been determined), at least one of whom was not on duty that night and was also in civilian clothes, and four young Socialists in civilian clothes, most or all of whom were connected with "La Motorizada." The open assembly and public dispatch of orders at the Pontejos barracks would tend to discount the possibility of any prearranged conspiracy, as later charged.

Condés's squad proceeded to the apartment building of Calvo Sotelo not far from the center of Madrid and had no difficulty gaining entry. (There is some evidence that this or other squads also made an attempt to arrest such figures as Gil Robles and Lerroux, but both were out of the city.) At the apartment door Condés showed the monarchist leader his Civil Guard identity card and assured him that he was not being arrested — since he had parliamentary immunity — but was being taken to an urgent meeting with the Director General de Seguridad. Calvo Sotelo could see the official Assault Guard truck by street lamp in the street below, and without great resistance agreed to go. Condés ordered the driver to take them back to the Pontejos barracks. After the truck had carried them only a few blocks, a highly excitable young Socialist militant named Luis Cuenca (aka "Victoriano Cuenca" and "El Cubano"), one of those who had earlier been given Assault Guard identity cards for the Cuenca elections, abruptly shot Calvo Sotelo twice in the back of the head, killing him almost instantly. The incomplete evidence indicates that this was a spur-of-the-moment act, totally contradicting the mission's goal to arrest the chief monarchist leader, and leaving a police scandal of the greatest magnitude. To gain time, Calvo Sotelo's body was abandoned at the morgue of the Almudena, Madrid's main cemetery.

Though the government immediately imposed censorship,[69] the news spread rapidly on the morning of the thirteenth. As some of the facts became known, all the right and many moderates became convinced that they provided the most flagrant and decisive illustration of all the charges about partisan and politicized administration of public order. Never before in the history of parliamentary regimes had a leader of the parliamentary opposition been murdered by a detachment of state police. Condés quickly realized that he had presided over an enormous blunder of incalculable consequence, turning himself in immediately to Socialist Party headquarters and later talking with Prieto, who advised him to go into hiding, since the situation could no longer be redeemed.[70] The first political response came from the leaders of the Communist Party, who decided that morning to urge the government publicly to dissolve all rightist and fascist political parties, arrest all those known for important activities in such groups and to confiscate the leading conservative newspapers.[71]

The council of ministers met twice that day, agreed to suspend the opening of the Cortes, denounced the murder of Calvo Sotelo in a brief statement, and declared there would be a full public investigation and prosecution, but also announced a decision to close the centers of the monarchist Renovación Española and of the CNT in Madrid (though neither was involved in the murder) and to arrest many more rightists. On the fifteenth the director general of security announced that 185 provincial and local leaders of the Falange had been arrested in recent days, and on the following day all rightist centers in Barcelona were closed. Thus the only immediately effective response of the government was to begin a process of abolishing rightist political activity. *Claridad* complacently declared on 15 July: "They don't like this government? Then substitute a dictatorial government of the left. They don't like the state of alarm? Then let it be all-out civil war." The editors would very soon get more "all-out civil war" than they had bargained for. Prieto himself made no further move to rectify the situation, simply urging in *El Liberal* on the fourteenth the union of the left and threatening the right if they dared respond with further violence of their own.

On the fourteenth, Marcelino Domingo did talk to Martínez Barrio, who agreed to urge Azaña to replace the Casares Quiroga administration with a better government, but Azaña refused, saying that would be the same as making Casares Quiroga responsible for the assassination.[72] The judicial investigation did go forward, hampered by a cover-up in Assault Guard recordkeeping. Three minor Assault Guards were arrested, but none of the principals. Finally an order went out for the arrest of a number of the Guards in Condés's squad (who had apparently gone into hiding), though no such order was given regarding Condés, who was currently taking refuge in the home of a Socialist leader.

Whereas the UMRA saw the Castillo killing as one in a sequence of several murders of young leftist officers, rightists had no doubt that the Calvo Sotelo killing represented an organized leftist conspiracy. Many linked it with the two kidnap-murders by the left the preceding weekend as part of a new leftist tactic to sequester and then murder their victims. The funerals of both Castillo and Calvo Sotelo took place on the fourteenth. Afterward, young Falangists and rightists marched into the center of Madrid, where they were met by large numbers of aggressive police. There was more than a little gunfire, with between two and five demonstrators killed, according to various newspaper accounts. Though now complete breakdown between left and right was widely predicted, the government's actions against the CNT only encouraged further hostilities between the two labor organizations, and in one affray in Madrid that day a *cenetista* was killed. Not all Assault Guard officers were, however, political leftists, and apparently several protested the role of their corps in the killing of Calvo Sotelo and in opening fire on unarmed protestors that day. Their objections led to their arrest for insubordination.[73]

The government could not avoid convening a meeting of the Diputación Permanente of the Cortes at 11:30 A.M. on the fifteenth. This final session of a branch of the Republican parliament was opened by the monarchist Conde de Vallellano, who charged:

This crime, without precedent in our political history, has been made possible by the atmosphere created by the incitements to violence and personal assault on the deputies of the right repeated daily in parliament. . . . We cannot coexist one moment longer with the facilitators and moral accomplices of this act.

Whereupon he immediately walked out.

The main speech was delivered with aggressiveness and eloquence by Gil Robles. After giving his latest statistical resume of disorders, which he said included sixty-one deaths from politically related acts between 16 June and 13 July, he observed that every day he read in Popular Front newspapers phrases such as "the enemy must be smashed" or there must be "a policy of extermination."

> I know that you are carrying out a policy of persecution, violence and extermination against anything that is rightist. But you are profoundly mistaken: however great may be the violence, the reaction will be greater still. For everyone killed another combatant will rise up. . . . You who are today fostering violence will become the first victims of it. The phrase that revolutions, like Saturn, devour their own children is commonplace, but no less true for being so. Today you are complacent, because you see an adversary fall. But the day will come when the same violence that you have unleashed will be turned against you.

The rightist deputies did not charge that the government had planned or ordered the execution, but that it was responsible for the circumstances which made it possible.

Ventosa and Portela spoke for the center, the former asserting that the Casares Quiroga government was completely unfit to deal with the present crisis because of its self-confessed partisanship and refusal to apply the law equally to all, the prime minister being "a man more apt to touch off a civil war than to restore normalcy." Portela insisted that the government's constant litany explaining away all excesses and irregularities because of the alleged disorder it had inherited was pure fraud, since under Portela's government there had been, he said, constitutional freedom and equal justice for all.

The Role of Violence

Violence obviously played a major role in the life and death of the Second Republic, being proportionately more extensive than in the case of any other central or west European regime of the period. Beginning with election day on 16 February 1936, there had been a rapid reescalation of violence, culminating in the dramatic events of 12–13 July. The government had no interest in collecting and releasing political "crime statistics," and thus the only global data presented in the spring and summer of 1936 were those given by rightist leaders, especially Gil Robles, in parliamentary speeches denouncing the expanding chaos. Leaving aside the numerous instances of arson and destruction of property, religious and secular, rightist sources claimed to have counted 204 political killings between 16 February and the middle of May, 65 more in the next month, and another 61 between mid-June and 13 July.[74] Though these figures were largely rejected at the time, they were occasionally accepted in later years by some leftist writers as an approximately accurate reflection of the general state of affairs.[75]

The only detailed statistical study of political violence in this period (or for any other part of the Republic) is that made by Edward E. Malefakis, further re-elaborated by Ramiro Cibrián.[76] Given the lack of official records, this study relied on the leading Spanish newspaper of the Republican years, *El Sol,* supplemented by the extensive coverage of Spanish affairs in *La Nación* and *La Prensa* of Buenos Aires, to compensate for the limitations imposed by censorship in Spain itself. The research yielded a grand total of 273 political killings from 31 January to 17 July 1936, some 20 percent less than the figures presented by Gil Robles (330 for the period 16 February–13 July). A brief breakdown by district and category is presented in table 13.2.

In general, these data indicate two periods of peak violence, near the beginning and end of this final period of the Republic. The initial wave of lethal incidents which took place in the first month following the electoral victory of the Popular Front declined after the outlawing of the Falange in mid-March. The volume of incidents began to increase once more after mid-April, reaching a second high point around 25 May and continuing until the final breakdown. These data completely disprove the contention of the American historian Gabriel Jackson that a relative decline had set in during the last weeks before the Civil War.[77]

Table 13.2. Deaths in Political Conflicts, 3 February to 17 July 1936

Madrid	45
Barcelona	3
Seville, Malaga, and Granada	35
Other provincial capitals	54
Other cities	13
Total (urban centers)	150
Rural towns in 13 agrarian reform provinces	34
Villages in 13 agrarian reform provinces	32
Rural towns in other provinces	25
Villages in other provinces	28
Total (rural centers)	119
Grand total	269

Source: Data provided by E. E. Malefakis in J. J. Linz, "From Great Hopes to Civil War: The Breakdown of Democracy in Spain," in Linz and A. Stepan, eds., *The Breakdown of Democratic Regimes: Europe* (Baltimore, 1978), 188.

The killings were particularly centered in several major cities, led by Madrid, with Seville and Málaga next in line. There was also a high rate of disorder in certain parts of conservative Old Castile, led by Logroño. Conversely, there was no correlation between the incidence of violence in 1936 and the revolutionary insurrection of 1934. Of the main centers involved in the latter, Asturias registered only a middling index of violent incidents in 1936, while Catalonia and the Basque Country were among the most peaceful regions. Two of the regions exhibiting some of the highest concentrations of radical farmworker activity, Extremadura and eastern Andalusia, failed to register particularly high indices of violence.

Cibrián has formulated a theory to account for the regional distribution of violence in 1936 which combines the three variables of Socialist strength, political polarization, and political radicalization. Socialist strength is measured by the Socialist party vote in the February elections, polarization by adding the combined votes of all the parties clearly on the right or left, and radicalization by the combined number of candidates presented in a given district by Communists and Falangists. The combined measurements produced by these factors generally correlated closely with the differing regional levels of violence.[78]

Juan Linz has noted that the approximate total of 270 political killings in Spain within five and a half months in 1936 contrasts unfavorably with the volume of 207 political killings reported in Italy during the first four and a half months of 1921,[79] possibly the high point of violence there. Since Italy had a population nearly 50 percent greater than that of Spain, the Italian rate of violence was proportionately distinctly lower.

Tentative totals for political killings during the five years of the Republic would be approximately as presented in table 13.3.

The violence in Spain was proportionately more severe than in the internecine struggles prior to the breakdown of democracy in Italy, Germany,[80] and Austria,[81] with the possible exception of the first months of quasi–civil war of the Weimar Republic in 1918–19.[82] The sweeping legal powers exercised by the various Republican governments, the semi-militarization of the police and justice system, and the trigger-happy policies of the Civil Guard and Assault Guards were, even all taken together, inadequate to control the situation, amounting, as the Socialist Vidarte has said, to *palos de ciego* (flailings of a blind man).

It should be kept in mind that the extent of violence was much less during the first three years of the Republic and did not threaten to destabilize the regime. Truly serious violence developed only after political polarization became extreme in 1934. The shift by the Socialists to violence and insurrectionary tactics created a much more severe polarization in Spain

Table 13.3. Total Political Killings

Year	Month	Occurrence	Number of deaths
1931	April	Anarchist killings in Barcelona	22
	May	Quema de conventos	3
	May	San Sebastián	8
	July	Seville general strike	20
	Sept.	Barcelona general strike	6
	Sept.–Dec.	Various incidents	12
	Dec.	Castilblanco	5
1932	Jan.	Arnedo and other incidents	16
	Jan.	Anarchist insurrection	30
	Feb.	Various incidents	6
	March–April	"	7
	May–July	"	24
	Aug.	Sanjurjada	10
	Sept.–Dec.	Various incidents	9
1933	Jan.	Anarchist insurrection	80
	Feb.–May	Various incidents	23
	June–Sept.	"	4
	Oct.–Nov.	Electoral campaign and Madrid strike	9
	Dec.	Anarchist insurrection	89
1934	Nov.–June	Falangists killed by left	9
	June–Dec.	Slain by Falangists	5
	June	National Farm strike	13
	Oct.	Insurrection	1500
1935		Executions	2
		Various incidents	43
1936		Numerous incidents	270
Total			2225

Sources: Numerous newspapers, monographs, and other works, correlated by the author.

than ever developed in the other three countries, where the Socialists and even the Communists followed more moderate tactics. The character of violence in Spain also differed from the central European cases, the bulk of it stemming from one major revolutionary insurrection. The kind of *Zusammenstösse* (clashes between rival groups) so common in Germany and Italy were much less common in Spain because of the numerical weakness of Spanish fascists and the reluctance of the nonfascist right to engage in organized street violence. As Paul Preston has said, violence from the right was carried on by "isolated pistoleros rather than squads of Blackshirts or Stormtroopers,"[83] and to some extent this was true of the left as well.

Though the final spiral of violence in 1936 was extreme, other polities have undergone almost equal violence or disorder without breaking down. Crucial to the final events of the Republic was the character of government policy. From 1931 to 1935, varying Republican administrations had generally taken a strong stand against any major expression of violence, whether from left or right. Yet in 1936 the Azaña–Casares Quiroga government feared to adopt truly strong measures, partly because its own policy had become predicated on alliance with proto-revolutionary activity, and its leaders could see no way to overcome this contradiction. They did not even pursue a thoroughly and consistently partisan policy, for their only measures – mainly directed against the right – were too limited to repress effectively either Falangist activists or military conspirators. Thus both polarities became ever more violent and extreme, until the polity itself dissolved.

The final and climactic blow was the assassination of the rightist leader Calvo Sotelo by a combined group of insubordinate leftist state police and Socialist activists. This killing was the Spanish functional equivalent of the Matteotti affair in Italy. The latter produced a crisis that precipitated full dictatorship; the former was the final precipitant of civil war. That Matteotti was killed by Fascists and Calvo Sotelo by Socialists reflected the differences in the key source of violence within the two systems. There were, however, other equally important differences between the situations in Italy and Spain. In the former, the Fascist government had encouraged violence against the leftist opposition even though it probably had not ordered the killing of Matteotti, and its own followers forced it finally to take responsibility for the murder. In Spain, the left Republican government had never encouraged violence but had simply failed to restrain it and then proved totally ineffective in prosecuting those responsible.

Finally, the question may be asked why the violence under the Republic played so great a role in undermining the system when a continued high rate of deaths from terrorism completely failed to have such an effect on the democratic monarchy after 1975. The answer presumably lies in the refusal of the left Republican government to make a serious effort to repress disorder on both sides, all the while relying on the political and voting support of the Socialists, one of the major sources of the violence. The democratic monarchy after 1975 made energetic efforts to maintain civil rights for all and repress and prosecute political violence from all sources, while all the major political parties – eventually even including the main sectors of Basque nationalists – categorically repudiated violence. Thus under the democratic monarchy political violence, though extensive, has been limited to small terrorist groups acting in secret. Though more than seven hundred political killings (the great bulk of them by the Basque terrorist movement ETA) took place in the sixteen years between the begin-

ning of 1976 and the close of 1991, this could not be compared with the
more than 2200 deaths under the Republic in little more than five years,
including a major insurrection and the involvement of some of the main
political forces.

The Military Revolt of 17–20 July

The Spanish military conspiracy and revolt of 1936 may have been the
most widely written about, if not the most thoroughly investigated, in world
history. Numerous details were lovingly recounted, often with embellish-
ments and frequently with the masking of the whole truth, in the official
and unofficial historiography of the long Franco regime which followed.[84]
The conspiracy was extensive, complex, and also internally divided, and
it was long in maturing. As seen earlier, some commanders began to conspire at the first news of the Popular Front victory, and General Franco,
the circumspect chief of staff, was sufficiently alarmed to urge the political leadership to carry out a constitutional coup, if that were not a contradiction in terms, and even to consider for the first time direct action
by the military. Franco quickly concluded, however, that the latter was
not possible because the military leadership was too divided politically,
and his assessment was undoubtedly correct. Though the Azaña administration moved rapidly to place nearly all the top commands in the hands
of reliable generals, other rightist commanders agreed—albeit vaguely—
to make plans to move against the regime on 10 March. By April conspiracy abounded on the right. UME groups were plotting in garrisons
all over Spain with little coordination, the self-styled "junta of generals"
met periodically in Madrid trying ineffectually to coordinate whatever it
could, Calvo Sotelo and other leaders of the monarchist radical right were
inciting the military, the Carlists had formed their own Supreme Carlist
Military Junta across the border in St. Jean de Luz, and the Falangists were
also separately preparing for action. Some of the most moderate sectors
of the JAP, such as those connected with the Christian democratic Valencian branch (DRV), had begun to plot independently if ineffectively
within days of the Popular Front victory. More than a little of this was
known to government leaders, but not surprisingly they were skeptical
that this kaleidoscope of potential insurgency could ever be pulled together
successfully.

The senior commander who eventually emerged as organizer was Brig.
Gen. Emilio Mola, a veteran of the Moroccan campaigns and last national
police chief of the monarchy, who was first recognized in April by the leaders of various UME sections in the garrisons of north-central Spain as head

of planning for an antigovernment move. A national network of conspiracy nonetheless only began to take shape a month later, for the response of the military in general was slow but cumulative, as incidents multiplied and tension spread. Moreover, the question of authority and legitimacy was difficult to resolve. The senior military rebel under the Republic had been Sanjurjo, whose prominence and seniority had been established by his partial leadership of the abortive rebellion of August 1932. Since being amnestied he had lived in exile in Portugal, and he lacked either opportunity or ability to organize a successful conspiracy from abroad. Thus by the end of May he transferred his active authority to Mola, who planned to establish Sanjurjo as acting head of a military junta after the revolt materialized.

Mola engaged in rudimentary political planning and envisioned the result of a successful rebellion to be not a restored monarchy but a rightwing authoritarian republic. This would maintain certain vestiges of liberalism, such as separation of church and state, but greatly increase the authority of the government and probably establish some sort of corporative system, rather like the authoritarian republican Estado Novo of neighboring Portugal. He apparently intended to appeal to most of the center forces as well as the right.

The chief problem was the army itself. The officer corps was also a bureaucratic class, and the great majority of its members were not eager to involve themselves in a desperate undertaking that might easily lead to their ruin. They had to be concerned about their families and pensions. The Republican government still existed, and the Constitution was still the law of the land, even though less and less enforced. The revolutionaries had not yet tried to take over the government directly; after a few more months, they might begin to settle down, and then the crisis would ease. Military activism had been a disaster in Spanish politics between 1917 and 1931; most officers were aware of this and all the less eager to throw themselves into the fray. Furthermore, the ferocious propaganda of the left made it clear that in any radical confrontation, defeated military dissidents would not be treated as leniently as in earlier generations. Thus some of the leading would-be rebels apparently only committed themselves fully to the revolt after reaching the negative conclusion that it would be more dangerous for them if they did not, a situation that only matured in July.

Liaison between the military and civilian groups was poor. Mola eventually received financial support from the monarchists and the CEDA, but in fact never spent most of the money and had a low opinion of the rightist political forces.[85] They had little organized paramilitary strength to offer,[86] and Mola viewed them with distaste as untrustworthy failures.

Moreover, though Calvo Sotelo had always encouraged a military revolt, there is no clear indication that he played any role in the conspiracy. This may have been because Mola sought to avoid being compromised by the monarchist radical right, which enjoyed scant popular support.

The largest antileftist force engaging in direct action was the Falange. Yet despite his open letter at the beginning of May urging the military to rebel, José Antonio Primo de Rivera had the same opinion of the military that Mola had of civilian politicians. He did not agree to Falangist participation in a military revolt until 29 June and then limited it to a time-frame of eleven days. Mola tried to set a target date of 10 July but had to cancel it due to inadequate support and also because of the arrest of one of the chief Falangists involved. Carlist leaders were even stickier to deal with. After having to cancel his first projected date, Mola made one last effort to deal with the Carlists on 9 July and this time was successful: vague terms were worked out during the next six days.

Elsewhere the situation remained confused and problematic; as late as 12 July Franco is said to have sent an urgent message to Mola expressing reluctance to go through with a revolt at that time.[87] Most officers would act only on direct orders from above, which were not likely to be forthcoming. The conspiracy was further weakened by the fact that it was primarily based on preemptive considerations. A successful counterrevolution could be mobilized, it seemed, only in the face of a matured revolutionary threat, yet the revolutionary left kept hanging fire. Economic disorder was great, there was considerable violence in certain areas, and the government made it clear that it was a partisan of the left and would not provide impartial administration vis-à-vis the center and right. But the left was altogether disunited, and there was as yet no revolutionary action directly aimed at the immediate overthrow of the Republican state.

Hence the decisive importance of the murder of Calvo Sotelo. To many it symbolized a radicalism and government complicity out of control, an end to the constitutional system. For the next thirty years apologists for the military revolt would refer to fake documents alleging that the killing of Calvo Sotelo was but the prelude to a Communist plot to seize power by the end of July. In fact no concrete leftist plan to take over the government has ever been revealed, and it is absolutely implausible that the Communists — still a comparatively small force — could have dreamed of such a timetable. All the revolutionary groups, on the other hand, stated that they considered the days of a nominal parliamentary government to be numbered and expected some sort of revolutionary regime to follow in the near future. This was clearly explained in manifold public pronouncements during the spring and summer of 1936.

The military rebellion was rescheduled by Mola to begin on 18, 19, and 20 July in a series of zones, spreading from the strong army position in the Moroccan Protectorate to the southern part of the peninsula and then to the northern garrisons. It was precipitated in Morocco on the afternoon of the seventeenth because of an informer, but the rebels quickly gained control of the entire Protectorate, despite the fact that the majority of the small Spanish population there had voted for the Popular Front. Nonetheless, because of many loose ends and Mola's staggered timetable, no generalized revolt in the peninsula garrison took place for thirty-six hours.

Subsequently there was much speculation as to why the left Republican government did not take more stringent action to avert a major revolt. The conspiracy was not exactly a secret, for though the details were not known to the government, rumors had flown for months, certain civilian contacts had been arrested, and most of the active plotters were known to be hostile. The government had, in fact, taken more than a few measures to keep the Army under control. Nearly all the top command assignments had been changed, and most of the active senior commanders were, as events proved, loyal to the regime. Many civilian activists, mainly Falangist, had been arrested, and some of the top conspirators had been placed under at least partial surveillance.[88]

There were deep-seated reasons why Azaña and Casares Quiroga did not go further. Perhaps the most basic was that they felt themselves caught between two fires. All of Azaña's policy was staked on maintaining the Popular Front, yet the government was in danger of becoming its prisoner or hostage rather than ally. The possibility of some sort of break with the revolutionary left was not to be discounted, either, though Azaña and Casares Quiroga were themselves determined not to be responsible for precipitating it. Should that occur, the revolutionary left in the streets could only be neutralized by a comparatively strong army in the barracks. Azaña wished to be the ally of the revolutionary left, but not their prisoner. After becoming president of the Republic, he became increasingly anguished, frightened, and withdrawn. In a conversation with Gil Robles immediately after his elevation to head of state, he seemed already to have lost his customary arrogance and declared: "I don't know where we will end up. Your friends should give me a margin of confidence. They should not make trouble for me. I have enough problems on the other side."[89] One of the keenest students of the president declares that worries about the military conspiracy "did not play in Azaña's anguished mind the same role as the attitude and actions of the extreme left."[90]

Thus to Azaña and Casares Quiroga, their military policy seemed sensible and coherent. Some measures had been taken, while the danger from the right might easily be overestimated. The *sanjurjada* had been a feeble affair, and the military were known to be divided. The easiest time for them to have acted would have been between October 1934 and February 1936, yet they had done nothing. Indeed, an aggressive policy to neutralize the military might simply crystallize a determination which would otherwise remain latent at best, while also leaving the government increasingly defenseless before the revolutionary left. Casares Quiroga had begun to speak highly of the Civil Guard, whose discipline he now needed, and he pooh-poohed any worry about the military, which he put down to personal hysteria, or fear, or outmoded sectarian attitudes.[91] Spokesmen of the revolutionary left had frequently referred to Casares's role as that of Kerensky, so that, according to the Socialist Vidarte, he placed a photo of the Russian leader in his office to remind him that he must avoid such a fate.[92] Juan Moles, the independent Republican interior minister, thought it important not to provoke the military into a reactive sense of solidarity.[93] As a consequence, the leftist officers in the Assault Guard and UMRA had become strident critics of the prime minister and had been on the verge of mutiny for a few hours after the death of Castillo.

There is testimony that Casares first informed the council of ministers in a meeting on 10 July that a military conspiracy did indeed exist, and that it might break out within the next forty-eight hours. He provided more than a little information, though the government had not been able to identify "El Director" (Mola) who signed the main documents. They had the option of aborting the movement by a series of immediate arrests, yet they lacked conclusive proof of the ringleaders and thus would not be able to prosecute them effectively. The alternative was to wait for the movement to mature — always assuming that it would be little more than a repeat of the *sanjurjada* — and smash it completely once it began, which was the decision already taken by Azaña and himself.[94]

The cabinet met a week later on the afternoon of Friday the seventeenth, scarcely two hours after the revolt began in Morocco. According to one account, Casares admitted that it was possible that the rebels might be able to take over all the Protectorate, but he prophesied correctly that a loyal navy would prevent them from reaching the mainland. Beyond that limited conclusion, however, the prime minister proved paralyzed and took no significant action.[95] He would not play Kornilov, or even Noske, yet he seemed more determined than ever not to play Kerensky. During the next crucial twenty-four hours, the government did little more than temporize, as the revolt began to spread (somewhat slowly) to some of the peninsula garrisons.

Socialist and Communist patrols had been seen occasionally in the streets

of Madrid for three days, since the fifteenth, but neither of the two mass
worker movements had a true paramilitary militia. Though Largo Caballero had spoken on 16 June of the need to create a "red army," the Socialists had organized little more than the scant membership of their *Motorizada* in Madrid. Certain FAI-CNT groups had begun to collect arms, but
they did not possess regularly equipped and organized militia groups. Only
the Communists were better prepared, having already organized possibly
as many as two thousand men in their MAOC, mostly in the Madrid area,
with leaders such as Enrique Lister, who had undergone some training in
the Frunze Academy in Moscow,[96] while the chief organizer of the UMRA
was a Communist officer on the General Staff of the Republican Army,
Capt. Eleuterio Díaz Tendero.

By the afternoon of Saturday the eighteenth, Largo Caballero and other
revolutionary leaders began to demand the "arming of the people," meaning Socialists and Communists. This Casares still would not do, remaining in a state of semiparalysis. Finally Azaña's personal military secretary,
Lt. Col. Juan Hernández Saravia (who had just been actively reassigned
to the War Ministry) did take responsibility for the initial release of weapons to arm five battalions of volunteers from the Popular Front parties
in Madrid.[97]

About 10:00 P.M. that evening Casares resigned, and Azaña authorized
Martínez Barrio, as the leader of the "right wing" of the Popular Front,
to form a new and broader coalition of "all the Republican parties" of the
left and center, excluding only the Communists and POUM on the left,
the CEDA and the other rightist groups, and in the center only the Lliga.
It received virtual carte blanche terms to put down the rising and restore
order. Miguel Maura refused to participate on the grounds that it was too
little and too late, and Prieto also soon had to decline on instructions from
the Socialist Party, though the latter promised full support to the new
government.[98]

Around 4:00 A.M. on the nineteenth Martínez Barrio began to contact
the district military commanders in the peninsula by telephone. Though
he was not able to make contact with all, he found that several of those
loyal to the Republic had already been virtually deposed by younger officers. Martínez Barrio was also able to speak directly with Mola, and subsequently the main controversy over the abortive new government would
have to do with the terms of their conversation. Martínez Barrio has claimed
that he merely told Mola the new government would restore order and
justice and urged him not to rebel.[99] Other sources, however, claim that
he went much farther, even so far as suggesting a direct political deal with
the military, who could name their own candidates for the Ministries of

the War and Navy, and for the Ministry of the Interior as well. The weight of evidence would indicate that some such deal was indeed discussed,[100] and if Azaña had had the courage to authorize a lesser compromise a week earlier the full civil war might have been avoided. As it was, Mola replied that it was too late, for all the rebels had sworn not to be dissuaded by any political deals or compromises in accomplishing overthrow of the regime.

The great compromise had been attempted too late, though Martínez Barrio continued with the formation of a new left-center coalition that was completed around 5:00 A.M. on the nineteenth. He was relying especially on Felipe Sánchez Román and Marcelino Domingo as his chief lieutenants, and his coalition included five members of Unión Republicana, three of Izquierda Republicana, three from Sánchez Román's PNR, one member of the Esquerra, and a senior general, the pro-Republican José Miaja without party affiliation, in the Ministry of War. This coalition represented a shift away from the moderate left to the left-center, though it was not a broad national unity-type coalition. Even so, it was quickly rejected by some of the more radical members of Azaña's own party, and by 7:00 A.M. the Socialist left had already organized a demonstration in the streets against it. This was the last straw for Martínez Barrio, who had slept for only about one hour in the past forty-eight, and about 8:00 A.M. he resigned, later charging that "the Martínez Barrio government died at the hands of the Caballero Socialists, the Communists and also irresponsible Republicans."[101]

The attempt at compromise was over, the new government led by José Giral that soon followed being basically a reprise of the Casares Quiroga ministry. The Civil War had begun, and the constitutional life of the Republic had ended, replaced by what has varyingly been termed the "Third Republic,"[102] the "Spanish People's Republic,"[103] and the "revolutionary Republican confederation."[104] In differing degrees, the wartime Republic was all of the above, but not a continuation of the parliamentary regime of 1931–36.

14

Why Did the Republic Fail?

SINCE the drama of the Republic ended in one of the most notorious civil wars of the century, its own history has usually been overshadowed by the conflict which followed, the latter soon becoming part of international history, as well. Yet it is perfectly clear, to paraphrase Ortega,[1] that the Civil War cannot be understood without understanding the history of the Republic which preceded it. Common opinion has normally presented simplistic and reductionist explanations for the failure of the Republic, ranging from conspiracy theory — a plot by the left or the right, or by the Axis powers or the Soviet Union, in concert with one of the former — to, at the more abstract end, the irresistible extremism of the left or right (or both), or to the inevitable limitations of backwardness. While the alleged responsibility of foreign powers is a canard, the product of Civil War propaganda by both sides, the other standard explanations contain no more than an element of truth, which in each case falls short of a full and adequate explanation.

The founding of the democratic Republic in Spain can be seen in broader perspective as the final phase in the broad wave of liberalization following the end of World War I, which added ten new, in each case nominally democratic, republics in central and eastern Europe (as well as the Irish Free State) to those already existing in France, Switzerland, and Portugal. That the new wave of democratization did not fully impact Spain earlier was due above all to its neutrality in the war, which gave the established oligarchic regime a few more years of life than was the case elsewhere. Even the first impulses of post-war democratization had major repercussions in Spain, however, and contributed together with the colonial debacle to the downfall of the monarchist parliamentary system in 1923 and of the short-lived dictatorship which followed. The Spanish democratization was thus not totally distinct from the general European chronology, but Spain proceeded in two distinct phases, the second much more powerful than the first.

The paradox, as pointed out earlier, was that effective Republican democratization occurred only during the second year of the Great Depression, after the general tide of democratization had ebbed in Europe as a
whole and was flowing in the opposite direction. The reasons for this delay stemmed from Spain's unique geographic position and its aforemen-
tioned neutrality, combined with the weakness of all-Spanish nationalism
and the right in general, together with the cumulative effect of the Spanish
liberal and progressive tradition — a source of recurrent initiatives since
1810 — as stimulated by the political and economic events of the late 1920s.
Eventually, of course, all the new republican or nominally democratic regimes established after the end of the war failed, with the exceptions only
of Finland, Ireland, and Czechoslovakia. Though outcomes in no case were
predetermined, the times obviously did not favor success. Moreover, since
all the other new democratic systems in underdeveloped eastern and southern Europe gave way to more authoritarian regimes, the argument from
social and economic backwardness is not to be dismissed lightly. Yet levels
of development alone may not always be fully determinant, for democracy
also failed in a much more modern Germany and more recently in other
societies economically more advanced than was the Spain of 1936.[2] Conversely, the first liberal parliamentary systems were introduced and stabilized in countries then at a lower level of modernization than was the Spain
of the Second Republic.

Detlev Peukert has described the drama of Weimar Germany as consti-
tuting the "crisis years of the classically modern,"[3] that is, the period in
which the typical political, cultural, social, and economic forces of the
early twentieth century came into full expression and direct conflict. Such
a contention obviously could not be equally true of Spain, which was much
less advanced, yet Spain was in fact not so backward as has often been
supposed. Economic growth and social change during the 1920s had been
among the most rapid in the world, literacy was increasing fairly rapidly,
and the agrarian sector of the labor force was falling below 50 percent for
the first time. Moreover, Spain had a much longer history of modern liberal government than had Germany, though it possessed even less experience in direct democratization. The long course of constitutional government in Spain — however often honored only in the breach — had encouraged
a bewildering panoply of parties just as complicated, and offering at least
as many different social and ideological options, as those of Germany. To
that extent the Second Republic constituted a distinctively Spanish version of the mass political and cultural "crisis of the classically modern,"
as all the major political and ideological forces of the twentieth century
emerged and converged in Spain, albeit in a society considerably less ad-

vanced in educational and technological development than Germany. Movements such as neotraditionalism, anarchism, Trotskyist-Leninist communism, and mass-mobilized micronationalism were all more strongly developed in Spain than in Germany, though Spanish fascism was for some time quite weak. Altogether, at least twelve different leftist and liberal revolutionary or reform projects were pursued in Spain under the Republic, without counting the variety of counterrevolutionary proposals. A minimal list would include the following:

1. Moderate liberal democracy (the various center parties)
2. Regional nationalism and autonomy (PNV, Esquerra Catalana, and many other groups)
3. Moderate Republican left (Unión Republicana, Partido Nacional Republicano)
4. Radical Republican left (Izquierda Republicana, Radical Socialists)
5. Democratic evolutionary socialism (Besteiro)
6. Advanced social democracy (Prieto)
7. Semi-revolutionary socialism (Largo Caballero and the Socialist left)
8. Leninism (BOC-POUM)
9. Trotskyism (Izquierda Comunista)
10. Stalinism (PCE)
11. Syndicalism (Treintistas, Partido Sindicalista)
12. Anarchosyndicalism (FAI-CNT)

The Second Republic began with certain advantages over some of the new democratic regimes of eastern Europe. It was not necessary to build a newly united nation or construct a new state system from scratch, to reconstruct an economy devastated by World War I or absorb large numbers of refugees from irredentist territory, to face a mass populist monarchism or cope with a majoritarian peasant population (in the anthropological sense), even though the agrarian problems in Spain were obviously severe. And the proliferation and fragmentation of political parties were initially even more pronounced in an east European republic like that of Poland.[4]

In general, the main problems besetting the Republic may, for purposes of analysis, be divided into three categories: the structural, the conjunctural, and the more technically political. In each category grave deficiencies could be found. Social and economic structural problems were undoubtedly severe, the worst being the plight of the newly two million landless farmworkers and their families, a plight made much more conflictive by the fact that Spain was now a rapidly modernizing country with democratic mass mobilization. The low wages, limited productivity, and poor living conditions of four million more urban workers in industry and services were also a problem, even though not so acute in terms of sheer social misery. Though industry and finance had expanded rapidly during the 1920s, their ability to sustain new expansion and improvement during the depression was problematical at best. A special kind of structural problem was the incomplete integration of the major regions, with their disparate rates of modernization, producing modern regional nationalism, which added horizontal political cleavage to the vertical socio-political divisions. At the same time, it would be difficult to establish conclusively that these structural problems were decisive by themselves, some of them having been worse a generation earlier. Rapid development between 1915 and 1930 had not overcome any of these difficulties, but had had the somewhat para-doxical effect of sharpening them. Recent economic improvements, together with the growth of literacy and expanding mobilization, had raised the levels of consciousness and of expectations. A somewhat more modern, productive, and politically conscious society demanded even more rapid change than had recently occurred or than was, in fact, possible. By 1930 Spain had begun to enter the medium phase of expanding industrialization in which social conflicts were sharpest. It was a time when workers were sufficiently mobilized to demand much more, but also when the means to complete industrialization and the achievement of general prosperity were not yet at hand.

The conjuncture was more negative yet, for the 1930s constituted the climax of the "long generation" of world war and intense sociopolitical conflict that stretched from 1914 to 1945. This was the period of the most extreme internal and external strife in modern history, provoked by the climax of European nationalism and imperialism, and by mass social and political struggles over issues of modernization, democracy, and equality. Thus the depression years were scarcely propitious for new democratic experiments. In much of Europe they created conditions advantageous to the authoritarian right and to fascism, and such influence was felt in Spain from 1933 on, becoming a major factor in the political choices of both right and left. Yet it is difficult to demonstrate that the historical conjuncture necessarily determined the course of events in and of itself. Spain was for a long time remarkably immune to some of the major motivating forces of the great European conflict, such as intense nationalism (save for micro-nationalism) and major imperialism, while generic fascism remained weak until the final weeks of the Republic. The impact of the depression was proportionately less than in some other lands, and much of the economy was recovering by 1935, proportionately more than in France or the United States.

Yet the conjuncture did have a powerful effect through the radicalizing impact of key developments abroad, both in terms of positive inspirations and negative apprehensions. The left was increasingly attracted by the mirage of revolution, in part as represented by the Bolshevik Revolution and the Soviet Union. Though the anarchists marched to their own drummers, the Socialists and other Marxist groups were more and more drawn to the Leninist ideal (though not always convinced by it) and at the same time were sufficiently far from the grim reality of the Soviet Union under Stalin not to become disenchanted. Equally or more important was the left's revulsion against the victories of fascism and the authoritarian right in central Europe and elsewhere during 1933–34, which had a strong negative demonstration effect and greatly contributed to polarization in Spain.

It can also be argued that the worst and most decisive problems stemmed from the specific dynamics of political leadership, policy choices, and party conflicts, rather than from the inevitable effect of structural problems or international conjunctural influences. Certainly the Republican political system suffered from impressively poor leadership in all major sectors, though it enjoyed no monopoly over this negative characteristic, which was equally evident in a more modern country such as Germany.

The political problems of the Republic began first of all with the founding Republicans themselves. Though they claimed to represent — and in some respects did represent — a decisive break with the past, the left Republicans remained typical products of modern Spanish liberalism and radicalism. They reflected the tenacious sectarianism and personalism of old-style nineteenth-century factional politics and the insistence on government as a kind of patrimony rather than as a broad representation of all the diverse national interests. As was the case with so many of the leaders of regime changes in the nineteenth century, they did not represent an effort to overcome and transcend the divisions of the past so much as the zeal of a new group to impose its own values and take revenge on ousted predecessors.

This revival of nineteenth-century petit-bourgeois radicalism had been, of course, provoked by the Primo de Rivera dictatorship. Though Primo de Rivera's regime had constituted an unusually mild form of authoritarianism, it had destroyed constitutional continuity and its consequences lay like a dark shadow across the life of the Republic. It bore the responsibility for initiating the new politics of polarization and repression, to which the left Republicans responded partly in kind, unable to transcend the original breakdown of liberalism in 1923.

The new Constitution of 1931, while codifying important principles, followed in the mold of all preceding modern Spanish constitutions in being the creation of one significant sector of political society to be imposed on that portion which did not share its values. In certain key respects it was no more the product of broad consensus and national agreement than its nineteenth-century predecessors (with the partial exception of the 1876 constitution). Even worse, it soon turned out that those groups most responsible for writing the Constitution were not themselves committed to the rules which they had just set up. As soon as they lost the next election, they demanded the annulment of its outcome and the opportunity to try again, for their concept of the Republic was "patrimonial," insofar as they would not tolerate it representing policies other than their own. In fact, few sectors of Spanish politics were unreservedly loyal to the Republic as democratic procedure, and these were to be found in the ever narrowing center of the spectrum.[5] Lack of consensus about basic rules of the game was a handicap from the very beginning, and some later literature would suggest that basic agreement among elites is more important than sheer level of development in guaranteeing the stability of a new democracy.[6]

For key sectors of the founding Republican coalition, the new system did not represent a commitment to a set of constitutional rules so much as the decisive breakthrough and final hegemony of a basic left-liberal reformist process which involved not merely decisive political changes but also irreversible changes in church-state relations, education, culture, and the socioeconomic structure, together with the solution of key dilemmas in regional autonomy and military reform. Most of these reforms were salutary but should not have precluded equivalent respect for the democratic process, even at the cost of their partial or temporary reversal.

The question has frequently been asked if the original Republican leadership did not simply try to reform too much too fast, irremediably overloading the system. In terms of the way in which reforms were undertaken, the answer is undoubtedly yes, but it is not so clear that this need have been the case with the substance of many of the reforms themselves. The country was greatly in need of continuing modernizing reform, and a broad policy that concentrated on technical and practical reforms with obvious benefits — educational development, military reform, regional autonomy, public works, improvement of labor conditions, and some measure of agrarian reform — were in most respects such obvious national needs that it might not necessarily have been impossible to have built a national coalition in favor of them.

The Republican achievements in education, regional autonomy, public works, and labor were fruitful and impressive. The military reform was long overdue and in many respects positive, though subject to notable limitations. Nearly everyone agreed on the need for agrarian reform, though, as has been seen, the actual legislation was not well conceived in social and technical terms, though its goals were laudable. There was also need for separation and reform in church-state relations, where much might have been achieved at minimal cost.

Conversely, the political introduction and style of the reforms was badly handled from the beginning, due to the sectarian rhetoric and procedures of the left Republican-Socialist coalition. In some areas an originally non-existent opposition was stimulated gratuitously, due to the absence of any spirit of conciliation or desire for consensus on the part of the reformers. A generally sensible military policy was converted by Azaña's lack of tact into what was perceived (with considerable exaggeration) as an antimilitary vendetta, generating hostility among Army officers who were not originally hostile to the Republic. Worst of all, of course, were both the style and substance of the religious reforms, conceived as vengeance against religious interests — even though more Spaniards believed in Catholicism than in any philosophical or political creed — instituting not merely separation of church and state but infringement of civil rights and persecution of religious devotion.

There were also notable failures in economic policy. Fiscal reform was feebly addressed, while unnecessary amounts of money were to be consigned to replace the entire Catholic educational system. This would leave all the less for stimulating employment, adding necessary infrastructure, and encouraging economic expansion, not to speak of land reform. Most Republican leaders were too ignorant of — and also too disinterested in — economics to devote adequate attention to that area, though this was such a common failing of the decade that there was nothing particularly Spanish or Republican about it.

The approach to some of these problems as a zero-sum game was especially counterproductive. This perspective broadened the precedent that each new turn of the political wheel was to be used to exact vengeance on the previous holders of power, establishing retroactive new politicized jurisdictions and discouraging consensus. In this regard, the Republic, rather than representing an improvement on the old monarchist constitutional system prior to 1923, in key respects represented a regression to the extreme factionalism of the mid-nineteenth century. This was what Ortega had in mind in 1932–33 when he lamented that Republican leaders, rather than addressing the most important twentieth-century problems, represented instead a return to certain fixations of the past.

One of the most destructive consequences of the new "patrimonial Republicanism" was that it blurred the realities of Spanish society to most of the new leaders. They ignored the extent of conservative interests[7] and of popular Catholicism on the one hand and the potential of revolutionary extremism on the other, while optimistically exaggerating the likely appeal of their own forms of Republican progressivism. This overconfidence was due to the initial effects of the rupture in 1931, when conservative interests remained too uncertain and disoriented to contest the first elections effectively, resulting in a parliament and Constitution not representative of the country as a whole.[8] Conversely, a more genuinely representative parliament would probably have tried to produce a more moderate but progressive Constitution that might have made the Republic more acceptable to the great bulk of opinion. This would in certain respects have produced a more moderate social policy, alienating the workers even more rapidly than proved to be the case, but could have fostered a broader democratic liberalism among the middle classes, part of the agrarian population, and even among a minority of workers that might have produced more stable electoral majorities. There is no guarantee that such would have been the outcome — social antagonisms may have become so intense that no liberal democratic regime could have survived — but the moderate strategy offered a potentially viable alternative to the politics of polarization.

The functioning of the Republican system was further handicapped by a defective electoral system and an extremely high rate of turnover of political personnel. The electoral system overcorrected the potential problem of multiparty proportionality and created lopsided effects which translated any shift in public opinion or any major change in alliance strategies into massive polar swings in representation. Thus the political system came to suffer the effects of both fragmentation and polarization at one and the same time. Failure to move toward electoral reform during 1935 was a major mistake.

The drastic turnover in political personnel was another of the destructive consequences of the dictatorship, which had destroyed the older political forces and then left a void behind it not surprisingly filled with political novices. The drastic turnover in personnel that occurred in 1931 was repeated in each of the two following elections, partly due to the exaggerated consequences of the electoral law, and constituted one of the major liabilities of the new regime. The most tolerant figures in the Republic were usually found among the minority of centrists and moderate conservatives who had earlier gained experience under the preceding regime, though they were greatly outnumbered by the radicalized groups of novices who came to the fore after 1931.

Spanish economic interests behaved very much as major economic interests have done everywhere else in similar circumstances, supporting the center-right and moderate right, though in some cases with movement toward the radical right. Mercedes Cabrera, the principal student of interest group politics, concluded that they developed no real alternative of their own and hoped above all that a more stable and moderate Republican regime would preserve law and order. Large landowners constituted the principal sector more attracted by the radical right, yet even they as a whole played no corporate role in directly subverting the system.[9]

Openly subversive forces were at first not numerous or important, with the partial exception of the CNT. The latter was flanked on the extreme left by the Communists, while later the Republic would face the subversion of the monarchist radical right and the Falange. None of these were really significant save for the anarchists. The latter did constitute a mass movement, but their libertarian insurrectionist tactics never seriously threatened to overthrow the regime. Perhaps the main consequence of anarchist extremism was to maintain pressure on the UGT that weakened the Socialist commitment to social democratic reformism.

Much more important and decisive were the stances of what Juan Linz has called the major "semiloyal" parties: the Socialists and the CEDA. The ambiguity of the CEDA was fundamental, for the party would never commit itself to "Republicanism" or to the democratic system *tout court*. The contribution of the CEDA was not to Republicanize the right, but to secure the commitment of the bulk of the Catholic electorate to parliamentary and legalist procedures. This was of considerable importance to the Republic, yet it hardly solved the problem of the Republic's future, as the left incessantly pointed out. Though the CEDA was much more reluctant than the Socialists to engage in political violence, it remained ambiguous about ultimate goals, which for some members clearly were to replace the Republic with a corporative and more authoritarian system. This ambiguity was, in turn, used both by the centrist president and the left to deny the CEDA normal constitutional access to government.

The CEDA leadership was itself guilty of grave errors that helped to undermine the policy. More important even than the question of ambiguity about ultimate aims was what the CEDA did in 1935. Its excesses in pursuing the repression were totally counterproductive, merely helping to build a broader, stronger, and reunited left. It failed to implement constructive reform in key areas, concentrating on a reactionary policy of undoing aspects of the previous legislation. It failed to emphasize vital changes in the system that were already within its grasp, such as electoral reform — strongly supported by the otherwise antagonistic Alcalá Zamora — which might have had a fundamental impact in reducing polarization in the next elections. And at the close of the year Gil Robles and his colleagues adopted an arrogant and self-righteous policy that merely played into the hands of Alcalá Zamora's manipulations, a mistake compounded by their exclusive approach to the elections that divided the opposition to the Popular Front.

Despite all these failings, the exclusionist policy against the CEDA must be seriously questioned. The CEDA was not some small, violent revolutionary terrorist or fascist group that could simply be suppressed or ignored. It represented, in fact, the largest single specific political orientation found among Spanish citizens. No democratic system could ever function or survive without coming to terms with Catholic opinion, the preferred orientation of a plurality if not a majority of the population. The question must therefore be raised whether or not the correct course of action in 1934–35 would simply have been to follow constitutional due process, since a democracy cannot long function any other way. It is not convincing to view Alcalá Zamora's initial decision to admit the CEDA to limited participation in 1934 as other than fully justified, and the violent reaction of the left as other than unjustified and disastrous for the polity. At that time both the president and the prime minister, together with the dominant coalition party, were fully committed to parliamentary democracy. This situation offered a reasonable opportunity to broaden the base of government, create a stable majority, and build a broader democratic consensus, just as Lerroux planned. Subsequently, however, Alcalá Zamora refused to follow fully the logic of parliamentary democracy and allow the largest party to lead a government. Had he done so, a worst-case scenario would have ultimately led to a CEDA-dominated coalition producing drastic constitutional reform in 1936. Had this produced a semicorporative and more authoritarian system, it might have been the end of Republican democracy for a decade or so but would have avoided the horrors of the Civil War and the Franco regime. In hindsight, even the worse-case scenario for full CEDA inclusion would hardly have produced the worst outcome.

The Socialists on the left played a role somewhat similar to the CEDA on the right in their "semiloyalty." Their contribution to the coalition of the first biennium was noteworthy, marking a major step in the evolution, maturation, and expansion of the Socialist movement in Spain at a time when only in the more developed countries of Germany and northern Europe had Socialist parties advanced as far. Yet the PSOE lacked the maturity and unity of the German Social Democrats, its response to political adversity being the direct opposite of the latter.[10] Though it turned to government collaboration five years earlier than the French Socialists, its ambiguities more closely reflected those of the "two and a half" Austrian Social Democrats, for the French Socialists eventually committed themselves to full social democratic collaboration just as *caballerismo* was in the ascendant in Spain.

Polarization crystallized not so much with the triumph of the CEDA in 1933 as with the insurrrection of 1934, which revealed that the bulk of the worker left was committed to varying forms of revolutionary action. The richness and diversity of revolutionism under the Republic has had few equals anywhere in the world. Its extent and variety stemmed from the combination of a conflictive, underdeveloped social structure with a democratic, mobilized, and highly fragmented political system. Modern Spanish politics had regularly featured a rather unique conjunction of advanced political forms and institutions amid socioeconomic backwardness, a combination that differentiated Spain from, for example, most of eastern Europe and the Balkans. The opportunity for mass mobilization and untrammeled democracy amid the depression,[11] following an unprecedented generation of accelerated modernization, suddenly raised the classic "Spanish contradiction" to a new level that made revolutionary challenges almost inevitable, though not at all irresistible.

This did not mean that Spain was merely "ripe" for revolution, as many theorists held, for in key respects the society had already become too strong and complex for revolutionaries to conquer. If the urban and industrial labor force was proportionately much larger than that of Russia in 1917, so were the middle classes and the right in general. Some of the key conditions that encouraged successful revolution in more backward societies, such as foreign economic and political domination or the absence of free institutions, did not at all obtain in Spain, whose circumstances were much more similar to those of Italy after 1919. There the left had succumbed to a rightist-fascist coalition in some respects quite similar to the one that eventually won the Spanish Civil War, as moderates warned many times between 1934 and 1936, though most of the left was unwilling to listen. The political analyses carried out by the leaders and theorists of the revolutionary left, like many of those made by the left Republicans, often had the effect more of masking than illuminating key realities.

It is, nonetheless, beside the point to have expected those who basically rejected parliamentary democracy, whether on the left or right, to have taken responsibility for safeguarding parliamentary institutions. The principal responsibility for safeguarding constitutional democracy lay with those who created it in the first place – the liberal and left Republicans.

Of all the political sectors, only the centrist liberals – those of Alcalá Zamora, Maura, the Radicals, and the Catalan Lliga – took up positions primarily in defense of constitutional democracy and the rules of the game. Small parties such as those of Maura, Sánchez Román, and even the larger Lliga lacked the strength to influence the situation decisively, however, so that the major roles in the center were played by Alcalá Zamora and by

Lerroux and his Radicals. If the Second Republic in Spain was to become stabilized in the form of constitutional democracy like the Third Republic in France, it would probably have been necessary for the essentially moderate, middle-class Radicals to have played much the same stabilizing role as their French homonyms and counterparts, and this they certainly attempted to do during 1933–35. The Radicals obviously failed, though their sins were more of omission than commission. That is, they did not commit major mistakes that violated the letter and spirit of democratic practice, as did most other major parties, but they lacked strong organization or clear, productive goals. The Radicals quickly became the sole representative in Spain of what was much more common in established democracies elsewhere — a sizable political sector devoted to porkbarrel politics and a tolerant liberal philosophy of live-and-let-live. In the supercharged Spanish atmosphere, this had only limited appeal and was denounced as an absence of morality and purpose. Leadership in the Radicals was lacking, Lerroux being too old and lacking in energy and other party luminaries lacking in vision or ability. Thus the Radicals failed for not being more than they were, yet if they had possessed significant counterparts constitutional democracy might have endured.

In an increasingly polarized situation in which most major actors had limited or no commitment to democracy, President Alcalá Zamora saw himself as the ultimate guarantor of the liberal Republic. This was, of course, technically correct, and there was no doubt of the president's sincerity, yet he himself quickly became a major problem. Though Alcalá Zamora was a sincere liberal and constitutionalist, and a distinguished jurist, he was also a product of the older nineteenth-century liberal tradition and culture in Spain. This was an essentially elitist and oligarchic political culture populated by localist and party notables. It represented a form of transition from the traditional culture that had been based in good measure on status, aristocracy, and concepts of lineage and honor. Thus it had difficulty in overcoming a profound elitism and personalism, an obsession with status and egocentric concerns.

For whatever reasons — some of them objectively grounded fears concerning the strength of antidemocratic leftist and rightist forces — Alcalá Zamora quickly came to perceive his role as that of independent *poder moderador* in an almost royalist manner. It may be seriously argued that he himself interfered more overtly with the normal functioning of constitutional government than had the much criticized Alfonso XIII. As soon as the initial strength of the Azaña coalition began to wane, the president set to work, relieving the left Republican leader of power even before his parliamentary majority had technically disappeared. Alcalá Zamora's interference with the Azaña government was nonetheless less overt than his role with the second Cortes, during whose mandate he constantly acted to thwart the possibility of normal parliamentary majoritarian government, making and unmaking minoritarian or less than fully representative cabinets at will. In the process, he inevitably earned the hatred of both right and left, each of which aimed at removing him from office as soon as possible.

In certain respects it is perfectly understandable that the president felt the need to take action to restore some sort of balance or safeguard vis-à-vis the left and right. More dubious was his apparent willingness to help destroy the existing structure of the center — Lerroux and the Radicals — in order to reconstruct it in a new form subordinated indirectly to his own leadership. This was the sheerest folly and not surprisingly ended in disaster. That Alcalá Zamora seriously expected to rebuild a new center from the fulcrum of state power indicates the extent to which he remained culturally and psychologically a liberal of the old regime and failed fully to understand the character and force of the new political institutions and society which he himself had helped to build under the Republic.

The only other Republican leader who enjoyed responsibility equivalent to that of Alcalá Zamora was Manuel Azaña, the only other politician to have held roughly equivalent powers and initiative in leadership over almost as long a period. Azaña publicly confessed that he was "sectarian" and not a "liberal." He was, at least during his first government, forthright that Republican constitutionalism would have to be interpreted by essentially partisan rules in order to achieve his goals, but he did not understand until too late that such an approach made Republican democracy impossible. He himself recognized the extent of his pride and arrogance but had such faith in his own (sometimes very limited) powers of judgment that he became convinced of his own indispensability. His rejection of a more tolerant liberal democracy in favor of a policy of radicalism and polarization coincided with a mass mobilization and radicalization that greatly magnified the consequences of sectarianism. When the principal leaders of Republican politics in practice rejected the rules of the game they themselves had created, the polity could not long endure.

Though determined to represent a new politics, Azaña sometimes described himself privately as the "most traditionalist" man in Spanish public life. He was in fact much more a product of the old elitist and sectarian culture of the nineteenth century than he sometimes realized. A linear descendant of the *exaltados* of 1820, Azaña represented the old as much as the new. He was the last in a long line of nineteenth-century sectarian bourgeois politicians and might with little exaggeration be called the last great figure of traditional Castilian arrogance in the history of Spain.

Azaña always emphasized the crucial role of his own bourgeois left in the outcome of the Republic, declaring in a speech of 17 July 1931:

Note well, Republicans, that on the day of our failure we would not have at hand the facile excuse of casting the blame on our neighbor. No; if the Republic goes under, the blame will be ours. If we do not know how to govern, the blame will be ours. There is no one else on whom to cast the burden of responsibility. Note that freedom brings with it this tremendous consequence: unavoidable responsibility, not only before our fellow citizens, but before history.[12]

A much better writer than politician, a much better molder of words than leader of men, Azaña in fact had little genuine political ability, being virtually, in the words of Portela Valladares, more "antipolitical" than "political."[13] His extreme hubris cast him in the role of a protagonist of classical tragedy. Azaña's was only the most obvious example of the general failure of leadership under the Republic.[14]

Azaña claimed the need for "a radical policy" due to the lessons of recent history but, like many intellectuals of the early twentieth century, misread that history. Nearly two generations later, the next group of Spanish politicians who had the opportunity to establish a democratic regime read their history more accurately, emphasizing tolerance, equal rights, and consensus. Their task was easier amid a modern, urban, generally educated, and prosperous citizenry, and within the context of a prosperous, stable, and democratic Europe. Yet their success was not a foregone conclusion. It benefited decisively from able, adroit, and prudent leadership, which was determined to avoid the mistakes of the past and quietly repudiated the sectarian legacy of the Republic. The Second Republic probably had the odds against it from the start, but certainly it was badly served by its own principal leaders, who greatly facilitated the work of the Republic's enemies.

General Accounts of the Republic

Notes

Index

General Accounts of the Republic

THERE are numerous general accounts of the Second Republic in Spanish, mostly superficial and frequently tendentious. The first general treatments were journalistic or political in character (sometimes both). Thus, during the Civil War, Marco Alessi published an Italian Fascist critique in *La Spagna dalla monarchia al governo di Franco* (Milan, 1937), while Juan Guixé defended the reform program in *Le vrai visage de la République espagnole* (Paris, 1938).

The lengthiest accounts are four-volume works in Spanish, both entitled *Historia de la Segunda República española* and both strongly conservative critiques. The first was written by the prominent Catalan journalist and essayist José Pla in the immediate aftermath of the Civil War and published in Barcelona in 1940–41. It provided lengthy excerpts from speeches and parliamentary sessions and often included lists of disorders and violence without any source attribution. The second, by the veteran Francoist journalist Joaquín Arrarás (Madrid, 1956–63), had many of the same features but was more thorough and also lavishly illustrated, though its source references sometimes left much to be desired. Both of these lengthy accounts stressed political narrative to the neglect of other aspects. This was also true of the briefer synthesis by the well-known historian Melchor Fernández Almagro, *Historia de la República española (1931–1936)* (Madrid, 1940). The later *Historia secreta de la Segunda República* (Madrid, 1954–55), 2 vols., by the police writer Eduardo Comín Colomer and intended as an exposé, was not a history but a diatribe.

Serious studies in other languages have been rare. The first major treatment abroad was provided by the first half of Gabriel Jackson's *The Spanish Republic and Civil War* (Princeton, 1965), which was not a complete history but achieved a more rounded overview and became the classic statement of the moderate left's viewpoint. Carlos M. Rama, *La crisis española del siglo XX* (Mexico City-Buenos Aires, 1960), had many of the same features but tried to be even broader in scope, and was the first scholarly treatment by a Latin American. Jean Bécarud, *La Deuxième République espagnole 1931–1936* (Paris, 1962), was so brief that it constituted neither a history nor a real book, but a short analytic monograph on several key problems.

The first objective treatment to appear in Spanish was presented by Carlos Seco Serrano in volume 6 of the Editorial Gallach's *Historia de España* (Barcelona, 1968). This was soon followed by the much more lengthy work of Ricardo de la Cierva, *Historia de la Guerra Civil española, I. Antecedentes: Monarquía y República 1898–1936* (Madrid, 1969), devoted primarily to another complete political history of the Republic from a conservative viewpoint. La Cierva's detailed study took the place for the moderate right already held by that of Jackson for the moderate left and would stand as the best single-volume account until the censorship eased further.

The 1970s was the richest decade in general publications because of the growing freedom of expression, climaxed by the death of Franco in 1975 and the end of the dictatorship soon afterward. The best single general work to appear was Luis Romero's *Cara y cruz de la República 1931–1936* (Barcelona, 1980), an inquiring, well-written account that exploited some of the recent research and still stands as one of the two best balanced and most objective histories in Spanish. Other notable products of the liberation decade were Manuel Tuñón de Lara's *La II Republica* (Madrid, 1976), a more structural analysis, and Eduardo de Guzmán, *La Segunda República fue así* (Barcelona, 1977), a competently written narrative that generally avoided distortions and inaccuracies. Jesús Lozano González's ornate *La Segunda República* (Barcelona, 1973) treated the entire period down to the end of the Civil War.

Other general accounts in the 1970s had less to recommend them. Most extensive were Federico Bravo Morata's *La República* (Madrid, 1973), 5 vols., and *Historia de la República (1931–1936)* (Barcelona, 1977), 2 vols., which might as well have been written thirty years earlier. These works were deficient in perspective and critical analysis, defensive of the Republican leaders and based on the concept that "the people were not equal to their leaders"—a remarkably inane idea in view of the low caliber of most of the leadership.

In something of a class apart is Julio Gil Pecharromán's highly professional, meticulously informed *La Segunda República* (Madrid, 1989). Though the book consists of only 194 brief pages of text, it is word for word the most precise treatment available.

Notes

Chapter 1. The Ordeal of Modernization in Spain

1. Oswald Spengler, *The Decline of the West* (New York, 1926), 1:107–8, 148–50.

2. Leandro Prados de la Escosura, *De imperio a nación: Crecimiento y atraso económico en España (1780–1930)* (Madrid, 1988), 67–94.

3. Leandro Prados de la Escosura, *Comercio exterior y crecimiento económico en España, 1826–1913* (Madrid, 1982), and "Las relaciones reales de intercambio entre España y Gran Bretaña durante los siglos XVIII y XIX," in P. Martín Aceña and L. Prados, eds., *La nueva historia económica de España* (Madrid, 1985), 119–65.

4. These are among the principal conclusions of Prados, *De imperio.*

5. Ibid. See also Jordi Nadal, *El fracaso de la revolución industrial en España, 1814–1913* (Barcelona, 1975); N. Sánchez-Albornoz, ed., *La modernización económica de España, 1830–1930* (Madrid, 1985); and J. Nadal, A. Carreras, and C. Sudrià, eds., *La economía española en el siglo XX: Una perspectiva histórica* (Barcelona, 1987).

6. Albert Carreras, *Industrialización española: estudios de historia cuantitativa* (Madrid, 1990); Pedro Fraile, "Crecimiento económico y demanda de acero: España 1900–1950," in Martín Aceña and Prados, *La nueva historia económica*, 71–100; Rosa Vaccaro, "Industrialization in Spain and Italy (1860–1914)," *The Journal of European Economic History* 9 (Winter, 1980); and C. Molinas and L. Prados de la Escosura, "Was Spain Different? Historical Backwardness Revisited," *Explorations in Economic History* 26 (October, 1987): 385–402.

7. Jordi Nadal, "La industria fabril española en 1900," in Nadal, Carreras, and Sudrià, *La economía española*, 23–61.

8. See N. Sánchez Albornoz, ed., *Españoles hacia América: la emigración en masa, 1880–1930* (Madrid, 1988).

9. See the articles on late nineteenth-century Spanish agriculture by A. M. Bernal, J. Sanz Fernández, R. Robledo Hernández, and R. Garrabou in J. L. García Delgado, ed., *La España de la Restauración* (Madrid, 1985), as well as R. Garrabou, et al., ed., *Historia agraria de la España contemporánea* (Barcelona, 1986), vol. 2; R. Garrabou, *Un fals dilema: modernitat o endarreriment de l'agricultura valenciana (1850–1900)* (Valencia, 1985); and R. Garrabou, ed., *La crisis agraria de fines del siglo XIX* (Barcelona, 1988).

10. Prados, *De imperio*, 121.

389

11. Richard Lachmann, *From Manor to Market: Structural Change in England,
1536–1640* (Madison, 1987).

12. In 1797 the Spanish aristocracy held jurisdiction over about 50 percent of
Spanish land, the Church over 17 percent, while common lands, middle-class properties, and peasant smallholdings (under "royal domain") altogether accounted for
only about 33 percent. Ten years earlier in France peasants either owned or farmed
as quasi-property 40 percent of the land, bourgeois owners held another 20 percent, commons included an approximately equal amount, noble domains amounted
to only 16 percent, and the Church held 4 percent. Guy Hermet, *Le problème
meridional de l'Espagne* (Paris, 1965), 2.

13. Pascual Carrión, *Los latifundios en España* (Madrid, 1932), 51–52.

14. Prados, *De imperio,* 227.

15. Ibid., 224.

16. The structure of Restoration politics is laid bare in José Varela Ortega, *Los
amigos políticos* (Madrid, 1977); Javier Tusell, *Oligarquía y caciquismo en Andalucía* (Barcelona, 1976), 2 vols.; and Robert W. Kern, *Liberals, Reformers and Caciques in Restoration Spain 1875–1909* (Albuquerque, 1974). Carlos Serrano, *Le
tour du peuple* (Madrid, 1987), treats the failure of the first challenges to the system in the 1890s.

17. Cf. Gail Stokes, *Politics as Development: The Emergence of Political Parties
in Nineteenth-Century Serbia* (Durham, N.C., 1990).

18. The collective volume edited by C. Serrano and S. Solaun, *1900 en Espagne
(essai d'histoire culturelle)* (Bordeaux, 1988), provides a trenchant survey of Spanish culture at the turn of the century.

19. On Spanish Catholicism in the nineteenth century, see William J. Callahan,
Church, Politics and Society in Spain, 1750–1874 (Cambridge, 1984), and Frances
Lannon, *Privilege, Persecution, and Prophecy: The Catholic Church in Spain, 1875–
1975* (Oxford, 1987).

20. Joan C. Ullman, *The Tragic Week* (Cambridge, 1968), and Joaquín Romero
Maura, *"La rosa de fuego"* (Barcelona, 1975).

21. Catalan history may be approached through the eight volumes of the *Història de Catalunya* edited by P. Vilar (Barcelona, 1979–82), especially volume six
on the period from 1868 to 1939 by Josep Termes. On the twentieth century, see
Albert Balcells, *Historia contemporánea de Cataluña* (Barcelona, 1983). Catalan
nationalism now has a lengthy bibliography. See Jaume Rossinyol, *Le problème
national catalan* (Paris, 1974); J. M. Poblet, *Història básica del catalanisme* (Barcelona, 1975); J. A. González Casanova, *Federalisme i autonomia a Catalunya
(1868–1939)* (Barcelona, 1974); and the texts edited by F. Cucurull, *Panorámica
del nacionalisme català* (Paris, 1975), 6 vols.

The bibliography on Basque history and nationalism is also growing rapidly.
The *Diccionario histórico del País Vasco* (Bilbao, 1982), 2 vols., by F. García de
Cortázar and M. Montero, is a useful tool. My *Basque Nationalism* (Reno, 1975)
presents an account in English of the early nationalist movement through the Civil
War years.

22. The best brief introduction to the history of organized labor in Spain is Benjamin Martin, *The Agony of Modernization: Labor and Industrialization in Spain* (Ithaca, 1990). In Spanish there is a three-volume work by M. Tuñón de Lara, *El movimiento obrero en la historia de España* (Barcelona, 1972), somewhat one-sided and now dated.

The principal study of the origins of Spanish anarchism is Josep Termes, *Anarquismo y socialismo en España: La Primera Internacional (1864–1881)* (Barcelona, 1972), but see also Clara Lida, *Anarquismo y revolución en la España del siglo XIX* (Madrid, 1972). General accounts include Robert W. Kern, *Red Years/Black Years: A Political History of Spanish Anarchism, 1911–1937* (Philadelphia, 1978); César Lorenzo, *Les anarchistes espagnols et le pouvoir 1868–1939* (Paris, 1969); Manuel Buenacasa, *El movimiento obrero español 1886–1926* (Barcelona, 1928); A. Padilla Bolívar, *El movimiento anarquista español* (Barcelona, 1976); Jacques Maurice, *L'anarchisme espagnol* (Paris, 1973); and Juan Gómez Casas, *Historia del anarcosindicalismo español* (Madrid, 1968) and *Historia de la F. A. I.* (Bilbao, 1977). The latter work has been translated as *Anarchist Organization: The History of the F.A.I.* (Montreal-Buffalo, 1986). The most accurate and systematic treatment of anarchism in the south is Jacques Maurice, *El anarquismo andaluz* (Barcelona, 1990).

The leading works on early anarchist ideology are José Alvarez Junco, *La ideología política del anarquismo español (1868–1910)* (Madrid, 1976), and George R. Esenwein, *Anarchist Ideology and the Working-Class Movement in Spain, 1868–1898* (Berkeley-Los Angeles, 1989). Principal studies of the origins and early years of the CNT are J. Romero Maura, *"La Rosa de Fuego"* (Barcelona, 1975); Xavier Cuadrat, *Socialismo y anarquismo en Cataluña (1899–1911)* (Madrid, 1976); and Antonio Bar, *La CNT en los años rojos* (Madrid, 1981). For anarchist culture, see Lily Litvak, *La musa libertaria* (Barcelona, 1981) and *Espana 1900: Modernismo, anarquismo, y fin de siglo* (Barcelona, 1990), which may be compared with Richard D. Sonn, *Anarchism and Cultural Politics in Fin-de-siècle France* (Lincoln, Neb., 1989).

23. The principal history of Spanish Socialism is the five-volume *Historia del socialismo español* (Barcelona, 1989), edited by M. Tuñón de Lara, though sometimes general and uneven. On the early years, see V. M. Arbeloa, *Orígenes del PSOE (1873–1880)* (Madrid, 1972); A. Elorza and M. Ralle, *La formación del PSOE* (Barcelona, 1989); Francisco Mora, *Historia del socialismo obrero español* (Madrid, 1902); and J. J. Morato, *El Partido Socialista Obrero* (Madrid, 1918; repr. 1976). E. del Moral, ed., *Cien años de socialismo en España* (Madrid, 1977), presents the basic earlier bibliography. There are several brief general accounts, such as A. Padilla Bolívar, *El movimiento socialista español* (Barcelona, 1977).

The chief study of the early years of the UGT is Manuel Pérez Ledesma, "La Unión General de Trabajadores: Ideología y Organización (1888–1931)" (Ph.D. diss., Madrid Autonomous University, 1976). See also his *El obrero consciente* (Madrid, 1987); J. Aisa and V. M. Arbeloa, *Historia de la Unión General de Trabajadores, 1888–1931* (Bilbao, 1974); and the sometimes distorted account by Amaro del Rosal, *Historia de la UGT de España (1901–1939)* (Barcelona, 1977), 2 vols.

24. See Helen Nader, *Liberty in Absolutist Spain* (Baltimore, 1990).

25. Jacques Maurice, *El anarquismo andaluz* (Barcelona, 1990), and Temma Kaplan, *Anarchists of Andalusia, 1868-1903* (Princeton, 1977).

26. Javier Paniagua, *Anarquistas y socialistas* (Madrid, 1989), treats the early relations between the two movements.

27. Miquel Izard, *Revolució industrial i obrerisme: Les "Tres Classes de Vapor" a Catalunya (1869-1913)* (Barcelona, 1970).

28. The most extensive discussion, couched in somewhat different terms, will be found in Albert Balcell's lengthy introduction to his *El arraigo del anarquismo en Cataluña: Textos de 1926-1934* (Barcelona, 1973), which reprints the initial debate on this problem by Catalan Marxist and anarchist theorists in the journal *L'Opinió* during 1928. The inadequacies of the approach taken by the Socialist Party are discussed in some detail in Paul Heywood, *Marxism and the Failure of Organized Socialism in Spain, 1879-1936* (Cambridge, 1990), 1-84.

29. The fullest treatment of these first halting steps is J. I. Palacio Morena, *La institucionalización de la reforma social en España: La Comisión y el Instituto de Reformas Sociales* (Madrid, 1988).

30. Francisco Villacorta Baños, *Profesionales y burócratas: Estado y poder corporativo en la España del siglo XX, 1890-1923* (Madrid, 1989).

31. The fullest and most reliable one-volume treatment of twentieth-century Spain is Javier Tusell, *El siglo XX, Manual de historia de Espana,* VI (Madrid, 1990). The best general account in English is still Raymond Carr, *Spain 1808-1975* (Oxford, 1982). The best brief treatment in a third language is Guy Hermet, *L'Espagne au XXe siecle* (Paris, 1986). A Soviet perspective may be found in the Akademiya Nauk SSSR's *Ispaniya 1918-1972 gg. Istoricheskii ocherk* (Moscow, 1975), while Werner Krauss, ed., *Spanien 1900-1965* (Munich, 1972), is topical in approach.

32. Gerald Meaker, *The Revolutionary Left in Spain, 1914-1923* (Stanford, 1974), provides an excellent general account of the worker left in these years.

33. On the revolt of the middle classes, see Villacorta Baños, *Profesionales,* 331-502, and L. Rodríguez Camuñas, *El problema de las clases medias como principio de regeneración nacional* (Madrid, 1923).

34. Salvador de Madariaga addressed the interpretation in "Spain and Russia: A Parallel," *New Europe* 4 (1917): 198-204, and Ortega y Gasset later took it up briefly in *España invertebrada* (Madrid, 1921).

35. The best analysis in any language of the impact of World War I on Spain is Gerald H. Meaker, "Spain," in H. Schmitt, ed., *Neutral Europe Between War and Revolution 1917-23* (Charlottesville, Va., 1988), 1-65.

36. See Carolyn P. Boyd, *Pretorian Politics in Liberal Spain* (Durham, N.C., 1979).

37. J. A. Lacomba Avellán, *La crisis española de 1917* (Malaga, 1970), is the best single treatment.

38. On the problem of anarchist violence, sometimes called "terrorism," during the first quarter of the century, see Rafael Núñez Florencio, *El terrorismo anarquista, 1888-1909* (Madrid, 1983); J. Romero Maura, "Terrorism in Barcelona and Its Impact on Spanish Politics 1904-1909," *Past and Present* 41 (1968): 130-83;

Walther L. Bernecker, "Strategien der 'direkten Aktion' und der Gewaltanwendung im spanischen Anarchismus," in W. Mommsen and G. Hirschfeld, eds., *Sozialprotest, Gewalt, Terror* (Stuttgart, 1982), 107-34; Albert Balcells, "Violencia y terrorismo en la lucha de clases de Barcelona de 1913 a 1923," *Estudios de Historia Social* 3-4 (1987): 37-79; Angel Pestaña, *Lo que yo aprendí en la vida* (Barcelona, 1934), reprinted in his *Trayectoria sindicalista* (Madrid, 1974); and his *Terrorismo en Barcelona,* ed. J. Tusell (Barcelona, 1979); León-Ignacio, *Los años del pistolerismo* (Barcelona, 1981); Amaro del Rosal, *La violencia, enfermedad del anarquismo* (Barcelona, 1976); and Colin Winston, *Workers and the Right in Spain, 1900-1930* (Princeton, 1985).

39. See Antonio Barragán Moriana, *Conflictividad social y desarticulación política en la provincia de Córdoba 1918-1920* (Córdoba, 1920); M. Tuñón de Lara, *Luchas obreras y campesinas en la Andalucía del siglo XX: Jaén (1917-1920), Sevilla (1930-1932)* (Madrid, 1978); and J. M. Macarro, *Conflictos sociales en la ciudad de Sevilla en los años 1918-1920* (Córdoba, 1984).

40. José Alvarez Junco, *El emperador del Paralelo: Lerroux y la demagogia populista* (Madrid, 1990), J. B. Culla i. Clarà, *El republicanisme lerrouxista a Catalunya (1901-1923)* (Barcelona, 1986); and John R. Mosher, *The Birth of Mass Politics in Spain: Lerrouxismo in Barcelona, 1901-1909* (New York, 1991).

41. See Manuel Suárez Cortina, *El reformismo en España* (Madrid, 1986). On the party's leader, there are Mariano Cuber, *Melquiades Alvarez* (Madrid, 1985); Maximiano Garcia Venero, *Melquiades Alvarez: Historia de un liberal* (Madrid, 1974); and E. G. Gingold, "Melquiades Alvarez and the Reformist Party, 1901-1926" (Ph.D. diss., University of Wisconsin), 1973).

42. Javier Tusell, *Radiografía de un golpe de estado* (Madrid, 1987), presents a detailed account of the pronunciamiento and of the decomposition of the parliamentary government. The failure of the Liberals is studied in Thomas G. Trice, *Spanish Liberalism in Crisis: A Study of the Liberal Party during Spain's Parliamentary Collapse, 1913-1923* (New York, 1991).

A sympathetic treatment of the way D. Alfonso grappled with the severe problems facing Spanish government will be found in Carlos Seco Serrano, *Alfonso XIII y la crisis de la Restauración* (Madrid, 1979). See also Vicente Pilapil, *Alfonso XIII* (New York, 1969).

43. Shannon E. Fleming, *Primo de Rivera and Abd el-Krim: The Struggle in Spanish Morocco, 1923-1927* (New York, 1991), and S. E. Fleming and A. K. Fleming, "Primo de Rivera and Spain's Moroccan Problem, 1923-1927," *Journal of Contemporary History* (hereafter referred to as *JCH*) 12:1 (January, 1977): 85- 100.

44. James Rial, *Revolution from Above: The Primo de Rivera Dictatorship in Spain, 1923-1930* (Fairfax, 1986), focuses on the regime's economic policies.

45. The principal study of the dictatorship's politics is Shlomo Ben-Ami, *Fascism from Above: The Dictatorship of Primo de Rivera in Spain 1923-1930* (Oxford, 1983). See also J. L. Gómez Navarro, *El régimen de Primo de Rivera* (Madrid, 1991).

46. Anthony D. McIvor, "Spanish Labor Policy during the Dictablanda of Primo de Rivera" (Ph.D. diss., University of California, San Diego, 1982); Eduardo Aunós, *Política social de la dictadura* (Madrid, 1944); and Alfredo Montoya Melgar, *Ideología y lenguaje en las leyes laborales de España: La dictadura de Primo de Rivera* (Murcia, 1981).

47. See M. García Canales, *El problema constitucional en la dictadura de Primo de Rivera* (Madrid, 1980), and, on relations with Fascist Italy, G. Palomares Lerma, *Mussolini y Primo de Rivera* (Madrid, 1989).

48. José Andrés Gallego, *El socialismo durante la dictadura, 1923–1930* (Madrid, 1977), treats aspects of Socialist policy in these years.

49. The opposition of most of Spain's leading intellectuals is exhaustively studied in G. García Queipo de Llano, *Los intelectuales y la dictadura de Primo de Rivera* (Madrid, 1988).

Chapter 2. The Republican Transition, 1930–1931

1. This was pointed out by Shlomo Ben-Ami, "The Republican 'take-over': prelude to inevitable catastrophe?," in P. Preston, ed., *Revolution and War in Spain 1931–1939* (London 1984), 14–34.

2. During the boom of 1960–75, agricultural labor underwent a 19 percent decline in terms of the total national labor force.

3. The service sector of the Spanish labor force would not again undergo significant expansion until after 1960.

4. Some of these data are from M. Tuñón de Lara, *Historia de España: La población, la economía, la sociedad (1898–1931)* (Madrid, 1984), 601.

5. Shlomo Ben-Ami, *The Origins of the Second Republic in Spain* (Oxford, 1978), 26–36.

6. There is a detailed study of the defection of the old parliamentary leaders in Carlos Seco Serrano, "El cerco de la monarquía: La ruptura de los partidos dinásticos con Alfonso XIII durante la dictadura de Primo de Rivera," *Boletín de la Real Academia de la Historia* 187:2 (1987): 161–269.

7. Berenguer later published a memoir, *De la dictadura a la República* (Madrid, 1975).

8. Shlomo Ben-ami, "The Forerunners of Spanish Fascism: Unión Patriótica and Monárquica," *JCH* 9:1 (January, 1979): 49–79.

9. José Sánchez Guerra, *Al servicio de España* (Madrid, 1931).

10. The best general account of political maneuvering in 1930 will be found in Ben-Ami, *Origins*, though Eduardo de Guzmán, *1930; Historia política de un año decisivo* (Madrid, 1973), offers considerable detail.

11. M. Baras i Gómez, *Acció Catalana (1922–1936)* (Barcelona, 1984), presents the most complete account of Acció Catalana. Enrique Ucelay da Cal, "Estat Català" (Ph.D. diss., Columbia University, 1979), 2 vols., is the fullest study of that organization down to the death of its founder, Francesc Macià, in 1933. Formation of the Esquerra is treated in the broadest study of that coalition, M. D. Ivern

i Salvà, *Esquerra Republicana de Catalunya (1931–1936)* (Montserrat, 1988), 1:1–73. See also J. B. Culla i Clarà, *El catalanisme d'esquerra (1928–1936)*; Josep M. Poblet, *Historia de l'Esquerra Republicana de Catalunya* (Barcelona, 1976); and Da Cal, "La formació d'Esquerra Republicana de Catalunya," *L'Avenç* 4 (July–August, 1977), as well as further references in Ivern i Salvà, *Esquerra Republicana*, 1:51–52.

12. On the commitment to Catalan autonomy, see Adolfo Hernández Lafuente, *Autonomiá e integración en la Segunda República* (Madrid, 1980), 16–43.

13. *El Socialista*, February 5 and 13, 1924, quoted in Paul Preston, *The Coming of the Spanish Civil War* (London, 1978), 15.

14. Quoted in Maximiano García Venero, *Historia de las Internacionales en España* (Madrid, 1958), 3:423. A. C. Saiz Valdivielso, *Indalecio Prieto* (Barcelona, 1984), is the only biography, but see also the prologue by Edward Malefakis to Prieto's *Discursos fundamentales* (Madrid, 1975), 7–32.

15. Lerroux gives his version of this maneuvering in his memoir, *La pequeña historia* (Madrid, 1963), 60–67.

16. The Republican Committee had dispatched emissaries, led by the ORGA politician Santiago Casares Quiroga, to Jaca on the eve of the action to inform Galán and García Hernández that the date had been postponed. Casares Quiroga, in poor health, arrived in Jaca late the night before and promptly went to bed without making contact with the conspirators. Thus at the very outset of his republican political life he revealed what would manifest itself as persistent ineptitude in dealing with critical situations.

17. At least five soldiers and police were killed in the Jaca affair, and others were wounded. The text of revolutionary decrees, prepared by Galán but never actually posted, decreed summary execution of all who resisted. They asserted somewhat inaccurately that the movement was led by officers from the rank of captain downward, that senior ranks would be severely purged and the army supplemented by a broad new national guard. A special "producers' committee" was to be named to supervise each factory in Spain. This unpublished *bando* is given in full in Emilio Mola Vidal, *Tempestad, calma, intriga y crisis* (Madrid, n. d.), 56–57. See also Graco Marsá, *La sublevación de Jaca* (Madrid, 1931), but especially the recent study by J. M. Azpiroz Pascual and F. Elbot Broto, *La sublevación de Jaca* (Zaragoza, 1984).

18. Ramón Franco, younger brother of the already famous general, was a national hero in his own right, a sort of Spanish Charles Lindbergh who had flown the first trans-Atlantic flight from Spain to Argentina.

19. The republican military conspirators had formed a small "Uníon Militar Republicana." There are three memoirs from this group: Eduardo López de Ochoa, *De la dictadura a la República* (Madrid, 1931); Gonzalo Queipo de Llano, *El movimiento reinvindicativo de Cuatro Vientos* (Madrid, 1933); and Ramón Franco, *Madrid bajo las bombas* (Madrid, 1931).

20. The moderate and apolitical Julián Besteiro, president of the UGT's national committee, opposed a general strike and never issued any orders for one, as he later admitted in a Cortes debate on 11 April 1934. The division within the leader-

ship was later discussed at length in the Party congress of 1934. *Actas de las sesiones celebradas por el XIII Congreso ordinario del PSOE* (Madrid, 1934). A manuscript by Antonio Bartolomé y Más in the Sección Guerra Civil of the Archivo Historico Nacional gives a *lerrouxista* version of the events of December.

21. José Casado García, *Por qué condené a los capitanes Galán y García Hernández* (Madrid, 1935), presents the justification of the officer who presided over the courtmartial. J. Arderíus and J. Díaz Fernández, *Vida de Fermín Galán* (Madrid, 1931), is typical of republican literature on Galán, not a serious biography but a sort of novelized hagiography.

22. Quoted in Ben-Ami, *Origins*, 233.

23. *El Socialista*, April 5, 1931.

24. All data from the *Anuario Estadístico de España 1932*. For a local study, see A. M. Lorenzo Gorriz, *Movilización popular y burguesía republicana en Castelló de la Plana: Las elecciones del 12 de abril de 1931* (Castellón de la Plana, 1988).

25. *ABC* (Madrid), April 14, 1931.

26. Quoted in Ben-Ami, *Origins*, 241.

27. Ibid., 242.

28. Lerroux, *Pequeña historia*, 20: Francisco Largo Caballero, *Mis recuerdos* (Mexico City, 1954), 107–9.

29. *El Sol* (Madrid), April, 1931.

30. The only death was reported in Huelva, *ABC* (Seville), April 14, 1931.

31. Conde de Romanones, *Las últimas horas de una monarquía* (Madrid, 1931), 8.

32. *La Vanguardia* (Barcelona), April 15, 1931. Proclamation of the Republic in Barcelona is treated in detail in José Gaya Picón, *La jornada histórica de Barcelona* (Madrid, n.d.).

33. Romanones has given two somewhat different versions of these events in his *Ultimas horas* and in *Reflexiones y recuerdos: Historia de cuatro días* (Madrid, 1940). That of Alcalá Zamora appeared in *El Sol*, May 17, 1931.

34. The lengthiest memoir of these days by a Republican leader is Miguel Maura, *Así cayó Alfonso XIII* (Barcelona, 1966), 141–89. Key monarchist memoirs, in addition to those by Romanones, are by Emilio Mola Vidal in his *Obras completas* (Valladolid, 1940) and Juan de la Cierva y Peñafiel, *Notas de mi vida* (Madrid, 1955), 343–72.

There are two lengthy chronicles of these months: Fernando Díaz Plaja, *España, los años decisivos: 1931* (Madrid, 1970) and J. L. Fernández-Rua, *1931: La Segunda República* (Madrid, 1977). Three accounts of the last days of the monarchy, sympathetic to the crown, are Julián Cortés Cavanillas, *La caída de Alfonso XIII* (Madrid, 1932); Alvaro Alcalá Galiano, *La caída de un trono* (Madrid, 1933); and J. M. Tavera, *Los últimos días* (Barcelona, 1976). Other accounts include A. Piracés, *Por qué se proclamó la Segunda República en España* (Barcelona, 1931); Rafael Sánchez Guerra, *Proceso de un cambio de régimen* (Madrid, 1932); Nicola Pascazio, *La rivoluzione di Spagna* (Rome, 1933); and Julio Merino, *Todos contra la Monarquía 1930–1931* (Barcelona, 1985).

35. José Pla, the first historian of the Second Republic, ironically quoted similar words from Fernando VII on 19 July 1820, concerning the first restoration of liberalism, and by Estanislao Figuera, first president of the First Republic, on 11 February 1873. The latter had declaimed that "a people capable of carrying out this profound transformation without the slightest disorder shows that it is a people ready for liberty," famous last words in view of the doleful history of his new regime. José Pla, *Historia de la Segunda República española* (Barcelona, 1940), 1:102.

36. The chief historian of Spanish Masonry is J. A. Ferrer Benimeli. See his *Masonería española contemporánea* (Madrid, 1980), 2 vols., and his edited works *La Masonería en la historia de España* (Zaragoza, 1985) and *Masonería: Política y sociedad* (Madrid, 1989), 2 vols., as well as J. Ignacio Cruz, "Masonería y política en la II República," *Historia 16* 14:160 (August, 1989), 21–27. It might be further observed that various sectors of European Masonry were capable of quite diverse new political enthusiasms. Some lodges of Italian Scottish Rite Masons soon became ardent pro-Fascists, and in the first year of Mussolini's government no less than twelve of the twenty-eight members of the Fascist Grand Council were Masons, though the Duce soon forced them to choose between Fascism and Masonry. Cf. Claudio Segrè, *Italo Balbo; A Fascist Life* (Berkeley-Los Angeles, 1987), 139.

37. This is made clear in the principal study of Masonry during the Republic, M. D. Gómez Molleda's *La Masonería en la crisis española del siglo XX* (Madrid, 1986).

38. As Largo would declare in a later speech to Socialist youth: "Though we do have some ideas of theory, we have no time to expound them because our activity is absorbed by a more urgent task, which is facing the common enemy." Largo Caballero, *Posibilismo socialista en la democracia* (Madrid, 1933), 9.

39. Though there is no definitive biography, the literature on Macià is extensive, beginning with L. Aymamí i Baudina, *Macià* (Barcelona, 1933). There is a bibliography of subsequent works in Ivern i Salvà, *Esquerra*, 50, and, most recently, in Enric Jardí's brief *Francesc Macià* (Barcelona, 1991).

40. The initial relationship between Catalonia and the Provisional Government is treated in Hernández Lafuente, *Autonomía*, 47–66.

41. Colin Winston, *Workers and the Right in Spain, 1900–1936* (Princeton, 1985), presents a definitive study of the Sindicatos Libres.

42. These killings were all reported in the press. Winston has counted sixteen in Barcelona and three each in Badalona and Sabadell (ibid., 291–92).

43. *La Vanguardia*, May 3, 1931.

44. *Soldaridad Obrera*, April 24 and June 11, 1931, in Ben-Ami, *Origins*, 263.

45. Maura, *Así cayó*, 266, 267.

46. Ortega declared in *Crisol* on June 1, 1931: "There is no other people in the world capable of doing a similar thing, though all, in fact all, dream of doing it."

47. Three of the most militant young monarchists, the Miralles brothers, spent two years in jail as a result of this incident. They were finally tried and absolved in 1933. Joaquín Arrarás, *Historia de la Segunda República española* (Madrid, 1956–63), 2:185.

48. *El Sol*, May 11, 1931; Maura, *Así cayó*, 245. The incident also led to the arrest of more monarchists and the closure of *ABC* for a lengthy period.

49. Maura, *Así cayó*, 246-50.

50. Ibid., 251-52.

51. Church historians have compiled a list of 119 attacks on Church properties from May 11 to May 13, though the press did not report quite that many at the time. Antonio Montero Moreno, *Historia de la persecución religiosa en España* (Madrid, 1961), 25. Francisco Narbona, *La quema de conventos* (Madrid, 1959), and Arrarás, *Segunda República*, 2:74-100, present detailed descriptions from the Catholic viewpoint. See also Vicente Cárcel Ortí, *La persecución religiosa en España durante la Segunda República (1931-1939)* (Madrid, 1990), 107-14.

52. Attacks on Catholic buildings and property continued sporadically over the next two years and were revived on a large scale in 1936. Reportedly the first conviction took place in Zaragoza in April 1934, when an arsonist was sentenced to ten years imprisonment and a fine of 15,000 pesetas for having set fire to a church. Cárcel Ortí, *Persecución religiosa*, 113.

53. Marcelino Domingo, *La experiencia del poder* (Madrid, 1934), 88-90, expresses the anguish of some of the cabinet ministers over the lack of a more moderate and humane police force.

54. This should probably be translated as "riot police." The official name of Assault Guards was probably too belligerent, but expressed the government's pugnacity and determination in the face of any opposition.

Chapter 3. The Republican Constitution

1. Shlomo Ben-Ami, *The Origins of the Second Republic in Spain* (Oxford, 1978), 274, 275.

2. This account of the 1931 elections closely follows the careful study by Javier Tusell, *Las Constituyentes del 1931: unas elecciones de transición* (Madrid, 1982), 25-40.

3. Cf. Ben-Ami, *Origins*, 264-70, and the sardonic comments of Julio Camba, *Haciendo de República* (Madrid, 1968), 91-99.

4. Tusell, *Constituyentes*, 39-45.

5. The best treatments of the new Republican party system are in J. J. Linz, "The Party System of Spain: Past and Future," in S. Lipset and S. Rokkan, eds., *Party Systems and Voter Alignments* (New York, 1967), 197-282, and Santiago Varela, *Partidos y parlamento en la Segunda República* (Barcelona, 1978).

6. According to its campaign manager, Joaquín Chapaprieta, in his *La paz fue posible* (Barcelona, 1971), 150-56.

7. Quoted in Ben-Ami, *Origins*, 293.

8. The principal study is Eduardo Espín, *Azaña en el poder: El partido de Acción Republicana* (Madrid, 1980).

9. Quoted in Ben-Ami, *Origins*, 293.

10. Ibid., 281.

11. Concerning violence during the campaign, see Tusell, *Constituyentes*, 72–76. By far the most notorious incident was the supposed "complot de Tablada" having to do with the alleged conspiracy of Major Ramón Franco and leftist extremists in Andalusia (where Franco was a candidate) to initiate an armed uprising at Tablada airport outside Seville on 27 June and declare an independent "Republican state of Andalusia." Several of the accused were arrested before the twenty-seventh, while Franco broke a leg when a campaign platform collapsed beneath him, but it is not clear there was in fact any such conspiracy. See Blas Infante Pérez, *La verdad sobre el complot de Tablada y el Estado libre de Andalucía* (Seville, 1931); J. L. Ortiz de Lanzagorta, *Blas Infante* (Seville, 1979); and M. Tuñón de Lara, *Luchas obreras y campesinas en la Andalucía del siglo XX Jaén (1917–1920) Sevilla (1930–1932)* (Madrid, 1978), 169–78.

12. Numerous local electoral studies are now available for the Republican years, though with sufficient gaps to fuel dissertations for years to come. Listed alphabetically by city or province, these include S. de Pablo, *La Segunda República en Alava: Elecciones, partidos y vida pública* (Bilbao, 1989); J. Sánchez Sánchez and M. A. Mateos Rodríguez, *Elecciones y partidos en Albacete durante la Segunda República (1931–1936)* (Albacete, 1977); M. García Andreu, *Alicante en las elecciones republicanas 1931–1936* (Alicante, 1985); for Aragon: E. Fernández Clemente and C. Forcadell, *Estudios de historia contemporánea de Aragón* (Zaragoza, 1978), 141–90; A. Peiró Arroyo and E. Pinilla Navarro, *Nacionalismo y regionalismo en Aragón (1868–1942)* (Zaragoza, 1981), 125–204; and L. Germán Zubero, *Aragón en la II República* (Zaragoza, 1984), 225–303; J. A. González Casanova, *Elecciones en Barcelona (1931–1936)* (Madrid, 1969); L. Palacios Buñuelos, *Las elecciones en Burgos, 1931–1936* (Madrid, 1980); D. Caro Cancela, *La Segunda República en Cádiz: Elecciones y partidos políticos* (Cádiz, 1987); M. A. Cabrera Acosta, *Las elecciones a Cortes durante la II República en las Canarias occidentales* (Tenerife, 1990); Mercè Vilanova, *Atlas electoral de Catalunya durant la Segona República* (Barcelona, 1986); J. A. Sancho Calatrava, *Elecciones en la IIa República: Ciudad Real (1931–1936)* (Ciudad Real, 1989); Antonio Barragán, *Realidad política en Córdoba 1931* (Córdoba, 1980); P. Cornella i Roca, *Les eleccions de la Segona República a la ciutat de Girona 1931–1936* (Gerona, 1975); L. E. Esteban Barahona, *El comportamiento electoral de la ciudad de Guadalajara durante la Segunda República* (Guadalajara, 1988); A. Cillán Apalategui, *Sociología electoral de Guipúzcoa (1900–1936)* (San Sebastián, 1975); S. Hernández Armenteros, *Jaén ante la Segunda República* (Granada, 1988); E. Pardas Martínez, *La Segunda República y La Rioja (1931–1936)* (Logroño, 1982); A. Millares Cantero, *La Segunda República y las elecciones en la provincia de Las Palmas* (Las Palmas, 1982); Conxita Mir, *Lleida (1890–1936)* (Montserrat, 1985); F. Bermejo Martín, *La IIa República en Logroño* (Logroño, 1984); M. Mante Bartra, *La problemática de la Segunda República a través del estudio de una situación concreta: el Mataró de los años treinta* (Mataró, 1977); J. M. Quintana, *Menorca, siglo XX: De la Monarquía a la República* (Mallorca, 1976); J. A. Ayala, *Murcia y su huerta en la Segunda República, 1931–1939* (Murcia, 1978); J. Gómez Salvago, *La Segunda República: Elecciones y partidos*

políticos en Sevilla y provincia (Seville, 1986); L. Aguiló Lucia, *Las elecciones en Valencia durante la Segunda República* (Valencia, 1974); J. Serralonga Urquidi, *Eleccions i partits polítics a la Plana de Vic (1931–1936)* (Barcelona, 1977); F. Costa Vidal, *Villena durante la Segunda República: Vida política y elecciones* (Alicante, 1989); and J. Bueno, C. Gaudo, and L. Germán, *Elecciones en Zaragoza capital durante la Segunda República* (Zaragoza, 1980). Among the numerous articles on Republican elections, those by Mercedes Villanova Ribas on elections in Catalonia are noteworthy.

13. Tusell, *Constituyentes*, 141–54.

14. *Anuario Estadístico 1932* (Madrid, 1933); Tusell, *Constituyentes*, 133–39.

15. See Manuel Ballbé, *Orden público y militarismo en la España constitucional (1812–1983)* (Madrid, 1983), 319–20. The government was severely embarrassed and largely managed to suppress reporting of the incident, the only account published in Madrid appearing on the back pages of the Republican daily *La Voz*. Maura, the interior minister, who had refused "categorically" to reform the Civil Guard or "to alter a single comma of its ordinances," later wrote that "it was a real miracle that a heavy volley by such powerful weapons in such a narrow place did not cause a greater number of victims," and admitted that a different kind of police armed with clubs and pistols might have broken up the demonstration more peacefully. *Así cayó*, 279.

16. Anarchists were not the only source of concern in the electoral campaign. On 20 June two infantry regiments briefly patrolled the streets of Oviedo after Socialists violently disrupted a meeting of the Liberal Democratic Party.

17. The CNT published a *Memoria del Congreso extraordinario celebrado en Madrid, los días 11 al 16 de junio de 1931* (Barcelona, 1931). The principal account of the FAI-CNT under the Republic is still John Brademas, *Anarcosindicalismo y revolución en España, 1930–1937* (Barcelona, 1974). In English, see Robert W. Kern, *Red Years, Black Years* (Philadelphia, 1978), and, in French, Cesar Lorenzo, *Les anarchistes espagnols et le pouvoir, 1868–1939* (Paris, 1969).

18. FAI doctrines are treated in the lead article in Antonio Elorza, *La utopía anarquista bajo la Segunda República* (Madrid, 1973), and in Xavier Paniagua, *La sociedad libertaria: Agrarismo e industrialización en anarquismo español (1930–1939)* (Barcelona, 1982).

19. The chief study of the Spanish Communist Party under the Republic is Rafael de la Cruz, *El Partido Comunista de España en la Segunda República* (Madrid, 1987). See also Joan Estruch, *Historia del Partido Comunista de España* (Barcelona, 1978); Pelai Pagès, *Historia del Partido Comunista de España* (Barcelona, 1978); Antonio Padilla Bolívar, *El movimiento comunista español* (Barcelona, 1979); and Víctor Alba, *El Partido Comunista en España* (Barcelona, 1979).

20. The best account is J. M. Macarro, *La utopía revolucionaria: Sevilla en la Segunda República* (Seville, 1985), 13–14. According to his tally, these produced twenty new labor contracts and five improved contracts, thirteen of the strikes having been sparked by employers' efforts to reduce benefits. See also Macarro's *Sevilla*

la roja (Branes, Seville, 1989); N. Salas, *El Moscú sevillano: Sevilla la roja* (Seville, 1990); and, on developments in the countryside, M. Tuñón de Lara, *Luchas obreras y campesinas en la Andalucía del siglo XX: Jaén (1917–1920) Sevilla (1930–1932)* (Madrid, 1978).

21. Guillermo Cabanellas, *Cuatro generales* (Barcelona, 1979), 1:231–32.

22. Macarro, *Utopía*, 149–55.

23. The most famous of these was Buenaventura Durruti, the subject of several biographies, of which the most thorough is Abel Paz, *Durruti* (Barcelona, 1978).

24. There is a conservative but largely accurate description of the events of September, 1931, in Barcelona in José Pla, *Historia de la Segunda República española* (Barcelona, 1940), 1:190–99.

25. The principal studies of the conflict within the CNT are Eulalia Vega, *Anarquistas y sindicalistas, 1931–1936* (Valencia, 1987) and *El trentisme a Catalunya (1930–1933)* (Barcelona, 1980). Also important are Manuel Buenacasa, *La CNT, los "Treinta" y la FAI* (Barcelona, 1933), and two works by Albert Balcells, *Crisis económica y agitación social en Cataluña, 1930–1936* (Barcelona, 1971) and "La crisis del movimiento anarcosindicalista y el movimiento obrero en Sabadell entre 1930 y 1936," in his *Trabajo industrial y organización obrera en la Cataluña contemporánea (1900–1936)* (Barcelona, 1974). See also the biography *Angel Pestaña* by A. M. de Lera (Barcelona, 1978).

26. The issue was debated in Spanish historiography more than a generation later. See J. S. Pérez Garzón, "La revolución burguesa en España: Los inicios de un debate científico, 1966–1979," in M. Tuñón de Lara, et al., *Historiografía española contemporánea* (Madrid, 1980), 98–112.

27. The role and attitude of the UGT was explained by one of its leaders, Enrique de Santiago, in his *La UGT ante la revolución* (Madrid, 1932).

28. *El Socialista*, July 12, 1931.

29. Expressed, for example, in two books, Javier Bueno's *El Estado socialista: Nueva interpretación del comunismo* (Madrid), which appeared in June, 1931, and Gabriel Morón, *La ruta del socialismo en España* (Madrid, 1932).

30. He declared at the 1932 UGT congress: "Marxism is an idealist position that constitutes the reality of history studying economic movements," like the hypotheses of "the poets of science." Quoted in Marta Bizcarrondo, *Araquistain y la crisis socialista en la II República* (Madrid, 1975), 183.

31. Besteiro explained his position in his *Marxismo y anatimarxismo* (Madrid, 1935) and is the subject of a number of works. The first, Andrés Saborit's *Julián Besteiro* (Mexico City, 1961), is a political biography, while E. Lamo de Espinosa, *Filosofía y política en Julián Besteiro* (Madrid, 1973), and Carlos Díaz, *Besteiro: El socialismo en libertad* (Madrid, 1976), treat his political and philosophical ideas.

32. *El Socialista*, July 12, 1931.

33. According to his cabinet colleagues. Maura, *Así cayó*, 278–87; Manuel Azaña, *Obras completas* (Mexico City, 1965–68), 4:37.

34. Largo's main speeches from this period are collected in his *Posibilismo socialista en la democracia* (Madrid, 1933). For a biography of the third Socialist

minister, see Virgilio Zapatero, *Fernando de los Ríos* (Madrid, 1974). Enrique López Sevilla has provided a general account in *El Partido Socialista Obrero Español en las Cortes Constituyentes de la Segunda República* (Mexico City, 1969), while Juan-Simeón Vidarte has written a memoir, *Las Cortes Constituyentes de 1931–1933* (Barcelona, 1976). Of the numerous writings of Prieto's later years, the first volume of his three-volume *Convulsiones de España* (Mexico City, 1967–69) contains the most material on the period of the Republic.

35. Altogether, in all three Republican parliaments combined, only 11.7 percent of the total number of deputies had sat in the parliament of the constitutional monarchy. Juan J. Linz, "Continuidad y discontinuidad en la élite política española, de la Restauración al Régimen actual," in *Estudios de ciencia política y sociología: Homenaje al Profesor Carlos Ollero* (Guadalajara, 1972), 361–423.

36. Julio Gil Pecharromán, *La Segunda República* (Madrid, 1989), 43.

37. Ortega's political speeches and writings of this period have been collected in his *Rectificación de la República* (Madrid, 1973), those of his associate Ramón Pérez de Ayala in the latter's *Escritos políticos* (Madrid, 1967), and those of Unamuno in his *República española y España republicana* (Salamanca, 1979). The principal studies are Gonzalo Redondo, *Las empresas políticas de José Ortega y Gasset* (Madrid, 1970); Andrew Dobson, *An Introduction to the Politics and Philosophy of José Ortega y Gasset* (Cambridge, 1989); and Jean Becarud, *Miguel de Unamuno y la Segunda República* (Madrid, 1965). See also Gabriel Morón, *Historia política de José Ortega y Gasset* (Madrid, 1965); V. Romano García, *José Ortega y Gasset, publicista* (Madrid, 1976), 243–51; and M. Cabrera and A. Elorza, "Urgoiti-Ortega: El 'partido nacional' en 1931," in J. L. García Delgado, ed., *La II República española: El primer bienio* (Madrid, 1987), 233–63.

The role of the intellectuals as a whole is treated in J. Tusell and G. García Queipo de Llano, *Los intelectuales y la Segunda República* (Madrid, 1990); J. Becarud and E. López Campillo, *Los intelectuales españoles durante la II República* (Madrid, 1978); and Paul Aubert, "Los intelectuales en el poder (1931–1933)," in García Delgado, *La II República*, 169–231. A short anthology of diverse views of leading intellectuals is offered in V. M. Arbeloa and M. de Santiago, *Intelectuales ante la Segunda República* (Salamanca, 1981).

38. According to the claims, for example, of the Socialist journalist Luis Araquistain, a member of the commission, in *El Sol*, December 8, 1931.

39. See Ma. P. Villabona, "La Constitución mexicana de 1917 y la española de 1931," *Revista de Estudios Políticos* (hereafter referred to as *REP*) 31–32 (January–April, 1983), 199–208.

40. Though a comparative moderate, Asúa spoke favorably of the Soviet Union and sought to distinguish between the Red Terror of 1918–21 and what he liked to refer to as the Soviet "juridical regime," as though the latter had superseded the former. *Libertad* (Madrid), May 27, 1931.

41. On the development and application of this concept, see F. Tomás y Valiente, "El 'Estado integral': Nacimiento y virtualidad de una fórmula poco estudiada," in J. L. García Delgado, ed., *La II República española: El primer bienio* (Madrid, 1987), 379–95.

42. Quoted in Arrarás, *Segunda República*, 1:148–49.

43. Quoted in Arrarás, *Segunda República*, 1:156.

44. *Diario de las Sesiones de las Cortes Constituyentes* (October 15, 1931), 1666–72. Unless otherwise indicated, quotations from parliamentary speeches in this and subsequent chapters are drawn from the same source and will not be further referenced.

45. The fullest study of the debate over Article 26 is Fernando de Meer, *La cuestión religiosa en las Cortes de la Segunda República* (Pamplona, 1975). See also V. M. Arbeloa, *La semana trágica de la Iglesia en España (octubre de 1931)* (Barcelona, 1976); Cesare Marongiu Buonaiuti, *Spagna 1931: La Seconda Republica e la Chiesa* (Rome, 1976); and F. Astarloa Villena, *Región y religión en las Constituyentes de 1931* (Valencia, 1976).

46. See Joaquin Tomás Villarroya, "Presidente de la República y Gobierno: Sus relaciones," *REP* 31–32 (January–April, 1983): 71–99.

47. Gil Pecharromán has calculated that during the sixty-three months of the peacetime Republic there were eighteen different cabinets, averaging about three and a half months each. Of these, only two fell because of adverse parliamentary votes, three because the confidence of the president was withdrawn, three more as a result of the elections of new parliaments and a new president, and nine due to internal disagreement. Gil Pecharromán, *Segunda República*, 78. The last figure is symptomatic of the extreme fragmentation that soon developed.

48. M. Bassols, *La jurisprudencia del Tribunal de Garantías Constitucionales* (Madrid, 1981).

49. The principal contemporary study was Nicolás Pérez Serrano, *La Constitución española (9 diciembre 1931): Antecedentes, texto, comentarios* (Madrid, 1932). The published *Diario de las Sesiones de las Cortes Constituyentes, 1931–1933* (Madrid, 1933) comprises twenty-five volumes, while the *Crónica de las Cortes Constituyentes de la Segunda República* (Madrid, 1931–34), prepared by Arturo Mori, consists of twelve volumes. Detailed treatment of the debates may be found in Fernando de Meer, *La Constitución de la II República* (Pamplona, 1978). Luis Jiménez de Asúa later published *La constitución política de la democracia española* (Santiago de Chile, 1942), as well as the informal *Anécdotas de las Constituyentes* (Buenos Aires, 1942). The lexicon and vocabulary of the Constituent Cortes and of Republican politics in general are studied in J. F. García Santos, *Léxico y política de la Segunda República* (Salamanca, 1980), and M. A. Rebollo Torio, *Vocabulario político, republicano y franquista (1931–1971)* (Valencia, 1978). Alfonso García Valdecasas presents a brief account in "La elaboración del texto constitucional," *REP* 31–32 (January–April, 1983): 57–70, and a lengthy bibliography is provided by M. García Canales, "La Constitución española y su aplicación (Bibliografía comentada)," in *REP* 31–32 (January–April, 1983): 209–64. Luis de Sirval (pseud.), *Huellas de las Constituyentes* (Madrid, 1933), is an anecdotal approach by a contemporary journalist. For comparisons with previous Spanish constitutions, see F. Fernández Segado, *Las Constituciones históricas españolas* (Madrid, 1981), and J. F. Merino Merchán, *Regímenes históricos españoles* (Madrid, 1988).

50. The most detailed critique was published by Alcalá Zamora after his deposi-

tion as president under the title *Los defectos de la Constitución de 1931* (Madrid, 1936).

51. That day he wrote in *Crisol:* "An immense number of Spaniards who collaborated with the advent of the Republic with their actions, their votes or even more importantly, with their hopes, now say with discontent and uneasiness, 'It wasn't this! It wasn't this!' The Republic is one thing. 'Radicalism' is something else."

52. *Luz* (Madrid), July 16, 1932.

53. Immediately published as the pamphlet *Rectificación de la República* (Madrid, 1931).

54. Salvador de Madariaga, *Españoles de mi tiempo* (Barcelona, 1974), 293.

55. The first biographies of Azaña were Frank Sedwick, *The Tragedy of Manuel Azaña and the Fate of the Spanish Republic* (Columbus, Ohio, 1963), and Emiliano Aguado, *Don Manuel Azaña Díaz* (Barcelona, 1972), but the fullest political account is Santos Juliá, *Manuel Azaña, una biografía política* (Madrid, 1990). Cipriano de Rivas Cherif, *Retrato de un desconocido* (Barcelona, 1980), is a fond portrait by his brother-in-law and the best source for intimate details. J. M. Marco, *La inteligencia republicana: Manuel Azaña, 1897–1930* (Madrid, 1988), is good on his early years. José Montero, *El drama de la verdad en Manuel Azaña* (Seville, 1979), treats his intellectual life, and Manuel Muela, *Azaña, estadista* (Madrid, 1983), his political goals and projects. Also important are Juan Marichal's prologues to the four volumes of Azaña's *Obras completas* (Mexico City, 1965–68) and Marichal's *La vocación de Manuel Azaña* (Madrid, 1968). The collection *Azaña* (Madrid, 1980) and Josefina Carabias, *Los que le llamábamos Don Manuel* (Madrid, 1980), are publications by his admirers, though they are sometimes not uncritical. Other pertinent accounts may be found in five recent books, L. Arias, *Azaña o el sueño de la razón* (Madrid, 1990); J. M. Marco, *Azaña* (Madrid, 1990); Jesús Ferrer Solá, *Azaña: Una pasión intelectual* (Barcelona, 1991); J. Peña González, *Manuel Azaña: El hombre, el intelectual y el político* (Madrid, 1991); and Ministerio de Justicia, *Azaña, jurista* (Madrid, 1990); as well as in Carlos Rojas, *Dos presidentes: Azaña/Companys* (Barcelona, 1977); two books by Víctor Alba, *Los sepultureros de la República* (Barcelona, 1977) and *Los conservadores en España* (Barcelona, 1981); and three articles in *Historia contemporánea*, vol. 1 (1988).

56. Maura, *Así cayó,* 223–25.

57. From Manuel Fraga Iribarne's prologue to Rojas, *Dos presidentes.*

58. Marichal, *Vocación,* 133–34, 141–43.

59. Quoted in Alba, *Conservadores,* 253.

60. Maura, *Así cayó,* 229.

61. Ibid., 230.

62. Martínez de Anido, like several other principals, remained safely in exile. On this entire process, see Carolyn P. Boyd, "'Responsibilities' and the Second Republic, 1931–6," in M. Blinkhorn, ed., *Spain in Conflict 1931–1939* (London, 1986), 14–35.

63. Alcalá Zamora's major public addresses of the Republican period are collected in his *Discursos* (Madrid, 1979).

64. His associate Maura had gone a separate path, forming his own miniscule Conservative Republican Party, with which Ortega y Gasset briefly flirted.

65. This is discussed more fully in Juan Avilés Farré, *La izquierda burguesa en la Segunda República* (Madrid, 1985), 118–21.

66. *Obras completas*, 4:93.

67. Ibid., 4:185.

68. Cf. Gerhard Jasper, *Der Schutz der Republik: Studien zur staatlichen Sicherung der Demokratie in der Weimarer Republik, 1922–1930* (Tübingen, 1963).

69. *El Sol*, October 21, 1931.

70. The best discussion is in Ballbé, *Orden público*, 323–35.

71. Vidarte, *Cortes Constituyentes*, 293.

72. *Obras completas*, 2:871–72.

73. These incidents are detailed in Macarro, *Utopía*, 174–95.

74. The phrase is from Gabriel Jackson, *The Spanish Republic and the Civil War 1931–1939* (Princeton, 1965), 70. Accounts in the Madrid press were somewhat contradictory. Luis Jiménez de Asúa, et al., *Castilblanco* (Madrid, 1933), presents the Socialist version of these events.

Azaña's remarks in his diary, commenting on the "horrible barbarism" of Castilblanco, seem just: "The Civil Guard has always been harsh and, even worse, irresponsible. 'It pays with paper,' say the people, referring to its impunity. The Civil Guard always served well the old politics and its caciques, who used it both in elections and social issues, expanding not only its size, but the scope and frequency of its action. In small towns, the post commander is a little king, and the personal abuses innumerable. All this sows hatred.

Yet there are Socialists who are not enemies of the Civil Guard, for example Besteiro, who told me some time ago: 'It's an admirable machine. It should not be suppressed, but made to work in our favor.'" *Obras completas*, 4:294.

75. Press reports immediately following the incident vary with regard to casualties.

76. There are brief accounts of the insurrection in Kern, *Red Years*, 107–9, and in Arrarás, *Segunda República*, 1:255–59.

77. *Obras completas*, 2:139–44.

78. *Obras completas* 2:167–71. On 19 February, fourteen Madrid newspapers formed a "Liga Defensora de la Prensa" to protect themselves from the government. The rightist Domingo de Arrese, in his *Bajo la Ley de Defensa de la República* (Madrid, 1933), 9–14, presented a list of newspapers fined or suspended between 1931 and 1933.

79. *Obras completas*, 2:191–200.

80. The Christian democrat Ossorio y Gallardo (who would stand with the Republic during the Civil War) published a thoughtful commentary on what he termed "the worrisome case of Azaña":

Today Señor Azaña does not cultivate his personal power, but remains in contact with parliament. . . . He avoids the pompous and spectacular, so characteristic of all dictators, engages in dialogue and occasionally allows himself to be convinced. His concern over efficient rule sometimes leads him to forget the law and other times to violate his own legislation. If O'Donnell had not coined the phrase about not dying from an excess of legality, Azaña would have invented it. The honest ease with which he creates laws that are legitimate but not juridically appropriate; the rapidity with which he asks and obtains from parliament the power to impose his standards or those of his collaborators in basic issues; the disdain that he does not seek to hide toward the rule of law make of the prime minister something both more respectable and more dangerous than a dictator: a doctrinaire of arbitrary rule. . . . Spain needs him today, and depending on events, may need him for a long time. But for the same reason that his talents are excellent, his tendency toward abusive power may be the more destructive, since he does not employ it in anger so much as to convince people of its necessity. When someone interpellates him about the injustice of a certain policy, he limits himself to responding: the state has need of it. And all those who clamored yesterday for the rights of liberty today applaud such a subversive, anarchist thesis, and there are even those who say: 'I didn't hate the dictatorship but the dictator.' But that is the seed of fascism! Its evolution then appears fatal, unavoidable. The state is placed above the rights of the individual, because the nation is the state. Soon the abominable cycle will continue. The state is the government, the government is the party. The party is its leader. Louis XIV will walk among us without feathers, lace or a sword but adorned with a flexible common touch. That is how risky the policy of Azaña is. He directs it today; tomorrow he will be its prisoner." [*Luz* (Madrid), March 5, 1932.]

81. See the discussion in Tuñón de Lara, *Luchas obreras*, 245–46.

82. In fact, the French specialist Guy Hermet has judged that the extremism of anarchosyndicalism, combined with its ability to generate a mass following, was the primary obstacle to the consolidation of liberal democracy in Spain. Hermet, *L'Espagne au XXme siecle* (Paris, 1983).

Chapter 4. The Republican Reforms

1. Frances Lannon, *Privilege, Persecution and Prophecy: The Catholic Church in Spain 1875–1975* (Oxford, 1987), 182.

2. According to Arrarás, in 1932 there were 3,630 Spanish members of the order, 2,987 of whom lived in Spain. They inhabited 40 formal residences and operated 8 universities or advanced institutes, 21 *colegios* (secondary schools), 3 "colegios maximos," 6 novitiate centers, 2 astronomical observatories, and a total of 163 primary and professional schools, as well as directing 481 devotional associations and sending many missionaries abroad. A total of 6,798 students were enrolled in their (largely elite) secondary schools, while a Jesuit leprosarium housed 635 patients. Estimates of the Jesuit patrimony in Spain were in the neighborhood of 200 million pesetas (over twenty million dollars), and no more than a portion of it was seized. Ever since the Liberal Party offensive of 1910 the Jesuits had customarily transferred title to many of their holdings. Joaquin Arrarás, *Historia de la Segunda República española* (Madrid, 1956–63), 1: I, 281.

3. Niceto Alcalá Zamora, *Los defectos de la Constitución de 1931* (Madrid, 1936), 93.

4. Quoted in Arrarás, *Segunda República*, 2:123.

5. The six-volume *Arxiu Vidal i Barraquer* (Montserrat, 1976), edited by M.

Batllori and V. M. Arbeloa, provides a mass of vital material on the work of Vidal and on the principal personalities and problems in church-state relations.

6. The fullest account of the conflict between the Church and the Republic in one volume will be found in José M. Sánchez, *Reform and Reaction* (Chapel Hill, 1964). In addition to references cited in the preceding chapter, see C. Marongiu Buonaiuti, "La Santa Sede e la Republica Spagnola dopo la Constituzione (9 dicembre 1931–19 novembre 1933)," *Storia e Politica* 23:4 (1984): 600–44, and the surveys by Manuel Ramírez Jiménez in his *Los grupos de presión en la Segunda República española* (Madrid, 1969), 193–262, and his *Las reformas de la II República* (Madrid, 1977), 9–42. Literature on the topic is reviewed in F. García de Cortázar, "La Iglesia imposible de la Segunda República (Comentario bibliográfico)," *REP* 31–32 (January–April, 1983): 295–311.

Among contemporary accounts, the government's policy is presented in Alvaro de Albornoz, *La política religiosa de la República* (Madrid, 1935), while the Basque priest Antonio de Pildain, one of the few clergymen in the Constituent Cortes and one of the most articulate defenders of the Church, published a collection of his speeches, *En defensa de la Iglesia y la libertad de enseñanza* (Madrid, 1935). Alfred Mendizábal, *Aux origines d'une tragédie* (Paris, 1937), offers the viewpoint of one of the tiny minority of Catholic liberals, while E. Allison Peers, *Spain, the Church and the Orders* (London, 1945), is a defense of the Church by a leading British Hispanist.

7. See Barry R. Bergen, "Molding Citizens: Ideology, Class and Primary Education in Nineteenth-Century France" (Ph.D. diss., University of Pennsylvania, 1987), and older French works such as Mona Ozouf, *L'Ecole, l'Eglise et la République, 1871–1914* (Paris, 1982), and Pierre Chevalier, *La separation de l'Eglise et de l'école: Jules Ferry et Léon XIII* (Paris, 1981).

8. For further data, see Encarnación González, *Sociedad y educación en la España de Alfonso XIII* (Madrid, 1988).

9. The controversy over secondary education to this point is treated in E. Díaz de la Guardia Bueno, *Evolución y desarrollo de la Enseñanza Media en Espana, 1875–1930* (Madrid, 1988).

10. These data are drawn mostly from David V. Holtby's unpublished paper, "Education during the Second Republic: Toward a Reconsideration," with the permission of Professor Holtby.

11. Mariano Pérez Galán, *La enseñanza en la Segunda República española* (Madrid, 1975), 49–50, 339–40.

12. The Catholic position was presented in Teodoro Martínez, *Hacia una España comunista: La escuela única* (Valladolid, 1931), and, more cogently, in Enrique Herrera Oria, *Educación de una España nueva* (Madrid, 1934).

13. *Gaceta de la República*, February 29, 1936.

14. See also the data in chapters 7 and 8 of Mercedes Samaniego Boneu, *La política educativa de la Segunda República durante el bienio azañista* (Madrid, 1977).

15. There are now a number of studies on educational reform and expansion

under the Republic, perhaps the best being Pérez Galán, *Enseñanza en la Segunda República*. Others, in addition to Samaniego Boneu, *Política educativa*, include Antonio Molero Pintado, *La reforma educativa de la Segunda República española* (Madrid, 1977); the collection *La revolución laica* (Valencia, 1983); David V. Holtby, "Society and Primary Schools in Spain, 1898–1936" (Ph.D. diss., University of New Mexico, 1978); Manuel de Puelles Benítez, *Educación e ideología en la España contemporánea (1767–1975)* (Barcelona, 1980), 316–41; and Carlos Alba Tercedor, "La educación en la II República," in M. Ramírez Jiménez, ed., *Estudios Sobre la II República española* (Madrid, 1975), 49–85. There are also regional studies, such as E. Cortada Andrev, *Escuela mixta y coeducación en Cataluña durante la II República* (Madrid, 1988), and X. Cid Fernández, *Educación e ideología en Ourense na IIa Republica* (Santiago de Compostela, 1989). The Republican leaders of the educational reform presented their position in Marcelino Domingo, *La escuela en la República* (Madrid, 1932), and Rodolfo Llopis, *La revolución en la escuela* (Madrid, 1933).

16. As argued by Julián Marías, "La vida intelectual durante la República/2," *El País* (Madrid), August 10, 1981.

17. *Patronato de misiones pedagógicas* (Madrid, 1934–35), 2 vols., and Francisco Caudet, "Las misiones pedagógicas, 1931–1935," *Cuadernos hispanoamericanos* 453 (1988): 93–108.

18. Eduardo Huertas Vázquez, *La política cultural de la Segunda República española* (Madrid, 1988), surveys the Republic's broader cultural programs, and G. Santonja, *La República de los libros: El nuevo libro popular* (Barcelona, 1989), treats the expansion of publication. The experience of García Lorca's theatrical group "La Barraca" is described in Ian Gibson, *Federico García Lorca* (New York, 1989), 319–45, 407–12.

19. Gabriel Cardona, *El poder militar en la España contemporánea hasta la Guerra Civil* (Madrid, 1983), 139.

20. The most thorough study is Michael Alpert, *La reforma militar de Azaña (1931–1933)* (Madrid, 1982), which found that 7,613 out of a total of 20,576 officers retired, a percentage of 36.9 (p. 156). Apparently more than a thousand sergeants (also included in the provisions) also retired.

21. At first Azaña simply reconstituted the air "service," naming the Republican air hero Maj. Ramón Franco (younger brother of the general) the director general of aviation. However, the continuing political radicalization of the younger Franco and his possible connection with one of the first anarchist revolts (June 1931) prompted Azaña to replace him and reorganize the service as a distinct corps.

22. The full text was:

So long as there remain both in small towns and in the cities the economic and political plottings of those who for more than a century have monopolized and exploited the nation, so long as they have not been pulverized by the Republican parties and government, we cannot enjoy the security that some day they will not come back to surprise us, whether in elections or in the destruction of municipal organizations, or by taking over the government.

They must be defeated and pulverized from the government, and I can assure you that, if it becomes my responsibility some day, I shall pulverize them with the same energy and resolution I have used to pulverize other things no less menacing for the Republic. [*El Pueblo* (Valencia), June 9, 1931, quoted in Eduardo Espín, *Azaña en el poder: El partido de Acción Republicana* (Madrid, 1980), 330.]

23. The principal study is Alpert, *Reforma militar de Azaña*, while the most detailed account of the military under the Republic is Mariano Aguilar Olivencia, *El Ejército español durante la Segunda República* (Madrid, 1986). In addition to Cardona, *El poder militar*, Carolyn Boyd has provided an excellent and succinct analysis in her chapter "Las reformas militares" in L. Suárez Fernández, ed., *Historia General de España y América* (Madrid, 1986), vol. 17, 141–73. F. Bravo Morata, *La República y el Ejército* (Madrid, 1978), lacks objectivity, but the collection *Les Armées espagnoles et françaises: Modernisation et reforme entre les deux Guerres Mondiales* (Madrid, 1989) is worthwhile.

The principal contemporary accounts, which varied considerably with the perspective of the writer, include N. Cebreiros, *Las reformas militares* (Santander, 1931); J. García-Benítez, *Estudios de política militar contemporánea de España* (Madrid, 1931); Eduardo Benzo, *Al servicio del Ejército* (Madrid, 1931); Tomás Peire, *Una política militar expuesta ante las Cortes Constituyentes* (Madrid, 1933); and Guillermo Cabanellas, *Militarismo y militaradas* (Madrid, 1933); as well as Ramón Franco's *Decíamos ayer* (Barcelona, 1932) and the observations of Gen. E. Mola Vidal in his *Obras completas* (Valladolid, 1940). Azaña's own motivations and attitudes are revealed in his speeches and in his diary, in volumes two and four of his *Obras completas* (Mexico City, 1965–68).

24. Decades later, the air force general and military historian Ramón Salas Larrazábal expressed a common opinion:

With inconceivable contumacy, Azaña repeatedly committed the grave error, and even abuse, of mordant and wounding phrases, together with excessive bombast in speeches and public declarations, especially in the lengthy preambles to his reformist decrees in which he frequently accused all and sundry of any manner of ills which he proposed to rectify, announcing with pomp and circumstance immediate improvements, which not only often were not realized but sometimes had a totally opposite effect from what he intended. . . .

These measures were, in general terms, well intentioned and many of them correct, but they were tarnished by his conviction—so little justified at that point—that he had in the army an innate foe whom he must humiliate. [*Historia del Ejército Popular de la República* (Madrid, 1973), vol. 1, 22–23.]

Col. Segismundo Casado, last commander of Republican Madrid in the Civil War, lamented even later:

If Señor Azaña had held in due esteem the army, not merely for its patriotic mission but for its loyal obedience to the Republic, it is undeniable that the reforms would have won the support of the majority of officers. But unfortunately Señor Azaña was not well-balanced, suffering from a civilian inferiority complex that was reflected in the scorn and hatred that he felt for military men. This complex was fully demonstrated throughout his political career. [*Pueblo*, October 7, 1986, in Aguilar Olivencia, *El Ejército*, 235.]

25. Manuel Burgos y Mazo, *La Dictadura y los constitucionalistas* (Madrid, 1935), 4:195, and *Antología histórica* (Valencia, 1944), 157–64.

26. Lerroux's very guarded version of this is in *La pequeña historia* (Madrid, 1963), 144–45.

27. Azaña, *Obras completas,* 4:399.

28. Manuel Goded, *Un faccioso cien por cien* (Zaragoza, 1939), 18.

29. Azaña's account of this incident will be found in his diary (*Obras Completas,* 4:413–18) and in his speech to the Cortes on the following day.

30. Emilio Esteban Infantes, *La sublevación del general Sanjurjo* (Madrid, 1933), 31.

31. During the year that followed, widely distributed photos of Sanjurjo and several of his military colleagues in striped penitentiary uniforms among common criminals would spark indignation among many other officers, who had not been involved in the revolt.

32. There is a generally accurate and detailed account of the *sanjurjada* in Arrarás, *Segunda República,* 1:419–84. A sizable literature soon developed, much of it by the general's apologists. This included, in addition to the memoir by his aide, Esteban Infantes, *General Sanjurjo,* such publications as R. Gómez Fernández, *"El 52": De general a presidiario* (Madrid, 1932); Andrés Coll, *Memorias de un deportado* (Madrid, 1933); A. Cano y Sánchez Pastor, *Cautivos en las arenas* (Madrid, 1933); Luciano de Taxonera, *10 de agosto de 1932* (Madrid, 1933); and the subsequent *Sanjurjo* (Madrid, 1943) by C. González Ruano and E. R. Tarduchy. A little on Barrera's role may be gleaned from Julio Milego, *El general Barrera* (Madrid, 1935).

33. There is an excellent study by Isidre Molas, *Lliga Catalana* (Barcelona, 1972), 2 vols. The Lliga's outstanding leader, Francesc Cambó, was also a major figure in Spanish politics. There are two brief biographies, M. García Venero, *Vida de Cambó* (Barcelona, 1952), and Ignacio Buqueras, *Cambó* (Barcelona, 1987), but the major work is Jesús Pabon's magisterial *Cambó* (Barcelona, 1969), perhaps the outstanding single biography of any figure of twentieth-century Spain. There are also Cambó's posthumous *Memorias (1876–1936)* (Barcelona, 1987). Bernat Muniesa, *Burguesía catalana ante la República española (1931–1936),* 2 vols., is a highly critical account of Catalan conservatism under the Republic.

34. These municipal councils were composed either of Esquerra representatives elected on 12 April or of *comisiones gestoras* of the Esquerra appointed by the Republican government. The Esquerra thus gained two-thirds of the seats in the first Catalan legislature in a process boycotted by the Lliga and also by the Federalist Republicans and Republican Right of Alcalá Zamora. Rural agricultural interests, who feared the domination of Barcelona, also tended toward opposition. There were several contemporary accounts: Antoni Rovira i Virgili, *Catalunya i la Republica* (Barcelona, 1931); F. de Solá Cañizares, *El moviment revolucionari a Catalunya* (Barcelona, 1932); and Lliga Catalana, *Historia d'una politica 1901–1933* (Barcelona, 1933).

35. Quoted in Shlomo Ben-Ami, *The Origins of the Second Republic in Spain* (Oxford, 1978), 295.

36. Isidre Molas, *El sistema de partidos políticos en Cataluña, 1931–1936* (Barcelona, 1974), provides a good overview of the Catalan political system under the Republic.

37. Aguirre's version is given in his *Entre la libertad y la revolución, 1930–1935* (Bilbao, 1935), 152–53. The account of Ramón Sierra, *Euzkadi* (Madrid, 1941), 128–31, is somewhat tendentious.

38. The basic study is Ricardo Miralles Palencia, *El socialismo vasco durante la II República* (Bilbao, 1988).

39. Albert Balcells, "Anarquistas y socialistas ante la autonomía catalana, 1930–1936," in M. Tuñón de Lara, ed., *La crisis del Estado español 1898–1936* (Madrid, 1978), 81–108, provides an excellent overview of the problem.

40. Roger Arnau, *Marxisme català i qüestió nacional catalana, 1930–1936* (Paris, 1974), 2 vols., is a collection of basic texts. See also Andreu Nin, *Els moviments d'emancipació nacional* (Barcelona, 1935), and his *La cuestión nacional en el Estado español* (Barcelona, 1979), a posthumous collection of documents and writings.

41. *Euzkadi* (Bilbao), October 16, 1931. The speeches are collected and given in full or summarized in Domingo de Arrese, *El País Vasco y las Constituyentes de la Segunda República* (Madrid, 1931).

42. *El Pensamiento Navarro* (Pamplona), January 19–22, 1932, quoted in Martin Blinkhorn, *Carlism and Crisis in Spain 1931–1939* (Cambridge, 1975), 77.

43. There is an extensive discussion in Aguirre, *Entre la libertad,* 196–217.

44. *Euzkadi* (Bilbao), June 21, 1932. J. M. Jimeno Jurío, *Navarra jamás dijo no al Estatuto Vasco* (Pamplona, 1977), holds that the vote did not in fact represent a majority of Navarrese citizens. The mounting conflict between Basque nationalists and other Catholics is treated in J. M. Goñi Galárraga, *La Guerra Civil en el País Vasco: Una guerra entre católicos* (Vitoria, 1989), 37–114.

45. Blinkhorn, *Carlism and Crisis,* treats the dominant political force in Navarre. For an overview, see his "War on Two Fronts: Politics and Society in Navarre, 1931–6," in P. Preston, ed., *Revolution and War in Spain 1931–1939* (London, 1984), 59–84. In recent years the literature on the liberal and leftist minorities in Navarre has grown considerably: J. J. Virto Ibáñez, *Partidos republicanos de Navarra* (Pamplona, 1986) and "La Navarra que fue a la guerra," *Historia 16* (February 1989): 11–20; A. García Sanz, *Republicanos navarros* (Pamplona, 1985); and two books by E. Majuelo Gil, *La II República en Navarra* (Pamplona, 1986) and *Luchas de clases en Navarra (1931–1936)* (Pamplona, 1989).

46. Santiago de Pablo, *El nacionalismo vasco en Alava (1907–1936)* (Bilbao, 1988).

47. The fundamental account of Basque nationalism throughout this period is J. L. de la Granja, *Nacionalismo y II República en el País Vasco* (Madrid, 1986), while J. P. Fusi Aizpurúa, *El problema vasco en la II República* (Madrid, 1979), offers the most incisive analysis. For the key province of Vizcaya, see J. J. Díaz Freire, *Expectativas y frustraciones en la Segunda República (Vizcaya, 1931–1933)* (Bilbao, 1990).

48. The debate over the statute and its structure are treated in J. M. Roig i Rosich,

L'Estatut de Catalunya a les Corts Constituens (1932) (Barcelona, 1978) and Manuel Gerpe Landín, *L'Estatut d'autonomia de Catalunya i l'Estat integral* (Barcelona, 1977).

For the broader dimensions of autonomy in Catalonia and other regions, see Adolfo Hernández Lafuente, *Autonomía e integración en la Segunda República española* (Madrid, 1980) and his "En torno a la bibliografía sobre la cuestión autonómica en la Segunda República española, *REP,* 31–32 (January–April, 1983): 279–86, as well as Santiago Varela, *El problema regional en la Segunda República española* (Madrid, 1976). *Los nacionalismos en la Espana de la II Republica* (Madrid, 1991), edited by J. Beramendi and R. Maíz, contains useful articles on the various movements during these years. A pre-glasnost Soviet perspective may be found in L. V. Ponomaryova, "Natsionalyi vopros v Ispanii i osvoboditelnoe dvizhenie katalontsev v 1931–1933 gg.," in Institut Istorii Akademiya Nauk SSSR, *Iz istorii osvoboditelnoi borby ispanskogo naroda* (Moscow, 1959), 55–122.

49. Ismael E. Pitarch, *Sociologia dels polítics de la Generalitat (1931–1939)* (Barcelona, 1977), treats the Catalan political elite.

50. José Arias Velasco, *La Hacienda de la Generalidad, 1931–1938* (Barcelona, 1977). J. Camps i Arboix, *El parlament de Catalunya (1932–1932)* (Barcelona, 1976), provides broader treatment of the Catalan legislature.

51. X. Vilas Nogueira, "La primera fase del proceso estatuario gallego: Asamblea de La Coruña, de 4 de junio de 1931," *Boletín de Ciencia Política,* 11–12 (April, 1973): 185–204.

52. See Alfonso Bozzo, *Los partidos políticos y la autonomía en Galicia, 1931–1936* (Madrid, 1976). Emilio González López, *Memorias de un diputado de las Cortes de la República* (La Coruña, 1989), are the memoirs of one of the two key leaders of the ORGA. Some of the basic documents may be found in B. Cores Trasmonte, ed., *El Estatuto de Galicia* (La Coruña, 1976).

53. Alfons Cucó, *El valencianismo político, 1874–1939* (Barcelona, 1977), is the principal account.

54. See J. A. Lacomba Avellán, *Regionalismo y autonomía en la Andalucía contemporánea (1875–1936)* (Granada, 1988).

55. Santos Juliá, "Francisco Largo Caballero y la lucha de tendencias en el socialismo español," *Annali della Fondazione Giangiacomo Feltrinelli* (1983–84), 857–85, terms this a plan for "worker corporativism."

56. Ministerio de Trabajo y Previsión Social, *Labor realizada desde la proclamación de la República hasta el 8 de septiembre de 1932* (Madrid, n.d.).

57. Ibid.

58. There is a brief study by S. González Gómez and M. Redero San Juan, "La Ley de Contratos de Trabajo de 1931," in J. L. García Delgado, ed., *La II República española: el primer bienio* (Madrid, 1987), 75–93. J. de Hinojosa Ferrer, *El contrato de trabajo* (Madrid, 1932), is a contemporary study, while S. Gónzalez Gómez, "Antecedentes históricos de la ley de contrato de trabajo de la II República," *Studia Historica* 1:4 (1983): 89–103, treats the background.

59. A. Martín Valverde, "El proyecto de ley de intervención obrera de la Segunda República Española," in M. Alonso Olea, et al., *Estudios de Derecho del Trabajo. En memoria del profesor Gaspar Bayón Chacón* (Madrid, 1980), 279–93. Estudios Sociales y Económicos de la Asociación Patronal, *El control obrero* (Madrid, 1931), presented the employers' case.

60. The basic study is Mercedes Samaniego Boneu, *La unificación de los seguros sociales a debate: La Segunda República* (Madrid, 1988).

61. Julio Aróstegui, "Largo Caballero, ministro de trabajo," in J. L. García Celgado, ed., *La II República española: El primer bienio*, 59–74, presents a clear overview. A Montoya Melgar, *Ideología y lenguaje en las leyes laborales de la Segunda República* (Murcia, 1983), treats doctrine and terminology, while A. Mazueco Jiménez, "La política social socialista durante el primer bienio republicano," *Estudios de Historia Social* 14 (1980): 135–55, presents a critique from the left. The *Anuario Español de Política Social* for 1934 provides the texts of all the social and economic reform legislation.

62. Gloria Núñez, *Trabajadoras en la Segunda República* (Madrid, 1989), presents a wealth of data on problems of women workers.

63. Enrique Prieto Tejeiro, *Agricultura y atraso en la España contemporánea* (Madrid, 1988), 67.

64. The most detailed study is David W. Beck, "Public Works in Spain, 1926–1933" (Ph.D. diss., University of New Mexico, 1980).

65. Jose Sánchez Jiménez, "Política y agrarismo durante la Segunda República," *Cuadernos de Historia Moderna y Contemporánea* 8 (1987): 211–33, surveys diverse proposed solutions, which he variously categorizes as technical, collectivist, socialist, Catholic, conservative-monarchist, and fascist.

66. These data are from E. E. Malefakis, *Agrarian Reform and Peasant Revolution in Spain* (New Haven, 1970), 72, still the fundamental study of the Republican agrarian reform.

67. G. García-Badell, "La distribución de la propiedad agrícola de España en las diferentes categorías de fincas," *Revista de Estudios Agro-Sociales* 30 (January–March, 1960).

68. Ibid.

69. Malefakis, *Agrarian Reform*, 98. He adds that "if female day labor is taken into account, the proportion of the agricultural population formed by day laborers would rise to 50.2 percent in southern Spain as against only 21.8 percent in the rest of the nation."

70. The report commissioned by the Ministry of Labor, *La crisis agraria andaluza de 1930–1931* (Madrid, 1931), was somber in the extreme.

71. Malefakis, *Agrarian Reform*, 91.

72. Ibid., 166–79; Pascual Carrión, *Los latifundios en España* (Madrid, 1932), 420–34.

73. Juan Díaz del Moral and José Ortega y Gasset, *La reforma agraria y el Estatuto catalán* (Madrid, 1932).

74. Malefakis, *Agrarian Reform*, 179–85.

75. Ibid., 205–10.

76. Ibid., 210–18.

77. Ibid., 218–25.

78. The limited efforts at collective agriculture are treated in Julián Casanova, et al., *El sueño igualitario: Campesinos y colectivizaciones en la España republicana, 1931–1936* (Zaragoza, 1989), and Luis Garrido González, *Colectividades agrarias en Andalucía: Jaén (1931–1939)* (Madrid, 1979).

79. See, in addition to the classic study by Malefakis, Jacques Maurice, *La reforma agraria en España en el siglo XX (1900–1936)* (Madrid, 1975); M. Tuñón de Lara, *Tres claves de la Segunda República* (Madrid, 1985), 21–92; and the brief survey in Ramírez Jiménez, *Los grupos de presión*, 165–92. Alejandro López, *El boicot de las derechas a las reformas de la II República: La minoría agraria, el rechazo constitucional y la cuestión de la tierra* (Madrid, 1984), treats the rightist opposition.

80. On the growth of women's rights in Spain, see Condesa Campo-Alonge, *La mujer en España* (Madrid, 1964) and M. A. Capmany, *El feminismo ibérico* (Barcelona, 1970), and on the divorce legislation, see Ricardo Lezcano, *El divorcio en la II República* (Madrid, 1979).

81. Francisca Rosique Navarro, *La reforma agraria en Badajoz durante la IIa República* (Badajoz, 1988), 225–28.

82. See Sanford Elwitt, *The Third Republic Defended: Bourgeois Reform in France, 1880–1914* (Baton Rouge, 1986).

Chapter 5. Waning of the Left Republican Coalition

1. This involved *Luz, El Sol,* and *La Voz,* though their support was only temporary and soon veered into opposition. On the proliferation of the party press under the Republic, see the catalog by Antonio Checa Godoy, *Prensa y partidos políticos durante la II República* (Salamanca, 1989).

2. Juan Avilés Farré, *La izquierda burguesa en la II República* (Madrid, 1985), 159–65.

3. Joaquín Arrarás, *Historia de la Segunda República española* (Madrid, 1956–63), vol. 2, 53, notes that even the normally well-balanced liberal Marañón, in a prologue to the *Tópicos revolucionarios* of the Radical Socialist deputy Fernando Varela, circumstantially endorsed the fact that "judicial process" might sometimes become "arbitrary," declaring that "without such brief but opportune departures from normal judicial process, the latter would nullify itself." The Christian democratic Ossorio y Gallardo more wisely lamented that this way of thinking was dangerous and widespread among the governing Republicans, for "that is what they have believed and said, with absolute good faith!" *Ahora,* November 15, 1932.

4. The mini-insurrection received considerable press coverage. Brief synthetic accounts may be found in John Brademas, *Anarco-sindicalismo y revolución en España* (Madrid, 1974), 98–103, and in Robert W. Kern, *Red Years, Black Years* (Philadelphia, 1978), 115–18.

5. The basic facts were presented in the preliminary opposition report to the Cortes on 23 February and in the official report of the subsequent investigating commission on 10 March. A collection of materials has been edited by Manuel García Ceballos, *Casas Viejas: Un proceso que pertenece a la historia* (Madrid, 1965), but the fullest reconstruction is by Jerome Mintz, *The Anarchists of Casas Viejas* (Chicago, 1982). Other works include Gerard Brey and Jacques Maurice, *Historia y leyenda de Casas Viejas* (Madrid, 1977), and Antonio Ramos Espejo, *Después de Casas Viejas* (Barcelona, 1984).

6. The anarchist version is fully developed in Ramón Sender's *Viaje a la aldea del crimen* (Madrid, 1934). Federico Urales, *España, 1933: La barbarie gubernamental* (Barcelona, 1933), is a general indictment of the government repression.

7. J. Arrarás, ed., *Memorias íntimas de Azaña* (Madrid, 1939), January 15, 1933.

8. *El Sol*, May 23, 24, 27, 1934. Rojas was freed by Nationalist forces after the Civil War began and given an army commission. He participated in the brutal repression in Granada in 1936–37 and eventually earned the criticism even of his Nationalist comrades, resulting in his court-martial and dismissal from the army at the end of the Civil War, according to Ramón Salas Larrazábal in Mintz, *Anarchists*, 287, 307.

9. *Obras completas* (Mexico City, 1965–68), vol. 2, 635.

10. According to *El Sol*, April 25, 1933, the *Anuario Estadístico 1934*, and to other sources cited in William J. Irwin, *The 1933 Cortes Elections* (New York, 1991), 3. Somewhat different initial results were first reported by *El Sol* and other papers before all returns were in, and these more fragmentary results have been cited by a number of historians in referring to the elections.

11. Quoted in Emilio Salcedo, *Vida de Don Miguel* (Salamanca, 1964), 357.

12. *El Sol*, October 9, 1933. Political attitudes and trends among the intelligentsia in these months are examined in J. Becarud and E. López Campillo, "Radicalización y vacilaciones de los intelectuales españoles en 1933–1934," in M. Tuñón de Lara, ed., *La crisis del Estado español 1898–1936* (Madrid, 1978), 321–41.

13. He had even encouraged them to help the government complete the current legislative agenda and thus exhaust its political mandate, opening the way to restructuring of the coalition. See the detailed remarks of Diego Martínez Barrio of the Radicals, who met with Alcalá Zamora five times during this period, in Martínez Barrio's *Memorias* (Barcelona, 1983), 176–78.

14. There is a good brief discussion of the law in Manuel Ballbé, *Orden público y militarismo en la España constitucional 1812–1983* (Madrid, 1983), 359–63.

15. *El Sol*, October 23, 1932; *El Socialista* October 23, 25, 1932; Paul Preston, *The Coming of the Spanish Civil War* (London, 1978), 77–78 (*CSCW*), and Amaro del Rosal, *Historia de la UGT de España 1901–1939* (Barcelona, 1977), vol. 1, 350–52.

16. *El Socialista*, February 12, 1932.

17. On Socialist Party structure and membership, see Manuel Contreras, *El PSOE en la II República* (Madrid, 1981), 61–206. Two regional studies are Ricardo

Miralles, *El socialismo vasco durante la II República* (Bilbao, 1988), and J. M. Palomares Ibáñez, *El socialismo en Castilla: Partido y sindicato durante el primer tercio del s. XX* (Valladolid, 1988), and, for Valladolid, A. de Prado Moura, *El movimiento obrero en Valladolid durante la II República (1931–1936)* (Valladolid, 1985).

18. *Boletín del Ministerio de Trabajo y Previsión Social*, April, 1933, in Preston, *CSCW*, 71, 217.

19. Adrian Shubert, *The Road to Revolution in Spain: The Coal Miners of Asturias 1860–1934* (Urbana and Chicago, 1987), 141–49. Because of a number of wildcat strikes and the activism of the CNT minority, Asturias led the country in the total number of strikes proportionate to its worker population during 1932–33.

20. Salamanca was one of several districts in León and Old Castile where there was a sizable number of landless workers whose militancy sometimes equaled that of their counterparts in the south. See Carlos Hermida Revillas, *Economía agraria y agitaciones campesinas en Castilla la Vieja y León: 1900–1936* (Madrid, 1989), 216–70, who observes of the Salamanca strike (p. 250): "Incidents were very numerous, with demonstrations, confrontations with the Civil Guard, and blocking of highways and telephone service."

21. *El Socialista*, October 13, 1932, cited in Contreras, *El PSOE*, 245.

22. According to Avilés Farré, *Izquierda burguesa*, 187, a total of 22,670 of the approximately 35,000 settlements negotiated by the *jurados* during 1933 were categorized as favorable to workers. There remained the significant minority won by employers and the effects of increasing unemployment.

23. See the citations from the press in Preston, *CSCW*, 78.

24. *El Socialista*, July 25, 1933.

25. Ibid., July 4, 1933.

26. Both quotations are from Preston, *CSCW*, 85.

27. *El Socialista*, August 16, 1933. Largo's main speeches of this period were collected in his *Discursos a los trabajadores* (Madrid, 1934).

28. A brief overview of the process of radicalization of Spanish Socialism is presented in Andrés de Blas Guerrero, *El socialismo radical en la II República* (Madrid, 1978). A classic Soviet approach may be found in S. P. Pozharskaya, "Taktika ispanskoi sotsialisticheskoi rabochei partii v pervye gody burzhuazno-demokraticheskoi revoliutsii (1931–1933 gg.)," in Institut Istorii Akademiya Nauk SSSR, *Iz istorii osvoboditelnoi borby ispanskogo naroda* (Moscow, 1959), 263–307.

29. There is a detailed study by Santos Juliá, *Madrid 1931–1934: De la fiesta popular a la lucha de clases* (Madrid, 1984), and an English summary in his "Economic crisis, social conflict and the Popular Front: Madrid, 1931–6," in P. Preston, ed., *Revolution and War in Spain 1931–1939* (London, 1984), 137–58.

30. Gordón Ordás's main speeches and articles are collected in his two-volume *Mi política en España* (Mexico City, 1961–62).

31. The break up of the Radical Socialists is treated in Avilés Farré, *Izquierda burguesa*, 199–202, and in Manuel Ramírez Jiménez, *Las reformas de la II República* (Madrid, 1977), 91–124.

32. As early as Christmas day of 1932 he had written in his diary:

I am handicapped by my formation as an artist and my historical sensibility and fear that I transpose political action to an invulnerable dimension of esthetic values. Between my thought and, more exactly, my attitude, my state of mind and feeling and the reality of my country, there lies a distance that cannot be filled by my popularity and personal authority, though demonstrated daily.

Once more my revulsion is so severe that I feel nausea and an impulse to flee. . . . Nonetheless, the only course in this situation is to discipline oneself to work for the future of Spain. The future of Spain! . . . What a terrible secret!

Chapter 6. Economic Policy and Performance

1. C. Martí, J. Nadal, and J. Vicens Vives, "El moviment obrer a Espanya de 1929 a 1936 en relació amb la crisis económica," *Serra d'Or* (February, 1961).

2. The principal studies of the depression in Spain and of its relation to the world economy are Juan Hernández Andreu, *Depresión económica en España 1925–1934* (Madrid, 1980) and *España y la crisis de 1929* (Madrid, 1986). See also Leandro Benavides, *Política económica en la II República española* (Madrid, 1972), and, for further references, Francisco Comín, "Una guía bibliográfica para el estudio de la economía en la Segunda República," *REP* 31–32 (January–April, 1983): 313–34.

3. The industrial tariff is treated in F. Pelecha Zozaya, *El proteccionismo industrial en España (1914–1931)* (Barcelona, 1987), and in P. Fraile Balbín, *Industrialización y grupos de presión: la economía política de la protección en España 1900–1950* (Madrid, 1991).

4. Marcelino Domingo, the agriculture minister, gives his own account in his *La experiencia del poder* (Madrid, 1934), 240–48.

5. On these initial problems, see Juan Ventosa y Clavell, *La situación política y los problemas económicos de España* (Barcelona, 1932), and Charles Lefaucheux, *La peseta et l'économie espagnole depuis 1928* (Paris, 1935).

6. *El Sol*, April 22, 1931.

7. As Calvo Sotelo pointed out in his *En defensa propia* (Madrid, 1932), 64–65.

8. Ramírez Jiménez, *Las reformas de la II República* (Madrid, 1977), 171–84; Benavides, *Política económica*, 122–23. Per capita income that year was 1,075 pesetas.

9. "Resumenes estadísticos, 1931–34," cited in Hernández Andreu, *Depresión económica*, 195, and Benavides, *Política económica*, 122–42.

10. This is briefly summarized in Douglas W. Richmond, "The Politics of Spanish Financial and Economic Policies During the Second Republic, 1931–1933," *The Historian* 49:3 (May, 1987): 348–67. For a detailed history of finance, see Francisco Comín Comín, *Hacienda y economía en la España contemporánea (1800–1936)*. Vol. 2. *La Hacienda transicional (1875–1936)* (Madrid, 1988).

11. See especially Pablo Martín Aceña, *La política monetaria en España, 1919–1935* (Madrid, 1984).

12. The "Spanish Keynes" of the period was Germán Bernácer, who held the chair of physics and chemistry in the Escuela de Comercio. Bernácer was a disciple

of the eccentric American theorist Henry George, who held that economic distress stemmed from monopolies of land ownership and could be cured by the nationalization of land. Bernácer's first book, *Sociedad y felicidad: Ensayo de mecánica social* (1916), was long, detailed, and generally ignored. More important was the article "La teoría de las disponibilidades como interpretación de las crisis económicas y del problema social," which he published in the *Revista Nacional de Economía* in 1922, followed by his effort to present a new theory of interest and the business cycle in his second book *La teoría del interés* (1925). He argued that economic expansion might stem from a variety of factors, such as greater investment, growth of consumption, or monetary expansion. But whereas most pre-Keynesian economics tended to hold that crises were due, among other things, to tensions in the credit market, Bernácer argued that they were simply due to reduced consumption because of either inflation or greater savings. Moreover, he denied that self-correcting mechanisms existed any longer to limit the length of a depression. This theory of "effective demand," which largely ignored the role of investment, was developed further in numerous articles in the *Revista Nacional de Economía* and, beginning in 1933, in *Economía Española*. As a Georgist, Bernácer argued that income from land constituted the real source of interest on capital, so that public ownership of natural resources was the key to the economy, while other standard remedies such as public works, the interest rate, and so forth were secondary and would not basically solve the problem. With the coming of the Republic, Bernácer became Jefe del Servicio de Estudios del Banco de España. He later criticized both the American New Deal and the Spanish and French Popular Fronts for presenting secondary palliatives and not going to the heart of economic problems. See G. Ruiz, *Germán Bernácer, un economista anticipativo* (Madrid, 1984).

13. J. M. Canales Aliende, *La administración de la Segunda República: La organización central del Estado* (Madrid, 1986).

14. Francisco Comín, "La economía española en el periodo de entreguerras (1919–1935)," in J. Nadal, A. Carreras, and C. Sudrià, eds., *La economía española en el siglo XX* (Barcelona, 1987), 105–49.

15. There is no authoritative study concerning the extent of wage increases. Juan Avilés Farré, *La izquierda burguesa en la II República* (Madrid, 1985), 186, reports that the Cámaras de Comercio issued data in 1933 indicating that within the past three years (since 1930) wages had risen from an index of 107 to 124, or about 16 percent, which accords with the calculations of Albert Balcells, *Crisis económica*, 167. Mercedes Cabrera, *La patronal ante la II República* (Madrid, 1983), suggests about "20 percent in real terms," (p. 132), which is probably too high. However, Jordi Palofox, "La gran depresión de los años treinta y la crisis industrial española," *Investigaciones Económicas* no. 11 (1980): 5–46, concludes that overall the increase in real wages was somewhat higher than 20 percent. Certainly, as Malefakis, *Agrarian Reform*, says, individual categories of farm wages in some provinces temporarily doubled.

16. Comín, "La economía."

17. Benavides, *Política económica*, 137.

18. Ibid., 256.

19. Balcells, *Crisis económica*, 127.

20. According to data from various sources compiled by Benjamin Martin, *The Agony of Modernization* (Ithaca, 1990), 348–49.

Chapter 7. Foreign Policy

1. For a general introduction to the foreign policies of modern Spain, see James W. Cortada, ed., *Spain in the Twentieth-Century World* (Westport, Conn., 1980).

2. Speech of 19 April 1933 in Bilbao; the text is given in Manuel Azaña, *Obras completas* (Mexico City, 1966), 2: 689.

3. Salvador de Madariaga, *Bosquejo de Europa* (Mexico City, 1951).

4. Spanish foreign policy in the first Republican biennium is evaluated in Ismael Saz Campos, "La política exterior de la Segunda República en el primer bienio (1931–1933): Una valoración," *Revista de Estudios Internacionales* 6:4 (1985): 843–58.

5. Cf. C. Barcia Trelles, *Francisco de Vitoria, fundador del Derecho internacional moderno* (Madrid, 1928).

6. As Lerroux admits for his own tour of service, "international policy was the least important matter." *La pequeña historia* (Madrid, 1963), 99.

7. These principles are set forth by Madariaga in *Spain: A Modern History* (New York, 1958), 464–65, and, more broadly, in his memoir, *Memorias (1921–1936)* (Madrid, 1977). See also Carlos Fernández Santander, *Madariaga, ciudadano del mundo* (Madrid, 1991).

8. Madariaga, *Memorias*, 290–317, 344–54.

9. Madariaga had earlier published the book *Disarmament* (New York, 1928) on his proposals.

10. See the brief study by J. F. Pertierra, *Las relaciones hispano-británicas durante la República española (1931–1936)* (Madrid, 1984).

11. These problems are detailed by Douglas Little, *Malevolent Neutrality: The United States, Great Britain, and the Origins of the Spanish Civil War* (Ithaca, 1985). Despite its inflated title, this study has little or nothing to do with the "origins of the Civil War," mainly treating British and American economic relations with the Republic. A major bone of contention was the threat to nationalize the ITT telephone subsidiary which had been set up under the dictatorship. Some further light on American relations is shed by the memoir of the United States ambassador, the gentleman historian Claude G. Bowers, *My Mission to Spain* (New York, 1954).

12. Ma. A. Egido León, *La concepción de la política exterior durante la II República (1931–1936)* (Madrid, 1987), 329–39. This detailed study provides the best account of foreign policy positions and practice under the Republic.

13. See ibid. for an analysis of the foreign policy goals of the extreme left, 521–610.

14. See *ibid.* for a discussion of problems concerning building a pan-Hispanic federalism, 171–95, 296–99.

15. Ismael Saz Campos, *Mussolini contra la II República* (Valencia, 1986).

16. Hipólito de la Torre Gómez, *Do 'perigo espanhol' a amizade peninsular: Portugal-Espanha, 1919–1930* (Lisbon, 1985).

17. João Soares, *A revolta de Madeira* (Lisbon, n.d.).

18. H. de la Torre Gómez, *La relación peninsular en la antecámara de la guerra civil de España (1931–1936)* (Mérida, 1988); Cesar Oliveira, *Portugal e a II República de Espanha, 1931–1936* (Lisbon, 1985).

19. De la Torre, *La relación,* 32–33, based on documents in the Portuguese government's *A Espanha Vermelha contra Portugal* (Lisbon, 1937), 20–25, 106–9; J. L. Alcofar Nassaes, "Azaña frente a Oliveira Salazar," *Historia y Vida* 163 (October 1981): 92–106; and Manuel Azaña, *Obras completas* (Mexico City, 1965–68), 1:130–31, 265.

20. De la Torre, *La relación,* 39.

21. Ibid., 72–87.

22. Report of the Portuguese embassy, 1 April 1936, ibid., 110. Since 1933, foreign diplomats and businessmen had with increasing frequency prophesied a worst-case scenario for the outcome of the growing political polarization, sometimes in blood-curdling and chiliastic terms. (Cf. Little, *Malevolent Neutrality,* 132 et passim.) These jeremiads sadly proved to be correct.

Chapter 8. Resurgence of the Right, 1933–1934

1. The only general study of all the rightist groups under the Republic is Richard A. H. Robinson, *The Origins of Franco's Spain* (London, 1970). See also the collected articles in Paul Preston, *Las derechas españolas en el siglo II* (Madrid, 1986).

2. For a brief overview of modern Catholic religious culture and politics in Spain, see my *Spanish Catholicism* (Madison, 1984).

3. In the published papers of Vidal i Barraquer, *Esglesia i Estat durant la segona Republica espanyola* (Montserrat, 1971), 1:27–29.

4. Quoted in Robinson, *The Origins,* 81.

5. José Monge Bernal, *Acción Popular* (Madrid, 1936), is an early account by a supporter.

6. J. M. Gil Robles, *No fue posible la paz* (Barcelona, 1968), 79. There are also two books on the CEDA leader. Juan Arrabal's admiring *José María Gil Robles* (Avila, 1935) was a sort of campaign biography, while J. M. Gutiérrez Ravé's later *Gil Robles, caudillo frustrado* (Madrid, 1967), was an attack from the extreme right.

7. The most thorough study is José Ramón Montero, *La CEDA* (Madrid, 1977), 2 vols. Robinson has presented the most scholarly positive evaluation of the CEDA in *The Origins,* and Preston the most searing indictment in *The Coming of the Spanish Civil War* (London, 1978) (CSCW). The CEDA press and propaganda were active; a list of publications is given by Montero, *CEDA,* 1:495.

8. Quoted in Robinson, *The Origins,* 118, 124.

9. Ibid., 115.

10. *El Debate's* Berlin correspondent in 1932–33 was Antonio Bermúdez Cañete, who had participated in the first effort to found a Spanish fascist movement in 1931.

11. *ABC,* October 17, 1933. See also Montero, *CEDA,* 2:249–55.

12. Gil Robles visited Alfonso XIII in Paris in June 1933 to obtain his political blessing for the CEDA, which, at least circumstantially, he managed to obtain. At that point the king was skeptical that the new monarchist party Renovación Española would achieve anything and thus was willing to see what the CEDA might accomplish, since it did not formally compromise the monarchy. S. Galindo Herrero, *Los partidos monárquicos bajo la Segunda República* (Madrid, 1956), 115; J. Cortés Cavanillas, *Confesiones y muerte de Alfonso XIII* (Madrid, 1951), 32, 106.

13. See Oscar Alzaga, *La primera democracia cristiana en España* (Barcelona, 1973).

14. Raul Morodo, *Orígenes ideológicas del franquismo* (Madrid, 1985), is a thorough ideological study, superseding Luis Ma. Ansón, *Acción Española* (Zaragoza, 1960).

15. An inventory of backers is presented in Morodo, *Orígenes,* 65–73.

16. This critique was first articulated by Víctor Pradera, *Al servicio de la Patria: Las ocasiones perdidas* (Madrid, 1930).

17. *Obra de Ramiro de Maeztu* (Madrid, 1974) and, more concretely, *Frente a la República* (Madrid, 1955), an anthology of his writings from these years. The principal studies are Vicente Marrero, *Maeztu* (Madrid, 1955), and, more briefly, Ricardo Landeira, *Ramiro de Maeztu* (Boston, 1978). Douglas Foard presents a lucid overview in "Ramiro de Maeztu y el fascismo," *Historia 16* 4:37 (May, 1979): 106–16.

18. The principal study is Julio Gil Pecharromán, "Renovación Española: Una alternativa monárquica a la Segunda República" (Ph.D. diss., Universidad Complutense, 1985), 2 vols.

19. There is a considerable literature about Calvo Sotelo but no adequate study. He published two collections of his writings in the early 1930s, *En defensa propia* (Madrid, 1933), and *La voz de un perseguido* (Madrid, 1933), 2 vols., and outlined some of his economic concepts in *El capitalismo contemporáneo y su evolución* (Madrid, 1935). Two preliminary studies of the early part of his career are Manuel Pi y Navarro, *Los primeros veinticinco años de Calvo Sotelo* (Zaragoza, 1961), and J. Soriano Flores de Lemus, *Calvo Sotelo ante la Segunda República* (Madrid, 1975). All general biographical accounts have been written by admirers. The principal are Aurelio Joaniquet, *Calvo Sotelo* (Madrid, 1939); Eduardo Aunós, *Calvo Sotelo y la política de su tiempo* (Madrid, 1941); and General Felipe Acedo Colunga, *José Calvo Sotelo* (Barcelona, 1957). Eugenio Vegas Latapié, one of the leading *Acción Española* writers and activists, published *El pensamiento político de Calvo Sotelo* (Madrid, 1941), as well as his own *Escritos políticos* (Madrid, 1940), and subsequent *Memorias políticas* (Madrid, 1983).

Beginning in 1933 quite a number of books on corporative doctrine appeared in Spain. Perhaps the most notable were Eduardo Aunós, *La reforma corporativa del Estado* (Madrid, 1935), and Joaquín Azpiazu, *El Estado Corporativo* (Madrid, 1936).

20. The basic study is Martin Blinkhorn, *Carlism and Crisis in Spain, 1931–1939* (London, 1975), 1–206. A Carlist narrative will be found in Luis Redondo and Juan Zavala, *El Requeté* (Barcelona, 1957), 225–310.

21. Carmen Bassolas, *La ideología de los escritores: Literatura y política en "La Gaceta Literaria" (1927–1932)* (Barcelona, 1975).

22. See Douglas W. Foard, *The Revolt of the Aesthetes: Ernesto Giménez Caballero and the Origins of Spanish Fascism* (New York, 1989).

23. There are two full-length biographies entitled *Ramiro Ledesma Ramos*, the better one by José Ma. Sánchez Diana (Madrid, 1975).

24. The best study of original Falangist doctrine is Javier Jiménez Campos, *El fascismo en la crisis de la Segunda República española* (Madrid, 1979). See also Bernd Nellessen, *Die verbotene Revolution* (Hamburg, 1963).

25. There are numerous biographical accounts of José Antonio Primo de Rivera. New ones still continue to appear. The best is Ian Gibson, *En busca de José Antonio* (Barcelona, 1980).

26. A copy of the text of this agreement was given to me by Pedro Sainz Rodríguez in Lisbon in May 1959. It has since been published by Gil Robles in *No fue posible*, 442–43.

27. Pertinent documentation of this relationship was first published by Angel Viñas, *La Alemania nazi y el 18 de julio* (Madrid, 1974), and by John F. Coverdale, *Italian Intervention in the Spanish Civil War* (Princeton, 1975), 57–58. The fullest account, however, will be found in Ismael Saz Campos, *Mussolini contra la II República* (Valencia, 1986).

28. A detailed narrative of the party under the Republic will be found in my *Falange: A History of Spanish Fascism* (Stanford, 1961), 1–115.

29. See Mercedes Cabrera, *La patronal ante la II República* (Madrid, 1983), 61–71, 152–95, 274–86.

30. Ibid., 50–57, 215–18, 233–36.

31. This situation may be compared with diverse patterns of fragmentation among middle-class German social and economic interests during the Weimar Republic, as emphasized in the work of such diverse historians as Jurgen Kocka, Heinrich Winkler, Larry E. Jones, and Peter Fritzsche. In Spain the organized economic interests tended to be less effectively associated with political parties and to fragment more along regional lines. In France during the founding generation of the Third Republic, a very different environment prevailed, as presented by Herman Lebovics, *The Alliance of Iron and Wheat in the Third French Republic, 1860–1914: Origins of the New Conservatism* (Baton Rouge, 1988).

32. One being the call for "complete power" and the use of democracy as only a means to "make parliament disappear," if need be, on 15 October as quoted above (at n. 11), and a second *tremendista* speech on 2 November, in which he declared that "we are about to put democracy to the test, perhaps for the last time. . . . If

tomorrow parliament is against our ideals, we shall go against parliament," the latter quoted in Robinson, *The Origins*, 141.

33. R. M. Capel Martínez, *El sufragio femenino en la Segunda República española* (Granada, 1975).

34. In his *Oligarquía y enchufismo* (Madrid, 1933), 61–70, Joaquín del Moral claimed that the winners were the twenty-seven deputies of Azaña's Acción Republicana, whose total prebends amounted to 278,841 pesetas per month, or 9,943 per deputy, and the forty-one deputies of the Catalan Esquerra, whose various government positions held a combined monthly income of 476,000 pesetas, or an average of 11,609 per deputy.

35. Robinson, *The Origins*, 150. This figure, however, combines the deaths of three CEDA members, apparently killed by the left, during the final phase of the campaign in the provinces, and at least three people (including one *cedista*) reported killed on election day. *El Debate*, November 21, 1933, and Monge Bernal, *Acción Popular*, 217, 360–61, claim that twice as many *cedistas* were killed, but this number cannot be substantiated.

36. William J. Irwin has calculated approximately 545,000 *cenetista* abstentions, which would have amounted to 6.02 percent of the total vote. *The 1933 Cortes Elections* (New York, 1991), 270–71. Moreover, conservatives paid some *cenetistas* not to vote; Robinson, *The Origins*, 337, presents considerable evidence that this bribery occurred. The effect of anarchist abstention was arguably greatest in Cádiz province, where 62.7 percent of the electorate did not vote, enabling 25 percent or less of the electorate to vote in a center-right list that included the Falangist leader José Antonio Primo de Rivera.

37. The Socialist Party secretariat subsequently announced that by its calculations the various parties of the disunited left had actually gained some thirty thousand more combined popular votes than the united right in the first round of voting. This may be correct, for according to Irwin's figures in table 8.1, the percentages of the total vote would have been 33.97 percent for the former coalition and 33.40 for all the right, but this of course leaves out the 30 percent of the electorate who voted for the center, more commonly aligned with the moderate right. For further discussion of electoral behavior, see Barry B. Seldes, "Social Cleavages and Electoral Behavior: The Case of Republican Spain" (Ph.D. diss., Rutgers University, 1971).

38. Altogether, nearly two-thirds of all deputies under the Republic held seats in only one of the three Republican parliaments, while only 71 of 992 were members of all three. These tabulations are by J. J. Linz, "Continuidad y discontinuidad en la élite política española," in *Estudios de Ciencia Política y Sociología (Homenaje al profesor Carlos Ollero)* (Madrid, 1972), 362–94.

39. Santos Juliá, *Historia del socialismo español*, ed. M. Tuñón de Lara (Barcelona, 1989), 3:85.

40. Alcalá Zamora, *Memorias* (Barcelona, 1977), 259–60.

41. According to a document quoted in Santos Juliá, *Manuel Azaña* (Madrid, 1990), 311.

42. The text of this letter was somewhat more veiled, though its intention was fully clear, and it is quoted in toto in Diego Martínez Barrio, *Memorias* (Barcelona, 1983), 212. This proposal is corroborated in Alcalá Zamora, *Memorias*, 260. See the discussion by Carlos Seco Serrano, "De la democracia a la guerra civil," *Historia General de España y América* (Madrid, 1986), 17:xxii–xxiii.

43. Alcalá Zamora, *Memorias*, 260.

44. Zaragoza was the national headquarters of the FAI. See Graham Kelsey, "Anarchism in Aragon during the Second Republic: The emergence of a mass movement," in M. Blinkhorn, ed., *Spain in Conflict 1931–1939* (London, 1986), 60–82, and Enrique Montañés, *Anarcosindicalismo y cambio político: Zaragoza 1930–1936* (Zaragoza, 1989).

45. The *tres ochos* (three "eights") were the mini-insurrections of 18 January 1932, 8 January 1933, and 8 December 1933.

46. John Brademas, *Anarco-sindicalismo, y revolución en España* (Madrid, 1974), 112–17; Joaquín Arrarás, *Historia de la Segunda República española* (Madrid, 1956–63), 2:250–56; and Robert W. Kern, *Red Years, Black Years* (Philadelphia, 1978), 123–25.

47. Quoted in Jesús Pabón, *Palabras en la oposición* (Seville, 1965), 196.

48. The basic study of the party is Octavio Ruiz Manjón, *El Partido Republicano Radical 1908–1936* (Madrid, 1976). See also Andrés de Blas Guerrero, "El Partido Radical en la política española de la Segunda República," *REP*, 31–32 (January–April, 1983), 137–64. Antonio Marsá Bragado, *El republicanismo histórico* (Madrid, 1933), presented the Radical party's own self-image at this juncture.

49. The Liberal Democrats were the new party of Melquiades Alvarez, who was the subject in this period of Mariano Cuber's *Melquiades Alvarez* (Madrid, 1935), and has been treated more broadly in M. Garcia Venero's book of the same name (Madrid, 1974), and in E. G. Gingold, "Melquiades Alvarez and the Reformist Party, 1901–1936" (Ph.D. diss., University of Wisconsin, 1973).

50. The *yunteros* had been settled on land under the terms of the Law for the Intensification of Cultivation, not of the agrarian reform itself, and did not have the tenure guarantees provided by the latter.

51. As Preston has noted, *CSCW*, 107.

52. Lerroux later wrote in his memoirs that the 1933 elections might have been considered a defeat for Republicans, who should have been grateful that the CEDA and Agrarians were willing to support the next Republican government. *La pequeña historia* (Madrid, 1963), 210–12.

53. This is best treated in Ruiz Manjón, *El Partido*, 413–19.

54. On the Radical Party in Valencia, see Stephen Lynam, "'Moderate' Conservatism and the Second Republic: The case of Valencia," in M. Blinkhorn, ed., *Spain in Conflict 1931–1939* (London, 1986), 133–59, and L. Aguiló Lucia, "El sistema de partidos políticos en el País Valencià durante la Segunda República," in M. Tuñón, ed., *La Crisis del Estado español* (Madrid, 1978), 505–16.

55. Madariaga had been invited to join Lerroux's first government in September 1933 but had insisted that it maintain a working relationship with the Social-

ists and resist any amnesty for Sanjurjo, terms that Lerroux would not meet. Madariaga was nonetheless a conservative and elitist kind of liberal, as he soon made clear in a new prospectus for political reform, *Anarquía o jerarquía*, published in book form at the close of 1934. He declared direct universal suffrage democracy a prescription for demagogy and disaster, proposing instead that direct democracy be limited to the local level, with provincial and then national assemblies to be selected indirectly and organically by the representatives elected on the lower level, such "organic democracy" to be complemented by a corporative system of national economic administration. See also P. C. González Cuevas, "Salvador de Madariaga y la democracia orgánica," *Historia 16* 9:127 (November, 1986): 27–31, and G. Fernández de la Mora, *Los teóricos izquierdistas de la democracia orgánica* (Barcelona, 1985).

56. The fullest account is in Saz Campos, *Mussolini*, 66–85. Antonio de Lizarza Iribarren, *Memorias de la conspiración* (Pamplona, 1969), 34–36, is the memoir of one of the Spanish participants.

57. John F. Coverdale, *Italian Intervention in the Spanish Civil War* (Princeton, 1975), 64.

58. The most noted was the pamphlet by the canon Aniceto de Castro Albarrán, *El derecho a la rebeldía* (Madrid, 1934), but Eugenio Vegas Latapié's *Catolicismo y República* (Madrid, 1934) included an appendix on "Insurrection" to legitimize the concept.

59. Alcalá Zamora has presented his account of this in his *Memorias* (Barcelona, 1977), 271–74. Lerroux's version is in *Pequeña historia*, 248–52.

60. Manuel Azaña, *Mi rebelión en Barcelona* (Madrid, 1935), 82.

61. Some Radicals and conservatives began to call Alcalá Zamora an "Alfonso en rústica" ("Alfonso in paperback"; i.e., a cheap edition of the former king).

Chapter 9. The Revolutionary Insurrection of 1934

1. One of the most cogent statements of this interpretation will be found in J. M. Macarro Vera, "Causas de la radicalización socialista en la II República," *Revista de Historia Contemporánea*, no. 1 (December, 1982). Julio Merino, *Los socialistas rompen las urnas: 1933* (Barcelona, 1986), goes over many details but adds little.

2. Santos Juliá, *Historia del socialismo español (1931–1939)*, vol. 3 of M. Tuñón de Lara, ed., *Historia del socialismo español* (Barcelona, 1989), 79.

3. Paul Preston, *The Coming of the Spanish Civil War* (London, 1978) (*CSCW*), 100.

4. Quoted in Juliá, *Historia*, 85.

5. Texts of both projects may be found in Dolores Ibarruri, et al., *Guerra y revolución en España* (Moscow, 1967), 1:52–57, while that of the party is given in Juliá, *Historia*, 347–49. Largo's account is in Francisco Largo Caballero, *Mis recuerdos* (Mexico City, 1954), 134–35.

6. Much of the discussion there and at other top-level UGT meetings of the

two preceding months has been published by Amaro del Rosal in his *1934: Movimiento revolucionario de octubre* (Madrid, 1983), 34–204.

7. On the Madrid section, see A. Pastor Ugeña, *La Agrupación Socialista Madrileña durante la Segunda República* (Madrid, 1985), 2 vols.

8. See the remarks of Juliá, *Historia*, 101–6.

9. The most recent account of the downfall of Austrian Socialists is A. G. Rabinbach, *The Crisis of Austrian Socialism, 1927–1934* (Ithaca, 1983).

10. For this group, see A. Balcells, *Ideari de Rafael Campalans* (Barcelona, 1973).

11. According to Maurín, the BOC grew from approximately three thousand members in 1931 to five thousand by 1934, with notable membership outside Catalonia only in Castellón and Valencia. (Response to a questionnaire of February 24, 1968.) There is no adequate critical study of Maurín. See Antoni Monreal, *El pensamiento político de Joaquín Maurín* (Barcelona, 1984); Manuel Sánchez, *Maurín, gran enigma de la guerra y otros recuerdos* (Madrid, 1976): Víctor Alba, *Dos revolucionarios: Andreu Nin/Joaquín Maurín* (Madrid, 1975); and Maurín's own *La revolución española* (Barcelona, 1932; 1977). A history of the BOC constitutes volume one of Víctor Alba's series *El marxisme a Catalunya* (Barcelona, 1974–75), volumes three and four of which are devoted to Nin and Maurín. V. Alba, ed., *La Nueva Era 1930–36,* (Gijón, 1976), is an anthology of the main BOC journal, and J. Coll and J. Pané, *Josep Rovira* (Barcelona, 1978), the biography of one of the secondary leaders. An excellent analysis of the ideological maneuvers involved may be found in Paul Heywood, "The Development of Marxist Theory in Spain and the Frente Popular," in M. S. Alexander and H. Graham, eds., *The French and Spanish Popular Fronts* (Cambridge, 1989), 116–30. For the Socialist Party in Barcelona during the Republic, see Albert Balcells, "El socialismo en Cataluña durante la Segunda República (1931–1936)," in *Sociedad, política y cultura en la España de los siglos XIX–XX* (Madrid, 1973), 177–213.

12. The Izquierda Comunista is treated in Pelai Pagès, *El movimiento trotskista en España (1930–1935)* (Barcelona, 1977); Ignacio Iglesias, *Leon Trotski y España* (Madrid, 1977); and Francesc Bonamusa, *Andreu Nin y el movimiento comunista en España (1930–1937)* (Barcelona, 1977). The writings of its leader, Andreu Nin, have been variously anthologized under the titles *Los problemas de la revolución española (1931–1937)* (Paris, 1971); *Por la unificación marxista* (Madrid, 1978); and *La revolución española* (Barcelona, 1978).

13. Adrian Shubert, *The Road to Revolution in Spain* (Urbana-Chicago, 1987), 141–62; Juliá, *Historia,* 115–16.

14. Cf. J. M. Macarro Vera, "Octubre, un error de cálculo y perspectiva," in G. Ojeda, ed., *Octubre 1934* (Madrid, 1985), 269–82.

15. Rafael Salazar Alonso, *Bajo el signo de la revolución* (Madrid, 1935), 75–77, 122–28.

16. Preston, *CSCW,* 114–15, and E. E. Malefakis, *Agrarian Reform and Peasant Revolution in Spain* (New Haven, 1970) 317–42. George A. Collier, *Socialists of Rural Andalusia: Unacknowledged Revolutionaries of the Second Republic* (Stanford, 1987), is worth consideration in this regard. It is an anthropological study

of a town containing a thousand farmworkers in the sierra of northern Huelva province. There the Socialists won the municipal elections of April 1933 and ran the town and local district until October 1934. They seem to have had little interest in collectivization and real socialism, but sought instead radical changes in labor relations. They were fueled by a revolution of rising expectations, enormously stimulated by their apparent success. For a different example of peasants exhibiting many of the attitudes and behavior of proletarian workers, see Robert Edelman, *Proletarian Peasants: The Revolution of 1905 in Russia's Southwest* (Cornell, 1986).

17. Malefakis, *Agrarian Reform,* 337.

18. The best accounts of the strike are in Malefakis, *Agrarian Reform,* 338–42, and in M. Tuñón de Lara, *Tres claves de la República,* 130–53.

19. In the most prominent case, the deliberate murder of the Falangist student leader Matías Montero Rodríguez on 9 February 1934, the person responsible (not formally a member of the Socialist Youth) was arrested, convicted, and sentenced to twenty-three years, but released after the Popular Front victory in 1936.

20. This material is based on the reporting of these incidents in the Madrid Press, particularly *El Sol.*

21. Cf. *ABC,* February 13, 1934.

22. These incidents are treated in further detail in my *Falange: A History of Spanish Fascism* (Stanford, 1961), 51–58.

23. Indalecio Prieto, *Discursos en América* (Mexico City, 1944), 106. Or, as Largo later commented of the Socialist Youth, "they did whatever they felt like." *Mis recuerdos,* 141.

24. Preston, *CSCW,* 117.

25. *Boletín de la UGT,* August, 1934, ibid., 118.

26. The splintering of left Catalanism is treated in E. Ucelay da Cal, "Estat Català" (Ph.D. diss., Columbia University, 1979), 495–549, and M. D. Ivern i Salvà *Esquerra Republicana de Catalunya (1931–36)* (Montserrat, 1988), 1:265–428.

27. Dencàs declared:

Am I a communist? Am I a fascist? I myself don't know. What I do realize, however, is that any political line, to triumph, needs to move young forces, to give them a mystique, a discipline and bring them into action. That's what I want to do in Catalonia. I want to flee the old molds of republicanism. I don't want to enter the molds — untried at home — but old in other countries of dogmatic marxism. To form a strong and ardent political movement based on two fundamental principles: nationalism, socialism, is what I want. [Quoted in J. Miravitlles, *Crítica del 6 d'octubre* (Barcelona, 1935), 117, cited in Da Cal, "Estat Català," 541–42.]

28. The first biography was Angel Ossorio y Gallardo, *Vida y sacrificio de Companys* (Buenos Aires, 1943), but J. M. Poblet, *Vida i mort de Lluis Companys* (Barcelona, 1976), is a fuller account.

29. The development of this problem is treated in Albert Balcells, *El problema agrari a Catalunya (1890–1936): La qüestió rabassaire* (Barcelona, 1968).

30. The case was argued for the Generalitat by Amadeu Hurtado, as he recounts in his memoir *Quaranta anys d'advocat* (Esplugues de Llobregat, 1967), 2:256–98.

On the technical issues, see André Lubac, *Le Tribunal Espagnol des Garanties Constitutionelles* (Montpellier, 1936).

31. *Obras completas* (Mexico City, 1965–68), 2:977–82.

32. Jesús Pabón, *Cambó* (Barcelona, 1969), vol. 2, pt. 2, 356–58.

33. During the preceding year Dencàs had served effectively as councillor of sanitation and social assistance and deserves some of the credit for the government's new achievements in health and medical facilities. His Escamots had first appeared in a mass parade in their green shirts at Barcelona's Montjuich stadium in October, 1933. Since that time their opponents had talked increasingly of a "Catalan fascism," while the Escamots sometimes referred to themselves as a "Catalan liberation army." The only study is J. M. Morreres Boix, "El Enigma de Josep Dencàs," *Historia Nueva* 21 (October, 1978): 94–104.

34. Joaquín Arrarás, *Historia de la Segunda República española* (Madrid, 1956–63), 2:381–82.

35. Ibid., 395–96.

36. Alcalá Zamora, *Discursos* (Madrid, 1979), 638–45.

37. Alcalá Zamora, *Memorias*, (Barcelona, 1977), 279–84.

38. On the lengthy though poorly focused preparations for revolt, see the memoirs by Rosal, 1934, 205–56, and Juan Simeón Vidarte, *El Bienio Negro y la insurrección de Asturias* (Barcelona, 1978), 163–236, and, for the general context, the studies in the collection *Octubre 1934: Cincuenta años para la reflexión* (Madrid, 1985).

39. Preston, *CSCW*, 127.

40. Araquistain has been studied in Marta Bizcarrondo, *Araquistain y la crisis socialista en la II República: Leviatán (1934–1936)* (Madrid, 1975). See also the anthology edited by Paul Preston, *Leviatán* (Madrid, 1976), and Preston's "The Struggle against Fascism in Spain: *Leviatán* and the Contradictions of the Socialist Left, 1934–1936," in M. Blinkhorn, ed., *Spain in Conflict* (London, 1986), 40–59.

41. Juan Avilés Farré, *La izquierda burguesa en la II República* (Madrid, 1985), 232–36. This movement toward the economic left by Izquierda Republicana may be compared with the "New Radical Movement" in the French Radical Party between 1926 and 1932. The differences were, of course, that the French Radicals were a much stronger, more broadly based group and in the long run were not won over by the new economic leftism. See Mildred Schlesinger, "The Development of the Radical Party in the Third Republic: The New Radical Movement, 1926–1932," *Journal of Modern History* 46:3 (September, 1974): 476–501.

42. Avilés Farré, *Izquierda burguesa*, 243–44.

43. Ibid., 239–40.

44. Ibid., 245–46.

45. Ibid., 246–48.

46. Alcalá Zamora, *Memorias*, 277–78. Alcalá Zamora later wrote that he suffered a night of severe insomnia after Martínez Barrio's visit, for he then realized that the left would never accept the normal working of the Constitution if

it meant their exclusion from power, which made some kind of revolt or breakdown almost inevitable.

47. Arrarás, *Segunda República*, 2:410.

48. Prieto later gave his version of this in "Mi escapatoria de 1934," *El Socialista* (Toulouse), July 5, 1951. His inconsistencies as a Socialist leader have been denounced by Víctor Alba in the latter's *Los sepultureros de la República* (Barcelona, 1977), 105–95. The fullest reconstruction of the *Turquesa* incident will be found in P. I. Taibo II, *Asturias 1934* (Gijon, 1984), 1:81–96.

49. *El Sol*, September 18, 1934.

50. These developments are well summarized in Arrarás, *Segunda República*, 2:424–43.

51. J. M. Gil Robles, *No fue posible la paz* (Barcelona, 1968), 161; Salazar Alonso, *Bajo el signo*, 319–20.

52. My interviews with Eloy Vaquero in New York, May–June, 1958.

53. In Prieto's *El Liberal* (Bilbao), January 23, 1936.

54. Though some of them found the energy to assault the exterior of the home of their bête noire, Besteiro. Preston, *CSCW*, 133.

55. Alejandro Lerroux, *La pequeña historia* (Madrid, 1963), 302.

56. Elsa López, et al., *Diego Hidalgo* (Madrid, 1986), and Concha Muñoz Tinoco, *Diego Hidalgo* (Badajoz, 1986), are brief accounts of his career. Hidalgo published an instant memoir on his experience as minister of war, *¿Por que fui lanzado desde el Ministerio de la Guerra?* (Madrid, 1935).

57. The original Catalan text may be found in Lluis Aymamí i Baudina, *El 6 d'octubre tal com jo l'he vist* (Barcelona, 1935), 249–51.

58. There were several contemporary accounts of the farcical drama in Barcelona: L. Aymamí i. Baudina, *El 6 d'octubre tal com jo l'he vist* (Barcelona, 1935); Enrique de Angulo, *Diez horas de Estat Català* (Madrid, 1935); F. Gómez Hidalgo, *Cataluña-Companys* (Madrid, 1935); Angel Estivill, *6 d'octubre: L'ensulsiada dels jacobins* (Barcelona, 1935); Jaume Miravitlles, *Critica del 6 d'octubre* (Barcelona, 1935); and, more recently, Manuel Cruells, *El 6 d'octubre a Catalunya* (Barcelona, 1970), and J. Tarín-Iglesias, *La rebelión de la Generalidad* (Barcelona, 1988).

59. Sebastià Campos i Terre, *El d'octubre a les comarques* (Barcelona, 1935; reprint ed., Tortosa, 1987). There were also a few scattered disorders in the Catalan countryside during the weeks that followed. See also Ricard Vinyes i Ribes, *La Catalunya internacional: El frontpopulisme en l'exemple català* (Barcelona, 1983), 98–120.

60. Azaña's memoir is *Mi rebelión en Barcelona* (Madrid, 1935), reprinted in vol. III of his *Obras completas*. He reported that he was told by Catalanist leaders that a revolt would be used as no more than a bargaining chip (pp. 74–76), which is believable. The nineteenth-century pronunciamiento quality of all this is doubly ironic in Azaña's case. He would never endorse revolutionary violence but he would obviously want the illegal pronunciamiento to succeed, indicating that some of his political instincts were not so much different from the traditional Spanish military men for whom he expressed such supercilious disdain.

61. Cf. J. D. Carrión Iñíguez, *La insurrección de 1934 en la provincia de Albacete* (Albacete, 1990).

62. The best brief treatment of the revolt in the Basque provinces is J. P. Fusi, "Nacionalismo y revolución: Octubre de 1934 en el País Vasco," in G. Jackson, et al., *Octubre 1934* (Madrid, 1985), 177–96.

63. Cf. Ludolfo Paramio, "Revolución y conciencia preindustrial en octubre del 34," in Jackson, et al., *Octubre 1934*, 301–15.

64. The Asturian background is explained in Adrian Shubert's *The Road to Revolution in Spain: The Coal Miners of Asturias 1860–1934* (Urbana-Chicago, 1987). He concludes that mining, per se, does not necessarily produce a more united or radical labor force than other sectors of industrial employment and instead emphasizes the historical and economic context in Asturias. Asturian coal, though relatively abundant, is of low quality, and the industry was never adequately capitalized or efficient to achieve high productivity. Both the dictatorship and the Republic had tried and failed to provide a remedy, when the only true solution was greater development or diversification, virtually impossible during the depression. Contemporary Asturias is treated more generally in David Ruiz, et al., *Asturias contemporánea, 1808–1975* (Madrid, 1981). On the CNT in the region, see A. Barrio Alonso, *Anarquismo y anarcosindicalismo en Asturias (1890–1936)* (Madrid, 1988). Preparations for the revolt are detailed in Taibo, *Asturias 1934*, 1:17–112, and in Taibo's article "Las diferencias asturianas," in *Octubre 1934*, 231–42.

65. The use of Moroccan as well as elite Legion troops from the Protectorate was much criticized by the left, but Azaña had called in both the Tercio and Regulares in 1932. The Moroccans had no monopoly on atrocities compared with Spaniards on either side and should not be held primarily responsible for the summary executions that did take place.

66. According to Yagüe's remarks quoted in J. Arrarás, ed., *Historia de la Cruzada española* (Madrid, 1940), 7:259.

67. Some of the most precise estimates of fatalities will be found in Aurelio de Llano Roza de Ampudia, *Pequeños anales de quince días* (Oviedo, 1935), the best of the contemporary accounts; and also in Bernardo Díaz Nosty, *La comuna asturiana* (Madrid, 1974); and Taibo, *Asturias 1934*, 2:243.

68. A government report of 30 October 1934 reported 220 officers and troops killed and 43 missing, for a total of 263. The Civil Guard apparently suffered 111 fatalities, and other police a total of 81. See E. Barco Teruel, *El "golpe" socialista del 6 de octubre de 1934* (Madrid, 1984), 258, and F. Aguado Sánchez, *La revolución de octubre de 1934* (Madrid, 1972), 503.

The literature on Spain's "Red October" soon became extensive and has continued to grow. Gen. Eduardo López Ochoa published a memoir, *Campaña militar en Asturias en octubre de 1934* (Madrid, 1936). Other contemporary accounts, in addition to Llano Roza, include Reporteros reunidos, *Octubre rojo* (Madrid, 1934); Ignacio Núñez, *La revolución de octubre de 1934* (Barcelona, 1935), 2 vols.; "Un testigo imparcial" (author), *Revolución en Asturias* (Madrid, 1934); J. S. Valdivielso, *Farsa y tragedia de España en el 1934* (Oviedo, 1935); Heraclio Iglesia Somoza,

Asedio y defensa de la cárcel de Oviedo (Vitoria, 1935); Jenaro G. Geijo, *Episodios de la revolución* (Santander, 1935); M. Martínez de Aguiar, *¿A dónde va el Estado español?* *Rebelión socialista y separatista de 1934* (Madrid, 1935); Vicente Madera, *El Sindicato Católico de Moreda y la revolución de octubre* (Madrid, 1935); and the brief interview book by Luis Octavio Madero, *El octubre español* (Madrid, 1935).

Among the leading contemporary leftist accounts were Manuel Grossi, *La insurrección de Asturias* (Barcelona, 1935): Antonio Ramos Oliveira, *La revolución española de octubre* (Madrid, 1935); Manuel D. Benavides, *La revolución fue así* (Barcelona, 1937); "José Canel" (pseud.), *Octubre rojo en Asturias* (Madrid, 1935); Ramon González Peña, *Un hombre en la revolución* (Madrid, 1935); Marcelino Domingo, *La revolución de octubre* (Madrid, 1935); "Ignotus" (Manuel Villar), *El anarquismo en la insurrección de octubre* (Valencia, 1935); Solano Palacio, *La revolución de octubre* (Barcelona, 1935); and Julián Orbón, *Avilés en el movimiento revolucionario de Asturias* (Gijón, 1934).

Later detailed studies include, in addition to the works previously cited by Aguado Sánchez, Barco Teruel, Díaz Nosty, and Taibo, J. A. Sánchez G. Sauco, *La revolución de 1934 en Asturias* (Madrid, 1974), and David Ruiz, *Insurrección defensiva y revolución obrera: El octubre español de 1934* (Barcelona, 1988). Marta Bizcarrondo, *Octubre del 1934: Reflexiones sobre una revolución* (Madrid, 1977), collects a series of texts, with an introduction on the origins of the Alianza Obrera. More detailed bibliographies will be found in Jackson, et al., *Octubre 1934*, 320–44, and in Taibo, *Asturias 1934*, 2:245–51. Antonio Padilla Bolívar, *1934: Las semillas de una guerra* (Barcelona, 1988), presents a chronicle of the entire year.

69. Doval had lost his commission for involvement in the *sanjurjada* but had been readmitted to the Civil Guard in the recent amnesty. Franco seems to have encouraged his appointment to Asturias.

70. The total number of extra prisoners maintained in Spanish jails through 1935 was approximately fifteen thousand, but an additional number may have been temporarily arrested in October and November 1934.

71. Gabriel Jackson, *The Spanish Republic and the Civil War 1931–1939* (Princeton, 1965), 166, estimates about forty, which seems approximately correct. The principal study of the assaults on the clergy is A. Garralda, *La persecución religiosa del clero en Asturias (1934 y 1936–1937)* (Avilés, 1977), 2 vols. See also ACNP de Oviedo, *Asturias roja: Sacerdotes y releigiosos perseguidos y martirizados* (Oviedo, 1935), and the hagiographic *Los mártires de Turón* (Madrid, 1935).

Almost inevitably amid a violent revolution, a certain number of common crimes (murder, rape, theft) occurred under the cover of revolutionary turmoil. The government's report *En servicio a la República: La revolución de octubre en Asturias* (Madrid, 1935) refers to three women allegedly raped and killed by revolutionaries.

72. One of the fullest statements is "Ignotus" (Manuel Villar), *La represión de octubre* (Barcelona, 1936). Even after the Popular Front victory in 1936, however, no systematic investigation was completed, so that no reliable statistics are available.

73. *Spanish Republic,* 167.
74. Ramiro Ledesma Ramos, *¿Fascismo en España?* (Madrid, 1935), 38. (Italics in the original.)
75. Salvador de Madariaga, *Spain: A Modern History* (New York, 1958), 434–35.
76. Edward Malefakis, in R. Carr, ed., *The Republic and the Civil War in Spain* (London, 1971), 34.
77. Raymond Carr, ibid., 10. Richard Robinson puts it more strongly:

The Socialists and the CEDA both had ideals incompatible with liberal democracy, but whereas the evolutionary tactic was dogma for the CEDA it was not for the Socialists. The latter had accused the former of being Fascist in 1933, but whereas Largo Caballero had threatened to use violence since the autumn of 1931, Gil Robles did not make counter-threats until the autumn of 1933. It was the Socialists, not the CEDA, who turned against the democratic system." [Richard A. H. Robinson *The Origins of Franco's Spain* (London, 1970), 106.]

78. Indalecio Prieto, *Discursos en América* (Mexico City, 1944), 102.

Chapter 10. Government by the Center-Right, 1934–1935

1. Federico Escofet has published a memoir, *De una derrota a una victoria* (Barcelona, 1984), 69–143.
2. Alcalá Zamora, *Los defectos de la Constitución de 1931* (Madrid, 1936), 190–91.
3. Though the version he gave in his *Memorias* (Barcelona, 1977), 292–94, is compressed and misleading.
4. Gil Robles, *No fue posible la paz* (Barcelona, 1968), 145–48.
5. Two different accounts of the repression, not incongruent, may be found in Gabriel Jackson, *The Spanish Republic and the Civil War 1931–1939* (Princeton, 1965), 159–64, and Ricardo de la Cierva, *Historia de la Guerra Civil española,* vol. 1, *Perspectivas y antecedentes 1898–1936* (Madrid, 1969), 435–56.
6. A total of 1,116 out of 8,436, according to Rafael Salazar Alonso, *Bajo el signo de la revolución* (Madrid, 1935), 116–29.
7. Menéndez had suffered greatly in prison and had attempted suicide, though it was not clear that he had been subjected to physical torture.
8. Lerroux's brief account is in his *La pequeña historia* (Madrid, 1963), 373–74.
9. On the terms of repression in the Catalan countryside during 1935, see Unió de Rabassaires, *Els desnonaments rustics a Catalunya* (Barcelona, 1935), and Ricard Vinyes i Ribes, *La Catalunya internacional: El frontpopulisme en l'exemple catalá* (Barcelona, 1983), 98–138.
10. Alardo Prats, *El gobierno de la Generalidad en el banquillo* (Madrid, 1935), gives an account of the trial.
11. Joaquín Arrarás, *Historia de la Segunda República española* (Madrid, 1956–63), 3:153.
12. Quoted in Arrarás, *Segunda República,* 3:161. Cambó, as usual, had the most pertinent observation about the phenomenon of mass rallies. He pointed out that "the excitement of the masses is the indispensable prerequisite for a fascist

coup or a proletarian revolution. . . . These mass rallies can never be used by a party that wants to maintain a center position." Quoted in Jesus Pabón, *Cambó* (Barcelona, 1969), 2:433.

13. Lerroux's attitude was most graphically symbolized by a military parade and joint banquet attended by both himself and Gil Robles in the arch-CEDA city of Salamanca. He later wrote of this occasion:

I had reached the following conclusion: in order for the Republic to gain its balance and survive, it had to move from its sad experience of two years of demagogy with Azaña to the experience of two more years of balanced and moderate government that would in turn facilitate subsequent progressive and stable center goverments. The second experience requires power in the hands of the CEDA. Let it so [enjoy power], so that party may lose doctrinaire rigidity, learn to compromise, unify and organize itself and cleave to the Republic, however rightist it may be. Afterward, the political pendulum will resume its synchronic swing. [Lerroux, *Pequeña historia,* 393.]

This led wits to speak of a "Pact of Salamanca" that had supposedly replaced the original "Pact of San Sebastián."

14. Malefakis, *Agrarian Reform and Peasant Revolution in Spain* (New Haven, 1970), 343–55. See also J. Tusell and J. Calvo, *Giménez Fernández, precursor de la democracia española* (Seville, 1990), 70–100.

15. Malefakis, *Agrarian Reform,* 362.

16. La Cierva, *Historia,* 1:487.

17. Richard A. H. Robinson, *The Origins of Franco's Spain* (London, 1970), 226–27.

18. The best succinct treatment of military administration during 1935 will be found in Carolyn Boyd, *Historia General de España y América* (Madrid, 1986), 17:162–69, and the fullest account in Mariano Aguilar Olivencia, *El Ejército español durante la Segunda República* (Madrid, 1986), 365–468.

19. *Documents on German Foreign Policy* (Washington, D.C., 1950), series C, vol. 4, docs. 303, 330, 445, originally cited in Paul Preston, *The Coming of the Spanish Civil War* (London, 1978), 159 (*CSCW*).

20. Antonio Rodríguez de las Heras, *Filiberto Villalobos: Su obra social y política (1900–1936)* (Salamanca, 1985), 177–272, provides a detailed account of his work under the Samper and fourth Lerroux governments.

21. See Mariano Pérez Galán, *La enseñanza en la Segunda República española* (Madrid, 1975), 203–304, and Manuel de Puelles Benítez, *Educación e ideología en la España contemporánea (1767–1975)* (Barcelona, 1980), 342–45.

22. These were the proposals that Alcalá Zamora elaborated in his small book, *Los defectos de la Constitución de 1931* (Madrid, 1936). In his *Memorias,* he claims that Azaña eventually admitted to him that the Constitution was even more defective than the president claimed, but because reform had become such a polarizing issue between left and right he, Azaña, had to oppose reform.

During the first weeks of 1935 there appeared Madariaga's new book on representation *Jerarquía o anarquía (Hierarchy or Anarchy),* which proposed partially indirect and corporate representation together with limited direct voting. Its partial coincidence with the critique by the moderate right was noted, and the book received a certain amount of attention.

23. See Francesc Carreras, "Los intentos de reforma electoral durante la Segunda República," *REP* 31–32 (January–April, 1983): 165–97.

24. In various weekly articles of the journal *JAP* from November 1934 to March 1935.

25. Robinson, *The Origins*, 208–15.

26. Calvo Sotelo, who favored more deficit financing, observed that the Republic had had one twelve-month budget, one for nine months, two for six months, and five trimestral prorogations.

27. Quoted in Arrarás, *Segunda República*, 3:148.

28. Joaquín Chapaprieta, *La paz fue posible* (Barcelona, 1971), 165–201. See also "Las reformas tributarias en la II República española," in Manuel Ramírez Jiménez, *Las reformas de la II República* (Madrid, 1977), 185–98, and J. Gil Pecharromán, "La opinión pública ante las reformas haciendísticas de Joaquín Chapaprieta," *Hispania* 47, 167 (1987): 1001–26.

29. See the analysis by Carlos Seco Serrano in his prologue to Chapaprieta, *La paz*, 58–59.

30. "Straperlo" was a neologism combining the names of its two inventors and promoters, Strauss and Perle. The term quickly passed into common usage and became the national term for black-market dealing after the Civil War. The Straperlo wheel differed from conventional roulette in that it was not based on pure chance but followed complex yet regular procedures that might be calculated by nimble players (though the operator in turn had the means of further manipulating the outcome if he chose, to throw a winning calculation off). Theoretically this created a new game of "skill" rather than pure chance.

31. The initial contact man was said to have been the liberal Mexican journalist Martín Luis Guzmán, former administrator of *El Sol* and close friend of Azaña. Strauss's principal letter to Alcalá Zamora, accompanied by much alleged documentary evidence, was dated 5 September 1935. Chapaprieta, *La paz*, 267–68; Octavio Ruiz Manjón, *El Partido Republicano Radical 1908–1936* (Madrid, 1976), 503–4; Alcalá Zamora, *Memorias*, 312.

32. Gil Robles relates that in the period immediately after the 1933 elections he had a working agreement with Cambó that the CEDA and the Lliga would do their best to monitor the Radicals in power and adopt common measures if significant signs of financial corruption occurred. *No fue posible*, 144.

33. See the candid remarks of the Radical journalist and sometime minister César Jalón in his *Memorias políticas* (Madrid, 1973), 214–18 et passim.

34. Chapaprieta, *La paz*, 256–60.

35. Jalón, who had the greatest respect and admiration for Lerroux, referred to the adopted son and his coterie as "the clan Aurelio" and as *la aduana* (the customs house). *Memorias*, 223.

36. See especially the lengthy account in *El Debate*, October 26, 1935, and days following.

37. The impact of the Straperlo affair on the Radicals is treated in Ruiz Manjón, *El Partido*, 500–27.

38. As Alcalá Zamora admits in his *Memorias*, 311. He also states that the original Tayá contract had been properly cancelled for nonperformance of services, and this seems to be correct.

39. Chapaprieta, *La paz*, 307–9; Lerroux, *Pequeña historia*, 394–400.

40. The internal collapse is examined in Ruiz Manjón, *El Partido*, 529–59. This may be compared with the much different situation in Spain in 1990, when a strongly organized Socialist Party with a bare parliamentary majority was able to ride out more severe financial scandals, and even increase its vote in Andalusian regional elections.

41. Chapaprieta, *La paz*, 82.

42. Quoted in Arrarás, *Segunda República*, 3:267.

43. Gil Robles's account is in *No fue posible*, 361–64. Alcalá Zamora later justified his veto of Gil Robles by the latter's failure to curb the "fascist" authoritarian elements of his party, particularly the JAP. He claimed that Gil Robles justified to him his policy of not doing so on the grounds that such elements were less dangerous in the CEDA where they could be managed by him than if they went over to the Falange. *Memorias*, 341, 343.

44. Gil Robles gives his account of his maneuver in *No fue posible*, 362–66.

45. Franco reiterated his position of 11 December 1935 in a wartime letter to Gil Robles, making it clear that this was the stand of himself and other generals, and that Gil Robles was not to blame. The letter first appeared in *El Correo de Andalucia*, April 6, 1937.

46. The best discussion of alternative scenarios will be found in J. J. Linz, "From Great Hopes to Civil War: The Breakdown of Democracy in Spain," in J. Linz and A. Stepan, eds., *The Breakdown of Democratic Regimes: Europe* (Baltimore, 1978), 142–215.

47. Lerroux recognized the eclectic composition of his party under the Republic, emphasizing that it was doing a service in the incorporation of diverse elements into Republican democracy, and speculated about its possible ultimate disappearance after a true Republican left and right had become consolidated. A final evaluation of the Radicals may be found in Ruiz Manjón, *El Partido*, 677–85.

Chapter 11. The Elections of 1936

1. Manuel Portela Valladares, *Memorias* (Madrid, 1988), 160–61.

2. Joaquín Chapaprieta *La paz fue posible* (Barcelona, 1971), 353–60.

3. J. M. Gil Robles, *No fue posible la paz* (Barcelona, 1968), 386–90.

4. Quoted in Joaquín Arrarás, *Historia de la Segunda República española* (Madrid, 1956–63), 3:293.

5. *La Libertad* (Madrid), April 13, 1935; Diego Martínez Barrio, *Orígenes del Frente Popular español* (Buenos Aires, 1943), 24–31.

6. The best study is Santos Juliá, *Orígenes del Frente Popular en España (1934–1936)* (Madrid, 1979), 27–41.

7. The text was first published in Carlos de Baráibar, *Las falsas 'posiciones socialistas' de Indalecio Prieto* (Madrid, 1935), 139–45.

8. The text appeared in *La Libertad* (Madrid), March 30, 1935. See Juan-Simeón Vidarte, *El bienio negro y la insurrección de Asturias* (Barcelona, 1978), 387–98.

9. Juliá, *Historia*, 147–48.

10. Julián Besteiro, *Marxismo y anti-marxismo* (Madrid, 1935). Preston notes that "his insinuations that the violence of the Socialist left was hardly distinguishable from fascism did not endear him to the Caballerists." Paul Preston, *The Coming of the Spanish Civil War* (London, 1978) (*CSCW*), 138. The *besteiristas* published their own weekly *Democracia* from June to December 1935. It should be noted that a true "Socialist right," such as Déat's Neosocialism in France or de Man's "Planism" in Belgium, did not exist in Spain. *Besteirismo* was essentially a return to Kautskyism.

11. The most detailed examination of Socialist radicalization is Santos Juliá, *La izquierda del PSOE 1935–1936* (Madrid, 1977). See also Andrés de Blas Guerrero, *El socialismo radical en la II República* (Madrid, 1978). Useful brief treatments may be found in Preston, *CSCW*, 131–50, and in his "The struggle against Fascism in Spain: *Leviatán* and the contradictions of the Socialist Left, 1934–6," in M. Blinkhorn, ed., *Spain in Conflict 1931–1939* (London, 1986), 40–59, while the broadest short overview is Helen Graham, "The Eclipse of the Socialist Left: 1934–1937," in F. Lannon and P. Preston, eds., *Elites and Power in Twentieth-Century Spain* (Oxford, 1990), 127–51.

12. On these maneuvers, see Juliá, *Orígenes*, 12–26, and Rafael Cruz, *El Partido Comunista de España en la Segunda República* (Madrid, 1987), 217–47.

13. The most recent, and possibly the best, study of the Popular Front in France is Julian Jackson, *The Popular Front in France 1934–1938* (Cambridge, 1988). See also Karl G. Harr, Jr., *The Genesis and Effect of the Popular Front in France* (Lanham, Md., 1987), and Georges Lefranc, *Histoire du Front Populaire* (Paris, 1974). Víctor Alba, *El Frente Popular* (Barcelona, 1976), is a very general account. The development of the French Popular Front and its influence in Spain, and in Europe as a whole, are treated in M. S. Alexander and H. Graham, eds., *The French and Spanish Popular Fronts: Comparative Perspectives* (Cambridge, 1989), and H. Graham and P. Preston, eds., *The Popular Front in Europe* (New York, 1987).

14. Azaña's three major speeches of 1935 were published as *Discursos en campo abierto* (Madrid, 1936). The Comillas rally is described by an eyewitness, Henry Buckley, in his *The Life and Death of the Spanish Republic* (London, 1940), 179–88, and by Frank Sedwick, *The Tragedy of Manuel Azaña and the Fate of the Spanish Republic* (Athens, Ohio, 1963), 145–50.

15. Somewhat varying accounts of this meeting and the split may be found in *Claridad*, December 23, 1935; *El Socialista*, December 20–25, 1935; Francisco Largo Caballero, *Mis recuerdos* (Mexico City, 1954), 146–48; Vidarte, *El bienio negro*, 26; and G. Mario de Coca, *Anti-Caballero* (Madrid, 1936), 152–54, 193–98.

16. Joaquín Maurín, leader of the BOC, still adhered basically to his two-class theory of the Spanish revolution, according to which the bourgeoisie could no longer play a progressive role. Only the broad working class could guarantee a democratic-socialist revolution, which would very soon have to enter a revolutionary socialist phase, though the small progressivist sectors of the petite bourgeoisie might cooperate with the worker left in the initial democratic phase.

Andreu Nin's Izquierda Communista had finally broken with Trotsky in the autumn of 1934 when it rejected the latter's insistence on "entryism," meaning fusion with the Socialist Party, which Nin and his colleagues viewed as too social democratic and compromised by bourgeois Republicanism. The decision of Maurín and Nin to form a new party in 1935 rather than join the Socialists had destructive consequences, for it left the Socialists weaker and the POUM isolated, while making it easier for the Communists to take over the Socialist Youth and the smaller Catalan socialist groups in 1936. Maurín and Nin would have preferred above all a revolutionary bloc of the non-Stalinist worker left but joined the Popular Front as the best option available. On the formation of the POUM and its revolutionary stance, see Joaquín Maurín, *Revolución y contrarevolución en España* (Barcelona, 1935; Paris, 1966); Víctor Alba, *Historia del P.O.U.M.*, vol. 2 of *El marxisme a Catalunya* (Barcelona, 1974); and in English, V. Alba and S. Schwartz, *Spanish Marxism versus Soviet Communism: A History of the POUM* (New Brunswick, N.J., 1988), 87–110.

17. The manifesto was carried in the press on 16 January 1935.

18. Juliá, *Los orígenes*, 134–49.

19. Adrian Shubert, "A Reinterpretation of the Spanish Popular Front: The Case of Asturias," in Alexander and Graham, *The French and Spanish Popular Fronts*, 213–25. Cf. Diego Abad de Santillán, *Por qué perdimos la guera* (Buenos Aires, 1940), 36, and César M. Lorenzo, *Les anarchistes espagnols et le pouvoir 1868–1939* (Paris, 1969), 89–92.

20. *El Sol*, January 14, 1936.

21. The prison population in Spain officially listed for 15 February 1936, was 34,526. The average prior to mid-1934 had been approximately 20,000, and thus the number of new prisoners dating from the insurrection was presumably in the neighborhood of 15,000. Benito Pabón, one of the two deputies elected by Pestaña's Partido Sindicalista, admitted as much in the Cortes on 2 July 1936.

22. Portela Valladares, *Memorias*, 167–68.

23. Ibid.

24. Portela indicates that a more indirect understanding was also reached with Martínez Barrio in Seville. Ibid., 166.

25. Though in Badajoz province Portela was able to make a deal with the Socialists, as J. S. Vidarte explains in *Todos fuimos culpables* (Barcelona, 1977), 38–41.

26. According to Joaquín Chapaprieta, *La paz fue posible* (Barcelona, 1971), 390–96.

27. Octavio Ruiz Manjón, *El Partido Republicano Radical 1908–1936* (Madrid, 1976), 559–72.

28. The best brief account of the campaign of the right will be found in Richard A. H. Robinson, *The Origins of Franco's Spain* (London, 1970), 241–47.

29. *La Publicidad* (Granada), January 23, 1936, in Miguel Pertíñez Díaz, *Granada 1936: Elecciones a Cortes* (Granada, 1987), 46.

30. The only study is Pertíñez Díaz, *Granada 1936* (cited in the preceding footnote), and it is limited primarily to citations of mutually hostile partisan local newspaper accounts.

31. Javier Tusell has found that, of the major historical accounts, the one nearest the correct figures was the highly rightist *Historia de la Cruzada española* (Madrid, 1940), directed by Joaquín Arrarás. Estimates by various writers are given in Tusell, et al., *Las elecciones del Frente Popular* (Madrid, 1971), 2:15.

32. This is the nearest to a definitive study that we shall probably ever have and computes totals for each district in terms of the highest number of votes for the leading candidate on each list (presumably the absolute total number of voters voting that particular list in the district), with some correction when one ticket gained both the majority and minority in a given district.

33. Juan J. Linz and Jesús M. de Miguel, "Hacia un análisis regional de las elecciones de 1936 en España," *Revista Española de la Opinión Pública*, no. 48 (April–June, 1977): 27–67.

34. Following the breakdown in Linz and De Miguel, "Las elecciones de 1936."

35. Ruiz Manjón, *El Partido*, 572–88.

36. In Badajoz, where in 1933 the Socialists had drawn 139,000 votes compared with 8,000 for Azaña's party, the left Republicans had been given four of ten places on the Popular Front ticket in order to deny representation to the *besteiristas*, according to Preston, *CSCW*, 148. Shubert, in "A Reinterpretation," 221, states that in Asturias "each candidature given the Republicans represented 8,552 votes, while each Socialist place represented 12,775."

37. The main differences after the start of the Civil War would be found in New Castile and Galicia, both of which reversed identities. New Castile had mostly voted for the right but was held in the Republican zone by the pull of Madrid and its military strength, while Galicia, which returned more Popular Front deputies than any other region, was won by the insurgents. The popular vote in Galicia was in fact distinctly more triangulated than in most regions and the outcome therefore heavily influenced by the alliance system, so that the actual Popular Front plurality there was considerably smaller than the number of deputies made it seem.

38. Portela Valladares's account is in his *Memorias*, 175–82, and that of Gil Robles in *No fue posible*, 492–97.

39. Franco's version is presented in Arrarás, *La Segunda República*, 4:50–51.

40. Portela Valladares, *Memorias*, 182–84.

41. Ibid., 184–85.

42. Arrarás, *La Segunda República*, 4:57–58.

43. Portela Valladares, *Memorias*, 186–87.

44. Ibid., 188–90. A different perspective may be found in J. S. Vidarte, *Todos fuimos culpables* (Barcelona, 1977), 40–50.

45. He adds somewhat cryptically after narrating Franco's offer to bring in the elite units: "In this he [Franco] was correct. The most recent news reaching the ministry only confirmed and expanded on what had been received earlier," presumably referring to the expansion of disorder. Portela Valladares, *Memorias*, 192.

46. As might be expected, there is some variance between the lengthy version of Portela Valladares, *Memorias*, 192–96, and the more terse account of Alcalá Zamora, *Memorias* (Barcelona, 1977), 347–48, who terms this brief section of his narrative "The Resignation-Flight of Portela." Alcalá Zamora claims that, until the last minute, Portela was convinced that his centrist electoral maneuver would succeed, but that his nerve totally collapsed on the evening of the sixteenth. He contends that Portela was most concerned about leftist riots on the seventeenth, and then became increasingly alarmed over military pressures on the eighteenth, only to be finally panicked by more leftist disorders into immediate resignation on the nineteenth. Alcalá Zamora has been quoted as claiming a month later in private conversation that Portela "failed me in everything, and through his desertion, despite my efforts, allowed the revolutionary front to carry off unjustly sixty more seats through postelectoral abuses." J. Tusell and J. Calvo, *Giménez Fernández, precursor de la democracia española* (Seville, 1990), 201.

Chapter 12. The Left Returns to Power, February to May 1936

1. When the news of Portela's resignation first reached him, Azaña wrote in his diary (*Obras completas* [Mexico City, 1965–68], 4:564):

The normal thing would have been for the government to wait until the Cortes meets before resigning. Today we do not even know the precise electoral results or how much of a majority we have. . . . We take over unexpectedly, a month before the Cortes convenes, and our situation will be the more delicate and difficult without the support of parliament. . . . I always feared that we would return to power in difficult conditions. They could not be worse. Once more we must harvest grain while it is still green.

Concerning Azaña's virtual fear of victory and of heading a new government, see Marichal's introduction to volume three of Azaña's *Obras completas*, pp. xxvii–xxix.

2. Azaña noted that the tone of the speech "had been agreed upon in the Council to calm the disordered surge of the Popular Front and urge calm for everyone." Ibid., 4:566.

3. *El Sol*, February 21, 1936.

4. Cf. the remarks of Manuel Portela Valladares in his *Memorias* (Madrid, 1988), 197–98.

5. *El Socialista* announced on 18 February that some Popular Front groups had already managed to open a number of prisons the day before, and similar announcements were made in several other leftist papers.

6. *El Sol*, February 26, 1933.

7. Catalonia under the Popular Front is treated in Ricard Vinyes, *La Catalunya Internacional: el frontpopulisme en l'exemple català* (Barcelona, 1983).

8. It was typical of the distance between leaders of left and right that Azaña

could record in his diary that he had personally met Giménez Fernández for the first time on 20 February, adding that "he tells me that nothing separates him from me except religious policy. I have never heard him speak nor read anything of his. I have no idea if he is any good. . . . He seems to me a utopian conservative, fit only for speeches at the floral games." Azaña wrote that the right "are now terribly afraid. They want pacification, . . . but if they had won the elections, . . . rather than granting amnesty they would have jailed everyone who was still at liberty." When Giménez Fernández complained of violent assaults on CEDA centers and newspapers, Azaña shrugged it off with a standard rhetorical flourish, telling him that "you must come to understand that the right wing of the Republic is me, while you are simply wayward apprentices." *Obras completas*, 4:570, 572.

9. *El Debate*, 6 March 1933; Gil Robles, *No fue*, 575.

10. Gil Robles, *No fue* 576.

11. See Miguel Pertíñez Díaz, *Granada 1936: Elecciones a Cortes* (Granada, 1987), 102–6 and the lurid propaganda piece by Angel Gollonet and José Morales, *Rojo y azul en Granada* (Granada, 1937).

12. Many but far from all of these incidents can be reconstructed from the partially censored press. Lengthy narratives of the disorders will be found in José Pla, *Historia de la Segunda República española* (Barcelona, 1940), vol. 4, and Joaquín Arrarás, *Historia de la Segunda República española* (Madrid, 1908), vol. 4, and also in Fernando Rivas, *El Frente Popular* (Madrid, 1976).

13. Davis Jato, *La rebelión de los estudiantes* (Madrid, 1967), 285–89, narrates these incidents from the Falangist viewpoint. Juan Antonio Ansaldo, ¿*Para que . . . ?* (Buenos Aires, 1953), recounts flying the Falangist gunmen to Biarritz.

14. The only historian of the Republic to place this in objective perspective is Luis Romero, *Por qué y cómo mataron a Calvo Sotelo* (Barcelona, 1982), 40–42.

15. According to Rivas, *El Frente*, 122.

16. As Luis Romero wrote of leftists engaged in violence, "the police never arrested them." *Historia 16* 100 (August, 1984): 55.

17. Luis Romero, *Por qué y cómo*, 56–58.

18. Ibid., 59. Though, as shown above, Azaña himself derived no personal satisfaction from the anticlerical outbursts.

The most spectacular case of arson in March, aside from the riot in Granada, occurred in the town of Yecla, where fourteen churches and other religious buildings were torched in one day. The large-scale arson and disorder provoked the temporary flight of part of the local population, but prompted the Communist *Mundo Obrero* to inquire rhetorically on 21 March how many churches there were to be burnt in all Spain, if there were so many to be torched in one comparatively small town.

19. Claudio Sánchez Albornoz, *De mi anecdotario político* (Buenos Aires, 1972), 116.

20. *Mundo Obrero* (Madrid), March 2, 1936.

21. Rivas, *El Frente*, 149–51.

22. Arrarás, *Segunda República*, 4:87–88.

23. Antonio Cacho Zabalza, *La Unión Militar Española* (Alicante, 1940), is not an altogether reliable account.

24. Juan-Simeón Vidarte, *Todos fuimos culpables* (Barcelona, 1977), 1:50–51. On the tiny leftist minority in the officer corps, see the first part of the memoirs of Antonio Cordón, *Trayectoria* (Barcelona, 1977).

25. Of the eight generals attending, only two held active commands and five were retired. Two monarchist colonels (Galarza and Varela) were also present.

26. See F. Olaya Morales, *La conspiración contra la República* (Barcelona, 1979), 314–23, and Daniel Sueiro, "Sublevación contra la República," pt. 2, *Historia 16* 8:90 (October, 1983): 21–32.

27. On Basque Socialists in this final phase, see, in addition to the book by Miralles cited earlier, his article "La crisis del movimiento socialista en el País Vasco, 1935–1936," *Estudios de Historia Social* 3–4 (1987): 275–87.

28. *El Socialista*, February 12, 1936.

29. *Mundo Obrero*, March 5, 1936. This was essentially the same thirteen-point program that *Mundo Obrero* had published on February 15, the eve of the elections.

30. *Claridad*, January 25, 1936.

31. Gabriel Mario de Coca, *Anti-Caballero: Crítica marxista de la bolchevización del Partido Socialista* (Madrid, 1936), 207, 211.

32. Ricard Viñas, *La formación de las Juventudes Socialistas Unificadas* (Madrid, 1978). The memoir of the former Socialist Youth activist, Angel Merino Galán, *Mi guerra empezó antes* (Madrid, 1976), 73–99, points out that the unification was carried out exclusively by the top leadership without consultation.

33. See Rafael Cruz, *El Partido Comunista de Espana en la Segunda República* (Madrid, 1987), 248–93, and the same author's "El Partido Comunista y el Frente Popular, 1935–1936," *Historia 16* 11:123 (July, 1986): 22–28.

34. *Solidaridad Obrera*, April 15, 1936.

35. Ibid., April 24, 1936.

36. As mentioned in *Claridad*, April 6 and May 30, 1936, and noted by Paul Preston, *The Coming of the Spanish Civil War* (London, 1978; *CSCW*).

37. Many of these incidents were not recorded in the *Diario de las Sesiones*, though they were sometimes picked up by the press.

38. *Mundo Obrero* presented its list on 19 February.

39. Carlos Seco Serrano in the *Historia de España* (Barcelona, 1968), 6:158.

40. Salvador de Madariaga, *España* (Buenos Aires, 1964), 359–60.

41. Cf. Preston, *CSCW*, 175.

42. The most pertinent treatment is that of Pertíñez Díaz, *Granada 1936*, 106–22.

43. The right certainly had more money to try to corrupt the electoral process in several areas than did the left, but, with the exception of Granada, the principal interference probably came from the machinations of the ministry of the interior, favoring the center.

44. See Prieto's prologue to Luis Solano Palacio, *Vísperas de la guerra de España* (Mexico City, n.d.), 6–7.

45. Javier Tusell Gomez, et al., *Las elecciones del Frente Popular en España* (Madrid, 1971), 2:190.

46. Alcalá Zamora, *Memorias* (Barcelona, 1977), 351.

47. *Boletín del Ministerio de Trabajo*, in Preston, *CSCW*, 178.

48. Malefakis, *Agrarian Reform and Peasant Revolution in Spain* (New Haven, 1970), 367–68.

49. Quoted in Mercedes Cabrera, *La patronal ante la II República* (Madrid, 1983), 293.

50. Malefakis, *Agrarian Reform*, 369.

51. Ibid., 373.

52. *El Sol*, June 23, 1936.

53. The best brief treatment of the economic policy of the last Republican government is J. M. Macarro Vera, "Social and Economic Policies of the Spanish Left in Theory and in Practice," in M. S. Alexander and H. Graham, eds., *The French and Spanish Popular Fronts* (Cambridge, 1989), 171–84.

54. On the restoration of the *jurados mixtos* and the problem of labor costs, see J. Montero, *Los Tribunales de Trabajo (1908–1938)* (Valencia, 1976), 193–98.

55. Mariano Pérez Galán, *La enseñanza en la Segunda República española* (Madrid, 1975), 309–22; Manuel de Puelles Benítez, *Educación e ideología en la España contemporanea (1767–1975)* (Barcelona, 1980), 345–47.

56. Salvador de Madariaga, *Spain: A Modern History* (New York, 1958), 475.

57. Madariaga, *Spain*, 452–53.

58. One province among a number where landowners became aggressive was Guadalajara. See A. R. Díez Torres, "Guadalajara 1936: La primera crisis del caciquismo," *Estudios de Historia Social* (1987): 3–4, 289–305.

59. Most of this was described in the press. The lengthiest accounts are in Rivas, *El Frente*, 172–90, and in Ian Gibson, *La noche en que mataron a Calvo Sotelo* (Madrid, 1982), 250–53. The Madrid police authorities endeavored to behave responsibly, arresting numerous workers as suspects in firing on the procession, and even briefly detaining for interrogation the Assault Guard lieutenant and militant Socialist José Castillo, who was aggressive in repressing the demonstration, shooting point-blank and seriously wounding one of its militants.

60. On the afternoon of 16 April, Azaña remarked angrily to the Socialist Vidarte, "With your heckling of the Civil Guard, you [Socialists] are turning them against the Republic, just like you did in the parade two days ago." Vidarte, *Todos fuimos*, 90–91.

61. Ibid., 103.

62. Romero, *Por qué y cómo*, 87; Arrarás, *Segunda República*, 4:242.

63. Antonio Ramos Oliveira, *Historia de España* (Mexico City, 1952), 3:244.

64. Alcalá Zamora, *Memorias*, 353.

65. According to his letters to his brother-in-law, Cipriano de Rivas Cherif, quoted in the latter's *Retrato de un desconocido* (Barcelona, 1980), 667–72. Azaña later reminisced during the Civil War that Alcalá Zamora acted as though he were "the leader of the anti-Republican opposition." *Obras completas* (Mexico City, 1965–68),

4:719. Here, as usual, Azaña employs the term "Republican" in his customary sectarian sense.

66. And, Alcalá Zamora adds, apparently with good reason, for four members of the family were killed in the mass executions in Jaén during the first part of the Civil War. *Memorias*, 353.

67. Ibid., 352.

68. Ibid., 357.

69. Ibid.

70. Ibid., 358.

71. Ibid., 359.

72. Joaquín Chapaprieta, *La paz fue posible* (Barcelona, 1971), 407–12.

73. Letter of Azaña in Rivas Cherif, *Retrato*, 674.

74. Chapaprieta, *La paz*, 414, noted scornfully that "Azaña spoke of economic problems with his customary ignorance of them."

75. Or so Giménez Fernández told Gabriel Jackson years later, *The Spanish Republic and the Civil War, 1931–1939* (Princeton, 1965), 215.

76. The fullest account of the constitutional problems involved and of the session of 3 April will be found in Joaquín Tomás Villarroya, *La destitución de Alcalá Zamora* (Valencia, 1988), 85–106.

77. Azaña to Rivas Cherif, in *Retrato*, 676.

78. Madariaga, *Spain*, 454. Julián Besteiro is quoted as having told the Socialist parliamentary delegation: "It seems to me that we are the ones least entitled to say that the CEDA Cortes was not properly dissolved, since in meetings, in the press and on every hand we never stopped asking for that very thing." Vidarte, *Todos fuimos*, 75.

79. Alcalá Zamora, *Memorias*, 360–73.

80. Ibid., 372.

81. Gil Robles, *No fue posible*, 559–60.

82. This episode is explained variously by Franco's brother-in-law and go-between Ramón Serrano Súñer, in the latter's *Memorias* (Barcelona, 1977), 56–58; José Gutiérrez Rave, *Gil Robles, caudillo frustrado* (Madrid, 1967), 165; Gil Robles, *No fue posible*, 563–67; and Maximiano García Venero, *El general Fanjul* (Madrid, 1967), 227.

83. The only organized armed force of Madrid Socialists was a group known as "La Motorizada," from their habit of traveling about by car, bus, or truck. Its membership was drawn especially from the UGT syndicate of "Artes Blancas" (composed especially of bakers) and also from some members of the JSU. Organized around the first of March, its members seem in fact to have been as much beholden to Prieto as to Largo Caballero, indicating how simplistic it is to attribute all activism to *caballeristas*.

The Communists in the Madrid area had organized their own Milicias Antifascistas Obreras y Campesinas (MAOC—Workers and Peasants Antifascist Militia), which, though small, was more overtly paramilitary and received some weekend instruction from officers of the UMRA. Cf. Enrique Líster, *Memorias de un luchador* (Madrid, 1977), 67.

84. Regina García, *Yo he sido marxista* (Madrid, 1953), 115, is an account by the sometime Socialist daughter of one of the principal victims.

85. Romero observes with his customary cogency: "Then and now—more in the left than in the right—it has been a fairly general habit to cast the blame for shameful and criminal acts on mysterious agents provocateurs who are presumed to belong to and work for the opposing side. Note that these agents provocateurs are never caught, and when in certain cases the guilty are found and identified, they belong to the same or related organizations of those making such charges, not to the opposing side, and are then defended energetically. If all these agents provocateurs really existed they would then be unmasked by the groups they have supposedly infiltrated. . . . What actually exist are certain people who are extreme and excitable by nature and are swept along by a fanaticism that limits their reason and induces them to commit destructive and counterproductive deeds which cause shame and indignation among their own coreligionists." *Por qué y cómo*, 103.

86. Indalecio Prieto, *Cartas a un escultor* (Buenos Aires, 1961), 94.

87. José Pla, *Historia de la Segunda República española* (Barcelona, 1940), 4:437–38. Prieto subsequently considered this one of the most important speeches of his career, having it reprinted twice during the Civil War and citing it numerous times in later writings. But its message was totally rejected by *Claridad* on 4 May, which declared the most fundamental need was for greater intensification of the class struggle.

88. Romero, *Por qué*, 100.

89. Primo de Rivera, *Obras completas* (Madrid, 1952), 919–23.

Chapter 13. Breakdown, May to July 1936

1. Gil Robles relates: "The pallor of Azaña's face was cadaverous and his nervousness impressed us all. In spite of his extraordinary facility of speech, he stumbled several times in repeating the brief oath of loyalty to the Republic. . . . During his entrance into the limousine that would carry him to the presidential palace he was cold and aloof. He did not smile or bat an eyelash even once." *No fue posible la paz* (Barcelona, 1968), 605. Gil Robles may not have been able to remember each detail as precisely as he narrated it, but it was clear that by this time Azaña had become greatly alarmed.

2. See Marichal's introduction to volume three of Azaña's *Obras completas* (Mexico City, 1965–68), xxxi–xxxii.

3. For example, Juan-Simeón Vidarte, *Todos fuimos culpables* (Barcelona, 1977), 1:74–80; Julián Zugazagoitia, *Guerra y vicisitudes de los españoles* (Paris, 1968), 1:20; and even Francisco Largo Caballero, *Mis recuerdos* (Mexico City, 1954), 155.

4. Claudio Sánchez Albornoz, *De mi anecdotario* (Buenos Aires, 1972), 127.

5. Though Azaña has left no documentation on this point, his brother-in-law and confidant Cipriano de Rivas Cherif asserts that he seriously backed the Prieto option. *Retrato de un desconocido* (Barcelona, 1980), 328.

6. Though this proposal was scarcely plausible, in a letter to the author of 30 October 1959, Prieto expressed nostalgic regret that he had not made a stronger effort to reach an understanding with the more broad-minded elements to the right of the Socialists.

7. Paul Preston, *The Coming of the Spanish Civil War* (London, 1978), 178 (*CSCW*).

8. Ibid.

9. Largo Caballero, *Mis memorias*, 145.

10. Vidarte, *Todos fuimos*, 117–26; Indalecio Prieto, *Convulsiones de España* (Mexico City, 1967), 1:164, 3:135–36; Amaro del Rosal, *Historia de la U. G. T. de España 1901–1939* (Barcelona, 1977), 1:479.

11. According to the version of José Larraz, who participated in the talks, *ABC*, June 16, 1965.

12. *Obras completas*, 4:570–71.

13. Diego Martínez Barrio, *Memorias* (Barcelona, 1983), 329. Cf. Josefina Carabias, *Azaña: Los que le llamábamos don Manuel* (Barcelona, 1980), 230–33. (It should be mentioned, however, that the Martínez Barrio memoirs are among the more misleading and incomplete memoirs by politicians of the period.)

14. *Retrato*, 328–29.

15. Cf. the remarks of the financially austere Alcalá Zamora, *Memorias* (Barcelona, 1977), 378.

16. The left Republican Mariano Ansó would write years later that Casares's stance declaring himself "in a state of war with a sizable fraction of national society" was "totally unaccustomed in a prime minister." *Yo fui ministro de Negrín* (Barcelona, 1976), 118. In the same vein see Félix Gordón Ordás, *Mi política en España* (Mexico City, 1962), 2:526.

17. Gil Robles, *No fue posible*, 618–19; Joaquín Arrarás, *Historia de la Segunda República española*, 4:275; Vidarte, *Todos fuimos*, 135–36; and Juan Avilés Farré, *La izquierda burguesa en la II República* (Madrid, 1985), 305. Years later, shortly before his death, Giménez Fernández wrote:

from April 1936 Besteiro, Maura, Sánchez Albornoz and myself discussed and pondered the possibility of a parliamentary government of the center that would extend from the Socialist "right" of Besteiro to the Christian democrat CEDA "left" of Lucia, to combat the demagogy of the fascists and of the Popular Front. Unfortunately, this plan, which in principle did not seem bad either to Prieto or Gil Robles, failed to take form due to the following obstacles: a) The political myopia of Martínez Barrio, who, in exchange for gaining the seven seats stolen from the right [by the Comisión de Actas] and passing from 35 to 42 deputies, failed to realize that his group had passed from being the balance wheel . . . and had become completely inoperative. b) The fear of Azaña, who realized that he was losing control of the left and had therefore accepted the presidency . . . , without understanding that by deposing Alcalá Zamora he had lost a major support for his own suddenly more moderate views. . . . c) The stubbornness of Prieto who, in order not to be labeled a traitor by his own party, refused to split the Socialist parliamentary delegation so long as he lacked the support of a majority of it, for though later in May he increased from 30 to 45 votes — especially after the attack on Negrín in Ecija — he still lacked eight deputies, who could not bring themselves to decide in enough time to bring about a split and a parliamentary crisis which, according to Sánchez Albornoz, Azaña would have accepted in order to appoint a Prieto government since, also out of fear, Sánchez Román would not accept the task. d) The pressure on the right in favor of civil war, where the JAP, outraged by the attacks of the extreme left and the lenience with which these were treated by the authorities, was passing in waves to the fascists and Carlists, the financiers were showering with money those who planned a revolt and, finally, Gil Robles made clear to Lucia and myself at the end of May the impossibility of continuing to plan for a center solution, since there were very few of us who really wanted it and the mystique of civil war had unfortunately taken hold of the great majority of Spaniards. [Quoted by Carlos Seco Serrano in his prologue to Javier Tusell Gomez, et al., *Las elecciones del Frente Popular en España* (Madrid, 1971), 1:xvii–xviii.]

18. Richard A. H. Robinson, *The Origins of Franco's Spain* (London, 1970), 226–67. All Catholic schools were officially taken over by decree on 28 July, after the Civil War began.

19. *Información*, May 14, 1936, in Mercedes Cabrera, *La patronal ante la II República* (Madrid, 1983), 30-3-04.

20. Cf. Alberto Balcells, *Crisis económica y agitacion social en Cataluña de 1930 a 1936* (Esplugues de Llobregat, 1971), 233–34.

21. Again, see the discussion by J. M. Macarro Vera, "Social and Economic Policies of the Spanish Left in Theory and in Practice," in M. S. Alexander and H. Graham, eds., *The French and Spanish Popular Fronts* (Cambridge, 1989), 171–84.

22. Cabrera, *La patronal*, 291.

23. *Hoy* (Badajoz), May 27, 1936, in Francisca Rosique Navarro, *La reforma agraria en Badajoz durante la IIa República* (Badajoz, 1988), 304.

24. M. Pérez Yruela, *La conflictividad campesina en la provincia de Córdoba 1931–1936* (Madrid, 1979), 204.

25. *Caspe: Un estatuto de autonomía* (Zaragoza, 1977): Luis Germán Zubero, *Aragón en la II República* (Zaragoza, 1984), 189–206; and R. Sainz de Varanda, "La autonomía de Aragón en el periodo del Frente Popular," in M. Tuñón de Lara, ed., *La crisis del Estado español* (Madrid, 1978), 517–33.

26. X. Vilas Nogueira, *O Estatuto Galego* (Pontevedra, 1975); Alfonso Bozzo, *Los partidos políticos y la autonomía de Galicia (1931–1936)* (Madrid, 1976); Xavier Castro, *O galeguismo na encrucillada republicana* (Orense, 1985); Bernardo Maíz, *Galicia na IIa Republica e baixo o franquismo* (Vigo, 1987); Adolfo Hernández Lafuente, *Autonomía e integración en la Segunda República* (Madrid, 1980), 386–90.

27. *El Congreso confederal de Zaragoza (mayo, 1936)* (Toulouse, 1955). CNT figures for 1 May 1936 showed little more than 30 percent of Catalan industrial workers in their syndicates, compared with more than 60 percent at the end of 1931. Balcells, *Crisis económica*, 198.

28. *Solidaridad Obrera*, May 11, 1936. See also the commentary by John Brademas, *Anarcosindicalismo y revolución en España (1930–1937)* (Esplugues de Llobregat, 1974), 168–70.

29. *Solidaridad Obrera*, May 13, 1936.

30. The best analysis is Santos Juliá, *La izquierda del PSOE (1935–1936)* (Madrid, 1977).

31. *New York Times*, June 26, 1936.

32. *El Socialista*, July 1, 1936, and the memoir by Vidarte, who was in charge of the secretariat, *Todos fuimos*, 195–208. He maintains that he also invalidated some of the votes from his native Badajoz for the same reasons.

33. *Claridad*, July 10, 1936.

34. Ibid., July 13, 1936.

35. See J. L. Martín i Ramos, *Els origens del Partit Socialist Unificat de Catalunya* (Barcelona, 1977), and, on the earlier history of its components, Montserrat Roig, *Rafael Vidiella* (Barcelona, 1976), and Imma Tubella, *Jaume Compte i el Partit Català Proletari* (Barcelona, 1979).

36. Angel Ossorio y Gallardo, *Vida y sacrificio de Companys* (Buenos Aires, 1943), 148–55; M. D. Ivern i Salvà, *Esquerra Republicana de Catalunya (1931–1936)* (Montserrat, 1988), 2:177–210; Jesus Pabón, *Cambó* (Barcelona, 1969), 2:486–89; and M. García Venero, *Historia del nacionalismo catalán* (Madrid, 1967), 2:417–19.

In his chapter "L'oasi català: Un miratge," Ricard Vinyes i Ribes (*La Catalunya internacional* [Barcelona, 1983], 303–35), dissents from this view, pointing out that the concept of "Catalan oasis" was first suggested by Manuel Brunet as a proposal for improvement in *La Veu de Catalunya* on March 4, 1936. Certainly there were many strikes and considerable disorder in Catalonia, but the difference was notable on two levels: government policy and administration, and the distinctly lower rate of political homicide.

37. At the end of 1935 various Catholic labor groups had come together in a "Frente Nacional Unido de Trabajo," claiming 276,389 members, at that moment technically nearly 20 percent of organized labor in Spain. In June 1936 their Madrid headquarters was closed by the government because of alleged "provocations," part of the government's de facto policy of progressively shutting down rightist organizations, as the Communists periodically urged publicly.

38. *El Sol*, May 26, 1936.

39. Francisco Sánchez Pérez, "La huelga de la construcción en Madrid (junio–julio, 1936)," *Historia 16* 14:154 (February 1989): 21–26.

40. Because of this pronounced variation, a clear understanding of the situation will be achieved only after monographic study of each major region. One partial example of the latter is found in the research of J. A. Alarcón Caballero, *El movimiento obrero en Granada en la II República (1931–1936)* (Granada, 1990), 420–26.

41. As in the terms of 26 June established by the *jurado mixto* of Cordoba, studied in M. Pérez Yruela, *La conflictividad campesina en la provincia de Córdoba, 1931–1936* (Madrid, 1979), 412–29.

42. E. E. Malefakis, *Agrarian Reform and Peasant Revolution in Spain* (New Haven, 1970), 384.

43. Ibid., 383. Baldomero Díaz de Entresotos, *Seis meses de anarquía en Ex-*

tremadura (Caceres, 1937), is a melodramatic account published after the Civil War began, but the reality was serious enough.

44. Manuel Tuñón de Lara, *Tres claves de la Segunda República* (Madrid, 1985), 194–95.

45. Almost all the forms of radical agrarian activity attending the Russian revolution of 1905, as detailed by Teodor Shanin, *Russia, 1905–07: Revolution as a Moment of Truth* (New Haven, 1986), 84–90, found expression in southern Spain during the spring of 1936. This is not an indication that conditions were generally equivalent in the two countries as a whole, but there were some clear parallels between Russia and the agrarian unrest in the south.

46. The fullest account is in Fernando Rivas, *El Frente Popular* (Madrid, 1976), 275–80.

47. Calvo Sotelo charged in the Cortes on 6 May that eight to ten thousand Falangists and rightists were then in jail, possibly an exaggeration. Falangists claimed that seventy of their members had died violent deaths between November 1933 and 1 June 1936, while *cedistas* claimed to have lost twenty-six members to violence before 1936. Both claims are probably approximately correct.

What was undeniable was the sudden growth in support for the now illegal organization, and the extent of the reaction among the right in general. The Christian democrat Ossorio y Gallardo lamented on 10 June in *Ahora* that the behavior of the left had become irrational and destructive, with no positive outcome in view: "The Popular Front was created to combat fascism, but the way things are going in Spain the only fascism will be the one engendered by the Popular Front itself."

Agustín Calvet ("Gaziel"), the respected conservative editor of Barcelona's *La Vanguardia*, wrote in the latter on 12 June:

How many votes did the fascists have in Spain in the last election? Nothing: a ridiculously small amount. . . . Today, on the other hand, travellers returning from different parts of Spain are saying: "There everybody is becoming a fascist." What kind of change is this? What had happened? What has happened is simply that it is no longer possible to live, that there is no government. . . . In such a situation, people instinctively look for a way out. . . . What is the new political form that radically represses all these insufferable excesses? A dictatorship, fascism. And thus almost without wanting to, almost without realizing it, people begin *to feel themselves* fascist. They know nothing about all the inconveniences of a dictatorship, which is natural. They will learn about those later on, when they have to suffer them.

. . . Fascism is, in the cases of France and Spain, the sinister shadow projected across the land by democracy itself, when its internal decomposition turns it into anarchy. The more the rot spreads, the more fascism expands. And therefore the deluded concern that the triumphant Popular Front shows about a defeated fascism is nothing more than the fear of its own shadow.

48. Frank Manuel, *The Politics of Modern Spain* (New York, 1938), 168.

49. Joaquín Arrarás, *Historia de la Segunda República española* (Madrid, 1956–63), 4:280.

50. Maximiano García Venero, *Historia de las Internacionales en España* (Madrid, 1958), 3:106–8. This document was never published by the PNR, but García Venero claims to have seen the original and had "no doubt of its authenticity."

51. Avilés Farré, *La izquierda*, 306–7; Gil Robles, *No fue posible*, 680.

52. Alcalá Zamora, *Memorias*, 376–78, says that he was forced to hand over money twice.

53. Zugazagoitia, *Historia de la guerra de España* (Buenos Aires, 1940), 9.

54. Referring to the special administrative boards appointed by the government in certain provinces where the right had predominated.

55. The colors of the United Socialist Youth.

56. Hans Buchheim has noted: "Dictatorship is a legitimate aspect of republican constitutions," not to be confused with an "authoritarian regime" that functions as "a dictator without temporal limits." During crises of the Roman republic, a dictatorship was named "who was vested with unlimited powers and who was not required to account for his administration. . . . However, his term of office was limited to a maximum of six months." *Totalitarian Rule* (Middletown, Conn., 1968), 21.

57. *La Libertad*, June 28, 1936.

58. *Le Petit Journal* (Paris), July 2, 1936, in Gil Robles, *No fue posible*, 681.

59. Ossorio added: "And if this is the case, who is really in favor of the present frenzy? Whose interests does it serve? What we are seeing would only make sense if the revolutionaries could be sure of winning the revolution. But they are blind if they believe that. In Spain the outcome will not be won by the first revolution, but by the second: that of reconstruction." *Ahora*, June 30, 1936.

60. Luis Romero, *Por qué y cómo mataron a Calvo Sotelo* (Barcelona, 1982), 165–66.

61. *Claridad*, July 3, 1936.

62. *Mundo Obrero*, July 10, 1936.

63. C. Santacana and X. Pujadas, *L'altra olimpiada: Barcelona '36* (Badalona, 1990).

64. All these events were reported in the Madrid press. There are summaries in Luis Romero, *Por qué y cómo*, 167–70, and Rivas, *El Frente*, 350–51.

65. It has long been assumed that Falangist gunmen killed Castillo, a natural assumption in that the former were responsible for nearly all killings of Socialists in the Madrid area. However, the most objective study, Ian Gibson's *La noche en que mataron a Calvo Sotelo* (Madrid, 1982), uncovered some evidence which indicates that the deed may have been done by Carlists in revenge for the shooting on 16 April (pp. 204–14).

66. The suspicions of more moderate left Republicans, such as the Galicianist leader Emilio González López, later fell on Ossorio for his role in the affair. Interview with González López in New York, 10 June 1958.

67. The most accurate reconstruction of these events is the work by Ian Gibson, *La noche en que mataron a Calvo Sotelo* (Madrid, 1982). Many valid details, along with much interpretation and distortion, will be found in the *Comisión sobre ilegitimidad de los poderes actuantes en 18 de julio de 1936* (Barcelona, 1939), App. I, and the *Causa General: La dominación roja en España* (Madrid, 1943), both prepared by special commissions of the Franco regime.

68. At least one Communist militia leader has admitted participating in the organization of the arrest assignments, further indication of the breakdown of normal police procedure. Juan Tagüeña, *Testimonio de dos guerras* (Barcelona, 1978), 72.

69. The rightist *Ya* and *La Epoca* published that day what little information was available and were immediately suspended by the government indefinitely.

70. Vidarte, *Todos fuimos*, 213–14; Prieto, *Convulsiones*, I, 162.

71. *Mundo Obrero*, July 14, 1935.

72. Avilés Farré, *La izquierda*, 311.

73. According to Romero, *Cómo y por qué*, 252.

74. In the speeches of Gil Robles and Calvo Sotelo, frequently cited here and elsewhere, and reproduced extensively in the longer multi-volume histories and in R. de la Cierva, ed., *Los documentos de la primavera trágica* (Madrid, 1967).

Brief general accounts such as P. Vicente Murga, *Determinación de la Guerra Civil española* (San Juan, Puerto Rico, 1936), and Hugh R. Wilson, *Descent into Violence — Spain January–July, 1936* (Ilfracombe, Devon, 1969), are at best partisan and impressionistic.

75. Cf. José Peirats, *La C. N. T. en la revolución española* (Toulouse, 1951), 1:121.

76. Ramiro Cibrián, "Violencia política y crisis democrática: España en 1936," REP 6 (November–December, 1978): 81–115.

77. *The Spanish Republic and Civil War* (Princeton, 1965), 222.

78. Cibrián, "Violencia política."

79. Renzo de Felice, *Mussolini il fascista: La conquista del potere* (Turin, 1966), 35–39, 87.

80. For data on the Weimar Republic, see Eve Rosenhaft, *Beating the Fascists? The German Communists and Political Violence 1929–1933* (Cambridge, 1983) and Richard Bessel, *Political Violence and the Rise of Nazism: The Storm Troopers in Eastern Germany, 1925–1934* (London, 1984).

81. Gerhard Botz, *Gewalt in der Politik: Attentäte, Zusammenstösse, Putschversuche, Unruhen in Österreich 1918 bis 1934* (2d ed., Vienna, 1983).

82. Hannsjoachim W. Koch, *Der deutsche Bürgerkrieg: Eine Geschichte der deutschen und österreichischen Freikorps 1918–1923* (Berlin, 1978); the anonymous account *Die Münchner Tragödie: Entstehung, Verlauf und Zusammenbruch der Räte-Republik München* (Berlin, 1919); Heinrich Hillmayr, *Roter und Weisser Terror in Bayern nach 1918* (Munich, 1974); and H. A. Winkler, *Von der Revolution zur Stabilisierung: Arbeiter und Arbeiterbewegung in der Weimarer Republik 1918 bis 1924* (Berlin and Bonn, 1984).

83. Paul Preston, *The Spanish Right Under the Second Republic* (Reading, 1971), 6.

84. The serious historiography is much less lengthy, but nonetheless detailed. The broadest account is F. Olaya Morales, *La conspiración contra la República* (Barcelona, 1979), though partly vitiated by being itself a partisan account written from the opposite perspective. The best treatment in Spanish is still Ricardo de la Cierva, *Historia de la guerra civil española: Antecedentes* (Madrid, 1969), 735–816. In English there are treatments in my *Politics and the Military in Modern*

Spain (Stanford, 1967), 314–40, and *The Franco Regime* (Madison, 1987), 78–100.

85. Gil Robles has declared that the CEDA provided a subsidy "shortly before" the revolt, but that he himself had no direct contacts with the leading military conspirators. Though this sounds somewhat ingenuous, it may be technically correct. Gil Robles states that the instructions he gave to party members were "for each individual to act according to his conscience without implicating the party; to establish direct contact with the military authorities, not form an autonomous party militia and, above all, to await concrete orders whenever the uprising began." *No fue posible,* 730, 798.

86. In June the secretary of the Valencian section, the DRV, allegedly promised Mola 1,250 militia volunteers at the beginning of a revolt and 50,000 after five days. La Cierva, *Historia,* 743–44. In most areas, however, the CEDA and JAP could not convincingly make such promises.

87. Cf. Romero, *Por qué y cómo,* 238; Ramon Garriga, *Los validos de Franco* (Barcelona, 1981), 25; and Ramón Serrano Súñer, *Memorias* (Barcelona, 1977), 52–60.

In later years, Franco would emphasize his reluctance to rebel. As he observed on 29 June 1965, "I always told my companions: 'As long as there is any hope that the Republican government can avoid anarchy or the clutches of Moscow, one must continue to support the Republic, which was accepted first by the king, secondly by the monarchist government and thirdly by the Army.'" Francisco Franco Salgado-Araujo, *Mis conversaciones privadas con Franco* (Barcelona, 1979), 452. Thus hardcore conspirators in Pamplona had come to refer to Franco derisively as "Miss Canarias de 1936" for his "coquetry."

88. For fuller discussion, see Vicente Palacio Atard, "El Gobierno ante la conspiración de 1936," in *Aproximación histórica a la guerra de España* (Madrid, 1970), 133–65.

89. Gil Robles, *No fue posible,* 608.

90. Juan Marichal, in his introduction to Azaña's *Obras completas,* 3:xxxii.

91. Zugazagoitia, *Historia,* 5–6; Prieto, *Convulsiones,* 1:163, 3:143–44; Vidarte, *Todos fuimos,* 146–47, 190–92; Largo Caballero, *Mis memorias,* 161–63.

92. Vidarte, *Todos fuimos,* 151–52.

93. Ibid., 192.

94. Ibid., 252–55.

95. Ibid., 255–56; Martínez Barrio, *Memorias* (Barcelona, 1983), 358–59.

96. The MAOC was intended to become "the organizational basis for the future worker-peasant Red Army." *Material de discusión para el Congreso Provincial del Partido Comunista que se celebrará en Madrid, durante los días 20, 21 y 22 de junio de 1936.*

97. Eligio de Mateo Sousa, "La sublevación en Madrid," *Historia 16* 15:165 (January, 1990): 111–16. In addition, one or two other senior leftist army officers began to hand over weapons that night, according to the various sources cited in Burnett Bolloten, *The Spanish Civil War* (Chapel Hill, 1991), 39, 754.

98. Martínez Barrio, *Memorias,* 361–63; Azaña, *Obras completas,* 4:714–15.

There is some disagreement between Martínez Barrio and Azaña on the breadth of the new coalition, which Azaña says was to have extended "from the Republican right to the Communists," while Martínez Barrio contradicts himself in this respect in other statements.

99. Martínez Barrio, *Memorias*, 363–64, and Antonio Alonso Baño, *Homenaje a Diego Martínez Barrio* (Paris, 1978), 67–107.

100. Vidarte, *Todos fuimos*, 236–38, 252–53, 280–84, confirms this according to the reports of government monitors who listened in on the conversations, as did Sánchez Román (who had been in the room with Martínez Barrio at the time) to a third party, as cited in Gil Robles, *No fue posible*, 791. An edition of *El Pensamiento Navarro* (Pamplona) which appeared later that day claimed that Mola had been offered the Ministry of War. Further references may be found in Bolloten, *Spanish Civil War*, 755. See also J. M. Iribarren, *Con el general Mola* (Madrid, 1945), 102–3; Zugazagoitia, *Historia*, 58–65; Luis Romero, *Tres días de julio* (Barcelona, 1967), 158, 193; Maximiano García Venero, *El general Fanjul* (Madrid, 1970), 287–90; Largo Caballero, *Mis memorias*, 156–57; and J. Pérez Madrigal, *Memorias de un converso* (Madrid, 1943–51), 7:65–68.

101. In a letter to Madariaga, quoted in the prologue to the fourth edition of Madariaga's *España* (Buenos Aires, 1944). Martínez Barrio has written that in striving to form the coalition he felt that "the military rebellion was no longer our worst enemy. Graver yet was the problem within our ranks created by irresolution, disorientation and the fear of courageous decisions." *Memorias*, 361.

102. The term coined by Burnett Bolloten, especially in chapter four of *Spanish Civil War*, entitled "The Revolution and the Rise of the Third Republic."

103. The standard Comintern title, first employed by the Spanish Communist leadership in reference to the Republic in March 1937, and later elaborated ad infinitum in the official Spanish Communist journal *Nuestra Bandera* in the years immediately following World War II.

104. The phrase invented for the first year of the Civil War by Carlos M. Rama, *La crisis española del siglo XX* (Mexico City, 1960).

Chapter 14. Why Did the Republic Fail?

1. As Ortega put it in the "Epílogo para ingleses" of the later editions of his *La rebelión de las masas:* "The Englishman or American has every right to think whatever he wants about what has happened or ought to happen in Spain, but that right is insulting unless he accepts the corresponding obligation of becoming well informed about the reality of the Spanish Civil War, in which the first and most important step is to understand its origins, the causes that produced it."

2. The extent to which, for example, the French Third Republic was endangered is still debated by historians. See Philippe Bernard and Henri Dubief, *The Decline of the Third Republic, 1914–1938* (Cambridge, 1988).

3. Detlev Peukert, *Die Weimarer Republik: Krisenjahre der klassischen Moderne* (Frankfurt, 1987).

4. In this regard, see the cogent remarks by Edward Malefakis, "La Segunda República española: Algunas observaciones personales en su 50 aniversario," *La IIa República española* (Barcelona, 1983), 97–109.

5. Conversely, it might be argued that the judiciary constituted an element of apparent strength, for the court system remained largely free of overt politicization, in the process drawing criticism from both right and left. It did not discriminate unfairly on behalf of those guilty of political crimes or violence either on the left or (as in Weimar Germany) on the right. The pressing concern of the left to pass new legislation for the political purging of the judiciary indicated that it had remained to a considerable degree free of the partisan leftist hegemony of 1936.

6. Dankwart Rustow has emphasized the crucial importance of agreement among political elites at the outset of a new system, since the "hardest struggles are against the birth defects of the political community." "Transitions to Democracy: Toward a Dynamic Model," *Comparative Politics* 2 (April, 1970): 337–63. Cf. Herbert J. Spiro, *Government by Constitution* (New York, 1959), 361–83; Robert A. Dahl, *Polyarchy: Participation and Oppression* (New Haven, 1971), 71; Samuel P. Huntington, "Will More Countries Become Democratic?", *Political Science Quarterly* 99 (Summer, 1984): 193–218; and J. Higley and R. Gunther, *Elites and Democratic Consolidation in Latin America and Southern Europe* (Cambridge, 1992).

7. Both left Republicans and Socialists initially tended to confuse the middle-class leftist intelligentsia and small progressive sectors with broad bourgeois interests generally, a massive sociopolitical miscalculation that recapitulated at a surprisingly late date and admittedly in a different form the same confusion found in Russia in 1905. Cf. Teodor Shanin, *Russia, 1905–07: Revolution as a Moment of Truth* (New Haven, 1986), 73 et passim.

8. In Germany, for example, the Weimar constitution was created by an acting coalition of moderate Socialists, middle-class democrats, and the Catholic Center (the latter sector participating because political Catholicism, always minoritarian in Germany, was more liberal and progressive there than in Spain).

9. Mercedes Cabrera, *La patronal ante la II República* (Madrid, 1983), 307–12.

10. H. A. Winkler, "Choosing the Lesser Evil: The German Social Democrats and the Fall of the Weimar Republic" *JCH* 25:2–3 (May–June, 1990): 205–7, and Winkler's *Der Weg in die Katastrophe: Arbeiter und Arbeiterbewegung in der Weimarer Republik 1930–1933* (Berlin, 1990).

11. As Sydney Tarrow has observed of a later period of conflict in Italy, crises tend to develop as "social conflict is transparent and political opportunities are expanding," rather than in times of the restriction of political rights and opportunities. *Democracy and Disorder: Protest and Politics In Italy, 1965–1975* (New York, 1989), 48–49.

12. Joaquín Arrarás, *Historia de la Segunda República española* (Madrid, 1956–63), 1:231–32.

13. Manuel Portela Valladares, *Memorias* (Madrid, 1988), 211.

14. The leadership must take much of the blame for the very low score of the

Republic in the operational measurements of T. R. Gurr and M. McClellan, *Political Performance: A Twelve-Nation Study* (Beverly Hills, 1981), 72. The summary score for the Republic was −7.80, compared with −6.01 for Germany between 1923 and 1932, and −3.95 for Yugoslavia from 1921 to 1929. The Republic also ranked highest in polarization, scoring 15.9 on that measurement compared with 6.16 for Weimar Germany. Moreover, the average cabinet duration of only 101 days in Spain compared unfavorably even with Austria during the depression crisis (149 days), and was more than twice as bad as in Germany or Italy.

Index

455